Studies in Church History

34

GENDER AND CHRISTIAN RELIGION

GENDER AND CHRISTIAN RELIGION

PAPERS READ AT
THE 1996 SUMMER MEETING AND
THE 1997 WINTER MEETING OF
THE ECCLESIASTICAL HISTORY SOCIETY

EDITED BY

R. N. SWANSON

PUBLISHED FOR
THE ECCLESIASTICAL HISTORY SOCIETY
BY
THE BOYDELL PRESS
1998

BR
141
.S84
Vol.34

First published 1998

A publication of the Ecclesiastical History Society
in association with The Boydell Press
an imprint of Boydell & Brewer Ltd
PO Box 9, Woodbridge, Suffolk IP12 3DF, UK
and of Boydell & Brewer Inc.
PO Box 41026, Rochester, NY 14604-4126, USA

ISBN 0 9529733 1 6

ISSN 0424-2084

A catalogue record for this book is available
from the British Library

Library of Congress Cataloging-in-Publication Data
Data applied for

Details of previous volumes available from Boydell & Brewer Ltd

This book is printed on acid-free paper

Printed in Great Britain by
St Edmundsbury Press Limited, Bury St Edmunds, Suffolk

IN MEMORY OF
ROSALIND M. T. HILL

CONTENTS

PREFACE

'Gender and Christian Religion' was the theme chosen by Professor Anthony Fletcher for his Presidency of the Ecclesiastical History Society in 1996–7. Predictably, it stimulated considerable and wide-ranging interest, resulting in the submission of over sixty communications for the Summer Conference. The contents of the present volume comprise the seven main papers delivered at the summer conference of 1996 and the January meeting in 1997, and a selection of the communications offered in the summer. As usual, the process of making decisions about which papers should be published has forced the editor to make harsh choices, to ensure a reasonable chronological balance and a volume which reflects the wide range of issues and debates stimulated by the main theme.

The Society wishes to thank the University of Kent at Canterbury, and especially the staff of Rutherford College, for their co-operation and care at the summer conference. Richard Eales has our sincere thanks for acting as local liaison and organizing the outings. As usual, we thank King's College, London, for hospitality at the January gathering.

* * *

As the editing of this volume was in progress, the death was announced of Professor Rosalind Hill. One of the first members of the Society, and a former President, her constant support has been much valued over the years. Back in 1978 the Festschrift in her honour, *Medieval Women*, initiated the series of subsidia volumes to *Studies in Church History*. Her presence at the summer conferences (often, in recent years, after somewhat hair-raising drives back from Austria) will be greatly missed.

Robert Swanson

LIST OF CONTRIBUTORS

Anthony FLETCHER (*President*)
Professor of History, University of Essex

Stewart J. BROWN
Professor of Ecclesiastical History, University of Edinburgh

Alison M. BUCKNALL
Research Student, University of Birmingham

Gillian CLARK
Senior Lecturer in Classics, University of Liverpool

Simon COATES
British Academy Postdoctoral Research Fellow, King's College London

Krista COWMAN
Tutor, Department of History, University of York

Greg CUTHBERTSON
Associate Professor, Department of History, University of South Africa

Jacqueline EALES
Reader in History, Christ Church College, Canterbury

Sean GILL
Senior Lecturer in Theology and Religious Studies, University of Bristol

Jeremy GREGORY
Principal Lecturer in History, University of Northumbria

Catherine HALL
Professor of Modern British Social and Cultural History, University College London

Susan HARDMAN MOORE
Lecturer in Reformation Studies, King's College London

David HILLIARD
Reader in History, The Flinders University of South Australia

Anders JARLERT
Professor in Church History, Lund University

Margaret P. JONES
Tutor, Wesley House, Cambridge

Louise KRETZSCHMAR
Senior Lecturer, Department of Systematic Theology and
Theological Ethics, University of South Africa

Katherine J. LEWIS
Research Associate, Centre for Medieval Studies, University of
York

Conrad LEYSER
Lecturer in Medieval History, University of Manchester

Charlotte METHUEN
Assistentin for Church History, Evangelisch-Theologische
Fakultät, Ruhr-Universität Bochum

Sue MORGAN
Lecturer in Gender History, Chichester Institute of Higher
Education

Rachel MORIARTY
Research Fellow in Theology, La Sainte Union College,
Southampton

Christine PETERS
Lecturer in History, The Queen's College, Oxford

Kate PETERS
Lecturer in Records and Archives Management, University
College London

Richard M. PRICE
Lecturer in Church History, Heythrop College, University of
London

Peter van ROODEN
Lecturer, Research Centre Religion and Society, University of
Amsterdam

Constance M. ROUSSEAU
Associate Professor of History, Providence College, Providence,
Rhode Island

David SHORNEY
    Honorary Visiting Research Fellow, University of Bradford
Julia M.H. SMITH
    Reader in Medieaval History, University of St Andrews
Jo SPREADBURY
    Research Student, King's College, University of London
Rowan STRONG
    Lecturer in Church History, Murdoch University, Perth,
    Australia
Brian TAYLOR
John TOSH
    Professor of History, University of North London
Linda WILSON
    Tutor in Church History, Open Theological College,
    Cheltenham

ABBREVIATIONS

Abbreviated titles are adopted within each paper after the first full citation. In addition, the following abbreviations are used throughout the volume.

ActaSS	*Acta sanctorum*, ed. J. Bolland and G. Henschen (Antwerp, etc., 1643–)
AHR	*American Historical Review* (New York, 1895–)
Annales	*Annales: Economies, Sociétés, Civilisations* (Paris, 1946–)
BL	London, British Library
CathHR	*Catholic Historical Review* (Washington, D.C., 1915–)
CChr.CM	*Corpus Christianorum, continuatio medievalis* (Turnhout, 1966–)
CChr.SL	*Corpus Christianorum, series Latina* (Turnhout, 1953–)
ChH	*Church History* (New York/Chicago, 1932–)
CIC	*Corpus iuris canonici*, ed. E. Richter and E. Friedberg, 2 vols (Leipzig, 1879–81)
CUL	Cambridge, University Library
DNB	*Dictionary of National Biography* (London, 1885–)
EETS	Early English Text Society (London, 1864–)
EHR	*English Historical Review* (London, 1886–)
es	extra series
HistJ	*Historical Journal* (Cambridge, 1958–)
HThR	*Harvard Theological Review* (New York/Cambridge, MA, 1908–)
HWJ	*History Workshop Journal* (Oxford, 1976–)
JBS	*Journal of British Studies* (Hartford, Conn., 1961–)
JEH	*Journal of Ecclesiastical History* (Cambridge, 1950–)
JFHS	*Journal of the Friends' Historical Society* (London/Philadelphia, 1903–)
JMedH	*Journal of Medieval History* (Amsterdam, 1975–)
JThS	*Journal of Theological Studies* (London, 1899–)
MGH	*Monumenta Germaniae historica inde ab a. 500 usque ad a. 1500*, ed. G.H. Pertz *et al.* (Hanover, Berlin, etc., 1826–)
Cap.	*Leges 2, Leges in Quart 2: Capitularia regum Francorum*
Conc.	*Leges 2, Leges in Quart 3: Concilia*

SS	*Scriptores*
SRM	*Scriptores rerum merovingicarum*
SRG	*Scriptores rerum germanicarum in usum scholarium*
nd	no date
np	no place of publication
os	old series/original series
P&P	*Past and Present: A Journal of Scientific History* (London, 1952–)
PG	*Patrologia Graeca*, ed. J. P. Migne, 161 vols (Paris, 1857–66)
PL	*Patrologia Latina*, ed. J. P. Migne, 217 vols + 4 index vols (Paris, 1841–61)
PRO	London, Public Record Office
SC	Sources chrétiennes (Paris, 1942–)
SCH	*Studies in Church History* (London/Oxford/Woodbridge, 1964–)
SCH.S	*Studies in Church History: Subsidia* (Oxford, 1978–)
Speculum	*Speculum: A Journal of Medieval Studies* (Cambridge, MA, 1925–)
ss	supplementary series
Traditio	*Traditio: Studies in Ancient and Medieval History, Thought, and Religion* (New York, etc., 1943–)
TRHS	*Transactions of the Royal Historical Society* (London, 1871–)

* * *

Canon law citations are laid out according to the 'modern form' (see James A. Brundage, *Medieval canon law* [London and New York, 1995], app. 1), with quotations from *CIC*.

INTRODUCTION

A reading of the thirty-two contributions to this volume brings home the sheer complexity of the issues surrounding gender in relation to Christian tradition, practice, and experience. Historians are at an early stage in unravelling these. The volume presents an exciting and diverse series of sparks from the anvil of historical research in this field. It cannot hope to provide a comprehensive or conclusive view of the matter. Yet a number of prominent themes emerge, all of them demanding further work, which it will be the business of this Introduction to identify. If the gendering of history as a whole has only just begun, this volume, taken overall, must stand as a signal initiative in the process of the gendering of Christian history over two millennia.

Issues surrounding concepts of gender run through the essays in the volume. Rachel Moriarty, at its start, deals penetratingly with the key phrase 'playing the man' as it summarizes a component of masculinity and was applied by a Victorian cleric to an ancient martyrdom. Sean Gill explores at length how Thomas Hughes handled the dilemma of Muscular Christianity, seeking a portrayal of Christ which combined the highest attributes of both masculine and feminine nature in an age when English society was somewhat obsessed by a sharp polarization of gender difference. Sue Morgan's essay is a distinctive contribution in this field. She shows how Ellice Hopkins, the founder of the Victorian male purity movement known as the White Cross Army, sought to re-educate men in rigorous moral virtue. She denied the double standard and erected a discourse of moral Darwinism in which sexual purity was associated with moral courage and mature strength of character as the ultimate manifestation of man's spiritual progress.

Several medievalist contributions to the volume explicate the origins and development of Christian thinking about gender. Gillian Clark's reflections upon Augustine's discussion of the creation narrative remind us of the abiding power of a tradition which identified maleness with reason and femaleness with the body and desire. Julia Smith's explication of the *Etymologiae* of Isidore of Seville shows how the notions of male strength and female softness were developed into definitions of 'man' and 'woman' of 'virtually canonical status' and how early medieval writers 'delineated a coherent code of gendered moral conduct' which remained powerful throughout the medieval and early modern periods. Conrad Leyser's exploration of gender in the context of eleventh-century reform spells out how remote thinking about it was then from our own time since, while no positive and universal conception of the feminine existed and the modern notion of individuality was meaningless, women were bound to be judged entirely within the confines of their subordinate status. Gender becomes a deceptive category of historical analysis at a time when men were judged by other men in terms of how effectively they exercised control over their women and resisted being swayed by them. Misogyny, in this mental world, disinherited women both socially and personally.

The question of misogyny is bound to be close to the surface in a series of essays which are discussing a patriarchal church order. Constance Rousseau, however, offers a reconsideration of Innocent III's misogyny which complicates any monolithic view of papal attitudes to women. Yet we should not forget, as R. M. Price concludes in an essay on one of the grosser misogynist texts of the *Golden Legend*, that the patriarchal imperative was not 'simply accepted by Christianity in its formative period but justified and reinforced by a theological argument unparalleled in paganism or classical philosophy'. Several contributors explore aspects of how this patriarchal imperative worked itself out in practice and was adapted to the changing conditions of the Church and society. Charlotte Methuen discusses the *Didascalia Apostolorum*, a church order written in Syria in the third century as part of a process of imposing both patriarchal hierarchy and the subjection of all its members to the control of the bishop. She argues that it is too simple to see a scheme of this kind merely in terms of men as winners and women as losers. Jacqueline Eales, in an essay on a celebrated seventeenth-century puritan commentator on marriage, reflects upon the importance of his own experience as one of a first generation of married clergy in setting out precepts for male and female relationship and conduct. She finds his innate traditionalism informed and enlarged by that experience. Stewart Brown traces the breakdown of the Church of Scotland's form of corporate discipline known as 'standing the session' under the pressure of changing attitudes to gender relations: with the double standard becoming increasingly contentious, this involved young pregnant women being judged and admonished by older male elders, which was much less acceptable at the end of the nineteenth century than it had been early in the eighteenth. He finds a 'less patriarchal and judgemental Church of Scotland' emerging in the early years of the present century. These contributions exemplify the complex attitudes and shifts of practice that have characterized patriarchal Christianity over the centuries.

Another series of papers on the clerical profession has fascinating things to say about how men saw themselves facing the constrictions of gender stereotyping when they identified their ministerial roles and aspirations. As Jeremy Gregory puts it well, the clergy were always in a liminal position regarding gender. Susan Hardman Moore argues that puritan writers were happy 'to adopt a feminine identity in spiritual experience'. Her investigation of the feminized language of male puritan devotion shows how marriage, newly hallowed by Protestantism, provided a perfect metaphor for the clergy's intimacy with God. Emotion that would elsewhere have been conspicuously unmanly was acceptable in this context. Jeremy Gregory concludes, from his research into sermons preached before the eighteenth-century annual meetings annual meetings in the of the Corporation of the Sons of the Clergy, that Anglican clergy prided themselves on being pious, charitable, and moderate. These were exactly the qualities, he notes, which contemporary commentators praised as feminine virtues. Peter van Rooden's revealing investigation of manuals for the ministry in the Dutch Protestant Church around 1800 brings to light a set of virtues and an idealized comportment which is quite markedly feminine. He discusses why this gendered identity of the Dutch ministers was not seen as a problem, concluding that they found the badge of their masculinity in a sense of cultural superiority and moral leadership which enabled them to envisage themselves as creating the nation.

Women over the ages have been portrayed and have portrayed themselves as brides of Christ. Yet at the same time, as Jo Spreadbury's intriguing essay shows, the female medieval image of *Ecclesia* as a woman holding the chalice allowed visionary women who were virgins to bypass clerical control and claim access to the sacrament. Two essays in the volume deal directly with gender and female sainthood. Simon Coates suggests that the hagiographers of Radegund, a saint of Merovingian Gaul, made a flexible use of male and female models of sanctity to construct a third gender whose religious ideal was based upon a rejection of sexuality and 'the desire to appear as angels'. Katherine Lewis considers a series of texts and wall paintings relating to the life of the virgin martyr St Margaret of Antioch. She finds

Margaret constructed as drawing strength from rather than negating her femininity in her fight for Christ, a member of a domestic community in which Christianity was being passed from woman to woman in private in defiance of the public and patriarchal structure. Her exemplary femininity is presented as a strength in the fourth-century clash with paganism. Lewis concludes that in this sense St Margaret could and did 'function as a role model for women', particularly the young and unmarried for whom she provided an example of chastity.

Women, so the dominant gender ideology of the period from 1600 to 1900 in England taught, were weaker than men, more emotional yet at the same time more naturally religious. Men recognized this, and a central theme of the latter part of the volume is how groups of women sought and found space for the expression of their religious commitment and energy within patriarchal churches and sects. Kate Peters stresses the very prominent role of women in the early stages of the Quaker movement yet, at the same time, argues that the movement's male leaders quickly established disciplinary strategies for the control of members famed for their public activity. Whereas Quakers justified women's preaching role in ungendered terms, their view of family and social relations more broadly was fairly traditional and in line with contemporary patriarchal expectations. Margaret Jones's interesting analysis of women's accounts of their spiritual experience in the Methodist *Arminian Magazine* reveals that female autobiographies, included through John Wesley's deliberate patronage, focus largely on states of soul and mind while male ones tend to provide a narrative of achievements and actions. She provides striking evidence of the sharply differentiated gendered experience of religion in the late eighteenth and early nineteenth centuries. David Shorney expounds the role of women acting as evangelists on equal terms with men in the Bible Christian societies in the early nineteenth century, but sees limits being placed on their role in governmental matters. More privately, Anders Jarlert explores the writings of three urban middle class women in western Sweden who in the course of the nineteenth century found fulfilment through spiritual counselling in a revivalist mode. Rowan Strong's essay looks at the work of the aristocratic Lady Lothian, arguing from the evidence of the Jedburgh Tractarian project that a single woman could be powerfully influential in such a context even given a degree of dependence on the men around her. Alison Bucknall considers issues concerning women's roles in active ministry among

Victorian Evangelicals as they emerged in the debates of the Mildmay Conference and the Keswick Convention between 1856 and 1900. She finds the Mildmay women seeking to avoid offence to contemporary ideas of womanhood, yet combining ideals of gentleness and strength, whereas Keswick moved its participants away from the domestic model of service, bringing them out of their separate sphere to join men in the practical world of foreign mission as well as providing them with a more closed personal world of spiritual contemplation.

Three papers in the volume deal with gender in the context of domestic religion. In my Presidential essay, I contribute a series of case studies of women's spiritual experience in the home from the seventeenth and nineteenth centuries. Contrastingly, John Tosh contributes a pathbreaking essay which, focusing upon masculinity in truly relational terms, explores in fascinating detail 'how religion was experienced through domesticity and how domesticity was understood in religious terms'. The protagonists are three nineteenth-century middle-class men, all of them Methodists, and the essay establishes what the home, marriage and childrearing meant to them as central elements in their lives. Linda Wilson uses a large number of women's obituaries from four denominational magazines published between 1825 and 1875 to investigate the patterns of nonconformist domestic spirituality in this period. She concludes that, despite a sense of tension between a contemporary ideology of passivity and their urge to activism, these Victorian women succeeded in developing a many-sided and practical form of spiritual guardianship in their homes.

The growth in recent times of feminist consciousness receives attention in two pieces. In a case study of the activities of the Liverpool Church League for Women's Suffrage between 1913 and 1918, Krista Cowman discusses its attention to issues of gendered space, noting in particular the brief experiment in 1914 of a Woman's Church in which the gender roles were reversed. David Hilliard's vigorous account of the confrontation between evangelical religion, feminism, and gay activism in Sydney since the 1970s portrays a joint challenge to hegemonic masculinity that has produced an atmosphere of intense debate in the diocese unparalleled elsewhere in Australia. He neatly defines the central issue at stake as 'the idea that gender differences and the subordination of women to men are clearly defined in the New Testament and are part of the God-created order for both family and Church', arguing convincingly that in Sydney more than anywhere else in the Anglican world the issues of the ordination of women to the priesthood and homosexual equality have been seen as 'interconnected and consecutive'.

The excursions to Australia and Sweden are not the only occasions on which the volume moves away from its British moorings. Other contributions provide illuminating insights into gender and Christianity in Moldavia and Wallachia, Jamaica, Sarawak, and South Africa. Christine Peters ponders the gender implications of an iconographical language in votive images, having discovered that Eve is depicted as a saint in the Orthodox wall paintings of sixteenth-century Moldavia. Catherine Hall, in a stimulating account of missionary activity in early nineteenth-century Jamaica, shows Christian manhood and sense of destiny under strain, and discusses how emancipation of slaves created newly constructed women as gendered beings together with a form of manhood which had previously been impossible for the black slave. Brian Taylor accounts for the beginnings of professional women's missionary activity in Sarawak during the 1850s and traces women's religious roles and activity there through the subsequent decades to the 1970s. Greg Cuthbertson and Louise Kretzschmar contribute a useful historiographical survey of work on gender and religion in South Africa, commenting upon the construction of African women's religious identities and showing how the reception of Christian missionary activity by African women raises important issues about the meanings of their femininity. So all in all this volume ranges very widely indeed. The high quality of the work it contains is a tribute to the liveliness and good health of the Society and of its scholarship.

Anthony Fletcher

'PLAYING THE MAN': THE COURAGE OF CHRISTIAN MARTYRS, TRANSLATED AND TRANSPOSED

by RACHEL MORIARTY

THE aged Bishop Polycarp was burnt to death in the arena at Smyrna in the afternoon of 23 February 155 (or 156), in front of a hostile crowd. The terrible story was lovingly recorded, copied and passed round the churches; it is probably the first non-biblical record of a martyrdom, and survives by itself and in Eusebius' *History*. As Polycarp entered the arena Christian eyewitnesses heard a voice from heaven, saying in Greek, for all to understand, ''Ίσχυε, Πολύκαρπε, καὶ ἀνδείζου'. The first word means 'be strong'; the last shares a root with two other Greek words, ἀνδρεία, which means courage, and ἀνήρ, which means a male person, a man. We shall consider later how Polycarp's contemporaries understood this; centuries later, about the 1880s, an Anglican academic clergyman, Joseph Lightfoot, who was soon to be a bishop himself, translated Polycarp's story into English. He found an apt English idiom: 'Be strong, Polycarp,' he wrote, 'and play the man.'[1]

In this paper this masculine metaphor will be discussed, together with other gender images, in second-century martyrdoms and in a few much more recent English translations. Early Christians do not come out well in current debate on gender, and idioms which identify courage with manliness seem to confirm the worst about them, reinforced in English translation. Trailing the patriarchal assumptions of Judaism and classical antiquity, it seems that early Christians soon abandoned the promise of equality suggested by Paul to the Galatians, that 'in Christ there is no male nor female' (Gal. 3.28), and certainly did not establish an inclusive tradition in the Church they founded. In a usually depressing picture of patristic gender-priorities, men and women martyrs represent a fleeting equality.[2]

[1] *The Martyrdom of Polycarp*, ix; text, translation, and notes in J. B. Lightfoot, ed. J. R. Harmer, *The Apostolic Fathers* (London, 1891 and later edns), pp. 186–99 (introd. and Greek text) and 203–11 (translation); originally translated in J. B. Lightfoot, *The Apostolic Fathers*, Part II, 3 vols (London, 1885), 3. The story appears in Eusebius' *Ecclesiastical History*, IV, xv, 17 – see below, n. 15 for versions.

[2] Stuart G. Hall, 'Women among the early martyrs', *SCH*, 30 (1993), pp. 1–22.

I

Though patriarchal structures soon closed in, Perpetua and Blandina join Polycarp, Justin, and Alban as continuing models of heroism, independent of sex. Does the imagery of martyrdom support this inclusive picture? The enquiry is twofold. The first question concerns the language and culture of the original stories: are these images signs of an underlying male bias, or are they dead metaphors revealing no more than a quirk of vocabulary? The second concerns the process of translation, in its widest sense: how far is our understanding of early Christianity and its idiom shaped (even if we know Greek) by associations transposed to and from our own language, history, and culture? In other words, we shall discuss the rhetoric of gender and the history of metaphor.

We must begin by briefly setting the discussion in the wider debate on gender and language in the early Church. Feminist theologians, especially Elisabeth Schüssler Fiorenza, Elizabeth A. Clark, Rosemary Radford Ruether, and recently Grace M. Jantzen, have effectively directed attention to 'the story about women'.[3] They identify 'a conceptual error of vast proportions', in which men's stories have stood for the whole of human experience, and women's for a sub-set, the 'disabling gender-construction' of patristic stereotypes, and its frequent assumption that women can only attain to Christian perfection by, in effect, becoming male.[4] Their approach has prompted a re-reading of early texts, with closer attention to their gender overtones; and this process joins study of the dynamics of language and metaphor and the communities using them, and particularly of religious language, through the work of such scholars as Janet Martin Soskice and Sallie McFague.[5] Averil Cameron has united the two areas

---

[3] See Elisabeth Schüssler Fiorenza, *In Memory of Her* (London, 1983); Elizabeth A. Clark, *Women in the Early Church* (Wilmington, DE, 1983); Rosemary Radford Ruether, *Sexism and God-Talk* (London, 1983); Grace M. Jantzen, *Power, Gender and Christian Mysticism* (Cambridge, 1995). There is a valuable selection of material in Ann Loades, ed., *Feminist Theology: A Reader* (London, 1990), esp. her introduction.

[4] Loades, *Feminist Theology*, introduction, pp. 1–11: she quotes (p. 3) Gerda Lerner, *The Creation of Patriarchy* (New York, 1986), pp. 236–67. See also Kari Vogt, '"Becoming male": a Gnostic and early Christian metaphor', in Kari Børreson, ed., *Image of God and Gender Models in Judaeo-Christian Tradition* (Oslo, 1991), pp. 172–87.

[5] Janet Martin Soskice, *Metaphor and Religious Language* (Oxford, 1985), and Sallie McFague, *Metaphorical Theology: Models of God in Religious Language* (Philadelphia, PA, 1982). For a valuable recent account of the whole field see Dan R. Stiver, *The Philosophy of Religious Language: Sign, Symbol and Story* (Oxford, 1996), esp. pp. 112–33.

in a brilliant study of the rhetoric of early Christian discourse on women in connection with virginity.[6]

The effect of translation is less noticed. Analysing gender assumptions is more complicated when the texts are moved to new languages and cultures – for this purpose, into English, in Britain at three different points in its history. Clearly modern English draws on a different world of metaphor from that of second-century Asia Minor – but there is more to it than that. A Victorian translation reveals assumptions which are neither ours nor Polycarp's, and uses some imagery which, as we shall see, has roots in English Protestant mythology as well as the early Church. Perhaps, as Rosemary Radford Ruether suggests, we rely too much on 'our grandmothers' vocabulary' in our understanding of the foundations of Christianity.[7] Yet our own ideas of gender metaphor are changing under our feet, and the English words 'he' and 'men' are particularly sensitive to the charge of excluding women – though some still defend an earlier inclusive understanding. With this ambivalence now, can we judge of 'exclusive language' in the past? How faithful is an 'inclusive' patristic translation? The best that can be done is to be aware of the layers of meaning behind our own understanding, and approach the past through the present.

Polycarp and his co-martyrs offer a case-study as a footnote to this debate. Their stories are literary constructions, but their significance is historical because of the assumptions they reveal and the patterns they set for later tradition of the understanding and presentation of faith and events. We start with our picture – it can be no more – of his classical vocabulary.

* * *

The words Polycarp's spectators heard are a quotation from the Septuagint (LXX) version of Joshua 1.6.[8] In these words God sends Joshua forth to lead his people into the Promised Land, with the

---

[6] Averil Cameron, 'Virginity as metaphor: women and the rhetoric of early Christianity', in eadem, ed., *History as Text* (London, 1989), pp. 181–205; eadem, *Christianity and the Rhetoric of Empire: the Development of Christian Discourse* (Berkeley, Los Angeles, and London, 1991).

[7] Rosemary Radford Ruether, in discussion after a lecture, 'Ecofeminism: first and third world women', given at La Sainte Union College, Southampton, 25 May 1996.

[8] LXX quotations are from Henry Barclay Swete, ed., *The Old Testament in Greek according to the Septuagint*, 3 vols (Cambridge, 1887).

guarantee of divine protection; Moses had already commissioned him
as his successor (Deut. 31.6, 7 and 23) in the same terms. The word
ἀνδρίζου had a masculine ring, as we have seen. But there were other,
perhaps stronger, connotations for the Smyrnaean audience, who knew
their Old Testament scripture in the Greek of the LXX. The whole
phrase conveys scriptural, if male, authority, and also serves a literary
and a spiritual purpose: how better to begin this account, in which
Polycarp enters the heavenly kingdom closely identified with Christ in
his passion, than with an echo of Joshua, whose name in Greek is Jesus?
The audience might also have recalled Paul's similar use of the word in
the First Letter to the Corinthians, where he exhorts his readers to
show vigilance, faith, and manly courage (I Cor. 16.13).

What are we to make of the masculinity? Does it reveal a deep-
seated sexism, a dead metaphor for simple courage, or a interesting
model of manhood? Classical method looks to the literary uses of the
word, in works which would be familiar to educated Greeks from the
standard curriculum. ἀνδρεία did not always mean courage in a good
sense, and could mean 'stubbornness'. It did not always apply literally
to men: educated readers might recall that Sophocles' Electra hoped to
be admired for her (manly) courage; or that Aristotle noted five
different kinds of courage (ἀνδρεία again), and concluded that men's
was that of leadership, ἀρχική, while women's, like their function, was
'subordinate', ὑπηρετική; Socrates, he said, took a different view, that
courage, like wisdom and justice, was the same for men and women.[9]
The relationship of virtue and gender was the subject of active classical
debate, still going on, if inconclusively, in Christian circles at least a
century after Polycarp's death. Clement of Alexandria maintains that
'the woman does not possess one nature, and the man exhibit another,
but the same: so also with virtue', and denies that 'it belongs to the
male alone to be virtuous, and to the woman to be licentious and
unjust. It is offensive even to say this.' Good for him: but a little later,
he declares: 'is not woman translated into man, when she is become . . .
unfeminine, and manly, and perfect?'[10]

---

[9] Sophocles, *Electra*, l.983; Aristotle, *Ethica Nicomachea*, 1116^{a}15–1117^{b}21, in Aristotle, *Ethica Nicomachea*, trans. W. D. Ross (Oxford, 1925), III.8; Aristotle, *Politics*, 1260^{a}22, in W. L. Newman, *The Politics of Aristotle*, 2 vols (Oxford, 1887), 2, pp. 20 (Greek text), 219–20 (notes); other examples are quoted in Liddell and Scott, *A Greek-English Lexicon*, new edn, ed. Henry Stuart Jones and Roderick McKenzie (Oxford, 1948).

[10] Clement of Alexandria, *Stromateis*, iv, 8, and vi, 12, in Alexander Roberts and James Donaldson, ed. and trans., A. Cleveland Coxe, rev., *The Ante-Nicene Fathers*, 8 vols (Grand

For the male Polycarp there is something else to notice: men could presumably fall short of the truly manly, as women might occasionally achieve it. It was theoretically possible to be less than a man, aspiring to but not achieving ἀνδρεία – otherwise there would be no need for exhortation. This seems important: here is a gender model for classical and early Christian men, but its manliness does not come automatically to those of the male sex. The model is active and dominant, as women's models were not; but it may in its own way have been constricting and disabling. Re-reading early texts may make us take a more sympathetic view of classical and early Christian men as well as women.

Another point may escape English speakers, unused to gender in modern language: most ancient abstract nouns are grammatically feminine, even though the words for courage and virtue regularly have roots in words with male or masculine meanings. Besides ἀνδρεία, there is the Latin word regularly used for physical courage, *virtus* (linked with *vir*, a male person), with its plural *virtutes*, virtues, and the Greek feminine noun ἀρετή, goodness and virtue, rooted in another Greek word for male. It is not clear exactly how sex is linked with gender in language, but it is not straightforward.

The English translation presents a new set of issues. The Victorian Anglican Lightfoot would have known his classical grammar; but he would also have been familiar with the Authorized Version of the Bible. There, the Joshua text reads, 'Be strong and of a good courage', and is translated not from Greek but from the Hebrew *'amats*, which does not have connotations of maleness.[11] But the Pauline text (I Cor. 16.13), originally in Greek, appears, as it does in Tyndale's version, as 'Quit you like men.'[12] Gender overtones appear in Greek originals, and that was what Lightfoot had before him. His version reduced the scriptural impact for his English readers; but it called up a different set of Anglican images.

Rapids, MI, 1962), 2, pp. 419²–20¹ and 503¹; and see also Clark, *Women*, p. 18; Rosemary Radford Ruether, 'The liberation of Christology from patriarchy', in Loades, *Feminist Theology*, pp. 138–48; Vogt, 'Becoming male'; and Jantzen, *Power, Gender and Christian Mysticism*, p. 53.
[11] I am grateful to my colleague Stephen Greenhalgh, of La Sainte Union College, Southampton, for help with this.
[12] Both James Moffat in *The New Testament: A New Translation*, new edn, rev. (London, 1934) and Ronald A. Knox, in *The New Testament Newly Translated into English* (London, 1945) render this verse 'play the man'; modern translations, including the New English Bible, the Jerusalem Bible, the Revised Standard Version, the Revised English Bible and the Good News Bible, prefer variants on being brave, valiant, and courageous.

'Be of good comfort, Master Ridley, and play the man', said Bishop Hugh Latimer to Bishop Nicholas Ridley as they stood together at the stake in Oxford on 16 October 1555; and John Foxe noted it in his *Acts and Monuments* of 1570.[13] Latimer was himself quoting Polycarp, whose story is something of a *topos* for Reformation martyrologies.[14] Foxe's book was to shape the attitudes and language of English Protestants for centuries. The Victorian Lightfoot and his successors inherited this religious and literary tradition, and 'play the man' sprang to their lips and pens in martyrological contexts; with its overtones of the stage, the stake, and the playing-field, it reminds us also of the romantic masculine idealism of poems like Kipling's 'If', where becoming a man is the prize for achieving human virtues. It may be that the nineteenth-century combination of public schools, classical education, and patristic literature have left behind a tradition of masculinity which has shaped British perceptions of all three.

There is another possibility to consider. It is reasonable to ask whether 'man' in this sense and in this instance has the inclusive sense of 'humanity' it often carries in the Book of Common Prayer and the Authorized Version of the Bible, as in 'man shall not live by bread alone' (Deut. 8.3; Matt. 4.4). This does not seem convincing. In this use of 'play the man', the Greek root is male, as we have seen, and translators, as classical scholars, would be likely to reflect this. The inclusive sense is less effective here. It is, however, true that until the last few years it was assumed, as grammarians asserted, that 'man embraces woman', and how far this metaphorical embrace meant a wider overlap in understanding is for speculation. It is hard to draw conclusions from this masculine context.

'Play the man' appears in most English translations of Polycarp, including revisions and selections in recent standard source-books, at least up to 1989;[15] so English students usually meet Polycarp locked to

---

[13] In John Foxe, *The Acts and Monuments of these Latter and Perilous Days*, ed. G. Townsend and S. R. Cattley, 8 vols (London, 1837–41), 7, p. 550.

[14] Prof. Susan Wabuda in her paper 'To be promoted above the Angels: Hugh Latimer's understanding of Martyrdom', presented at the 65th Anglo-American Conference of Historians on 'Religion and Society', London, 3–6 July 1996, argues from Latimer's letters that he saw and described himself as a martyr before his death. I am grateful to her, and to Prof. David Loades and Dr Andrew Pettegree, for discussion on this point.

[15] For instance, in Eusebius, Bishop of Caesarea, *The Ecclesiastical History and the Martyrs of Palestine*, ed. and trans. Hugh Jackson Lawlor and John Ernest Leonard Oulton, 2 vols (London, 1927, repr. 1954), 1, p. 119; G. A. Williamson, in Eusebius, *The History of the Church* (Harmondsworth, 1965), p. 171 – it remains in the 2nd edn, rev. and intro. Andrew Louth

the English Reformation by masculine imagery reinforced by Victorian translation. Versions by American translators tend to avoid the phrase, and have 'contend manfully', or 'have courage'. In 1989, Michael Holmes modernized Lightfoot for reasons of 'clarity, readability and contemporary [American] English usage', and replaced it with 'Act like a man!'[16] Either way, gender is evident to modern ears. For anyone alert to inclusive language in the 1990s, the phrase seems more exclusively male, and less historically evocative, than it did a generation ago. In time, archaic language changes its resonance, and different aspects of metaphor gain significance and prominence; ancient texts are overlaid with layers of shifting connotations.

* * *

The martyrological gender-view can be widened to include both sexes in two more texts. Twenty years after Polycarp's death, a group of men and women martyrs went to their deaths in Lyons, and their story was again circulated to the Churches.[17] Here the use of gender imagery is very different. The martyrs' courage is much praised, but not usually with the word ἀνδρεία: other words, without gender overtones, are preferred, like χαρά, patient endurance, or ἀτρομία, steadfastness. In spite of their mixed sex, the martyrs are collectively given the usually male title of 'athletes', and the pagans taunt them with being 'unmanly' and 'cowards', ἀνάνδροι. Some were called murderers, ἀνδροφόνοι, killers of men, without, it seems, particular reference to the sex of their victims. Pagans, however, are guilty of ἀπανθρωπία, inhuman behaviour. The sharp distinction between ἀνήρ and ἄνθρωπος, which we, from a non-gendered language background, assume was precise, was in practice probably fairly flexible.

Later the gender image gets its own back when a man figuratively gives birth. In the arena, the popular doctor, Alexander, delivers himself of his final confession of faith: 'it was clear to those standing

(Harmondsworth, 1989); and see, for instance, Kirsopp Lake, *The Apostolic Fathers* (Loeb edition), 2 vols (London and New York, 1924), 2, p. 322. Source-books which use the phrase include the standard selections: Henry Bettenson, *Documents of the Christian Church* (originally 1943), 2nd edn (Oxford, 1967), p. 10; J. Stevenson, ed., *A New Eusebius*, new edn, ed. W. H. C. Frend (London, 1987), p. 25.

[16] See, for example, Eusebius Pamphilus, *The Ecclesiastical History*, IV, xv, 17, trans. Revd C. F. Crusé (London, 1865); Herbert Musurillo, trans., *The Acts of the Christian Martyrs* (Oxford, 1972), p. 9; and *The Apostolic Fathers*, 2nd edn, trans. J. B. Lightfoot and J. R. Harmer, ed. and rev. Michael W. Holmes (English edn, Leicester, 1989), p.viii.

[17] 'The Martyrs of Lyons', in Musurillo, *Acts*, pp. 65–84.

around the platform that he was, as it were, suffering in the pain of giving birth'.[18] The phrase is specifically obstetric, ὥσπερ ὠδίνων, in labour-pains; but it had a long and full metaphorical history, going back to Homer's account of the Cyclops,[19] as familiar to educated Greeks as the Authorized Version of the Bible was to Lightfoot. Elsewhere, those who fail to go through with martyrdom are described as 'stillborn'. These gynaecological metaphors are hardly to be taken literally, but that makes it harder to draw precise conclusions about gender-construction.

The most striking case of confused gender boundaries comes with the heroine Blandina. As a slave, small, frail, and despised, she reveals God's power to reverse the natural order; hanging in a cross-shape in agony before the beasts, she appears as Christ to her comrades in suffering: 'they saw in the person of their sister him who was crucified for them'.[20] Even in paradox the female Blandina represents the male Christ. She also evokes another female model of martyrdom, the mother of the Maccabees, whose story may have inspired Christian martyrdom accounts. In what seems to be an echo of that text, Blandina is 'like a noble mother encouraging her children and sending them forth as victors to the King'.[21] The Maccabees text goes on to show the mother firing 'her woman's reasoning with a man's courage (RSV)' (τὸν θῆλυν λογισμὸν ἄρσενι θυμῷ: II Macc. 7.20–3), in words with coarser sexual overtones. There is no such crude suggestion for the Christ-like Blandina.

Modern readers may well find this ambivalent gender-imagery more acceptable than the assumption that courage is male. This text shows that to some extent the root-senses of such words were weakened as metaphors of courage and production. In English, where we do not as a rule use images of childbirth for males (except in the stylized example of delivery I have just used), the words strike with an original and creative force, and translation brings in no added baggage; they may have been different, dead metaphors or even clichés, in Greek.

* * *

[18] Ibid., pp. 76–7, l. 30, 78–9, l. 1.
[19] Homer, *Odyssey*, ix, 415.
[20] Musurillo, *Acts*, pp. 74–5, l. 18.
[21] Ibid., pp. 78–9, l. 30; W. H. C. Frend, *Martyrdom and Persecution in the Early Church* (Oxford, 1965), p. 19, sees the Maccabees text as earlier than this martyrdom, but others place it later.

A last example comes from a martyr from nearly thirty years later, the noble Vibia Perpetua, in Latin-speaking Carthage. Before her death, she had a series of visions, and her (evidently) first-hand record of them survives. She saw herself led out to fight with a hideous Egyptian, and rubbed down with oil by her seconds: 'facta sum masculus', she wrote. Much has been made of this image and its Freudian and Jungian overtones; it has been seen as showing Perpetua's wish to avoid the customary rape of female victims, as a sign of her status as 'virago', or of the usual Graeco-Roman premium on masculinity. Brent Shaw is surely right in seeing it as a symbol of 'empowerment', and Grace Jantzen as ensuring her 'courage and spiritual integrity'; as Averil Cameron points out, she 'draws on contemporary expectations of gender'.[22]

All the same, perhaps too much has been made of it. Perpetua remains grammatically feminine throughout, and is greeted by the 'trainer', Christ, as a 'daughter', *filia*; if she has had a sex-change, he hasn't noticed. Here again, translation can slant perception. Most modern versions have something like Musurillo's 'suddenly I was a man', Elizabeth Clark's 'I was made a man', or Grace Jantzen's quotation 'I was changed into a man.'[23] The Latin words, at a minimum, need only mean 'I became male.' *Masculus*, like English 'male' (and 'female'), can have a mechanical sense with reference to shape;[24] in English 'man' can also mean strong, as in a regular architectural and building metaphor, 'is it man enough to bear the weight?' Although all the heavier gender assumptions are undoubtedly present at some level for Perpetua, *masculus*, so interpreted, calls up a less drastic image than those containing the English vocabulary of sex-change. Could this be a case where a modern translator's metaphorical apparatus adds something to the original text? Our own literary mythology shows us Jo March, Nancy Blackett, and schoolgirl heroines wishing they were boys to avoid the constricting convention and dress required of girls; and our medical knowledge includes historical sex-changes. These images from our past and

---

[22] See Brent Shaw, 'The passion of Perpetua', *P&P*, 139 (May, 1983), pp. 1–46; Jantzen, *Power, Gender and Christian Mysticism*, pp. 49–51; Cameron, 'Virginity as metaphor', p. 194, and Luise Schottroff, *Lydia's Impatient Sisters* (London, 1995), p. 113 and n.

[23] Musurillo, *Acts*, p. 119; Clark, *Women*, p. 101; Jantzen, *Power, Gender and Christian Mysticism*, p. 50, where this phrase is attributed to Musurillo (sic).

[24] Lewis and Short, *A Latin Dictionary* (Oxford, 1879, and later edns), under *masculus*, II, A.

present may perhaps colour our reading of Perpetua's much older story.

* * *

In conclusion, we return to our original questions. As far as we can interpret the original texts, martyrs' stories show some familiar patriarchal assumptions of masculinity, power, and courage; but there is also more ambiguous language, cross-gender images, moribund male and female words, and also a model of maleness with its own limitations. Exactly how they worked in antiquity we cannot be sure, since we all (classicists included) see them through a filter of our own culture and time, with several layers of historical gendered language between us and the texts, some of it preserved in translations. Martyrs' stories are hard to isolate from other texts on this basis, but they seem originally to have presented a rather more mixed set of images than one might expect; while their English translation reflects older usage, with overtones we have now largely forgotten or rejected as exclusive.

So there may be no more chance to play the man. It is appropriate to end with another martyrological text with its Victorian translator. This is a sixth-century hymn for an anonymous martyr, translated by Lightfoot's older contemporary John Mason Neale. The Latin text, which includes the telling word *viriliter*, 'manfully,' runs as follows:

> poenas cucurrit fortiter
> et sustulit viriliter;
> pro te effundens sanguinem
> aeterna dona possidet,

and Neale elegantly turned it thus:

> For thee through many a woe he ran,
> In many a fight he played the man;
> For thee his blood he dared to pour.
> And thence hath joy for evermore.[25]

[25] The Latin text of the hymn 'Deus, tuorum militum' (with an edited translation) appears in *Hymns Ancient and Modern, Historical Edition* (London, 1909), no. 200, as well as in the Latin Breviary, where it is the regular hymn for the feast-day of a single martyr, 'commune unius martyris' (see, for instance, the Benedictine *Breviarium Monasticum, pro*

When the text was revised by the editors of the *New English Hymnal* in 1986, a new and less literal understanding prevailed:

> Right valiantly they kept the faith,
> And glorified thee unto death;
> For thee their blood they dared to pour,
> And thence have joy for evermore.[26]

The new inclusive version marks the discreet elimination of a piece of Christian metaphor and gender history.

La Sainte Union College of Higher Education, Southampton

omnibus sub regula S. Patris Benedicti militantibus, 2 vols [Bruges, 1930], 1, p. 28*). The translation quoted is from *The English Hymnal* (Oxford, 1906 and later edns), no. 181, 'O God, thy soldiers' crown and guard'.

[26] *The New English Hymnal* (Norwich, 1986), no. 218; the translation is attributed to 'J. M. Neale 1816–66 and editors', whose names are listed on p. vi of the introduction.

ADAM'S ENGENDERING: AUGUSTINE ON GENDER
AND CREATION

by GILLIAN CLARK

I N *Confessions* 13, Augustine discusses the right interpretation of the creation narrative in Genesis.[1] His exegesis is allegorical, relating spiritual truth to its expression in the physical world. This physical expression was needed because Adam fell:

> All things are beautiful because you make them, and you who made all things are inexpressibly more beautiful. If Adam had not fallen from you, there would not have come forth from his womb [*utero eius*] that salt sea-water the human race, profoundly curious, stormily swelling, unstable and in flux, and so there would have been no need for your agents, in many waters, to perform mystic actions and sayings in the corporeal and perceptible mode.[2]

But how can Adam have a womb? Especially, how can Adam have a womb in the context of the Fall, when the separation of male and female is established and the bearing of children in pain is the specifically female penalty? Translators elide or rework the image, but Augustine chooses words attentively, and he really does mean 'womb'. In some fourth-century authors *uterus* refers more generally to the abdominal cavity, but Augustine's usage can easily be documented.[3] It is also possible to trace some of the texts of Scripture,

---

[1] I am much indebted to Gerald Bonner for his prompt and helpful comments on this paper. I am of course responsible for errors or misinterpretations.

[2] *Confessions*, XIII, xx, 28: 'et pulchra sunt omnia faciente te, et ecce tu inenarrabiliter pulchrior, qui fecisti omnia. a quo si non esset lapsus Adam, non diffunderetur ex utero eius salsugo maris, genus humanum profunde curiosum et procellose tumidum et instabiliter fluidum, atque ita non opus esset ut in aquis multis corporaliter et sensibiliter operarentur dispensatores tui mystica facta et dicta.'

[3] CETEDOC makes it possible to trace Augustine's use of *uterus* and alternative words. For other senses of *uterus*, and other Latin words for 'womb', see J. N. Adams, *The Latin Sexual Vocabulary* (London, 1982), pp. 100–9, and J. André, *Le vocabulaire latin de l'anatomie* (Paris, 1991), pp. 188–93. I have yet to find a translation of *Conf.*, XIII, xx, 28 which has 'womb'.

and themes of the *Confessions*, which influenced his language here.[4] But that leaves an exegetical puzzle, of a kind which would have delighted Augustine because it combines a problem of textual interpretation with much wider implications: is it possible to imagine a human body which is not gendered; is the human soul also gendered; and how are human beings, male and female, made in the image of God who is not constrained by gender?

These are problems which concerned the late fourth as well as the late twentieth century, but there is an important difference of approach. Most modern exegetes of the creation narrative in Genesis start from the assumption that it includes different versions.[5] Patristic exegetes started from the assumption that Scripture is a unity and that seeming contradictions can always be explained so as to instruct us further. (This was not a Christian peculiarity. Rabbinic exegesis does the same, and late antique commentators on Plato also started from the assumption that everything he said is consistent: he never changed his mind or tried out an idea which he later abandoned, nor did Aristotle ever disagree with him.) So these patristic exegetes tried to integrate the various accounts, in Genesis 1–3, of the creation of human beings. In the Old Latin version of Genesis 1.26–8, so far as it can be reconstructed, Augustine read

God said, 'Let us make man in our image and likeness, and let [him] rule over the fish of the sea and the birds of the air and all cattle and all the earth and all creeping things which crawl upon the earth.' And God made man in the image of God: male and female he made them. And God blessed them, saying, 'Increase and multiply and fill the earth and rule over it.'[6]

[4] See on this aspect G. Clark, 'Adam's womb and the salty sea', *Proceedings of the Cambridge Philological Society*, 42 (1996), pp. 89–105.

[5] A good example is Phyllis A. Bird, 'Male and female he created them: Genesis 1.27b in the context of the priestly account of creation', *HThR*, 74 (1981), pp. 129–59.

[6] This is a close translation of the text probably read by Augustine in the *Vetus Latina*, as reconstructed by James O'Donnell, *Augustine: Confessions*, 3 vols (Oxford, 1992), 3, p. 345: 'et dixit deus, "faciamus hominem ad imaginem et similitudinem nostram, et dominetur piscium maris et volatilium caeli et omnium pecorum et omnis terrae et omnium repentium quae repunt super terram." et fecit deus hominem ad imaginem dei: masculum et feminam fecit eos. et benedixit eos deus dicens, "crescite et multiplicamini et inplete terram et dominamini eius."' In the translation [him] is bracketed because there is no pronoun in the Latin (or the Greek).

Exegetes had to integrate this account with Genesis 2.7, in which God makes man from the mud of the earth; with Genesis 2.18–25, in which God puts Adam to sleep and makes Eve from his rib; and with I Corinthians 11.7, in which Paul says that man is the image and glory of God, woman the glory of man. These passages presented them with several problems. It was understandable and satisfactory that woman was made from and for man, a secondary and subordinate creation. But Genesis 1.27 says that the original human creation was male and female. Is this a spiritual or a physical distinction? If it is a spiritual distinction, does it imply that femaleness is a characteristic of the soul as well as the body? Were human bodies made only as a consequence of sin, or were they made even before sin, because God knew they would be needed for reproduction? Does Paul mean that femaleness is not in the image of God, and is he talking about bodies or souls? The answers to these questions entailed different exegeses of the Genesis narratives. Perhaps Genesis 2.7–25 recapitulates in greater detail the creation reported in Genesis 1.27; or perhaps Genesis 1.27 refers to a spiritual creation and Genesis 2 to a subsequent physical creation, an actualization of that which in Genesis 1.27 is potential. Or the two halves of Genesis 1.27 may refer to spiritual creation in the image of God, followed by physical creation as male and female.[7]

Language is an important aspect of the problems. In Genesis 2 Adam recognizes Eve, saying that she shall be called woman because she was taken from man. This is the first use, in Greek and Latin texts, of the word which means 'man' in the sense of 'male human being' (*anêr, vir*), as distinct from the word which can mean 'human being' without distinction of gender (*anthrôpos, homo*). Greek and Latin do not easily reproduce the Hebrew word-play on *ish/ishah*, 'man/woman',[8] but there was a more general difficulty. The use of *anthrôpos* or *homo, anêr* or *vir*, ought to make it clear at what point in the creation narrative there is a male human being. Unfortunately, it does not, because both *anthrôpos* and *homo* are habitually used where only a male human being can be in question. Even when they refer to both sexes, they can, like

---

[7] Maryanne Cline Horowitz, 'The image of God in man – is woman excluded?', *HThR*, 72 (1979), pp. 175–206, discusses a range of patristic interpretations.
[8] Augustine comments on the difficulty in *De Genesi contra Manichaeos*, II, xiii, and Jerome discusses it in *Quaestiones Hebraicae in Genesim*, II, xxiii: he suggests *vir/virago* (a forced usage, because *virago* usually means a fierce warrior-woman), and remarks that the translator Symmachus used a Greek word *andris* to parallel *andros*, the genitive of *anêr*. See C. T. R. Hayward, *Jerome's Hebrew Questions on Genesis* (Oxford, 1995), pp. 32, 113.

the English generic use of 'man', make everyone forget about women. Thus, in the Genesis 2 account, *anêr* or *vir* is not used of Adam until Eve has been formed from him; but the continuity of the name Adam, and the need to provide Adam with a suitable helper, strongly suggest that the preceding *anthrôpos* or *homo* is a man. Latin does not have a definite article to give the game away (though it does have gendered pronouns), but in Greek, *anthrôpos* always has the masculine article unless there is – unusually – a specific reference to a woman. Was the masculine gender in the grammatical sense heard as the masculine gender in the social sense? This is a difficult question, especially for those whose native language does not have grammatical genders;[9] and it is made more difficult by the almost total absence of writing by women in the patristic, or indeed the classical, period. The answer may be that, like the generic use of 'man' before the 1960s, masculine genders were taken as the norm and went unnoticed unless someone wanted to make a point. But the creation narrative is just the context in which points were made, because its language was so closely studied and its implications were so important.

Augustine in Latin, and Basil in Greek, habitually use masculine genders, but both on occasion recognize the problems of masculine language. Basil cites Genesis 1.27, *kai epoiêsen ho theos ton anthrôpon. kat' eikona theou epoiêsen auton*, in its standard form, using the masculine article with *anthrôpos* and the masculine pronoun *auton*. He then comments:

Perhaps the woman may say here, 'What has this saying to do with me? At that time the man came into being. For it did not say *tên anthrôpon* [with the feminine article], or just *anthrôpon*, but by the addition of the article it indicated the male.'[10]

But, says Basil, Scripture immediately removes this possible misunderstanding by continuing 'male and female he created them'; women are therefore the spiritual equals of men, created together with men, and morally just as capable if not more so. Similarly Augustine, in *City of*

---

[9] See on this question George Lakoff, *Women, Fire and Dangerous Things: What Categories Reveal about the Mind* (Chicago, 1987).

[10] Basil, *De hominis structura*, I, xxii (also recognized as *Homily 10 on the Hexaemeron*), *PG* 30, col. 33. The work has sometimes been ascribed to his brother Gregory, and Migne therefore prints it also in *PG* 44, cols 257–98.

God, deals with an argument that because woman was made out of man, all human beings will be resurrected as men: this seemed to be supported by Paul's saying (Ephesians 4.13) that we shall attain perfect manhood. Augustine prefers the opinion that there will be both sexes in the Resurrection, though of course they will experience no sexual desire. Femaleness, he says, is not one of the defects which will be removed from the resurrected body, for God created woman as well as man, and the creation of woman out of man emphasises the unity between them and prophesies the relation of Christ and the Church. As for Paul, Augustine invokes Psalm 112.1, *beatus vir qui timet Dominum*, 'blessed is the man who fears the Lord'. This shows, he says, that Scripture can use *vir* to mean *homo*, since women who fear the Lord are also blessed.[11]

In both these examples, the use of masculine language had been taken to imply that women, *qua* women, are not God's creation. The fourth century – not just the late twentieth century – asked a range of questions about the gendering (verbal and physical) of the first human beings and its implication for those of the present day. These questions provide a context for the problem in *Confessions* 13, where Augustine presents readers with the further question of when, on any interpretation of the Genesis narrative, Adam could have a womb. One possibility is that Adam, in this passage, continues to be the name of humanity in general:[12] 'the *adam*' in the Hebrew text of Genesis 1.26, rather than the name of the male human being who appropriates it in Genesis 2.18–25. In Latin, conveniently, *de utero eius* could mean 'from her womb' as much as 'from his womb'. This interpretation seems to be supported by Augustine in *City of God*, when he argues from the wording of Genesis 5.2 ('he made them male and female and blessed them and called their name Adam') that whereas Eve was a personal name, Adam was the name of both. Adam, he says, is translated into Latin as *homo*.[13] Elsewhere in *City of God* he says that Eve herself was not created like Adam but came into being from Adam, so that the whole human race should come forth (*diffunderetur*, the verb also used

---

[11] *De civitate Dei* xxii, xviii.
[12] This is the explanation suggested by J. Gibb and W. Montgomery in their commentary, *The Confessions of Augustine* (Cambridge, 1908); they also observe that this passage is a remarkable instance of 'catachresis', the extended use of words. James O'Donnell, *Augustine*, 3, p. 388, gives some endorsement to their suggestion, but emphasises the oddity.
[13] *De civitate Dei*, XV, xvii.

in *Confessions* 13) from one human being.[14] If Adam is the representative and origin of the entire human race, and Adam is also Eve's name, then a reference to Adam's womb need cause no more than a temporary shock until the reader remembers. But does the reader remember? Augustine makes his point about the name Adam, in *City of God*, not because he is interested in the relation of Adam and Eve, but for a particular and somewhat eccentric exegetical purpose: as a contrast with the name Enos. This name, he says, according to Hebraists, is also translated *homo*, but *enos* cannot be used as the name of a woman. Enos was the son of Seth, which means 'resurrection', and in the Resurrection there will be no marriage.[15]

So perhaps Adam's womb continues to startle, or at least to demand that the reader reflects on Adam as representative human, and asks how a generic human can have a sex-specific organ. This problem connects with questions about the creation and embodiment of humanity which concerned Augustine at the time of writing *Confessions* 13. He had made two attempts on the exegesis of Genesis 1–3, and was either working on a third or engaging in thought which contributed to it.[16] He says in *Retractations* that he wrote *On Genesis against the Manichaeans* soon after his return from Italy to Africa (so in 388 or 389). Its two books deal with the Creation and the Fall, ending with the expulsion of Adam and Eve from Paradise. It was an allegorical interpretation, and after it he decided to try a historical interpretation: to judge from the sequence of books discussed in *Retractations*, this was about 393, quite soon after his ordination. The task proved to be very difficult for what he describes, probably rightly, as his inexperience (he had asked for a sabbatical to study Scripture before starting his pastoral work), and he abandoned it after one book. He rediscovered the manuscript only when working on the *Retractations*, in 427. It ended at 'and God said, Let us make man in our image and likeness'. Augustine decided to add two paragraphs offering a Trinitarian interpretation, but otherwise to let it stand as *Literal Interpretation of Genesis: an unfinished book*. He thought it was useful as evidence of his early attempts at understanding; but he recommended his later work, the twelve books of *Literal Interpretation of*

[14] *De civitate Dei* XII, xxii.

[15] For the importance of etymology in exegesis of this period, see Hayward, *Jerome's Hebrew Questions*, pp. 93–4.

[16] See further G. Bonner, 'Adam', in C. Mayer *et al.*, eds, *Augustinus-Lexikon*, 1 (Basle, 1994), pp. 63–87.

Genesis.[17] It is difficult to decide how this longer *Literal Interpretation* relates to the sustained allegorizing of *Confessions* 13, because there is no consensus on when either was written. Augustine tells us that *Literal Interpretation* was begun after *On the Trinity* (so after 404) but finished first; both took a long time to write. *Confessions* was begun in 397, but some scholars think that only books 1–9 were completed then, and that books 10–13 are a later addition, or that book 10 is one later instalment and books 11–13 another. Moreover, Augustine may well have worked on allegorical and literal interpretations together: his two earlier attempts do not imply a progression from the allegorical to the literal, and he does not, in any case, make a clear distinction between the two.[18]

Confessions 13, on any plausible dating between 397 and (say) 404, belongs to a time when Augustine was modifying his beliefs about human sexuality and embodiment, and therefore his exegesis. In *Genesis against the Manichaeans* 1.19.30 he argues that the command to increase and multiply, given before sin, may be understood spiritually, as the union of 'manly reason' (*virilis ratio*) with the active soul over which it rules, to bring forth spiritual children. Carnal fecundity comes after sin, and carnal generation is inferior to the life of resurrection. This position appears to underlie *Confessions* 13.28. If Adam had not fallen, the human race would not have come forth from his womb and there would have been no need for corporeal signs and sacraments: that is, there would be no material world of generation. *Confessions* 13.27 interprets the command to increase and multiply in terms of the fecundity of human reason. But Augustine later rejected this belief. His comment in *Retractations* on *Genesis against the Manichaeans* 1.19.30 is that unless he can be understood as saying something other than 'human beings would not have had human children if they had not sinned', he absolutely does not endorse it (*omnino non adprobo*).[19] The controversies of the late fourth and early fifth centuries, and his own pastoral work, had made him realize the danger of devaluing the physical world, including the relationship of man and woman in marriage, which God had created.[20] Book 3 of

[17] *Retractationes*, I, ix and I, xvii.
[18] See the introduction by Roland J. Teske to his translation, *St Augustine on Genesis*, Fathers of the Church, 44 (Washington, DC, 1991), esp. pp. 17, 27–31; and R. A. Markus, *Signs and Meanings: World and Text in Ancient Christianity* (Liverpool, 1996), ch. 1.
[19] *Retractationes*, I, ix, 2.
[20] These controversies have been extensively discussed: see especially Elizabeth A. Clark,

Literal Interpretation offers a different possibility. With Genesis 1.26–31 as his lemma, Augustine promises (3.19) a fuller discussion of the creation of humanity. (He provides this in book 6, where he argues that Genesis 2 is the unfolding in time of the timeless creation.) In book 3 he is concerned especially with the Trinitarian implications of the plural 'let us make man in our image', but at 3.21 he raises the question of why God assigns food to these as yet immortal human beings. This, Augustine says, is a problem. The command 'increase and multiply' may also seem to imply mortal bodies, for increase, it seems, can happen only by the intercourse of male and female – but perhaps it could happen in immortal bodies without the corruption of lust. This suggestion is repeated and expanded in book 9, which was written perhaps as early as 402.[21] Augustine suggests further that the genitals, like other members of the body, could have been under rational control, and in *City of God* he goes into greater detail on how physical reproduction could occur without lust or pain.[22] But uncorrupt physical reproduction does not solve the problem he started with: how could anyone claim that immortal bodies require food to sustain them?[23]

One suggestion is rejected in ch. 22: that Genesis 1.26 refers only to the creation of the *homo interior*, the 'inward man', and Genesis 2.7 refers to the later creation of bodies from mud. This cannot be right, Augustine says, because 'male and female he created them' must refer to bodies. He considers an argument that the human mind shows a male-female division between the contemplation of eternal truth and the administration of temporal things, the male guiding and the female obeying. This gendering of reason, the identification of maleness with reason and femaleness with perception or with desire, is found in

'Adam's only companion: Augustine and the early Christian debate on marriage', *Recherches Augustiniennes*, 21 (1986), pp. 139–62, and, for their effect on Augustine's exegesis, eadem, 'Heresy, asceticism, Adam and Eve: interpretations of Genesis 1–3 in the later Latin fathers', in her *Ascetic Piety and Women's Faith* (Lewiston, NY, 1986), pp. 353–86. See also David G. Hunter, 'Helvidius, Jovinian and the Virginity of Mary in late fourth-century Rome', *Journal of Early Christian Studies*, 1 (1993), pp. 47–71, with references to his earlier articles.

[21] For the dating, see Clark, 'Adam's only companion', pp. 370–1. She points to Augustine's comment in *De Genesi ad litteram*, IX, vii, 12 that he has 'recently' written *De bono nuptiarum* (401).

[22] *De Genesi ad litteram*, IX, x; *De civitate Dei* XIV, xxii–xxiii, on which see further G. Clark, 'The bright frontier of friendship: Augustine and the Christian body in late antiquity', in R. Mathisen and H. Sivan, eds, *Shifting Frontiers in Late Antiquity* (Aldershot, 1996), pp. 212–23.

[23] *De civitate Dei* XIII, xx, says that it was to prevent any distress from hunger and thirst.

Ambrose, who took it from Philo, and relates to cultural perceptions of femaleness as sensuous and irrational.[24] Augustine came close to it in *Genesis against the Manichaeans* (2.11.15): 'virile reason should make subject to itself its animal part, through the help of which it gives orders to the body, and the woman, whom the order of things makes subject to the man, was made as an example of this'. But, Augustine now says, it is male and female bodies which symbolize this division. The mind cannot do so, because it is in God's image in so far as it contemplates eternal truth, not in so far as it is concerned with temporal things, and both male and female were created in God's image; so a human being who is female in body may be renewed in mind, for there is neither male nor female in the image of God.[25] So, Augustine argues, 'male and female he created them' must mean bodies: this rules out the interpretation that only the spirit was then made, though it is only the spirit which is in God's image. He also argues that the singular *homo* in 'let us make man' is used 'because of the unity of the joining', *propter coniunctionis unitatem*; and that the creation of female from male, which will be spelled out later in Genesis, rules out the interpretation that both sexes were apparent in one human being, as sometimes occurs in androgynes.[26] This seems a less convincing argument: it could equally be argued that the male did not exist until the female had been separated out of the previous androgyne. But it does show that Augustine, in book 3 of *Literal Interpretation of Genesis*, thinks God made two human embodied beings, male and female.

Augustine's exegesis of Genesis changed, but does not appear at any time to leave the option of a womb for Adam. Perhaps, then, we should use an Augustinian tactic and move from literal to figurative explanation of a seeming contradiction. Augustine is notorious for his account of sin as a sexually transmitted disease, carried in the corrupted seed of Adam, in whom all future humanity was present at the time of sin. Late in his life, Julian of Eclanum accused him (or so Augustine says) of

---

[24] See further Horowitz, 'Image of God in man', pp. 191–2, 199–200.

[25] See further R. J. McGovan, 'Augustine and spiritual equality: the allegory of man and woman with regard to *imago Dei*', *Revue des études Augustiniennes*, 33 (1987), pp. 255–64, and the careful discussion by Kim Power, *Veiled Desire: Augustine's Writing on Women* (London, 1995), pp. 131–68, of the mistaken charge that Augustine said women are not in God's image.

[26] Philo might have been interpreted as thinking that the *anthrôpos* of Gen. 1.27 was androgyne: Horowitz, 'Image of God in man', p. 191.

putting all the blame for human inherited sin on the male: Augustine had said *omnes ille unus fuerunt*, 'everyone was that one [man]', but Augustine could not count, for Adam and Eve were two. Augustine defends his use of *ille unus* with an argument like that of *Literal Interpretation*: Adam and Eve were one flesh, and at the time when sin was committed, no descendant of Adam had yet been 'transfused by semination to the mother'.[27] When he wrote the *Confessions*, Augustine's theory of sin was not fully worked out, but he was already using the idea that all humanity was present in Adam,[28] and he always (so far as the evidence goes) shared the common Graeco-Roman assumption that it is the male seed which starts a new human life. Why, then, does the human race comes forth from Adam's womb, not from Adam's contaminated seed? Is Augustine deliberately conflating the genders?[29] If so, what is his purpose? Two linked possibilities come to mind. One is that mixing and confusion are characteristic of the fallen material world, the flux and turmoil which Augustine here associates with the human race; whereas clarity and definition come from God.[30] Another is that the human race had its origin in sexual division, which must be overcome in the return to unity. Adam's womb is a deliberately startling reminder of that division. Perhaps it may prompt a more general reflection. Augustine often unthinkingly reproduces the values and prejudices of his culture, late Graeco-Roman antiquity; but when he applies his intellect and his linguistic awareness to the language of Scripture, he is not constrained by ideologies of gender.

University of Liverpool

---

[27] *Opus imperfectum contra Iulianum*, II, clxxviii.

[28] Notably in *Ad Simplicianum*, 1 (written in 396, just before the *Confessions*): see further Paula Fredriksen, '*Excaecati occulta justitia Dei*: Augustine on Jews and Judaism', *Journal of Early Christian Studies*, 3 (1995), pp. 299–324, especially pp. 299–313.

[29] This is the suggestion of Margaret Miles, *Desire and Delight: a New Reading of Augustine's Confessions* (New York, 1992), pp. 114–15.

[30] On the importance of *modus*, 'limit' or 'defining form', for Augustine, see O'Donnell, *Augustine*, 2, pp. 47–8.

'FOR PAGANS LAUGH TO HEAR WOMEN TEACH': GENDER STEREOTYPES IN THE *DIDASCALIA APOSTOLORUM*[1]

by CHARLOTTE METHUEN

THE broader theme of gender and Christian religion presupposes three definitions: of Christianity, of religion, and of gender. Probably none of these is as simple as it might first appear, but that of gender is perhaps the most critical for our theme. Although there are still some who would use the terms 'gender' and 'sex' interchangeably, there is a growing tendency to recognize an important distinction between gender – that is, femininity and masculinity, regarded as largely socially constructed – and sex, the biological distinction between male and female human beings.[2] Gender is best considered as born out of interactions between men and women. This means that the gender roles which make up what we experience as masculinity and femininity cannot be defined by looking only at men or at women, although ideas about both can be gained from looking at one group or the other. That is why gender history is different from women's history, and that is why both women's history and gender history are essential enterprises. We need women's history because we need to know where women were as well as where they were not. We need to know what spaces women found for their self-expression, and

---

[1] Paraphrased from *Didascalia Apostolorum* [hereafter *Did. Ap.*], ch. 15, R. Hugh Connolly, *Didascalia Apostolorum* (Oxford, 1929), pp. 132–3. The standard English translations of the text are R. Hugh Connolly, *Didascalia Apostolorum* (Oxford, 1929) and Arthur Vööbus, *The Didascalia in Syriac* (Louvain, 1979), Corpus Scriptorum Christianorum Orientalium [hereafter CSCO]: text vols 401, 407, translation vols 402, 408. This article will hereafter refer to the translation by Vööbus.

[2] I recognize that there is a serious discussion about the extent to which both gender and sex are constructed, and also a historiographical debate about the ability of historians to analyse these constructs. A detailed discussion of these questions cannot be offered here, but see for instance Ursula King, 'Gender and the Study of Religion', in Ursula King, ed., *Religion and Gender* (Oxford, 1995), pp. 1–38, Lyndal Roper, *Oedipus and the Devil* (London, 1994), pp. 1–34 (discussing the early modern period, but nevertheless important for the wider historical debate), Natalie Zemon Davies, '"Women's history" in transition: the European case', and Joan Wallach Scott, 'Gender: a useful category of historical analysis', both in Joan Wallach Scott, ed., *Feminism and History* (Oxford, 1996), pp. 79–104 and 152–80 respectively.

how these traditions were transmitted or lost. But we must understand this against a background of what women and men themselves saw as possible openings and avenues and expressions of their femininity and masculinity respectively. The project of gender history, it seems, must seek to look away from leadership roles if it is to understand the way in which men and women interacted with, were defined by, and transcended the norms and ideas of the societies in which they lived. If such a project is so fraught with difficulties as to be virtually impossible even in studies of our own culture, then it most certainly cannot be fulfilled when writing the history of the early Church where our sources are not only restricted in number but come from an age which had radically different biological understandings from ours of what it meant to be male or female and when social structures such as marriage had a very different meaning.[3] Even if we can transcend our own expectations of what gender roles should look like, we are in many cases never going to get away from one man's idealization of his own congregation or church. If we must accept that it is necessary to apply what Elisabeth Schüssler-Fiorenza has called a 'hermeneutic of suspicion' to uncover even the existence of women, how much more difficult it will be to gain a proper understanding of the role of gender in the establishment of the structures and practices of the church, to understand the 'masculinizing' as well as the masculinity (or at least maleness) of those who have almost entirely led the Church after its earliest years. For this was a process; it is beginning to be more widely recognized that, as Margaret Miles concludes in her brief study of the establishment of the Church in Carthage,

> patriarchal order was not, as we may have come to think of it, inevitable, God-ordained, and scripturally based. It was the gradual implementation of women's subordination, in churches and in society, over women who understood Christian faith to render obsolete the gender stipulations of their culture, who experienced the freedom of Christ specifically as freedom from the cultivation of a lifestyle and spiritual life undefined by males.[4]

---

[3] For a discussion of the philosophical and medical understanding of sex and gender, see Thomas Laqueur, *Making Sex: Body and Gender from the Greeks to Freud* (Cambridge, MA, 1990); for the changing understanding of marriage, see John Boswell, *The Marriage of Likeness: Same Sex Unions in Pre-modern Europe* (London, 1995), pp. 3–52 and 162–198.

[4] Margaret R. Miles, 'Patriarchy as political theology: the establishment of North African

It is easy to look no further, to conclude with a heavy sigh that patriarchy simply won the day and to leave it at that. But I think it is necessary to look at this process more carefully. There is a danger here that we may be over-simplifying a very complex phenomenon, and doing so in a way which reflects our own understanding of conservative views of gender. Miles's interpretation of the writings of Tertullian, Cyprian, and Augustine suggests that in the ideology which triumphed in Christianity women's role is subordinate: men lead while women follow. Or, as Ulrike Wagener puts it in her analysis of the 'house of God' metaphor in I Timothy, women learn while men teach, and this polarity is parallel to the polarity of 'ruler-subject'.[5] Of course, this does on one level represent an accurate assessment of the process, or at least of part of it; but we also need to recognize that the early Church seems to have been confronted with – and to have held together – a variety of understandings of the roles of men and women. While it remains a scandal and a tragedy that, as one of my students recently put it, 'Die Herren haben sich die konservativsten [gesellschaftlichen Normen] ausgesucht', to see this process only in terms of this dichotomy of man/woman, male/female, ruler/subject, teacher/learner, simply to see men as winners and women as losers, may be historiographically somewhat short-sighted.

This becomes apparent upon a detailed examination of the *Didascalia Apostolorum*, a church order which was written in Syria some time in the third century. The *Didascalia* is almost certainly the product of a process of imposing patriarchal hierarchy very similar to those identified by Miles as taking place in Carthage and by Wagener as exemplified in the Pastoral Epistles. Arguably, it represents an attempt to introduce a monarchical episcopate into a particular church or group of churches, a process which involves the exclusion of women (and particularly widows) from leadership functions within the congregation.[6] However, the *Didascalia* retains women in the church hierarchy as deaconesses who exercise a (restricted) authority.

Christianity', in Leroy S. Rouner, ed., *Civil Religion and Political Theology* (Notre Dame, IL, 1986), pp. 169–86, here p. 184.

[5] Ulrike Wagener, *Die Ordnung des 'Hauses Gottes'. Der Ort von Frauen in der Ekklesiologie und Ethik der Pastoralbriefe* (Tübingen, 1994), pp. 92–104, also p. 237.

[6] Charlotte Methuen, 'Widows, bishops and the struggle for authority in the *Didascalia Apostolorum*', *JEH*, 46 (1995), pp. 197–213. For the role of the bishop, see Georg Schöllgen, 'Die Anfänge der Professionalisierung des Klerus und das kirchliche Amt in der Syrischen Didaskalie' (University of Bonn, Habilitation thesis, 1991).

Deaconesses anoint women at baptism; they are responsible for teaching women after baptism; and they are needed 'for the houses of the pagans where there are believing women'.[7] At the same time, the majority of men are also explicitly excluded from teaching and liturgical functions in the church. In the church hierarchy, the congregation is told,

> the bishop sits for you in the place of God Almighty. But the deacon stands in the place of Christ, and you should love him. The deaconess, however, shall be honoured by you in the place of the Holy Spirit. But the presbyters shall be to you in the likeness of the apostles, and the (orphans and) widows shall be reckoned by you in the likeness of the altar.[8]

This metaphor renders the widows static and reduces their consequence, while assigning to the deaconesses a place in the Godhead;[9] but it places both deaconesses and widows above the men and women of the congregation. Women's authority is certainly being restricted here, but what results is not a simple pattern in which men are rulers over subordinate women. Instead, the church portrayed by the *Didascalia* is a hierarchical organization in which one man stands at the pinnacle of a hierarchy in which some women at least have a distinct place. This paper will seek to demonstrate that this organization is shaped by the interaction between a particular theology and a clash of gender roles.

Both theologically and practically, the *Didascalia* focuses not so much on strategies by which men may control women as on the way in which one man, the bishop, may control the members of his church. Correct – that is, non-heretical – Christianity is witnessed by the Christian's lifestyle, and correct church order centres upon the definition of who is within the fold and who is outside; the bishop's main task is to control the borders of his congregation. His control of

---

[7] For the functions of deaconesses, see *Did. Ap.*, Vööbus, 408, pp. 156–8.

[8] *Did. Ap.*, Vööbus, 402, p. 100. In view of the undoubted importance of the widows in his congregation and the author's later use of the altar metaphor to restrict the movement of the widows, I think it is correct to view the orphans as of minor importance here, included only to emphasise the picture of widows as the receivers of charity, especially since the older recension speaks only of widows (Vööbus, 402, p. 48*).

[9] See Methuen, 'Widows, bishops and the struggle for authority', p. 202, and, for the widow as altar in other early Christian texts, Carolyn Osiek, 'The widow as altar: the rise and fall of a symbol', *Second Century*, 3 (1983), pp. 159–69.

the actions and the behaviour of the members of the church extends far beyond the walls of the church and into their daily lives. The author of the *Didascalia* encourages the bishop to control where his church members spend their time, and what they do there; to control with whom they consort, with whom they bathe, and with whom they sleep. This author is no promoter of sexual asceticism, for although he is adamantly opposed to 'fornication' in this case the term seems to mean adultery. He is keen that the children of Christians, and especially their sons, should be married off as soon as possible to avoid the temptation of such relationships.[10] He restricts sexual intercourse to marriage; but within marriage he seems to instruct that husbands and wives should be sleeping with one another. A man should 'please [his wife] with honour'; a woman is to 'be ready for [her husband's] service'.[11] The author's primary concern here seems to be to control the sexual expression of members of his congregation by restricting it to marriage; but it is notable that although his view of marriage is Pauline, and thus distinctly hierarchical,[12] he seeks to exert the same control over both men and women.

The author's apparent emphasis on the man as the initiator of sexual intercourse and his insistence that the man is the head of the woman and thus of the marriage does not, however, mean that he views

---

[10] *Did. Ap.*, Vööbus, 408, p. 203 and see also p. 160, recommending that the fathers of sons should adopt girl orphans as suitable future wives for their sons. The insistence that men should marry as early as possible probably means that the terms 'husband' and 'man' cannot really be distinguished, although this is a difficult conclusion since the terms 'wife' and 'widow' – and hence 'wife' and 'woman' – clearly can be.

[11] *Did. Ap.*, Vööbus, 402, pp. 12 and 20. Here the author of the *Didascalia* seems to be opposing the ascetic trend which is generally associated with Syriac Christianity. See Robert Murray, *Symbols of Church and Kingdom: Early Syriac Tradition* (Cambridge, 1975), pp. 11–15, and, for a detailed discussion of asceticism in the Syrian Church, Arthur Vööbus, *A History of Asceticism in the Syrian Orient*, 2 vols, CSCO 184, 197 (Louvain, 1958–60).

[12] The author repeats – and clearly accepts – Paul's statement that the man is the head of the woman, so that although he instructs husbands that they are to care for their wives (*Did. Ap.*, Vööbus, 402, p. 12), he reminds wives that they are subject to their husbands, 'because the head of the woman is the man and the head of the man that walks in the way of righteousness is Christ' (p. 20). In the marital relationship it is, theoretically at least, the man who takes the initiative: 'A husband shall not condemn or despise his wife, and shall not be lifted up against her, but let him be merciful and let his hand be open to give. And let him court his wife alone, and please her with honour' (p. 12). Wives are particularly enjoined not to quarrel, 'especially with your husband, lest your husband, if he is a heathen, because of you be offended and blaspheme against God . . . Or again, if your husband is a believer, that he be constrained as one who knows the scriptures, and shall say to you the saying from Wisdom: "It is better to sit upon a corner of the roof than to dwell with a talkative and contentious woman within the house"' (pp. 26–7).

women as more likely to be tempted to adultery or flirtation than men. He urges both women and men to be aware of the dangers of dressing so as to attract the opposite sex; and warns both women and men that they themselves are guilty if a person not their spouse finds them attractive.[13] There are distinctions here: women, and not men, are warned that 'when you have sinned with one you become slack and go also to others', and a woman, but not a man, is guilty of the soul of her sexual partner if they actually commit adultery together.[14] However, men's behaviour is of equal concern to the author; indeed, it seems that it is really the adulterous behaviour of husbands and the danger that men's dress might attract women other than their wives which are the focus of his attention.

The instructions to wives do include instructions on dress: women are to be veiled in the street and should walk with downcast looks,[15] 'and you shall not be plaited with the dresses of harlotry, nor clothe yourself in the garment of harlotry nor be shod with shoes so that you resemble those who are this way'.[16] Thus a woman's dress and behaviour are to be interpreted as an expression of her sexuality. To some extent, a man's dress and hairstyle have the same function, and so men too should be careful how they dress and adorn themselves:

you shall not grow the hair upon your head but cut it off; and you shall not comb and adorn it nor perfume it, so that you do not bring upon you those women who are out to capture or are captured by lust. You also shall not clothe yourself in a beautiful garment and also not be shod upon your feet with shoes whose workmanship is of the lust of foolishness. You also shall not put rings of gold work upon your fingers – because all of these things are the devices of harlotry and everything that you do apart from nature. For to you, a believing man of God, it is not lawful to grow the hair of your head and to comb it and wipe it, for this is a pleasure of lust. And you shall not arrange and adorn it, and you shall not fashion it so that it shall be beautiful.[17]

[13] *Did. Ap.*, Vööbus, 402, pp. 13 (concerning husbands) and 24 (concerning wives).
[14] Ibid., p. 24.
[15] Ibid., p. 26
[16] Ibid., p. 24.
[17] Ibid., pp. 13–14.

Like that of a woman, a man's apparel may be a cause of sexual temptation. Male clothing seems, however, to be indicative of status to a much greater extent than that of women, so that this instruction to men means also that they should not try to achieve status in the world. To pluck the beard or to 'alter the form of your face and change it beyond God's creation' is to 'please men' and to try to impress;[18] instead men should 'in the humility of neglect pretend to be poor before men'.[19] Clothes for men are outward signs not only of the sexuality which both men and women must control, but also of the status from which they, as Christians, are supposed to hold themselves distant.[20]

Although the author of the *Didascalia* does not explicitly address the question of household arrangements, what he seems envisage is a household in which women are to lead a secluded but busy life at home, where a woman's 'hand shall be for the wool and [her] mind upon the spindle'.[21] In contrast most men have work and leisure to take them outside the house. Where possible, women and men are to be kept separate; they should bathe separately and should sit separately in church.[22] The author seems here to have in mind the Greek pattern of household structure, in which houses had separate men's and women's quarters, with little communication between them.[23] He seems too to be driven by two somewhat divergent impulses: Christianity should

---

[18] Ibid., p. 14.

[19] Ibid., p. 13.

[20] Miles has suggested that such concern about clothing reveals 'a disagreement over the issue of acculturation versus separation', with the supporters of a separatist theology promoting 'a distinguishing drabness of dress': Miles, 'Patriarchy as political theology', p. 174. Although the *Didascalia* is unusual in discussing men's clothing and appearance in such detail, there is no doubt that its author is promoting a separatist theology.

[21] *Did. Ap.*, Vööbus, 402, p. 21.

[22] Ibid., pp. 16 (men bathing), 26 (women bathing); *Did. Ap.*, Vööbus, 408, pp. 131-3 (seating in the church).

[23] See Wendy Cotter, 'Women's authority roles in Paul's churches: countercultural or conventional?', *Novum Testamentum*, 36 (1994), pp. 350-72, esp. 358-66, for the architecture of the women's quarters in classical Greek houses, Susan Walker, 'Women and housing in classical Greece: the archaeological evidence', in Averil Cameron and Amélie Kuhrt, eds, *Images of Women in Antiquity* (London and Canberra, 1983), pp. 81-91. Cotter recommends that caution be exercised in describing the role of women in 'Graeco-Roman' culture, since there were important differences in the role of women in Greek and Roman households. Roman women were accorded a good deal more freedom than Greek women in interacting with men in household and society. Roman houses were not divided into men's quarters and women's quarters, while Greek houses were; Roman women accompanied their husbands to private functions, while the Greek women were expected to remain secluded in the house and dinner parties were for men only.

not call women and men to an ascetic lifestyle and they should, therefore, live and sleep together, but the fact that women and men are sexually susceptible to each other means that they must be kept apart. This latter concern probably accounts for his insistence that the Church needs deaconesses to visit Christian – and potentially Christian – women, especially in pagan households. The author's concern to keep women segregated from men also necessitates the appointment of women to a particular role in the congregation's hierarchy.

Nevertheless, the *Didascalia*'s author explicitly seeks to exclude women from participation in the main teaching function of the Church and he emphasises that they may not baptize.[24] One of the reasons he gives for this is that it goes against 'the pagan' view of women's proper place in society. Women should not teach because non-Christians will not believe what women say:

> Indeed, when the gentiles, those who are being instructed, hear the word of God spoken not firmly, as it ought to be, unto edification of life everlasting – and especially because it is spoken to them by a woman – about how our Lord clothed himself in the body, and about the passion of Christ, they will deride and mock, instead of praising the word of doctrine.[25]

Similarly, as has already been noted, wives of pagan husbands are instructed not to argue with their husbands because this will give the husband the wrong idea about Christianity. If Christianity is to appeal to a particular pagan community, as the *Didascalia*'s author is keen that it should, it must be preached in such a way as not to contradict the social mores of that community, and that means the silencing of women except when speaking to women.

However, the introduction of the monarchical episcopate, as required by the author's theology, results not only in the silencing of women. Socially, men have more freedom, but this too is to be curtailed:

> You shall not roam and go idly about in the streets and see the empty spectacle of those who behave themselves evilly; but persevere in your craft and your work, look for and be willing to

---

[24] *Did. Ap.*, Vööbus, 408, pp. 144–5, 151.
[25] Ibid., pp. 144–5.

do those things that are pleasing to God. You should also meditate continually upon the utterings of the Lord. However, if you are rich and have no need for a craft to live by, you shall not roam and go about vainly, but be ever constant in coming near to the faithful and to them that are likeminded with you, meditating and learning with them through the living words. And if not, sit at home and read the Law and the Book of Kings and the Prophets and the Gospel [which is] the fulfilment of these.[26]

Rather than studying pagan philosophy or reading stories, men should read only the Bible, which contains writings enough to satisfy any wish for narratives, philosophy, or songs.[27] Studying and following the teachings of wisdom will 'keep [men] from the strange and adulterous woman whose words are seducing',[28] that is, both actual adultery with a human woman and metaphysical adultery by succumbing to the teachings of other groups, whether heretical Christian or heathen. The people of God, and particularly the men, are to avoid any 'assembly of the gentiles', and especially the theatre, 'the assembly of error and destruction'.[29] It is only by attending church, remaining within the 'assembly of the church' and pursuing religion as his true work that a man can avoid other seductions and attain salvation and eternal life.[30]

Although these instructions that men should stay at home have no parallel in the instructions for wives they exactly match the instructions that the *Didascalia* issues for devout widows:

let a widow know that she is the altar of God. . . . The altar of God indeed never wanders or runs about anywhere, but is fixed in one place. A widow must not therefore wander or run about among the houses; . . . A widow who wishes to please God sits at home and reflects on the Lord day and night, and without

---

[26] *Did. Ap.*, Vööbus, 402, p. 14.
[27] Ibid., pp. 14–15. The expectation seems to be that only men will be literate, and that not all of them will be (the bishop should, if possible, be a man of learning: Ibid., p. 44). There is no suggestion that women are literate, although it is of course possible that those who had been teaching were.
[28] Ibid., p. 17.
[29] *Did. Ap.*, Vööbus, 408, pp. 137–8.
[30] *Did. Ap.*, Vööbus, 402, pp. 137–9. These latter instructions are addressed to 'the people' but the references to handicrafts and work suggest that they are actually addressed to the men of the Church.

ceasing at all times offers intercession and praise purely before the Lord.[31]

Like men, widows are to remain at home and contemplate God; although men may read the Bible, while widows should pray, the effect is the same. Given the author's view of the place of wives, it is difficult not to conclude that if widows here are being urged to behave as women should, then lay men are too. Widows and men outside the Church hierarchy are removed from circulation; like wives, they are to stay at home.

A similar parallel may be observed in the restrictions of the teaching role which exclude not only women but also lay men:

It is not right for widows to teach nor for a layman. About punishment and the rest, and about the kingdom of the name of Christ, and about His dispensation, neither a widow nor a layman ought to speak. Indeed, when they speak without the knowledge of doctrine, they bring blasphemy against the word. For our Lord likened the word of his Gospel to mustard. But mustard if it is not prepared with skill, is bitter and sharp to those who use it. On this account the Lord said in the Gospel, to widows and to all the laity: 'Do not throw your pearls before swine, lest they trample upon them and turn against you and rend you.'[32]

The prohibition of teaching is effectively a prohibition for all except those who hold an office in the Church hierarchy. Widows are doubly disadvantaged, for they are disqualified automatically by their sex. Apostolic tradition as well as common practice requires this ban for, as the author of the *Didascalia* puts it (claiming to speak for the apostles):

He, the Lord God, Jesus Christ, our teacher, sent us the Twelve to instruct the people and the nations. And there were with us women disciples, Mary Magdalene, and Mary the daughter of James, and the other Mary, and he did not send [them] to instruct the people with us. If it were required, indeed, that

---

[31] *Did. Ap.*, Vööbus, 408, pp. 146, 148.
[32] *Did. Ap.*, Vööbus, 402, pp. 144–5.

women should teach, our teacher Himself would have commanded these to give instruction with us.[33]

This theological ban can be relaxed for the deaconess, since the
author's understanding of gender roles requires women to minister to
women. A similar ban on men's teaching would clearly be impossible
since men do hold the teaching functions in the Church. However,
only men who have been appointed to do so should actually teach; the
ban on teaching excludes most men as well as (technically) all women
from the Church's teaching functions. Thus, the introduction of a
hierarchically organized leadership does not only affect the role of
women; it sets laymen under control and restricts their movements.
While these men will continue to exercise authority within their own
households, in the Church as a whole their role is not significantly
different from that of the women.

Perhaps it is no coincidence that although the elect Church of God
is 'a royal priesthood, a holy assembly, a people for inheritance', it is
also the 'bride adorned for the Lord God'.[34] Although this metaphor is
not developed in the *Didascalia*, it is one of the dominant ecclesiological metaphors in Syriac Christianity, and in the *Acts of Thomas* serves
as a liberating motif for women. A woman who is the Bride of Christ
is, to a certain extent at least, freed from her attachment to an earthly
bridegroom or husband and can abandon her household to lead her
own life.[35] The author of the *Didascalia* sees this differently. For him
the role of the Bride of Christ is that of the dutiful wife, a role
associated with seclusion and restriction. As the Bride of Christ, the
Church as a whole should shut itself away; the place of the wife
becomes the place of all Christian women and lay men. And just as a
household is represented in public by the father of the household, so
too only the bishop can properly represent the Church in the public
sphere.[36]

---

[33] *Did. Ap.*, Vööbus, 408, p. 145. A similar argument is offered against baptizing by
women: if women could lawfully baptize, Jesus would have been baptized by his mother
(p. 151).

[34] *Did. Ap.*, Vööbus, 402, p. 99.

[35] For the Bride of Christ as an ecclesiological motif, see Murray, *Symbols of Church and
Kingdom*, pp. 131-3. For this motif as a liberation for women, see Methuen, 'Widows,
bishops and the struggle for authority', pp. 208-9.

[36] The bishop also takes over perhaps the only feminine authority role recognized by the
author, for he is not only father but also mother of the congregation: *Did. Ap.*, Vööbus, 402,
p. 104, and see Schöllgen, 'Die Anfänge der Professionalisierung des Klerus', pp. 261-2.

The *Didascalia*'s definition of the authority and role of the bishop and the consequent exclusion of almost all women and most men from the hierarchy of the Church seems to take place as a response to an interplay of theological and cultural concerns. The author's cultural understanding, apparently important to the group to which he wishes to appeal, that proper behaviour for women means staying secluded at home and not teaching or baptizing or playing a leadership role in the church community, is reinforced and extended to men by his interpretation of both biblical texts and the theological motif of the Church as the Bride of Christ.[37] The *Didascalia*'s exclusion of women does not, however, seem to be simply a corollary of the Church's 'going public', as, for instance, Karen Jo Torjesen argues in the case of Tertullian:

> In Tertullian's new vision of the church as a political body, the church's ministries had become legal rights to be exercised only by full members of the political body. Since according to the public–versus–private gender ideology, women could not hold office, participate in debate, or exercise any public functions, neither could they do any of these things in the body politic of the church. The right to minister was a right restricted not to the clergy but to citizens who were members of the body politic; and women could not be members of the body politic. Tertullian justified his prohibitions against women's leadership by labelling these functions 'manly'.[38]

This is certainly one factor which motivated the *Didascalia*'s author, in that his concern that the Church should not lose face before the pagans is one of his reasons for banning the teaching of women. But his central concern seems to be not that the Church should act as a proper public institution, but that it should represent the right kind of household with the right kind of social roles.

---

[37] The author may be seeking to counteract a social structure in which women had more freedom. Susan Ashbrook Harvey believes that 'Syrian society before its Christianisation provided for its upper-class women a relative degree of freedom and respect, resulting from and dependent upon the advantages of an affluent society.' See Susan Ashbrook Harvey, 'Women in early Syrian Christianity', in Cameron and Kuhrt, *Images of Women*, pp. 288–98, especially pp. 293–4.

[38] Karen Jo Torjesen, *When Women were Priests: Women's Leadership in the Church and the Scandal of their Subordination in the Rise of Christianity* (San Francisco, 1995), pp. 164–5.

The *Didascalia* is not a church order which restricts only women. The movements of widows and men are to be restricted; the teaching of widows and laymen is frowned upon. It follows that it is the freedom not only of widows but also of the laymen of the congregation which the author is trying to curtail. All the people of the Church are urged to bow to the authority of the bishop and deacons, to accept them as their teachers, to appeal to them in matters of faith, and to allow them to decide disputes. If the dichotomy of ruler/subordinate, teacher/learner, male/female is to be imposed here, it is only possible to conclude that the great majority of the men of the Church are being urged to behave as women, in a manner consonant to the Church's status as the Bride of Christ. That this holds only to a degree can, however, be seen from the distinctions between the roles of men and women, husbands and wives. Men and women – husbands, wives and widows – are being shown to particular places in the Church; a Church which is ruled by men, certainly, but one in which all the members are subject to the control of the bishop and to the restrictions imposed by a theology which sees the Church as the Bride of Christ in a social context which keeps brides as much as possible secluded within the household.

Ruhr-Universität Bochum

REGENDERING RADEGUND? FORTUNATUS, BAUDONIVIA AND THE PROBLEM OF FEMALE SANCTITY IN MEROVINGIAN GAUL[1]

by SIMON COATES

I N the prologue of her *De vita sancti Radegundis*, Baudonivia, an inhabitant of Radegund's community of the Holy Cross at Poitiers, adopted a phrase from Venantius Fortunatus' *Vita Hilarii* to express her unworthiness for the task: 'I can as easily touch heaven with my fingers as perform the task you have imposed on me.'[2] Baudonivia, the first female hagiographer in Merovingian Gaul, was here drawing from the *Life* of a male saint to introduce her work. She was thus, like all hagiographers, not alone in her task. This was doubly the case, since immediately prior to the composition of her own work Venantius Fortunatus had himself composed a *Vita* of the saint.[3] Radegund was thus a focus of both male and female interest. This paper will examine the two *Lives* from a gendered perspective, exploring the manner in which gender, a constructed rather than a physiological form of sexual differentiation, may illumine Radegund's sanctity. It will also explore the extent to which the texts reveal

[1] An early version of this paper was presented to the Denys Hay Seminar at Edinburgh University in May 1996. Its final version was completed during a period of research funded by the British Academy. I wish to thank Marilyn Dunn, Judith George, Julia Smith, Janet Nelson, and Conrad Leyser for comments on previous drafts. I am grateful to the President and Members of the Ecclesiastical History Society for a bursary to attend the Canterbury conference.
[2] Baudonivia, *De vita sanctae Radegundis liber II* [hereafter *VR2*], ed. B. Krusch, *MGH SRM*, II (Hanover, 1888), p. 377. The *Vita* was composed during the years 609–14. Translation in *Sainted Women of the Dark Ages*, ed. and trans. Jo Ann McNamara and John E. Halborg with E. Gordon Whatley (Durham, NC, 1992), p. 86. The literature on Radegund is extensive: see R. Aigrain, *Sainte Radegonde vers 522–587*, 3rd edn (Paris, 1924); Brian Brennan, 'St Radegund and the early development of her cult at Poitiers', *Journal of Religious History*, 13 (1985), pp. 340–54; Christina Papa, 'Radegunde e Balthilde: modele di santita regia feminile nel regno merovingio', *Benedictina*, 36 (1989), pp. 13–33; Sabine Gäbe, 'Radegundis: sancta regina, ancilla. Zum Heiligkeitsideal der Ragundisviten von Fortunat und Baudonivia', *Francia*, 16/1 (1989), pp. 1–30; Joan M. Petersen, 'The spirituality and miracles of St Radegunde', in Judith Loades, ed., *Monastic Studies: The Continuity of Tradition* (Bangor, 1990), pp. 34–47; and studies in *Études mérovingiennes, Actes des Journées de Poitiers, 1–3 Mai 1952* (Paris, 1953).
[3] Venantius Fortunatus, *De vita sanctae Radegundis Liber I* [hereafter *VR1*], ed. B. Krusch, *MGH SRM*, II, pp. 364–77; trans. *Sainted Women of the Dark Ages*, pp. 70–86.

different traditions about the saint, and the underlying unity which they also possessed.

Early medieval Francia has provided fruitful soil for a rich crop of studies of female saints and authors. Alongside the studies of Wemple and McNamara there now stands a body of work by British and European female historians identifying women as authors of anonymous works, emphasising their political role and, more problematically, seeking to establish the femininity of a historical narrative.[4] Gender, however, allows males to enter the fold more easily. By admitting the social into the sexual, it describes the behaviour expected of men and women and the behaviour not expected by them. It also links the feminine to the masculine, recognizing that it is impossible to view one without the other.[5] It is clear that Radegund particularly lends herself to this form of analysis, since she was a saint viewed through male and female eyes. Presumably, it would be thought, a male would bring a different perspective to the manner in which he viewed a saint than a female would. This is the view of much of the extant work on the two *Lives* of Radegund: let us consider it further.

* * *

The models upon which Fortunatus could draw for the composition of his *Life* of Radegund were the *Lives* which had shaped the composition

---

[4] Suzanne Fonay Wemple, *Women in Frankish Society: Marriage and the Cloister, 500–900* (Philadelphia, PA, 1981); eadem, 'Female spirituality and mysticism in Frankish monasticism: Radegund, Balthild and Aldegund', in John A. Nichols and Lilian T. Shank, eds, *Medieval Religious Women*, vol. 2, *Peace Weavers* (Kalamazoo, MI, 1987), pp. 39–54; Jo Ann McNamara, 'The need to give: suffering and female sanctity in the Middle Ages', in Renate Blumenfeld-Kosinski and Timea Szell, eds, *Images of Sainthood in Medieval Europe* (Ithaca, NY, 1991), pp. 199–221; eadem, 'A legacy of miracles: hagiography and nunneries in Merovingian Gaul', in Julius Kirschner and Suzanne Wemple, eds, *Women of the Medieval World: Essays in Honour of John H. Mundy* (Oxford, 1985), pp. 36–52; eadem, 'The ordeal of community: hagiography and discipline in Merovingian convents', *Vox Benedictina*, 3–4 (1986), pp. 293–326; Janet L. Nelson, 'Perceptions du pouvoir chez les historiennes du Haut Moyen Age', in M. Rouche, ed., *La Femme au Moyen Age* (Maubeuge, 1990), pp. 75–85; eadem, 'Women and the word in the earlier Middle Ages', *SCH*, 27 (1991), pp. 53–78; Rosamond McKitterick, 'Women and literacy in the Middle Ages', in her *Books, Scribes and Learning in the Frankish Kingdoms Sixth to Ninth Centuries* (Aldershot, 1994), ch. XIII; Julia M. H. Smith, 'The problem of female sanctity in Carolingian Europe c.780–920', *P&P* 146 (Jan., 1995), pp. 1–37; Pauline Stafford, *Queens, Concubines and Dowagers: The King's Wife in the Early Middle Ages* (Athens, GA, 1983). A survey of recent literature on women may be found in Elisabeth Van Houts, 'The state of research: women in medieval history and literature', *JMedH*, 20 (1994), pp. 277–92.

[5] J. W. Scott, 'Gender: a useful category of historical analysis', *AHR*, 91 (1986), pp. 1053–75; Allen J. Frantzen, 'When women aren't enough', *Speculum*, 68 (1993), pp. 445–71.

of hagiography in late antiquity: the writings of Jerome, Sulpicius Severus, and Athanasius. Within this general corpus of writings lay a separate thread of writing concerning women, most prominently those women such as Perpetua who had suffered agonizing deaths as martyrs.[6] In the fourth century, the focus shifted, and *Lives* of pious women were written emphasising their holy lives rather than their gruesome deaths. In the West, Jerome's *Life* of Paula followed this tradition. The chief focus of these *Vitae* was on virginity and chastity. This emphasis upon chaste female spirituality locked women away in bodies without histories; entombed in ascetic cells they were largely immune to outer event and physiological change.[7]

It is commonly assumed that the ideal of the virago, the asexual saint whose greatest achievement was to imitate male virtues, lay at the heart of Fortunatus' narrative.[8] In order to understand the manner in which the ideal of the virago took shape in late antiquity and the early medieval West, the sexual attitudes of the Fathers themselves must be considered before turning to the text of Fortunatus' *Life*.

The early Fathers divided the world into the spiritual and the carnal.[9] Cyprian recognized that in this framework the body could be drawn either way.[10] Similarly, according to Ambrose and Jerome, the body could be a 'temple of God' or a 'brothel'.[11] On some occasions the

---

[6] Martin Heinzelmann, 'Neue Aspeckte der biographischen Literatur in der lateinischen Welt (1.-6 Jh.)', *Francia*, 1 (1973), pp. 27–44; René Aigrain, *L'hagiographie: ses sources, ses méthodes, son histoire* (Paris, 1953). On Perpetua see Brent D. Shaw, 'The Passion of Perpetua', *P&P* 139 (May, 1993), pp. 3–45.

[7] Jerome, *Epitaphion Sanctae Paulae: Sancti Eusebii Hieronymi Epistulae*, ed. Isidor Hillberg, 3 vols, Corpus Scriptorum Ecclesiasticorum Latinorum, 54–6 (Vienna, 1910–18), 2, pp. 306–51. On late antique virginity see Peter Brown, *The Body and Society: Men, Women and Sexual Renunciation in Early Christianity* (New York, 1988); Susanna Elm, '*Virgins of God': The Making of Asceticism in Late Antiquity* (Oxford, 1994); Averil Cameron, 'Virginity as metaphor: women and the rhetoric of early Christianity', in A. Cameron, ed., *History as Text: The Writing of Ancient History* (London, 1989), pp. 181–205; John Bugge, *Virginitas: An Essay on the History of a Medieval Ideal* (The Hague, 1975).

[8] Wemple, *Women in Frankish Society*, pp. 183–5; eadem, 'Female spirituality and mysticism', pp. 43–5. For the *virago* see Elena Giannarelli, *La tipologia femminile nella biographia e nell'autobiografia cristiana del IVo secolo*, Studi Storici, 127 (Rome, 1980), pp. 18–25.

[9] Joyce E. Salisbury, *Church Fathers, Independent Virgins* (London, 1991), provides a useful survey. Further material in eadem, 'The Latin doctors of the Church on sexuality', *JMedH*, 12 (1986), pp. 279–89.

[10] Cyprian, *The Dress of Virgins*, in *Treatises*, trans. R. J. Deferrari (New York, 1958), p. 34.

[11] Ambrose, *Concerning Virgins*, in *A Select Library of Nicene and Post-Nicene Fathers, Second Series*, ed. P. Schaff and H. Wace, 14 vols (Oxford and New York, 1890–1900), 10, p. 376; Jerome, *To Eustochium*, ibid., 6, pp. 24, 31.

Fathers could explicitly link males with the spiritual and females with the carnal. In his *Etymologiae*, Isidore of Seville described women according to their sexuality: 'femina' had the Greek force of fire, concupiscence was passionate and women inhabited a carnal realm. Furthermore, the menstrual blood of women could cause wine to turn sour, plants to parch, trees to lose fruit, iron to be corroded, and dogs to become rabid.[12]

Alongside this explicit linking of women with sexual sin, the Fathers constructed an ideal of virginity based upon the cultivation of masculine virtues. In rejecting their sexuality women transcended their gender and gained the souls of men. Thus in Jerome's *Commentarium in epistolam ad ephesios libri 3* he remarked that 'as long as woman is for birth and children, she is different from men as body is from soul. But if she wishes to serve Christ more than the world, then she will cease to be a woman and will be called man.'[13] Similarly, Ambrose commented, 'she who believes progresses to complete manhood . . . she then does without worldly name, gender of body, youthful seductiveness and garrulousness of old age'.[14] In contrast to the withering and decay found in Isidore's *Etymologiae*, Ambrose's *De institutione virginitate* viewed virginity as a closed garden, characterized by growth and reproduction marked by an abundance of lilies.[15]

Turning to Fortunatus' *Life*, it would appear that the preface belongs firmly in this tradition. The eulogistic tone explicitly links Radegund to a glorious company of pious virgins.

> Christ makes them strong who were born weak so that, when those who appeared to be imbeciles are crowned with their merits by Him who made them, they garner praise for their Creator who hid heavenly treasure in earthen vessels. For Christ the king dwells with his riches in their bowels.[16]

Ascetic virtue is celebrated throughout Fortunatus' *Vita*. As a child, Radegund conversed about the desire to be a martyr and, along with

---

[12] Isidore of Seville, *Etimologias*, xi.1, 24, 141, ed. J. Oroz Reta and M. Marcos Casquero, 2 vols (Madrid, 1982), 1, pp. 37–43.

[13] Jerome, *Commentarium in epistolam ad ephesios libri 3*, PL 26, col. 533.

[14] Ambrose, *Expositio evangeliis secundum Lucam*, PL 15, col. 1844.

[15] Ambrose, *De institutione virginitate*, PL 16, cols 335, 384.

[16] *VR1*, Praefatio; trans. *Sainted Women of the Dark Ages*, p. 70.

Samuel, a youthful cleric, would carry a cross and sing psalms.[17] After her marriage she would rise from her bed to 'prostrate herself under a hair cloak by the privy'[18] so that the cold pierced her body. As a result the king claimed he had married a *monacha* rather than a queen. She cultivated the friendship of ascetic nuns such as Pia, who would send her a hair cloth which she wore under her royal garments.[19] After renouncing the court to live the ascetic life more fully she ate nothing but vegetables, drank only honeyed water, and would not touch wine.[20] At Poitiers, she lay on a bed of ashes covered by a hair cloth, binding her neck and arms with iron circlets so tightly that they cut her flesh. She was also known to heat a brass plate up in her cell and press it on to her body, roasting her flesh.[21] Wemple and Gäbe argue that these ascetic practices are at the centre of Fortunatus' *Life*, analysing Radegund from an interior perspective, moving her as quickly as possible away from the public world of the court and placing her in the secluded, sacred, world of the community.[22] Fortunatus' *Life* also might be considered to have conformed to an essentially male ideal of female sanctity through its emphasis upon Radegund's likeness to St Martin, whose cult by the sixth century had developed to the extent that he was viewed as the apostle of Gaul.

Radegund's devotion to the Martinian cult began as soon as she entered the religious life. Martin may appear an awkward hagiographical mould into which Radegund could be poured. He was, after all, a former soldier and a bishop, not a queen. For Fortunatus, however, Martin epitomized the manner in which a saint should live. Renouncing arms and fornication, he had turned his back on societal norms.[23] Radegund followed him both literally and metaphorically. Fleeing from the world of the court, 'her fortunate sails approached Tours', where she 'conducted herself around the courts, shrines and basilica of

[17] *VR1*, c. 2, pp. 365–6.
[18] *VR1*, c.5, pp. 366–7; trans. *Sainted Women of the Dark Ages*, p. 73.
[19] *VR1*, c.6, p. 367.
[20] Ibid., c.15, p. 369.
[21] Ibid., c.22, 25, 26, pp. 371–3.
[22] Wemple, *Women in Frankish Society*, pp. 183–5; eadem, 'Female spirituality and mysticism', pp. 43–5; Gäbe, 'Radegundis', pp. 1–30.
[23] Sulpicius Severus, *Vita Sancti Martini*, ed. J. Fontaine, *Vie de Saint Martin*, SC, 133–5 (Paris, 1967–9); Clare Stancliffe, *Saint Martin and His Hagiographer* (Oxford, 1983). For the development of the Martinian cult in fifth- and sixth-century Gaul see Raymond Van Dam, *Saints and their Miracles in Late Antique Gaul* (Princeton, 1993); idem, 'Images of Saint Martin in late Roman and early Merovingian Gaul', *Viator*, 19 (1988), pp. 1–27.

Saint Martin weeping unchecked tears'.[24] Fortunatus again likened her specifically to Martin when he described a miracle whereby she restored a fellow member of her community to life.[25] This Martinian model had also formulated further male perceptions of Radegund's sanctity. Writing to support the saint after she had founded her convent in Poitiers, seven bishops in Gregory of Tours' *Libri historiarum* explicitly connected her with the Martinian cult, 'In that you came to us from well-nigh that same region whence Saint Martin came, for so we learn, it is no marvel if in your work you seem to mirror him whom we believe to have been your guide.'[26]

It would thus seem that Fortunatus' status as a male cleric consciously conditioned the manner in which he viewed the sanctity of a female saint. Along with his fellow males he constructed an image of Radegund which placed together pieces of an older, male jigsaw. This phenomenon has parallels elsewhere in other near-contemporary texts composed in Ireland. The *Codex Salamanticensis* arguably contains the oldest materials associated with the *Life* of Mo Ninne and her foundation of Cell Schléibe, Killeevy in County Armagh. In the Salamanca *Life*, Mo Ninne is described as possessing a masculine soul, sowing the female earth with masculine seeds. Similarly Brigit is described as acting 'uiriliter' in the hymn *Audite uirginis laudes*.[27]

With the image of the virago in mind, let us now turn to Baudonivia's *Life* of Radegund to consider how she, as a female, may have approached her subject from the inside, rendering Radegund an active peace weaver and mother figure.

* * *

Baudonivia begins her work with the claim that she will 'not repeat what the apostolic Bishop Fortunatus recorded'.[28] Wemple and others

---

[24] *VR1*, c.14, p. 369; trans. *Sainted Women of the Dark Ages*, p. 76.

[25] *VR1*, c.37, p. 376; Sulpicius Severus, *Vita Sancti Martini*, c.7, SC, 133, pp. 266–9.

[26] Gregory of Tours, *Libri Historiarum* [hereafter *LH*], ed. B. Krusch and W. Levison, MGH SRM, I.i (Hanover, 1951), IX.39, pp. 393–6.

[27] *Vita sanctorum Hiberniae ex codice olim Salamanticensi nunc Bruxellensi*, ed. W. W. Heist (Brussels, 1965), pp. 83–95, at p. 89. The *Life* was probably composed in the latter half of the seventh century but drew on lost materials of earlier origin. On its dating see Richard Sharpe, *Medieval Irish Saints' Lives: An Introduction to the Vitae Sanctorum Hiberniae* (Oxford, 1991), pp. 243–6; Mario Esposito, 'The sources for Conchubranus' Life of St Monenna', in Mario Esposito, *Irish Books and Learning in Mediaeval Europe*, ed. M. Lapidge (London, 1990), pp. 73–8. On the Brigit hymn see *Liber hymnorum*, ed. J. H. Bernard and R. Atkinson, 2 vols, Henry Bradshaw Society, 13–14 (London, 1897–8), 2, p. 15.

[28] *VR2*, Praefatio, MGH SRM II, p. 378; trans. *Sainted Women of the Dark Ages*, p. 86.

have therefore stressed that Baudonivia's chief aim was to overturn the ideal of the virago espoused by Fortunatus, and to put in its place an active, self-consciously female, image of sanctity. Since Baudonivia was a woman it is assumed that she was more concerned with Radegund as an outgoing and emotional woman than as a withdrawn and ascetic former queen. Baudonivia's *Life* shows Radegund actively engaged in acts of charity and spiritual motherhood, energetically nurturing the sisters. The opening chapter shows her to be 'energetic in redeeming captives and profusely generous with alms to the needy'.[29] She preached on the psalms and diligently read the Fathers. Similarly, the *Life* conveys a consistent interest in direct speech and the female voice, to the extent that she preached unceasingly.[30] Furthermore, in the tenth chapter she is praised as a peace maker, concerned for the welfare of the *patria*. She prayed diligently for kings, teaching her flock to do likewise in an attempt to halt the long civil war between Chramn and Childebert. She prayed for the community's safety and exercised a strong, female authority, inflicting punishment on a former servant girl for occupying her throne. The girl caught fire, smoke rising from her, and the flames could only be quenched by Radegund's intervention.[31]

Discussion of the femininity of Baudonivia's narrative has also centred around further material which is absent from Fortunatus' *Life*, namely Radegund's concern to collect relics, and particularly her initiation of a mission to procure the True Cross from the imperial court. In chapter thirteen, Radegund is informed in a vision that relics which she had collected and subsequently lost were to be miraculously found at Saix. The following chapter records her interest in the eastern martyr Mamas and the despatching of the physician, Reovalis, to the patriarch at Jerusalem in search of the saint's relics. Reovalis successfully procured Mamas' little finger, but this serves merely as the prelude to Radegund's single-minded mission to acquire the wood of the Cross at Constantinople.[32]

Baudonivia interprets Radegund's mission by comparing her with the original discoverer of the Cross, St Helena. In acting like Helena, Radegund brought salvation to Gaul and spread abroad the fame of her

---

[29] *VR2*, c.1, pp. 379–80; trans. *Sainted Women of the Dark Ages*, p. 87.
[30] *VR2*, cc.8–10, 17, 19, pp. 382–5, 389–90, 391–2.
[31] Ibid., cc.10–12, pp. 384–6.
[32] Ibid., cc.13–14, 16–17, pp. 386–90.

own community: 'What Helena did in oriental lands, Radegund the blessed did in Gaul.'[33] The arrival of the Cross was marked by dissension and conflict when Bishop Maroveus refused to install the relic. Moreira and Fontaine have argued that this was central to Baudonivia's portrait of Radegund as a zealous guardian of the relic, who was able to quell the factional infighting and turn the arrival of the Cross into a triumph for both her community and, on a wider scale, her *patria*.[34]

The fullest account of Maroveus' hostility to the arrival of the relic is found in Gregory of Tours' *Libri historiarum*.[35] The relic's arrival threatened to alter the balance of spiritual power in Poitiers, undermining Maroveus' status. Radegund therefore appealed to her nephew, King Sigibert, begging him to order a bishop to deposit the relic in Poitiers. A ceremony was duly performed by Bishop Eufronius of Tours, and the relic installed in defiance of Maroveus' authority. Baudonivia interprets these events by once again using the model of Helena, and comparing the initial rejection of the Cross to the manner in which the Jews of Jerusalem rejected Helena's efforts. The story of Radegund's triumph over her enemies also effectively re-enacts the Passion in Gaul as rejection and scorn are turned into glorious victory. In contrast, Fortunatus wrote closer to the climactic political events that marked the arrival of the Cross and therefore avoided all discussion of these contentious issues, concentrating upon Radegund's interior asceticism rather than her status as a national saint.

* * *

Radegund's sanctity has thus been explained by an interpretative framework that is concerned with politics and the sexual status of her hagiographers. The problem, however, does not end here. It is compounded by the work of a male historian, Jean Leclercq, whose analysis basically reverses the interpretation offered by the work of females.[36] For Leclercq, Fortunatus was unable fully to understand the

---

[33] *VR2*, c.16, pp. 387–9; trans. *Sainted Women of the Dark Ages*, p. 97; Isobel Moreira, 'Provisatrix optima: St Radegund of Poitiers' relic petitions to the east', *JMedH*, 19 (1993), pp. 300–3. On Helena herself see Jan Willem Drijvers, *Helena Augusta: The Mother of Constantine the Great and the Legend of her Finding of the True Cross* (Leiden, 1995).

[34] Fontaine, 'Hagiographie et politique de Sulpice Sévère à Venance Fortunat', *Revue de l'histoire de l'eglise de France*, 62 (1976), pp. 113–40; Moreira, 'Provisatrix optima', *passim*.

[35] *LH*, IX.40, pp. 396–8.

[36] Jean Leclercq, 'La Sainte Radegonde de Venance Fortunat et celle de Baudovinie: essai

interior spirituality of Radegund and instead concentrated on her exterior attributes, emphasising her charity, her concern to clean the latrines and chop wood, and her ability to heal lepers and the sick.[37] In contrast, Baudonivia as a member of the community which Radegund had founded concentrated on her diligence in practising the night-office; the manner in which she prayed diligently all night, preaching in her sleep; and how she summoned Eodegunde, the portress of the community, by shouting 'Alleluia instead of her name'.[38] Closer inspection, however, reveals marked similarities between the images of sanctity created by Baudonivia and Fortunatus.

* * *

Further analysis of the two *Lives* of Radegund reveals that it is difficult to conceive of a strict dichotomy between male and female perceptions of the saint. Baudonivia was equally aware of the power of the Martinian cult and anxious to portray Radegund in a Martinian mould. This is evident from the second chapter of her *Life* where Radegund is shown actively destroying a pagan Frankish temple by fire in a manner which clearly recalls Martin's own campaigns against idolatry in the vicinity of Tours.[39] The rebuking of the housemaid Vinoberga, who had been presumptuous enough to sit in Radegund's throne, bears marked similarities to the account in Sulpicius Severus' *Dialogues* of how Martin caused the imperial throne to catch fire and burn the emperor Valentinian.[40] Similarly, there are other instances where Baudonivia draws upon earlier hagiographical works describing male saints in order to construct her image of Radegund's sanctity. In addition to quoting Fortunatus' own *Vita Hilarii*, and thereby directly relating Radegund's sanctity to that of Poitiers' most notable male saint, she quoted almost verbatim from the *Life* of Caesarius of Arles in describing the manner in which, due to the saint's death, her tireless

d'hagiographie comparée', in A. A. R. Bastiaensen, A. Hilhorst, and C. H. Kneepkens, eds, *Fructus Centesimus. Mélanges offerts à Gerard J. M. Bartelink à l'occasion de son soixante-cinquième anniversaire* (Steenbrugge, 1989), pp. 207–16.

[37] *VR1*, cc.17–19, 23–4, 27–30, 34–5, 37–8, pp. 370–1, 372, 373–4, 375, 376.

[38] *VR2*, cc.8–9, 14, 17–19, pp. 367–8, 369, 370–1.

[39] Ibid., c.2, p. 380; Sulpicius Severus, *Vita sancti Martini*, c.14, *SC*, 133, pp. 282–5. Moreira, '*Provisatrix optima*', p. 303 wrongly asserts that this incident occurs in Fortunatus' *Life*.

[40] *VR2*, c.12, pp. 385–6; Sulpicius Severus, *Dialogi*, II.5, ed. C. Halm, Corpus Scriptorum Ecclesiasticorum Latinorum, 1 (Vienna, 1866), pp. 186–7.

preaching voice had ceased its discourse.[41] This has the effect not only of constructing Radegund in accordance with a male model, but also of reinforcing the community's own debt to Caesarius expressed in its adoption of his *Regula virginum* to govern its internal affairs at the time of the conflict with Maroveus.[42] Baudonivia was not alone in her focus on Radegund as a new Helena, since this motif had appeared in an earlier hagiographical work composed by a male, Gregory of Tours' *Liber in gloria martyrum*. There, in a concise account of Radegund's acquisition of the True Cross, she is named as 'comparable to Helena in both merit and faith'.[43]

The idea that Baudonivia consciously sought to overturn the ideal of the virago and replace it with a picture of Radegund as a powerful *domina* and peace maker fails to understand the diverse manner in which the early Fathers discussed the relationship between virginity and asceticism by assuming that they promulgated a monolithic spiritual ethic which was decidedly misogynist in tone. The diversity of their language and belief thus needs to be considered.

Asceticism is 'in essence a statement about the relationship between the body, the soul, and the human potential for salvation'.[44] It cannot be understood in isolation from the manner in which the power of God is conceived to be mediated on earth. According to Origen all created beings were connected to their creator through their soul, which occupied a higher position than the created matter of the body. The soul, however, was enmeshed in the body, and the individual's free will could cause moral decline. Nevertheless, due to such individual free will the soul could rise above the limits of the body and progress towards God. In Origen's thought the imitation of Christ through asceticism therefore transcended the boundaries imposed on the body by gender.[45] As a result, communities of men and women in Asia Minor and Egypt practised ascetic perfection in common, living as angels on earth.

Writing after the Council of Nicaea, however, Athanasius posited that all creation was chaotic and unstable. This view of creation meant that he perceived the soul as well as the body to be marked by

---

[41] *VR2*, c.19, pp. 390–1; *Vitae Caesarii episcopi Arelatensis libri duo* [hereafter *Vitae Caesarii*], II.32, ed. B. Krusch, *MGH SRM*, III (Hanover, 1896), pp. 495–6.

[42] *LH*, IX.40, pp. 396–8.

[43] Gregory of Tours, *Liber in Gloria Martyrum*, c.5, *MGH SRM*, I.i, pp. 489–92.

[44] Elm, 'Virgins of God', p. 373.

[45] Ibid., pp. 367–78; Brown, *Body and Society*, p. 171.

weakness, lowering the individual's potential to possess free will. As a result, a different conception of asceticism came to develop, which involved the transformation of the body rather than its transcendence. In this form of practice the soul was not separate from the body, and could not transcend it. This brought with it a renewed emphasis upon gender and the constraints imposed by the body. In this ascetic model, which was also evident in Ambrose's thought, the clear division between the creator and creation meant that the pursuit of virginity, imitating the unpolluted body of Christ, was the means by which the Church could be constructed on earth.[46] Sexual differentiation, however, remained.

As the body and its gender began to be seen less as a passing stage and ultimately as more important in the cultivation of ascetic virtues, this led to a concern for the greater separation of male and female ascetics. Whereas the asceticism expounded by Origen was concerned with the means by which men and women may transcend the limitations of their humanity, the asceticism of the later Roman Empire came to symbolize the manner in which, by embracing the religious life, men and women could surpass human weakness. They would only be transformed eschatologically, never immediately, because whilst Christians lived in the world the *civitas mundi* and the *civitas diaboli* co-existed and would only be separated at the Last Judgement. Due to the fracture of their will caused by the Fall, men and women remained prone to lustfulness and bodily desire. As a result they were to be institutionally separated for the avoidance of temptation.[47]

The institutionalization of female ascetic communities in Gaul found expression in the *Regula virginum* of Caesarius of Arles.[48] This Rule created a strictly regulated cloister prohibiting nuns from leaving the community for any reason.[49] The Rule, which was much

---

[46] Elm, 'Virgins of God', pp. 378-83; Brown, *Body and Society*, pp. 341-65; V. Harrison, 'Male and female in Cappadocian theology', *JThS*, 41 (1990), pp. 441-71.

[47] Elm, 'Virgins of God', pp. 381-5.

[48] This was the first Rule written specifically for a women's monastery in East and West, see W. E. Klingshirn, 'Caesarius's monastery for women in Arles and the composition and function of the "Vita Caesarii"', *Revue Bénédictine*, 100 (1990), pp. 441-81; idem, *Caesarius of Arles: The Making of a Christian Community in Late Antique Gaul* (Cambridge, 1994), pp. 104-10, 117-24; D. Hochstetler, 'The meaning of monastic cloister for women according to Caesarius of Arles', in T. F. X. Noble and J. J. Contreni, eds, *Religion, Culture and Society in the Early Middle Ages* (Kalamazoo, MI, 1987), pp. 27-40.

[49] Caesarius of Arles, *Regula Virginum*, ed. J. Courreau and A. de Vogüé, *Césaire d'Arles. Oeuvres Monastiques I*, SC, 345 (Paris, 1988), pp. 35-273, at pp. 71-81.

influenced by Augustine, emphasised charity and the common ownership of property. Furthermore, the entire daily routine of the community was designed to encourage prayerful devotion, spiritual reading, work, and fasting.[50] Prayer included the obligation to pray not only for the community but also for the populace as a whole.[51] It thus seems clear, therefore, that Baudonivia's emphasis upon Radegund's constant praying for the well-being of the *patria* was related less to any specific femininity in her text and more to her knowledge of the manner in which Radegund's community had adopted a monastic rule for women written by a man and designed to create a model of perfect Christian living. An awareness of the community's adoption of strict enclosure is evident from Baudonivia's account of Radegund's death where 'since it was ordained that no living person should issue out of the gates of the monastery, the whole flock stood on the walls'[52] to watch the burial.

The manner in which Caesarius' *Regula virginum* had emphasised charity and service is manifest in both Fortunatus' and Baudonivia's *Lives*. Baudonivia praised Radegund's ability to feed pilgrims 'from her own table' and to wash and cleanse the sick, as well as her almsgiving.[53] Similarly, in Fortunatus' *Life*, she washed the putrid flesh of beggars, 'busy as a new Martha', whilst at Saix.[54] This concern did not cease even after she secluded herself more fully at Poitiers, since she would diligently scrub vegetables and clean the community's kitchens.[55]

Furthermore, both texts are marked by a concern for Radegund's ability to transform the limitations of her body. In Fortunatus' *Life* this is expressed in terms of her active commitment to fasting, clinging to Christ and satiating her hunger with tears. 'She had contempt for the food of the belly, for Christ was her only nourishment.'[56] Enclosed in her cell, 'she ate no bread, except on Sundays',[57] sleeping on a hair cloth. Baudonivia similarly wrote of her bodily austerities, describing

---

[50] Ibid., cc.5–6, 9, 18–22, 30–1, 71, pp. 182–7, 186–9, 192–9, 208–11, 268–9.

[51] *Vita Caesarii* I.28, p. 467. 'The man of God formulated the idea by divine inspiration from the ever-reigning Lord that the church of Arles should be adorned and the city protected not only with countless troops of clergy but also by choirs of virgins': trans. W. E. Klingshirn, *Caesarius of Arles: Life, Testament, Letters* (Liverpool, 1994), p. 22.

[52] *VR2*, c.24, p. 393; trans. *Sainted Women of the Dark Ages*, p. 103.

[53] *VR2*, cc.8, 17, pp. 382–3, 389–90.

[54] *VR1*, c.17, p. 370.

[55] Ibid., c.24, p. 372.

[56] Ibid., c.6, p. 367; trans. *Sainted Women of the Dark Ages*, p. 73.

[57] *VR1*, c.22, pp. 371–2; trans. *Sainted Women of the Dark Ages*, p. 79.

how she did not cover her arms but wore only fingerless gloves, sackcloth, and ashes.[58] The emphasis on the body is again apparent in Baudonivia's description of the sisters' lament for her passing: 'Indeed it is painful to remember what she was like. For we humbled ones long for her teaching, the form and face, person, knowledge, piety, goodness and sweetness that she had in herself from the Lord that made her special among her people.'[59] Similarly, her 'holy life was as sweet and pure as her face'[60] and, in recounting Gregory of Tours' memory of her death, Baudonivia records how, as he approached the body, 'he saw an angel's face in human form, a face refulgent with roses and lilies'.[61]

* * *

Radegund shows that the problem of female sanctity in Merovingian Gaul cannot be explained by rigid gender stereotyping. Instead it must be approached as a religious problem, since both Fortunatus and Baudonivia wrote primarily for the spiritual edification of Radegund's own community. Instead of constructing an image of female sanctity based upon the transcending of gender, Fortunatus sought to show how, by embracing the ascetic life, Radegund was able to transcend the limitations imposed on her by her body and live a life detached from worldly concerns. The attempt to establish the femininity of Baudonivia's narrative fails to understand her own debt to patristic accounts of female asceticism and her use of male, as well as female, models of sanctity. Furthermore, it fails to understand the extent to which Radegund's own community at Poitiers was shaped by the *Regula virginum* of Caesarius of Arles as it sought to reflect Caesarius' criteria for the construction of a Christian community. To both Fortunatus and Baudonivia, Radegund remained physically a woman. However, their texts sought to replace the aristocratic social ideal of gender which viewed women as devoted wives and child bearers with a religious ideal based upon a rejection of sexuality and the desire to appear as angels. This amounted to an attempt to construct a third gender, that of the clergy. Baudonivia's expression of her own humility in her preface was a recognition of Radegund's own sanctity. She was aware that whilst fingers could not touch the sky, fingers from the sky

---

[58] *VR2*, c.8, pp. 382–3.
[59] *VR2*, c.19, pp. 390–1; trans. *Sainted Women of the Dark Ages*, p. 101.
[60] *VR2*, c.20, pp. 391–2; trans. *Sainted Women of the Dark Ages*, p. 101.
[61] *VR2*, c.23, p. 392, citing Gregory of Tours, *Liber in gloria confessorum*, 104.

could touch earth as divine grace transformed a captive queen into a holy saint. In both *Lives*, the message which is conveyed is therefore characterized as much by its unity as its diversity. Radegund's status as a religious woman who had left the world to become a nun was intended to edify and encourage the sisters she had nurtured. The image of her sanctity, created by Baudonivia and Fortunatus, was ultimately aimed at promoting her ability to reflect the values of the heavenly kingdom where 'there is neither Jew nor Greek, slave nor free, male nor female, for you are all one in Christ Jesus'.[62]

King's College, University of London

---

[62] Gal. 3.28.

GENDER AND IDEOLOGY IN THE EARLY MIDDLE AGES

by JULIA M. H. SMITH

O N 29 June 824, a woman named Dhuoda went to Aachen to be married in the imperial palace.[1] She herself tells us about the wedding, yet it is characteristic of the Carolingian age that we know far more of the groom, Bernard of Septimania, than of the bride. His career and connections can be pieced together from a wide range of sources, but she is only known from the manual of moral and spiritual advice which she composed in 841–3 for her absent fifteen-year-old son William. Bernard's life can be reconstructed as a coherent narrative, but Dhuoda's only emerges from a few tattered snapshots, without even a family album to contain them.[2] Famous as she is as the only lay woman among the tiny handful of women writers known to us by name from the early Middle Ages, Dhuoda's isolation must be stressed.[3] Not merely her personal sense of loneliness, powerfully conveyed, nor even the difficulty of placing her within any secure literary context, but also her historiographical isolation mark her out, for we know all too little about the women of the early medieval aristocracy to which Dhuoda belonged. We can neither sketch with any precision the lifestyle of Dhuoda's peer group, nor assess whether she is typical of it – or exceptional. The married women of the Carolingian aristocracy remain largely occluded from our sight, chronicled only in disjunct fragments of evidence which do not permit of any extended or systematic analysis. When we can find them, aristocratic women more often appear enveloped within the bonds of

---

[1] Dhuoda, *Liber Manualis*, praefatio. Pierre Riché, ed., *Manuel pour mon fils, SC*, 225b (Paris, 1991), p. 84 (also available in English translation by Carol Neel under the title *Handbook for William: a Carolingian Noblewoman's Counsel for her Son* [Lincoln, NE, 1991]). In preparing this paper I am very grateful to David Ganz and Mayke de Jong for sage advice, and to Kate Cooper, Ann Matter, Jinty Nelson, and Tom Noble who have all shared unpublished work with me.

[2] Carolyn G. Heilbrun, *Writing a Woman's Life* (London, 1989). On Bernard, see Joachim Wollasch, 'Eine adlige Familie des frühen Mittelalters, ihr Selbstverständnis und ihre Wirklichkeit', *Archiv für Kulturgeschichte*, 39 (1957), pp. 150–88; Janet L. Nelson, *Charles the Bald* (London, 1992), pp. 80–1, 88–91, 102–3, 120–1, 139–41.

[3] Peter Dronke, *Women Writers of the Middle Ages: a Critical Study of the Texts from Perpetua to Marguerite Porete* (Cambridge 1984), pp. 36–54.

family and kinship than independent individuals within political contexts. But there remains the unsettling image of the young Dhuoda, briefly translated out of her familial and domestic setting into the shadowy corridors of imperial power: and the scene prompts questions about the place of wives and marriage within the Carolingian polity.

Historians are by now sensitive to the elusiveness of women within the political record, the strategies needed to locate them and the dangers of reverting to over-reliance on notable or notorious women at the expense of their more ordinary and typical sisters.[4] For no part of the early Middle Ages is this more true than in the Carolingian period. Whether the contrast is drawn with Anglo-Saxon England, Merovingian Gaul, or the Ottonian empire, the Carolingian centuries present themselves as a world of overwhelmingly male power politics, whether secular or ecclesiastical.[5] We do not hear of powerful abbesses who counselled bishops and guided kings or of charismatic, wonderworking women ascetics such as those recorded in Bede or Gregory of Tours. Nor do we find kings' wives who determinedly controlled the succession to the throne, or widowed queens who ruled on behalf of child kings as we do in tenth-century England and Germany. Far less can be said about aristocratic women's access to landed property in Carolingian Francia than it can in Anglo-Saxon England, and the political significance of the landed endowments of communities of Carolingian women religious seems negligible in comparison with those of the Ottonian empire. However, if we are to give the women of the Carolingian aristocracy their due, we must look for them not only in the *res gestae* of kings and courtiers but also in the ideological constructs which inform those sources. Rather than asking what role

---

[4] Cf. the comments of C. Dauphin, A. Farge, G. Fraisse, *et al.*, 'Culture et pouvoir des femmes: essai d'historiographie', *Annales*, 41 (1986), pp. 271–93; Amanda Vickery, 'Golden age to separate spheres? A review of the categories and chronology of English women's history', *HistJ*, 36 (1993), pp. 383–414; Pauline Stafford, 'Women and the Norman Conquest', *TRHS*, 6th ser., 4 (1995), pp. 221–50; Hans-Werner Goetz, *Frauen im frühen Mittelalter* (Cologne, 1995), pp. 13–30.

[5] Of the growing literature on women and gender in the early Middle Ages, the following are fruitful avenues into the more specialist literature: Nancy Partner, *Studying Medieval Women: Sex, Gender, Feminism* (Cambridge, MA, 1993); Janet L. Nelson, 'Family, gender and sexuality in the Middle Ages', in Michael Bentley, ed., *Companion to Historiography* (London, 1997), pp. 153–76; Werner Affeldt and Annette Kuhn, eds, *Interdisziplinare Studien zur Geschichte der Frauen im Frühmittelalter* (Düsseldorf, 1986); Werner Affeldt, ed., *Frauen in Spätantike und Frühmittelalter: Lebensbedingungen – Lebensnormen – Lebensformen* (Sigmaringen, 1990).

aristocratic wives played in Carolingian society and finding only fragments and frustration as the answer, it is far more fruitful to turn to the place of women within the Carolingian rhetoric of power and within discourses about the right ordering of society. We need instead to ask how women's role was conceptualized and related to wider issues of appropriate social organization. In this vein of enquiry, distinctions between men and women interlink with ideas about social order to form a gendered discourse about the proper location of authority and about women's place in the characteristically Carolingian search for peace, concord, and order.

Carolingian ideas about gender and about moral or political ideology intersected and combined most fruitfully around the subject of wives. As I shall show, there developed a coherent strand of thinking about wives' moral obligations and social importance. It is, to be sure, only one thread out of many in the early medieval web of ideas about the relationship between men and women, but nevertheless one whose implications were far-reaching. To the extent that the place of women within medieval political thinking has been examined at all, analysis has hitherto concentrated upon the scholastic ideas of the thirteenth century, when the recovery of the Aristotelian corpus transformed both the premises and methods of debate.[6] To shift focus to the early Middle Ages is to enter uncharted waters, and thereby to emphasise the range and complexity of medieval ideas about wives, gender, and social order.

We must start by noting the intellectual resources available to Carolingian writers who contemplated the contribution of married women to Christian society. From the classical and patristic heritage of late antiquity, early medieval writers had access to a huge range of texts, ideas, and assumptions. Whether concerning legal or moral relationships between men and women, ideas of sexuality and self-discipline, the theological distinction between man and woman, or classical scientific treatment of sexual difference, that heritage was vast, and neither coherent nor consistent. It embraced many genres, including biblical commentary, works of didactic and pastoral exhortation, and scientific treatises, each of which incorporated a distinctive discourse on

---

[6] Jean Bethke Elshtain, *Public Man, Private Woman: Women in Social and Political Thought* (Princeton, NJ, 1981); D. H. Coole, *Women in Political Theory: From Ancient Misogyny to Contemporary Feminism*, 2nd edn (New York, 1993); James M. Blythe, 'Family, government and the medieval Aristotelians', *History of Political Thought*, 10 (1989), pp. 1–16.

gender and social relations. In effect, the Middle Ages inherited a plurality of opinions and approaches.[7] Each idea had had its origin in a particular social and intellectual milieu, and as a contribution to a particular debate, yet all were transmitted to the early Middle Ages in ways which disarticulated them from their own original contexts, and, in the case of patristic arguments about the importance of virginity for example, often transformed pointed political arguments into generalized and authoritative statements.[8] Moreover, those ideas had been formulated in an environment of religious and philosophical pluralism, and as Christianity became the single acceptable religion of the early medieval West, codes of Christian conduct originally intended to identify a religious elite became transformed into the generally applicable and normative standards of a compulsory Christian society with profoundly different forms of political and social organization.

As early medieval writers wrestled to make sense of this heritage and to repackage it (often in simplified form) in more easily accessible digests, handbooks, and florilegia, two complementary ways of thinking came to dominate all forms of argument. The one took biblical texts as the point of departure for discussions of any and every moral, social, or political issue; the other brought the verbal tools of a late antique education to bear on the challenge of elucidating the meaning of scripture. In this, grammar and etymology occupied a crucial role, for by grounding the meaning of words in their (real or purported) philological derivations and linguistic cognates and/or in fundamental grammatical principles such as number and gender, grammar and etymology became particularly important keys to the inner allegorical or typological sense of the *verba sacra*. The point is a commonplace one to students of early medieval thought, perhaps most famously exemplified by the aphorism that rulers (sic: kings) are so called because they rule, *reges a regendo vocati*.[9] Commonplace though it

[7] The literature is vast, but is usefully approached via Joan Cadden, *Meanings of Sex Difference in the Middle Ages: Medicine, Science, and Culture* (Cambridge, 1993) and Peter Brown, *The Body and Society: Men, Women and Sexual Renunciation in Early Christianity* (New York, 1988).

[8] J. Bugge, *Virginitas: an Essay on the History of a Medieval Ideal* (The Hague, 1975); Averil Cameron, 'Virginity as metaphor: women and the rhetoric of early Christianity', in Averil Cameron, ed., *History as Text: The Writing of Ancient History* (London, 1989), pp. 181–205; Kate Cooper, 'Insinuations of womanly influence: an aspect of the Christianization of the Roman aristocracy', *Journal of Roman Studies*, 82 (1992), pp. 150–64.

[9] The original phrase is to be found in Isidore, *Etymologiae*, IX.iii.4, ed. W. M. Lindsay (Oxford, 1911), but soon became a commonplace of early medieval political thought.

may be, this habit of mind is of fundamental importance to an understanding of early medieval ideas of gender distinctions and the social *mores* to be derived therefrom.

Nothing illustrates this better than a discussion held at the Council of Mâcon in 585. Gregory of Tours – but not the official conciliar *acta* – reports that one of the bishops present asserted that 'woman', *mulier*, could not be called 'man', *homo*.[10] As a statement about the etymology of the two nouns, the point seems a fair one; as a statement about their gender it may well have had its origin in the compound meaning of *homo* as 'man' in both the sense of humankind and in the sense of male. The other bishops present countered their colleague by citing Genesis 5.2, that in the beginning God created humankind, *homo*, and that 'male and female created he them . . . and called their name Adam': hence the bishops opined that for this reason Christ was called 'son of man' although born from a virgin woman. Patristic writers had indeed held conflicting opinions about how to interpret Genesis 1.27 and 5.2 and about whether female as well as male had been created in God's image, and these controversies found echoes in medieval biblical commentaries.[11] For Gregory, however, the point was that the correct interpretation of scripture meant bringing grammar and theological truth into alignment with each other.[12]

The bishops assembled at Mâcon did not have available to them one of the most influential works in the transmission of late antique learning to the early Middle Ages, the *Etymologiae* of Isidore of Seville, published on his death in 636. A concise but comprehensive encyclopedia of classical culture, the *Etymologiae* provided succinct definitions and interpretations of a huge range of subjects ranging from geology and wool-working to law and theology.[13] Its rapid and widespread dissemination ensured its popularity as one of the most

---

[10] *Libri Historiarum*, VIII.20 (*MGH SRM*, I, pt 1, pp. 386–7). On this passage, see Godefroid Kurth, 'Le Concile de Mâcon et l'âme des femmes', in his *Etudes Franques*, 2 vols (Brussels, 1919), 2, pp. 161–7.

[11] K. E. Børreson, '*Imago Dei*, privilège masculin? Interprétation augustinienne et pseudo-augustinienne de Gen. 1.27 et I Cor. 11.7', *Augustinianum*, 25 (1985), pp. 213–34; H.-W. Goetz, *Frauen im frühen Mittelalter* (Cologne, 1995), pp. 82–90. Cf. Maria L. Arduini, 'Il tema *vir* e *mulier* nell'esegesi patristica e medioevale de Eccli. XLII.14. A proposito di una interpretazione di Ruperto di Deutz', *Aevum*, 54 (1980), pp. 315–30, 55 (1981), pp. 246–61.

[12] And similarly in the preface to his *Liber Vitae Patrum* (*MGH SRM*, I, pt 2, p. 662).

[13] Jacques Fontaine, 'Isidore de Séville et la mutation de l'encyclopédisme antique', *Cahiers d'Histoire Mondiale*, 9 (1966), pp. 519–38; Peter Brown, *The Rise of Western Christendom* (Oxford, 1996), pp. 218–19, 221.

vital of all early medieval guides to knowledge. As such, it provides us with definitions of 'man' and 'woman' of virtually canonical status. Isidore's significance in this context is that from the etymology of *vir* and *mulier* he derived normative views of the social conduct expected of men and women respectively. His definitions are worth quoting in full:

> Man [*vir*] is named because there is greater force [*vis*] in him than in women, whence also strength [*virtus* – both physical and moral strength] takes its name, or because he rules over women by force.
>
> Woman [*mulier*] however is named from softness [*mollities*], as if 'softer' [*mollier*] with a letter changed and one taken away were 'woman' [*mulier*]. They differ from each other in bodily strength and weakness, for the man's strength [*virtus*] is greatest and the woman's is less, so that she may be subject to the man. This is lest, repelled by women, lust were to drive men to seek others, or to fall upon their own sex . . . .
>
> The female person [*femina*] is derived from those parts of the thighs [*partibus femorum*] where this sex is distinguished from men. Others think that 'female person' [*femina*] is derived by Greek etymology from 'fiery force' [*ab ignea vi*] because she lusts so strongly, for the female [*feminas*] is much more sensual than the male [*viris*], among women [*in mulieribus*] just as among animals. Hence excessive love among the ancients was called womanly love [*femineus amor*].[14]

Strength and softness (both physical and moral), domination and subjection, sexual excess, and the fear of homosexual relationships are all encoded here in the three words *vir, mulier, femina*. For Isidore and his many early medieval readers, etymology subsumed social ideologies: the meanings of words acquired their own, autonomous moral force.

The implications of Isidore's definitions are clear. The binary distinction of male and female described everything from genital physiology to sexual activity and social behaviour. The distinction central to much recent feminist thinking between the biological and

---

[14] *Etymologiae*, IX.ii.17–19, 24.

the cultural, in other words between sex and gender, has no purchase here: for Isidore, the shift from male:female to masculine:feminine was instantaneous.[15] Nor did this permit of any other vocabulary for describing human behaviour. Women who acted with physical strength, firm and resolute behaviour, or who displayed moral courage, were described as acting in manly fashion. Thus, for example, Gregory of Tours told the tale of a woman whom the drunken Duke Amalo tried to rape. Dragged, resisting and injured, into his bed she managed to seize his sword and 'as Judith did to Holofernes', cut off his head with a 'virile blow' [*ictu virili*].[16] Similarly, when a Catholic Merovingian princess was sent in marriage to Visigothic Spain, her refusal to be rebaptized as an Arian earned her behaviour the adverb 'manly' [*viriliter*].[17] Manly behaviour in a woman was generally praiseworthy: indeed it made her a *virago*, a woman of masculine strength, and this was the epithet bestowed on holy women who pursued a life of extreme ascetic rigour.[18]

If masculine behaviour stood at the positive end of a spectrum of behaviours, the feminine pole carried a more negative charge. Battle exemplified this most dramatically: victories were won 'manfully', but those who fled were 'womanly'.[19] Other forms of behaviour might be similarly gendered. Two ninth-century clerics who quarrelled over the ownership of relics of Vincent of Saragossa did so in an undignified way 'in the manner of women' [*muliebriter*].[20] From womanly speech,

---

[15] Henrietta L. Moore, 'Understanding sex and gender', in Tim Ingold, ed., *Companion Encyclopaedia to Anthropology: Humanity, Culture and Social Life* (London, 1994), pp. 813–30.

[16] *Libri Historiarum* IX.27 (*MGH SRM*, I, pt 1, pp. 445–6).

[17] *Libri Historiarum* V.38 (*MGH SRM*, I, pt 1, p. 244).

[18] Isidore, *Etymologiae*, IX.ii.22. For a discussion of the term in hagiographical contexts see Julia M. H. Smith, 'The problem of female sanctity in Carolingian Europe, c.780–920', *P&P*, 146 (Feb. 1995), pp. 1–37 at pp. 18–20. I am aware of one example of a woman whose masculine behaviour earned criticism. When Gerald of Aurillac found a peasant woman ploughing because her husband was too ill, he gave her the money to hire a labourer to do this *opus virile*. Gerald's biographer, Odo of Cluny, described the woman's situation as a *calamitas*, and explains Gerald's response on the grounds that a woman doing man's work was contrary to nature and therefore abominable to God. Odo of Cluny, *Vita Geraldi*, I.21: *PL* 133, col. 656. On the gendered distribution of tasks in peasant communities, see further Ludolf Kuchenbuch, '*Opus feminile*: das Geschlechtverhältnis im Spiegel von Frauenarbeiten im früheren Mittelalter', in Hans-Werner Goetz, ed., *Weibliche Lebensgestaltung im frühen Mittelalter* (Cologne, 1991), pp. 139–75.

[19] See especially the account of the West Saxon victory over Viking marauders in 860 in *Asser's Life of King Alfred*, ed. W. H. Stevenson with introduction by Dorothy Whitelock (Oxford, 1959), ch. 18, pp. 17–18: 'Osric, Hamtunensium comes, cum suis et Æthelwulf comes, cum Bearrocensibus, viriliter obviaverunt . . . [pagani] muliebriter fugam arripiunt.'

[20] Aimoin of Saint-Germain-des-Prés, *Translatio Vincentii* ch. 8 (*PL* 126, col. 1018B).

through hair and dress to sexual actions and religious deviance was a slide from worse to worse. Nature, acording to Hrabanus Maurus, deliberately provided different clothing for each sex, and to wear the clothing of the other sex was abominable to God and led to a confusion of roles, of begetting with birthing. Through a loss of the distinction between the sexes, wearing the garments of the other sex also led to the abandonment of chaste behaviour. 'How deformed is a man doing woman's work', he exclaimed.[21] Men whose strength and constancy degenerated into feminine softness were *effeminati* in the opinion of Haimo of Auxerre and such, he added, were the Jewish leaders of his own day.[22] For the author of a commentary on the Apocalypse, on the other hand, it was the customs of heretics which were 'effeminate'.[23] And Walahfrid Strabo caught the essence of Carolingian attitudes when he commented that being 'effeminate' was all in the mind.[24] But those who lived 'softly', Hrabanus opined, were eunuchs and therefore debarred from the kingdom of heaven,[25] and few can have forgotten that the effeminate were among those whom St Paul had explicitly debarred from inheriting the kingdom of God.[26] In short, men whose behaviour turned them, socially speaking, into women contravened the God-given natural order.

Drawing on the patristic legacy of biblical commentary and on the characteristic early medieval fascination with words as the signifiers of a hidden, inner meaning, early medieval writers delineated a coherent code of gendered moral conduct and mapped out consistent norms of social behaviour. But the playing field was not a level one, for although a woman might be uplifted by masculine resolve even to the point of becoming a *virago*, the name Adam had given to the woman created from his flesh who dwelt with him in paradise (cf. Genesis 2.23), men could only fall into softness, weakness, sin, and ultimately damnation.

---

[21] Hrabanus Maurus, *Ennarationes super Deuteronomium*, II.29 (PL 108, cols 922–3), commenting on Deut. 22.5.

[22] Haimo of Auxerre, *Commentarium in Isaia*, 3.4 (PL 116, col. 737D): 'Effeminati autem sunt, qui fortitudinem stabilitatemque virilem in femineam mollitiem habent redactam. Tales sunt hodie principes Judaeorum, pueriliter videlicet cuncta agentes, nulliusque virtutis existentes.'

[23] Alcuin(?), *In Apocalypsin*, 9.8 (PL 100, col. 1140).

[24] Walahfrid Strabo, *In Isaia prophetam*, 59.16 (PL 113, col. 1302): '"quia not est vir": mente omnes effeminati sunt'.

[25] Hrabanus Maurus, *Ennarationes super Deuteronomium*, III.7 (PL 108, col. 929C) commenting on Deut. 23.1, here quoting Bede on the same verse.

[26] I Cor. 6.9.

Carol Clover's conclusion apropos early Scandinavian society, that 'sexual difference . . . [was] less a wall than a permeable membrane', is equally applicable to the Christian culture of Latin Christendom in the seventh, eighth, and ninth centuries.[27] Those who were biologically male could become socially women, and *vice versa*. But unlike heroic Scandinavia, the consequences might be momentous in early medieval Christendom, for the fate of the individual soul was at stake.

Some of Isidore of Seville's earliest readers were Irish. Among them was the anonymous author who *c.* 630 × 650 wrote a tract on *De duodecim abusivis saeculi*. 'The Twelve Abuses of the Age' (or better, 'The Twelve Reprehensible Personalities of the World') include the *rex iniquus* who cannot rule others because he does not rule himself. Under him, justice is lacking, peace is not maintained, the earth is barren, flocks perish, enemies invade, death is everywhere. He is the anti-type of everything a king should be: 'the peace of the people, the safety of the fatherland, the bulwark of the nations, the cure of illness, the joy of humankind, the temperateness of the climate, the serenity of the sea, the solace of the poor'.[28] Fifth among the other abuses comes the 'woman without modesty'.[29] The *femina sine pudicitia* is in many ways the female equivalent of the *rex iniquus*: the two passages contain verbal echoes of each other and deploy very similar rhetorical strategies to make their point. Her modesty 'preserves chastity, restrains avarice, deflects strife, calms anger, attacks lust, tempers cupidity, punishes lasciviousness, warns against drunkenness, does not multiply words, opposes gluttony and condemns deceit'. In an extension of Pauline thoughts, *pudicitia* is both an inner and an outer virtue, affecting both the appearance of the body and the condition of the soul. In summary, 'modesty is the ornament of the noble, the exaltation of the humble, the nobility of the ignorant, the beauty of the base, the prosperity of the worker, the solace of those who suffer, the augmentation of all

---

[27] Carol Clover, 'Regardless of sex: men, women and power in early northern Europe', *Speculum*, 68 (1993), pp. 363–87, quotation from p. 387 (and reprinted in Nancy F. Partner, ed., *Studying Medieval Women: Sex, Gender and Feminism* [Cambridge, MA, 1993], pp. 61–85).

[28] Pseudo-Cyprian, *De duodecim abusivis saeculi*, ed. Siegmund Hellmann, Texte und Untersuchungen zur Geschichte der altchristlichen Literatur, ser. 3, 4 (Leipzig, 1910), pp. 51–3 with quotation on p. 53. On the sources and diffusion of this work, Hans Hubert Anton, 'Pseudo-Cyprian, *De duodecim abusivis saeculi* und seine Einfluss auf dem Kontinent, inbesondere auf die karolingische Fürstenspiegel', in Heinz Löwe, ed., *Die Iren und Europa im frühen Mittelalter*, 2 vols (Stuttgart, 1986), 2, pp. 568–617.

[29] *De duodecim abusivis saeculi*, ed. Hellmann, pp. 40–3.

beauty, the multiplication of all merits, the friendship of God the creator'.[30] For this Irish writer, modesty was to women what prudence was to men, the guide to good conduct and morality; and the image of the *femina sine pudicitia* travelled throughout the early Middle Ages alongside that of the *rex iniquus*.

Pseudonymously attributed to Cyprian, *De duodecim abusivis saeculi* was one of the most-copied, if not *the* most-copied, of all early medieval works. Rapidly and widely disseminated in Anglo-Saxon England and on the continent, the twinned portraits of the righteous and the wicked king are justly famous as one of the fundamental cornerstones of early medieval political thought. These succinctly formulated, easily comprehensible ideas on just kingship struck a deep chord, and the influence of this little Irish treatise runs throughout all Carolingian political writing. And the Carolingian writers whose views on the social role and moral obligations of wives will shortly be discussed all knew their Pseudo-Cyprian.

* * *

Before we come to focus on the ways in which wives found a place within Carolingian expositions of social order, a brief word on their menfolk is needed. The Carolingian leaders, first as Mayors of the Palace and after 751 as kings, established their empire with the co-operation of an aggressive and wealthy aristocracy whose power, status and riches were vastly increased in the process.[31] The pride and code of honour of this 'super-aristocracy' revolved around military prowess but, beneath the triumphalist chronicles of Frankish expansionism, there lurks a bleaker picture of this intensely proud and belligerent warrior caste. As a group, they were given to worldly ambition and lust,[32] to lavish displays of conspicuous consumption, including heavy drinking and all its attendant consequences,[33] to corruption and favouritism in the use or abuse of power, and to wanton violence particularly against women and church property.[34]

---

[30] Ibid., quotations from pp. 40–1, 42–3.

[31] Stuart Airlie, 'The aristocracy', in Rosamond McKitterick ed., *New Cambridge Medieval History*, vol. 2, *c.700–900* (Cambridge, 1995), pp. 431–50.

[32] The two vices singled out by Alcuin, *De virtutibus et vitiis*, ch. 18 (*PL* 101, col. 627B).

[33] D. A. Bullough, *Friends, Neighbours and Fellow-Drinkers: Aspects of Community and Conflict in the Early Medieval West* (Cambridge, 1991).

[34] See in particular Hincmar of Rheims' *De coercendo et exstirpando raptu viduarum, puellarum ac sanctimonialium* (*PL* 125, cols 1017–32) for a powerful description of some

As Charlemagne and his churchmen began to formulate a trenchantly articulate vision of a more deeply Christian society, and from *c.* 780 developed a legislative programme to work towards this, the behaviour of these aristocratic thugs became increasingly open to criticism and attack. Efforts to constrain their behaviour took the form of a series of public rituals designed to humiliate and abase those whose transgressions of good order were particularly heinous. Those found guilty of offences such as parricide, incest, the murder of a priest or false coining were subject to a form of public penance which, by removing their swordbelt and stripping them of the right to bear arms, and halting all marital relations, left the offender to stand at the door of the church, ritually emasculated and socially dead. Another form of penance ordered the offender to seek reconciliation at distant shrines and sent him nearly naked, barefoot, and laden with chains to journey alone in search of forgiveness. And in an equivalent secular ritual, about which we know much less, the king could order the guilty one to carry a saddle around on his back at the king's pleasure.[35] Pride, in the opinion of many early medieval monastic writers, was the worst of all sins; and these forms of public humiliation struck at the heart of the armed warrior's honour code and crushed his spirit beneath the weight of social opprobrium.[36]

To complement humiliating rituals as a means of curbing lawlessness and violence, Carolingian moralists turned their attention to developing a new aristocratic honour code, one designed to temper the vices of aristocratic power with Christian virtues in a palatable mixture of military and religious ideals.[37] This series of 'moral breviaries for lay

aspects of this and, in general, Jean Devisse, *Hincmar, archevêque de Reims, 845–882*, 3 vols (Paris, 1975–6), I, pp. 526–34.

[35] On public penance, see Jean Chélini, *L'Aube du moyen âge: naissance de la chrétienté occidentale* (Paris, 1991), pp. 362–409, and Mayke De Jong, 'Power and humility in Carolingian society: the public penance of Louis the Pious', *Early Medieval Europe*, 1 (1992), pp. 29–52 (she also deals with *harmiscara*, the saddle punishment). On penitential pilgrimage, see C. Vogel, 'Le Pèlerinage penitentiel', *Revue des sciences religieuses*, 38 (1964), pp. 113–53.

[36] Lester K. Little, 'Pride goes before avarice: social change and the vices in Latin Christendom', *AHR*, 76 (1971), pp. 16–49, cf. R. Newhauser, 'Towards a modus in habendo: transformations in the idea of avarice', *Zeitschrift der Savigny-Stiftung für Rechtsgeschichte, kanonistische Abteilung*, 106 (1989), pp. 1–22.

[37] Pierre Toubert, 'une potion buvable de l'idéal chrétien et l'idéal militaire', 'La Théorie du mariage chez les moralistes carolingiens', *Settimane*, 24 (1976), pp. 233–82 at p. 247. On the genre as a whole, see Michel Rouche, 'Miroirs du prince ou miroirs du clergé?',

aristocrats', of which Dhuoda's *Handbook* for William is one, drew heavily on the fifth- and sixth-century literature on virtues and vices, most notably Cassian, Gregory the Great, and Prudentius, but reframed this ascetic ethic in a way which made it directly applicable to lay behaviour.[38] In one of the earliest examples of the genre (composed around the year 800), Alcuin wrote to Wido, Count of the Breton march, who he knew was 'preoccupied with thoughts of worldly affairs', and reassured him that if he followed this simple guidance on what to do and what to avoid, his lay condition would not debar him from eternal life.[39] At much the same time, Paulinus of Aquileia pointed out to Eric of Friuli the concordance between the life of the warrior, the *miles terrenus*, and that of the monk, the *miles spiritalis*, and furnished him with comparable advice.[40] And when Dhuoda wrote for young William, he was in the same situation, 'soldiering on amidst the throng of earthly troubles'.[41]

Whether the formulation of a Christianized honour code made any practical difference to aristocratic behaviour is not the point here – although it may be doubted that it did in any other than a tiny handful of instances.[42] Rather, all these treatises present a consistent and coherent ideology which transforms the power and status of an aristocrat into a ministry, a *ministerium*, with its own moral obligations and social responsibilities. This Carolingian thought-world about the responsible use of power and the maintenance of a divinely instituted social order proposes that the powerful warrior has a duty and a function in this world and can achieve salvation without abandoning his martial profession. To do so, he must exercise his power with justice, use his wealth for the benefit of the poor and needy, turn his

---

Settimane, 39 (1992), pp. 341–64; Thomas F. X. Noble, 'Secular sanctity: forging an ethos for the Carolingian nobility' (forthcoming), to which I am greatly indebted.

[38] 'Moral breviaries for lay aristocrats': the phrase is Toubert's, 'Théorie du mariage', p. 244. For a demonstration of the way that the most widely-read of these treatises drew on the patristic and ascetic tradition, see Liutpold Wallach, 'Alcuin on virtues and vices: a manual for a Carolingian soldier', *HThR*, 48 (1955), pp. 175–95.

[39] 'Sciens te in multis saecularium rerum cogitationibus occupatum': Alcuin, *De virtutibus et vitiis*, prefatory epistle (*PL* 101, col. 613). For reassurance that laity could enter the kingdom of heaven, see below, n. 46.

[40] Paulinus of Aquileia, *Liber exhortationis*, ch. 20 (*PL* 99, cols 212–14).

[41] Dhuoda, *Liber manualis*, IV.2, ed. Riché, *Manuel pour mon fils*, p. 204: 'Tu, tamen, fili, dum in saeculo militaris inter mundanas actionum turmas.'

[42] Most notably the case of Gerald of Aurillac, who remained in the world but did renounce both arms and marriage. Cf. Stuart Airlie, 'The anxiety of sanctity: St Gerald of Aurillac and his maker', *JEH*, 43 (1992), pp. 372–95.

sword against the enemies of Christ, discipline his own conduct, exercise sexual restraint both within and outside marriage, and undertake penance for his sins. Ascetic conversion to a life away from the bustle of the world had been a highly publicized route to salvation for the late Roman nobleman anxious for his soul: for his Carolingian equivalent, salvation was this-worldly and quotidian.[43]

As Notker of St Gall remarked late in the ninth century, 'life in this world cannot be carried out without marriage and the practice of arms'.[44] The employment of arms, of course, pertained to men. But marriage implies a wife, and it is finally here, in Carolingian discussions of conduct within marriage, that aristocratic wives may be found. Ninth-century clergy expended much effort to define and enforce a theory of marriage which stressed its indissoluble and monogamous nature, and which rigorously defined those who were not permitted to marry each other on the basis of close kinship, whether biological or other. The resulting legislation and legal disputes constitute one of the decisive moments in the history of western marriage, and modern scholars have expended considerable energy in elucidating the intentions, inconsistencies, and consequences of Carolingian marriage law.[45] But much less attention has been given to Carolingian views about good conduct and moral worth within a legal marriage, and the relationship between a woman and her husband on the one hand and her children on the other.

In addressing his advice to Wido, Alcuin had reassured the count that, according to their individual merits, people of every age, sex, and occupation might enter the kingdom of heaven, women as well as men, lay as well as clerical.[46] Paulinus of Aquileia made it clear to Eric of Friuli that the route to salvation began in the household, and that it

---

[43] On the piety of married late Roman aristocrats who did not undergo a monastic conversion, see Kate Cooper, 'The "silent majority" in the early medieval period', in W. E. Klingshirn, ed., *The Limits of Ancient Christianity* (forthcoming).

[44] Notker the Stammerer, *Gesta Karoli magni imperatoris*, II.10, ed. Hans F. Haefele, *MGH SRG*, ns 12 (Berlin, 1962), p. 66.

[45] Jean Gaudemet, *Le Mariage en occident: les moeurs et le droit* (Paris, 1987), pp. 91–132; Suzanne Fonay Wemple, *Women in Frankish Society: Marriage and the Cloister, 500–900* (Philadelphia, 1981), pp. 75–123; and, controversially, Jack Goody, *The Development of the Family and Marriage in Europe* (Cambridge, 1983).

[46] Alcuin, *De virtutibus et vitiis*, ch. 36 (*PL* 101, col. 638): 'igitur sicut omnibus aequaliter regni Dei praedicata est beatitudo, ita omni sexui, aetati et personae aequaliter secundum meritorum dignitatem regni Dei patet introitus. Ubi non est distinctio, quis esset in saeculo laicus vel clericus, dives vel pauper, junior vel senior, servus vel dominus: sed unusquisque secundum meritum boni operis perpetua coronabitur gloria.'

was his responsibility to lead all his dependents, from the greatest to the least, along that road. Within his own house he was to 'announce, exhort, order and persuade' his family and retainers that they should avoid 'pride, slander, drunkenness, fornication, luxury, anger, perjury, and greed, the root of all evils'.[47] Paulinus here struck an Augustinian note, for Augustine had argued that peace – social order in harmony with divine law – began in the household, and that it was the responsibility of the paterfamilias to correct all members of the household and lead them towards God.[48] Two decades or so after Paulinus, Jonas of Orleans spelled out the full implications of this. Bishop, courtier, and imperialist ideologue, Jonas was decisive in the formulation of the political ideas promulgated in the 820s and 830s. Not only kings and councils engaged his attention; he also wrote 818 × 828 a didactic handbook to guide Matfrid, Count of Orleans in the exercise of virtue whilst holding royal office.[49]

Within the *De institutione laicali* is contained a semi–independent treatise on marriage. Here, Jonas not only outlined the new Carolingian norms and values attached to marriage but also sketched out a wifely *ministerium* that closely resembled the role and responsibilities which Jonas' exact contemporary Dhuoda herself assumed.[50] His intention, he reminded Matfrid, was to provide him with a 'mirror' which he could read and reread to show him how to lead an honourable married life.[51] Drawing very heavily on Augustine's *De bono coniugali* and on Isidore of Seville, Jonas argued that marriage was among the good things made by God at the creation of the world.[52] It was the very bedrock of earthly society, the place where the faith which Augustine had identified as the core of the holy marriage bond met and merged with the faith between humankind and God, and with

---

[47] *Liber exhortationis*, ch. 29 (PL 99, cols 225–6).

[48] *De civitate Dei*, xix,16 (*CChr. SL*, 48, p. 683). Cf. Roger Bonnaud Delamare, *L'Idée de paix à l'époque carolingienne* (Paris, 1939).

[49] *De institutione laicali* (PL 106, cols 121–278). On Jonas' career see the introduction to the new edition of his *De institutione regia*, ed. A. Dubreucq, *Le Métier du roi*, SC, 407 (Paris, 1995), pp. 9–42, esp. pp. 28–31. On the two different recensions of *De institutione laicali*, their date and dissemination, see Isolde Schröder, 'Zur Überlieferung von De institutione laicali des Jonas von Orleans', *Deutsches Archiv*, 44 (1988), pp. 83–97.

[50] *De institutione laicali*, II.1–16 (PL 106, cols 167–99). It must also be stressed that despite the great similarities of thought between Dhuoda and Jonas, there is no evidence that Dhuoda knew Jonas' treatise. They had, however, read many of the same works, including Augustine's *Enchiridion* and Alcuin's *De virtutibus et vitiis*.

[51] *De institutione laicali*, prefatory letter (PL 106, cols 123–4).

[52] Ibid., II.1 (PL 106, col. 167).

the faithfulness owed by a warrior to his king. In contrast to the tradition which emphasised that marriage contained within it hierarchy and subordination, Jonas followed Augustine and saw it more nearly as a partnership between equals.[53] The same standards of conduct, morality, and sexual fidelity applied to both spouses: men could not demand that their wives refrain from adultery if they did not do so themselves. The *fides* at the heart of marriage demanded *equal* modesty [*pudicitia*] from both.[54]

Within this relationship, women set the moral standard which men should emulate. If a man's wife became afflicted with mental or physical incapacity, or lost her family inheritance, he should not put her aside and take another endowed with greater lineage, intelligence, beauty, or wealth. Instead, he should follow the example of 'modest and honourable women' who 'sit assiduously at their husbands' bedsides during their long illnesses, succour them and do nothing to detract from the faithfulness of the marriage'.[55] Jonas envisioned women within the familial setting in which we do indeed find them in the historical record, but in so doing, he proposed that wives represented the true faithfulness that kept a Christian society together. Virtuous wives, Jonas argued, were moral guides and exemplars.

For Jonas as for Augustine, marriage was for the begetting and raising of children: in becoming a wife, a woman almost inevitably became a mother as well. Here too women's role was central. Parents must love their offspring more in the spirit than in the flesh, and teach them to observe heavenly values more than earthly ones.[56] Job, Tobias, and David showed how to do this. Although among both sexes were to be found people more dedicated to the pursuit of spiritual than earthly profit, Jonas commented, there were 'some noble men and also some noble women' who were driven by earthly greed and who neglected the welfare of their souls, but all people – men and women – who had young children in their care had a moral responsibility and must fulfil the 'office of a pastor'. Only through parental solicitude could sin

---

[53] Ideas about hierarchy and subordination within marriage are discussed briefly by Goetz, *Frauen im frühen Mittelalter*, pp. 330-1.

[54] *De institutione laicali*, II.4: 'Patet nempe quod inter virum et uxorem par pudicitiae forma et conjugalis tori fides sit conservanda' (*PL* 106, cols 174-7, esp col. 177).

[55] Ibid., II.12, cols 188-91. 'Et sicut pudicis et honestis feminis moris est, virorum suorum infirmantium, et longa aegritudine tabescentium lectulis jugiter assidere, eisque famulari, et pro viribus opitulari et in nullo a conjugali thori fide deficere' (col. 191).

[56] Ibid., II.14, col. 192.

inspired by the devil be kept away.[57] Here, then, is the wifely *ministerium*: to nurture and share responsibility for training children and dependents in upright Christian conduct.

Shrewd pastor that he was, Jonas had described the wife's role in such a way as to counter one of the main ways in which women's behaviour threatened Carolingian social cohesion. On the occasions when women were implicated in serious offences against public order, their usual crime was one particular form of homicide: infanticide.[58] By focusing wifely obligations around the raising of children, Jonas mapped out a morality specifically designed to counter women's sin, just as his masculine ethic attacked the roots of men's sin.

Jonas' image of the moral duties of a wife may nevertheless have been little more than a conceptual and schematic rendition of the role regularly undertaken by many aristocratic wives. The guiding influence of early medieval mothers can be traced in sources from at least the seventh century. Take, for example, Erchenfreda, mother of Desiderius (Bishop of Cahors, 630–55): her letters of spiritual guidance to her son were preserved by his hagiographer, and their tone is one of clear moral authority.[59] Nor were the *matronae* of the seventh- and eighth-century Arnulfing dynasty any different. Begga, *gloriosa genetrix* of Pippin II (of Herstal), raised her son to rule with her daily salutary conversation; a generation later the widowed Neustrian noblewoman Ansfled, 'a pious and energetic woman . . . filled with the spirit of prudence and thoughtful diligence', raised her grandson Hugo and taught him with her daily admonitions to serve God.[60]

In the ninth century, Dhuoda provides the best example of a noble wife who lavished moral and spiritual guidance on her son, fulfilling the wifely *ministerium* sketched by Jonas. She certainly administered her husband's estates during his absences at court, although her relationship with Bernard seems strained by their long periods of separation –

---

[57] *De institutione laicali*, II.16, cols 197–9, quotations from col. 197.

[58] Schmitz, 'Schuld und Strafe. Eine unbekannte Stellungnahme des Rathramnus von Corbie zur Kindestötung', *Deutsches Archiv*, 38 (1982), pp. 363–87 discusses the relevant legislation. I am only aware of a single instance of what happened in practice: see letter of Stephen V to Lambert, Bishop of Le Mans, *Epistolae Stephanae papae V*, no. 24: PL 129, col. 807, where it is misattributed to Stephen IV.

[59] *Vita Desiderii Cadurcae urbis episcopi*, 9–11 (*MGH SRM*, IV, pp. 569–70).

[60] *Annales Mettenses priores*, aa. 678, 693, ed. B. de Simson, *MGH SRG* (Hanover, 1905), pp. 3, 16. Cf. Janet L. Nelson, 'Gender and genre in women historians of the early Middle Ages', in eadem, *The Frankish World, 750–900* (London, 1996), pp. 183–97, at p. 193.

and quite possibly also by the political scandals which swirled around him in the 830s.[61] In educating William in how to conduct himself honourably at court, Dhuoda offered her son a 'mirror' and urged him to study it as assiduously as women who 'are absorbed in examining their faces in mirrors in order to cover their blemishes and enhance their beauty ... to please their husbands'.[62] It has recently been claimed that, in setting out a code of prayer and practical conduct for William, Dhuoda arrogated to herself her husband's paternal authority.[63] Certainly, as she wrote, she put into her own mouth the words of St Paul and of the Rule of St Benedict; but in claiming a maternal right to propound moral insights and to guide her son in his passage to adulthood, Dhuoda was doing no more than what Jonas had envisaged a wife would do in any truly Christian marriage. The only difference was that Dhuoda had to instruct her absent son by writing to him. Indeed we should be grateful for this, because her words offer us the only real clue to the way in which the ethic propounded by the clerical elite accorded with the needs and aspirations of the laity.

Jonas' novelty was to establish as normative a pattern of female probity and moral leadership which had hitherto been individual, familial, and pragmatic. By opening up a discourse about married women, Jonas encouraged a revaluation of their social and religious significance. Moreover, his ideas were influential, for they became the hallmark of many subsequent Carolingian writers' attitudes towards women and marriage. For example, we can trace their impact in later texts of lay moral guidance, such as those by Hrabanus Maurus and Hincmar of Rheims.[64] They also had a legislative impact, for in 845 (a year or two after the deaths of both Jonas and Dhuoda) the bishops assembled at the Council of Meaux/Paris put into law the wifely office urged by Jonas, and indeed went even further than he had done by emphasising that responsibility for the moral probity of the household fell most especially to noble wives.[65] In appointing *potentes feminae* as

[61] Dhuoda, *Liber Manualis*, praef. and X.4, ed. Riché, pp. 84–6, 350–2.

[62] Ibid., prologus, p. 80.

[63] M. A. Claussen, 'Fathers of power and mothers of authority: Dhuoda and the *Liber Manualis*', *French Historical Studies*, 19 (1996), pp. 785–809, with full discussion of the quotations from the Bible and the Rule of St Benedict which Dhuoda uses. I am grateful to Janice Farnham for drawing my attention to this article.

[64] Toubert, 'Théorie du mariage', pp. 259–60.

[65] Council of Meaux/Paris, cl. 77 (*MGH Conc.*, III, p. 124). Cf. Janet L. Nelson, 'Women and the word in the earlier Middle Ages', *SCH*, 27 (1990), pp. 53–78.

the guardians of rectitude and good conduct and as the teachers of fundamental Christian texts and tenets, the Church confirmed and extended Jonas' vision.[66]

If wives' obligations were to form the taproot of the search for order and stability, we must do a little more historical digging to locate the direction of its growth. We can find it in a couple of directions. One is hagiographical, and that is significant because early medieval saints' lives are more usually an indication of implicit cultural expectations and values than they are a guide to what any individual might have ever said or done. The female saints of the early Middle Ages were either virgins or widows who entered the religious life after the death of their spouses. Whereas Merovingian hagiographers had taken their cue from Jerome's fulminations against marriage, and had been quick to stress that virginity was the more rewarded condition, fulsome descriptions of nurturing mothers occur in saints' lives from the later ninth century onwards. Their subject may be either the mother of the saint or the widowed saint herself during her earlier, married life. One such was Rictrude of Marchiennes. The *vita* composed in 907 not only presents her as model of holy matrimony in exact conformity with Jonas' views but also describes how she continued to nurture her children and guide their spiritual growth from her own monastic retirement in her widowhood.[67] This hagiographical exaltation of motherhood culminated at the turn of the millenium, when a life of Matilda, mother of Otto I, was written. In this, marriage and motherhood formed the essential frame for her life and her claim to sanctity. Within her marriage, she conformed to the Carolingian ideal of sexual self-discipline and 'chaste conjugality' which Jonas and others had elaborated. For Matilda's hagiographer, marriage was a state of spiritual value, a sanctified condition of reciprocity and co-operation between spouses: through Matilda's good counsel and her prayers, her

---

[66] Contrast the lack of differentiation between the roles of mother and father in earlier legislation, *MGH Cap.*, I, no. 121, p. 240.

[67] Hucbald of Saint-Amand, *Vita Rictrudis*, chs 5, 15, 17 (*PL* 132, cols 833–4, 841–3, 844–5). For Hucbald's use of Jonas' *De institutione laicali* in describing Rictrude's marriage, see Julia M. H. Smith, 'A hagiographer at work: Hucbald and the library of Saint-Amand', *Revue Bénédictine*, 106 (1996), pp. 151–71 at p. 156. For further hagiographical examples, see Toubert, 'Théorie du mariage', p. 259 n. 69. On motherhood as nurturing, see the introduction to John Carmi Parsons and Bonnie Wheeler, eds, *Medieval Mothering* (New York, 1996), pp. ix–xvii.

husband was helped towards salvation.[68] To the rhetorical question, 'Surely a woman will be more saved if she persists in chastity?', Haimo of Auxerre had replied: 'Undoubtedly, but [she will also be saved] if she bears children and raises them in faith and worship of the omnipotent God and leads them to the perfection of the good life.'[69] When mothering an emperor became the grounds for sanctity, the moral revaluation of married women's importance was complete.

Jonas' ideas on wives and marriage also left their impact on more conventional forms of political discourse, notably mirrors for kings. In turning to these, we need to recall Pseudo-Cyprian's influence on Carolingian formulations of ideas of good kingship. Jonas was one of those whose own tract on kingship, *De institutione regia*, made great use of the ideas contained in Pseudo-Cyprian's discussion of the *rex iniquus*.[70] Whether Jonas had read the fifth abuse condemning the woman without modesty when he composed his handbook for Matfrid is uncertain, for there is no textual trace of it in his language, although arguably his image of the ideal wife is the precise inverse of the reprehensible 'woman without modesty'. We can do no more than note that, within a very few years of Jonas completing his aristocratic mirror, the moral conduct of the king's wife first became a political issue. When Louis the Pious' sons rebelled against him in 830, accusations that the empress Judith had been sleeping with Dhuoda's husband Bernard lay at the centre of the ideological maelstrom.[71] In a culture where government took place in and through the imperial household, and in a political environment where Jonas had put his ideas on conjugal chastity and a social order founded on matrimony before a royal council only the previous year, it became easily possible to attack the emperor by hurling allegations of sexual misconduct and lack of modesty against his wife.[72] Jonas had successfully integrated women's moral probity into the political discourse of the day: there-

---

[68] Patrick Corbet, *Les Saints ottoniens: sainteté dynastique, sainteté royale et sainteté féminine autour de l'an Mil*, Beihefte der Francia, 15 (Sigmaringen, 1986), pp. 204–6.

[69] Haimo of Auxerre, *In epistolam I ad Timotheum*, 2.15 (PL 117, col. 791). This passage may be a rethinking of Jerome, *Adv. Jovinianum*, I.27 (PL 23, col. 249).

[70] *De institutione regia*, III.57–109, ed. Dubreucq, *Le Métier du roi*, pp. 188–92, quoting the ninth abuse verbatim.

[71] Carefully analysed by Elizabeth Ward, 'Caesar's wife: the career of the Empress Judith, 819–29', in Peter Godman and Roger Collins, eds, *Charlemagne's Heir: New Perspectives on the Reign of Louis the Pious* (Oxford, 1990), pp. 205–27; and eadem, 'Agobard of Lyons and Paschasius Radbertus as critics of the Empress Judith', *SCH*, 27 (1990), pp. 15–25.

[72] 829 Council of Paris, cl. 69 (*MGH Conc.*, II, pt 2, at pp. 670–1).

after, allegations of queenly adultery echoed repeatedly in Carolingian politics.[73]

Such accusations were used with powerful effect in the storm raised in 860 by Lothar II's attempt to divorce his childless wife and marry his beloved mistress by whom he already had a son.[74] In this climate, ideas of kingly behaviour became firmly and explicitly bound in with norms of the moral rectitude appropriate for a queen. For the decisive enunciation of this, we must turn to the '*Fürstenspiegel*' of the Irish poet Sedulius Scottus.[75] Sedulius was amongst those who had read Pseudo-Cyprian's views on kingship; and he had thought too about the image of the woman without modesty. The latter Sedulius excerpted into his commonplace book, in a way which stripped *pudicitia* of any specifically female association and turned it instead into a virtue of general applicability.[76] He also had it in mind when he turned his attention to the household dimension of royal governance. In his *Liber de rectoribus christianis*, Sedulius dissected the relationship between a ruler and his wife, children and household in a manner more indebted to Pseudo-Cyprian than to Jonas. Unlike Jonas in that he explicitly placed the wife under the authority and rule of the head of household (in this case the king), Sedulius nevertheless stresses the queen's capacity for moral good or harm.

> For so much a wife is closer [to a man] in law, to that extent she becomes either noxious with the poison of wickedness or pleasing with the sweetness of morals. To be sure, the foolish wife is the ruin of a household, the exhaustion of wealth, the fullness of crimes, and the abode of all evils and vices, who

---

[73] Details in Geneviève Bührer-Thierry, 'La Reine adultère', *Cahiers de civilisation médiévale*, 35 (1992), pp. 299–312.

[74] The strategies and rhetoric of this bitter dispute have been recently analysed by Stuart Airlie, 'The virgin secrets of girls and women: private bodies and the body politic in the Carolingian age' in a paper delivered to the Anglo-American Conference, July 1996.

[75] *De rectoribus christianis*, ed. Siegmund Hellmann, Quellen und Untersuchungen zur lateinischen Philologie des Mittelalters, 1 (Munich, 1906), pp. 19–91. There is no agreement whether Sedulius wrote this work between 855 and 859 for Lothar II (as argued by Hans Hubert Anton, *Fürstenspiegel und Herrscherethos in der Karolingerzeit*, Bonner Historische Forschung, 32 [Bonn, 1968], pp. 261–3) or for Charles the Bald in perhaps 869 (as claimed by Nikolaus Staubach, *Rex Christianus. Hofkultur und Herrschaftspropaganda im Reich Karl des Kahlen* [Cologne, 1993], pp. 109–12, 168–97).

[76] *Sedulii Scotti Collectaneum miscellaneum*, XIII.19–20, ed. Dean Simpson, CChr. CM, 67 (Turnhout, 1988), pp. 68–9. On Sedulius' indebtedness to Pseudo-Cyprian and other insular texts in his ideas on kings, see Anton, *Fürstenspiegel*, pp. 263–81.

adorns her exterior mien with diverse observances, but knows not how to adorn the interior beauty of her soul. . . . However, a chaste and prudent wife, diligently attending to useful matters with a humble demeanour and cheerful speech, peacefully manages her children and family; and, on behalf of her husband's welfare, if necessary, she sets her life against death and defends his wealth with an honourable reputation.[77]

Such a queen gives good counsel to the king and, in language redolent of Pseudo-Cyprian, is 'the increase of wealth, the support of the household, the delight of her husband, the glory of the family, and the union of all virtues'.[78] A royal marriage may not be quite an equal partnership, but Sedulius' virtuous queen nevertheless brings to her marriage the same wifely virtues which Jonas had praised – chastity, prudence, and moral probity.[79] If, as Augustine had argued, the household was the microcosm of the state, and if, as Jonas had urged, the right moral ordering of the household was the equal responsibility of wife as well as husband, then *a fortiori* the same applied to the royal palace. A wife's moral contribution to building a Christian society defined a queen's political role. A queen without modesty led to disorder throughout the polity.

* * *

In 936, the bishop of Verona languished in the royal prison at Pavia. He consoled himself by expounding at length the ways in which God's commands to humankind pertained differently according to times, ranks, conditions, ages, morals, emotions, sexes, and reasons.[80] In casting his acute eye at everyone from beggar to king, Rather of

---

[77] Sedulius Scottus, *De rectoribus christianis*, ch. 5, ed. Hellmann, p. 35, translated by Edward Gerard Doyle, *Sedulius Scottus: On Christian Rulers and the Poems*, Medieval and Renaissance Texts and Studies, 17 (Binghampton, NY, 1983), pp. 59–60. For a possible West Saxon reflection of Sedulius' ideas on good and bad queens, see Anton Scharer, 'The writing of history at King Alfred's court', *Early Medieval Europe*, 5 (1996), pp. 177–206, at p. 206.

[78] Sedulius Scottus, *De rectoribus christianis*, ch. 5, ed. Hellmann, p. 35.

[79] Ibid., p. 35: 'Is ergo perspicaciter procuret ut non solum nobilem pulchram ac divitem, sed et castam, prudentem atque in sanctis virtutibus morigeram habeat coniugem.' Cf Jonas, *De institutione laicali*, II.5 (*PL* 106, col. 179): 'Perpendant itaque conjugati, quod . . . exterior pulchritudo, et carnalis uxorum delectatio, earum interiori casto amore nullatenus sit praeferenda. Non sunt igitur in uxoribus divitiae tantum et pulchritudo, sed potius pudicitia et morum probitas quaerenda.'

[80] Rather of Verona, *Praeloquia* I.1, ed. P. L. D. Reid, *CChr. CM*, 46A (Turnhout, 1984), p. 5.

Verona did what no Carolingian writer had done before: he addressed married women directly. '*Uxor es?*' 'Are you a wife?' he asked, and proceeded to set out his own blend of scriptural examplars combined with the modesty demanded by Pseudo-Cyprian.[81] The wife should also note everything he had already said about women and about spouses. A woman, Rather had pointed out, should recall 'the softness [*mollitiem*] which you bear in your name' – and use it in the virtue of obedience, not the vice of sexual licence. She should remember too that at the creation she had been called *virago*, strong woman, and in this find the strength to obey divine precepts.[82] As a wife, she should keep in mind the faith which she owed equally to her husband and to Christ, and that marriage is a good, which should not be violated.[83] Men too should know that the name 'man' implied manliness, vigour, strength, force, and rule [*virtus, vireo, vires, vi+rego*], and that 'feminine softness' [*femineam mollitiem*] imperilled a man's soul.[84]

In Rather, the various strands in early medieval thinking about women and gender finally came together. As it had been propounded by Augustine, the household of a married couple formed one of the building blocks of earthly society. Jonas and subsequent Carolingian writers looked within marriage, and found there a wife's social place and her contribution to the realization of divine law. In addition, the late antique and early medieval emphasis on etymology suggested that a woman's moral characteristics, inherent in her name, nevertheless included the possibility of approximating to the strength of men. And finally, from the formulations of the most influential early medieval treatise on kingship came the detailed elaboration on modesty as the key to inward condition and outward behaviour. The route to salvation for an aristocratic wife and mother had been fully established.

When Rather wrote, allegations about queens' behaviour still surfaced from time to time.[85] It was probably inevitable that they did, for wives had come to bear a heavy weight of moral responsibility, and no lay woman was either more visible or in a position of greater moral authority than a queen. Carolingian thinkers had created an

---

[81] Rather of Verona, *Praeloquia* II.11–12, pp. 54–6, including quotation from Ps. Cyprian's fifth abuse.

[82] Ibid., II.3, p. 47.

[83] Ibid., II.4–10, pp. 47–54.

[84] Ibid., II.2, pp. 46–7.

[85] Bührer-Thierry, 'Reine adultère'.

aristocratic ideology where morality mattered both for men and for their wives. Picking and choosing from the range of classical, biblical, and patristic ideas available to them, they formulated opinions about married women's social worth and moral responsibilities. Frustrated though we may be at the meagrely thin evidence for what aristocratic women actually did in the early Middle Ages, we can assure ourselves that legislators and moralists did not forget them. During the early Middle Ages, women were not only 'good to think with':[86] they were also important to think about.[87]

University of St Andrews

---

[86] Brown, *Body and Society*, p. 153; Nelson, 'Women and the word', p. 58.

[87] For further general discussion of some of the issues raised in this paper, see Katrien Heene, *The Legacy of Paradise: Marriage, Motherhood, and Woman in Carolingian Edifying Literature* (Frankfurt, 1997), which appeared too late to be incorporated into the present text.

CUSTOM, TRUTH, AND GENDER IN
ELEVENTH-CENTURY REFORM

by CONRAD LEYSER

'THE Lord did not say, "I am custom", but "I am Truth".' So, allegedly, Pope Gregory VII, in words that – among medievalists at least – have become almost as well known as the Scriptural text to which they refer, 'I am the way, the truth, and the life' (John 14.6).[1] The Gregorian *dictum* embodies the paradox at the centre of the movement for Church Reform in the eleventh century, a paradox which continues to shape historiographical discussion of the period. On the one hand, Gregory and his circle presented themselves as uncompromising fighters for the truth of their vision of the Church, prepared to dismiss any appeal to established practice, however venerable; on the other, and in the same moment, however, they themselves appealed explicitly to past precedent in broadcasting their manifesto. In the comment attributed to Gregory, the authority of 'the blessed Cyprian' (mediated in turn by Augustine) is invoked to sanction the rejection of custom. To 'custom', then, the reformers opposed not 'truth' as a timeless absolute, but a notion of truth embedded in a tradition of moral language. Like many revolutionaries, they saw themselves as restoring their society to a pristine state from which it had fallen away – deaf to the accusation of their opponents that such 'reform' was in fact irreparably destructive of the peace of the community. In part because eleventh-century questions about the moral, and in particular the sexual, behaviour of the priesthood continue to be relevant in modern churches, modern scholars continue to take sides over Reform, depicting Gregory VII either as faithful restorer or as demonic innovator. This interpretative deadlock suggests, perhaps, that we should look again at the reformers' paradoxical notion of truth as it emerges through their use of inherited language. My suggestion is that crucial to the truth of

[1] H. E. J. Cowdrey, ed., *The 'Epistolae vagantes' of Pope Gregory VII* (Oxford, 1972), p. 151, and the references there on the question of attribution. My thanks to Kate Cooper, Kathleen Cushing, Mary Douglas, Henrietta Leyser, Janet Nelson, R. I. Moore, Frederick Paxton, and to the editor for their kindness and advice.

Reform in the eleventh century was its reassertion of a very ancient rhetoric of gender.

No-one would deny that, restoration or revolution, the Reform movement made a drastic intervention in the history of gender, and also of the body and sexuality, family and marriage, in western Europe – at least in theory.[2] The reformers aimed to create anew the body of the faithful. As they saw it, the community of Christians would henceforth reproduce itself through sexual unions solemnized in a church, involving partners who were distant enough from each other to avoid the pollution of incest. The sacrament of marriage would be solemnized by a priest who had himself chosen the opposite sexual path, namely that of avowed celibacy. Symbolically, the priest was tied to no human family: in imitation of Christ, his bride was rather the Church as a whole, all the faithful. From the 1050s a generation of brilliant polemicists, led by Peter Damian and Humbert of Silva Candida, assumed a public platform from which to articulate these demands – which were to be given definitive shape in the canons of the Lateran Council of 1215. Reform, in short, envisaged a radical clarity of division of sexual labour among human beings, and in particular among men.

This was the vision: the reality which it attempted to alter was one in which the practice of marriage was not under the control of the Church; incest prohibitions were not regularly or accurately enforced as kin joined with kin; and priests, if not formally married themselves, were, through concubinage, as fully involved in these family couplings as their lay siblings, with whom they also bought and sold, fought and killed. An early twelfth-century writer so characterized Manasses, Archbishop of Rheims in the 1070s: 'Manasses paid a great deal of attention to the military class and neglected the clergy. He is reported to have said on one occasion, "The archbishopric of Rheims would be a fine thing if one did not have to sing mass for it".'[3]

In the eyes of the reformers, such bishops were polluted. Their pollution was contagious, and it was sexual. Even when, as in the case of Manasses, the priest's transgression involved money or

---

[2] See the contrasting accounts of J. Goody, *The Development of the Family and Marriage in Europe* (Cambridge, 1983), esp. pp. 133–46, and D. Herlihy, *Medieval Households* (Cambridge, MA, 1985) esp. pp. 79–111.

[3] Guibert of Nogent, *Monodiae*, 1.11, J. F. Benton, ed., *Self and Society in Medieval France* (New York, 1970), p. 59.

violence rather than sex, the reformers used sexual language in order to evoke the contamination of the Church that followed from all priestly moral failure. Thus Gregory VII on the simony of Bishop Gottfried of Milan: 'He dared to buy, as if she were a vile servant woman, the bride of Christ and to prostitute her to the devil. Trying to separate her from the catholic faith, he strove to stain her with the crime of the heresy of simony.'[4] As the dispute between Gregory VII and Henry IV over the appointment to the see of Milan escalated into what we know as the 'Investiture Conflict', Pope and King each accused the other of anarchic sexual misconduct, including adultery and incest.[5]

As scholars have observed, we are here in the presence of pollution language, and it is a language spoken by and about celibate men for whom women and sex often represent abomination.[6] If we can explain this phenomenon – why it was that long-established practices such as clerical concubinage, or the giving and receiving of ecclesiastical office in return for money and favours were seen suddenly as foul and dangerous – then we understand Reform. A modern reflex is to understand such language psychologically, as a register of fear. This in turn produces an account of, say, priestly celibacy couched in terms of male neurosis and/or misogyny.[7] But such an approach is unlikely to

---

[4] Gregory VII, *Epistolae*, 1.15, E. Caspar, ed., *MGH Epistolae selectae* 2, p. 24; trans. A. G. Remensnyder, 'Pollution, purity, and peace: an aspect of social reform between the late tenth century and 1076', in T. Head and R. Landes, eds, *The Peace of God: Social Violence and Religious Response in France around the Year 1000* (Ithaca, NY, 1992), pp. 280–307 at pp. 298–9. My debts to Remensnyder's study go far beyond the use of this quotation.

[5] For Gregory's accusation of Henry, see K. Leyser, 'Early medieval canon law and the beginnings of knighthood', now in T. Reuter, ed., *Communications and Power in Medieval Europe: the Carolingian and Ottonian Centuries* (London, 1994), pp. 64–5 and nn. 64–7. For Henry's accusation of Gregory, involving his relationship with Matilda of Tuscany, see the decree of the Synod of Worms, *Die Briefe Heinrichs IV*, ed. C. Erdmann (Leipzig, 1937), pp. 65–8. I am grateful to Henrietta Leyser and Kathleen Cushing for these references.

[6] See in particular, Remensnyder, 'Pollution, purity, and peace', and R. I. Moore, 'Family, community, and cult on the eve of the Gregorian reform', *TRHS*, 5th ser., 30 (1980), pp. 49–69. The vilest pollution of all, in the eyes of Peter Damian at least, was represented by sexual relations among the clergy themselves. See C. Leyser, 'Cities of the Plain: the rhetoric of sodomy in Peter Damian's *Book of Gomorrah*', *Romanic Review*, 86 (1995), pp. 191–211.

[7] See e.g. A. Barstow, *Married Priests and the Reforming Papacy: the Eleventh-Century Debates* (New York and Toronto, 1982), pp. 22, 58, and the ground-breaking essay by J. A. McNamara, 'The *Herrenfrage*: the restructuring of the gender system, 1050–1150', in C. A. Lees, ed., *Medieval Masculinities: Regarding Men in the Middle Ages* (Minneapolis, 1994), pp. 3–29. Cf. the classic study of H. C. Lea, *Sacerdotal Celibacy in the Christian Church* (4th edn, London, 1932) which, while not considering the politics of gender, does not hesitate to

produce a historically specific explanation of Reform. An anthropology of pollution, as pioneered by Mary Douglas, is more likely to illuminate the structural context in which claims to purity are made and accusations of filthiness levied.[8]

* * *

The work of Georges Duby and of R. I. Moore has given us a social historical and an anthropologically informed logic of the programme for clerical Reform.[9] The division of masculine sexual labour, the regulation of marriage, and the extension of incest prohibitions: the key to the plot is land, its division, regulation, and extension. As Moore noted over a decade ago, it was Duby's great contribution to have offered a compelling narrative of the way in which the landed elites of western Europe reinvented themselves in the course of the eleventh century, in no small part via Reform.[10] To put it crudely, the knight and the priest, both in newly-defined roles, conspired to preserve the continuity of aristocratic power through land-holding at the expense of their womenfolk. What this view basically does is to take the reformers' language of misogyny as truly and directly reflecting a historically specific disinheritance of women.

Duby's account of the patriarchal transformation of the eleventh century, developed since the early 1950s by two generations of French scholars, is currently under critical discussion, both in France and in Anglo-American contexts.[11] This critique has not, however, developed to the point where Duby's basic model is redundant; and a brief sketch of this remains essential.[12] According to Duby, towards the end of the tenth century, a subsistence crisis afflicted the landed families of Carolingian Europe. The plunder that had sustained them under Charlemagne and his sons and grandsons had drained away, as had Carolingian power itself, not coincidentally. To the east, on the Elbe

understand clerical celibacy in terms of the 'impalpable but irresistible power' of the medieval Church (p. 2).

[8] M. Douglas, *Purity and Danger: An Analysis of the Concepts of Pollution and Taboo* (London, 1966).

[9] See in particular, G. Duby, *The Knight, the Lady, and the Priest*, trans. B. Bray (New York, 1983), and R. I. Moore, 'Family, community, and cult'.

[10] R. I. Moore, 'Duby's eleventh century', *History*, 69 (1984), pp. 36–49.

[11] See e.g. most recently D. Barthelemy and S. D. White, 'Debate: the "feudal revolution"', *P&P*, 152 (Aug. 1996), pp. 196–223.

[12] See e.g. G. Duby, *The Three Orders: Feudal Society Imagined*, trans. A. Goldhammer (Chicago, 1980), pp. 147–66.

frontier, the plunder economy had been reconstituted under Ottonian leadership; but for families further west there was a problem of survival. Their solution was to seek to exact from the peasantry with far greater consistency than before a surplus of agricultural production – or to put it another way, to continue plundering, only with far greater intensity and with far more control of detail. Hence for Duby, the eleventh century was the age of castles and of castellans. Groups of armed men on horseback usurped the imperial power to command and constrain (known as the 'ban', and properly exercised by counts as public officials) and exacted what justice they pleased from a virtually powerless population. This gang rule was feudal 'custom': our clearest evidence for the regime of exploitation which the castellans now operated are the so-called 'customaries', which set down in writing what the poor now owed to the powerful.[13] This invention of tradition brooked little argument. To the question by what right did he do these things, Ralph of Evreux responded by cutting off the hands and feet of those peasants who had risen in anger to ask him.[14]

The castellan revolution was not conducted without sacrifice on the part of the landed elite itself. If land was to be farmed intensively, then it had to be kept together, not dispersed among the various family members who, according to pre-existing practice, would all receive a share. The ultimate survival of the family, however, now required a shift from partible inheritance to primogeniture – meaning the substantial disinheritance of younger sons and of daughters, the reduction of the daughter's dowry and of the son's marriage portion (the property which he would give over to his wife). The eldest son would now receive the bulk of the family property and would do his best to increase it.

The social logic of Reform starts here as a drama of disinheritance. The tight definition of marriage, the extension of incest prohibitions, and the enforcement of clerical celibacy: all of these measures would prevent the proliferation of claims to inheritance so characteristic of the Carolingian or Ottonian periods. Of the disinherited, the younger sons had more options. The daughters, in Duby's somewhat phallo-cratic imagination, were at the mercy of their violent menfolk, and could only seek refuge or endure captivity in nunneries. For the

[13] See J.-F. Lemarignier, 'La dislocation du *pagus* et le problème des *consuetudines* (x^e–xie siècles)', in *Mélanges dédiés à la mémoire de Louis Halphen* (Paris, 1950), pp. 401–10.
[14] R. H. Hilton, *Bond Men Made Free* (London, 1973), pp. 70–1.

younger brothers, however, there were two options: *le rouge et le noir*. They could either become knights errant, leaving behind natal family and roaming the countryside fantasizing about one day meeting a rich heiress; or they could become priests, again leaving family behind and, as it were, marrying the rich heiress that was the Church. Both knight and priest were bound by an ethic of sexual restraint, chivalric self-control in the case of the former, ascetic celibacy in the case of the latter. The more permanent sexual restraint of the priest carried with it a greater, or at least a more certain, social status – in effect a kind of compensation for the original disinheritance.

Not the least striking aspect of Duby's account for our purposes is the way that it inverts conventional assumptions about the meaning of Reform. The famous and violent conflict between popes and kings, and between Pope Gregory VII and King Henry IV in particular, leads us instinctively to cast Reform as a battle between Church and State, clergy and laity. In Duby's perspective, however, the clash between Pope and King which dominates the media in fact conceals a fundamental collusion between clerical and lay interests, or at least a negotiated settlement, over the distribution of property. The division of sexual labour between men – that is to say, the sharp differentiation between clergy and laity – in fact served the needs of the landed elite for the indivisibility of landed property. In this sense, the Truth that reformers stood for was, unwittingly or otherwise, all too compatible with the 'custom' of the lay *seigneurie*.

This can only be part of the story (especially in northern Italy, where primogeniture was not the means used to resolve heightened competition over land). As Duby affirmed, and as R. I. Moore has pre-eminently demonstrated, Reform was also a popular movement of protest against the arbitrary exercise of seigneurial power. In his trenchant 1980 article in particular, 'Family, community and cult on the eve of the Gregorian Reform', Moore explains why it was that crowds of people gathered in cities like Florence or Milan, Arras or Cambrai, in explosive demonstrations against the uncleanness they perceived in the lives of their priests and bishops.[15] Drawing on the work of Mary Douglas, Moore argues that the society of eleventh-century Europe exemplifies a case of 'the system at war with itself' in

---

[15] Moore, 'Family, community, and cult'; see also his *The Origins of European Dissent* (London, 1977), pp. 36–168.

Douglas's terms.[16] In families and communities split apart by quarrels over land and by the migration of labour necessary to support the agrarian boom, priests, women, and especially priests' wives assumed an unprecedented social importance as mediators in the resulting conflicts. The possibility that priests and their families might abuse their power – or rather, the impossibility of preventing them from doing so – meant that socially vulnerable groups invoked the language of pollution and taboo to guard against the eventuality that new-found powers would corrupt their moral arbiters. In groups aspiring to a system of primogeniture, the activities of those in theory disenfranchised were likely to attract pollution fears: priests, women, and especially priest's wives might become socially 'dirty' because they were 'matter out of place', because their actual power continued to exceed the subdued role they were now supposed to play.

The crowd was the key instrument through which accusations of pollution were voiced and adjudicated. In the Milan in the 1050s, a 'popular front', known as the Pataria, boycotted the masses of priests accused of simony or sexual misdemeanour; they beat and sometimes killed the priests themselves and their concubines.[17] Conversely, the crowd looked for leadership to such religious specialists as had demonstrated their perfect disengagement from the networks of sex, money, and violence that represented the abusive power of the castellans. Through his non-violence, his celibacy, his refusal to purchase his office, or to exploit it for financial gain, a pure priest could demonstrate that he was not a lord's man.[18] Here the truth of Reform is indeed in voluble protest against the custom of the castellans.

On the one hand, then, we have Duby and Reform as seigneurial hegemony, on the other Moore and Reform as popular protest: both scenarios are of course right. Not the least important legacy of the eleventh century is to have established or, at the very least, to have focused one of the central dilemmas for the Church: whether it sides with or against the powers that be.

* * *

[16] Douglas, *Purity and Danger*, ch. 9.
[17] For a narrative account of the Patarenes, see J. P. Whitney, *Hildebrandine Essays* (Cambridge, 1932), pp. 143–57; for an analysis, H. E. J. Cowdrey, 'The papacy, the Patarenes, and the church of Milan', *TRHS*, 5th ser., 18 (1968), pp. 25–48.
[18] Moore, 'Family, community, and cult', pp. 64–5 and *passim*.

The foregoing views are based on the premise that the language of Reform accurately described social reality.[19] Take the well-known case at Florence, as recounted by Andrew of Strumi, one of the chief publicists of the Pataria. An abbot, Guarino, brings a case to the Bishop of Florence. The Bishop's wife Alberga, sitting beside her husband, pronounces on the case; the abbot in turn denounces her: 'Vile Jezebel, do you dare to speak before a meeting of good men and clerks?'[20] This would seem to be – and is often taken as – a perfect illustration of the state of the unreformed Church, the corruption to which the Reformers wished to put an end. As Moore's own work on heresy eloquently demonstrates, however, eleventh-century sources may flatter to deceive their hasty readers.[21] The minds of eleventh-century writers were full of language from the fifth century, if not even earlier. Thus it is, Moore shows, that we have Manichees in Aquitaine in the first decade of the century – not because there are any dualist groups actually in operation there, but because the reporter concerned turned instinctively to Augustine to describe the popular dissent around Limoges. *Mutatis mutandis*, the same may be true of Alberga the Jezebel: we meet her in the course of a polemical narrative, not a detached description of the state of the Church.

No less than the rhetoric of heresy, the rhetoric of gender as deployed by the Reformers demands reading with critical suspicion. In her recent *The Virgin and the Bride*, Kate Cooper demonstrates that the social dynamics of the Christianization of the Roman Empire have been misunderstood, because of a basic historiographical failure to parse the ancient rhetoric of gender.[22] We have entirely under-estimated the extent to which the men and (in particular) the women in the sources refer not to human subjects, but to a symbolic rhetorical economy for discussing the distribution of power among the elite. Whether or not it actually happened, the story of Alberga the bishop's wife conforms to an extremely traditional rhetorical pattern for defaming a man's character by depicting him as unduly swayed by the counsels of his wife. The woman in the story, in other words, is a

---

[19] See e.g. ibid., p. 51.
[20] Andrew of Strumi, *Vita Gualberti*, MGH SS 30, 2, p. 1105, cited by Moore, 'Family, community, and cult', p. 68.
[21] See Moore, *Origins of European Dissent*, pp. 8–20.
[22] K. Cooper, *The Virgin and the Bride: Idealized Womanhood in Late Antiquity* (Cambridge, MA, 1996).

woman 'to think with',[23] and we should beware before making any immediate decisions about her historical agency. The text may in fact tell us far more about the positions of the men involved in the circulation of the story.

Cooper's fundamental premise is that 'gender' as commonly understood by modern scholars is a deceptive category of historical analysis where ancient and medieval social relations are concerned. Our notions of gender as a social or rhetorical construct, however assiduously anti-essentialist, nonetheless continue to trade on a post-Enlightenment understanding of the individual (if only to demonstrate the fictive quality of this idea of subjectivity). Cooper insists that this idea of individuality is meaningless in pre-industrial society, where the basic unit of production, both economic or cultural, and the primary site of identification, is the household. 'The male and female members of a household would have been seen, and would have understood themselves, as two representative dimensions, two *personae*, by which a household might project its quality and claim its rightful standing.'[24] Gender, then, was a relatively weak constraint upon a person's sense of selfhood or agency; and the concept of 'female/male solidarity' cutting across social status was all but empty of meaning. Granted that she was his subordinate, an aristocratic woman had far more in common with her husband or with male kin than with the other women who served her in the household. Her relationships with her female kin would have determined by relative standing in familial terms. The same point is made with aplomb by Sara Suleri in *Meatless Days*, her account of her childhood in Pakistan. Having set out stories of her grandmother, mother, sisters, she must regretfully conclude, '[T]here are no women in the third world.'[25]

What this means is that texts which appeal to universalized notions of 'women' or 'womanly influence' – as texts do from the 'Epic of Gilgamesh' onwards – do not map directly on to a social reality which knew no universal feminine. We need some other way of making sense of these narratives. Cooper suggests that the basic political question governing the ancient rhetoric of gender was not a contest for power between men and women, but between rival families for control of the

---

[23] See P. R. L. Brown, *The Body and Society: Men, Women, and Sexual Renunciation in Early Christianity* (New York, 1988), p. 153 and n. 57.

[24] Cooper, *Virgin and Bride*, p. 4.

[25] S. Suleri, *Meatless Days* (London, 1990), p. 20.

city. This was a competition played out largely, though not at all exclusively, between men. In assessing a man's fitness for power in the city the key question was: was he likely to put his own family's interests ahead of those of the common good? Could he be trusted to administer public moneys without feathering his own dynastic nest? This central question was – and is – often posed and answered not by a careful examination of the candidate's financial transactions, but by a rhetorically charged, if no less meticulous, discussion of his sexual track record. The ancient Romans, like the American (if not also the British) electorate, took marital concord in the household to signify that the candidate could be trusted to administer the city wisely. A man's sexual self-control and his judicious attention to the counsels of his spouse epitomized his capacities of civic government and administration. Conversely, a man who could plausibly be accused of failing to maintain a stable sexual partnership with his wife – either because of his own unstable desires, or because of her overweening influence upon him – was at a disadvantage in the competition for public power. In this compelling metaphorical discourse, sex stood for money, and women stood in for men. As Cooper puts it, let us 'assume for the sake of argument that when a woman is mentioned, a man's character is being judged' by other men.[26]

The relevance of this hermeneutic to the eleventh-century texts is heightened by Cooper's account of the triumph of Christianity, and, in particular, of the ideal of celibacy. While most Roman Christians would have shared instinctively in the ancient moral economy of marital concord, a minority seem deliberately to have set out to subvert it in order to stage a competition between Christians and pagans for public power. The classical code of concord prized sexual restraint within marriage as an index of self-control: taking this premise to the extreme, radical ascetic Christians began to argue that complete eradication of sexual desire, that is, total renunciation of the pleasures of the marriage bed in the name of Christ, was the sign of a more complete self-control, and thus political integrity, than that demonstrated by any pagan senator. Against the figure of the chaste and fertile bride as a symbol of male trustworthiness, the ascetics promoted the icon of the entirely celibate virgin. In so doing they meant to signal their own sexual status, their complete immunity from

[26] Cooper, *Virgin and Bride*, p. 19.

womanly influence and from the ties of family. Fixed as they claimed to be on an otherworldly kingdom, they were morally superior candidates for power in this world. By the early fifth century, the Christian ascetics promoting this ideal – men such as Ambrose and Jerome – had managed permanently to alter the terms of the language in which the public power of men would be discussed.

This is not to say that what Robert Markus has called 'the ascetic invasion' was completely successful.[27] Although we hear disproportionately little from the silent majority who were unpersuaded of the necessity of celibacy, we can hardly doubt their existence, and their continuing commitment to marriage, reproduction, and questions of inheritance. This is not to say, however, that the ascetic moral minority and the sexually active laity lived in separate worlds. Monasteries were never very far away in any sense from secular households, proving from the start an invaluable resource in the disposition of family property.[28] Ascetics and their lay kin inhabited the same moral universe, in particular when it came to questions of power and its proper use. Ascetics themselves sought to explain that their message did not involve spectacular feats of renunciation, but the application of extremely traditional moral principles. The displacement of pagan senators completed, it became less important, perhaps, to accent the rhetoric of gender. By the death of Pope Gregory the Great in 604, a version of ascetic purity was available to all in power, married or not. Gregory's *Pastoral Rule*, a treatise on what sort of person should come to power, and how they should exercise it, has nothing to say about celibacy on the part of the ruler, who is defined in studiously neutral terms: Gregory has in mind any kind of ruler. As Julia Smith shows elsewhere in this volume,[29] when the laity do come into fuller textual view in the Carolingian period, we can see the extent to which there is a live moral tradition, both for men and for women, outside the cloister.

* * *

If we return to the eleventh century, the first effect of this rhetorical perspective on the function of gender must be to alter our approach to the sources. It ought to be possible to foreclose discussion of knightly

[27] R. A. Markus, *The End of Ancient Christianity* (Cambridge, 1990), ch. 11.
[28] See C. Leyser, *Family and Monastery in Early Medieval Europe* (in preparation).
[29] Above, pp. 51–73.

or priestly culture as neurotic or misogynist in its intentions: although these may have been the effect, fear of sex or hatred of women were not the purpose of the heavily-coded language employed by all parties. The disinheritance of women as depicted in charters or in patrilineal genealogies may connote not a direct change in the distribution of property, but a shift in the way families represented themselves.[30] While we may dissent from Duby's 'alarming sympathy for the psychology of sexual dominance'[31] in asserting the victory of the castellans, we may be in a position to extend his original insight that the eleventh century witnessed not a new nobility, but a reinvention – through patrilineal rhetoric rather than primogeniture – of the already established Carolingian families. Encrypted as it may be in an ancient pattern, the evidence does not suggest a bland continuity across the period 800–1200: in a highly rhetorical culture, a change in self-presentation is an event of the first importance.

This is not, however, to say that real women, and real younger sons, were not disinherited – that the reality did not on occasion accord with the rhetoric. It is simply that we may be unable to tell from the available evidence. Pauline Stafford has called for caution before presuming the victory of primogeniture, having found plentiful evidence of landholding and inheritance by aristocratic women.[32] Their presence is easier to account for if we do not assume that the rhetoric of misogyny of relates directly to disinheritance of women. The career of someone like Emma, who was relatively remote from Reform, or of Matilda of Tuscany, who was central, shows how a woman might seek to manipulate the tropes of womanly influence to her own advantage. Matilda's achievement in managing to ride out the accusation of evil counsellor of Gregory VII surely demands further study.[33]

If it is the case that, when a woman is mentioned, a man's character is being judged by his peers, we might start looking for the men concerned. In Duby's scenario, the men in competition are, typically, fathers and sons, or elder brothers and younger brothers. These conflicts may in turn resolve into an institutional dialogue between

---

[30] D. Herlihy, 'Land, family, and women in continental Europe, 700–1201', *Traditio*, 18 (1962), pp. 89–120 on the difficulty of interpreting matronymics in charters.

[31] The phrase is Cooper's, describing the work of Paul Veyne: *Virgin and Bride*, p. 2.

[32] Stafford, 'La mutation familiale: a suitable case for caution', paper delivered at the International Medieval Congress, Leeds, 1995.

[33] Above, n. 5.

the sexually active laity and the infertile clergy. Here again rhetorical criticism allows us to extend Duby's argument. We can see the tense collaboration between clergy and laity as a function of their heightening rhetorical battle. In a context where a rhetorical 'edge' could be decisive in resolving a property dispute, it was in lay interests to aspire to a demonstration of concord within marriage, as it was in clerical interests to continue to claim the supreme moral superiority of celibacy. Elder and younger sons each compelled the other into a declaration of sexual probity from which it was difficult to retreat.

Also amplified is R. I. Moore's sense of the involvement of the crowd. The patrician families of the ancient world had always competed with each other before an audience: their best rhetorical efforts were aimed at persuading not only other aristocrats, but an unpredictable popular following. By the mid-eleventh century, classical politics had, perhaps, returned to the cities of northern Italy and the Low Countries. It was once more the *plebs* whose loyalties those in power attempted to capture through their stylized moral self-promotion.

At the heart of Reform, perhaps, was not so much a conflict between clergy and laity, as among the ambiguously defined order of the 'prayingmen'.[34] It is the intensity of competition between religious specialists that most vividly explains the flourishing of the rhetoric of womanly influence in the eleventh century. Accusations of impurity were not simply levelled by celibate priests at their conjugally bound colleagues. Ian Robinson, nearly twenty years ago, demonstrated the way in which claims to purity and accusations of pollution were generated from within the circle of Gregory VII.[35] This had more than a little to do with Gregory's capacity to isolate himself precisely by insisting on ever more extravagant demonstrations of loyalty, but these cases are structurally, as well as personally, revealing. In the very eye of the reforming hurricane, we may see with some clarity the terms on which male religious competed for the moral highground.

Robinson's most telling example concerns Manasses, Archbishop of Rheims from 1069 until his deposition by Gregory in 1080. As we saw earlier, Manasses was, within a generation, a byword for flagrant

---

[34] The formulation is Janet Nelson's: 'Monks, secular men, and masculinity, c. 900', in D. M. Hadley, ed., *Images of Masculinity in the Middle Ages* (forthcoming).

[35] I. S. Robinson, 'The friendship network of Gregory VII', *History*, 63 (1978), pp. 1–23; idem, '*Periculosus homo*: Pope Gregory VII and episcopal authority', *Viator*, 9 (1978), pp. 103–31.

simony – but he had originally been a friend of Gregory's.[36] How did this reversal of fortune come about? In his earlier incarnation as Archdeacon Hildebrand, Gregory had backed Manasses against the Bishop of Laon for the see of Rheims. Manasses accordingly showed himself eager to support Gregory's papacy, coming to Lenten synods, and holding councils himself to promulgate papal decrees. But a chorus of accusers was massing against him. To name but three: Helinand, the still-rankled Bishop of Laon, the scholar Bruno, then chancellor of the school of Rheims, who was to leave and found the Carthusians, and thirdly the cathedral provost, also called Manasses, who was later himself to ascend the archiepiscopal throne at Rheims. These men pestered the Archbishop, and sought to undermine his position at Rome by accusing him of simony. Gregory seems throughout to have resisted this charge; indeed, in 1076 the Pope heard from his legate in France, Hugh of Die, that the provost – not the Archbishop – was a simoniac and had begged pardon for having obtained his office improperly. The following year, Archbishop Manasses attempted to reinforce this impression by writing to Gregory of his provost's uncontrolled violence and sexual activities – in particular, his incestuous union with his own sister, a nun and abbess.[37] But the provost Manasses, although accused of the complete portfolio of pollutions, now had a powerful friend in the legate Hugh of Die, who represented his apparent disgrace as a simoniac as a dutiful submission to legatine authority. It was this virtue of obedience which Archbishop Manasses was, by contrast, loath to demonstrate, and which proved his undoing. When the Archbishop refused repeatedly to attend councils called by Hugh, Gregory no longer felt inclined to resist the overall weight of accusations against his former protégé. In 1080, at Hugh's behest, Manasses was deposed. The following year, we hear of him at Rome with King Henry IV. By the time Guibert of Nogent wrote in 1115, Manasses was remembered not only as a simoniac, but as one 'totally lacking that tranquillity of temper which is most becoming to a gentleman'.[38] The lack of self-control which the Archbishop had attributed to his

---

[36] For this and what follows, see Robinson, 'Friendship network', pp. 15–18 and the references there given; also J. R. Williams, 'Archbishop Manasses I of Rheims and Pope Gregory VII', *AHR*, 54 (1948–9), pp. 804–24.
[37] For this letter see MGH, *Die Briefe der deutschen Kaiserzeit*, 5, pp. 178–82, esp. p. 179.
[38] Guibert, *Monodiae*, 1.11, trans. Benton, p. 59.

provost had now rebounded, and had come to rest on Manasses in perpetuity.

Manasses's case illustrates to perfection the volatility of the claims and accusations raised by reformers. The drama is played out in the white heat of Gregory's conflict with Henry IV, when we might expect that the issue of allegiance would subsume all other tests of probity. Manasses was not, however, an isolated casualty of the engine of Reform.[39] It was in the nature of Reform to scrutinize minutely a man's character, to consider all possible slurs against him. As clerics, both accusers and accused were specialists in the genre of scrutiny: we should not be surprised to find the rhetoric of womanly influence, the classic instrument for character scrutiny, running wild in this period.

The basic structural problem, as contemporaries had observed from the early decades of the century, was that there were rival groups of religious specialists. When he came in the late 1020s to rearticulate the traditional scheme of the tripartite division of human society, Bishop Adalbero of Laon faced a problem in classifying those responsible for the spiritual wellbeing of the community.[40] It was not difficult to identify those who worked, or those who fought, but the third group could be represented either by the clergy or by cloistered ascetics. In the end, Adalbero chose a generic description – 'those who prayed' – that obfuscated the issue of division. In other contexts, however, notably at the court of King Robert the Pious, Adalbero waxed voluble on the subject of the dissension that split the ranks of the *oratores*, or more precisely, the insubordination of monks to episcopal authority. Several scholars have worked to unravel the knot of accusations entangling Robert and his entourage in the 1020s, including womanly influence, monkish flattery, and – fatally for selected clerks at Orleans – heresy.[41]

Rather than attempt to revisit this complex scene, we may return to the simpler story of Abbot Guarino and Alberga the bishop's wife. What this story illustrates is, perhaps, less the condition of the unreformed Church, than the archetypal conditions under which the

---

[39] See Robinson, 'Friendship network', for several other instances.

[40] See C. Carozzi, 'Les fondements de la tripartition sociale chez Adalbéron de Laon', *Annales*, 33 (1978), pp. 683–702; Moore, 'Family, community, and cult', pp. 55–6.

[41] See e.g. R.-H. Bautier, 'L'hérésie d'Orleans et le mouvement intellectuel au débuts du XIe siècle: documents et hypothèses', in *Enseignement et vie intellectuelle, IXᵉ-XVIᵉ siècle. Actes du 95e Congrès national des sociétés savants (Rheims, 1970): section de philologie et d'histoire jusqu'à 1610 tome 1* (Paris, 1974), I, pp. 63–88; Duby, *Three Orders*, pp. 21–54.

rhetoric of Reform is generated. Reform begins when monks accuse bishops of being susceptible to womanly influence. They thereby assert that they are the truly celibate, the truly expert, as against the concubine-ridden priesthood.

Reform is often thought of as the moment at which standards of monastic holiness break out of the cloister into the wider clerical and lay world beyond; but the claim to moral superiority had never been confined to the cloister. Gregory the Great, for one, had ensured precisely that monks could claim no monopoly on spiritual authority. What Reform represents, therefore, is just the reverse – the attempt by (initially) cloistered men to reassert their supreme integrity, to reappropriate the moral highground from the bishops who had stolen it in the early middle ages.

Eleventh-century monks then, as Frederick Paxton has put it, staged their own revolt against the Carolingian authorities: they played the castellans to the bishops' counts.[42] This was not, or not only, spiritual warfare: land was at stake, just as in secular conflicts. Very often, disputes between monks and bishops started with discussion of dispute over monastic immunities. In their defence of their property rights monks were unabashed, every bit as assertive as their lay counterparts. Thus Abbo of Fleury, who conclusively defeated Arcbishop Arnulf of Rheims in his defence of monastic property rights: 'I am more powerful than our Lord the king of the Franks in these lands where no one fears his rule.'[43] More extravagant still was the boast of Odilo of Cluny that he had found Cluny of wood and left it of marble, exactly as had the Emperor Augustus in Rome. In their appropriation of the classical rhetoric of gender against their clerical contemporaries, the ascetic reformers of the eleventh century could boast with similar confidence of emulating the Roman past.[44]

*　*　*

[42] F. Paxton, '*Abbas* and *Rex*: image of authority in the biographical literature of Fleury (987–1044)' (unpublished paper). My thanks to the author for making available a copy of this paper.

[43] Aimo of Fleury, *Vita s. Abbonis*, 20, PL 139, col. 410. For discussion see T. Head, *Hagiography and the Cult of the Saints: the Diocese of Orleans, 800–1200* (Cambridge, 1990), pp. 236–57; and also idem, 'The judgement of God: Andrew of Fleury's account of the Peace League of Bourges', in T. Head and R. Landes, eds, *The Peace of God: Social Violence and Religious Response in France around the Year 1000* (Ithaca, NY, 1992), pp. 219–38.

[44] Jotsald, *Vita s. Odilonis*, 1.13, PL 142, col. 908.

The woman in the texts of Reform is, therefore, like the woman in the courtly romances, or the woman who is Jesus as Mother: she is not an historical agent, but a woman to think with. This does not mean the end of the historical inquiry itself. We need, on the contrary, to be still more precise about why actors in the drama of Reform should have called upon this rhetorical tradition when they did. That men can use women to think with, and have done so at many different points in the Christian and other traditions, makes all the more urgent the question of why the ancient rhetoric of gender was used to enforce a division of male sexual labour in eleventh-century Europe.

In this analysis of rhetorical timing, the model of social change proposed by Duby remains relevant as an explanory framework. While being more cautious about who is doing what to whom, we can still imagine a context in which the rhetoric of womanly influence flourishes because of heightened competition between and among families over the distribution of landed property. The meaning of clerical celibacy may still be related at the level of reality to the fact of inheritance disputes; the meaning of simony to the fact of the circulation of money; and the meaning of peace from the incidence of arbitrary violence which, for one recent commentator, lies at the centre of the eleventh-century revolution.[45]

The current critique of Duby takes rhetorical criticism one step further. Dominique Barthelemy and others have argued that the whole of the 'transformation of the year 1000' is, in effect, an optical illusion; that what Duby sees in the charters as evidence for a breakdown in comital justice, the rise of private and militarized power of the castellans, is no more than a change in scribal practice.[46] If this critique is accurate, it renders all the more pressing the task of explaining how men in the eleventh century came to formulate their languages of custom and of truth.

University of Manchester

---

[45] T. N. Bisson, 'The "feudal revolution"', *P&P*, 142 (Feb. 1994), pp. 8–42.

[46] See above, n. 11; see also J. L. Nelson, reviewing Head and Landes, *Peace of God* in *Speculum*, 69 (1994), pp. 163–9, on the possibility that 'the crowd', at least in the early eleventh century, is a rhetorical construct.

THE GENDER OF THE CHURCH: THE FEMALE IMAGE OF *ECCLESIA* IN THE MIDDLE AGES

by JO SPREADBURY

IN a famous eucharistic vision, recorded in the *Scivias*, Hildegard of Bingen saw what she calls the 'image of a woman' ('*muliebris imago*') approaching the Cross so that she was sprinkled by the blood from Christ's side. In the Eibingen miniature which accompanies this vision, the woman is shown not only sprinkled with Christ's blood but catching it in a chalice. Below the Cross an altar bearing a chalice is shown and the same woman stands beside it, her arms outstretched in prayer. Hildegard says in the text that the woman 'frequently approached' the altar and there 'devotedly offers her dowry, which is the body and blood of the Son of God'. The illustration shows nothing of the vested priest who is described in the text approaching the altar after the woman to celebrate the divine mysteries; but it appears that the woman herself is celebrating the mysteries of Christ's passion which are recalled in the Eucharist and pictured around the altar. The interpretation of this vision says that the woman is *Ecclesia*, the Church, the Bride of Christ.[1]

The aim of this paper is to explore the conceptual implications which lie behind such a vision, to examine the image of the Church as a gender-specific female figure and to compare this with ecclesiastical teaching on the role of women. To this end it will look first at late Antique and early medieval 'theory' about the Church, and then at later medieval 'practice': how this theory was made concrete in iconography, and what influence it may have had. This presupposes that the female form of *Ecclesia* is to be understood as more than just a linguistic accident, based on the feminine gender of the noun. Such a supposition is supported by the weight of iconographic evidence and devotional writing in which the Church is represented as a woman.[2]

---

[1] Hildegard of Bingen, *Scivias*, trans. Columba Hart and Jane Bishop (New York, 1990), ii, vision 6, p. 237 (illus. p. 235).

[2] See, e.g., S. Tromp, 'Ecclesia sponsa virgo mater', *Gregorianum*, 18 (1937), pp. 3–29; Claude Chavasse, *The Bride of Christ, an Enquiry into the Nuptial Element in Early Christianity* (London, 1939); J. C. Plumpe, *Mater Ecclesia. An Inquiry into the Concept of the Church as*

The ultimate source of this hypostasis is the Pauline argument in the Epistle to the Ephesians (5.21–33) that the union of husband and wife is modelled on the mystery of the relationship between Christ and his Church, a relationship which echoes the nuptial language used for the Old Testament covenant between God and his people Israel. That the Church is the Bride of Christ became a commonplace of early Christian and medieval theology, and many writers developed the theme with reference to the Song of Songs or the wedding feast of the Lamb which St John describes in Revelation. As Bride, the 'female' Church is duly subject to Christ as a wife to her husband, according to the Pauline view of 'headship'.

However, the interpretation in Ephesians of the phrase from Genesis (2.24) that 'the two shall become one flesh', as a 'profound mystery ... that refers to Christ and the Church', also gives rise to St Paul's fundamental concept of the Church as the Body of Christ.[3] Expressions such as 'corpus quod est Ecclesia', or 'corpus scilicet Ecclesia', are standard ways of referring to this.[4] To underline that they were truly 'one flesh', the Church was said to have been born from the side of Jesus as he 'slept' in death on the Cross, just as the first Eve had been formed from Adam's side.[5] Thus the blood and water which issued from Jesus' side are seen both as a type of the Sacrament, and also as a type of the Church as she is the Body of Christ.[6]

The Church is also said to participate in the offering of the Eucharistic Body of Christ. For example in the Carolingian period, following the influential writings of Isidore of Seville and Bede especially, *Ecclesia* is frequently described as 'celebrating' or 'offering' the sacrifice to God. To quote one example from Bede, 'the Church is never separated from Christ ... but rising to offer the sacrifice of the Mass on solemn feastdays, she enacts within herself the mysteries of his flesh and blood in the wine and bread'.[7] Bede even says that the power

---

Mother in Early Christianity, Catholic University of America Studies in Christian Antiquity, 51 (Washington, DC, 1943); A. Müller, *Ecclesia-Maria* (Fribourg, 1951).

[3] E.g. Eph. 1.22, 5.23; Col. 1.18, 24.

[4] H. de Lubac, *Corpus mysticum. L'eucharistie et l'église au moyen âge: étude historique*, Théologie, 3, 2nd edn (Paris, 1949), p. 94.

[5] E.g. Tertullian, *De anima*, 43: Eve coming from Adam's side is 'a type of the Church, the true mother of all living' (*PL* 2, col. 723). See S. Tromp, 'De nativitate Ecclesiae ex corde Iesu in cruce', *Gregorianum*, 13 (1932), pp. 489–527.

[6] E.g. Augustine, *In Iohannis evangelium tractatus*, IX.10: 'the dead Christ's side is pierced with a spear, that the sacraments may flow forth to form the Church' (*PL* 35, col. 1463).

[7] *Expositio in Samuelem*, I, v (*PL* 91, col. 514): 'Et Ecclesia nunquam a Christo deserta ...

of the keys was committed to *Ecclesia* by Jesus.[8] The Church as Christ's Body is one with him in his priesthood and so shares in his self-offering. An extreme expression of this is Paschasius Radbertus' argument that 'Christ and *Ecclesia* are one body. Therefore Christ without *Ecclesia* is not the eternal high priest, nor is *Ecclesia* offered to God the Father without Christ.'[9]

Clearly when the Church is described in terms of a priest offering the sacrifice of the Mass she is in some cases meant to represent the 'universal Church', the 'priesthood of all believers';[10] and Isidore for instance uses 'Christians', 'the faithful', or simply 'we', as the subject of *offere* as well as *Ecclesia*.[11] There is this corporate sense in the way Paul refers to the Church, but it still does not inhibit his use of the single figure for the Bride of Christ: writing to the Corinthians he says (II Cor. 11.2): 'I betrothed you [*vos*] to Christ . . . as a pure virgin to her one husband.' So when the concept of *Ecclesia* becomes concrete in iconography, the dominant image is the literal one: the figure of a woman such as Hildegard saw.

The main attribute of *Ecclesia* in iconography, consequently, is a chalice, as shown in an early seventh-century Egyptian mural where *Mater Ecclesia* (named) holds a cup in her left hand and points to the red liquid it contains with her right hand.[12] The sacramental significance of *Ecclesia*'s chalice is even more clearly demonstrated in scenes of the crucifixion where, from the late eighth or early ninth century until the fifteenth, she is shown (as in Hildegard's picture) catching Jesus' blood in a cup,[13] and she sometimes manages this even as she is being

---

solemnibus missarum diebus ad immolandum ascendens, carnis eius et sanguinis in vino ac pane secum mysteria defert.' See P. Raphael Schulte, *Die Messe als Opfer der Kirche*, Liturgiewissenschaftliche Quellen und Forschungen, 35 (Münster, 1959).

[8] *PL* 91, col. 1016: 'Dominus eidem Ecclesiae dicit, Quaecunque alligaveris super terram . . .'; *PL* 93, col. 163: 'Data est Ecclesiae in Christo omnis potestas in coelo et in terra, clavibus ei ligandi atque solvendi dimissis.'

[9] *Epistola de corpore et sanguine domini* (PL 120, cols 1352–3): 'Christus et Ecclesia unum corpus. Itaque nec Christus sine Ecclesia pontifex in aeternum, nec Ecclesia sine Christo Deo Patri offertur.'

[10] Cf. Walafrid Strabo: 'unum panem esse et sanguinem, quem universalis offert ecclesia', cited in Schulte, *Die Messe*, p. 142; Mozarabic liturgy: 'Ecclesia ecce tua . . . voce imprecatur unica, et sacrificiorum oblata offert devotione cernua', ibid., p. 55.

[11] Schulte, *Die Messe*, p. 36.

[12] Gertrud Schiller, *Die Ikonographie der Christlichen Kunst*, 5 vols in 6 (Gütersloh, 1966–91), 4.1, fig. 98. For ease of reference, most of my iconographic examples are taken from this one work, although I do not necessarily cite all her relevant illustrations.

[13] Ibid., 2, figs 364–5, 367, 371–3 etc.; 4.1, figs 100–1, 107–11 etc.

born from his wounded side.[14] The salvific effect of Christ's sacrifice is thus encapsulated in images that just show *Ecclesia* with a chalice: the Body of Christ ministering the Blood of Christ, as the Church makes the sacrament of the Eucharist present for the faithful. Although *Ecclesia* in crucifixion scenes is at first most frequently found in sacramentaries and liturgical books, she becomes popular in monumental art from the twelfth century onwards and thus would have been familiar to a far wider audience.[15]

However, these concrete, public representations of *Ecclesia* highlight the inherent conflict between the iconographic type of the Church and the role allowed to women in the medieval Church. Church councils and canon law repeatedly forbade women, even consecrated religious, from touching sacred vessels, carrying communion to the sick, or even approaching the altar. These prohibitions are expressed in the strongest language. Gratian, for example, some twenty years before Hildegard recorded her vision, reiterated

> that consecrated women and nuns handle sacred vessels and altar cloths . . . is utterly blameworthy and reprehensible . . . this pestilence must be blotted out.[16] . . . [S]acred vessels may not be touched except by consecrated [men] dedicated to God, lest God be angered at such presumption and strike down his people.[17] . . . [S]ome priests have so little regard for the divine mysteries that they entrust the holy of holies to those lay people and women who are prohibited from entering the sacrarium and approaching the altar. How dreadful and detestable this is.[18]

---

[14] Schiller, *Ikonographie*, 4.1, figs 217–20.

[15] Ibid., 4.1, figs 113, 116, 126, 129, 132–3, 135 etc.

[16] D.23 c.25 (*CIC*, 1, col. 86): 'Sacratas Deo feminas vel monachas sacra vasa vel sacratas pallas penes vos contingere, et incensum circa altaria deferre, perlatum est ad apostolicam sedem; que omnia vituperatione et reprehensione plena esse, nulli recte sapientum dubium est. . . . Et ne pestis hec latius divulgetur, per omnes provincias abstergi citissime mandamus.'

[17] D.1 de cons. c.41 (*CIC*, 1, cols 1304–5): 'In sancta apostolica sede statutum est, ut sacra vasa non ab aliis, quam a sacratis Dominoque dicatis contrectentur hominibus. Ne pro talibus presumptionibus iratus Dominus plagam inponat populo suo, et hi etiam, qui non peccaverunt, pereant, quia perit iustus sepissime pro inpio.' Note the gender distinction implicit in these last two examples between the 'consecration' of men and women: the participle *sacratus* is used of both, yet women are not thereby 'qualified' in the same way as men.

[18] D.2 de cons. c.29 (*CIC*, 1, col. 1323): 'Pervenit ad notitiam nostram, quod quidam presbiteri in tantum parvipendant divina misteria, ut laico aut feminae sacrum corpus

Yet at this period *Ecclesia* as a woman was shown holding a Eucharistic chalice, and in some illustrations, like Hildegard's, she is shown at the altar. In several of the liturgical *Exultet* Rolls, a woman representing the Church is shown standing in the apse of the sanctuary.[19] In one case she stands behind an altar on which the eucharistic elements are placed, with her arms outstretched in the *orans* posture which, due to the position of the altar and elements, evokes the stance of a priest at the 'Sursum corda'.[20] In other cases she sits on a structure which doubles as both a church building and an altar, with candlesticks ranged either side of her as the sacramental Body of Christ.[21]

These representations which show the Church on her own escape a qualification which could be imposed on the image of *Ecclesia* when she is paired with *Synagoga*. The latter is often shown turning away from the Cross in unbelief, her crown slipping from her head and her banner, or the tablets of the Old Law, broken. Here the positive image of 'woman' is qualified by the negative image, as the two female figures, like the Virgin Mary and Eve, between them demonstrate the ambivalence of many early writers towards women, capable of great sanctity and redemptive power or sinfulness

Domini tradant ad deferendum infirmis, et quibus prohibetur, ne sacrarium ingrediantur, nec ad altare appropinquent, illis sancta sanctorum conmittuntur. Quod quam sit horribile quamque detestabile, omnium religiosorum animadvertit prudentia.' Cf. the letter from three Gallican bishops admonishing two Irish priests in Brittany in the sixth century for allowing women to administer the chalice: 'adhibitis mulieribus in sacrificio divino, quas conhospitas nominastis, facere praesumastis, sic ut erogantibus vobis eucharistiam illae vobis positis calices teneant et sanguinem Christi populo administrare praesumant. Cuius rei novitas et inaudita superstitio nos non leviter contristavit': L. Duchesne, 'Lovocat et Catihern, prêtres bretons du temps de sainte Melaine', *Revue de Bretagne et de Vendée*, 6th ser., 7 (1885), pp. 5–6.

[19] These illustrations to the proclamation sung when the Paschal candle was lit were clearly intended to be seen by the congregation. They are placed upside down in relation to the text so that they become visible as the deacon recites and the manuscript unrolls over the back of the lectern.

[20] Myrtilla Avery, *The Exultet Rolls of South Italy* (Princeton, NJ, 1936), pl. LXIV (MS originally from Sorrento, *c.* 1105–18, now in the archives at Montecassino). This interpretation assumes either a late attestation of westward-facing celebration, or that *Ecclesia* is represented from the east during the prayer of consecration. Cf. pl. XLV (also in Schiller, *Ikonographie*, 4.1, fig. 209), CXLIX, both late eleventh-century, where the altar is not shown and *Ecclesia*'s gesture is correspondingly less hieratic.

[21] Avery, *Exultet Rolls*, pl. CXL (MS Vat. Lat. 9820, dated *c.* 981–7, from S. Vincenzo al Volturno, also in Schiller, *Ikonographie*, 4.1, fig. 208), CLXXXIX (late eleventh-century from South Italy, now in the museum at Velletri). A late thirteenth-century roll does 'revise' this image to show a bearded man wearing a mitre (or perhaps a papal tiara) in place of the female figure (Avery, *Exultet Rolls*, pl. CLVIII).

and corrupting temptation.[22] Such ambivalence is also shown in commentaries on Revelation, where both the woman clothed in the sun and the scarlet whore were considered in medieval thought to represent the Church, either faithful or sinful.[23] It is notable that the whore of Babylon is both described (Rev. 17.4) and depicted as holding a cup;[24] yet this did not inhibit the representation of the Bride of Christ with her chalice. Indeed *Ecclesia* is even shown by some artists riding on a beast with the four heads of the Gospel creatures, which is close as a type to the seven-headed beast of the scarlet whore.[25] This overlap of imagery clearly presented problems for some medieval writers. In the patristic period theologians employed the idea that the Church could be represented by sinful women who were redeemed, like Rahab or Hosea's prostitute wife.[26] Ambrose said with reference to the woman of the city who anointed Jesus in Luke 7: 'it is fitting that the Church took on the form of a sinner [*peccatrix*] since Christ also took on the form of a sinner [*peccator*]'.[27] However, by the Middle Ages the problem of heretical sects meant that the Church had to be seen as pure and uncorrupt, and some heretics clearly tried to argue that the whore of Babylon represented the Roman Church in contrast to their own pure beliefs. The Dominican Moneta of Cremona was even forced to assert, in response to Cathar claims, that the scarlet whore in Revelation could not have been intended to portray the *Ecclesia Romana* because the Church as such did not exist at the time St John wrote.[28] One wonders if the image of the prostitute with the cup was a particular focus for Cathar criticism of the Church because of their views about the catholic sacraments.[29]

---

[22] See E. Guldan, *Eva und Maria, eine Antithese als Bildmotiv* (Graz and Cologne, 1966).

[23] Marie-Louise Therel, 'La "femme à la coupe" dans les images inspirées de l'Apocalypse', in *Actes du 96e congrès national des sociétés savantes (Toulouse, 1971), Section d'archéologie et d'histoire de l'art. Archéologie occitane*, tome I, préhistoire et varia (Paris, 1976), pp. 373–94.

[24] Ibid.; Schiller, *Ikonographie*, 5, figs 598–600, 610–13, 617–22, etc.

[25] Cf. ibid., 4.1, figs 111, 113, 227; 5, figs 600, 622, 625 etc. (N.b. fig. 624, where the prostitute is pictured on a stumbling donkey in the manner of *Synagoga*.)

[26] Jean Danielou, *From Shadows to Reality. Studies in the Biblical Typology of the Fathers*, trans. W. Hibberd (London, 1960), pp. 244–60.

[27] *Expositio evangelii secundum Lucam*, vi, 21 (*PL* 15, col. 1674): '[Ecclesia] merito speciem accipit peccatricis, quia Christus quoque formam peccatoribus accepit.'

[28] *Adversus Catharos et Valdenses*, ed. T. Ricchini (Rome, 1743), V, i–ii, pp. 399–401.

[29] See Peter of Vaux-de-Cernay, *Hystoria Albigensis*, P. Guebin and E. Lyons, eds, 3 vols (Paris, 1926–39), I, 12, p. 12, for a juxtaposition of these two concerns.

Another more serious qualification of the positive value of this image of the Church for redressing the balance weighed down by medieval misogyny would be that the figure is simply an abstract allegory, with little or no relevance for the position of real women. Arguably, however, the iconographic type of *Ecclesia* did influence the representation of other more concrete female saints where such a qualification does not apply. In some crucifixion scenes from the eleventh century onwards which reflect Byzantine influence, the Church is pictured kneeling rather than standing at the foot of the Cross.[30] That attitude came to be used as standard for Mary Magdalen, who was herself frequently regarded by patristic and early medieval writers as a type of the Church. In later portraits of the Magdalen, her usual attribute, the jar of ointment, is depicted as an ornate vessel like a chalice or ciborium, and art historians have remarked that in some paintings she lifts the lid of the jar as if its contents were precious, 'as if she were revealing a mystery'.[31] Sometimes (as in the picture known as the Mansi Magdalen) she is shown holding the lid vertically over the jar between thumb and forefinger in a curiously sacerdotal stance, reminiscent of a priest when he turns to the congregation with the host and chalice and proclaims 'Ecce Agnus Dei'.[32] In a late print of 1530, by the 'Monogramist RB', a rather florid Magdalen kneels at the foot of the Cross actually catching Christ's blood in a chalice over which a small host hovers.[33] The image of *Ecclesia* with her chalice also seems to have paved the way for depictions like those which show St Barbara holding chalice and host, to represent the opportunity she would grant to her devotees to receive Communion before they died;[34] or those of

---

[30] See H. V. Sauerland and A. Haseloff, *Der Psalter Erzbischof Egberts von Trier* (Trier, 1901), pp. 179–84.

[31] M. J. Friedländer on Quentin Massys' Antwerp Magdalen: *Die altniederlandische Malerei*, 14 vols (Berlin, 1924–37), 7, p. 35 (fig. 61, pl. XXXIII).

[32] Ibid., 7, fig. 87, pl. LXI. Note the similarity in posture and background between this painting and the artist's full-length portrait of the risen Christ in the Johnson collection in Philadelphia (ibid., 7, fig. 95, pl. LXIV).

[33] I have only seen this reproduced in the Warburg Institute photographic collection, but it is described by J. D. Passavant, *Le peintre-graveur*, 6 vols (Leipzig, 1860–4), 4, p. 135, no. 14. Passavant, however, does not mention the presence of the host in the Magdalen's chalice. A twelfth-century *Vita*, echoing a sermon of Gregory the Great, describes in sacramental imagery how the Magdalen, as *apostola apostolorum*, compensated for the guilt of Eve: 'Then with a poisoned cup Eve inebriated a man in paradise; now the Magdalen gives the chalice of eternal life to the apostles to drink' (*PL* 106, col. 1475; wrongly attributed to Hrabanus Maurus).

[34] See J. de Lapparent, *Sainte Barbe* (Paris, 1926); and for the literary sources of this image

more historical women saints like Odilia, Abbess of Hohenburg in Alsace, who was said to have revived after her death when an angel brought her the sacrament, which she then administered to herself.[35] Even St Clare holding her monstrance in token of her legendary routing of the Saracens from the walls of Assisi may owe something to the iconographic type of *Ecclesia* who may also be shown with a monstrance.

At the level of personal devotion, the image of *Ecclesia* seems to have influenced the experience of women in many ways as more than an abstract allegory. The cult of the Sacred Blood was of particular importance to women, and this may be connected to the access they saw for the female figure of Ecclesia to Christ's blood in crucifixion scenes. Catherine of Siena, who is known to have been susceptible to visual images,[36] frequently exhorts her correspondents to stand at the foot of the Cross to be bathed and inebriated in the blood of Christ, although she cites Mary Magdalen rather than invoking *Ecclesia* directly as her exemplar in this.[37] It does not seem coincidental that women frequently experienced visions in which they received communion in a manner that bypassed clerical authority.[38] Many of these incidents date from the thirteenth century, in direct response to increasing prohibition of the chalice to women,[39] a fact that would have thrown the ambiguity of *Ecclesia* as a woman with a chalice into even starker relief. Ida of Léau, grieving with her sisters when even the ablutions cup was prohibited to them, tried to go up to the altar to take the sacrament in both kinds and could scarcely be dragged back to the choir by two other nuns who were aware that women should not approach the altar. As a result, however, Ida was visited by the Lord every Sunday and received 'more sweetness and savour' than she had obtained from the sacrament itself.[40] Lutgard of Aywières standing

---

Baudouin de Gaiffier, 'Le triptyque du Maître de la Légende de Sainte Barbe, sources littéraires de l'iconographie', *Revue belge d'archéologie et d'histoire de l'art*, 28 (1959), pp. 3–23.

[35] A. M. Raggi, 'Odilia', *Bibliotheca Sanctorum*, 13 vols (Rome, 1961–70), 9, cols 1110–16.

[36] Millard Meiss, *Painting in Florence and Siena after the Black Death* (Princeton, NJ, 1951), pp. 105–6.

[37] E.g. Suzanne Noffke, *The Letters of Catherine of Siena, Volume 1* (New York, 1988), letter 2, p. 42.

[38] Caroline Walker Bynum, *Holy Feast and Holy Fast. The Religious Significance of Food to Medieval Women* (Berkeley, Los Angeles, and London, 1987), esp. pp. 227–37.

[39] Joseph A. Jungman, *The Mass of the Roman Rite: its Origins and Development*, trans. Francis A. Brunner, 2 vols (New York, 1951–5), 2, pp. 381–6, 412–14.

[40] *Vita B. Idae Lewensis*, ch. 2, paras 19–20, ActaSS, Oct., 13, pp. 113–14. After this experience Ida is said to have written verse in the vernacular extolling spiritual communion

before the crucifix (in the manner of *Ecclesia*) was embraced by 'Christ all bloody on the Cross', and drank sweetness from the wound in his side.[41] Angela of Foligno also had a vision of Christ bleeding and drank from his wound; on another occasion she was told by angels that 'he is given to you in order that you may present and administer him to others'.[42] Such cases can be multiplied from the many examples quoted in recent studies of women's visions and eucharistic experience.[43]

In some thirteenth-century visions which specifically involve a chalice, the influence of the figure of *Ecclesia* is felt even more strongly, as by the late Middle Ages women would have had no direct experience of receiving from the consecrated chalice, let alone of administering it or seeing other women do so. Hadewijch of Helfta received a chalice full of blood from which she drank.[44] Gertrude the Great, who described Jesus as 'flesh of my flesh and bone of my bone', received the spiritual imprint of his wounds and said to him that 'By those wounds you healed my soul and gave me the cup of the nectar of love to drink.'[45] Gertrude was also entrusted with the power of binding and loosing by Christ in a vision, and he equates her in this with 'all the ministers of his Church'.[46] Mechtild of Hackeborn was given Christ's heart in the form of a beautifully chiseled cup at communion, and he commanded her to go and 'offer to all the saints the drink of life from my heart'.[47] After Juliana of Cornillon's death in 1258, a woman who had loved her saw the saint assisting Christ while he celebrated mass; the woman approached the altar and received a beautiful and excellent chalice from the High Priest and his virgin

---

and the 'cup' which God gives himself, to the detriment of the 'pocula quae tradunt gentes Christi'.

[41] Thomas of Cantimpré, *Vita S. Lutgardis*, ii, 1: *ActaSS*, June, 4, p. 193.

[42] Angela of Foligno, *Le Livre de l'expérience des vrais fidèles: texte latin publié d'après le manuscrit d'Assise*, ed. and trans. M.-J. Ferré and L. Baudry (Paris, 1927), para. 17, p. 16 and para. 151, p. 326.

[43] E.g. Bynum, *Holy Feast and Holy Fast, passim*.

[44] *Hadewijch: the Complete Works*, trans. Columba Hart (New York, 1980), vision 1, para. 177, p. 266; cf. vision 7, paras 57, 64, p. 281.

[45] Gertrude, *The Herald of God's Loving-Kindness, Books One and Two*, trans. A. Barratt (Kalamazoo, MI, 1991), ii, 4, para. 3, p. 110. Her devotional focus on images of the crucifixion is shown by her later experience of being pierced by a shaft of love 'like a ray of the sun' which issued from 'the side of the crucified Christ painted on the page' of a book she kept in her stall in choir: ibid., ii, 5, para. 2, p. 113.

[46] Ibid., i, 14, para. 4, p. 83.

[47] *Sanctae Mechtildis virginis ordinis sancti Benedicti liber specialis gratiae* (Paris, 1877), i, 1, pp. 7–10.

assistant.[48] When a priest who had criticized Ida of Louvain was celebrating, she seems to have approached the altar and stood behind him, and it is said that in her ecstasy she 'was robed in sacerdotal vestments', as if she were a concelebrant, and she received the sacrament miraculously.[49] *Ecclesia* is shown in some images in what appear to be clerical vestments including a bishop's mitre,[50] as is the Virgin Mary, the type of the Church *par excellence*, who was seen in visions by at least two women administering the chalice.[51]

So what can be made of the tensions apparent between the image of *Ecclesia* as a woman holding a chalice and the medieval circumscription of women's ministry and access to the sacrament? In a sense this problem parallels that of the legends that described Mary Magdalen as a preacher and apostle, which achieved a wide popularity in the later Middle Ages despite the Pauline prohibitions on women teaching and speaking publicly which were enshrined in canon law.[52] The representation of *Ecclesia* as a woman holding a chalice was clearly acceptable to ecclesiastical authority as a self-image, since it was promoted in public decorative schemes. Although male clerics in some sense represented Christ in their priestly role, and could be seen as themselves being espoused to the Church, they were still part of the Body of Christ, that is the Church which is represented as female. The female nurturing images used of abbots and clergy giving spiritual instruction have been highlighted recently, so it seems that male clerics and religious accepted that their role was appropriately represented by the female figure of *Ecclesia* administering the sacraments to nourish

---

[48] *Vita S. Julianae Corneliensi*, ii, 9, para. 54: *ActaSS*, April, 1, p. 475.

[49] *Vita Ven. Idae Lovaniensi*, iii, 1: *ActaSS*, April, 2, p. 183. Medieval concelebration generally assumed a principal celebrant assisted by the other priests in this manner: Jungmann, *Mass of the Roman Rite*, 1, pp. 195–9. The phrase used of Ida's position in relation to the priest, 'stans retro secus pedes illius', is that used by Luke (7.38) of the woman who anointed Jesus, who was identified with Mary Magdalen in medieval thought. This usage implies that the dinner at the house of the Pharisee described by Luke had sacramental associations for Ida's biographer, with the Magdalen, like Ida, approaching Christ at the (altar) table. Such associations had been notably highlighted by Paulinus of Nola, *Epistola iv ad Severum*: *PL* 61, col. 278.

[50] Schiller, *Ikonographie*, 3, fig. 491. See also Avery, *Exultet Rolls*, plates cited above nn. 18–19.

[51] *Vita Benevenutae*, c.6, para. 51: *ActaSS*, Oct., 13, p. 163; Mechtild of Hackeborn, *Liber specialis gratiae*, i, 7, p. 96.

[52] This is the subject of my doctoral research: '*Gloriosa praedicatrix*: the origins, development and influence of the medieval legends about St Mary Magdalen as preacher and apostle' (University of London, Ph. D. thesis, 1998).

the faithful.[53] Women, on the other hand, were portrayed and portrayed themselves literally as brides of Christ. They do not appear to have identified outright with 'the' Bride of Christ, however, and did not claim direct sacerdotal functions in reponse to her image, even though this step might in theory have been taken. Hildegard records God saying that in general 'those of female sex should not approach the office of My altar',[54] yet God goes on to say that a consecrated virgin 'has the priesthood and all the ministry of My altar in her Bridegroom, and with him possesses all its riches'. The twelfth-century *Speculum virginum* says similarly of virgins, that 'The bride of Christ . . . has preferred the Lord's chalice to the golden chalice of Babylon, offering herself and her own to God . . . a living sacrifice.'[55]

The image of *Ecclesia* in practice seems rather to lie behind the authorizing visions which women experienced and which allowed them to bypass clerical control and claim access to the sacrament, albeit indirectly, in their own right. There are no comparable cases where lay men received visions in which they performed those sacerdotal activities forbidden to them by canon law, nor any examples to my knowledge of lay men being represented pictorially and publicly handling the eucharistic elements. Unlike women, men were at least considered ontologically capable of receiving ordination, and laymen could legitimately express a sense of vocation to sacramental ministry. So while the Church ultimately represents the whole company of the faithful, men and women alike, the medieval response to the gendered image of *Ecclesia* as a woman shows a gendered reading. The ultimate indifference to gender implied by Christ and the Church being 'one flesh' was neither explored nor exploited.

Westcott House, Cambridge

---

[53] See Caroline Walker Bynum, *Jesus as Mother, Studies in the Spirituality of the High Middle Ages* (Berkeley, CA, 1981), pp. 110–69; eadem, *Fragmentation and Redemption* (Berkeley, CA, 1991), pp. 165–6, 177–8. Ann W. Astell, *The Song of Songs in the Middle Ages* (Ithaca, NY, 1990), p. 96, notes St Bernard's 'concern to feminize his auditors, to lead them into a personal identification with the *Sponsa*'.

[54] Although it can be argued that this prohibition refers only to married women (rather than virgins or widows) who are 'appointed to bear children and diligently nurture them': Hildegard, *Scivias*, ii, vision 6, para. 76, p. 278.

[55] BL, MS Arundel 44, fol. 94r.

GENDER DIFFERENCE AND INDIFFERENCE IN THE WRITINGS OF POPE INNOCENT III

by CONSTANCE M. ROUSSEAU

BOTH R. Howard Bloch and Jean Leclercq have recently included the name of Pope Innocent III (1198–1216) among the ranks of medieval misogynistic writers.[1] Such an anti-feminist designation results from his treatise *De miseria humanae conditionis* (1195), which he authored whilst a cardinal deacon, as Lothario de Segni.[2] However, the passages cited by Bloch and Leclercq only appear misogynistic when we consider them super-ficially. If we look at the entire corpus of Innocent's writings and his actions, in their proper contexts, we discover that this Pope can not be so easily categorized. Rather, our analysis will show that there is much more diversity in his perspective on gender than originally thought.[3]

The *De miseria* should be seen in its unique context when evaluating

---

[1] I would like to thank Norma Kroll and Joseph Goering for their helpful suggestions in sharpening and clarifying the argument in earlier versions of this paper.

R. Howard Bloch, *Medieval Misogyny and the Invention of Western Romantic Love* (Chicago, 1991), pp. 19–21, 25; Jean Leclercq, *Women and St. Bernard of Clairvaux*, trans. Marie-Bernard Said, Cistercian Studies Ser., 104 (Kalamazoo, MI, 1989), pp. 139–45. For a general discussion of misogyny see Marie Thérèse d'Alverny, 'Comment les théologiens et les philosophes voient la femme', *Cahiers de civilisation médiévale*, 20 (1977), pp. 105–29; Vern L. Bullough, 'Medieval medical and scientific views of women', *Viator*, 4 (1973), pp. 485–501. An older but still useful survey of misogyny is Katherine M. Rodgers, *The Troublesome Helpmate: a History of Misogyny in Literature* (Seattle, WA, 1966).

[2] Lothario dei Segni, *On the Misery of the Human Condition*, trans. Margaret Mary Dietz, The Library of Liberal Arts (Indianapolis, IN, 1969) and the Latin critical edition *De miseria humane conditionis*, ed. Michele Maccarrone (Lugano, 1955). On Innocent III's pontificate in general see, Brenda Bolton, *Innocent III: Studies on Papal Authority and Pastoral Care*, Collected Studies Series (Aldershot, 1995); Helene Tillmann, *Pope Innocent III*, trans. Walter Sax (Amsterdam, 1980); Christopher R. Cheney, *Innocent III and England*, Papste und Papsttum, 9 (Stuttgart, 1976).

[3] On a general discussion of gender theory and its uses in historical writing, see the seminal article by Joan W. Scott, 'Gender: a useful category of historical analysis', *AHR*, 91 (1986), pp. 1053–75. On sexual differences in the Middle Ages and their implication for gender construction, see Joan Cadden, *The Meanings of Sex Differences in the Middle Ages: Medicine, Science, and Culture* (Cambridge, 1993), and Joyce E. Salisbury, 'Gendered sexuality', in Vern L. Bullough and James A. Brundage, eds, *Handbook for Medieval Sexuality* (New York, 1996), pp. 81–102.

its attitude towards women. Books I and III of the treatise belonged to the *contemptus mundi* tradition which emphasised the vileness and misery of human existence.[4] Moreover, John C. Moore has recently proposed that Book II is a *speculum curialis* which reflected the questionable moral practices Innocent observed during his career in the Roman Curia.[5]

Both Bloch and Leclercq cited the following passage in the treatise referring to the tribulations of wifely duplicity and married life as evidence of Innocent's misogyny:

> There are three things which keep a man from staying home: smoke, a leaky roof, and a shrewish wife . . . If she be beautiful, men readily go after her; if she be ugly, she goes as readily after them. It is hard to keep what many want, and annoying to have what no one cares about. . . . When you buy a horse, an ass, an ox, a dog, clothes and a bed, even a cup and a pitcher, you first get a chance to look them over. But no one displays a bride, lest she displease before the marriage.[6]

Other unsavoury aspects of a wife not quoted by Bloch but mentioned in this passage are her desires for extremely expensive clothing and jewels, for her husband's total attention and praise, and for mastery over the household.[7]

Bloch further discusses the Pope's anti-feminist etymological word-play on the consequences of female sin. The pontiff said that a female infant cries 'E' and the male 'Ah' since they are born of E-va. This name 'E-va' is composed of two interjections of 'Eu' and 'Ah', expressing much sorrow and pain. Hence, the Pope concluded, before the Fall, the female was called 'woman' since she was created from man, but after, she deserved to be called 'Eva'. He thus implied

---

[4] Robert Bultot, 'Mépris du monde, misère et dignité de l'homme dans la pensée d'Innocent III', *Cahiers de civilisation médiévale*, 4 (1961), p. 441. See also Jean Delumeau, *Sin and Fear: the Emergence of a Western Guilt Culture, 13th-18th Centuries*, trans. Eric Nicholson (New York, 1990), pp. 14, 16, 21-3, 42-7.

[5] John C. Moore, 'Innocent III's *De miseria humanae conditionis*: a *speculum curiae?*', *CathHR*, 67 (1981), pp. 556-7, 563.

[6] Bloch, *Medieval Misogyny*, pp. 20-1, and Leclercq, *Women and St. Bernard*, p. 145 n. 25, citing Dietz, *Misery*, 1.17, p. 20; Maccarrone, *De miseria*, 1.17, pp. 23-4.

[7] Dietz, *Misery*, 1.17, pp. 20-1, Maccarrone, *De miseria*, 1.17, pp. 23-4.

that woman was the cause of the grief and anguish humans experienced after the Fall.[8]

We can have little doubt that these two passages from the *De miseria* indicate medieval antifeminism, but the very nature of this source as wholly negative toward earthly things also offers some explanation for its harsh attitude towards women. The admittedly negative perspective of Books I and III results from an implicit comparison between life on earth and that with God. Inevitably, given this point of view, all aspects of human life, including women and marriage, fall short when compared to those of eternal bliss.

In this context, the female sex was not the only target for vituperative attack in this treatise. The *De miseria* reviled human beings for their creation from dust, slime and ashes. The text also claimed that deformed and handicapped children were better never to have been born; criticized the aged for their nostalgia, miserliness, querulousness, and physical deterioration, and denounced the debauchery and corruption of the rich.[9] Furthermore, it stated generally that men – and according to Moore, Innocent was especially referring to male members of the papal curia – were overly proud and ambitious, covetous, and avaricious. They sought riches, pleasures, and honours; and were inclined to gluttony, drunkenness, and lust.[10]

We can further account for the decidedly negative bias in the *De miseria* by Innocent's plan to pair this text with a second treatise which would discuss the dignity of the human condition.[11] Thus, the *De miseria* was not representative of the Pope's entire perspective. However, this projected second treatise was never written[12] and thus scholarly evaluations can be skewed.

Of course, one might argue that Lothario's citation of misogynistic authorities signified his agreement with them. However, evidence concerning whether women should enter the church immediately after giving birth demonstrates that later on, as Pope, he did not necessarily

[8] Bloch, *Medieval Misogyny*, p. 25, citing Dietz, *Misery*, 1.6, p. 10; Maccarrone, *De miseria*, 1.6, p. 13.
[9] Dietz, *Misery*, 1.1, p. 6; 1.5, pp. 9–10; 1.10, p. 13; 1.15, pp. 17–18 and Maccarrone, *De miseria*, 1.1, p. 8; 1.5, p. 12; 1.10, p. 16; 1.15, pp. 20–1.
[10] Dietz, *Misery*, 2.2, p. 33; 2.14, p. 43; 2.17–22, pp. 45–9; 2.26–33, pp. 51–7; Maccarrone, *De miseria*, 2.2, p. 39; 2.14, pp. 49–50; 2.17–22, pp. 51–7; 2.26–33, pp. 59–65.
[11] Dietz, *Misery*, Prologue, p. 3; Maccarrone, *De miseria*, Prologus, p. 4; Bultot, 'Mépris', pp. 442, 448. Bultot attempts to reconstruct the treatise on man's dignity by using other Innocentian works on pp. 448–53.
[12] Bultot, 'Mépris', p. 442.

or consistently support the attitudes quoted in this treatise as a deacon. The *De miseria* referred to Mosaic Law, whereby because of the effusion of blood, parturient women were forbidden to enter the temple for forty days should they bear a male infant and eighty if a female.[13] Nevertheless, Innocent recommended the opposite in a letter of 1198 to the Archbishop of Armagh advocating the immediate entrance of these women into church. The Pope stipulated that the Gospel of Christ superseded the Old Law. The Archbishop should not deny the women access to the church if they desired to give thanks, for otherwise they would appear to be penalized for their labour pains, as if for a fault (*'ne poenam illis in culpam convertere videamur'*). However, women who desired to wait a while out of reverence were also praiseworthy for their devotion.[14] The papal letter thus revealed a more humane and sensitive attitude toward these women. Perhaps Innocent's dealing with real-life pastoral situations modified his previous strictness concerning the taboo of Leviticus 12.2–5.[15] Such epistolary proof in itself calls into question whether the *De miseria* can be considered the last word on Innocent's attitudes toward women.

The results are much more mixed when we examine another source, the eighty sermons authored by Innocent for holy days and feast days of certain saints. These texts were compiled probably during 1201–5.[16] Not surprisingly, Innocent's discourse on individual holy women of the Old and New Testaments is usually laudatory, but constructed on a symbolic level. When comparing the Church to women of the Old Testament, Innocent assigned the qualities of maturity to Sara, prudence to Rebecca, fecundity to Leah, grace to Rachel, devotedness

---

[13] Dietz, *Misery*, 1.4, p. 9; Maccarrone, *De miseria*, 1.4, p. 12.

[14] O. Hageneder and A. Haidacher, eds, *Die Register Innocenz' III, Bd. I, Pontifikatsjahr 1198/99* (Graz and Cologne, 1964), 63, pp. 93–4 [hereafter *Register*, I]; *PL* 214, col. 55; *Regesta pontificium Romanorum inde ab. a post Christum natum 1198 ad 1304*, ed. A. Potthast, 2 vols (Berlin, 1874–5, repr. Graz, 1957) [hereafter Potthast], I, no. 517.

[15] Innocent's answer is very similar to that of Pope Gregory the Great who had clearly pointed out that a woman could enter the Church even immediately after birth. See D.5 c.2: *CIC*, I, cols 7–8. Despite this repeated statement, the notion of uncleanness persisted. See Waltar von Arx, 'The churching of women after childbirth: history and signification', *Concilium*, 112 (1979), pp. 63–72, for an historical discussion of this practice of churching.

[16] *PL* 217, cols 310–688; For an analysis of all the sermons, see John C. Moore, 'The sermons of Pope Innocent III', *Römische historische Mitteilungen*, 36 (1994), pp. 81–142, on dating see esp. pp. 85–7; C. J. Vause, 'The sermons of Innocent III: a rhetorical analysis' (University of California Ph. D. dissertation, Santa Barbara, 1984) and the much older study by G. Scuppa, 'I Sermoni di Innocenzo III' (Pontificia Universitas Lateranense dissertation, Rome, 1961).

to Anna, chastity to Susanna, courage to Judith, and beauty to Esther.[17] Referring to the New Testament, the Pope likened Mary's eternal virginity to a spiritual fortress which withstood the buffets of pride and lust, and portrayed the mother of Christ as the restorer of new life to the world; he regarded Elizabeth as a new Sara, fecund in old age because of divine intervention; Martha and Mary as exemplars of the active and contemplative life; and Mary Magdalene as exemplifying the Christian penitent.[18]

Besides discussing individual holy women, Innocent treated women collectively in his sermons. These passages reveal what we might call a 'tempered misogyny', tempered in the sense that while not as virulent as the descriptions of the *De miseria*, the Pope does consider women as sinful and as a cause for sin. Yet he simultaneously points to the moral guilt of men who transgress. For instance, he emphasised the culpability of Eve as the first sinner, in whom all women sinned; but then noted that through Adam, all men also sinned.[19] According to Thérèse d'Alverny, this Augustinian stress on the equal blame of both sexes in the Fall was rarely expressed in twelfth-century theological and philosophical treatises.[20] Innocent's Ash Wednesday Sermon similarly depicted the moral failings of his clerical contemporaries in sexual situations with women:

> The bonds of lust hold us so that we are not ashamed to keep girls publicly in our houses. . . . Those who are not clean of union with women cannot worthily take the sacred bread. . . . Indeed they spend the night in their chamber with the son of Venus; in the morning they offer at the altar the son of the Virgin. At night they embrace Venus; in the morning they venerate the Virgin.[21]

Nor did Innocent only castigate clergy. He also reproved laymen who fornicated with women rather than followed Christ.[22]

Within the licit context of marriage, when the Pope considered the

---

[17] *PL* 217, col. 662. I would like to thank John Doran for this reference.

[18] *PL* 217, cols 581, 577–8, 531, 580, 562. On Innocent's mariology see Wilhelm Imkamp, '*Virginitas quam ornavit humilitas*: Die Verehrung der Gottesmutter in den *Sermones* Papst Innocenz III', *Lateranum*, 46 (1980), pp. 344–78.

[19] *PL* 217, col. 400, 'et in Eva peccaverunt caeterae mulieres, in Adam vero caeteri viri'.

[20] D'Alverny, 'Comment les théologiens', pp. 107, 110.

[21] *PL* 217, col. 368; translation in Moore, 'The sermons', p. 95.

[22] *PL* 217, cols 528–9; Moore, 'The sermons', pp. 97–9, has doubts about the authenticity of this text.

relations of husband and wife, he alluded to the scriptural concept of male headship and domination of woman. He also maintained the Augustinian bipolar opposition of soul/body to male/female.[23] We can interpret the following passage describing the marriage of Zachariah and Elizabeth as somewhat antifeminist since the rational soul is gendered as 'masculine': 'Just as a husband corrects and rules over his wife, so should the spirit correct and rule over the flesh, so that it will not be wanton and fall into the sin of fornication.'[24] Nonetheless, his attitude is still not so easily categorized, because the gender of the human soul was flexible for Innocent. In his theological treatise, *De quadripartite specie nuptiarum*, he portrayed the soul espoused to God as feminine, which accorded with scriptural bridal imagery as well as heterosexual norms. Still, he does depict this soul as sinful and in need of divine love.[25]

So far, our investigation of Innocent's attitudes toward gender has been based solely on texts in which the Pope constructed an image of woman. Our assessment of his misogyny will be further nuanced if we consider Innocent's treatment of actual women in everyday practice as found in the papal correspondence. These letters provided instruction and adjudication for the problems and queries of the Christian faithful, practices which grew during the twelfth and thirteenth centuries.[26] The texts give evidence of papal reactions toward women extending over the whole spectrum from 'tempered misogyny' in the sermons to papal compassion and sensitivity, even to gender indifference in certain instances.

We discover another aspect of the Pope's modified antifeminism in his treatment of female religious superiors. Innocent lived in a cultural milieu which excluded women from many opportunities; and for the most part the Pope accepted these limitations. Since, according to ecclesiastical law, women were excluded from the sacrament of orders, not even an abbess could exercise sacerdotal or episcopal powers.[27]

---

[23] Rosemary Radford Ruether, 'Misogynism and virginal feminism in the Fathers of the Church', in Rosemary Radford Ruether, ed., *Religion and Sexism: Images of Woman in Jewish and Christian Traditions* (New York, 1974), pp. 156–8.

[24] *PL* 217, col. 542.

[25] *PL* 217, col. 929.

[26] A good introduction to the registers, their manuscript tradition, and printed editions can be found in C. R. Cheney and Mary G. Cheney, *The Letters of Pope Innocent III (1198–1216) concerning England and Wales: A Calendar with an Appendix of Texts* (Oxford, 1967), pp. ix–xxiv.

[27] Renée Metz, 'Le statut de la femme en droit canonique médiéval', in her *La femme et*

However, in a letter of 11 December 1210, Innocent dealt with the abbesses in the dioceses of Burgos and Placencia in Spain who persisted in blessing their nuns, hearing their confessions, and even preaching the Gospel.[28] The Pope deemed these actions as unsuitable (*absonum*), and commanded his bishops to prohibit them in the future. He justified his decision on the basis of ecclesiastical tradition; for 'although the blessed Virgin Mary was more excellent and worthy than all the apostles, the Lord still committed the keys of the kingdom to them rather than to her'.[29] Clearly gender was a factor here for Innocent but his misogynistic viewpoint is somewhat ameliorated by his implied recognition of the spiritual excellence of religious women, especially the abbesses, whose analogue was the Virgin Mary.

A 'tempered misogyny' is likewise seen in Innocent's application of the conjugal debt in cases involving married women. According to the Pauline concept of the conjugal debt, marriage established a sexual duty between spouses whereby the husband and wife no longer had sole jurisdiction over their own bodies, but gained power over and access to that of their partner. The debt offered the only area of marriage where theoretically women had equal rights with their husbands.[30]

However, it seems that Innocent disregarded the sexual rights and needs of married women in three instances. Such papal indifference suggests misogyny and even insinuates the desire to remove married women from an active sexuality. Yet these three cases represented unusual exceptions and circumstances. The first case concerned times of dire military need. Up to the time of Innocent's pontificate, canon law, following the principle of the conjugal debt, required the couple's mutual consent before the husband could take a vow to go on crusade which would cause a long spousal separation.[31] In a letter of 9 September 1213 to Conrad, Dean of Speyer,[32] the Pope implied

---

l'enfant dans le droit canonique médiéval, Variorum Collected Studies (Aldershot, 1985), ch. IV, pp. 97–102.

[28] *PL* 216, col. 356; Potthast, I, no. 4143.

[29] *PL* 216, col. 356.

[30] I Cor. 7.3–6; Elizabeth M. Makowski, 'The conjugal debt and medieval canon law', *JMedH*, 3 (1977), pp. 99–100; James A. Brundage, 'Sexual equality in medieval canon law', in Joel T. Rosenthal, ed., *Medieval Women and the Sources of Medieval History* (Athens, GA, and London, 1990), pp. 66–79.

[31] James A. Brundage, 'The crusader's wife: a canonistic quandary', *Studia Gratiana*, 12 (1967), pp. 428–30.

[32] *PL* 216, cols 904–5; Potthast, I, no. 4807.

that military necessity and his own view of marital cohabitation were more important than a wife's consent to her husband's crusading venture. According to Innocent, the lack of sexual relations did not dissolve the marriage, but rather conjugal union had to give way during difficult times.[33]

Mortal sin was a second factor which could interfere with a wife's sexual rights to the marriage debt. According to Innocent, when a man knew with certainty of a canonical impediment hindering his marriage, he should refrain from sexual union which would result in serious sin. Here, the Pope, motivated by pastoral concern, considered that the couple's eternal salvation superseded any momentary marital embrace.[34]

Advanced age was the final factor which could adjust the demands of the conjugal debt. Alexander III (1159–81) had stipulated that in a consummated marriage a spouse could enter religious life only with the free consent of his partner.[35] According to a letter of Innocent of 9 April 1205, Juliana had been forced to consent to her husband's desire to enter the monastic life after being physically abused by him.[36] When her husband later left the Cistercian monastery of Warden but refused to take her back at her request, the Pope decreed that if the woman were of an age where sexual sin threatened, her husband should receive her and treat her with marital affection.[37] By this condition, the Pope implied that if the woman was so elderly there would be little probability of carnal sin she would remain separated from her spouse. These three instances of extremely mitigating circumstances do not vindicate the Pope's decisions but do to some degree explain his actions, which at first glance could be described as blatantly antifeminist.[38]

To call Innocent III a 'feminist' would be incorrect, but we do find in the letters a papal attitude toward women which is based to some degree on compassion, pastoral care, and Christian charity. From the beginning of the eleventh century, Gregorian reform, the papacy's

---

[33] Ibid.: 'cum per hoc matrimoniale vinculum non solvatur, sed subtrahatur ad tempus cohabitatio conjugalis: quod in multis aliis casibus fieri frequenter oportet.'

[34] *PL* 215, col. 1583; Potthast, I, no. 3668 (1–21 Feb. 1209).

[35] X.3.32.4–6: *CIC*, 2, cols 579–80.

[36] *PL* 215, cols 593–4; Potthast, I, no. 2470 (9 April 1205).

[37] Ibid.

[38] For a complete description of these three cases, see my article, 'The spousal relationship: marital society and sexuality in the letters of Pope Innocent III', *Mediaeval Studies*, 56 (1994), pp. 98–103.

attempt to impose clerical celibacy on clergy of major rank and on religious, inevitably touched the personal lives of their female partners. The loss of their status as clerical wives gravely threatened the women's welfare. After the conciliar decrees of Lateran II (1139), ecclesiastical authorities viewed them as concubines and a major reason for the lack of moral discipline in the Church.[39]

We might expect that as a supporter of the Gregorian reform, Innocent would be severely misogynist in his treatment of clerical concubines. However, the opposite is true. The Pope's actions also contrast even more significantly with the somewhat misogynistic words about the clergy's women found in his sermons. Innocent's directive in 1203 to Archbishop Andreas of Lund did continue to uphold the Gregorian ideals by ordering his clerics and cathedral canons to be celibate on pain of suspension from office and deprivation of benefice. However, the Pope also enjoined that the kin of the clerical concubines should provide support for the women dismissed from the ecclesiastical households.[40] This papal compassion for the plight of these women who could be left without any support when separated from their clerical partners is remarkable when compared to the retributory policies of some earlier popes such as Leo IX (1049-54), who was said to have commanded that concubines of Roman priests would become unfree handmaids (*ancillae*) of the Lateran palace.[41]

Moreover, Innocent compassionately encouraged Christian men to marry prostitutes to save their souls. On 29 April 1198, the Pope exhorted all Christian faithful to remove prostitutes from the brothels and make them wives, so they would lead chaste lives.[42] In this policy,

---

[39] Norman P. Tanner, ed., *Decrees of the Ecumenical Councils*, 2 vols (London and Washington, DC, 1990), 1, p. 198: c.7, Lateran II; see Anne L. Barstow, *Married Priests and the Reforming Papacy: The Eleventh-Century Debates*, Texts and Studies in Religion, 12 (New York, 1982), pp. 47-104, and John E. Lynch, 'Marriage and celibacy of the clergy: an historico-canonical synopsis, Part II', *The Jurist*, 32 (1972), pp. 189-201, for discussions of the problem of clerical marriage with some reference to the status and situation of concubines.

[40] O. Hageneder *et al.*, eds, *Die Register Innocenz' III, Bd VI, Pontifikatsjahr 1203/1204* (Vienna, 1995), no. 196, p. 333 [hereafter *Register*, VI]; *PL* 215, col. 223; Potthast, I, no. 2060. 'Ad recipiendas autem huiusmodi mulieres patres, fratres et consanguineos moneas diligentius et inducas et cogas etiam, prout videris expedire.'

[41] This was reported by Peter Damian, *PL* 145, col. 411, cited by Bernhard Schimmelpfennig, '*Ex fornicatione nati*: studies on the position of priests' sons from the twelfth to the fourteenth century', *Studies in Medieval and Renaissance History*, ns 2 (1979), p. 17.

[42] *Register*, I, no. 112, pp. 169-70; *PL* 214, cols 102-3; Potthast, I, no. 114.

Innocent neither condemned these women as tainted for their previous carnal transactions nor denied their sexual needs; rather, he attempted to channel and regulate them by the institution of legitimate marriage. In this way, he could also aid in the women's salvation and prevent their sexual exploitation.

Similarly, Innocent demonstrates his pastoral concern and sensitivity in cases involving a legitimate wife and her sexual needs. A letter of 24 February 1203 to the Prior of Osney described a woman married to an Englishman, W., who later committed adultery with her sister.[43] Given the establishment of the canonical impediment of supervenient affinity and the problem of public decency, the question arose about the future sexual relations of the couple. Here 'supervenient affinity' meant a particularly serious form of relationship which was established between spouses when a person had adulterous and incestuous relations with a relative of his/her spouse after the expression of marital consent.[44] The Pope decreed that, ideally, and where no risk of sexual transgression existed, the innocent wife should remain continent for the lifetime of her husband due to the canonical impediment. However, if the woman did not desire to abstain from conjugal intercourse, then she could exact the debt from W., since the impediment arising from her husband's crime should not victimize the innocent woman.[45]

Following a strict interpretation of canon law, the Pope's decision counselled celibacy; nonetheless, and most importantly, the guiltless woman was given a personal choice of whether to resume conjugal relations. In this sense, her desires could even supersede canon law. Innocent's decision disregarded certain distinctions drawn by Alexander III which previously would have determined the woman's sexual rights on the basis of whether the marriage was consummated or not, whether the adultery was publicly known or secret, and the proximity of the relationship between the victimized party and the adulterous relative.[46] Instead, Innocent's solution gave a sympathetic alternative,

---

[43] *Register*, VI, no. 2, pp. 5–6; *PL* 215, cols 10–11; Potthast, I, no. 1836. See also *PL* 215, cols 765–7, Potthast, I, no. 2656 (13 Jan. 1206), where in a similar case of adultery, the same twofold solution was given.

[44] See Jean Dauvillier, *Le mariage dans le droit classique de l'église depuis le Décret de Gratien (1140) jusqu'à la mort de Clément V (1314)* (Paris, 1933), p. 293.

[45] *Register*, VI, no. 2, pp. 5–6; *PL* 215, cols 10–11; Potthast, I, no. 1836.

[46] X. 4.13.2: *CIC*, 2, cols 696–7.

clearly based on the woman's individual preference and his pastoral care for her human frailties.[47]

In the previous cases, gender helped to determine the papal response, whether that response was somewhat negative or positive toward women. Gender did not play a role when the Pope dealt with the carnal misdeeds of both husband and wife, and here we can suggest that he possessed a certain 'gender indifference'. In a letter of 20 June 1203 we learn that B. de Belloloco and Agnes had separated, and had sworn not to seek future restitution of each other. However, B. later discovered he did not wish to remain continent and so sought restoration of Agnes, who had taken a lover in the interim.[48] The Pope instructed that either the couple both promise to observe continence or, if B. was unwilling to be chaste, his wife should return to him and render conjugal services since their vow was imprudent and they might both commit adultery. The fact that Agnes did not particularly desire a reconciliation did not influence the Pope's decision.[49] Agnes was committing sin; her husband was likely to follow. Innocent was here pastorally concerned with the moral disintegration of both spouses, where he recognized that sexual sin was not gender-related.

A comparison of two quite different adultery cases indicates that gender blindness continued to be the basis of the Pope's attitude toward the punishment of this crime. Innocent followed traditional principles of canon law where both men and women were equally culpable and should receive the same penalty for adultery.[50] In one case, of 3 April 1209, a man, L., had entered monastic life with the reluctant consent of his wife, who remained in the world and took several paramours. When Innocent was asked by L. whether his spouse's sexual sins could be attributed to him, the Pope declared

---

[47] A similar twofold solution was given for a woman in an unconsummated marriage impeded by supervenient affinity where a husband, without consummating the union, handed his unwilling wife over to a relative for sexual intercourse. Once again, the Alexandrine distinctions did not hold. See *PL* 216, col. 1264; X.4.13.6: *CIC*, 2, col. 698; Potthast, I, no. 1182 (Nov.-Dec. 1200).

[48] *Register*, VI, no. 108, p. 174; *PL* 215, cols 113–14; Potthast, I, no. 1946.

[49] Ibid.: 'cum et temerarium fuerit hujusmodi juramentum, et adulterium sit utrimque commissum.'

[50] James A. Brundage, *Law, Sex and Christian Society in Medieval Europe* (Chicago, IL, 1987), p. 247, noted the canonist Gratian's position here. However, refer to pp. 307, 320–1, where some decretists such as Rufinus, Sicard of Cremona, and Johannes Faventinus said that some of the penalties of husband and wife differed in practice.

that the woman had consented to L.'s vocation and her past sexual misdeeds precluded her from recalling her husband from the monastery, especially since she had not sought him before she fornicated.[51] If the woman had sought her husband before her carnal deeds, she would have probably regained him.[52] Her subsequent adultery hindered any restoration of her sexual rights.

A similar loss of sexual rights was imposed upon a man in the diocese of Roeskilde who solemnly married one woman in church, and then abandoned her and united publicly with a second in another region.[53] In his decision, Innocent ruled no second marriage existed, the man had committed adultery and therefore had to return to his first wife. He would expiate his sin by his obedient rendering of the debt at his wife's request, but lost any right to exact it himself.[54] If the Pope had been a thoroughly misogynistic judge, his contempt for women could have coloured his thinking with a double standard; however, Innocent implemented the canon law and punished perpetrators regardless of gender by prohibiting their exercise of sexual rights.

If we look at Innocent's actions during his pontificate as we have his writings, we find that the Pope was not merely applying canon law as it was written, but indeed was gender blind in certain instances. The Pope's anonymous biographer in the *Gesta* noted that, among his many acts of charity, he frequently gave contributions to indigent nuns as well as monks, indicating here that for Innocent, Christian charity was gender neutral.[55] But the most telling piece of proof is the rule that Innocent approved for the brothers and sisters of his foundation of the Hospital of the Holy Spirit which is remarkably egalitarian. Such an ideal is explicitly stated in c.97, which noted that the rule applied to both the brothers and sisters since it would be unsuitable (*indignum*) if there were two different ways for them to be received into the

---

[51] *PL* 216, col. 24; Potthast, I, no. 3698.

[52] See Alexander III's decree in X.3.32.1: *CIC*, 2, col. 529.

[53] Jacob Langebek, ed., *Scriptores rerum Danicarum medii aevi*, 9 vols (Hauniae, 1772–1834), 6, p. 12; Potthast, I, no. 536 (20 Sept.–31 Dec. 1198).

[54] Ibid.

[55] *PL* 214, col. 196. For Innocent's patronage of religious women in particular, see Brenda Bolton, 'Daughters of Rome: all one in Christ Jesus', in her *Innocent III*, also *SCH*, 27 (1990), pp. 101–15. On the Pope's financial assistance to Cistercian monasteries see also her article 'For the see of St. Peter: the Cistercians at Innocent III's nearest frontier', *Innocent III*, ch. 2, pp. 1–20, esp. pp. 10–12.

community and corrected for offences.[56] The Rule's equal treatment of the sexes is concretely demonstrated in the penalties for their fornication: a six-day fast on bread and water with a year-long abstention from meat and wine.[57]

Misogynist, feminist, or gender indifferent? From this exploration of Innocent's perspectives towards women, we are left with an impression of overall diversity. The severely misogynistic rhetoric which fits so neatly into a work like the *De miseria* does not appear in his sermons or letters. Innocent indeed shared some of the uncomplimentary views of women common to his society but did not emphasise them in his later writings which sometimes contain a 'tempered misogyny'. 'Feminist' is a distorted appellation, but this Pope did possess some degree of personal compassion and sympathy for the plight of individual women, usually in a pastoral context. Finally, in some instances gender did not matter. These exceptions were based sometimes on canon law or Christian doctrine, where there was 'neither male nor female in Jesus Christ'.[58] This reconsideration of Innocent's misogyny therefore offers a caveat for any interpretation which relies on a single text.

Providence College, Providence, Rhode Island, USA

---

[56] *PL* 217, col. 1154: 'Quidquid in Regula constitutum est, de fratribus et sororibus intelligitur, ut eidem Regulae subjaceant quia indignum satis videretur, si in domo Sancti Spiritus acceptio vel correctio fratrum et sororum duobus modis fieret; unde ordinatum est, ut sicut sub una Regula vivimus, ita sub eisdem judiciis Regulae subjecti esse debemus.' Brenda Bolton says that despite many probable revisions, part of the primitive text of this rule is datable to 1213. On Innocent's hospital see her article, '"Received in his Name": Rome's busy baby box', in *Innocent III*, and *SCH*, 31 (1994), pp. 153–67.

[57] *PL* 217, col. 1144.

[58] Gal. 3.28.

'GOD IS MORE WEARY OF WOMAN THAN OF MAN': REFLECTIONS ON A TEXT IN THE *GOLDEN LEGEND*

by RICHARD M. PRICE

THE presence of a malodorous taint of misogyny in Christian literature, both ancient and medieval, is a familiar fact that feminist writers, more than male chauvinists, have been keen to push under our noses. What is its explanation? The inferiority of women is a standard theme in male-dominated cultures. Christian literature, for so long the virtual preserve of male celibates, inevitably reflected their anxieties and their need for reassurance. But was there also a genuine theological component, however misconceived, arising from basic Christian convictions about human nature and the moral law?

* * *

One of the more gross but less familiar misogynist texts of the Middle Ages may be found in that thirteenth-century classic, the *Golden Legend* of Jacobus de Voragine. In his chapter on the Feast of the Purification of the Blessed Virgin Mary he notes that according to the twelfth chapter of Leviticus a woman who has given birth to a child is unclean and cannot enter the Temple for a period of time dependent on the sex of the child – forty days in the case of a male and eighty days in the case of a female. The text continues:

> The male child is brought into the Temple on the fortieth day just as the soul most frequently enters the body, as into its temple, on the fortieth day after conception . . . In the case of a woman who gives birth to a female child the number of days is doubled as regards both entering the Temple and the formation of the female body. The male body takes forty days to develop its organs and the soul is infused most often on the fortieth day, but the formation of the female body and the infusion of its soul take eighty days. There are three reasons (omitting the natural ones) for the female body taking twice as long to be formed and to be animated. First, since Christ was to take flesh in the male sex, he willed that the child should be formed and the mother cleansed

sooner, in order to honour the male sex and give himself more grace. Secondly, since woman sinned more than man, so her troubles were doubled above those of man in the outer world and were appropriately doubled inside the womb. Thirdly, this makes it clear that God is in some sense more 'weary' of woman than of man, since she has sinned more.[1]

The teaching of Leviticus that the birth of a girl causes uncleanness for twice as long as the birth of a boy continues to intrigue and puzzle scholars. *The Woman's Bible Commentary* (1992) is typical in observing, 'No satisfactory explanation of this discrepancy has yet been found.'[2] It was not in the nature of pre-modern biblical exegesis to raise a problem and then leave it unsolved. It was widely noted, as in the text before us, that there was a striking coincidence between the period of uncleanness and the time in the womb between conception and animation: in both the period was forty days in the case of a male child and eighty days in the case of a female one. The rules for uncleanness were among the laws of God, while the time of animation was one of the laws of nature: both, it was observed, discriminated between the two sexes in a similar way and to the same degree. Medieval and later Christian tradition increased the precision of the correspondence by some tidying up of the figures. It was Aristotle in his *Historia animalium* (583b) who had first dated the attainment of form and the 'first movement' to around forty days after conception in the case of male foetuses and ninety (not eighty) for the female. His evidence was careful observation of aborted foetuses. Since he balanced his claim that females develop more slowly in the womb with the claim that they develop more rapidly after birth, we may acquit him of gross sexism. Later writers, such as Pliny the Elder (*Natural History*, VII.6.41), were happy to repeat these figures without further investigation. If later Christian tradition reduced the ninety days to eighty, this

---

[1] *Legenda aurea*, ed. T. Graesse (Leipzig, 1850), ch. XXXVII, pp. 158–9. This edifying passage was lacking from the text translated by Caxton. My own version makes use of that of W. G. Ryan, *The Golden Legend*, 2 vols (Princeton, NJ, 1993), 1, pp. 143–4.

[2] A. Newson and S. H. Ringe, eds, *The Woman's Bible Commentary* (London, 1992), p. 40. Rupert of Deutz (d. 1129) linked the greater length of purification in the case of a girl to a greater flow of blood from the mother (*PL* 167, col. 802), following a long tradition going back to Hippocrates and Aristotle (*Historia animalium*, 583a) and paralleled in Rabbinic sources. Similar discrimination between male and female births is to be found in many cultures. See D. I. Macht, 'A scientific appreciation of Leviticus 12:1–5', *Journal of Biblical Literature*, 52 (1933), pp. 253–60.

was partly, no doubt, to make the figure more tidy but principally, we may surmise, to perfect the parallel with the Leviticus text we are discussing.[3]

Medieval moralizing was not content, however, with pointing out the concordance between Leviticus and the laws of nature, but sought to base both on a decree of divine justice. In the words of Rupert of Deutz (d. 1129),

> Both the written and the natural law place a greater burden on a woman than on a male because, of course, in the occurrence of the sin that introduced death into this world woman stood nearer than man did to that vessel of the devil, the serpent . . . For it was not woman through man but man through woman who was stained by the deceit of the devil.[4]

This text illustrates the misogynist interpretation of the temptation of Adam and Eve that we find recurrently in the Church Fathers and which has been repeatedly investigated in recent years.[5] Augustine lent the weight of his authority to the view already advanced by Tertullian and Ambrose that the serpent in choosing to corrupt Eve rather than Adam sagaciously selected the weaker vessel. The woman, in Augustine's words, 'had limited understanding and perhaps was living according to the spirit of the flesh and not according to the spirit of the mind'.[6] Adam had the strength to resist the devil's blandishments, but consented to share in the sin of Eve in order to remain with her and not deprive her of the comfort of his support and guidance. Is it surprising if women today find this story less than comforting?

So woman, according to this line of thought, is morally weaker than man. Doubtless this is why Bruno of Segni (d. 1123), in his allegorical exegesis of the same twelfth chapter of Leviticus, interprets the birth of a male child as a symbol of good works, and the birth of 'an impure

---

[3] The linking of the Aristotelian and Levitical figures occurs already in Hrabanus Maurus (d. 856), who followed the fifth-century Hesychius of Jerusalem (*PL* 108, cols 368–70). This link was so well established by the early modern period that the Leviticus text was used as evidence in support of the Aristotelian tradition on the time of animation: see *Dictionnaire de théologie catholique*, 1 (Paris 1909), col. 1309.

[4] *In Leviticum*, II.16, *PL* 167, col. 802. For this commentary see John H. van Eugen, *Rupert of Deutz* (Berkeley, CA, 1983), pp. 263–5.

[5] E.g., Margaret Miles, *Carnal Knowing* (Tunbridge Wells, 1992), ch. 4.

[6] *De Genesi ad litteram* XI.42.

girl' as a symbol of sin and unbelief.[7] Since woman is weaker than man, naturally she has sinned more, as the *Golden Legend* confidently asserts with reference, but without restriction, to the sin of Eve.

The text adds, for good measure, that in view of the Incarnation, where Christ assumed not simply human nature but maleness, he has endowed males with greater honour, so as to give himself more grace.[8] This claim also derives from the Augustinian inheritance. In the Christian faith it is far more important that the Word became flesh than that he became a male. Theologians have felt no special need to explain Christ's maleness. Aquinas in his *Summa Theologica* touches on the matter only incidentally, in the context of explaining why Christ took his flesh from a woman – which, oddly, he considers more problematic. Here he quotes Augustine:

> The redemption of mankind had to be displayed in both sexes. Therefore, since [the Son] had to assume maleness, this being the more honourable sex, it was appropriate for the redemption of the female sex to be displayed by the fact that this man was born of a woman.[9]

The implication of this argument is that in itself Christ's maleness binds him closer to men than to women. The claim that the male sex is the more honourable seemed uncontroversial; and it enjoyed the endorsement of St Paul, with his teaching that man 'is the image and reflection [literally, glory] of God but woman is the reflection of man' (I Corinthians 11.7). The picture of the Fathers and later the Schoolmen as grossly misogynist needs to be corrected in view of their general reluctance to push this text. Augustine and his successors reiterated that the image of God is located in the soul of every human being, the soul itself being sexless. But they followed St Paul in admitting that woman *qua* woman is not in the image of God.[10] In the

---

[7] *PL* 164, cols 419–20. Compare St Ambrose, 'She who does not believe is "woman"' (*Commentary on Luke* X.161, with reference to Christ's address to Mary Magdalene at John 20.15).

[8] This becomes still more grossly sexist in W. G. Ryan's version (n.1, above): Christ 'willed to endow it [the male sex] with more grace'. But in the Latin ('ut ampliorem sibi gratiam faceret') it is Christ, not the male sex as a whole, that receives more grace.

[9] Augustine, *De diversis quaestionibus LXXXIII*, 1.10, cited by Aquinas at *Summa Theologica*, 3a., 31.4.

[10] Kim Power, *Veiled Desire: Augustine's Writing on Woman* (London, 1995), pp. 131–57.

words of Aquinas, 'the image of God is found in man in a way in which it is not found in woman, for man is the beginning and end of woman, just as God is the beginning and end of all creation'.[11] If souls are sexless, then it is the woman's body that makes her inferior to man. The adult male body was viewed as normative of physical perfection in the human race, while the female body and the related peculiarities of feminine psychology (in the modern sense of the word) were treated as inferior, almost as defective. What is it in the female body that periodically down the centuries has fed misogyny?

* * *

Let us go all the way back to the ancient Greeks. Anne Carson in a fine article has set out the negative view of the female body that we find in the Greek philosophers and in classical Greek literature generally.[12] The female body was thought to be more liquid than the male. This wetness was associated with the supposed intensity of women's sexual drive: contrary to the nineteenth-century insistence on the greater purity and chastity of women, the Greeks were convinced that male lust is a pale shadow of female desire, just as female orgasm is far more intense than its male equivalent (as the sage Tiresias was supposed to have discovered when, through an unsettling metamorphosis, he became for a time a woman).

Because of her stronger sexual drive, woman is nearer than man to the untamed forces of nature. Particularly threatening is her kinship to prime matter, boundless and without form. In conception it is man who determines the form, while woman provides the raw, unshaped material. While man is the perfected human being, woman is 'a deficient male', in Aristotle's notorious phrase.[13] Woman is pliant and mutable: in myth it is most often women who change their shape. Moreover, women, being more liquid than men, lack a boundary of their own: their bodies tend to 'leak' and are also more permeable to physical forces from outside. In all, the proper boundaries between a human person and the outside world are insecure in the case of women. This makes them, in the Greek view, the prime source of mixture and contamination, and therefore of dirt and pollution.

---

[11] *Summa Theologica*, 1a., 93.4.
[12] A. Carson, 'Putting her in her place: woman, dirt and desire', in D. M. Halperin, J. J. Winkler, and F. I. Zeitlin, eds, *Before Sexuality* (Princeton, NJ, 1990), pp. 135–69.
[13] *De generatione animalium*, 775a.

Psychologically, this greater wetness and pliability of woman was linked to her supposedly more passionate nature and to the weakness of her reason: woman was thought to reason less clearly than man, and to be far inferior in the ability to determine action by rational deliberation. The Greeks, like ourselves, thought of reason as dry; it followed for them that it is weak in woman. If society was to follow to any degree the dictates of reason, women had to be under the rule of men. Women were married off young, immediately at puberty, so that the discipline of a husband might provide the floodgates without which human society would sink into the dissoluteness bordering on dissolution that was seen as the natural element of woman unrestrained.

How much of this web of dubious physiology and misogynist *Angst* recurs in medieval Christendom? Aristotle's physiology was widely known in the universities from the twelfth century onwards. But in any case the traditional clichés about the dampness of women and their dangerous malleability were by now firmly established.[14] So we read in Guido delle Colonne (writing in 1287),

> Is it wise to trust to feminine constancy or the female sex, which has never been able, through all the ages, to remain constant? . . . Just as it is known that matter proceeds from form to form, so the dissolute desire of woman proceeds from man to man, so that it may be believed without limit, since it is of unfathomable depth.[15]

Or, in the words of Andreas Capellanus, 'Woman is like melting wax, always ready to assume fresh shape.'[16] In a singularly repulsive passage Boccaccio writes of women's faces and bellies as sagging and malleable like dough, and dirty and leaky like manure.[17]

Still stronger than the echoes of the ancient understanding of female physiology was the constant repetition of ancient ideas of female psychology. Yes, women are more passionate than men; and woman needs to be subject to man's authority since, in the words of Aquinas,

---

[14] Claude Thomasset, 'The nature of woman', in Christiane Klapisch-Zuber, ed., *A History of Women in the West, II: Silences of the Middle Ages* (Cambridge, MA, 1992), pp. 43–69.

[15] Alcuin Blamires, *Woman Defamed and Woman Defended: An Anthology of Medieval Texts* (Oxford, 1992), p. 48.

[16] Ibid., p. 120.

[17] Ibid., pp. 173–5.

'the power of rational discernment is by nature stronger in man'.[18] Even Hildegard of Bingen, whose originality is now widely appreciated, repeated the clichés that women, in their softness and pliability, are subject to 'contemptible vacillation' and need the protection and guidance of the stronger, more steadfast sex.[19]

Some degree of subtlety and flexibility was introduced into this crude picture by a recognition that virtue, though 'masculine', is not denied to all women any more than weakness, though primarily feminine, is unknown in men. The two sexes, it was held, form a single continuum, allowing such combinations as the union of a female body with a male temperament. Medieval denigration of the feminine did not imply the condemnation of all women.[20] Unfortunately, this refinement served to enable the basic stereotype to survive refutation from experience: a self-controlled woman was seen as evidence not of the falsity of the stereotype but of the ability of some women to develop masculine traits of character. Moreover, there remained an unease over any blurring of the sexual divide.[21] In consequence, the 'virago' (a woman with the courage of a man) came to be viewed negatively, as a 'serpent under femininity', a 'feigned woman', and the 'nest of every vice', to use the vivid expressions of Geoffrey Chaucer.[22]

Before we simply dismiss all this as misogyny at its most objectionable and at times hysterical, we would do well to remind ourselves of two facts. First, notions of the female psyche as more intuitive and less rational than the male are alive and kicking even today. Indeed, feminists sometimes argue that society would function better if it were less dominated by male objectivity and obsession with general principles and more inspired by the virtues, supposedly stronger in women, of sympathy and accommodation.

Secondly, Christianity inherited from its Judaic roots a view of virtue as pondered and deliberate obedience to divine law. Together with this goes a distrust of the irrational in human nature, of the drives and passions customarily located in the body. The classic text is the Epistle to the Romans 7.22–3: 'I delight in the law of God in the inner

---

[18] *Summa Theologica*, 1a., 92,1.

[19] B. W. Scholz, 'Hildegard von Bingen on the nature of woman', *American Benedictine Review*, 31 (1980), pp. 361–83.

[20] Joan Cadden, *Meanings of Sex Difference in the Middle Ages* (Cambridge, 1993), pp. 202–9.

[21] Ibid., pp. 209–27.

[22] Chaucer, *Canterbury Tales: The Man of Law's Tale*, ll.359–64.

man, but I see in my limbs another law at war with the law of my mind and making me captive to the law of sin which is in my limbs.' Attempts to explain away the anthropological dualism of this text fail, since the word 'limbs' ($\mu\acute{\epsilon}\lambda\eta$ in the Greek) refers unmistakably to the body.[23] Such dualism has parallels in Greek thought but equally in Judaism, as in the following early Rabbinic text: 'The body of a human being is earthly, but his soul is heavenly; therefore if he fulfils the Law, and does the will of his Father in heaven, then he is like the creatures above; but if not, then he is like the creatures below.'[24] The Augustinian doctrine of original sin and concupiscence still further reinforced this tendency to view the reasoning faculty as the seat of morality, since (with the aid of divine grace) it can recognize the Law of God and apply general moral principles, while the emotions and bodily drives are looked upon with intense anxiety. If women are considered less likely than men to be guided by universal maxims acknowledged by the reason, and more inclined to be spurred by emotion and instinct, it will follow that woman will appear morally weaker than man, and still less inclined than man to acknowledge and obey the Law of God.[25]

In a thirteenth-century English text, the *Ancrene Riwle*, the appointment of a woman as doorkeeper at 2 Kings 4.5–6 is interpreted as follows: '"Woman" is Reason grown weak, when it should be manful, stalwart and bold in true faith. The keeper of the door lies down to sleep as soon as one begins to consent to sin and to allow desire to enter and enjoyment to develop.'[26] On the one hand we have the association of reason, virtue, and maleness, and on the other an association between desire, sin, and the womanly. A moralism that exaggerates the role of correct rational choice forms an unholy alliance with traditional sexual stereotypes.

There is an obvious contrast between passages such as this and the tendency in the nineteenth century to set up and reverence an idealized and sentimentalized picture of woman, and to claim (in the words of a character in Bernard Shaw) that 'a woman's moral

---

[23] The fashionable holistic interpretation of St Paul was refuted by R. H. Gundry, *Sôma in Biblical Theology* (Cambridge, 1976).

[24] Rabbi Simai (sixth century), quoted in C. G. Montefiore and H. Loewe, *A Rabbinic Anthology* (London, 1938), p. 314.

[25] 'Feminine unreason usually meant the inability of the higher faculties to control the passions of the flesh': Cadden, *Meanings of Sex Difference*, p. 207.

[26] *The Ancrene Riwle*, trans. M. B. Salu (London, 1955), p. 121.

number is higher than a man's'. The Victorians accepted that woman is more emotional and less rational than man, but saw this as a positive advantage, since it fostered the virtues of sympathy and self-sacrifice and provided a counterweight to the harsh mercantile spirit of the age.[27] But in earlier centuries it was the woman who appeared the sinner, and man when he betrays his sex by taking on the weakness of woman. Yes, as the *Golden Legend* puts it so trenchantly, 'God is more weary of woman than of man, since she has sinned more.'

It is of course the case that discrimination against women in the Christian tradition has many arrows in its sheaf. Theologically, the notion of one God invited from the first a new stress on rule by the head of each social unit, inevitably male, as a way to strengthen the image of God in society; the authority of ruler over subject, master over slave, father over son, and husband over wife was not simply accepted by Christianity in its formative period, but justified and reinforced by a theological argument unparalleled in paganism or classical philosophy.[28] The theme of this paper has been the similar implications of traditional Christian ethics. Most misogynist texts from the early centuries or the medieval period strike us today as merely silly, and the passage from the *Golden Legend* that has formed the basis of the present discussion is no exception. But behind texts such as these lies a coherent set of convictions about morality on the one hand and female psychology on the other, convictions which, though shaken in the last two centuries, are not wholly defunct, but continue subtly to undermine the position of women. The feminists are right to stress the need for searching self-criticism in the Church, if we are to see the creation of a Christianity for the twenty-first century free of sexual stereotypes and genuinely supportive of sexual equality.

Heythrop College, University of London

---

[27] W. E. Houghton, *The Victorian Frame of Mind* (New Haven, CT, and London, 1957), pp. 348–53.
[28] G. E. M. de Ste Croix, *The Class Struggle in the Ancient Greek World* (London, 1981), pp. 103–11, 418–25.

THE LIFE OF ST MARGARET OF ANTIOCH IN LATE
MEDIEVAL ENGLAND: A GENDERED READING

by KATHERINE J. LEWIS

THIS paper explores the possibilities of a feminist reading of the Middle English life of St Margaret of Antioch, whose status as a virgin-martyr is sometimes held to have made her an unattainable role model, suitable only for virgins who had dedicated themselves to God. Using both written and painted English narratives of St Margaret's life dating mainly from the fourteenth and fifteenth centuries, it shows that many elements of these could have been interpreted by all women as a validation of themselves and their experiences. The paper uncovers certain common themes and similarities of presentation, to see how far a general picture of Margaret emerges from them and what they say about the construction of femininity and the female. Although the narrative of the legend takes a variety of forms, both written and painted, it is sufficiently stable (largely 'controlled' by the *Legenda Aurea*) to allow different versions to be drawn on in this way.[1]

Some of these lives would have been encountered by women within their parish churches, either as sermons or as part of the internal decoration.[2] Others are found in manuscripts which appear to have

---

[1] This paper is based on the second chapter of my M. A. thesis, '"The ruler of the world is present, woman, in you": The life of St Margaret of Antioch; validation of the female and feminine experience' (University of York, 1992). I am extremely grateful to Felicity Riddy and Jeremy Goldberg for their constructive criticism of this paper in its various incarnations. I am also very grateful to Marcus Jones for photographing St Margaret for me.

[2] For extant wall painting narratives see E. W. Tristram, *English Medieval Wall Paintings of the Fourteenth Century* (Oxford, 1954), also C. E. Keyser, *A List of Buildings in Great Britain and Ireland Having Mural and Other Painted Decorations*, 3rd edn (London, 1883); A. Caiger-Smith, *English Medieval Mural Paintings* (Oxford, 1963); E. Clive Rouse, *Medieval Wall Paintings*, 4th edn (Haverford West, 1991). For the life of St Margaret contained in the *South English Legendary*, written 1270–85 (hereafter *SEL*), see Charlotte D'Evelyn and Anna J. Mills, eds, *The South English Legendary*, vol. 1, EETS, os 235 (London, 1956), pp. 291–302. Although this life was written in the thirteenth century I include it here because the seventeen extant manuscripts which contain it date from the fourteenth or fifteenth centuries; see Manfred Gorlach: *The Textual Tradition of the South English Legendary* (Leeds, 1974). For John Mirk's sermon life of St Margaret, written at the end of the fourteenth century and extant in at least twelve fifteenth-century manuscripts [hereafter *F*] see Theodor Erbe, ed., *Mirk's Festial: A Collection of Homilies by Johannes Mirkus (John Mirk)*, EETS, es 96 (London, 1905), pp. 199–202.

been read and used within a private context, both that of the household and, in the case of Bokenham's *Legendys of Hooly Wummen*, the nunnery.[3] At least two of the narratives considered here were specifically created for a female audience. Lydgate's *Legend of Saynte Margarete* was commissioned from him by Anne, Countess of March, between 1415 and 1426.[4] The Church of St Mary's at Tarrant Crawford, Dorset, was once part of a Cistercian nunnery, suggesting that the mid-fourteenth-century wall-painting cycle of St Margaret's life to be found there was painted for the nuns.[5] The different locations of the lives and the status of the various women who would have had access to them has important ramifications for the meaning and function of St Margaret and of her cult. The authors of these lives were probably all men, and in the case of the literary lives, clerks. This paper does not suggest that St Margaret was deliberately presented as a positive role model for women by these men, or that the authors actively tried to empower or liberate them. Rather, it suggests that this

---

[3] For *Meidan Margarete* [hereafter *MM*] see C. Horstmann, ed., *Altenglische Legenden, Neue Folge* (Heilbronn, 1881), pp. 489–98. This life is extant in five manuscripts dating from the thirteenth to the fifteenth centuries. Horstmann edited the text from Cambridge, Trinity College, MS 323. For the life of St Margaret contained in the Auchinleck manuscript, compiled at the beginning of the fourteenth century [hereafter *A*], see ibid., pp. 225–35. For the life of St Margaret in short couplets, extant in two fifteenth-century manuscripts [hereafter *AB*], see ibid., pp. 236–41 (text from Oxford, Bodleian Library, MS Ashmole 61). This version is also to be found in the Brome Commonplace Book; see Lucy Toulmin Smith, ed., *A Commonplace Book of the Fifteenth Century* (London, 1886), pp. 107–18. I shall refer to Horstmann's edition. For the life of St Margaret contained in the *Scottish Legendary*, composed in the late fourteenth century and extant in a unique late fifteenth-century manuscript [hereafter *ScL*], see W. M. Metcalf, ed., *Legends of the Saints in the Scottish Dialect of the Fourteenth Century: Part 3*, Scottish Text Society, 24 (Edinburgh, 1890), pp. 47–68. For the life composed by Osbern Bokenham in 1443 [hereafter *OB*], see Mary S. Serjeantson, ed., *Legendys of Hooly Wummen*, EETS, os 206 (London, 1938), pp. 7–38.
[4] For John Lydgate's *Legend of Saynte Margarete* [hereafter *L*] see Henry Noble MacCracken, ed., *The Minor Poems of John Lydgate: Part 1*, EETS, es 107 (London, 1911), pp. 173–92. For Lydgate and his female patrons, including Lady March, see Carol M. Meale, '"... alle the bokes that I haue in latyn, englisch, and frensch": laywomen and their books in late medieval England', in Carol M. Meale, ed., *Women and Literature in Britain, 1100–1500* (Cambridge, 1993), pp. 128–58. Bokenham's life of St Margaret was originally written for Thomas Burgh, who subsequently arranged for the compilation of Bokenham's female saints' lives into a manuscript for his sister's nunnery in Cambridge: Serjeantson, *Legendys of Hooly Wummen*, p. xx.
[5] For the nunnery at Tarrant Crawford and its putative connection with the wall paintings of St Margaret see E. Clive Rouse, 'St Mary's Church Tarrant Crawford' (pamphlet), and Roberta Gilchrist, *Gender and Material Culture: The Archaeology of Religious Women* (London, 1994), pp. 179–80, fig. 70. For Tristram's description of the cycle see his *Fourteenth Century*, p. 261.

may have been the way that women responded to St Margaret and the narratives of her life.

The paper concentrates on the early life of St Margaret and her upbringing by the Christian Nurse, and the subsequent opposition between paganism gendered as masculine and Christianity gendered as feminine, in order to demonstrate that Margaret's example of strength, faith, and fortitude derives from her feminine context and qualities. It must be stressed that there is no assumption of any absolute correlation between gender and biological sex in this investigation. However, virtually all virgin martyr narratives seem to involve the gendering of Christianity and paganism described above, and in all but one case this is reflected in the sex of the protagonists: the Christians are female, the pagans male.[6] Margaret does not have to negate her femininity to fight for Christ, rather she draws strength from it. This positive reading is contextualized by showing how the patterns of women's learning and reading constructed by the narratives relate to the actual practices of contemporary women.

Margaret functions as a paradigm of the devout young woman, one of many maidens who receives her education from a mother figure within a domestic context. The narratives further construct Margaret as an exemplar of the feminine by contrasting her with Olibrius, an exemplar of the masculine. Both characters are given clearly gendered attributes and activities to heighten the dichotomy between them, and ultimately to privilege femininity over masculinity, in a divinely sanctioned reversal of the gender hierarchy of this world.

St Margaret is born into the pagan world of fourth-century Asia Minor. All the texts begin by presenting a picture of the alternative evil, patriarchal hierarchy which Margaret rejects, partially by forcing it to reject her.[7] Paganism, represented as it is by the Father and Olibrius, is constructed as wholly masculine. It is also defended by the

---

[6] I have found Joan Cadden's *Meanings of Sex Difference in the Middle Ages: Medicine, Science and Culture* (Cambridge, 1993) a very useful introduction to medieval theories of sex and gender. My reading of virgin martyr lives has also been influenced by Judith Butler's theory of performative gender, see her *Gender Trouble: Feminism and the Subversion of Identity* (New York and London, 1990), especially pp. 1–34. The exception to the rule is the life of St Katherine of Alexandria which includes some male pagans whose conversion to Christianity is seen to entail their feminization. This issue is discussed at length in ch. 4 of my D. Phil. thesis, 'The cult of St Katherine of Alexandria in later medieval England' (University of York, 1996).

[7] For the introduction of Margaret's status and her father: *SEL*, pp. 291–2; *MM*, p. 489; *A*, p. 226; *AB*, p. 236; *ScL*, pp. 48–9; *F*, p. 200; *L*, p. 176; *OB*, p. 10.

male soldiers who take her into custody, the male torturers who tear her body so cruelly, and by the Devil himself, who is seen to possess demonstrably male attributes. Since these adherents of paganism are all ignorant and doomed to punishment, Margaret cannot be allowed to be tainted by any of them, so provision is made for her to be taken out of Antioch and raised by a third party: the Nurse. St Margaret is displaced from the pagan city to a precise distance of fifteen miles.[8] She is given an alternative female space from which to reject masculine pagan control and to embrace Christianity. The early fourteenth-century cycle of paintings at Battle, Sussex, shows the moment of transition from pagan to Christian as the baby Margaret is handed over to the Nurse.[9]

The texts give various explanations for this transition. Three of them recount that Margaret's mother died young: 'þis maide was þo hure moder deide ʒong and tendre inou.'[10] This provides a practical reason for Margaret's displacement and allows the Nurse to fill a maternal role in contrast to the biological and displaced paternalism of the Father and Olibrius respectively. *Meidan Margarete*, the Auchinleck life, and the Ashmole life all assign Margaret's mother a role in her daughter's fostering out to the Nurse; the baby Margaret is in danger because her father would rather have his daughter killed than risk her becoming a Christian: 'Hyre fader comandyd . . . that, none as sche was borne, To þe Deth sche schuld be brouʒht.'[11] So her mother sends Margaret into Asia to be brought up by a Nurse: 'ho sende it into Asye wid messengers ful yare To a norice, þat hire wiste and sette hire to lore'.[12] This reading of the episode further enhances the opposition between the cruelty of the male protagonists and the compassion of the female.

The various explanations have different implications, but all lead to the same end result: Margaret is provided with a liminal space in which to prepare for her inevitable fate. The first step of this preparation is the conversion itself. The texts construct Margaret's conversion as

---

[8] *SEL*, p. 292; *MM*, p. 489; *A*, p. 227; *AB*, p. 236; *ScL*, p. 49; *F*, p. 200; *L*, p. 176; *OB*, p. 11.

[9] For original photographs of the Battle cycle see Lewis, 'The life of St Margaret of Antioch', appendix, figs 26–9. St Margaret is handed over to the Nurse in fig. 26. For a schematic diagram of the paintings see E. Clive Rouse, 'Wall paintings in St Mary's Church Battle', *Sussex Archaeological Collections*, 117 (1979), pp. 154–5. This is the most complete extant wall-painting cycle of St Margaret's life to be found in England and Rouse's article provides the most detailed description of it.

[10] *SEL*, p. 292. See also *F*, p. 49; *OB*, p. 11.

[11] *AB*, p. 236. See also *MM*, p. 489; *A*, p. 226.

[12] *MM*, p. 489. See also *A*, p. 226; *AB*, p. 236.

having been directed or instructed in some way. Although, as Margaret was never really a pagan in the first place, drawn as she is towards some higher truth despite her pagan heritage, there is no sense of a process of debate and consideration culminating in conversion. Margaret is provided with the means to learn the truth. And as God's chosen representative she is empowered to recognize and accept it as such straight away. Margaret is aware of the pagan heritage which she has rejected. For example, in the *South English Legendary* life she describes her father as 'gret man inou among 3ou here ikud, Teodose þe hexte maister þat of oure temple is'.[13]

In some of the texts the Nurse is explicitly named as the transmitter of Christianity. In *Meidan Margarete*, the Auchinleck life, and the Ashmole life she achieves this in a typically feminine way, communicating Christianity orally, in the home: 'Fulle gode tayles sche cuthe telle . . . [of saints] how þei merterdome gane take All fore Jhesu Crystys sake.'[14] Bokenham's life portrays a virtuous Christian woman 'wyhs & sage', capable of teaching the tenets of Christianity to her charge: 'And priuyly a cristene wumman was she And in al hyr conuersacyoun bothe pure & clene.'[15] If the Nurse is not specifically named in the other texts her influence is certainly implied and it is safe to say that the Nurse is generally presented as having been responsible for the transmission of Christianity to the heroine.[16]

This accords with the atmosphere of male paganism previously described. As God does not choose to illuminate any of the male characters it is only natural that Margaret should be taught by a woman. That the medieval audience of Margaret's life made the same deduction is borne out by the evidence of the wall paintings. The cycle of paintings at Tarrant Crawford begins with an image of Margaret kneeling before her Nurse, whose arm is upraised in an unmistakable gesture of instruction.[17]

Christianity is thus seen being propagated by women, in private, in defiance of the patriarchal religious and social structures of the

[13] SEL, pp. 293-4.
[14] AB, p. 236. See also MM, p. 490; A, p. 226.
[15] OB, p. 11.
[16] The Scottish life alone does not impute Margaret's education to the Nurse (who is present in the text), but to an unidentified man. He plays no further part in her life or passion, however, and so does not significantly affect my argument: ScL, p. 49.
[17] For this image and the rest of the Tarrant Crawford cycle see Lewis, 'The life of St Margaret of Antioch', appendix, figs 13a-22.

masculine Empire. Christianity is passed from woman to woman and
this idea is further elaborated in the texts by the inclusion of an
amorphous group of maidens: 'So whyl þat scho was long þer among
oþer maydyns, scho herde speke of God and of oure Lorde Jhesu
Crist.'[18] If Margaret is educated in Christianity by the Nurse then it is
reasonable to suppose that the inclusion of the maidens is intended to
further the construction of Christianity as an all-female network. This
is certainly how the artist of the early fourteenth-century cycle at
Wendens Ambo, Essex, interpreted the episode since he (or possibly she)
begins the cycle with a fascinating picture which represents just this.[19]

The Nurse, seated on a bench, forms the centre of the picture, her
attention and instructive gesture directed towards a fragmentary figure
holding a book. The prominence thus given to this sole standing figure
indicates that it is St Margaret. In addition the artist has included three
obviously female figures (two of them are wearing some kind of head-
dress), sitting or kneeling at the Nurse's feet and all holding or reading
from open books. This image elaborates on what the texts leave
unstated: that these women form a Christian community united by the
female figure of the mistress as teacher. Women play an expanded role
in some of the other wall painting narratives too. At Battle, below the
depiction of Margaret's birth (an episode not so far found represented
in any other visual cycle) is the representation of Margaret's burial.[20]
Both scenes are directed by women. In the late fourteenth-century
cycle at Limpenhoe (now destroyed) Margaret's burial was attended by
sorrowing women, perhaps the 'maydyns'?[21] Women are also present at
Margaret's execution and burial as depicted in the early fourteenth-
century Queen Mary's Psalter.[22]

The image presented is thus deliberately one of a female textual
community. The Nurse does not just instruct by word of mouth, as
might be expected, but uses the written word. This is a very important

---

[18] F, p. 200. See also SEL, p. 293; MM, p. 490; A, p. 226; AB, p. 236; L, p. 177.

[19] Unfortunately, the paintings are in a poor state of preservation, and although the
elements which will be pointed out are visible in the original, they are not easy to make out
from a photograph. For ease of reference the sketches of this cycle made by Tristram should
be consulted. For the immediate instance, see Tristram, Fourteenth Century, pl. 50b. Tristram
dated the cycle to c. 1330.

[20] Lewis, 'The life of St Margaret of Antioch', appendix, fig. 26.

[21] F. C. Husenbeth, 'On some mural paintings discovered in Limpenhoe Church,
Norfolk', Norfolk Archaeology, 5 (1859), fig. 3.

[22] George Warner, Queen Mary's Psalter: Miniatures and Drawings by an English Artist of the
Fourteenth Century (London, 1912), p. 314.

image as it can be located in the context of contemporary women's literacy and reading practices. The notion of woman as educator fits into a more general context too. Another, and much more frequent, representation of an older woman teaching a young charge is to be found in the many images of St Anne teaching the Virgin. This was the most widely known image of the saint in England, and indeed was apparently invented there in the early fourteenth century.[23] It has been suggested that this subject was intended to perform a specific function; to promote or authorize the education of girls by their mothers.[24] That the relationship between Margaret and her Nurse is shown as that of teacher and pupil suggests that this image served the same purpose as that of St Anne and the Virgin. Both images demonstrate that women were perceived as chiefly responsible for devotional instruction within the domestic sphere, and indeed that this was a religious obligation inherent in motherhood.[25]

The life of St Margaret is often to be found in manuscripts whose contents (such as moral and devotional lyrics, courtesy texts, and versified articles of faith) suggest that they functioned as household books and were used for reading and instruction within the home; for example Cambridge University Library, MS Ff.II.38, the Auchinleck Manuscript, and Oxford, Bodleian Library, MS Ashmole 61.[26] Thus it seems likely that the life sometimes formed part of a domestic education programme, paralleled in the Nurse's practice of relating stories of saints to the maidens. That the life of St Katherine often appears alongside that of St Margaret in such manuscripts suggests that both were seen to have particular value for purposes of instruction within the household.[27]

[23] S. J. E. Riches, ' "The pot of oure hope": images of St Anne in the late medieval world' (University of York, D. Phil. thesis, 1991), p. 67; Christopher Norton, David Park and Paul Binski, *Dominican Painting in East Anglia: The Thornham Parva Retable and the Musée de Cluny Frontal* (Woodbridge, 1987), pp. 51–2.

[24] Riches, 'Images of St Anne', p. 66.

[25] Ibid. See also Pamela Sheingorn, ' "The wise mother": the image of St Anne teaching the Virgin Mary', *Gesta*, 32 (1993), pp. 69–80; Wendy Scase, 'St Anne and the education of the Virgin: literary and artistic traditions and their implications', in Nicholas Rogers, ed., *England in the Fourteenth Century: Proceedings of the 1991 Harlaxton Symposium* (Stamford, 1993), pp. 81–96.

[26] For the contents of these manuscripts see Gisela Guddat-Figge, *Catalogue of Manuscripts Containing Middle English Romances* (Munich, 1976), pp. 94–9, 121–7, 249–52.

[27] Both saints' lives appear in the Auchinleck Manuscript and CUL, MS Ff.2.38; also in Oxford, Bodleian Library, MS 14528 (Rawlinson Poet 34); Oxford, Corpus Christi College, MS 237; Cambridge, Corpus Christi College, MS 142; and BL, MS Harley 4012.

The image of Margaret and her companions as literate women reading and sharing books can also be contextualized. The work of Anne Dutton, Felicity Riddy, and Carol Meale establishes that women did indeed form book-lending, -giving, and -reading networks of the kind illustrated at Wendens Ambo.[28] Will evidence shows that many women who list books in wills leave them to other women, and there is evidence that both Lollard women and nuns formed themselves into reading groups often gathered around a 'teacher' like the Nurse.[29] Women as domestic instructors are familiar and authorized, and the texts and images make use of the distinction between public and private; paganism is public and therefore masculine, Christianity is private and therefore feminine.

That Margaret is taught the tenets of Christianity by her Nurse is not merely a device to set masculine against feminine, although it certainly has that effect; but it is a situation that would have been recognized and appreciated by the audience, especially its female component. Community among women is represented sympathetically much less often than the idea of community among men. A group of women usually signified gossips, slanderers, and drunks, whose speech was subversive. An example of this is to be found in the representation of Uxor Noe and the Good Gossopes in the Chester play of the Flood.[30] It must have been both refreshing and reassuring for women to be presented with positive images of themselves congregating to worship God and learn more about him.

The lives of virgin martyrs such as Margaret are often read as representing their heroines as prescribed by their sex, always vulnerable, suffering torture to expunge their weak and inherently sinful femininity, or else they are seen to eschew their femininity altogether and adopt masculine traits in order to authorize their activities.[31]

[28] Anne Dutton, 'Women's use of religious literature in late medieval England' (University of York, D. Phil. thesis, 1995); Felicity Riddy, '"Women talking about the things of God": a late-medieval sub-culture', in Meale, *Women and Literature*, pp. 104–27; Meale, ' . . . alle the bokes that I haue'.
[29] Riddy, 'Women talking about the things of God', pp. 109–10; Claire Cross, '"Great reasoners in Scripture": the activities of women Lollards 1380–1530', in Derek Baker, ed., *Medieval Women*, SCH. S, 1 (Oxford, 1978), pp. 359–80. For the most recent examination of the role of women in Lollardy see Shannon McSheffrey, *Gender and Heresy: Women and Men in Lollard Communities, 1520–1530* (Philadelphia, PA, 1996).
[30] Peter Happe, ed., *English Mystery Plays* (Harmondsworth, 1975), pp. 126–7.
[31] For examples of such readings see Marina Warner, *Alone of All Her Sex: The Myth and Cult of the Virgin Mary*, 2nd edn (London, 1991), p. 71; Margaret R. Miles, '"Becoming

Arguably, however, such readings do not take into account the experiences of the women who made up part of the audience to these lives and the ways in which the account of Margaret's liminal pre-martyrdom period relates to that experience. In this respect the work of Jocelyn Wogan-Browne on virgin martyr hagiography suggests a possibility of resistant readings of these texts, which in particular contexts may constitute relative empowerment or recuperation.[32] An important element in the popularity of virgin martyrs and their cults was undoubtedly their powers of intercession.[33] However, this does not account for the fact that these saints were presented and perceived as role models for the audiences of these lives. In the confrontation between Margaret and Olibrius, Margaret's exemplary femininity is presented not as weakness, but as strength. Margaret is inspirational and paradigmatic because she demonstrates that a woman can withdraw from male authority to define her own religious space.

The last picture of Margaret that we are given before the intrusion of Olibrius and paganism is one of feminine, pastoral simplicity. Margaret, who is of noble birth, humbly tends her Nurse's sheep out in the fields: 'Humble of hir porte, this gracyous creature Kepte of hir Noryce the shepe in theire pasture',[34] an archetypal occupation of peasant women and children, thus confirming Margaret's complete rejection of her worldly heritage and all that it entails.[35] It is also a conventional feature of the 'good' woman to be humble, so the woman in her is set in a wholly orthodox place. The image of her guarding sheep also invites comparison with Christ, the good shepherd who 'giveth his life for the sheep' (John 10.11). This is only the first of several ways in which Margaret's life is represented as an *imitatio Christi*.

Male": women martyrs and ascetics', in her *Carnal Knowing: Female Nakedness and Religious Meaning in the Christian West* (Boston, MA, 1989), pp. 359–80.

[32] Jocelyn Wogan-Browne, 'The Virgin's Tale', in Ruth Evans and Lesley Johnson, eds, *The Wife of Bath and All Her Sect: Feminist Readings in Middle English Literature* (London and New York, 1994), pp. 165–94, esp. p. 180.

[33] Eamon Duffy argues that virgin martyrs were perceived solely as conduits of intercessory power by the vast majority of medieval devotees; see his 'Holy maydens, holy wyfes: the cult of women saints in fifteenth- and sixteenth-century England', *SCH*, 27 (1990), pp. 175–96.

[34] *L*, p. 177. See also *SEL*, p. 293; *MM*, p. 490; *A*, p. 226; *AB*, p. 236; *ScL*, p. 49; *F*, p. 200; *OB*, p. 13.

[35] Judith M. Bennett, *Women in the Medieval English Countryside: Gender and Household in Brigstock before the Plague* (New York and Oxford, 1987), pp. 116–17.

Margaret awaits her fate with feminine passivity, which in this context is presented as a strength, not a weakness. She has been prepared for it in the female world and now she waits for male action to initiate her passion. This happens in the shape of Olibrius and his entourage riding past on their way to persecute Christians in Antioch. Olibrius sees and instantly desires Margaret: 'Anon riȝt in fole loue is herte to hure drou Him longede sore after hure.'[36] The irony is that Margaret, far from being his wife, is to be his first victim. The traditional gendered dichotomy between the sexes is thus made manifest in the two main protagonists: male is active, female is passive. The clash between masculine and feminine is made particularly explicit in the visual renderings of the scene which use markedly gendered activities to establish the differences between them. In the wall-painting cycles of the life of St Margaret at Wendens Ambo, Limpenhoe, Battle, and Charlwood (painted in about 1350) the iconography is identical.[37] Further examples in manuscript, embroidery, and stained glass versions, suggest that it was absolutely standard from at least the thirteenth century onwards.[38]

Margaret sits to the left raised up slightly, visually signifying her ascendancy over Olibrius and his world. She is surrounded by sheep, as described in the lives. Approaching from the right are Olibrius and various men armed with spears and clubs, representing both Olibrius' imperial power and the implied threat of their own virility, made manifest by their subsequent abduction of Margaret.[39] The presence of macho sexuality is further signalled by the depiction of the two rams at her feet, butting each other in a battle to establish superior potency.[40]

[36] *SEL*, p. 293. See also *MM*, p. 490; *A*, p. 227; *AB*, p. 236; *ScL*, pp. 49–50; *F*, p. 200; *OB*, p. 13.

[37] See Husenbeth, 'Limpenhoe Church', fig. 1. For the Battle version see Lewis, 'Life of St Margaret of Antioch', appendix, fig. 27. For a description of the cycle at Charlwood in Surrey see Tristram, *Fourteenth Century*, pp. 155–6. For photographs of the cycle see Lewis, 'Life of St Margaret of Antioch', appendix, figs 5–7. The fragmentary life of St Margaret to be found in Wiston Church, Suffolk contains part of this scene, showing Margaret spinning with sheep at her feet, looking up to a non-extant figure in front of her. See E. W. Tristram, *English Medieval Wall Painting: The Thirteenth Century* (Oxford, 1950), pl. 18b.

[38] Warner, *Queen Mary's Psalter*, p. 307. The Pienza Cope (1315–35) has a representation of this scene, A. G. I. Christie, *English Medieval Embroidery* (Oxford, 1938), pp. 178–83, pls 139–42. A panel of stained glass dating from the early fifteenth century, now in the west window of North Tuddenham Church, Norfolk, also depicts this scene: C. Woodforde, *The Norwich School of Glass-Painting in the Fifteenth Century* (London, 1955), p. 55.

[39] For Tristram's sketch of this painting see her *Fourteenth Century*, pl. 49.

[40] This reading was suggested to me by Delbert Russell. This element is barely visible in

Margaret is thus seen to be at risk both from ideological as well as physical attack, but remains impervious to both. One of the men traverses the space between the two protagonists, making visually explicit Olibrius' desire for her by holding out a large bejewelled ring in one hand, and a spear in the other. Thus Margaret is made to reiterate her rejection of worldly wealth and the other implications of this offer. She has chosen maidenhood and humility, not had it thrust upon her, and this lends her the power over Olibrius visually represented by her elevated position.

Interestingly, this scene includes two elements which do not occur in the textual accounts, both of which serve further to highlight the gendered distinction between the two main protagonists. Firstly, Olibrius and his men are shown, by the inclusion of a dog and a hare (visible below the ringbearer's feet) to be hunting. This serves to give a visual explanation for their presence not provided by the texts, where it is stated that Olibrius happens by on official business, rather than while indulging in leisure pursuits. The nature of the medium demands a visual explanation; but showing the men as hunters provides interesting undertones of chase, conquest and death which sum up Olibrius' intentions for Margaret herself. The male world is thus established as physically powerful and potentially brutal in this scene. This is underlined in the literary texts as Margaret is carried off to Antioch by Olibrius' henchmen, fulfilling their master's orders.[41]

The second additional element provides a positive counter to this: Margaret is holding a distaff and is clearly seen to be spinning. This does not occur in any of the written texts. Spinning is, of course, the archetypal feminine activity, from Eve onwards; as witness the words of the men of Beverley to Margery Kempe: 'Damsel, forsake þis lyfe that þu hast, go spynne and carde as other women dou.'[42] The female

the painting at Wendens Ambo, but does feature in Tristram's sketch. The two rams can still be seen in the glass panel at Tuddenham and at Battle, however, indicating that it was a fairly standard ingredient in the iconography of this scene. For a lengthier discussion of the significance of the rams within this context see Cordelia Beattie, '"For I see myself, Lord, harassed and beset like a lamb among rabid wolves": a study of a stained glass panel in North Tuddenham' (unpublished paper). I am grateful to Cordelia Beattie for sharing with me her observations on this scene.

[41] *SEL*, p. 293; *MM*, p. 491; *A*, p. 228; *AB*, p. 237; *ScL*, p. 53; *F*, p. 200; *L*, p. 173; *OB*, p. 14.
[42] Sanford Brown Meech and Hope Emily Allen, eds, *The Book of Margery Kempe*, EETS, os 212 (Oxford, 1940), p. 129; see also Bennett, *Women in the Medieval English Countryside*, p. 117. Beattie provides a more detailed discussion of the spinning motif, 'A study of a stained glass panel in North Tuddenham', pp. 9–12.

world is represented as private and constructive rather than public and destructive. This scene of contrast appears at the beginning of Margaret's visual life, thus setting the tone of conflict for the action to follow. This depiction of Margaret as typically feminine is also deliberately misleading in physical terms, as it makes her subsequent physical fortitude appear all the more miraculous.

Unlike a passage from a book, the scenes in these wall paintings were on constant display to the worshipper and were designed to be meditated on and ultimately participated in.[43] It must have been obvious that Margaret is firmly aligned with the female world, both from the images and from the texts with their suggestions of an autonomous female community.

Margaret is sent into this female community, directly or indirectly, by the male authority represented by her Father, but she does not fulfil his expectations, becoming a Christian and therefore subversive. Margaret does not need to resort to an assumption of masculine qualities; when faced with the threatening power of the male world, she visibly draws strength from her female background in order to distance herself as far as possible from Olibrius and all that he stands for. In so doing she sanctions the power of a female who is directly authorized by God.

While the female signifies knowledge, the male signifies ignorance, as Olibrius tries to convince Margaret that she is misguided in her beliefs; but there is a wider issue at stake. Margaret, as a woman, has no right to choose an alternative role to that dictated by her noble status. But Margaret refuses to live according to social expectations and the values of the world. She has been brought up away from the pagan world in a wholly feminine, Christian environment. Her reintroduction into the pagan space of Antioch necessarily causes great disruption; she flouts both social and religious convention and she defends her person and her beliefs with physical fortitude and reasoned arguments.[44] Her behaviour serves further to expose the inadequacy of her male opponents; the challenge of her impervious body and her unswerving, well-informed faith renders Olibrius more and more

---

[43] Margaret R. Miles, *Image as Insight: Visual Understanding in Western Christianity and Secular Culture* (Boston, MA, 1985), pp. 65–75; Sixten Ringbon, 'Devotional images and imaginative devotions: notes on the place of art in late medieval private piety', *Gazette des beaux arts*, 73 (1969), pp. 159–70.

[44] For examples of Margaret's rhetorical excellence see *SEL*, p. 295; *MM*, pp. 492–3; *A*, p. 228; *AB*, p. 237; *ScL*, pp. 53–4; *L*, pp. 180–1; *OB*, p. 22.

bestial and inhuman. By the end of the narrative the contrast between them is complete. Margaret has become the figurative type of Christ, suffering to obtain divine favour for her followers and ultimately taking her place in Heaven. Olibrius, on the other hand, faced with an imperfectly socialized woman who draws her strength from her female body and her feminine context, becomes diabolic in his frustration as he is rendered impotent in more ways than one.[45] There can be no doubt about his afterlife destination.

This feminist interpretation of the life of St Margaret reads it as a didactic yet validating reinforcement of female gender roles, taking into account the interests and experiences of the women who would have heard, read, or seen it. The life may have been particularly pertinent for young unmarried women; the visual narrative could be read as a defence against sexual temptation.[46] This observation is borne out by *The Book of the Knight of the Tower*, translated into English by Caxton and printed by him in 1484.[47] In one chapter the Knight exhorts his daughters, for whom the book was written, to remember the lives of saints Katherine, Margaret, and other virgin martyrs, 'For they surmounted many grete temptacions'.[48] They are thus used as examples of chastity which will become, in the case of the Knight's three daughters, wifely chastity. The Knight's use of virgin martyrs as role models for his daughters is a reminder that they were not perceived as exemplary for virgins alone. Similarly Christine de Pisan in her *The Treasure of the City of Ladies* recommends the lives of virgin martyrs as part of a training programme for girls who will be wives, writing that 'Young girls taught and brought up in this way are much sought after by men.'[49]

Margaret's upbringing and education by the Nurse reflect and authorize contemporary patterns of female literacy and learning, and Margaret demonstrates that knowledge can affect the power balance between male and female, a belief held very firmly by Christine de Pisan and which directed many of her writings. It would appear

---

[45] For Olibrius' rage and the tortures he inflicts upon Margaret see, e.g., *SEL*, p. 295; *MM*, p. 496; *A*, p. 233; *AB*, p. 240; *ScL*, pp. 62–3; *F*, p. 200; *L*, pp. 62–3; *OB*, p. 22.

[46] I am indebted to Jeremy Goldberg for this suggestion.

[47] M. Y. Offord, ed., *The Book of the Knight of the Tower, translated by William Caxton*, EETS, ss 2 (1971), p. xiv.

[48] Ibid., p. 91.

[49] Christine de Pisan, *The Treasure of the City of Ladies*, trans. Sarah Lawson (Harmondsworth, 1985), pp. 161–2.

therefore that within certain contexts St Margaret could and did function as a role model for women, validating themselves and their experiences and proving that given the right training they have it in them to vanquish the Devil himself.

University of York

ACCESS TO THE DIVINE: GENDER AND VOTIVE IMAGES IN MOLDAVIA AND WALLACHIA

by CHRISTINE PETERS

I N Orthodox Last Judgements in sixteenth-century Moldavia, both Adam and Eve appear as saintly intercessors on behalf of mankind. The presence of these suppliant figures, on either side of the throne of hetimasia (Plate 1),[1] suggests that Orthodoxy and Catholicism differed significantly in their evaluations of the gender implications of the Fall. In medieval Catholicism the portrayal of a nimbed figure of Eve, or even of Adam, was inconceivable. In the West the ideas of the Fall as the cause of the crucifixion and of Mary as the antithesis of Eve produced a powerful set of negative views of women's nature. The weaker sex was inherently vulnerable to temptation, flattery, and persuasion, endangering not only women's souls but those of all mankind. The veneration of Mary tempered this negative image, but Mary's extraordinary nature could never entirely erase the assumptions of innate female inferiority based on the role of Eve in the Fall. The depiction of Eve as a saint in Orthodox wall painting appears to offer an unexpected challenge to the view that such gender associations are the only possible outcome of the Genesis account. It is also tempting to relate the presence of such representations in Moldavia to the highly unusual social position of women in Moldavian society, based on inheritance customs which divided estates equally between both sons and daughters.[2]

The ways in which social and religious conceptions of female status intersect can be seen most clearly in votive images which depict the act of donation. As the greatest secular intrusion into sacred space, the votive image is a fundamental source for the study of the relationship

[1] The Orthodox iconographical theme of the throne of hetimasia represents and symbolizes the equality of the three hypostases of the Trinity.

[2] G. Fotino, *Étude sur la situation de la femme dans l'ancien droit roumain* (Paris, 1931), and 'Droit romain et droit oriental: phénomenes d'interpénétration de la représentation en matière de successions féminines dans l'ancien droit roumain', *Mélanges in memoria lui Vasile Parvan* (Bucharest, 1934), pp. 5–13; A. I. Gonța, *Satul in Moldova medievală-Instituțiile* (Bucharest, 1986), pp. 249–50. Women in Moldavia also retained significant control over their dowry during marriage.

Plate 1 Voroneţ (Moldavia): Detail of the Last Judgement. Adam and Eve kneel either side of the throne of hetimasia. [Photo: Institute for the History of Art, Bucharest]

144

between the human and the divine. Envisaged in Moldavia as a process of communication, these images include a saintly figure, usually the patron of the church, as a mediator between the donor and an enthroned Christ (Plate 2). The actual act of donation is limited to the male head of the family.[3] It is the husband who holds the church model, sometimes assisted by the saintly intercessor but never by his wife. She is merely portrayed as one of the procession of family members attending the act of donation. By contrast, in Wallachia both the husband and wife are normally depicted holding the model of the church (Plate 3).

This contrast in the portrayal of women in votive images in Moldavia and Wallachia is hard to reconcile with evidence for the different status of women in the two principalities. Wallachian society did not share the unusually generous inheritance provisions for women which were characteristic of Moldavia, and yet it is in Wallachia that we find the greater recognition of the joint role of the couple in the visualization of the act of donation. This paper will explore this apparent contradiction, and will begin by examining the nature of votive images and the portrayal of female donors. It will then seek to place this in the broader context of ideas of Eve as a saintly intercessor and of the potential for female sanctity.

* * *

The access to the divine illustrated by the votive image represents a particular possibility of communication, one that is individual, or at most familial, and is inscribed within the conventions of donation.[4] Its clear connection with issues of property and endowment means that it is in this type of image that we would expect the unusual legal status of Moldavian women to be visualized. The distinctive nature of the votive image can be seen by comparison with other representations of

---

[3] Depiction of women as active donors was only possible when no male co-donors were portrayed. This seems to be the case at the church of St Nicholas Rădăuți. The paintings in this church have subsequently been very much overpainted, but Marina Sabados suggests that the votive image on the east wall of the pronaos dates from the sixteenth century. Interestingly, the donor in this image does not hold a model of the church, but relies solely on the scroll of commendation held by the female saint who stands behind her with her right hand protectively on the donor's shoulder.

[4] For a more detailed discussion see C. Peters, 'The relationship between the human and the divine: towards a context for votive images in mural painting in Moldavia and Wallachia', *Revue des études sud-est européenes* [hereafter *RÉSEE*], 32 (1994), pp. 35-43.

Plate 2   Humor (Moldavia): The voievode Petru Rareş offers a model of the church to Christ with the intercession of the

intercessory communication. At Curtea de Argeş (Wallachia) the portrayal of the voievode Nicolae Alexandru as a humbly kneeling figure in the Deisis[5] contrasts with the stately sumptuosity of the donors in the principal votive image. At Probota (Moldavia) the iconography of the funerary portrait of Ion, son of Petru Rareş, resembles the accompanying votive image more closely; but in the former the portrayal of St Nicholas rather than Christ enthroned reduces the level of communication with the divine.[6] Acts of donation permit greater lay familiarity with the higher ranks of the divine. Furthermore, some acts of donation appear to grant more equality than others. The well-known image of Ştefan cel Mare presenting the gospels of Humor (1473) shows him kneeling in the lower register of the composition below the central image of Mary enthroned with the Christ Child. In contrast, votive images in mural paintings depicting the same voievode and his successors reject this assumption of humility and show them offering models of their ecclesiastical foundations almost with the presumption of equals. It is the specific relationship between the lay person and the divine, created by the act of donation of a church, monastery, or scheme of wall painting, which represents the conception of the upper limit of communication possible for a member of the laity.

The most cursory survey of votive images in Moldavia and Wallachia reveals a striking difference in the conception of the relationship between the human and the divine. Moldavian images include a portrayal of a saintly figure, usually the patron of the church, as a mediator between the donor and an enthroned Christ, whereas Wallachian images depict a symbolic representation of the divine emerging from the upper border of the composition.[7] In Moldavia, the approach to the divine can only be made through an intercessor who,

---

[5] At its simplest the composition of the Deisis consists of an enthroned figure of Christ flanked by the Virgin Mary and St John the Baptist as intercessors.

[6] D. Barbu, *Pictura murală în Ţara Românească în secolul al XIV-lea* (Bucharest, 1986), pp. 18–22; M. A. Musicescu and G. Ionescu, *Biserica Domnească din Curtea de Argeş* (Bucharest, 1976), p. 11; S. Ulea, 'Portretul funerar al lui Ion – un fiu necunoscut al lui Petru Rareş – şi datarea ansamblului de pictura de la Probota', *Studii şi Cercetării de Istoria Artei (Artă Plastică)*, 6/1 (1959), pp. 61–9. A similar contrast can be seen at Bistriţa-Neamţ: M. I. Sabados, 'Sur un portrait votif inédit de Bistriţa-Neamţ', *RÉSEE*, 30 (1992), pp. 89–96.

[7] I. D. Ştefănescu, *Iconografia artei bizantine şi a picturii feudale româneşti* (Bucharest, 1973), pp. 162–3; M. A. Musicescu, 'Byzance et le portrait roumain au Moyen Age', *Études Byzantines et Post-Byzantines*, 1 (1979), pp. 153–79, labels the Moldavian iconography of the votive image as the 'portrait à l'intercesseur' (p. 158).

Plate 3   Curtea de Argeş (Wallachia): Votive image of voievode Neagoe Basarab, his wife Despina, and their children. [Photo: Institute for the History of Art, Bucharest]

as a saint, shows both human and divine characteristics. The reward for enlisting the help of a saint is the possibility of a direct approach to Christ. Significantly, in a rare instance in which a saintly mediator is absent in Moldavian painting, at Dobrovaţ, the enthroned Christ is removed into a higher plane of the composition.[8] In contrast, Wallachian painting, with the exception of the votive image of Mircea cel Bătrîn at Cozia, rejects the solution of a saintly mediator between the human and the divine. Instead, in opting for a schematic representation of divine power, the votive image in Wallachia lacks the narrative emphasis and becomes more evidently symbolic and a validation of earthly power. The presence of the divine seems to set the seal of approval on earthly position and on earthly acts of donation.[9]

This iconographical distinction reflects significantly different conceptions in the two Romanian principalities, which cannot be dismissed as merely the product of emulation and adoption of external artistic influences. The closest parallels to the iconography of the Moldavian votive image with an intercessory saint can be found in medieval Serbia.[10] Thus, at Studenica, a female saint takes the donor by the hand and presents him to Christ enthroned. At Miliseva, the Virgin Mary similarly takes the hand of the founder, Vladislav, and presents him to Christ. However, despite the conceptual similarities between these Serbian and Moldavian images, artists in Moldavia did not slavishly imitate Serbian models. The Virgin at Miliseva is not the patron of the church, and the action of the saint leading the donor by the hand is adopted only rarely in Moldavia, as at Sfîntul Ilie lînga Suceava. Similarly, the position of the church held in the crook of the donor's arm is not the disposition usually adopted in Moldavia, where a greater emphasis is given to the act of donation and presentation, which makes possible the commendation of the lay person to the

---

[8] The church of Dobrovaţ is dedicated to the Descent of the Holy Spirit, which may explain the unusual absence of a mediatory saint. The votive image is described and discussed, mainly with respect to genealogy and dating, in V. Drăguţ, *Dobrovaţ* (Bucharest, 1984), pp. 7–9.

[9] C. L. Dumitrescu, *Pictura murală din Ţara Românească în veacul al XVI-lea* (Bucharest, 1978), pp. 44–65. A further Wallachian feature, first introduced at Bolniţa Coziei in 1542, was the inclusion of a small angel in the act of crowning the voievode.

[10] R. V. Petković, *La Peinture serbe du moyen âge* (Belgrade, 1930); M. Tatic-Djurić, 'L'iconographie de la donation dans l'ancien art serbe', in M. Berza and E. Stanescu, eds, *Actes du XIVe congrès international des études Byzantines – Bucarest 1971* (Bucharest, 1976), pp. 311–22.

divine. Finally, it is curious that the Serbian compositions position the throne of Christ to the viewer's left rather than to the right as in Moldavia. These differences do not invalidate the suggestion of a Serbian inspiration for the votive images of Moldavia. In their conceptions of the possible representation of a donor and the divine, Moldavian painters clearly preferred the Serbian solution of a saintly intercessor to the direct approach to Christ enthroned but, in doing so, they did not simply reflect the strength of the Serbian cultural connection. Not only did they choose to alter many of the details of the Serbian prototypes, but they also rejected other, and more contemporary, Serbian solutions which show the founders jointly participating in the act of donation.

This brief survey of the models available to the painters of the Moldavian images demonstrates that the iconographical contrast in the portrayal of the donors in Moldavia and Wallachia was not simply due to the strength of connections with the Serbian kingdom. In any case, Wallachian links with Serbia were not insubstantial. Dynastic links explain the presence of Serbian-type icons including lay donor figures in Wallachia; but such images are not known from Moldavia.[11] The example of Probota shows that a Serbian marriage alliance could influence the iconography of a Moldavian votive image. But the effect is limited to the replacement of the enthroned Christ with an image of Christ blessing from a segment of heaven whilst retaining the figure of a saintly mediator and the separation of husband and wife.[12] Both Moldavia and Wallachia borrowed different elements from Serbia, as appropriate for their own cultures. The lack of similarity in these

[11] A. Efremov, 'Portrete de donatori în pictura de icoane din Ţara Românească', *Buletinul Monumentelor Istorice*, 40/1 (1971), pp. 41–2; M. A. Musicescu, 'Byzance et le portrait roumain', p. 170, details the three icons commissioned by the Serbian princess Despina, wife of the voievode Neagoe Basarab. The icon of the Descent from the Cross (c. 1522) includes Despina in mourning holding her dead son. In another icon (c. 1522) Despina and her two daughters kneel at the feet of the Serbian royal saints, Simeon and Sava. The icon of St Nicholas (c. 1518) includes Despina, her husband, and her children.

[12] Elena was the daughter of John, despot of Srem (d. 1502) and married Petru Rareş, voievode of Moldavia, in 1529. After his death in 1546 she built two churches on her estate at Botoşani and one at Suceava. Some authorities maintain that Elena was also the sister of Despina, wife of Neagoe Basarab, voievode of Wallachia. If true, the limited nature of contemporary Serbian influence at Probota is all the more surprising. The ancestry of Despina is uncertain. She may have been the daughter of Domka, the first wife of despot Iovan Brankovitch, and at least some connection with the Brankovitch family seems certain: I.-R. Mircea, 'Relations culturelles roumano-serbes au xvie siècle', *RÉSEE*, 1 (1963), pp. 377–419.

adaptations shows that in the vital question of the relationship between the human and the divine, Orthodoxy in the two Romanian principalities was far from homogeneous.

* * *

Given this flexibility of the Orthodox religious cultures in Moldavia and Wallachia in adopting elements which suited local demands, the lack of correlation between the social status of women and their portrayal in votive images in a religious context seems all the more surprising. But it is inadequate to conclude simply that devotional differences imposed iconographical constraints. The presence of a saintly mediator and a more direct approach to Christ in Moldavian votive images reflected the strength of the cult of the saints and the emphasis on Christ as person and sacrament in Moldavian religious culture. These themes were taken up and developed in Moldavian exterior wall painting in the sixteenth century, and were combined in the portrayal of the prayer of all the saints on the eastern apse, which converges on the images of the various hypostases of Christ on the central axis.[13] These aspects can explain the Moldavian preference for the portrayal of a saintly figure commending the donor to Christ enthroned, instead of the more distant hand of God. But the concern to include a saintly mediator does not rule out iconographical solutions giving greater recognition to the wife's role. The example of the votive image at Moldoviţa in which the saint helps the donor to support the church model shows that there was no aesthetic barrier to the direct physical association of the wife in the act of donation (Plate 4).[14]

The lack of recognition of women's legal status in representations of women in Moldavian votive images is even harder to explain, since it is clear that these same images are very concerned to show levels of social status. The best example of this is the paintings of Humor.[15] Here the founder, the logofat Toader Bubuiog, deemed it prudent to include a

---

[13] The absence of exterior painting in Wallachia in this period means that a more detailed theological analysis of the total assemblage is required before we can fully appreciate the nature of the religious difference between the two regions.

[14] The second church at Moldoviţa was begun in 1532, and the paintings are thought to date from 1537. Saints interceding with Christ on behalf of the donor usually only hold an intercessory scroll. A possible composition would therefore have been for the husband and wife to hold the church model jointly whilst the saint held the scroll of commendation.

[15] The church was built in 1530, and the paintings completed in 1535.

Plate 4 Moldoviţa (Moldavia): The donor, Petru Rareş, and the Virgin Mary offer a model of the church to Christ. [Photo: Institute for the History of Art, Bucharest]

votive image of the ruler Petru Rareş and his family in the naos of the church (see Plate 2) and to relegate his own votive image to a more humble position in the *gropniţa* (tomb room). The hierarchical distinction is not, however, simply provided by the location of these two images, but is emphasised by the iconographical disposition of the figures. In the first image, the voievode Petru Rareş holds the model of the church and partly behind him stands the figure of Mary holding the intercessory scroll in one hand and apparently touching the roof of the church with her other hand. Mary looks back towards Petru Rareş, whilst Christ, seated on a throne, actively leans forward in the act of blessing the voievode. In the votive image of Toader Bubuiog, Mary is portrayed standing behind the throne of Christ and holds the model of the church with the donor. Compared to the voievodal tableau, Mary is now much more clearly associated with Christ than with the lay figure. It is almost as if Toader is presenting the church to both Mary and Christ, and significantly it is he who is depicted carrying his own scroll of recommendation.

The same mechanisms of subtle iconographical differentiation used to delineate social status were available to artists in representing the gender order. The presence of some changes in iconography which suggest a desire to associate the family of the donor more closely with the act of donation demonstrate that there was some flexibility, but they also show its essentially limited nature. In the earlier images, as at Humor and Voroneţ, the painter leaves a small gap between the voievode and the members of his family, whereas later examples like the one at Suceviţa show a continuous procession.[16] In all the images, the role of the wife is clearly less important than that of her donor husband. But there is one in which we can see an innovative attempt to reduce this difference. At Arbore the votive image of the founder, Luca Arbore, follows the usual Moldavian model with the patron of the church, St John the Baptist, commending the donor, who presents the model of the church to Christ and is followed by members of his family. The remarkable innovation here is the introduction of a second

---

[16] For Humor see n. 15. The church of Voroneţ was built in 1488, and the paintings of the sanctuary and naos date from the reign of Ştefan cel Mare (before 1496). An inscription dates the paintings of the narthex to 1550, but this is now thought to refer to a repainting of a scheme contemporary with the paintings in the sanctuary and the naos. The exonarthex was added and painted in 1547. E. Cincheza-Buculei, 'Le programme iconographique du narthex de l'église du monastère de Voroneţ', *Revue roumaine de l'histoire de l'art*, 30 (1993), pp. 6–7. Suceviţa was painted in 1595–6.

saintly figure, behind the first, who looks back towards Iuliana, the wife of Luca Arbore.[17] In giving Iuliana her own intercessory saint, but in failing to show her jointly holding the model of the church, the artist Dragoş Coman preserves the hierarchy of husband and wife common to all Moldavian images, and at the same time illustrates an unprecedented degree of association of husband and wife in the pious act of foundation.

This analysis of the votive images therefore confirms that the representation of donation and communication with the divine in Moldavia embodied a view of gender inequality which conflicts with the evidence for the unusually high legal status of women in this society. Examples such as Arbore demonstrate that some flexibility in portrayal was possible, but perhaps also serve to underline the limited freedom of manoeuvre. The problem of the representation of women in a religious context goes deeper than a reluctance to acknowledge women's joint contribution to a public act of religious donation. Funerary images, which make less overt claims for public behaviour qualifying the individual for an audience with the divine, also seem to

---

[17] The church of Arbore was built by Luca Arbore, pâracălab of Suceava, in 1502. The date of painting is less clear. An inscription in the naos gives the name of the painter, Dragoş, and the date 1541. For Balş this referred to a repainting, and he noted that all the figures in the naos votive images, except Christ and the saints, had been removed and replaced during the sixteenth century, probably after enemy destruction. The second votive image, which is in the pronaos above the tomb of Luca Arbore, depicts two not five children. If the convention of depicting only those in life was followed, this would suggest different dates of painting. More recently Drăguţ has taken the 1541 date of painting at face value, although recognizing the hand of more than one artist. This has the interesting result of making the patron of the paintings Ana, the niece of Luca Arbore who had lost his life for his part in a conspiracy against the voievode in 1523. However, it seems quite unlikely that the church would have remained unpainted for almost forty years, especially as Luca Arbore was clearly prospering in the first two decades of the sixteenth century. He invested large sums in purchasing villages, built a church at Sipote close to another of his residences, and in 1517 became tutor to the young prince Ştefăniţa.

Traces of painting to the left of the second saintly figure in the naos votive image at Arbore suggest the possibility of identification of an angel. The closest parallel to this composition is the votive image at Balineşti. Here, in the background behind the donor's wife a standing figure of an angel gestures towards Christ. The church of Balineşti was built by the logofat Ioan Tăutu and, according to the dedication inscription, was completed in 1499. It is probable that the votive image was completed before the death of Tăutu in 1511 by the artist Gavril Ieromanhul. G. Balş, *Bisericile lui Ştefan cel Mare*, Buletinul Com. Mon. Istorice (Bucharest, 1926), pp. 15, 111–17, 133–8, 253, 262; V. Drăguţ, *Arbore* (Bucharest, 1969), pp. 15–17; C. Popa, *Balineşti* (Bucharest, 1981), pp. 9–10; S. Ulea, 'Gavril Ieromonahul, autorul frescelor de la Balineşti', in *Cultura moldovenească in timpul lui Ştefan cel Mare* (Bucharest, 1964), pp. 424–61.

differentiate along gender lines. At Humor, Anastasia, the wife of the founder Toader Bubuiog, is portrayed above her tomb, kneeling before the Virgin and Christ Child. At Probota the funerary image depicts Ion, the son of the voievode Petru Rareş, with an enthroned figure of St Nicholas, the patron of the church. However, unlike Anastasia in the votive image at Humor, Ion is shown standing, rather than kneeling, in front of the saint. Even outside the special context of donation the portrayal of communication with the saintly could be defined along gender lines.[18]

* * *

This strength of gender differentiation in images where the religious meets the secular suggests that explanations should be sought primarily in the religious culture. At first glance, the portrayal of both Adam and Eve as saintly intercessors might seem to contradict this. But since the figure of Eve is so central to the development of gender distinctions within Christian cultures, her role needs to be examined more closely and to be placed in the wider context of religious belief in Moldavia.

The ability of Adam and Eve to act as intercessors for mankind at the Last Judgement is due to the prominence in Orthodox theology of the Anastasis or Resurrection, which is equated with the Descent into Hell. In contrast to Catholicism, the Anastasis is perceived as the culmination and most significant part of a continuous process beginning with the Crucifixion. Iconographically this stress is encapsulated in the standard illustrations for the front and back covers of gospel books: the Crucifixion and the Anastasis. As in Catholic doctrine, the redemption of Adam and Eve is prior to the Last Judgement, but the prominence of this moment in Orthodoxy seems to highlight the possibility of mankind enlisting their help at the blowing of the last trump. However, although saintly, the first parents of mankind have a more earthbound position in the saintly hierarchy. It is in the heavenly tier above that the Virgin Mary and St John the Baptist intercede on either side of Christ. Below, and framing the

---

[18] Very few funerary images survive, and of these not all take the form of the commendation of the individual to a divine or saintly figure. Gender differentiation is also expressed more subtly in the contrast between the two votive images at Arbore discussed above. Here the association of the wife in the act of donation is emphasised more in the votive image than in the funerary image. This rather paradoxical conclusion may simply reflect the position of the funerary image above the tomb of Luca Arbore.

throne of hetimasia which contains the instruments of the Passion, are the suppliant figures of Adam and Eve. This hierarchy is scarcely surprising. The history of Adam and Eve is more clearly rooted in the sphere of human frailty.

Common human frailty does not necessarily imply an equality in the status and role of Adam and Eve. Some hints of this inequality are already visible in the image of Adam and Eve as intercessors in the Last Judgement. Flanking the throne of hetimasia, it is Eve who is portrayed on the side of the damned. More significantly, in most representations Eve, unlike Adam, is depicted interceding with cloth-covered hands, unworthy of direct physical contact with the sacred.[19]

In images of the Fall itself misogynistic elements are muted. The portrayal of the serpent with a female head, familiar in western Catholicism, is unknown. It seems unlikely that this is simply because the Greek word for serpent is masculine: in the Old Slavonic used in the inscriptions both masculine and feminine forms of the word are possible.[20] Adam is also deliberately associated with the Fall. Despite the use of developed sequences of narrative scenes, none of the examples reserves a separate scene for Eve's temptation by the serpent. At Moldoviţa Adam and Eve stand either side of the tree, and both stretch out an arm equally to each other to give and to receive the forbidden fruit. At Voroneţ both Adam and Eve are shown in the act of eating, but the artist also seems to be trying to show Eve's temptation and Adam's responsibility simultaneously. The serpent is coiled around a tree close to Eve with its head close to her face, whilst Adam stands with his hand possessively clasped round the trunk of a second tree. At Suceviţa Adam is present to the right of the tree whilst the serpent whispers in Eve's ear, and in the next scene, when the couple have become aware of their nakedness, they both stand with a hand around the trunk of the tree. Finally, at Arbore the scene of the couple standing on each side of the tree illustrates not the Fall itself but the moment immediately afterwards.

Adam's association does not completely exonerate Eve, but it is significant that the opportunity for a more negative portrayal of Eve's

---

[19] For example, Eve is shown with cloth-covered hands in the Last Judgements at Arbore, Humor, Voroneţ, Moldoviţa, and St Demetrius, Suceava, but not at Probota.

[20] E. Levin, *Sex and Society in the World of the Orthodox Slavs, 900–1700* (Ithaca, NY, and London, 1989). By the mid-seventeenth century, under the influence of Catholicism, images of the Fall depicting the serpent with a female head can be found in Russia.

role was not seized by these artists. The emphasis on Adam's presence in all episodes of the Fall contrasts with the absence of Eve from the later scene of Adam's contract with the devil. Drawn from folklore, and yet in the mid-sixteenth century gaining sufficient ecclesiastical approval to be portrayed on the walls of monastic churches, the story of Adam's contract provides a counterweight to Eve's responsibility for the Fall. After the expulsion Adam struggles to feed his family by the sweat of his brow and succumbs to the blandishments of the devil, who promises greater rewards for his labour in exchange for authority over his children at death. The sequence of events is perhaps most vividly portrayed at Voroneţ, where Adam is shown first ploughing a barren field and then sitting down and writing a contract dictated by the devil.[21]

The introduction of the balancing story of Adam's contract with the devil does not seem to result in a completely equal perception of the human frailty of Adam and Eve. It appears that, even together with the association of Adam with the events of the Fall, the contract with the devil does not create an assumption of equal culpability. This may be partly due to a perceived dissimilarity in the two 'Falls'. The diabolical compact is, after all, made after the effects of original sin. Furthermore, in Christian history the resolution of these two faults is chronologically separate. According to the tradition, the devil hides the tablet with Adam's contract in the depths of the River Jordan where it is broken when Christ stands on it during his baptism. The fault of Eve can only be rectified by Christ's descent into Hell after the Crucifixion.

Most representations of the Anastasis clearly differentiate the roles of Adam and Eve. As in the Last Judgements, Eve, unlike Adam, is usually shown with cloth-covered hands, and Christ is portrayed holding the wrist of Adam as he steps out of his tomb. Thus at Balineşti, where Adam and Eve are both depicted to the right, Adam is in the foreground stepping out of the tomb as Christ holds his right wrist, whilst Eve kneels behind him waiting her turn with her cloth-covered hands upraised. Sixteenth-century portrayals of the Anastasis show some variation which can be more favourable to Eve. At Arbore Christ holds the wrists of the kneeling figures of Adam and Eve to his right and left.[22] Perhaps the most extensive treatment of the Anastasis

---

[21] P. Henry, *Folklore et iconographie religieuse* (Bucharest, 1928), pp. 21–30.

[22] The placing of the Anastasis in the context of the Acathist hymn in praise of the

is at Suceviţa, where the scene is portrayed at the entrance gate as the dedication of the church. Here Adam and Eve kneel on either side of Christ, both with cloth-covered hands stretched towards him. But this apparent equality is undermined by the fact that it is Eve who is followed by the crowd of pleading laity: Adam is on the side of the saintly. This same division is also adopted in other images of the Anastasis and fits with the view of the role of Eve in the Last Judgement. Adam and Eve may both be saintly, but Eve is closer to fallen humanity.

This gender hierarchy is not confined to Adam and Eve. In the ranks of the saints entering the Garden of Paradise in the scene of the Last Judgement an order of precedence is strictly observed. After the apostles, prophets, bishops, and male martyrs, it is the female martyrs and saints who bring up the rear. It is even more striking that in the elaborate scene of the Prayer of All Saints, which converges on the most sacred position of the axis of the eastern apse, the idea of *all* the saints is almost always interpreted as male. The one exception to this rule, the squeezing in of four female saints towards the end of the lowest tier of the north wall at Suceviţa, serves to underline the significance of this general omission.[23]

The lesser position, and even absence, of female saints in the ranks of the holy company of heaven contrasts with the development of devotion to the Virgin Mary. The extraordinary nature of Mary always makes her a problematic model for female spiritual capability and diminishes the practical impact of her presence on the lives of women. In sixteenth-century Moldavia, as in the Western Church, the potential for this positive relationship is affected by the distance of the Virgin Mary from laywomen. But in Moldavia the perception of this distance is also enhanced by the inability of other female saints to approach the status of Mary in the heavenly hierarchy. The important chain of spiritual potential from the laywoman through female saints and martyrs to the Virgin Mary is broken. Thus, although much of the decoration of the exterior surface of Moldavian churches is dedicated to the glorification of the Virgin Mary in the elaborate depiction of the verses of the Acathist hymn, this is perceived as having little direct relation to women. In scenes

Virgin Mary may contribute to a more egalitarian representation, as in the examples at Arbore and Suceviţa.
[23] The four female saints are Pelagia, Theodora, Barbara, and Mary the Egyptian.

showing the Virgin being adored by the laity, the worshippers are usually male.

Mary's isolation from both female saints and laity is also illustrated by two iconographical developments which become more common in the sixteenth century. In scenes of the Last Judgement and the Dormition, Mary's status is subject to redefinition and elevation. Orthodox depictions of Paradise in the Last Judgement show seated figures of Abraham, Isaac, and Jacob together with the Virgin Mary and, usually in the background, the thief who repented on the cross. In sixteenth-century Moldavian examples Mary tends to be portrayed seated on a separate throne, sometimes flanked with adoring angels, and even where she is still seated on the same bench as Abraham, Isaac, and Jacob her distinction is signified by small details such as a cushion or by resting her feet on a small platform (Plate 5).

This elevation of the status of Mary in depictions of the Last Judgement is developed in another direction in the iconography of the Dormition. From the end of the fifteenth century, scenes of the Dormition increasingly include the episode of the Jew Jephonias. Denying Mary's sanctity, his sacrilegious attempt to overturn the bier results in his hands adhering to the sides of the coffin and being severed from his arms by the sword of St Michael the Archangel. The Orthodox interpretation of this apocryphal story differs from the version current in medieval Catholicism. In the West the brutal severing of the hands of the Jew is omitted and the emphasis is on the possibility of the repentant and converted Jew being restored to his former health by the intervention of St Peter.[24] In the Orthodox world, by contrast, the story demonstrates that insufficient veneration and presumptuous familiarity with the divine will meet with retribution. In all Orthodox portrayals Christ stands behind the bier in a mandorla of light holding the nimbed, swaddled soul of the Virgin, but the addition of the Jew scene increases the emphasis on the sanctity of Mary's earthly body as well as her soul. Mary's corporeality, her closest point of contact with mankind, is being removed from the sphere of earthly human existence, and

---

[24] M. R. James, ed., *The Apocryphal New Testament, being the Apocryphal Gospels, Acts, Epistles, and Apocalypses* (Oxford, 1926), pp. 208, 214. The Greek narrative reads: 'And behold as they bare her [Mary], a certain Hebrew named Jephonias, mighty of body, ran forth and set upon the bed, as the apostles bare it, and lo, an angel of the Lord with invisible power smote his two hands from off his shoulders with a sword of fire and left them hanging about the bed.' The Latin narrative of Pseudo-Melito states: 'And he came near and would have overthrown the bier and cast the body on the earth. And forthwith his hands dried up from his elbows and clave to the bier.'

Plate 5   Voroneţ (Moldavia): The Garden of Paradise. The Virgin Mary seated on a separate throne, flanked by angels and the three Patriarchs. [Photo: Institute for the History of Art, Bucharest]

represents a further consolidation of the distance between Mary and female experience.

* * *

The starting point for this study was the expectation that the high legal status of women in sixteenth-century Moldavian society should have been conducive to a recognition of the joint participation of men and women in the act of donation, an expectation strengthened by the role of Adam and Eve as nimbed intercessors at the Last Judgement. The fact that Moldavian votive images conspicuously failed to confirm this expectation suggested the need to re-examine the gender implications of Moldavian religious culture, especially the Adam and Eve iconography.

Eve, although an intercessor, is less worthy than Adam to approach the sacred and, despite the introduction of Adam's contract with the devil, equal culpability cannot be recognized. Consequently, although perhaps less overtly than in Catholicism, Eve is still available as a religious justification for the gender hierarchy in Moldavia. This more nuanced view of the roles of Adam and Eve and perceptions of the limited status of female sanctity were mutually reinforcing. The possibility of the omission of female saints from the heavenly hierarchy, or their relegation to its lowest ranks, served to strengthen the view that Mary's nature was exceptional and to marginalize her role in the definition of lay gender relations.

The resulting imbalance between religious and secular conceptions of female status was resolved, at least in the context of the votive image, in favour of the religious view of inequality. This does not reflect the relative strengths of religious and secular spheres in Moldavia. Secular views will always be more vulnerable in a religious context. Moreover, it seems to have been easier to transpose the political order rather than the gender order into sacred space. At the same time it would be wrong to envisage a strictly rigid view of gender within the religious sphere. A certain degree of flexibility was possible, both in the recognition of women's role in the acts of donation and in the portrayal and understanding of the theological significance of female religious figures. In sixteenth-century Moldavia religious ideas of gender were significant in structuring access to the divine, but conceptions of gender roles, even in the heavenly sphere, were not absolutely fixed.

The Queen's College, Oxford

GENDER CONSTRUCTION IN EARLY MODERN ENGLAND AND THE CONDUCT BOOKS OF WILLIAM WHATELY (1583-1639)

by JACQUELINE EALES

CONDUCT books, or household manuals offering advice about marriage and the ordering of domestic relationships, attained their greatest popularity in early modern England between the late sixteenth century and the Civil War. Many of these works, including William Whately's popular *A Bride-Bush*, which ran into three editions between 1617 and 1623, and William Gouge's influential *Of Domesticall Duties*, which first appeared in 1622, originated as sermons and were written by puritan preachers. They are also a valuable source of information about the construction of ideal masculine and feminine behaviour in the early modern period. At the start of *A Bride-Bush*, which was based on a marriage sermon, Whately asserted 'I will make the ground of all my speech, those words of the Apostle Paul, Ephes. 5. 23. where hee saith, The Husband is the Wives head.' Towards the end of the book he noted that the male sex is 'preferred before the female in degree of place & dignity, as all men will yeeld that read what the Scriptures speake in that behalfe'.[1]

The gender order and social order were thus seen as interdependent and both were grounded in scriptural precept. In keeping with the general tenor of other household manuals of the time, Whately elaborated at length in *A Bride-Bush* on the conventional analogy between the exercise of authority within the state and within the family, which was the foundation of the contemporary political theory of patriarchy.[2] In both cases authority was derived from God and, as

[1] William Whately, *A Bride-Bush, or a Wedding Sermon: compendiously describing the Duties of Married Persons: by performing whereof, Marriage shall be to them a great Helpe, which now finde it a Little Hell* (London, 1617), pp. 1, 40. I would like to thank Mrs S. Crabtree, Special Collections Librarian at the University of Kent, Mrs Sheila Hingley, Canterbury Cathedral Librarian, and the Cathedral Library staff for their help in the preparation of this paper, which was written with the aid of a research grant from Christ Church College, Canterbury.

[2] G. J. Schochet, *Patriarchalism in Political Thought* (Oxford, 1975); J. P. Sommerville, *Politics and Ideology in England, 1603–1640* (London, 1986); Susan Dwyer Amussen, *An Ordered Society: Gender and Class in Early Modern England* (Oxford, 1988); eadem, 'Gender, family and

governor of the household, the husband was owed obedience in the same way that the monarch was to be obeyed by the people. The superiority of the husband was seen both as the will of God and as a part of the natural order. For Whately it was not enough for a wife to behave in a dutiful manner towards her husband; she had to be convinced that she was inferior and in the words of St Paul she must 'fear her husband'. This was not to be a slavish fear, but a 'loving fear', and Whately was particularly fond of using the metaphor of a rider and his well-broken horse to describe the ideal relationship between man and wife.[3]

Whately was dealing here in highly conventional contemporary constructs of gender, but recent work by Anthony Fletcher, Laura Gowing, Linda Pollock, Alison Wall, and Diane Willen, amongst others, has demonstrated that in practice the prescribed boundaries of gender were negotiable.[4] Both men and women might subscribe to the rhetoric of the gender order, whilst also circumventing its edicts. Similarly, by emphasising the importance of marital love as well as wifely subordination, Whately set up a series of tensions and inconsistencies in his work which he never really resolved. These inconsistencies were further compounded by Whately's own experience of marriage, which as a cleric was somewhat different from the experiences of the laity, as we shall see.

Although all conduct books contained much that was conventional in terms of political theory and of prescriptive attitudes towards gender roles, their contents have been variously interpreted. Recent historical debate has focused on the extent to which their authors framed a distinctively Protestant, or even puritan, view of marriage and whether this entailed any measure of equality between the genders. Even the

---

the social order, 1560–1725', in Anthony Fletcher and John Stevenson, eds, *Order and Disorder in Early Modern England* (Cambridge, 1985), pp. 196–217. For conduct books more generally see Daniel M. Doriani, 'The Godly Household in Puritan Theology, 1560–1640' (Westminster Theological Seminary [USA], Ph. D. thesis, 1986). I am grateful to Prof. Conrad Russell for drawing this thesis to my attention.

[3] Whately, *Bride-Bush* (1617), pp. 36–7, 43.

[4] Anthony Fletcher, *Gender, Sex and Subordination in England 1500–1800* (New Haven and London, 1995); Laura Gowing, *Domestic Dangers: Women, Words and Sex in Early Modern London* (Oxford, 1996); Linda Pollock, '"Teach her to live under obedience": the making of women in the upper ranks of early modern England', *Continuity and Change*, 4 (1989), pp. 231–58; Alison Wall, 'Elizabethan precept and feminine practice: the Thynne family of Longleat', *History*, 75 (1990), pp. 23–38; Diane Willen, 'Godly women in early modern England: puritanism and gender', *JEH*, 43 (1992), pp. 561–80.

contributions of individual authors, such as Whately, have been the subject of academic disagreement. Kathleen Davies has asserted that there was not a great deal that was new or unusual in Whately's writings whereas Anthony Fletcher sees Whately as being in the forefront of new developments in Protestant thinking about marriage in his handling of the subjects of conjugal love and sexual equality between husband and wife.[5]

Along with denying that marriage was a sacrament, English and continental reformers also rejected both the Catholic belief that celibacy was a more honourable state than marriage, and the theological tradition that held that all sexual activity, even within marriage, was potentially sinful and corrupting. It was not so much the case that the English clergy were introducing novel ideas about marriage (indeed in some respects, notably the subject of divorce, they were remarkably conservative), but they were rearranging and, importantly, extending traditional views in order to fit their own situation.[6] One long-term result of the legitimization of clerical marriage by statute under Edward VI was that the English clergy began to give much greater emphasis to the companionate element of marriage, as well its reproductive functions. The repeal of this legislation by Queen Mary created ambiguity surrounding the legal basis for clerical marriage, and calls for new positive laws continued until the outbreak of the Civil War, despite the Jacobean reinstatement of the Edwardian statutes.[7] Nevertheless, clerical marriage became the norm and the early seventeenth century saw the establishment of the second and third generations of married ministers.[8] The creation of clerical dynasties had also started to make a social impact, and the English reformed clergy generally believed that they held marriage and

[5] Kathleen M. Davies, 'The sacred condition of equality – how original were puritan doctrines of marriage?', *Social History*, 5 (1977), p. 578; Anthony Fletcher, 'The Protestant idea of marriage in early modern England', in A. J. Fletcher and Peter Roberts, eds, *Religion, Culture and Society in Early Modern Britain* (Cambridge, 1994), p. 180.

[6] For the medieval inheritance on the subjects of sex and marriage see James A. Brundage, *Law, Sex and Christian Society in Medieval Europe* (Chicago, 1987); for the changes contingent on the Reformation in England see Eric Josef Carlson, *Marriage and the English Reformation* (Oxford, 1994).

[7] *To the King's Most Excellent Majestie, The Humble Petition of the Ministers of the Church of England, Desiring Reformation of Certain Ceremonies and Abuses of the Church* (London, 1641), BL Thomason Tracts E170 (4), which asks for 'King Edwards statute for the lawfulness of ministers marriage to be revived', p. 3.

[8] Rosemary O'Day, *The English Clergy, the Emergence and Consolidation of a Profession, 1558–1642* (Leicester, 1979), p. 162.

wives in greater esteem than did their celibate Catholic counterparts. Their own assessment of their writings and social behaviour has dominated subsequent historical analysis, and by the 1960s it was accepted that the Reformation had generated a new theory of domestic relations, which elevated the role of women.[9] This belief was based on the Protestant emphasis on the spiritual equality of all believers and on the novel stress on marital love articulated by a clerisy which, for the first time, was able to write legitimately about marriage from personal experience.

The certainty of this interpretation has, however, been gradually eroded. Christopher Hill anticipated later developments in gender studies when he wrote in 1964 that 'the theology of Protestantism was patriarchal', and argued that the father's powers as governor of the family were reinforced by Protestant precept.[10] His insights were developed by Kathleen Davies, who argued against a distinctly 'Puritan' theory of domestic relations and posited instead that the Protestant conduct book writers were drawing on traditional advice offered to the laity by pre-Reformation Catholic authors. These findings have been supported by Margo Todd's work on humanist thought and by Margaret Sommerville's more general investigation into the attitudes of sixteenth- and seventeenth-century theorists.[11] The analysis first offered by Davies could well have taken on the revered mantle of orthodoxy had it not been for Anthony Fletcher's recent revival of the argument that the conduct book writers did enunciate a distinctive English version of the Protestant idea of marriage. Fletcher argues that this was based on their innovative advocacy of mutual sexual fulfilment within marriage, which along with the Protestant emphasis on spiritual equality brought the authors close to abandoning the traditional belief in female inferiority.[12]

At this stage in the debate it seems appropriate to consider the contribution made to the genre by individual writers in greater depth.

---

[9] Levin L. Schücking, *The Puritan Family* (London, 1969); W. and M. Haller, 'The puritan art of love', *Huntington Library Quarterly*, 5 (1941–2), pp. 235–72.

[10] Christopher Hill, *Society and Puritanism in Pre-revolutionary England* (London, 1964), pp. 450–1.

[11] Davies, 'Sacred condition of equality', see also the revised version, 'Continuity and change in literary advice on marriage', in R. B. Outhwaite, ed., *Marriage and Society: Studies in the Social History of Marriage* (London, 1981), pp. 58–80; Margo Todd, 'Humanists, puritans and the spiritualized household', *ChH*, 49 (1980), pp. 18–34; Margaret Sommerville, *Sex and Subjection: Attitudes to Women in Early-Modern Society* (London, 1995).

[12] Fletcher, 'Protestant idea of marriage', p. 179.

William Whately, the subject of this case study, was one of the most well-known of the conduct book authors. From 1610 until his death in 1639 he was vicar of Banbury in Oxfordshire, where his puritan sermons earned him the title of the 'roaring boy of Banbury'.[13] In *Bartholomew Fair*, first acted in 1614 and printed in 1631, Ben Jonson satirized the Banbury puritans in his comic creation of the hypocritical character of Zeal of the Land Busy. Whately's reputation as a preacher thus ensured that there was a keen market for his two marriage treatises: *A Bride-Bush*, and *A Care-Cloth: Or A Treatise of the Cumbers and Troubles of Marriage* (which appeared in 1624). Of the two works, *A Care-Cloth* is perhaps the more straightforward. The first quarter of the work is taken up with a justification of the lawfulness of marriage for all men and women. Although Whately does not specifically direct this section of the book at Catholic rejection of clerical marriage, this was part of his intention and he argued that to deny marriage to any sort of men would provoke them to 'filthinesse and vncleannesse, and all viciousnesse', a conventional Protestant slur against Catholic clerics.[14] The vast majority of the book is devoted to outlining the pitfalls of marriage in order to persuade those who would embark upon the married state to do so responsibly. Apart from illness, the death of a spouse, financial problems, and problems with children, there were also the character failings of one's spouse with which to contend.[15]

Whately's advice on how to avoid the cares of marriage included primarily the fear of God and godliness, and secondly the cultivation of love between man and wife.[16] As a cleric, Whately's chief aim in writing both *A Care-Cloth* and *A Bride-Bush* was to persuade the laity to turn to godliness in order to achieve domestic order but, as has already been argued here, a sub-text of both works was the justification of clerical marriage. As Whately argued in *A Care-Cloth* 'if the condemning of marriage be from the Deuill, the allowing of it is from God, and so haue all sorts of men vniuersally a full allowance from God to take the benefit of this estate'.[17]

A Bride-Bush is the more complex work, and two distinct versions of it survive. The first edition was prepared for the press in 1608, but was

---

[13] *DNB*, William Whately.

[14] William Whately, *A Care-Cloth: Or a Treatise of the Cumbers and Troubles of Marriage* (1624), p. 23.

[15] Ibid., pp. 43, 44.

[16] Ibid., pp. 77–8.

[17] Ibid., p. 22.

not printed until 1617. This version was later disowned by Whately in the second edition of 1619, as having been published without his knowledge by a friend to whom he had lent the manuscript. Whately's prime objective in reissuing the sermon seems to have been to enlarge upon his thoughts at length, and the second version was four times as long as the first.[18] A third edition appeared in 1623 and carried a withdrawal of the opinion expressed in both of the earlier editions that divorce and remarriage by the innocent party were allowable on the grounds of adultery or desertion. In supporting divorce in these cases Whately was in line with continental Reformed theory and practice; but as Martin Ingram has pointed out, these more radical measures had not been adopted in England, where it was only possible to obtain a separation on the grounds of adultery or cruel behaviour and the marriage remained undissolved.[19] Whately was forced by the High Commission to recant his more radical opinions in 1621. Yet they appeared in full once again in 1623, and in the preface to the third edition Whately unconvincingly claimed that although he had agreed to remove these arguments from the book, the printer had carelessly lost the corrections. Thus the second and third editions are to all intents and purposes identical, except for the two-page disclaimer about divorce of 1623.[20]

One of the most dramatic differences between the two texts is Whately's *volte face* on the subject of whether the husband could use physical correction on his wife. In 1617 Whately adamantly rejected this, saying 'we dare not allow him to proceede so farre as to correct by blowes'.[21] Here Whately was following orthodox Church teaching. The *Homily on Marriage* similarly forbade the husband to strike his wife and the great majority of marriage and household treatises agreed, although evidence from court cases suggests that Church teaching was not always observed by the laity. By 1619 Whately had substantially changed his mind and he then argued that a husband could use blows as a corrective if his wife had repeatedly and wilfully disobeyed him and refused to comply with reasonable commands. Whately was

---

[18] Whately, *Bride-Bush* (1619), sig. A1r. Whately refers here to 'certaine larger notes, which I had lying by me of that subiect'.

[19] Steven Ozment, *When Fathers Ruled: Family Life in Reformation Europe* (Cambridge, MA, 1983), pp. 80–99; Martin Ingram, *Church Courts, Sex and Marriage in England, 1570–1640* (Cambridge, 1987), p. 146.

[20] PRO, SP14/121/7; Whately, *Bride-Bush* (1623), sig. A3r-v.

[21] Whately, *Bride-Bush* (1617), p. 22.

clearly not entirely comfortable with this doctrine, which now placed him at odds with the majority of English clerical opinion of the time.[22] In the second edition of *A Bride-Bush* Whately returned to the subject repeatedly as if he had not quite said the last word on the matter. Above all he wanted to emphasise that husbands should not take his words as a licence to beat their wives for trifles. Thus he softened this prescription by arguing that of course no truly godly wife would provoke her husband to violence in the first place and, moreover, that husbands were not allowed to resort to force for the slightest disagreement. Yet, if a wife were groundlessly beaten by her husband, she could have recourse to the magistrate; but she must also remember her subordinate position and accept the punishment unfairly offered to her.[23]

Despite the extreme stance adopted by Whately on the subject of wife-beating, Fletcher is indeed right in arguing that Whately also saw the sexual relationship between husband and wife as an important element of the marriage bond. In keeping with Protestant thinking, Whately described the two chief ends of marriage as chastity and propagation. To achieve these ends the two main duties of marriage were 'the chaste keeping of each ones body each for other' and cohabitation, without which husband and wife could not consummate their physical relationship. If these two duties were not observed, he argued, then the marriage bond was broken although, as we have seen, he was later forced to recant these opinions.[24]

Whately not only adopted a radical stance on divorce, he was also, according to Fletcher, the author of one of the 'warmest' of the marriage treatises when it came to the subject of marital love. According to the earliest biographer of Whately, he had married in 1601 or 1602[25] and therefore we might assume that he spoke from personal experience when he described love as 'the life, the soule of

---

[22] Doriani, 'Godly Household', pp. 304–13; Sommerville, *Sex and Subjection*, pp. 93–6, which points out (at p. 95) that continental Catholic casuists permitted 'moderate' beating of wives and that this is 'one of the few areas of marital relations in which a Catholic-Protestant divide can be detected'. For church court cases involving wife-beating see Ingram, *Church Courts, Sex and Marriage*, p. 144, and A. J. Willis, *Church Life in Kent, being Church Court Records of the Canterbury Diocese, 1559–1565* (London, 1975), p. 61.

[23] Whately, *Bride-Bush* (1619), pp. 106–9, 123–5, 169–73, 198, 210–16.

[24] Whately, *Bride-Bush* (1617), pp. 2–3.

[25] William Whately, *Prototypes, or the Primarie Precedent Presidents out of Genesis* (London, 1640), sig. A2r [Life of Whately by Henry Scudder].

marriage, without which it is no more it selfe, than a carcasse is a man'. Married love was to be 'first spiritual, then matrimonial', and was to be achieved by the consideration by the married couple of the providence of God in their match and by the use of prayer. In Whately's exhortations to spouses to cultivate love he emphasised the closeness of the husband and wife: 'marriage-love admits of no equall, but placeth the yoke-fellow next of all to the soule of the party louing; it will know none dearer, none so deare'. For Whately it followed from this that the wife should be an equal partner in the husband's estate and that even after his death he should provide a competency for her according to his means, so that 'shee be not inferiour to her children . . . ouer whom she should command'.[26] In the second and third editions of *A Bride-Bush* Whately enlarged on this considerably, and argued that the husband should not limit his bequests to his wife for fear she would remarry and spend the wealth for which he had laboured. Whately pointed to the fact that some wise and discreet widows remarried with benefit both to the first husband's kindred and his children. On this point Whately followed his own advice, and in his will the majority of his bequests to his wife Martha were made during her natural life, without any limitation should she remarry.[27]

Whately's depiction of a close relationship between husband and wife creates some apparent tensions in his works, because although he was dealing with some radical ideas about divorce and the treatment of widows, at the same time traditional attitudes towards gender underpinned his work. In all of the editions of *A Bride-Bush* Whately was adamant that there was no equality between man and wife – 'the wiues iudgement must be conuinced, that she is not her husband's equall, yea that her husband is her better by farre, else there can be no contentment, either in her heart, or in her house'. Whately was also at pains to explain that his use of the word 'mutual' to describe the common duties of husband and wife did not imply equality: 'wee call them not therefore common or mutuall, because both should have like quantity of them; but because both must have some of all, and the husband most of all'.[28] Men were reminded that they were dealing with 'the weaker vessell' and should therefore be patient, mild, and loving towards their wives in order to elicit obedience. Whately

[26] Whately, *Bride-Bush* (1617), pp. 7–9, 33.
[27] Whately, *Bride-Bush* (1619), pp. 184–8; PRO, Prob. 11/180, fols 298v–299r.
[28] Whately, *Bride-Bush* (1617), pp. 36, 6.

likened authority to the arts of logic and rhetoric, which are at their most persuasive when their use is concealed. The husband should therefore praise his wife as well as correct her, and his reproofs should be administered gently and in private. A man who is unable to control his wife should not blame her for abusing his authority, for he has thrown away his power through 'folly & indiscretion'. Whately thus advised that a man's authority be maintained by godly example and by skill, not by overblown masculine behaviour in the use of commands, force, violence, 'big looks, & great words, & cruel behaviour', all of which would embitter and alienate his wife. Skill was all the more necessary because of the characteristics that Whately ascribed to the female sex. Women were subject to 'disreverent behaviour', which made them both loathsome and unwomanly. In order to curb this inclination the wife was advised both to acknowledge her inferiority and to carry herself reverently and obediently towards her husband. This included the use of moderate and quiet speech in front of not only the husband, but 'before any men'.

Whately linked excessive use of the female tongue and disobedience with sexual dishonesty, and asserted that women who inverted the natural order by scolding and chastizing their husbands were 'blemishes of their sexe' and 'next to harlots'.[29] In the second and third editions of *A Bride-Bush* Whately went so far as to argue that a woman who could not convince herself of her subordinate position could not attain salvation. He admitted that it was possible for a wife to have greater wealth or better parentage than her husband, or to have more 'wit and understanding, more readinesse of speech, more dexteritie of managing affaires'. Nevertheless, a woman's chief ornament, he argued, was 'lowliness of mind, which should cause her to maintain in her selfe a meane account of her selfe, and of her owne abilities' and thus she still had to acknowledge her husband's superiority in place and power. If she did not do so, then she could not have the qualities of grace 'so long as her pride is so predominant'.[30]

Some of the inconsistencies in Whately's work can be explained by the fact that he tended to emphasise spiritual and marital equality when addressing the husband, and laid greater stress on the differences between man and wife when addressing the wife. Inconsistencies also arose because of the conceptual basis of Whately's model of the ideal

[29] Ibid., pp. 29, 19, 39, 41, 39.
[30] Whately, *Bride-Bush* (1619), pp. 191–2.

marriage. Although Kathleen Davies has suggested that the conduct book writers were describing the marriage of what she terms the 'urban bourgeoisie',[31] the crucial point is that the organization of clerical marriage was more important to them as a model than has previously been recognized. Indeed, the perceived need to defend clerical marriage against Catholic detractors was one reason why conduct book writers turned so frequently to the analysis of marriage from the Reformation onwards.[32]

Whately for one claimed to have been entirely self-referential in his consideration of marriage, and both the second and third editions of *A Bride-Bush* were dedicated to his father-in-law, George Hunt, in thanks for having 'educated for me, and bestowed upon me a most excellent and vertuous wife'. Hunt was minister at Collingbourne Ducis in Wiltshire, and the training that his daughter Martha received from him doubtless served to fit her for the role of a virtuous wife. Indeed, in *A Bride-Bush* Whately claimed to be able to describe what a good wife should do 'finding the full dutie of a wife, in as exact compleatnesse, as mortality can affoord, daily and continually performed unto me in mine owne house'.[33] The ideal family in which wives, children and servants were benignly ruled by a wise, patient, God-fearing patriarch may well have appealed to the gentry and the urban middling sort alike; but it found its fullest expression in the homes of the clergy, where the God-given authority of the father was doubly reinforced. Children who were raised in clerical households were given an exceptional training. Elizabeth Joceline, whose *The Mothers Legacie* of 1624 is widely cited as evidence of female piety and humility, was raised in the home of her maternal grandfather, the Bishop of Chester, where she was taught languages (including Latin), history, and 'some arts', but principally studies of piety.[34] After she was orphaned, Elizabeth, later the wife of another famed conduct book writer, William Gouge, boarded at the house of an Essex minister, John Huckle of Hatfield Broad Oak, 'whose wife had a great name, and that

---

[31] Davies, 'Sacred condition of equality', p. 577.

[32] Heinrich Bullinger's *The Christen State of Matrimonye*, which was translated into English by Coverdale in 1541, provided the starting-point for later marriage treatises in England and it contained an entire chapter (12) centred on the argument that 'the pope in forbyddinge/ the spiritualitie to mary/ hath done agaynst God/ agaynst honestie and agaynst right'.

[33] Whately, *Bride-Bush* (1619), sigs A1r–A2v.

[34] Elizabeth Joceline, *The Mothers Legacie to her unborne Childe* (London, 1624), sig. A1r–v.

not without just desert, for skill and faithful care in training up young gentlewomen'. When Elizabeth Gouge died in 1626 she was characterized as 'a pious, prudent, provident, painful, careful, faithful, helpful, grave, modest, sober, tender, loving wife, mother, mistress, [and] neighbour'.[35] Amongst other authors of household manuals or marriage sermons who married daughters of the clergy we can count John Dod, whose first wife was a step-daughter of Richard Greenham, and Thomas Gataker, whose second wife (of four) was the daughter of the Revd Charles Pinner.[36]

The boundaries of gender construction may well have been negotiable for gentry wives with dowries and large estates to administer in their husbands' absences, or for city wives such as Gouge's parishioners, who took him to task for saying that women could not dispose of the common goods of the family without or against their husband's consent.[37] For the wives of the clergy such negotiation was more limited. There were, for example, no opportunities for a cleric's wife to share in his ministerial functions, and unlike many other wives she could not continue his work if she were widowed.[38] This goes some way towards explaining why conduct book writers, such as Whately, put such great stress on the division between the public duties of the husband and the private domestic duties of the wife. In public the minister's wife had to be a paragon of wifely obedience, and indeed the unsuitability of some early clergy wives has been cited by Eric Carlson as one reason why Elizabeth I was wary of clerical marriage.[39] As Thomas Taylor noted in a marriage sermon for a clerical colleague in 1625, 'it was expected that Elizabeth should shine in grace and godlinesse aboue ordinarie women, because she was Zacharies wife, the Priests wife, the wife of so holy a man'.[40]

In writing about marriage, clerical conduct book writers were not writing from the same base of experience as that of the married laity. Alison Wall has pointed out that the conduct book writers of the

[35] Nicholas Guy, *Pieties Pillar: Or a Sermon Preached at the Funerall of Mistresse Elizabeth Gouge* (London, 1626), pp. 39, 41.
[36] William Haller, *The Rise of Puritanism* (Philadelphia, PA, 1972; reprint of 1938 edn), p. 56; *DNB*, Thomas Gataker.
[37] Cited in Amussen, *An Ordered Society*, pp. 44–5.
[38] This last point may explain why Whately was so concerned for the provision of widows.
[39] Carlson, *Marriage and the English Reformation*, p. 59.
[40] Thomas Taylor, *A Good Husband and a Good Wife* (London, 1625), p. 16.

sixteenth century were young men, or even bachelors such as Henry Smith.[41] In contrast, by the Jacobean period the practice of clerical marriage had become fully established and the most influential of the early-seventeenth-century conduct book writers, Whately and Gouge, were married. As we have seen, their wives had also both received an atypical training for their future roles as wives and mothers inside clerical households. Moreover, the English clergy were still concerned about the status of clerical marriage and the need to vindicate it against Catholic attack.[42] In defining and defending marriage, the Protestant clergy drew on traditional concepts of social and gender order that would enhance their own authority as legitimate heads of patriarchal households. In advising their parishioners about the ideals of marriage, it was not the example of lay marriage which they offered as a model, it was their own construction of domestic order and of gender roles that they propounded as the ideal. It depended for its greatest success on husbands and wives who had internalized the precepts of early modern gender construction better than most and they were to be found amongst the clergy and the young women whom they had trained within their own households. The inconsistencies in Whately's work, which have led to such disparate interpretations of it, were based partly on his own personal doubts and changes of mind. They also reflect the wider tensions implicit in setting up a model derived from the exceptional experience of clerical marriage as a general paradigm for the conduct of all men and women.

Christ Church College, Canterbury

---

[41] Wall, 'Elizabethan precept and feminine practice', pp. 37–8.

[42] See for example, Joseph Hall, *The Honour of the Married Clergy, Maintained Against the Malicious Challenges of C. E. Mass-Priest* (London, 1628).

SEXING THE SOUL: GENDER AND THE RHETORIC
OF PURITAN PIETY

by SUSAN HARDMAN MOORE

P ATRIARCHS at home, but brides of Christ in spirit: it is an
intriguing fact that while puritan writers opposed any confusion
of gender roles in everyday life, they were happy for men to
adopt a feminine identity in spiritual experience. On one hand,
seventeenth-century conduct books and sermons hammered home
the divinely-ordained place of husbands and wives in marriage.
William Whately (1583–1639) argued that wives should always have
on their lips the refrain 'Mine husband is my superior, my better', and
that

> as our Lord Jesus Christ is to his Church . . . so must [the
> husband] be to his wife an head and Saviour . . . the Lord in his
> Word hath intitled him by the name of head: wherefore hee
> must not stand lower than the shoulders. . . . That house is a . . .
> crump-shouldered or hutcht-backt house, where the husband
> hath made himself an underling to his wife, and given away his
> power to an inferior.[1]

On the other hand, preachers encouraged men to think of themselves
as 'brides of Christ', and elaborated enthusiastically on the Christian
tradition of sexing the soul as female: 'the Son of God so loved the
soules of men, that he would make them a wife and marry them'.[2] We
find male fervour for Christ as 'my sweet loving husband' in sermons

---

[1] William Whately, *A Bride-Bush. Or, A Direction for Married Persons*, 3rd edn (London,
1623), pp. 97–8. For Whately, see *DNB*. See also the paper by Jacqueline Eales elsewhere in
this volume, pp. 163–74.
[2] Francis Rous, *The Mysticall Marriage. Experimentall Discourses of the Heavenly Marriage
betweene a Soule and her Saviour* (London, 1631), pp. 10–11. On the soul as female, see Ann
W. Astell, *The Song of Songs in the Middle Ages* (Ithaca, NY, 1990), pp. 10–12; Caroline
Walker Bynum, *Jesus as Mother* (Berkeley, CA, 1981), p. 138, and *Fragmentation and
Redemption* (Berkeley, CA, 1991), p. 165. Despite this feminization, Christian thought
ranked souls by gender: Caroline Walker Bynum, *The Resurrection of the Body in Western
Christianity, 200–1336* (New York, 1995), pp. 8–11, discusses the soul's need for attributes of
bodiliness to express individuality.

and biblical commentaries, in private diaries and records of spiritual experience. Men's double duty as patriarch and bride is well illustrated by the message of two eminent London preachers, William Gouge (1578–1653) and Richard Sibbes (1577–1635). Gouge expounded 'Domesticall Duties' from his pulpit at Blackfriars, making a careful distinction between male and female roles. Sibbes, up the road at Gray's Inn, delighted in female metaphors for religious experience, instructing his hearers to respond to Christ as their Bridegroom: 'this is the desire . . . of every Christian soul, that Christ would . . . "kiss her with the kisses of his mouth"'.[3]

Why did male puritans use the feminine images of bride and wife to express and define their religious experience, when in other respects they were keen to make a strict division between gender roles? Although women also spoke of themselves as brides of Christ, the focus here is on the significance of the imagery for men, to see how the apparent incongruity of their understanding of themselves as patriarchs and brides casts light on the interaction of gendered thinking with spirituality and theology.[4] Male identification with female symbols recurs often in puritan spiritual writings, and need not be seen as a particularly clerical phenomenon. Though ministers promoted the idea, so did laymen, and images of the self as Christ's bride are scattered through the reflections of layman and cleric alike.[5] However,

---

[3] William Gouge, *Of Domesticall Duties* (London, 1622); Richard Sibbes, 'The Spouse, her Earnest Desire after Christ', *The Complete Works of Richard Sibbes*, ed. A. B. Grosart, 6 vols (Edinburgh, 1862–4), 2, p. 203. Gouge's preaching was controversial with his female parishioners: Anthony Fletcher, 'The Protestant idea of marriage in early modern England', in A. Fletcher and Peter Roberts, eds, *Religion, Culture and Society in Early Modern Britain* (Cambridge, 1994), p. 167. For Gouge and Sibbes, see *DNB*.

[4] On women, see n. 28. Male advocacy of men becoming brides of Christ captures the issues best, but we could explore a range of female images adopted by men (all derived from the Bible): woman as nurse and midwife representing preachers, her breasts and milk the nurturing Word of God; woman as harlot representing unfaithfulness; the 'menstruous cloth' (Isa. 30.22) an image of uncleanness.

[5] The relative power of the imagery for laymen and clerics is impossible to quantify (ministerial writing on spirituality inevitably predominates). However, two substantial and influential tracts on the theme come from laymen, Henry Finch (1558–1625, *DNB*) and Francis Rous (1579–1659, *DNB*). Finch's *An Exposition of the Song of Solomon called Canticles* (London, 1615) was published anonymously by the agency of William Gouge: for Gouge's attribution of the work to Finch, see A. W. Pollard and G. R. Redgrave, *A Short-Title Catalogue of Books Printed in England . . . 1475–1640* (London, 1986), no. 10874.5. For Rous's *Mysticall Marriage* see Jerald C. Brauer, 'Types of puritan piety', *ChH*, 56 (1987), pp. 53–6. The spiritual journal of the layman John Winthrop provides a striking example of a meditation that moves from the experience of human marriage to marriage with Christ: see n. 18.

recent debate on gender in early modern Britain has overlooked the feminized language of male puritan devotion, and while studies of puritan spirituality recognize the importance of mystical marriage, they are silent on how the passion of male puritans for their divine Bridegroom relates to the construction of gender identity.[6] So what are we to make of what we might irreverently call 'spiritual cross-dressing'?

Feminized language runs riot in the letters of Samuel Rutherford (1600?–61), a Scottish presbyterian divine who played an important role in English religious politics during the Civil War. 'Many a sweet, sweet soft kisse, many perfumed well smelled kisses and embracements, have I received of my royall Master: He and I have had much love together'; 'Wee cannot rest till we be in other's arms – and o, how sweet is a fresh kiss from his holy mouth.'[7] Rutherford's language, according to the *Dictionary of National Biography*, 'is sometimes coarse and indelicate'. For us, it provides a full-blooded example of the male puritan's freedom to cross the gender divide in spirit. Like many others, Rutherford found his female voice through the imagery of the Song of Songs. Commentaries and sermons on Canticles abound in England from the 1580s – the more one looks, the more one finds.[8]

---

[6] On gender see, for example, Susan Amussen, *Gender and Class in Early Modern England* (Oxford, 1988); Anthony Fletcher, *Gender, Sex and Subordination in England, 1500–1800* (New Haven, CT, and London, 1995). Male use of female imagery has received more attention in studies of colonial America: Philip Greven, *The Protestant Temperament: Patterns of Child-Rearing, Religious Experience and the Self in Early America* (New York, 1977), pp. 124–40; Phyllis Jones, 'Biblical rhetoric and the pulpit literature of early New England', *Early American Literature*, 11 (1976–7), pp. 245–58; David Leverenz, *The Language of Puritan Feeling: An Exploration in Literature, Psychology, and Social History* (New Brunswick, NJ, 1980), pp. 83–7, 127–30; Margaret Masson, 'The typology of the female as a model for the regenerate: puritan preaching, 1690–1730', *Signs: Journal of Women in Culture and Society*, 2 (1976), pp. 304–15; E. S. Morgan, 'The puritan's marriage with God', *The South Atlantic Quarterly*, 48 (1949), pp. 107–12; Amanda Porterfield, *Female Piety in Puritan New England: the Emergence of Religious Humanism* (New York and Oxford, 1992), pp. 14–79; Ivy Schweitzer, *The Work of Self-Representation. Lyric Poetry in Colonial New England* (Chapel Hill, NC, and London, 1991). On puritan spirituality, Jerald C. Brauer, 'Types of Puritan piety', *ChH*, 56 (1987), pp. 39–58; Charles E. Hambrick-Stowe, *The Practice of Piety: Puritan Devotional Disciplines in Seventeenth-Century New England* (Chapel Hill, NC, 1982); G. F. Nuttall, 'Puritan and Quaker mysticism', *Theology*, 78 (1975), pp. 518–31; R. Tudur Jones, 'Union with Christ: the existential nerve of puritan piety', *Tyndale Bulletin*, 41 (1990), pp. 186–208; G. Wakefield, *Puritan Devotion* (London, 1957). Brauer, Nuttall, and Wakefield discuss the varied character of puritan mysticism, which is beyond our scope here.

[7] Samuel Rutherford, *Joshua Redivivus: or, Three Hundred and Fifty Two Religious Letters* (London, 1671), p. 39; Tudur Jones, 'Union with Christ', p. 201.

[8] Interest began with Theodore Beza, *Master Bezaes Sermons upon the Three First Chapters*

Puritan exegesis saw no conflict between interpreting 'bride' in a corporate sense as Church, and personal, sensual language about the soul and her Bridegroom. As one writer put it,

> What admirable comfort, and consolation utterly incomprehens-
> ible, the reading of this part of Scripture may bring every
> Christian, what peace . . . it may breed . . . what incomparable
> joy it may worke . . . is easier to consider by the spouse herself . . .
> representing not only the whole but every . . . member of the
> Church of God. My beloved, saith she, is mine, and I am his.[9]

A psycho-sexual approach may help to explain male puritans' vivid thoughts of union with Christ. Men who cast themselves in a female role betray guilt and ambivalence about their sexual identity: 'by becoming brides of Christ [they] . . . reconcile some of the conflicting elements at war within the self'. This was a line pursued in the 1970s, and the idea that we are dealing here with sexual repression, sexual turbulence, has truth in it.[10] But I think we can make more general and telling points about the interaction of gender-roles and spirituality if we take male identification with female roles out of the realm of psychoanalysis (where the focus is primarily on the individual), and instead see how men's use of feminized language fits in with their views on gender.

---

of the Canticle of Canticles, trans. John Harmar (Oxford, 1587); major treatments thereafter include George Gifford, *Fifteene Sermons upon the Song of Salomon* (London, 1598); William Gouge [Sir Henry Finch], *An Exposition of the Song of Solomon called Canticles* (London, 1615); Rous, *Mysticall Marriage*; Richard Sibbes, *Bowels Opened: or a Discovery of the Neere and Deere Love, Union and Communion betwixt Christ and his Church* (London, 1639); John Cotton, *A Brief Exposition of the Whole Book of Canticles* (London, 1642); John Collinges, *The Spouses Hidden Glory, and Faithful Leaning upon her Welbeloved* (London, 1648); John Preston, *The Mysticall Match between Christ and his Church* (London, 1648); John Robotham, *An Exposition of the Whole of Solomon's Song* (London, 1652); James Durham, *Clavis Cantici: or an Exposition of the Song of Solomon* (London, 1668); Rowland Stedman, *A Treatise of the Mystical Union of Believers with Christ* (London, 1668); Edward Polhill, *Christus in Corde: or the Mystical Union between Christ and Believers* (London, 1680). On contemporary interpretations of the Song of Songs, see Mason I. Lowance, *The Language of Canaan. Metaphor and Symbol in New England from the Puritans to the Transcendentalists* (Cambridge, MA, and London, 1980), pp. 41–54. The Song's sensual imagery nourished a wide range of devotional writing: Hambrick-Stowe, *Practice of Piety*, pp. 28–9; Stanley Stewart, *The Enclosed Garden* (Madison, WI, 1966), pp. 3–30. For its use in radical religion, 1640–60, see Nigel Smith, *Perfection Proclaimed. Language and Literature in English Radical Religion 1640–1660* (Oxford, 1989), passim.

[9] Beza, *Master Bezaes Sermons*, 'Epistle Dedicatory'.
[10] Greven, *Protestant Temperament*, p. 124.

The dynamic of the bridal language we encounter here is different from what has gone before: the imagery is being ardently adopted by Protestants who saw the union of husband and wife as a precious Christian calling, a lynchpin of religious and social order. It could be argued that puritan spirituality merely echoes the Christian tradition of reading the Song of Songs as an allegory for the marriage of Christ and the soul, an interpretation built on the New Testament's use of the metaphor of marriage for the union of Christ and the Church (Ephesians 5.22–33). However, this fails to take account of the impact of Protestantism on gender values. The honour given to marriage in the new movement, and the rejection of celibacy as a spiritual ideal, did much to win over hearts and minds: gender relations were not tangential to the Reformation, but crucial for its success.[11] Thus interpretations of the Song of Songs in newly Protestant England had a distinctive setting. 'Spiritual marriage' meant the wooing and winning of the soul by Christ, in a framework of thought that also heartily commended the sexual union of husband and wife. In contrast, medieval interpreters worked within a spirituality that honoured celibate Christians more than those who enjoyed married pleasures – a spirituality where the drive to transform sexuality into spiritual passion could equate 'spiritual marriage' not only with the union of Christ and believer but also with sexual abstinence in wedlock. The puritans' priorities were different, and set a higher premium on gender. They made God's gift of marital union an argument for defining the gender-roles of husband and wife, and then read these gendered roles back into their theology of spiritual marriage. We might note in passing that in both periods, enthusiasm for intimate exegesis of the Song of Songs owes much to an increased level of sexual experience among expositors: in early modern England, the advent of married clergy; in medieval times, to patterns of recruitment into new orders such as the Cistercians, which took in not child novices but adults who had been married or who knew

---

[11] Lyndal Roper, *The Holy Household: Women and Morals in Reformation Augsburg* (Oxford, 1989). Puritan commentators made much of the connection between the Song of Songs and Ephesians. The Epistle is actually rather reticent about Christ as husband of the soul: the author makes no explicit reference to spiritual marriage, but only to the phrase 'the two shall become one flesh' as a 'great truth, which I take it to refer to Christ and to the church' (Eph. 5.31–2). Other important texts for spiritual marriage include Pss 45, 62.5; Isa. 54.5–6; Hos. 2.20; I Cor. 6.17.

secular love literature.[12] But the values each period attached to sexuality and gender-relations differ sharply. So although the language we are considering has a long genealogy in Christian tradition, the social and cultural conventions that inform the imagery are rooted in a particular time. How, then, did puritan views of gender shape what it meant to be a bride of Christ? What purpose did it serve for men to see themselves in that role?

Contemporary ideas about gender relations pervade the theology of spiritual marriage. To counter what men perceived as threats to gender order and 'masculinity', puritan conduct books and sermons set out well-defined gender roles.[13] These stereotypes colour discussions of union with Christ. Puritan commentators moved easily from Solomon's Wisdom (Proverbs), with its code of conduct for a good wife, to Solomon's love-song (the Song of Songs) and its portrait of the soul as bride.[14] Human marriage existed as a model for spiritual union: 'the marriage of Adam and Eve was intended as a type and shadow of Christ and his church'.[15] This argument reversed the logic of Ephesians 5.22–33, which presents union with Christ as the pattern for human marriage. But by allowing the logic to run from the human to the divine, rather than the other way round, preachers created a rationale for projecting gender relations on to spiritual marriage. Step-by-step comparisons were made between events in earthly and spiritual marriage, from leaving one's parents (Christ had left his Father in heaven and his mother on earth) to the gift of children (spiritual graces). 'Til death us do part' had no counterpart in spiritual marriage, because union with Christ reached full consummation beyond the grave: 'the day of death is . . . a day of marriage', as Richard Sibbes put it.[16] Christ appears as the benevolent patriarch, a provider and ruler

---

[12] Astell, *Song of Songs*, p. 9, citing the work of Jean Leclercq.

[13] Fletcher, *Gender, Sex and Subordination*, esp. pp. 3–29, 101–23, 204–22.

[14] For elaborations on Proverbs, see Thomas Gataker, *A Good Wife Gods Gift: and A Wife Indeed* (London, 1623); Stephen Geree, *The Ornament of Women* (London, 1639); John Wing, *The Crown Conjugal or Spouse Royal: A Discovery of the True Honour and Happiness of Christian Matrimony* (London, 1620).

[15] Thomas Goodwin, 'A sermon on Ephesians 5:30–32', *The Works of Thomas Goodwin*, 12 vols (Edinburgh 1861), 2, p. 418.

[16] Richard Sibbes, *The Bride's Longing for her Bride-groomes Second Comming* (London, 1638), p. 98. In this life, 'spiritual conjunction' is 'made by the promise of the Bridegroom and the faith of the spouse', but 'real and entire actual union' will come after death: Beza, *Master Bezaes Sermons*, p. 21. For a comparison between human marriage and marriage with Christ, see Preston, *Mysticall Match*, pp. 2–21.

who bears with the infirmities of his wife, the 'weaker vessel'. Assumptions about women's lower place in the gender order sprang naturally to men's minds in interpreting the relation of Christ and his bride. Though he could have tackled the text differently, Sibbes discussed the bride's words of desire for the bridegroom, 'let him kiss me', in terms of superiority and inferiority: 'There are divers sorts of kisses spoken of in Scripture ... there is an holy kiss, Rom xvi 16, 1 Cor xvi 20, and an hypocritical kiss ... as Judas to Christ Matt.26.49. There are kisses of love, so Jonathan kissed David, 1 Sam 20.41 ... But here is the kiss of a superior to an inferior.'[17] The Suffolk gentleman John Winthrop, who later became the first governor of Massachusetts, loved his wife despite her inferior capacities, and found that

> when I considered of suche letters as my wife had written to me, and observed the scriblinge hand, the meane congruitye, the false orthog[raphy]; and broken sentences ... and yet founde my heart not onely acceptinge of them but delighting in them ... It made me thinke with myselfe ... will not my Lord and husband Christ Jesus ... accept ... the poorest testimonies of my love and dutye towards him? ... the more I thought [on this], the more sensible I grewe of the most sweet love of my heavenly husband, Jesus Christ.[18]

In public rhetoric and private prayer, the norms of patriarchy governed the relationship between bridal soul and Christ. Gender relations defined spiritual marriage.

Taking gender relations into theology opened the doors to a marvellous intimacy with God, which puritan piety badly craved. Marriage, with its newly-hallowed role in Protestantism, provided a perfect metaphor. At the same time, however, the patriarchal gloss on spiritual marriage meant that the bounds of intimacy were always well-defined: gender order structured the encounter with God. At issue here is the theological question of how Christians can legitimately express and experience God's immanence. This is a theme we need to set in the context of broad shifts in Christian thought at the Reformation. The stress in Calvinism on God's

[17] Sibbes, *Works*, 2, p. 202 (on Song of Songs 1.2).
[18] 'John Winthrop's Experiencia, 1616–18', *Winthrop Papers*, 5 vols (Boston, MA, 1929–47), 1, p. 203. For Winthrop (1588–1649) see *DNB*.

transcendent sovereignty, expressed in (for example) the decrees of election and predestination, and in the rejection of images, arose in reaction to a medieval tendency to humanize and materialize God's presence. The Calvinist God, however, could appear remote and arbitrary: a Judge who divided the saved from the damned on unfathomable grounds. The puritan search for assurance was a quest for intimacy with this God. Marriage gave a pattern for the soul's yielding to God, and emphasised the mutuality of love between Christ and the soul. It gave a vocabulary for expressing God's closeness that did not threaten his transcendence: 'he that is the Judge of the world, is your Husband, your beloved, and you are his: let nothing therefore dismay your hearts'.[19] The invitation to marriage was an invitation to intimacy. John Cotton (d. 1652), preacher at Boston, Massachusetts, urged Christians to enter Christ's marriage bed:

> looke what affection there is between Husband and Wife, hath there been the same affection in your soules towards the Lord Jesus Christ? Have you a strong and hearty desire to meet him in the bed of loves ... desire you to have the seeds of his grace shed abroad in your hearts . . . will you accept him . . . as your Husband?[20]

Intimacy, however, was governed by the rules of gender relations. When a man wedded himself to Christ, he took the bride's vow to 'love, honour and obey'. Thomas Doolittle made a solemn marriage covenant with Christ in his private devotions, promising

> I do here, with willingness of heart ... sincerely, and gladly take thee for my Lord, Head and Husband, to love honour and obey thee, whether I shall be rich or poor, in sickness or in health, in better or worse condition in this world, till death shall separate my soul from my body, for thee to be mine also after death, knowing that death shall not separate thee and me.[21]

---

[19] Thomas Hooker, *The Soules Exaltation* (London, 1638), p. 10. Calvin's theology stressed union with Christ (*Institutes*, III, i, 1) but puritans elaborated its intimate meaning.
[20] John Cotton, *Christ the Fountain of Life* (London, 1651), pp. 36–7.
[21] From a memoir prefixed to Thomas Doolittle, *A Complete Body of Practical Divinity* (London, 1723); cited by Tudur Jones, 'Union with Christ', p. 197. For Doolittle (1632?-

Thus the honoured place of marriage in Protestantism created a powerful language for spiritual intimacy. At the same time, the nature of intimacy was tightly defined by the gendered order.

Are there ways in which men's adoption of a female spiritual identity compensates for the straitjacket of gender roles?[22] When certainties are shouted loudly, to hide insecurity, certainties tend, paradoxically, to subvert themselves. Male identification with the bridal soul subverted the gender stereotype to the extent that it allowed men a safe place to express emotions and roles which were otherwise 'unmanly'. Wifely passion provided a compelling metaphor for the soul's ardent response to Christ, who, Thomas Goodwin assured his hearers, was 'the most fond and perfect lover that ever was'. In the words of Richard Baxter,

> See what a Sea of love is here before thee; cast thyself in, and swim with the arms of thy love in this Ocean of his love ... 'I am thine ... thy Lord ... thy husband ... wouldst thou have me? why then take me ... if thou be willing, I am willing.' ... Lord, I yield, I am unable, I am overcome.

For John Winthrop, thoughts of his wife led to a defining moment of spiritual surrender:

> God brought me ... in to suche a heavenly meditation of the love betweene Christ and me, as ravished my heart with unspeakable joye; methought my soule had as familiar and sensible society with him, as my wife could have with the kindest husbande. ... O my Lord howe did my soule melt with joye when thou spakest to the heart of thy poore unworthy handmayd! ... O my Lord, my love, how wholly delectable are thou! lett him kisse me with the kisses of his mouthe, for his love

---

1707) see *DNB*. Records of formal marriage covenants are rare, but illustrate men's deep engagement with the imagery. In 1741 Joseph Bean resorted to marriage with Christ to tame his 'unchast and immodist thoughts': at the wedding of a friend, he left the room and went 'up stars by my Self alone and there pleded with God that this Night be the Weden Night betwen Christ and my soul'; soon afterwards, his diary records a marriage covenant. Cited by Greven, *Protestant Temperament*, p. 126.

[22] Gerda Lerner, *The Creation of Patriarchy* (Oxford, 1986), p. 238: 'Gender is a set of cultural roles. It is a costume, a mask, a straitjacket in which men and women dance their unequal dance.'

is sweeter than wine: how lovely is thy countenance! how pleasant are thy embracings! my heart leaps within me for joye when I heare the voice of thee my Lord, my love, when thou sayest to my soule, thou are hir salvation . . . thou didst trimme me as a bride prepared for hir husband. . . . Wholye thine I am (my sweet Lord Jesus), unworthy . . . to wipe the dust off the feet of my Lord . . . yet thou wilt honor me with the societye of thy mariage chamber.[23]

Puritan spirituality has been described as a tradition that 'welcomes the power of feeling . . . delights in the amorous and sensory . . . demands the full responsiveness of emotional and sentient beings'.[24] Spiritual gender reversal was fundamental to this 'heart religion'. Crossing the gender line in spirit gave men a language for intimacy with God that went beyond the conventions of male behaviour.

Yet gender reversal was by no means an escape from gender. On the contrary, the power of feminized imagery for men derived precisely from the male understanding of what it meant to be a woman. Richard Sibbes, whose sermons popularized spiritual marriage, argued that 'for the most part women have sweet affections to religion, and therein they oft go beyond men'. Two of his reasons for this opinion bear on our case: that 'religion is strongly seated in the affections; and [women] have sweet and strong affections'; and that women are 'subject to weakness, and God delights to shew "his strength in weakness"'.[25] Sibbes's belief that women were more open to God helps to explain his enthusiasm for telling men to become brides of Christ. He thought of himself as a matchmaker: 'to preach is to woo'. Walter Cradock told his flock that Christ 'sends us not to hire servants. . . . We are not sent to get Gally-slaves to the Oares, or a Beare to the Stake: but he sends us to wooe you as spouses, to marrie you to Christ.'[26] When men could be persuaded to adopt feminine affections, they experienced the emotions

---

[23] Goodwin, *Works*, 2, p. 425; Richard Baxter, *The Saints Everlasting Rest* (London, 1650), pp. 797, 799–801; *Winthrop Papers*, 1, pp. 202–4.

[24] N. H. Keeble, *The Literary Culture of Nonconformity* (Leicester, 1987), p. 213.

[25] Sibbes, *Works*, 6, p. 520: from a sermon on 'Lydia's conversion', originally published in *The Riches of Mercie* (London, 1638). Sibbes offers a third reason for women's religiosity: child-bearing brings them close to death, and therefore closer to God.

[26] Sibbes, *Works*, 5, pp. 505–6; Walter Cradock, *Gospel-Libertie* (London, 1648), p. 28. Both cited by Tudur Jones, 'Union with Christ', pp. 198–9. For Cradock (1606?–59), see *DNB*.

that led to conversion. It is as if men had to shed their masculinity to be saved. In this context, the weak and inferior nature of women provided a strong incentive for men to identify themselves as brides of Christ. Men who believed in strict division of gender roles found spiritual gender-reversal a potent metaphor for extraordinary experiences of renunciation and conversion. The Quaker Isaac Penington spoke of 'my nothingness, my emptiness, my manifold infirmities . . . the Lord has broken the man's part in me'. When a man identified himself spiritually as woman, he took on a lowly role that emphasised his otherness from the divine Bridegroom, a role that robbed him of the status he enjoyed 'in the world', and 'of the flesh'.[27]

We have arrived at some answers to the question of why male puritans used female imagery to express and define their religious experience: a quest for intimacy with God that found a perfect metaphor in marriage; a drive towards gendered thinking that infected spirituality and theology as well as conduct books. Spiritual gender-reversal, which at first sight might appear to allow men to depart from their gender role, subverts the gendered order only superficially. When men became brides of Christ in spirit, they took on female roles they themselves had devised. There is a sad irony in the fact that men needed feminized language to express spiritual intimacy and the drama of conversion: the gender stereotypes they were creating left them with no other language for what, in terms of the conventions, was 'unmanly'. However positive the female imagery they used might be – we have after all been looking at 'brides of Christ', not 'unfaithful harlots' – it was still rooted in negative assumptions about women's inferiority and weakness, which ultimately provide a hollow way to define the encounter with God. And what of women in all this? Preachers advocated spiritual marriage to men and women alike. We

---

[27] See Bynum's comments on medieval males' use of female imagery, *Fragmentation and Redemption*, pp. 165–6, 177–8. For Penington, see Greven, *Protestant Temperament*, p. 125, and *DNB*. Schweitzer, *Work of Self-Representation*, pp. 1–35, argues that the puritan theology of conversion required men to undergo first a 'feminized subjection' to God, then a re-conversion to masculinity by being adopted as a son of God; women were excluded from this discourse. It seems to me that she over-systematizes puritans' free use of a wide range of biblical imagery, and simplifies the dynamic of gender relations in puritanism by ignoring the powerful puritan tradition of ministry to women. Janice Knight, *Orthodoxies in Massachusetts* (Boston, MA, 1994), pp. 225–6, rightly qualifies Schweitzer's case by stressing masculine themes in conversion preaching. However, the crucial issue is not whether masculine or feminine imagery predominates, but differences in the use and value of gendered imagery for men and women.

have established that male use of female imagery has a complex relation to men's gender role. What the dynamics are when women use bridal language is beyond our scope here, but we have seen enough to realize that a woman could not use the language like a man: identifying herself as Christ's bride carried no connotations of gender-reversal.[28] Let the last word go to Thomasine Winthrop, wife of John. As she lay dying, John Winthrop spoke to her of their marriage, and for him this led on naturally to talk of spiritual marriage, and of the consummation of her union with Christ. Thomasine, however, was bewildered, and could not identify with the logic that led from the human husband to the divine:

When I tould hir that the day before was 12 monthes [since] she was maried to me, and now this day she should be maried to Christ Jesus, who would embrace her with another manner of love than I could, 'O husband (said she, and spake as if she were offended, for I perceived she did mistake me) I must not love thee as I love Christ.'[29]

King's College, University of London

---

[28] For examples of women's use of the imagery, see Sara Heller Mendelson, 'Stuart women's diaries and occasional memoirs', in Mary Prior, ed., *Women in English Society, 1500–1800* (London and New York, 1985), pp. 194–5. For discussions of female spiritual experience, see Patricia Crawford, *Women and Religion in England, 1550–1720* (London, 1993), pp. 75–85, 112–15; Fletcher, *Gender, Sex and Subordination*, pp. 347–63; Peter Lake, 'Feminine piety and personal potency: the emancipation of Mrs. Jane Ratcliffe', *The Seventeenth Century*, 2 (1987), p. 147; P. Mack, *Visionary Women: Ecstatic Prophecy in Seventeenth Century England* (Berkeley, CA, 1992), pp. 172–86. Caroline Walker Bynum's comparisons of male and female use of symbols in medieval devotion are relevant here: *Holy Feast and Holy Fast. The Religious Significance of Food for Medieval Women* (Berkeley, CA, 1987), pp. 276–94; eadem, *Fragmentation and Redemption*, pp. 151–79.

[29] *Winthrop Papers*, 1, p. 189.

BEYOND THE CHURCH: WOMEN'S SPIRITUAL EXPERIENCE AT HOME AND IN THE COMMUNITY 1600-1900

by ANTHONY FLETCHER

THE Christian tradition has been elaborated and developed over many centuries in the context of gender, which provides the bedrock and framework of social order, powerfully influencing men and women's conduct of every aspect of their daily lives. The dynamic relationship between gender and religious experience – a relationship that may at times channel, control, confine, or liberate – is bound to be complex for the historian to unravel. This paper attempts the beginning of such an unravelling, albeit confined to the experience of women and to England. It focuses upon 1600 to 1900, to argue that the effective gender system – the patriarchy – of this period was being revised by men in a radical way which had major implications for the possibilities open for women to find the space they needed for their spirituality. We cannot of course speak of patriarchy as something given and permanent in Western Christendom, only of patriarchies; for, if we take the term to refer to men's institutionalized dominance over women and children in the family and the subordination of women outside it, men were bound to need constantly to adapt and adjust their means of achieving this end over the centuries.[1] The objective here is as follows: the paper begins by exploring how the meaning of gender and therefore the patriarchal system was revised between 1600 and 1900; it will then offer an outline, with illustrative examples, of the patterns of women's spirituality in that period. It starts with the home and within the home with the privacy of the closet, besides the family world of the hall and parlour. It will also look at some women who, through visions or prophecy, sought a national platform. If we are to begin to map women's personal religious experience from the Civil War to the end of the Victorian age, then, while appreciating how deeply some at times found themselves fed by clerical ministrations, we shall have to look largely beyond the

---

[1] For an account of this process over the period from 1500-1800 see my *Gender, Sex and Subordination in England 1500 to 1800* (London, 1995).

Church. The large question running through the paper is how far did the changing development of the gender system over these three hundred years constrict or release women's spiritual potential?

Gender in 1600 was still a cosmological principle which was given shape and substance by the humoral body: woman was distinct from and inferior to man, distinguished by her lesser heat. For heat was the source of strength, and strength, whether of mind, body, or moral faculties, in the traditional formulation was what gender was all about.[2] Woman was the 'weaker vessel': more lustful, irrational, and emotional because her body was more wet and spongey. At the same time she was more moody, passionate, impulsive, and emotionally powerful because she was more moist. Thus Richard Baxter advised husbands to be patient towards wives who 'by a natural passionate weakness, or by melancholy or crazedness, are wilful . . . your passion and sourness to a person that cannot cure her own unpleasing carriage, is a more inexcusable fault and folly than hers, who hath not the power of reason as you have'.[3] Phyllis Mack puts the point well when she says that 'since there was no strong inner scaffolding, no reliable central core or conscience', a woman's mind was believed to be 'easily permeated not only by outside influences but by her own strong inner drives'. Women were seen and portrayed as liminal creatures inhabiting what Mack calls 'a no man's land of natural and spiritual forces', possessed of 'an inner essence or imagination that could career over the widest emotional and spiritual landscape'.[4] A crucial difference, therefore, between men and women in the early modern gender system was that women were thought to be more open than men to both God and the devil. Their greater natural religiosity was generally taken for granted as a feature of their mutable temperaments, which could take them, as they emptied themselves of the self, close to God himself; just as it could lead them too easily into the pacts with the devil which marked the triumph of appetite over reason and morality.[5] Yet, at the same time, in early modern patriarchy women were told that they were men's spiritual equals in respect of the status of their

---

[2] T. Laqueur, *Making Sex* (Cambridge, MA, 1990); L. Schiebinger, *The Mind has no Sex?* (Cambridge, MA, 1989).

[3] Cited in P. Mack, *Visionary Women: Ecstatic Prophecy in Seventeenth-Century England* (Berkeley, CA, 1992), p. 26.

[4] Mack, *Visionary Women*, pp. 24–7.

[5] P. Crawford, *Women and Religion in England 1500–1720* (London, 1993), pp. 73–5; Fletcher, *Gender, Sex and Subordination*, p. 347.

souls. The puritan advice book writers and other commentators constantly asserted this.[6] Women were less fully endowed with moral apparatus than men, they were subordinate to men on earth and thus disqualified from full participation in parochial spiritual life, but they would share equally in the joys of paradise. In theological terms, as Ian Maclean summarizes these arguments, woman was 'the inferior of the male by nature, his equal by grace'.[7] George Fox recorded an incident in his *Journal* in 1675: 'I met with a sort of people that held women have no souls, adding in a light manner, no more than a goose. But I reproved them and told them that was not right, for Mary said "My soul doth magnify the Lord".'[8]

As the misogynist case against women lost its impetus and the old cosmology collapsed during the late seventeenth century, men sought a revised basis for patriarchy in a new construction of womanhood. In medical terms, this put more emphasis on the nervous system and women's greater sensibility and less on their reproductive system.[9] In sexual terms, it involved the practice of a learnt inner virtue as the bulwark of chastity.[10] In emotional terms, it anticipated the modern romantic notion of woman, elaborated between 1700 and 1850, as man's helpmeet and companion, as a devoted mother, and as the manager of a privatized home, which came to exercise a powerful moral force.[11] The process overall, it may be suggested, altered the whole notion of what a woman is. We can characterize it in terms of a gradual internalization of social roles as inherent personality traits.

In early modern England gender was still role-playing, adopting conventions of masculine or feminine behaviour. And the soul meanwhile could still go free, rising through vision or prophecy, as we shall

[6] A. J. Fletcher, 'The Protestant idea of marriage in early modern England' in A. J. Fletcher and P. R. Roberts, eds, *Religion, Culture and Society in Early Modern Britain* (Cambridge, 1994), pp. 179–80.

[7] I. Maclean, *The Renaissance Notion of Woman: A Study in the Fortunes of Scholasticism and Medical Science in European Intellectual Life* (Cambridge, 1980), p. 1.

[8] N. H. Keeble, ed., *The Cultural Identity of Seventeenth-Century Woman: A Reader* (London, 1994), p. 46.

[9] R. Martensen, 'The transformation of Eve: women's bodies, medicine and culture in early modern England', in R. Porter and M. Teich, eds, *Sexual Knowledge, Sexual Science: The History of Attitudes to Sexuality* (Cambridge, 1994), pp. 107–33; Fletcher, *Gender, Sex and Subordination*, pp. 291–3.

[10] Fletcher, *Gender, Sex and Subordination*, pp. 384–400.

[11] L. Davidoff and C. Hall, *Family Fortunes: Men and Women of the English Middle Class 1780–1850* (London, 1987), pp. 115–16; A. Giddens, *The Transformation of Intimacy: Sexuality, Love and Eroticism in Modern Societies* (London, 1992), pp. 38–47.

see, above gender altogether.[12] Between the Restoration and the accession of Queen Victoria, however, the possession of a gender was, step by step, invading the whole person. Femininity – belonging to 'the sex' as people began to say – came, in the words of Denise Riley, 'to colour existence to the point of suffusion'. What women lost when an ideological construction of their nature became fastened upon them, what was crowded out, was the wholly autonomous and sexually democratic soul. Respect for the female soul was often asserted in the nineteenth century, but arguably it was now a distinctly womanly soul that was spoken about in which the outstanding and supreme qualities of femininity were seen as being refined. 'That the soul before God had no sex', suggests Denise Riley, 'was not an argument available for feminist deployment after the eighteenth century's revisions of Nature and Reason.' The crucial point here is that, by the nineteenth century, women were being generally conceptualized as persons who were thoroughly sexed through all the regions of their being.[13] This is fundamentally important as a starting point in our investigation of their religious experience which, it follows, was assumed to be in some sense different from that of men. It had a new kind of distinctiveness. A seventeenth-century woman could still deconstruct herself, in a way not open to rational men, so as to become an empty vessel for God's grace or God's power. A nineteenth-century woman might have found this objective both inconceivable and incomprehensible. Instead she could learn from other women and practise an intensive pattern of domestic observance and piety which brought her life both meaning and purpose. If we are sometimes tempted to regard that pattern as tarnished by both sentiment and excess, we must remember that Victorian patriarchy confined the female spirit in a manner which gave it a narrow channel to run within.

Printed versions of seventeenth-century funeral sermons about godly women and the writings of some of these women themselves – in the form of diaries, poetry, and meditative reflections – enable us to make some kind of entry into their mental world. The locus of the godly woman's daily life and spiritual growth at this time lay in her private closet. One of the best documented examples is Jane Ratcliffe, wife of a Chester brewer, whose pattern of piety was set out by her

---

[12] Mack, *Visionary Women*, pp. 6–7.
[13] D. Riley, *'Am I That Name?': Feminism and the Category of Woman in History* (London, 1988), pp. 18–19, 42–3.

friend, counsellor, and minister John Ley in a funeral sermon of 1640. Peter Lake has argued that she created for herself 'a persona of some potency' by a process of sublimation and internalization of her religion: 'increasingly complete subjection to and possession by her God enabled her, if not to resist, then to circumvent the usual constraints of female existence'. What is especially interesting here, because it is explicit, is the male and clerical acceptance of Jane's spiritual potential in openly gendered terms. 'Great heat of devotion', wrote John Ley, 'if with little light of information in the lady (but in her truly there was both light and heat in a remarkable degree) may make them blessed, while great light of learning and little heat of zeal in the clergy may render them wretched.' One could hardly have a clearer statement of the mind-and-emotion dichotomy, or of the respect with which a conscientious moderate puritan minister could view a particular woman's closely observed spiritual pilgrimage. Ley saw in Jane a spiritual triumph of which he believed many of his fellow clerics were deprived, intent as they were on salvation through the medium of humane learning. The actual defects of her rationality, as he saw it, allowed her to achieve a better balance than they could between intellectual effort and spiritual enthusiasm. Thus Jane Ratcliffe exemplified the role of the empty vessel which the gender construction of her time allowed to the female. What Ley admired was her ardour: 'She was frequently and fervently covenant with God in her private supplications and therein was he most favourably familiar with her for he sent forth his spirit into her heart . . . which enabled her in an extraordinary manner and measure to put out her soul into his bosom.'[14]

The funeral sermons detailed the ways that godly women expressed their piety. Mary Gunter 'was thrice on her knees every day before God in secret'; Alice Lucy's 'first employment every day', we are told, 'was her humble address to Almighty God in secret; her next was to read some part of God's word'. Secretiveness was the essence of this devotional pattern. Much of the diary kept by Elizabeth Bury defeated her husband when he tried, after her death, to decipher its 'peculiar characters and abbreviations'. Elizabeth Walker, interrupted by her husband at her private writings, made him promise he would not look at her papers during her lifetime. After her death, he found in her desk memorials of God's providences to him, herself and their children, and

---

[14] P. Lake, 'Feminine piety and personal potency: the "emancipation" of Mrs Jane Ratcliffe', *The Seventeenth Century*, 2 (1987), pp. 150, 159, 163.

six pages of extracts from books about 'meekness of spirit'.[15] For the most part, we can assume, husbands were sympathetic towards or at least tolerant of their wives' spiritual independence. But where a relationship was deeply fraught, as a case in the Court of Arches in 1660 shows, private prayers could be a considerable bone of contention. Sir Oliver Boteler, a servant deposed, often 'took offence' at his wife Lady Ann 'for her piety and devotion', and said that 'he hated a wife that said her prayers and threatened to damn her body and soul and frequently disturbed and forced her from her closet when he knew she was at prayers'. On one occasion, this servant related:

> Sir Oliver in his mad mood and furious humour caused and forced his said wife to kneel down by his bed and say some prayers namely Our Father . . . which she endeavoured to do but was so distracted and distressed with such his usage and his insulting over her that she could not say them but by pieces and words here and there, at which he made himself sport and fell to laughing.[16]

Diary-keeping was a favourite aide memoire for these early modern godly women. Elizabeth Bury's diary provides one of the most complete records we have of their typical pattern of life.[17] She would often say, it was noted at her funeral, 'that, were it not for her diary, she would neither know what she was or what she did'. Three-quarters of surviving Stuart women's diaries contain considerable devotional material. Keeping a diary provided reassurance, a sense of personal identity, a kind of self-fashioning. 'It is the duty of every true Christian to remember and take notice of Almighty God our Heavenly Father's gracious acts of Providence over them, and merciful dealings with them', wrote Alice Thornton.[18] Meditative writings are a complementary genre to diaries: those of Lady Elizabeth Deleval and Alice Thornton, for example, recount incidents in their lives and sufferings in a theological context. The tension between secularity and spirituality is often evident in such accounts. Katherine Austen,

---

[15] Citations from Fletcher, *Gender, Sex and Subordination*, pp. 353–4.

[16] London, Lambeth Palace Library, Court of Arches, case 1041, Eee 4: Ann Boteler *v.* Oliver Boteler. I am grateful to Elizabeth Foyster for a transcript of these passages.

[17] M. Spufford, ed., *The World of Rural Dissenters 1520–1725* (Cambridge, 1995), pp. 25–7.

[18] Citation from S. H. Mendelson, 'Stuart women's diaries and occasional memoirs', in M. Prior, ed., *Women in English Society 1500–1800* (London, 1985), p. 187.

widowed at twenty-nine, is especially moving in the account she has left in her diary of her decision to remain single: 'As for my body it can be enjoyed but by one and I hope its the worst part of me and that which every servant maid and country wench may excel mine and can give the same satisfaction as mine. But that which my desire is should far excel my body is my soul and the virtues and qualities of that.'[19]

So the patriarchal society of seventeenth-century England, one is led to conclude, was certainly not one that crushed women's spiritual energy. On the contrary, in many instances, it allowed it full rein in this kind of private and household context. The better-known aspect of all this is the vigorous female leadership provided in the household devotions of gentry and middling sort homes by dedicated and well-read godly women. Instruction of children and servants was the foremost responsibility here, often exercised largely by a wife under a husband's watchful eye and ultimate control. The closet and the hall were the two sides of the godly woman's daily pattern of religion at the higher social levels.[20]

Spiritual striving and independence may, for all we know, have been nearly as common lower down the social scale. It is simply less well documented. Margaret Spufford discovered the case of Sister Sneesby of Over in Cambridgeshire, a woman who was in great spiritual distress in 1654 as she struggled to determine her own path, choosing between her Baptist principles and the new Quaker teachings. Baptist messengers who visited her found her

> in a very sad and deplorable condition . . . . We told her, that we heard that one of those commonly called Quakers was at her home and preached there and we were afraid his preaching had brought her into that condition. She answered that she could hear very little that he said but she said that she had read many of his books.

Perhaps Sister Sneesby was deaf. The Baptists, anyway, advised her to continue reading the Scriptures. But their hopes of reclaiming her were not fulfilled. For six years later, in 1660, the Widow Sneesby was one of

---

[19] Citations from Fletcher, *Gender, Sex and Subordination*, pp. 355–7.
[20] Crawford, *Women and Religion in England*, pp. 86–8; Fletcher, *Gender, Sex and Subordination*, pp. 351–2.

a small group who were imprisoned for not swearing the oath of allegiance. 'They were most of them poor women', the report of their detention noted, 'and had nothing to live on but what they did labour for.' As Margaret Spufford declares, one could hope for no more positive proof than this that the growth of literacy was a powerful weapon in spreading new opinions and making possible a personal pilgrimage even among the female poor. Sister Sneesby found her own way and held tenaciously to it.[21] The minds of those who have been discussed so far have to be understood in the context of living in a society which continually emphasised the otherness of women, not only in the kind of extreme behaviour where women were exalted as prophets or condemned as witches, but in day-to-day life with their menfolk and children. Whereas men were defined by their working role and their place in the social structure, women were defined in terms of their mysterious and occult power, which made appropriate their ascendancy in healing, the management of childbirth, and also the comfort of the dying. Women's nature was such that they always hovered on the edge of good and bad magic. At the same time it allowed them a remarkable spiritual potential, a potential to go free of socially constructed gender, to let God fill them as his passive and pure vessels with his divine energy and inspiration.[22] Let us turn to two women in seventeenth-century England who reached the heights of this. We know little about the life of Ann Collins, beyond what we can learn from her *Divine Songs and Meditations*, which was published in 1653. What is clear, though, as her recent anthologists put it, was that she 'interpreted and found purpose in her uncomfortable and withdrawn life by means of biblical precedent and a vocation to poetry'. She is much concerned with the vanity of earthly delights and sensual pleasures:

> But saved joy is like the sun's clear light
> Which may with clouds be sometimes overcast
> Yet breaks it forth anon and shines more bright
> Whose lively force continually doth last.

---

[21] M. Spufford, *Contrasting Communities: English Villagers in the Sixteenth and Seventeenth Centuries* (Cambridge, 1974), pp. 216–17. For further comment on literacy and religion among the poor in this period see Spufford, *World of Rural Dissenters*, pp. 64–85.

[22] Mack, *Visionary Women*, pp. 28–34.

One senses in reading Ann Collins's lyrical poems a life intertwined with God's grace as, with the rich Old Testament imagery of the female soul, she awaits the beloved: 'as a garden', she said, is 'her mind enclosed, fast being to safety, so confined from storm and blast, apt to produce a fruit most rare'. She denies this world in her aspiration for something 'not common with every woman that fruitful are' in the next one.[23]

Anne Bathurst's extensive private writings provide insight into the spiritual career and mentality of an ecstatic visionary who remained quite unknown in her own lifetime beyond the circle of the mystical Philadelphian Society to which she belonged. She sought God, she relates, from about ten years of age, but was oppressed by illnesses, fears, and sorrows until in 1678, at about forty, she found assurance. Around this time she was living with the Behmenist circle of John Pordage at Bradfield in Berkshire, but her mysticism, Brian Gibbons notes, remained 'primarily Christ centred' and she refused to indulge in the sophiological speculation which was so important to others of these English Behmenists.[24] Thenceforward her periods of devotion and dialogue with God in her closet formed the centrepiece of Anne Bathurst's life. The sexual language of her account exemplifies the way that she immersed her whole being in her union with God. She longed, she wrote on 8 September 1679, 'that I might lie in his arms as I had done the night before'. A few days later, she referred to herself as 'a spouse betrothed'. Earlier that summer, alternatively, she had written 'I saw myself as a little child at the feet of my dear Jesus.' In one especially interesting passage, Anne described what she called the 'divers operations' of the spirit:

> Sometimes it works as one drunk with love, sometimes by air, as the body is full of divine joyfulness and a body within a body carrying it very swift in motion to go on walking as without senses or feeling the ground or sense of weariness ... I speak now also of a spirit quick and powerful dividing betwixt the marrow and the bone and works in my heart . . . that I am like one drunk.[25]

---

[23] E. Graham *et al.*, eds, *Her Own Life: Autobiographical Writings by Seventeenth-Century Englishwomen* (London, 1989), pp. 54–70.

[24] B. J. Gibbons, *Gender in Mystical and Occult Thought: Behmenism and its Development in England* (Cambridge, 1996), pp. 107, 113–14.

[25] Crawford, *Women and Religion in England*, pp. 15, 82, 110–13; see also Mack, *Visionary Women*, pp. 8–9, 116–17.

The sheer force of this physical and emotional experience, at the height of this woman's ecstasy, comes across in these words. It is an experience, something to emphasise at this stage of the argument, that we can only fully appreciate by relating it to the world of gender in which Anne Bathurst lived. Her understanding of her own nature made it possible. This is not to say that such an ecstatic experience became totally impossible when the early modern mental world disappeared, but it almost certainly became much harder to achieve.

Puritan evangelicalism had nurtured the intense household piety which was the context of the individual spiritual careers we have been looking at.[26] But we are talking here about a tradition which largely dried up between the 1660s and the 1780s and which then found new life with the Anglican and Methodist evangelicalism of the late eighteenth and early nineteenth centuries. The argument takes a chronological leap at this point. James Obelkevitch has described the development of a Primitive Methodist movement in rural Lincolnshire between 1825 and 1875 which gloried in the expression of the emotions and established its own distinct liturgical year, with its summer lovefeasts and cycle of prayer and class meetings and chapel anniversaries. Lay people dominated the preaching, praying, singing, and shouting there. The family as a unit was also once more claimed for religion, with the household gathering for prayers often twice a day.[27] 'The shift to family worship across all denominations', argue Leonore Davidoff and Catherine Hall in their discussion of religion and the middle class between 1780 and 1850, 'marked the growing prominence given to the family.' The *Christian Observer* in 1820 echoed puritan commentators of two hundred years previously when it stated that the action of the patriarchal head in regularly gathering the household for prayer and Bible reading assisted 'the good order of families, to the discharge of relative duty, to the improvement of the young, to the morals of servants and to the welfare of the community at large'. 'Family celebrations could contribute to the building of the little kingdom of heaven above', noted an Essex Quaker in 1846.

---

[26] See e.g. C. Hill, *Society and Puritanism in Pre-Revolutionary England* (London, 1964), pp. 443–81; P. Collinson, *The Birthpangs of Protestant England: Religion and Cultural Change in the Sixteenth and Seventeenth Centuries* (London, 1988), pp. 60–93; M. Todd, *Christian Humanism and the Puritan Social Order* (Cambridge, 1987), pp. 96–117.

[27] J. Obelkevitch, *Religion and Rural Society: South Lindsey, 1825–1875* (Oxford, 1976), pp. 220–58.

Henry Thornton's *Family Prayers* went through thirty-one editions between 1834 and 1854.[28]

The *Christian Observer* emphasised 'relative' duties and by 1820 the doctrine of separate spheres had of course fully won the day. Serious Christian manhood involved the spiritual leadership of the household, but the actual day-to-day exercise of this leadership, with regard to children and servants, very often rested with the wife, female relatives, and governesses. Maria Marsh was married to the busy rector of St Peter's, Colchester, and her pattern of life in the 1820s is well documented. She was the exemplary clerical wife, taking responsibility for hospitality and instruction within the home while her husband evangelized abroad. She prayed individually by name, we are told, for each of her five children and three servants for their wrong doing. She taught the younger children daily religious lessons, giving them Bible instruction in addition on Sunday afternoons, either around the fireside in the winter, or in the garden in summer.[29] Mary Williams recounted the upbringing she had received as a child in the memoirs she wrote in old age when, as Mary Lucy, she was the retired mistress of Charlecote in Warwickshire. Her story, covering the period from 1803 to 1824, is of the feminine moral and religious influence of the chief figures in her life: her grandmother, mother, nurse and governess. 'After Grand Mamma's death, my own darling Mamma taught every-thing', she wrote, 'and heard me say my prayers. She bid me love God and try to be good and obedient and then God would love me and watch over me.' Her governess, Miss Blackburn, she recalled, was 'very handsome and very good but so strict'. Once in the schoolroom, Mary read the morning psalms with her mother downstairs and the evening ones upstairs in the company of her sister. Miss Blackburn, Mary Williams recalled, was 'a thoroughly religious woman' besides being 'very clever'.[30]

This was a very different social and mental world from the one encountered earlier. As I have stressed elsewhere, a whole new romantic ideology of womanhood was being successfully inculcated into these Hanoverian and Victorian girls and women.[31] At its core was a notion

---

[28] Citations from Davidoff and Hall, *Family Fortunes*, pp. 89–109.

[29] Ibid., pp. 79–80, 123–4.

[30] A. Fairfax-Lucy, ed., *Mistress of Charlecote: The Memoirs of Mary Elizabeth Lucy* (London, 1983), pp. 15–31.

[31] Fletcher, *Gender, Sex and Subordination*, pp. 364–400.

of destiny: that a woman was created not simply for man, but for the one man who chose her. It followed that the home, where she created a moral haven and provided a powerful moral force, was her proper scene of action and mission.[32] Women were still seen as more open to piety, more naturally inclined to devotion than men, but whereas in the seventeenth century that spiritual potential was allowed, even sometimes encouraged, to roam free, it had now been domesticated and tamed. The Victorian middle-class wife, loaded with spiritual and moral responsibility for families which were often large, besides running the home, could expect little space for private meditation and religious contemplation. One Essex shopkeeper noted this fact regretfully: 'a dear young family with a number of daily interruptions seems to allow very few opportunities for making memorandums of religious progress, and the state of the individual soul'.[33] This for both practical and ideological reasons was a narrower female space.

A good deal has been written by historians of Victorian Christianity about the various ways in which people expressed their faith in the Anglican and nonconformist traditions. When we look at public worship, the class and gender aspects of these denominational contrasts are striking. James Obelkevitch has remarked upon the distinctive tone and style to Anglican worship: 'its implicit virtues of order and restraint were also social values ... the tone of worship echoed certain secular values'. 'Indeed, the social manner of worship', he suggests, 'was more significant than the theological matter.' Primitive Methodism by contrast, boisterous in public, was at the same time a form of religion which gave direction to the inner religious life: 'a member was expected to have a spiritual career'.

Death, meanwhile, and the issue of holy dying, cut across denominational boundaries, as it did also across gender, age, and class ones. This, as we all know, was an age in which death was an obsessive presence, for the scene of the deathbed was most normally the home. The rituals and conventions of death in the family were at the core of the evangelical tradition. Obelkevitch studied a hundred obituaries of South Lindsey Primitive Methodists and found three major themes in the varied imagery of deathbed statements. These were triumph over affliction and temptation, joyous entry into heaven, and sheer exaltation.[34]

[32] Davidoff and Hall, *Family Fortunes*, pp. 114–15.
[33] Cited in ibid., p. 91.
[34] Obelkevitch, *Religion and Rural Society*, pp. 235–7.

But I want to take my main example here from an upper class family steeped in Anglican evangelism. Charlotte Bloomfield faced a lingering death in 1828, at the age of thirteen. Five years previously her father, Lord Bloomfield, had been appointed Minister Plenipotentiary at the court of King Charles XIII of Sweden. Aged almost sixty, he was called home, his memoirs record, 'to attend the deathbed of his dearly loved child'.[35] Charlotte's scrapbook, begun about two years previously and left unfinished with loose items ready for pasting, expresses the neatness and meticulous care of an aristocratic child reared in the conventional formulae of contemporary girlhood. A miniature, executed by the well-known portraitist Mrs Mee, shows a girl with small features and curly locks. Her elder sister, Georgiana, wrote an account of Charlotte's last days. What is striking about it is the way the women – mother, sister, nurse – managed and orchestrated the process of her death, seeking to make the leave-taking revelatory for both sides – Charlotte and her family – and suffusing it with piety and religious conviction. It was they, rather than the men, who displayed the emotional resourcefulness to match this crisis. Georgiana read and prayed with Charlotte each morning over the final period of two and a half weeks during which the doctor was visiting to apply poultices and blisters. The first Friday Charlotte 'spoke of the Rock of Ages to nurse'; the following Monday, Georgiana wrote, 'I gave her this text to think of at night: "my flesh and my heart faileth but God is the strength of my heart and my portion for ever"'; on the Thursday that week, she 'lay motionless all day' and on the Saturday 'knew nobody'. In what was to be her final week, she was tranquil on the Monday, 'kissed the hand of several of us' and 'certainly knew her Mama and testified her fondness'. When Lord Bloomfield visited her on the Wednesday 'she knew him, embraced him fondly and afterwards she attended to a prayer I said to her and kissed my hand'. On Thursday Charlotte enquired for her sister, 'Harriott . . . showed kindness to everyone . . . she understood several texts which at intervals were said to her.' She died peacefully on the Friday night, following a day on which she had bidden Georgiana 'say again a text she liked "Cast all thy care . . ."'. Other texts to which we are told she 'uniformly gave a smile' in her last days

---

[35] Georgiana Lady Bloomfield, ed., *Memoirs of Lord Bloomfield*, 2 vols (London, 1884), 1, p. 7.

included 'The Lord is very pitiful', and 'The Lord loveth whom he chasteneth.'[36]

Georgiana Bloomfield's memoir of her sister's last days is brief, episodic, and clearly intended only for the family's use. But there were mothers at this time who published memoirs of daughters who died young. In either case the motive and intention was recording for the sake of memory and example. The nineteenth century saw a huge output of spiritual writing by women, and only a small proportion of this appeared in print. Famous examples of women who published include Mary Sewell, whose text *Mother's Last Words* sold over a million copies, and Maria Charlesworth, wife of a Suffolk vicar, whose volume entitled *The Female Visitor to the Poor* offered a vision of a feminized paternalism in which the moral and religious vigour of a religious woman sustained the harmonious and hierarchical village community. It had become more acceptable than in the seventeenth century for women to publish their writings; and these, it has been suggested, 'provided a form of intervention for women at a time when other kinds of public speech were increasingly difficult'.[37] Yet the hundreds of commonplace books and private memoirs which remain in collections of family papers are probably much more typical of Victorian women's religious writings than the famous didactic texts. One of these is the commonplace book given in 1890 by Harriott Kingscote, the Harriott of Georgiana Bloomfield's narrative, to her niece Ethel Gore-Booth.

> Peace, perfect peace, in this dark world of sin?
> The blood of Jesus whispers peace within.
> Peace, perfect peace, by thronging duties pressed?
> To do the will of Jesus this is rest.

So run the first lines, transcribed from a contemporary poem, on the first page of the book. A mass of poetry and prose from Wordsworth, Longfellow, Rossetti, Browning, and Kipling follows, entered year by year by Ethel Gore-Booth, who remained a spinster throughout her life. The final entries are dated in the 1950s, shortly before her death.

---

[36] Papers relating to Charlotte Bloomfield in possession of the author. I am grateful to John Tosh for discussion of the issues raised by this material and to my mother, Delle Fletcher, for help with the Bloomfield family history.

[37] Davidoff and Hall, *Family Fortunes*, pp. 145–7.

Arguably this kind of material exemplifies what Victorian evangelism had fostered: an introverted female domestic piety, more passive than ecstatic or transcendent, emphasising Christian conviction, consolation, and endurance. Something fundamental has happened – there is a sense of a new world – between those fervent Stuart women discussed earlier and these equally but very different fervent Victorian ones. The story may be as much about changing attitudes to devotion in general as about changing conceptions of gender; but it is almost certainly not simply about one or the other.[38]

Let us return finally to the seventeenth century. The period of political upheaval between 1640 and 1660 saw the emergence of several women prophetesses as figures who gained national attention. The most important were Sarah Wight and Anna Trapnel. In his text *The Exceeding Riches of Grace Advanced*, which went through seven editions between 1647 and 1658, Henry Jessey told the story of the sixteen-year-old Sarah's period of ecstatic prophecy while bedridden. It ended, he related, after seventy-five days of fasting, with her sitting up, combing her hair, eating some boiled fish, and walking again. Jessey went through Sarah's outpourings and showed how they consisted of scriptually based passages, some of them close to the Hebrew or Greek of the original texts. She became an object of intense curiosity in the leading puritan circles of London in 1647, where the talk was all of whether she was mad, deluded, possessed by the devil, or inspired.

Seven years later, the visionary Anna Trapnel attracted a similar stream of visitors when she lay in her trance at Whitehall, offering prophesyings and predictive sayings at a time of acute political tension just after Oliver Cromwell had seized power as Lord Protector. Scribes around her took down every word they could gather.[39] The closest parallel in the eighteenth-century is Joanna Southcott, the most celebrated of a group of four women prophets who sought a national audience during the tense decade of the 1790s. The French Revolution had disrupted conventional political and moral orthodoxies and again created conditions in which a woman's millenarian spiritual claims might be taken seriously. Southcott, like Anna Trapnel 140 years

[38] Commonplace book of Ethel Gore-Booth, 1890–1965, in possession of the author.
[39] N. Smith, *Perfection Proclaimed: Language and Literature in English Radical Religion 1640–1660* (Oxford, 1989), pp. 45–53; Mack, *Visionary Women*, pp. 106–19; Crawford, *Women and Religion*, pp. 106–11; S. Hardman Moore, '"Such perfecting of praise out of the mouth of a babe": Sarah Wight as child prophet', *SCH*, 31 (1994), pp. 313–24.

before, spoke authoritatively about national events.[40] But the interesting difference is that whereas Trapnel proclaimed herself in entirely scriptural terms, Southcott's prophecies had a strong feminist bent to them. They abounded, Barbara Taylor has noted, 'in images of male villains and female defiance which aroused women to an anticipation of greater glory'.[41] Southcott articulated sexual antagonism, urging wives disappointed by marriage to find protection in the 'divine husband'. She could not have been more at odds with the doctrines of female passivity and submission which were by then dominant in both evangelical Anglican and Methodist circles.[42] So here from another angle we can see again how a sea-change in attitudes to gender separates the seventeenth century from the late eighteenth and nineteenth.

* * *

So what was happening between the 1660s and the 1820s? This has to be crucial to the overall argument. In the Quaker movement, between 1660 and 1700, women's leadership in the form of inspirational speech was checked and brought under control; in the Methodist movement after 1800 women's preaching was becoming unacceptable. This process of institutionalism was general and persistent. Radical evangelizing movements lost their impetus towards social transformation and became preoccupied with internal organization and with their own effectiveness.[43] While, in the late eighteenth century, the *Methodist Magazine* printed many biographies of female preachers, in the early nineteenth century these were replaced by accounts which extolled the homely virtues of clerical wives: women like Mrs Margaret Worrall, who, readers were told in 1820, excelled in 'domestic life . . . for which her mind was evidently focused'.[44]

The analysis advanced thus far can be summarized as follows. During the Interregnum women like Anna Trapnel, Mary Cary, and Katherine Chidley had defied gender, exploiting the construction at

---

[40] A. Clark, *The Struggle for the Breeches: Gender and the Making of the British Working Class* (London, 1995), pp. 109–11.
[41] B. Taylor, *Eve and the New Jerusalem: Socialism and Feminism in the Nineteenth Century* (New York, 1983), p. 164.
[42] J. K. Hopkins, *A Woman to Deliver her People: Joanna Southcott and English Millenarianism in an Era of Revolution* (Austin, TX, and London, 1982), pp. 77–86.
[43] Mack, *Visionary Women*, pp. 407–12; Crawford, *Women and Religion*, pp. 193–7.
[44] Cited in Clark, *The Struggle for the Breeches*, p. 98.

the heart of patriarchy of an emotional, intellectually empty, model of womanhood to their own ecstatic and visionary ends. Men could make sense of their prophetic careers in these terms, whereas Joanna Southcott's career no longer made any real sense in the 1790s. In so far as in the first years of Methodism women justified their preaching, they were merely stretching the constraints of gender by arguing that a few women's extraordinary gifts should not be denied. They could not defy patriarchy directly and comprehensively. The revision of patriarchy, carried out between the Restoration and the Victorian age, left women a confined religious space: in the home their place was a nurturing one at the centre of the household; beyond it they were confined to the village and neighbourhood where their traditional role as Lady Bountiful was preserved and enhanced. This, we may sense, could be an emotionally suffocating Christianity. Patricia Crawford has argued that a process of feminization of religion began between the Restoration and the mid-eighteenth century.[45] This, it may be suggested, went step-by-step with the development of the new polarization of gender roles and identities. Reason and faith were coming to stand in a more absolute relationship than previously to male and female. 'The natural softness of their dispositions along with the natural warmth of their imaginations', argued John Gregory in his best-selling conduct book *A Father's Legacy to his Daughter* of 1774, made women 'especially susceptible to feelings of devotion'.[46] There is a transformation here in the relationship between gender in English society and the practice of English Christianity, which requires much fuller investigation and unravelling.

University of Essex

---

[45] Crawford, *Women and Religion*, pp. 204–8.
[46] J. Gregory, *A Father's Legacy to his Daughters* (London, 1774), p. 10.

'WOMEN'S SPEAKING JUSTIFIED': WOMEN AND DISCIPLINE IN THE EARLY QUAKER MOVEMENT, 1652-56

by KATE PETERS

I N October 1655, two Quakers, Priscilla Cotton and Mary Cole, imprisoned in Exeter gaol, published a warning to the priests and people of England.[1] It was in many ways a typical Quaker tract, decrying the national Church of England, and urging people to turn to the inner light of Christ, rather than rely on the outward teachings of the national Church. But Priscilla Cotton and Mary Cole also levelled the following bitter accusation against England's ministry:

> thou tellest the people, Women must not speak in a Church, whereas it is not spoke onely of a Female, for we are all one both male and female in Christ Jesus, but it's weakness that is the woman by the Scriptures forbidden. . . . Indeed, you your selves are the women, that are forbidden to speak in the Church, that are become women.[2]

---

[1] I am grateful to Profs Patrick Collinson, Patricia Crawford, and Ann Hughes, all of whom have commented on drafts of this paper. Unless otherwise stated, all manuscript references are to material held at London, Friends' House Library.

[2] Priscilla Cotton and Mary Cole, *To the Priests and People of England, we Discharge our Consciences* (London, 1655), pp. 6-8. The London bookseller George Thomason dated his copy on 16 Oct. 1655. Many Quaker tracts were collected by Thomason, a bookseller and collector who literally bankrupted himself in an attempt to obtain a copy of everything published during the tumultuous years of the 1640s and 1650s. Beyond ensuring the survival of thousands of books from this period, the Thomason Collection is significant because he noted the date of acquisition on the title page of each tract he obtained. Thomason's dates are useful as an approximate guide to when tracts were published, or when they were in circulation in London. Where relevant, this essay will note Thomason's dating of the tracts under discussion. Details of his dating system, and of the history of the Thomason Collection as a whole, are given in the introduction in G. K. Fortescue, ed., *Catalogue of the Pamphlets, Books, Newspapers and Manuscripts relating to the Civil War, the Commonwealth, and Restoration, collected by George Thomason, 1640-1661*, 2 vols (London, 1908). For a more recent discussion of the Thomason Tracts, and especially the validity of using his dates, see Stephen J. Greenberg, 'Dating civil war pamphlets, 1641-1644', *Albion*, 20 (1988), pp. 387-401, and Michael Mendle, 'The Thomason Collection: a reply to Stephen J. Greenberg', *Albion*, 22 (1990), pp. 85-93.

This short Quaker tract may well have been sold and passed around the south west of England by Priscilla Cotton's husband, Arthur, who distributed other Quaker books in the area.[3] If so, he seems to have regretted it. The following year, Arthur Cotton wrote to the Quaker leader, George Fox, requesting more Quaker ministers for the two counties of Devon and Cornwall. His letter was unusually specific, asking Fox for preachers, 'which power and wisdom Guids', and then elaborating: 'and Rather men Friends For they doe nott Care to here any women Friends'.[4]

This paper is an examination of gender dynamics in the very early Quaker movement between the years 1652 and 1656, the first years for which we have any records of the movement, and a crucial period for its establishment as a national phenomenon. The kind of conflicts described in the opening cameo were an important dynamic in the development of the Quaker movement. Far from being a movement, as is often assumed, which was enabling of women like Priscilla Cotton and Mary Cole, it will be proposed that, from a very early date, leaders of the movement developed a series of ambiguous arguments about the status of women which served to legitimize and limit their presence in the Quaker movement. The attitudes of men like Arthur Cotton were central to the very early establishment of internal discipline and organizational structures. The perceived need to curb and control unruly women contributed in a very important way to the development of the movement's organization. This paper will argue that a doctrinal position on the spiritual equality of women, and on their fitness for public ministry, was very carefully presented in print; while at the same time practical, disciplinary strategies were developed for controlling the public role of women within the movement.

Quaker women have for a long time been a celebrated part of women's history. Hailed as 'Mothers of Feminism' and 'incipient feminists', they are remarkable for their public role in the developing Quaker movement.[5] Women preached and led meetings for worship;

---

[3] An example of this is in a letter from Arthur Cotton to George Fox, 20 Feb. 1656, Swarthmoor Transcript [hereafter Sw Tr] 1: 628. In 1664, one Nicholas Cole of Plymouth – probably a relative of Mary Cole – was named as a distributor of Quaker books. PRO, SP 29/109, fo. 44. I am grateful to Michael Frearson for this reference.

[4] Arthur Cotton to George Fox, 18 Nov. 1656, Sw Tr 1: 630.

[5] Margaret Hope Bacon, *Mothers of Feminism: the Story of Quaker Women in America* (San Francisco, CA, 1986); Christine Trevett, *Women and Quakerism in the Seventeenth Century* (York, 1991), p. 10.

they were prolific authors of published Quaker tracts; and they engaged audaciously in religious debate with ordained puritan ministers. In the seventeenth century, Quaker women preachers undertook itinerant preaching missions of staggering proportions; like the former servant, Mary Fisher, who travelled with Ann Austin to New England and Barbados, and later moved on to Turkey where she gained an interview with the Sultan.[6] The defiant public activity associated with Quaker women in the mid-seventeenth century has been described time and again by historians.

One of the reasons for this is that Quaker women are more accessible to historians than other women of the same period. Because of the unusually conscientious approach of early Quakers to recording their own history, we have access to autobiographies, spiritual testimonies, and printed tracts by early Quaker women. Accounts of their trials and imprisonments are recorded in Quaker books of sufferings; they wrote, and appear in, hundreds of Quaker letters still preserved at the Friends' House Library.[7]

The traditionally strong public role of Quaker women is reflected in their compelling presence in denominational histories. Mabel Brailsford wrote the first narrative history of seventeenth-century Quaker women in 1915, only four years after William Braithwaite's magisterial study of the beginnings of the movement as a whole.[8] In 1922, the first account of the social origins of early Quaker ministers included an analysis of the social status of women ministers; a subject which has not been attempted subsequently.[9] One woman in particular towers over the history of early Quakerism: Margaret Fell, the 'Mother of

---

[6] Phyllis Mack, *Visionary Women: Ecstatic Prophecy in Seventeenth-Century England* (Berkeley, CA, 1992), pp. 168–9.

[7] The role of women in recording Quaker history is in itself interesting, from Elizabeth Hooton and Margaret Fell keeping copies of their letters from 1652, to Emily Jermyn and Charlotte Fell Smith transcribing the Swarthmoor and Abram Barclay manuscripts in the nineteenth century. For Hooton's decision to keep copies of everything she wrote, see Thomas Aldam and Elizabeth Hooton to George Fox, Autumn 1652, A. R. Barclay Mss 1: 16, fo. 54.

[8] Mabel Brailsford, *Quaker Women* (London, 1915); W. C. Braithwaite, *The Beginnings of Quakerism* (London, 1911).

[9] Ernest E. Taylor, 'The first Publishers of Truth: a study', *JFHS*, 19 (1922), pp. 66–81. Compare with Barry Reay, 'The social origins of early Quakerism', *Journal of Interdisciplinary History*, 11 (1980), pp. 55–72; and also idem, 'Early Quaker activity and reactions to it, 1652–1664' (Oxford University D. Phil. thesis, 1979), pp. 37–8. Phyllis Mack argues that Quaker women from London tended to be of higher social status than those from the north of England: Mack, *Visionary Women*, pp. 186–96.

Quakerism', who ran the national headquarters of the movement from her home at Swarthmoor Hall, Lancashire, who organized national preaching missions, who helped to fund the movement, and who later lobbied hard for the setting up of separate women's meetings. Margaret Fell, never entirely forgotten by historians, has recently been revamped, and her latest biographer has reminded us of her central role in the developing Quaker movement.[10]

More recent studies of Quaker women reflect the expanding discipline of women's history. There is an increasing tendency to remove Quaker women from their immediate denominational context and to study them instead within the tradition of women's activism.[11] The roots of the Quaker movement lie in the turbulent years of the English revolution, in particular, in the atmosphere of increased religious toleration of the republican regimes of the 1650s. It is well known that women were active participants of many radical movements in the 1640s and 1650s. The sects and gathered churches which proliferated in the period provided a unique opportunity for women, and sometimes quite humble women, to play a significant public role.[12] Patricia Crawford's work on women's published writing shows a sharp rise in the number of women's publications, which addressed broad political and religious issues.[13] Patricia Higgins has examined women's petitions to parliaments and the political demonstrations mounted by women in London; and Phyllis Mack, Dorothy Ludlow, and Patricia Crawford have examined the activities of radical female sectaries.[14] This was the period of

---

[10] Isabel Ross, *Margaret Fell, Mother of Quakerism*, 2nd edn (York, 1984); Bonnelyn Young Kunze, *Margaret Fell and the Rise of Quakerism* (London, 1994). Margaret Fell is not the only early woman minister to have been the subject of a biography; see also E. Manners, *Elizabeth Hooton: First Quaker Woman Preacher (1600–1672)*, JFHS, Supplement series, 12 (London 1914); Lucy Hodgkin, *A Quaker Saint of Cornwall: Loveday Hambly and her Guests* (London, 1927).

[11] In 1991, Christine Trevett felt the need for a new feminist study on Quaker women in the seventeenth century, and, in her own words, wrote it, 'because no-one else had'. Trevett, *Women and Quakerism*, p. vii.

[12] This was famously argued by Keith Thomas nearly forty years ago in his seminal article, 'Women and the civil war sects', *P&P*, 13 (April, 1958), pp. 42–62. There has been an explosion in scholarship in this field over the past twenty years, much of it very usefully assimilated in Patricia Crawford, *Women and Religion in England, 1500–1720* (London, 1993), esp. pp. 119–82; eadem, 'The challenges to patriarchalism: how did the revolution affect women?', in John Morrill, ed., *Revolution and Restoration. England in the 1650s* (London, 1992), pp. 112–28.

[13] Patricia Crawford, 'Women's published writings, 1600–1700', in Mary Prior, ed., *Women in English Society, 1500–1800* (London, 1985), p. 269.

[14] Patricia Higgins, 'The reactions of women, with special reference to women

'the world turned upside down', 'when women preach and cobblers pray'.[15]

The activities of Quaker women have been integrated into this wider phenomenon of female activism in the English revolution; indeed, the extensive Quaker sources mean that Quaker women often form the mainstay of the argument that women were radical participants of the English revolution, threatening to 'shake patriarchy's foundations'. The numerous published writings of Quaker women have been singled out and studied by feminist literary critics as important examples of 'female' writing.[16] Most recently, Quaker women have been studied as examples of female spirituality and self-consciousness.[17]

Increasingly scholars argue that the public activities taken on by women in the revolutionary period ultimately reinforced rather than challenged patriarchal society.[18] Women justified and qualified their behaviour by affirming the inferiority of their sex, or claimed that their authority to act was based on spiritual, rather than actual worldly, equality with men.[19] They thus reinforced patriarchal assumptions that women, as women, should not behave in this way.

Discussions of female participation in the early Quaker movement also emphasise the spiritual impulse behind the women's extraordinary behaviour, and recognize it as equally limiting. Christine Trevett wrote

---

petitioners', in Brian Manning, ed., *Politics, Religion and the English Civil War* (London, 1973), pp. 179–222; Dorothy Ludlow, '"Arise and be doing": English preaching women, 1640–1660' (Indiana University Ph. D. thesis, 1978); eadem, 'Shaking patriarchy's foundations', in Richard L. Greaves, ed., *Triumph over Silence* (London, 1985); Phyllis Mack, 'Women as prophets during the English Civil War', *Feminist studies*, 8 (1982), pp. 19–45; Crawford, *Women and Religion in England*, chs 6–8.

[15] Anon., *Lucifers Lacky* (1641), sig. A3, cited in Michael Watts, *The Dissenters. From the Reformation to the French Revolution* (Oxford, 1985), p. 83.

[16] Elaine Hobby, *Virtue of Necessity: English Women's Writing 1649–88* (London, 1988); Margaret Ezell, 'Breaking the seventh seal: writings by early Quaker women', in her *Writing Women's Literary History* (Baltimore, MD, 1993), pp. 132–60; for a statistical analysis of Quaker women's writings within the context of other women's writing, see Crawford, 'Women's published writings, 1600–1700', pp. 265–74.

[17] Elaine C. Huber, '"A woman must not speak": Quaker women in the English left wing', in Rosemary Reuther and Eleanor McLaughlin, eds, *Women of Spirit: Female Leadership in the Jewish and Christian Traditions* (New York, 1979), pp. 154–81; the most substantial and authoritative study of this subject is Mack, *Visionary Women*.

[18] Patricia Crawford, echoing the question posed by Joan Kelly, 'Did women have a Renaissance?', wonders whether women in mid-seventeenth-century England had a revolution, and seems to think not: Crawford, *Women and Religion*, p. 5; see also eadem, 'The challenges to patriarchalism', pp. 112–28.

[19] Mack, 'Women as prophets', pp. 19–38.

in 1991: '[T]his was no brand of radical feminism which was being offered, revolutionary though it was in its way. . . . It was spiritual equality which was being held out to [Quaker women].'[20] Phyllis Mack, in a very important and extensive study, has argued that the ecstatic prophecy and public preaching of Quaker women was based on a negation of gender which was implicit to the whole of Quaker theology: both women and men in the Quaker movement insisted that they preached as 'disembodied spirits' in the Light of God, rejecting any worldly or carnal identity. At the same time, Mack argued that the non-spiritual, mundane existence of Quaker women was shaped by a celebration of women as 'nursing mothers of Israel'; and that the perception of them as providers and nurturers fed directly into the organizational and institutional developments in the Quaker movement as a whole.[21]

The focus on female religiosity or spirituality has had the effect of divorcing women from the immediate political context of the early Quaker movement. To some extent, non-denominational historians of Quaker women deny them agency in the development of Quaker ideas and fail to see them as active participants in the movement's growth. Recent works on Quaker women by Mack, Christine Trevett, and Elaine Huber all studied the 'Quaker doctrines' which shaped the women's spirituality as an established, immutable, and homogeneous mass. A major factor in the spiritual empowerment of women is seen to be George Fox himself. Christine Trevett was in no doubt that George Fox was the first Quaker proponent of women's preaching; Elaine Huber argued that George Fox should be credited for 'insisting on leadership roles for women'; Phyllis Mack wondered why Fox was 'so receptive to the authority of women'.[22]

Thus the argument is that Quaker women were at once empowered by the liberty they derived from their spirituality; and at the same time limited in the degree of female awakening this involved because the Quaker notion of spirituality was essentially ungendered: women had to stop being women in order to enter the public arena of the Quaker ministry.

---

[20] Trevett, *Women and Quakerism*, p. 52.
[21] Mack, *Visionary Women*, pp. 134, 236–61.
[22] Trevett, *Women and Quakerism*, pp. 13–14, 47–8; Huber, 'A woman must not speak', p. 160; Mack, *Visionary Women*, p. 240. Mabel Brailsford also devoted the whole first chapter of her book to the influence of the teachings of George Fox on the women of the Quaker movement: Brailsford, *Quaker Women*, ch. 1.

In this paper the issue is addressed somewhat differently. Rather than arguing that women were empowered in the Quaker movement by virtue of pre-existing, and implausibly enlightened, attitudes of leaders like George Fox, it examines the development of Quaker justifications for women's preaching as a dynamic feature of the early movement; and argues that the issue of women's preaching was incorporated into the nascent doctrines and disciplinary structures of the movement.

* * *

Those Quaker tracts which discussed the rights of women to preach constituted only a very small proportion of Quaker literature. Of the three hundred or so Quaker tracts printed between 1652 and 1656, only four addressed the issue at any length.[23] And although Quaker women were active ministers and remarkably prolific female authors of their time, none of them addressed the argument themselves. Despite this, the very existence of an argument in favour of women's preaching is rightly perceived as significant and has contributed to the view that the early Quaker movement was empowering of women.[24]

The argument over Quaker women's preaching has been dominated by the fact that the case was very famously propounded by Margaret Fell, in 1666. Fell's pamphlet, *Women's Speaking Justified, Proved and Allowed of by the Scriptures*, has attracted much attention from women's historians. An edition of it was reprinted in 1989. Moira Ferguson counted it a piece of feminist religious polemic. Isabel Ross, the Quaker biographer of Margaret Fell, hailed it as the first book to be written by a woman since the Reformation which argued for the spiritual equality of women.[25]

---

[23] The texts are: Richard Farnworth, *A Woman Forbidden to Speak in the Church* (London, 1654), reprinted in 1655; Ann Audland et al., *The Saints Testimony Finishing through Sufferings* (London, 1655); Priscilla Cotton and Mary Cole, *To the Priests and People of England* (London, 1655); George Fox, *A Woman Learning in Silence* (London, 1656).

[24] But note the important caveat that seventeenth-century texts about the role of women are frequently misread by historians: 'because they can so readily be situated in the context of gender politics, they are never fully situated in the political and discursive specificities of the early modern period'. Diane Purkiss, 'Material girls: the seventeenth-century woman debate', in Clare Brant and Diane Purkiss, eds, *Women, Texts and Histories 1575–1760* (London, 1992), p. 70.

[25] Margaret Fell, *Women's Speaking Justified, Proved and Allowed of by the Scriptures* (London, 1666, re-issued by Pythia Press, London, 1989); Moira Ferguson, ed., *First Feminists: British Women Writers 1578–1799* (Bloomington, IN, 1985), p. 114; Ross, *Margaret Fell*, p. 201.

It is problematic to equate Fell's work, written in 1666, with the emerging Quaker movement of the early 1650s. Margaret Fell was, by 1666, established as a major leader of the movement. Her wealth and social status were considerable: as wife and later widow of judge Thomas Fell, Margaret Fell oversaw a substantial farming estate and maintained her gentry status; after the Restoration she met Charles II to discuss religious toleration with him.[26] In 1669, she married George Fox, and together in the 1660s and 1670s it was their work which consolidated the Quaker movement into a respectable and disciplined Church. Fell's gentry status was very important in establishing the respectability of the Quakers, indeed on occasion more important than her gender as a significant counterweight to the perceived humble status of George Fox.[27] Fox and Fell collaborated over the establishment of separate women's meetings in the 1660s, in the face of serious internal opposition by other Quaker leaders; and both the Fox–Fell marriage, and the publication of *Women's Speaking Justified*, have been seen as part of the attempt to defend the meetings.[28] In this context, *Women's Speaking Justified* has been described as 'cautious' and lacking in the 'charm and wit' of other Quaker women's writing, and 'far more careful and conservative' than the actual preaching activities of women over the preceding decades.[29]

There are clear parallels between Fell's work and the handful of texts which actually posited the right of women to preach in the 1650s. In many ways Fell's work of 1666 was an expansion of these texts, and can be seen, like them, as part of an attempt by the Quaker leadership to normalize and legitimize the potentially disruptive public preaching of women in the Quaker movement.

The first Quaker pamphlet which posited the right of women to speak was written by a leading Quaker author, Richard Farnworth. It was circulating in London in the first half of January 1654, and so was probably written around the end of 1653; by all accounts, it can be

---

[26] Young Kunze, *Margaret Fell*, pp. 65–82, esp. pp. 78–9. Thomas Fell died in 1658.

[27] Bonnelyn Young Kunze, 'Religious authority and social status in seventeenth-century England: the friendship of Margaret Fell, George Fox, and William Penn', *ChH*, 57 (1988), pp. 170–86.

[28] Young Kunze, *Margaret Fell*, pp. 154–5.

[29] Trevett, *Women and Quakerism*, p. 54; Hobby, *Virtue of Necessity*, p. 45. Elaine Hobby is also quite correctly at pains to make mention of the earlier visionary Quaker works which vindicated women's preaching in far more extravagant terms before the Quaker 'official stance on the subject became ever more guarded' (ibid., p. 45).

considered a significantly early Quaker tract.[30] It was called, rather perversely, *A Woman Forbidden to Speak in the Church*, but despite the title was a case well argued from scriptural texts. Indeed, Farnworth rather modishly took on race, class, and gender on the frontispiece, quoting from Galatians 3.28: 'There is neither Jew nor Greek, there is neither bond nor free, there is neither male nor female, for ye are all one in Christ Jesus.' The point of the tract was to counter the argument from the Pauline edicts that a woman should not speak in the church; and that she should learn from her husband in silence and all subjection.[31] The central justification used by Farnworth for women's public speaking came from the book of Joel: 'And it shall come to pass, in the last dayes, saith the Lord, I will pour out my Spirit upon all Flesh; your Sons and Daughters shall prophesy.'[32]

Farnworth began his tract by considering the term 'church'. For him, it was not a physical or 'carnal' building, but 'is made all of living stones, elect and precious, [1 *Pet.* 2. 5.] and the Saints, their Bodyes are made fit Temples for the Holy Ghost to dwell in [2 *Cor* 6.16.]'.[33] By defining a church as the people who comprise its congregation, it would be more acceptable that women should be allowed to speak 'in the church': it established that women spoke first and foremost as spiritual beings.

From this, Farnworth very rapidly went on to dismiss gender as a significant criterion in determining who should be allowed to speak in the 'church':

> that which is flesh is flesh, and that knoweth not the things of God, neither in male nor female, but is adulterated from God, but that which is spirit is spirit, and is born of God, either in male or female, that knoweth him, and that is permitted to speak in the Temple.[34]

Farnworth also cited examples of female prophets from the Bible to show that women were likely to serve well as messengers of the holy spirit. Paul 'writ to the Romans to receive Phebe, which was a Servant

---

[30] The stationer George Thomason obtained a copy on 18 Jan. 1654.
[31] Cf. I Cor. 14.34; I Tim. 2.11.
[32] Cf. Joel 2.28; and also Acts 2.17–18.
[33] Farnworth, *A Woman Forbidden to Speak*, p. 2.
[34] Ibid., p. 3.

or Minister to the Church at Conchrea'; he had likewise commended Priscilla and Aquila; and also Mary 'who bestowed much labor on us'. Farnworth paid particular attention to Tryphena and Tryphos, 'delicious or delicate, two godly women, and beloved of the Lord, who laboured with Paul in the Gospel'.[35] Farnworth gathered all of his examples of female ministry from Romans 16, and so did not over-exert himself in his case study. His broader discussion conflated an attack on worldly wisdom and professional ministry with a justification of female ministry, arguing that spiritual integrity superseded gender: 'Let all carnal Wisdome in Male as well as in Female keep silence, for that is not permited [sic] to speak, it is adulterated from God; and the natural man knowes not the things of God.' From this, it was a short step to arguing that women's weaker natural state lent itself to their greater receptivity to God:

> all the Wisdom of the world it knoweth not God, who is a Spirit, and he chuseth the weak things of this world to confound the things which are mighty, I *Cor.* 1.27.28.29. and the Woman is counted the weaker Vessel, but the Lord is filling that Vessel full of his Wisdom, and ruleing it by his holy Spirit he dwelling in his Temple.[36]

Farnworth's argument appeared more pragmatic at the end of his tract when he finally returned rather neatly to his original dichotomy of the carnal and spiritual definition of the Church. He now provided – again referring to two biblical female prophets – a much more immediate and recognizable justification for the necessity of women to speak in the church, and one which referred to the actual nature of early Quaker worship:

> But to *Aquila* and *Priscilla* salute me, and to *the Church that is in their house*, I *Cor.*16.19, and let her speak by the Spirit of the Lord the things of God made manifest unto her, for if she be not permitted to speak in the Church, and the Church be in her house, she must not speak, but go out of her house.[37]

---

[35] Farnworth, *A Woman Forbidden to Speak*, p. 7. Compare with Romans 16.
[36] Ibid., p. 4.
[37] Ibid., p. 8.

Farnworth's conclusion was based on the fact that women held an important role in the early movement, of hosting meetings in their houses. The first pamphlet expounding the Quaker doctrine of 'allowing women to speak' was based on ideas of the spiritual equality of women and men, but also responded to a need to legitimize the existing functions carried out by Quaker women.

Farnworth's pamphlet was reprinted the following year, in 1655. In 1656 George Fox also published a tract which discussed the rights of women to speak. Like Farnworth's, this carried the similarly perverse title, *The Woman Learning in Silence*; and Fox spent his first page citing almost verbatim from the Pauline edict forbidding women to speak without apparently contradicting it.[38] Yet once under way, Fox's pamphlet reiterated the arguments of spiritual equality, scriptural precedent, and the fact that true preaching from the spirit essentially denied any worldly identity, as first expounded by Farnworth to justify women's preaching.

The intellectual presentation of spiritual equality in the Quakers' published writings was based, as Mack argued, on a negation of 'worldly' gender; the right of women to prophesy did not empower women, as women, with any worldly agency. These two tracts, placed in the context of other contemporary Quaker writings, contributed to the construction of a wider argument that placed other limitations on women.

Earlier, in April 1653, Richard Farnworth had written another tract which dealt more practically with the position of women in the Quaker movement. This tract, entitled *An Easter Reckoning*, contained a section called 'The Lords free love-offering to his own people', or 'How everyone is bound in duty to be in subjection to the Lord, and to walk in obedience to his commands'.[39] This outlined the proper social relations between God's own people in a godly commonwealth, beginning with children's 'dues or duty' to parents, servants' duties to their masters, magistrates' duties to God, and ending with instructions to alehouse keepers and warnings to 'whoremongers and adulterers'.[40] Under the heading 'Wives dues or duty to their husbands', Farnworth exhorted:

---

[38] Fox, *Woman Learning in Silence*.
[39] Richard Farnworth [and Thomas Aldam], *An Easter Reckoning* (London, 1653), sig. A1r.
[40] Ibid., pp. 17–20.

Wives, be in subjection to your own husbands, and love them in the Lord, walking in obedience to his commands, and be not angry, nor proud, nor stubborn, nor cross, nor hasty, nor peevish, nor perverse, do not scold, nor braul, nor lye, nor swear, for God doth forbid it; but be loving, and meek, gentle, and lowly minded, and be in subjection to the Lord, and live in love one with another; let not the woman usurpe authority over the man, but be in subjection, as Sarah was, who obeyed Abraham, and called him Lord; and be chast, and sober minded, and stay at home, and waite upon the Lord, and give glory to his name, in yeelding obedience to his commands, that he may be honoured and glorified for ever.[41]

To husbands, Farnworth was rather less exacting in his recommendations: 'Husbands, love your wives, as Christ loved his Church, and gave himself for it, and be loving and gentle to them, according to the command of the Lord.'[42]

An Easter Reckoning is an astounding tract because it appeared so early in the history of the Quaker movement, and yet established rules for the maintaining of Quaker discipline. It is clear from private correspondence that Farnworth and other Quaker leaders frequently circulated letters to be read at the local meetings which were springing up across the north of England. These similarly amount to a sort of early Quaker church discipline; yet for two reasons Farnworth's printed tract is more remarkable. First, the private manuscript exhortations between early Quakers more frequently related to forms of worship, urging friends not to lose their faith, and to meet often together for worship. Farnworth's printed tract, which was strongly reminiscent of the more common Christian conduct books, was concerned with real issues of social hierarchies and patriarchal control.[43] Secondly, Farnworth's tract was intended for a wider audience than isolated Quaker meetings. At least one hostile reader encountered the tract, for he referred to it in a printed work of his own attacking the Quakers; and we can be certain that other readers outside

---

[41] Richard Farnworth [and Thomas Aldam], *An Easter Reckoning*, pp. 18–19. Cf. Eph. 5.21, Col. 3.18–25, 4.1.

[42] Farnworth, *An Easter Reckoning*, p. 19.

[43] For a discussion of the genesis of the wider, but very similar 'protestant family', see Patrick Collinson, *The Birthpangs of Protestant England* (London, 1988), pp. 60–93.

the Quaker movement would have seen the tract.[44] *An Easter Reckoning* was a very early statement of Quaker conduct, intended to publicize Quaker doctrines to an audience who would undoubtedly be hostile, and in particular hostile to the predominance of unruly, outspoken women in the Quaker movement.

If the link between *An Easter Reckoning* and Farnworth's later publication of *A Woman Forbidden to Speak* seems tenuous, George Fox made it abundantly clear. In his own tract, *The Woman Learning in Silence*, he abandoned on page two his account of the wonders worked by women prophets in the Bible, to expound boldly on seventeenth-century patriarchy:

> Husbands love your Wives, and be not bitter against them. Wives submit your selves first to your Husbands as unto the Lord: The Husband is the head of the Wife, even as Christ is the head of the church, and is the Saviour of the body: Therefore as the church is subject to Christ, so let the Wives be subject to their own Husbands in everything. Husbands love your Wives, even as Christ loved the church, and gave himself for it, that he might sanctifie and cleanse it by the washing of water by the Word, that he might present it a glorious church, without spot or wrinckle, or any such thing, that it should be holy without blemish.[45]

In Fox's view, then, Quaker women, like all wives, were to be cleansed, and sanctified. They were to have their spots, wrinkles, and blemishes removed. There were thus very clear limitations to his 'receptivity of their authority'; and he stated them in the very tract in which he justifies their role as prophets.

The other printed Quaker tract of the early 1650s which defended women's public speaking affords a greater insight still into the influence of Quaker men in propounding the argument for the right of women to preach. Because it was written jointly by men and women, and described a series of events at a Quaker trial, it provides evidence of the very different attitudes of men and women in the Quaker movement to the activities of women, and to the perceived need to justify them to a hostile public.

---

[44] Luke Fawne *et al.*, *A Second Beacon Fired* (London, 1654).
[45] Fox, *Woman Learning in Silence*, p. 2. Cf. Eph. 5.25–7.

The tract, called *The Saints Testimony Finishing Through Sufferings*, was written by a group of Quaker prisoners at Banbury in 1655. Usually authorship is ascribed to the Quaker Ann Audland, although in fact many Quakers contributed to it.[46] The tight chronology leading up to the publication of the tract is important.

Ann Audland was wife of John Audland (*c.* 1630–64), a yeoman from Westmorland, who had served in the army in the Civil War, and had been a preacher to a group of Seekers since 1650.[47] Ann Audland herself, born in Kendal in 1627, had been educated for a time in London where she made contact with gathered churches, before returning to Kendal and the Preston Patrick Seekers, and marrying John Audland in 1650.[48] In September 1654, John Audland and his travelling companion John Camm travelled from London to Bristol on a Quaker preaching mission, passing through Banbury and Oxford. Once they arrived in Bristol they sent a letter to their wives in the north, Ann and Mabel, asking them to undertake a preaching mission to Banbury.[49] Ann Audland, leaving her young child behind at Kendal, travelled to Banbury with Mabel Camm and Mabel Camm's servant, Jane Waugh, arriving there on 13 January 1655; shortly afterwards, Ann Audland and Jane Waugh were imprisoned for assaulting the local minister and using 'blasphemous words'.[50] Ann Audland took issue with the grounds of her imprisonment, which she argued were unlawful; and on 5 February 1655 she explained why in her first tract, written in prison, and called *A True Declaration of the Suffering of the Innocent*. It was published in London and in circulation by early March.[51]

The recording of Quaker sufferings and trials in print was already an established genre of Quaker writing. Ann Audland would in all

<hr/>

[46] Audland, *The Saints Testimony*.

[47] For John Audland, see Richard Greaves and Robert Zaller, eds, *Biographical Dictionary of British Radicals in the Seventeenth Century*, 3 vols (Brighton, 1982–4), I.

[48] *DNB*; Dictionary of Quaker Biography (typescript index available at Friends' House Library, London).

[49] I infer this from a letter by John Audland and John Camm to Edward Burrough and Francis Howgill, 13 Sept. 1654, A. R. Barclay Mss 2: 157; see also 'The Journal of John Audland', in 'Letters of John Audland, 1653', Sw[arthmoor] Mss Box P2/15, pp. 32–4.

[50] Braithwaite, *Beginnings of Quakerism*, p. 199. Ann Audland requested of Burrough and Howgill: 'Let mee heare how the childe at Kendall doth' in a letter from Banbury. Ann Audland to Edward Burrough and Francis Howgill, [?6 April 1655], A. R. Barclay Mss 2: 175.

[51] Ann Audland, *A True Declaration of the Suffering of the Innocent* (London, 1655). George Thomason obtained a copy on 3 March 1655.

probability have seen many similar accounts, and was evidently confident of her purpose in writing: 'This', she explained to the local Justice of the Peace, 'was I moved to write to clear my conscience of thee, and leave thee without excuse, that when the Book of Conscience is opened, thou mayest remember that thou wast warned in thy lifetime.'[52]

Ann Audland made little reference to her sex in her first tract, of which she was the sole author, concentrating instead on the legal injustices wrought upon her, and by extension upon the nation. She subsumed her female identity as author under that of her identity as a Quaker, as did her male colleagues: the frontispiece stated that it was written: 'By *Anne Audland*, whom the world scornfully calls QUAKER'. The word Quaker appeared in large capitals on a single line, the largest word on the page.

Here we see the practical implications of the doctrine that it was through the spirit rather than the flesh that men and women were to prophesy. By emphasising that she was known to 'the world' as a Quaker, she was implying that she had another spiritual identity, which remained hidden from those who knew no better. The similarities with her male co-religionists must be stressed: the stylistic affectation of insisting in Quaker publications that they were known only 'to the world' as Quakers, or by their proper names, was by now widespread and an integral part of the Quakers' printed identity, which stressed the spiritual above the worldly. Ann Audland was perhaps more explicit than her male contemporaries in her use of this device in conjunction with reference to her gender, as the frontispiece also sported the citation from Acts 2.18: 'And on my servants and on my handmaidens, I will poure out in those dayes of my Spirit, and they shall prophesie.'

Inside the tract, she also stated that Christ 'is one in the male and in the female'.[53] Beyond referring to these biblical texts, however, Ann Audland developed the argument no further. If we can consider the brief reference to these texts as a justification for her behaviour as a woman, it was based on the negation of the significance of her gender, rather than on an attempt to qualify or normalize it.

Perhaps as a result of Ann Audland's alacrity in publishing an account of her sufferings, and also because of the very sophisticated

---

[52] Ibid., p. 2.
[53] Ibid., p. 5.

news network of Quaker correspondence, events at Banbury rapidly became a focal point for other Quaker missionaries.[54] A number of Quaker ministers, including Richard Farnworth and Robert Rich, as well as more women (Sarah Tims and Margaret Vivers), came to Banbury from Bristol, Gloucestershire, Berkshire, and elsewhere; and over the course of the summer of 1655 each was imprisoned in turn.[55] An account of their imprisonments and trial at Banbury Quarter Sessions in September 1655 was published in November. It was this jointly authored work, *The Saints Testimony Finishing Through Sufferings*, which proffered a further justification of women's public speaking. In this tract, indeed, a far more vivid picture was painted of the role played by women in the Quaker movement. The justification for women's preaching was juxtaposed to dramatic accounts of women's public activities in the movement. The account of the trial was clearly intended to demonstrate that public hostility to the Quakers was born out of an hostility to women: when Sarah Tims was called to the bar, apparently well versed in Quaker legal tactics:

> she desired to know by what Law they committed her; and one *Iohn Austine*, called Mayor, answered, *that sweeping the house, and washing the dishes was the first point of law to her* (or words to that effect) so sent her back again to the Prison, she not being charged with any breach of the Law.[56]

Margaret Vivers posed more of a problem to the court, and it was

> confessed that they had *Margaret Vivers* (who had spoken to the Priest in the *Steeplehouse* . . .) there, neither for whoredome, felony, nor theft, . . . yet it was the Mayors mind that she should be there, but whether she had committed any offence or no, they

---

[54] News of Ann Audland reached Kendal and thence Margaret Fell: Thomas Willan to Fell, 10 May 1655, Sw Mss 1: 235, 247. John Audland sent news of his wife to Edward Burrough and Francis Howgill in London: A. R. Barclay Mss 1: 116, 2: 175. Audland also informed John Wilkinson and John Storey of the prisoners in Banbury just as they were about to set off for London from Wiltshire in early April: John Audland to John Storey and Wilkinson, 1 April 1655, A. R. Barclay Mss 1: 28.

[55] Audland, *The Saints Testimony*, p. 2. See also John Audland to Margaret Fell, 1 Oct. 1655, Sw Mss 1: 391, who noted that Bristol heavyweights Captain Edward Pyott, Dennis Hollister, Thomas Gouldney, Walter Clement, John Camm, and Robert Rich had gone to Banbury for the assizes.

[56] Audland, *The Saints Testimony*, mispaginated, sig. Bv.

could not tel. . . . [T]he man that had kept her in custody, did object against a woman speaking in the church; it was asked whether the Spirit of God might not be permitted to speak in the Temple of God, yea or nay; the which by some was answered and granted that it might.[57]

At this point in the tract, the account of the trial was suspended, and there duly followed the familiar section proving the spiritual equality of men and women, and the biblical precedent for women prophets.[58] It is only later in the tract, when Richard Farnworth's trial is recorded, that it becomes clear that it was he who spoke in court on the right of women to prophesy:

there was a few words spoken concerning the Objection of the womans non-permission, . . . and when it was asked them on the Bench, if the Spirit of God might not speak in the Temple, they were then put to a stand, or partly silent about the same; and *R.F.* then and there said, if any of them would deny it, he would by plain Scripture prove that the Spirit of God might speak in his Temple (meaning either in the body of male or female).[59]

The presence of so many women in court had clearly raised the hackles of the authorities. The presentation of the trial in the Quakers' published account stressed the unsympathetic and unreasonable response of the prosecuting authorities: the women, like other Quaker prisoners, were not being tried under any law, and the justices' recourse to insulting the women was presented as petulant buffoonery. Even Farnworth's reasoned attempt to prove the legitimacy of his female colleagues' preaching was contrasted, in the tract, with the boorish inadequacy of the authorities' response:

when R.F. was there speaking about the Saints bodies being the Temples for God to dwel in . . . *Iohn Austine*, who is called a Justice, [said], if God did dwel in them, . . . where was his legs,

[57] Ibid., pp. 14–15.
[58] Ibid., pp. 15–16.
[59] Ibid., p. 24.

&c. for the which *William Allen*, called a Justice, gave a secret check, seeming to be troubled thereat.[60]

The presentation of the authorities as both crass and ridiculous made Farnworth's justification of his female colleagues easier. On one level, which must not be discounted, he was defending his silenced fellow prisoners' right to speak publicly, reiterating the by now well-rehearsed argument for spiritual equality.[61] But on another level, the tract was attempting to normalize the unusual public activities of the Quaker women. The exchange on the subject of the 'Women's non-permission' took place, in the published account of the trial, between men. It presented the women as fundamentally wronged by the justices, and thus suggested that they deserved to be defended. And, finally, the printed account of the trial with its justification of women's preaching, appeared in the wake of a highly charged public trial at which several women were present. Farnworth was already concerned with the public presentation of the position of women in the Quaker movement, as has been seen not only in *A Woman Forbidden to Speak*, but also when he had set out 'The wives dues or duty to their husbands' in 1653. In this context, his public defence of their behaviour in court can be understood as an attempt to defuse public criticism of unruly Quaker women.

* * *

If we turn to evidence beyond the published arguments defining or justifying women's right to speak in public, it is clear that women played a very important part in the early Quaker ministry. Whatever the problems of historians in explaining their active participation in the movement, it is nevertheless irrefutable that women were an accepted and even pre-existing component of the membership. The leaders of the movement, however, increasingly saw them as problematic and felt the need to constrain their behaviour; and the very first aspects of internal Quaker organization grew out of a need to curb their behaviour and enforce discipline on the movement.

---

[60] Audland, *The Saints Testimony*.

[61] The Quaker doctrine of spiritual equality was by now being discussed in Quaker meetings in Edinburgh. The puritan minister of Terling, John Stalham, who had visited Edinburgh in March 1655, was sufficiently well versed in the argument to be able to relay it in his tract, *Contradictions of the Quakers* (Edinburgh, 1655), p. 7.

Internal correspondence between Quakers describes an early movement in which women were active and accepted participants. The
itinerant Quaker minister Thomas Taylor wrote to George Fox from
Leicestershire in 1655, describing how he had met up on his travels
with the Yorkshire Quaker, Margaret Killam, who had been holding a
meeting at Swannington, and how they 'walked downe in the morning
to Nun Eaton to see frends and there is a pretty convincement upon
some women there, and a young man or two, but none come forth but
shee that was formerly'.[62]

Recruiting in this case, then, came largely from women. As
interesting as this was the apparent acceptance with which Thomas
Taylor viewed Margaret Killam's missionary work: 'But at Nun Eaton
we stayed not long [he explained], for shee M:K: was to be next day . . .
at Barrow at a meeting.'[63] This attitude was very common. Women
were very often described on the road, travelling from town to town,
arranging meetings, and sending news and greetings to their fellow
missionaries.

This kind of acceptance occasionally extended to a clear welcoming
of women. Francis Howgill spoke of an important conversion in
Ireland of

> the most emenent house in the towne and they are of the treue
> seed. She was a baptiste and they Cast her out for heresy . . ., a
> nouble woman she is, she declare agaynst the prest in publicke
> and was moved to declare agaynest the baptists and one day the
> markett day toke a load of Bookes of the highest prestes in the
> nation and burned them In the street, and these things are a good
> smell.[64]

William Dewsbery, writing to Margaret Fell with news that the
servant turned minister, Mary Fisher, had reached Barbados, in
addition related that 'Justice Crook's wife is prichous in her Measur
and many of the handmads of the lord is very betyfull in the power of
our god; who is Carying on his work all over.'[65]

---

[62] Thomas Taylor to George Fox, Lichfield, 16 March 1655, Sw Mss 3: 30.
[63] Ibid.
[64] Francis Howgill to Margaret Fell, c. Jan. 1656, A. R. Barclay Mss 1: 65, fo. 192.
[65] William Dewsbery to Margaret Fell, 15 Oct. 1655, Sw Mss 4: 141. Mack, *Visionary
Women*, pp. 168–70.

A very good reason for the acceptance by Quaker men of the participation of women in the movement is that they were already there. The term 'Quaker', it is often asserted, was first used with reference to a group of women in Southwark in 1647, who were reported to 'swell, shiver and shake'.[66] The rapid growth of the Quaker movement was achieved essentially by the linking up from around 1652 of established groups of radical sectarians and Seekers, whose ideas already reflected more or less the newly publicized Quaker beliefs. Among these were groups of women sectaries. An early centre in London to which northern Quakers first travelled was a meeting at the house of Simon Dring in Moorfields, where there was 'none but two women' who were preachers; and the link with them was probably the northern woman Isabel Buttery (a friend of James Nayler and other northern missionaries), who distributed some of the first Quaker tracts in London.[67]

This female network may well have extended beyond the Quaker movement.[68] In 1654 the prophet and Fifth Monarchist Anna Trapnel published an account of her journey from London to Cornwall. Women featured heavily in the account. Before she left, Anna Trapnel conferred with her 'sisters' about the necessity of her going; on the way, she dined at an 'old disciples house' in Exeter, belonging to widow Winters, who frequently entertained travelling 'saints'. Trapnel also stayed with the former Barebones M.P. Colonel Robert Bennett in Devon, and his wife and daughters travelled on with her for part of her journey, as far as the house belonging (as she described it) to the sister of Captain Langdon. She stayed, indeed, in a number of households where the women featured heavily. Upon her arrest and return to Bridewell in London, she described once again how her 'sisters' visited and stayed with her in prison.[69] The encountering of so many women, on a journey which was apparently spontaneous and ordered by the will of God, is in itself interesting. Two years later, however, two Quaker women from Bristol, Sarah Bennett and Mary Prince, travelled to Cornwall, passing through Devon and staying, apparently, in the same places. They too stopped off to see Colonel Bennett and his wife,

---

[66] Oxford, Bodleian Library, Clarendon State Papers 2624, MSS Clarendon vol. 30, fo. 140r.

[67] Alexander Delamain to Thomas Willan, 1654, Sw Mss 3: 93.

[68] Mack, *Visionary Women*, pp. 146–7.

[69] Anna Trapnel, *Anna Trapnel's Report and Plea* (London, 1654).

and expected to find Anna Trapnel there. On their confrontation with Colonel Bennett, Mary Prince described how 'love rose in him and he owned my words to be true and was brought tender', and they left some of their books with him. The two women had less success with Mrs Bennett, who listened, they reported, to 'all that was saide but theare is A hie sperite in her', which they attributed to the enduring influence of Anna Trapnel.[70] What is nonetheless clear is that there were known households which the itinerant godly of the 1650s would visit; that the women in these households were important targets; and that other women knew about them. It is out of exactly this milieu that the Quaker movement grew: it needs to be restated that women were a central part of this network.

More evidence of a sense of solidarity between Quaker women comes from their own correspondence. Letters between women typically salute exclusively women: the barely literate Sarah Bennett sent greetings in a letter to Margaret Fell and her daughters, to John Camm's wife, and to Ann Audland.[71] She had probably met Ann Audland at her trial in Banbury, and Mabel Camm and the daughters of Margaret Fell when they had travelled to Bristol; but it is highly unlikely that she had met Margaret Fell herself, whose name and reputation had clearly permeated south.[72] The significance of Margaret Fell, indeed, cannot be overstated as a clear inspiration to women ministers.[73] Ann Audland wrote to Margaret Fell: 'Blessed art thou amongst all women the standard of righteousness.'[74] Ann Dewsbery, a woman we hear little of otherwise, although her husband, William, was an active Quaker missionary, wrote in rapture to Margaret Fell after meeting her for the first time: 'blesed be the time that ever I saw thy face'. At the end of her letter, she gave news of her husband and explained, 'but I did not aquant him that I was to writ to you'.[75] Quaker women ministers

---

[70] Mary Prince and Sarah Bennett to George Fox, [June, 1656], Sw Mss 3: 116.

[71] Sarah Bennett to Margaret Fell, Bristol [1656], Sw Mss 4: 71.

[72] Margaret Fell's daughters Margaret and Sarah were in Bristol in June or July 1655: John Audland to Edward Burrough and Francis Howgill, 2 July 1655, A. R. Barclay Mss 1: 58.

[73] Phyllis Mack makes the important point that men also wrote to Margaret Fell, the main recipient of Quaker correspondence, in equally enthusiastic terms. This does not deny the fact that Quaker women ministers had a unique role model in Margaret Fell. Mack, *Visionary Women*, pp. 153–4.

[74] Ann Audland to Margaret Fell, [1655], Sw Mss 1: 22; cf. Luke 1.28.

[75] Ann Dewsbery to Margaret Fell, 1 March 1656, Sw Mss 4: 142.

corresponded autonomously with each other; and openly encouraged and inspired one another.

The organization of the early movement also supported women in very practical ways: again, the role of Fell is crucial. In 1654 Margaret Fell initiated the setting up of the central Quaker fund at Kendal, into which local groups from the northwest of England made donations of money. The Kendal Fund is central to the history of the early movement: it financed the itinerant ministry and Quaker publications, covering the cost of shoes and travelling cloaks, horses, books, and postage.[76] The accounts of money disbursed from the Kendal Fund also show a number of women receiving money for journeys and clothes. Ann Dixon from Grayrigg was given 10s. in April 1655 for going to London 'or into the south parts as moved', and thus was not only free to travel independently, but was clearly expected to travel where and how she wanted.[77] The Yorkshire minister Barbara Pattison, imprisoned in Plymouth gaol where she published a tract with Margaret Killan, received £1 5s. for clothes and 'other nessessaries'; in December 1654, Alice Birkett received 2s. 6d. for a pair of shoes, and 3s. for going to hear a Quaker trial at the Quarter Sessions in Cheshire.[78]

The existence of the Fund emboldened women. Rebecca Ward borrowed 20s. from the Quaker William Gandie of Frandley, Cheshire, and, when her father refused to pay him back, she arranged for William Gandie to be paid from the Kendal Fund. She also asked for some money to be given to her father, who 'was much burthened with friends passing upp and down', relying on his Welsh hospitality as they waited for a crossing to Ireland.[79] The servant Dorothy Waugh took off on a journey with Agnes Wilson which aroused the indignation of the keepers of the Fund, for she 'never Accquainted us of her Jorney and hath taken six or seven shillings of a friend and Bidd him tell us of it'.[80]

---

[76] For a more detailed account of the Kendal Fund and its significance, see M. Kate Peters, 'Quaker pamphleteering and the development of the Quaker movement, 1652–1656' (University of Cambridge Ph. D. thesis, 1996), pp. 92–6.

[77] George Taylor to Margaret Fell, Sw Mss 1: 215.

[78] George Taylor and Thomas Willan to Margaret Fell, [1655], Sw Tr 3: 543; Margaret Killin and Barbara Pattison, A Warning from the Lord to the Teachers and People of Plymouth (London, 1656). George Thomason dated his copy 29 Dec. 1655; George Taylor to Margaret Fell, 1654, Sw Mss 1: 215.

[79] George Taylor and Thomas Willan to Margaret Fell, [1655], Sw Mss 1: 238.

[80] Ibid. They found this particularly galling as Agnes Wilson had already been given 3s. for the journey, which they clearly considered adequate funding.

The accounts of the Kendal Fund are very revealing about the public activities of women in the Quaker movement. That money was given to women as well as to men underlines the acceptance of women's ministry within the movement, but also, more importantly, provides very real evidence as to how these women were given (and were sometimes bold enough to borrow in advance) the means to travel about the country.

In many ways, then, the organization of the early Quaker movement was very accommodating of women. Yet despite the expectation by men that women would act as preachers, there was frequently a sense, hinted at in the published account of the Banbury trial, that their presence was also fraught with difficulties. Much of the wariness of Quaker men, as has been seen in the printed tracts on the position of women, stemmed from the fear that women provided an easy target for public ridicule of the movement.

* * *

London's gutter-press equated the presence of women in the Quaker movement with suggestions of sexual depravity. A few weeks after the Quakers established a permanent presence in the capital, a quasi-Royalist journal, *Mercurius Fumigosus, or, The Smoking Nocturnal*, carried a titillating report in October 1654 about

> divers Erroneous Teachers, called *Quakers* that every day seek to delude *young Maides*, to innoculate their *spirits* into them, and make them young gods and Goddesses; no less than four they deverted not long since, *Who were so holy, they could know no sin, Yet quickly after became quick within.*[81]

One of the earliest serious puritan attacks on Quaker principles was that they held the doctrine 'of community in worldly things', which some of them '(did they speak out) extend to break marriage bonds'.[82] More specific still was the accusation that George Fox had seduced Margaret Fell and a number of other women, using a potent mixture of sexual charm, ribbons, and (it was hinted) witchcraft to attract women to him. Accusations such as these were rapidly and publicly

[81] *Mercurius Fumigosus, or, The Smoking Nocturnal*, 18–25 Oct. 1654, p. 186.
[82] Joseph Kellett *et al.*, *A Faithful Discovery of a Treacherous Design* (London, 1653), p. 42.

denounced by leaders of the Quaker movement, most dramatically when some of them presented themselves at the house of a London printer demanding substantiation of his allegations.[83]

Wariness about how women in the Quaker movement could be portrayed is clearly apparent in the development of internal discipline structures. The quashing of rumours began within the movement itself, and demanded strict controls by the leadership. In 1653 the Quaker Thomas Lawson was ordered by Fox to write a paper to 'send among friends' to clear his name of some rumours being 'tattled' about him. The rumour had sprung from his interruption of a sermon with an unnamed Quaker woman who had been denounced by the congregation as a whore, and the two of them had been accused of sexual depravity. Lawson – not apparently the woman – was asked to explain the allegations made against him to others in the movement. In the paper he duly submitted to Margaret Fell, Lawson, as well as denying any impropriety on his part, was very concerned to describe how the rumour had spread: 'the outward minde standing on looked forth at the reports of the world, and being at liberty tatled them abrode, without any ground, but onely by heresay, so things spread abrode, and are carried up and down'.[84]

James Nayler, who would later be associated with unruly women in a far more serious way, was deeply conscious of the need to refute public or published allegations of sexual impropriety in the movement. When two puritan ministers, William Cole and Thomas Welde, sneered at Christopher Atkinson's 'very immodest familiarity (to say no more) with a woman of his way, in the sight of a godly Minister at Kendale', James Nayler took up the taunt in his reply. '[T]o make a ground for your slander, ye say (to say no more) but why, to say no more? if ye know more, why doe you not speake the truth, but slander in secret?'[85] Within months of this confident public refutation of the accusations against Atkinson, private letters circulating between Quaker ministers reported, in scandalized tones, Christopher Atkinson's actual adultery with a woman in Norwich. Atkinson was formally ejected from the Quaker movement by a gathering of ministers at

[83] Thomas Aldam, *The Searching Out the Deceit* (London, 1655), pp. 1–4; see Peters, 'Quaker pamphleteering', pp. 160–3.

[84] Thomas Lawson to 'Friends', Sw Mss 1: 246.

[85] William Cole, Thomas Welde, *et al.*, *The Perfect Pharise under Monkish Holines* (London, 1654), p. 49; James Nayler, *An Answer to the Booke called The Perfect Pharisee* ([London], 1654), p. 27.

Norwich.[86] Substantiated internal reports of licentious behaviour were taken seriously, while publicly they were refuted or defused whenever possible. The case of Christopher Atkinson is an eloquent example of the Quaker movement's ability to present a virtuous public image, while at the same time developing disciplinary structures to control and contain unruly behaviour.

Phyllis Mack argues that the Quakers were bound by an extraordinary sense of community in which the role of women as nurturers and providers for the household was cherished and extended to the organization of the movement as a whole.[87] But in the concern of the early Quaker men to protect the movement, there is also a sense that women could do very real damage. In 1658, Richard Hubberthorne wrote to Fox with an account of a highly troubled meeting:

> yesterday wee had A meetinge at the bull and mouth and mildred was there in all Impudence and I haveinge spokne somthing in the livinge power of the lord to the people shee was tarmented and shee resolved soe to speake as that I should not speake any more to them and when she had spokne untill her naturell brith was spent she againe still did strive to speake and often tould the people that they should not heare A word from mee stay as longe as they would together for she intended to speake as longe as they stayed and in the livinge power of the lord I was cept and moved to stay: the meetinge begun at the 3 hower and wee stayed almost untill midnight for I was to stay and much of the lord was found in it for she did soe strive in her wickednes untill all her naturall parts was spent and her sences distracted that she was even realy mad and truth reaigned in pure dominion and in the life of truth was all freinds refreshed to see the deceipte to wast and destroy itselfe till it retained noe streingth and freinds in the life weare kept and reioyced over it: and the world was satisfied Concerninge it and Could see it and Judge it yet she said that the next meeting shee would Come in more power and we should not speake A word but the next meetinge shee did not come at all for shee hath soe destroyed her

[86] Richard Hubberthorne to George Fox and James Nayler, 10 Dec. 1654, Sw Tr 2: 569; Richard Clayton to Margaret Fell, 12 July 1655, Sw Tr 1: 564; George Taylor to Margaret Fell, 14 July 1655, Sw Mss 1: 239. See also Peters, 'Quaker pamphleteering', p. 33.
[87] Mack, *Visionary Women*, pp. 228–35, 236–61.

naturall parts that shee is soe horsie that shee Cannot speake at present: and it is like gods Judgments will Come upon her sudainly.[88]

This account suggests the intensity of the leadership struggle between Hubberthorne and 'Mildred'; the very clear distinction between the natural parts of the woman, which were wicked and distracted, and the spiritual responses of others at the meeting, epitomizes the distinction between carnal and spiritual, which in print Richard Farnworth had attributed to 'male' and 'female' in the opposite sense. Hubberthorne's letter is also very important because 'Mildred in all Impudence' was clearly known to Fox, and Hubberthorne was keeping him informed. In the same letter, Hubberthorne reported that Francis Howgill's sister Mary, for the past six months 'hath been much in these Counties of Essex suffolke and norfolke wheare she hath done hurt for she ministereth Confusion amonge freinds'. Hubberthorne's solution to the problem, he informed Fox, was to hold a general meeting in the area to reassure friends shaken by Mary Howgill's preaching.[89] We thus see emerging an early form of church discipline, with recognized leaders like George Fox and Margaret Fell, and intermediary scouts who reported on any ministerial deviance, or even implemented temporary measures to counter the ill effects on the movement.

There are frequent examples of this kind of early internal group discipline, centring on the potential threat posed by women. The Quaker minister Thomas Aldam, imprisoned in York Castle, was particularly meticulous: in 1652 he called in Richard Farnworth and William Dewsbery on two separate occasions to speak to his fellow prisoner Jane Holmes, who had fallen, he said, into 'pashon and Lowdnesse' – not a common problem reported among male Quaker preachers. But she refused to 'come to Judgement', and took a separate room in the prison, with Mary Fisher. Thomas Aldam described the situation very gravely in a letter to Margaret Fell, and asked, scrupulously, that any money sent to the prisoners should be expressly

---

[88] Richard Hubberthorne to Fox, 20 March 1656, Sw Tr 2: 593.

[89] Mary Howgill had been at the centre of controversial preaching for some time. In June 1656 she had visited Cromwell; in July of that year she travelled to Dover; and as a result published a piece of prophecy, *A Remarkable Letter of Mary Howgill to Oliver Cromwell, called Protector* (London, 1657).

directed to one group or the other as they no longer ate together.[90] Two years later, still in York Castle, Aldam sent another woman, Agnes Wilkinson, to Margaret Fell. She, Aldam said, had 'acted contrary to the light, in filthynes', and was 'cast out of the light with them who was partakers with her'. Aldam asked Fell to set a watch over her and 'keepe her out from Amongst Frends' until she repented.[91]

There were heightened fears about the role of women in the public ministry voiced around the time of the James Nayler crisis in late 1656. This, Patricia Crawford and Christine Trevett have both argued, centred around the assumption of leadership by Martha Simmonds as much as by James Nayler.[92] In July 1656 William Caton and George Fox discussed 'the women, or rather sisters', in Cornwall that had been 'fellow helpers in the Gospell'; George Fox said little to it, but suggested 'that some of them might Cease'.[93] In August 1656, Richard Clayton, a Quaker missionary in Ireland, sent back to Margaret Fell 'a filthy decetfull wench' lest 'she should have ca[u]sed the truth to have sufered'.[94] William Caton we find paralysed in Sussex in early 1657, refusing to go to Amsterdam because of rumours there of a woman 'gone distracted'. Edward Burrough wrote to Fox in February 1657, concerned by a 'short little maide', and urging him to take her out of the ministry and find her a more suitable post as a servant-girl somewhere, as many friends 'hath ben burdened by her as by her ministery . . . and to some she was an offence in bedfordshire'.[95]

The majority of early cases of internal Quaker discipline revolved around the perceived need to temper the behaviour of women, or indeed to 'cast them out' of the still nascent movement. Much early discipline of men, as in the case of Christopher Atkinson, touched on

---

[90] Thomas Aldam to 'Friends', [Nov. 1652], Sw Mss 3:40; Aldam to Thomas Towndrowe [1652/3], Portfolio 36:114; Brailsford, *Quaker Women*, p. 22.

[91] Thomas Aldam to Margaret Fell, 30 Oct. 1654, Sw Mss 4: 89.

[92] Crawford, *Women and Religion in England*, pp. 173–80. This paper deliberately avoids discussion of James Nayler's infamous fall from power in the Quaker movement, the ramifications of which were so cataclysmic. I would argue that the tension surrounding the status of women in the movement clearly pre-dated the spectacular events surrounding Nayler, Martha Simmonds, Hannah Stranger, and Dorcas Erbury. The Nayler case can be better understood against the background of a movement where gender was always an important and problematic dynamic.

[93] William Caton to Margaret Fell, 23 July 1656, Sw Mss 1: 313.

[94] Richard Clayton to Margaret Fell, 5 Aug. 1656, Sw Tr 1: 568.

[95] William Caton to Margaret Fell, Sw Mss 1: 314; 1: 366; Edward Burrough to George Fox, A. R. Barclay Mss 1: 36, fo. 100.

sexual transgression with women, or on rumours of it. The leaders of the early Quaker movement made very real and pragmatic decisions about the propriety of the ministry for many Quaker women. Their monitoring and ejection of wayward women foreshadowed developments in the systematic holding of meetings and circulation of epistles which characterized the Quaker movement of the 1660s and beyond. Public refutations of accusations of sexual transgression in the movement did not rehearse the right of women to preach. Private letters also made very few references to the spiritual equality of women and men. It becomes all the more convincing, in this context, that the tracts by Fox and Farnworth were written not as impassioned pleas for the right of their sisters to preach, but as a careful appropriation and legitimizing of their behaviour as women.

*　*　*

The current surge of interest in female spirituality or religiosity is a very important and welcome development for our understanding both of the experiences of women, and of the nature of religion in early modern European society. But we need to be very careful about how we contextualize women's religious experiences. The records surrounding Quaker women are very accessible, and highly seductive. As a result, the writings and doings of Quaker women have to some extent been plundered by historians as stirring examples of how strong religious convictions could empower women in the seventeenth century. It is very clear that the Quakers' emphasis on immediate spiritual religious experience had important implications for the role of women in the movement, allowing them equal authority with their male co-religionists.

There is a danger, though, in isolating women from the wider Quaker movement, which is the implicit and often unstated consequence of using Quaker women's records as a means of understanding female religiosity; in an important sense this detracts from the role of women in the Quaker movement. This paper began with a well-known extract from a piece of writing by Priscilla Cotton and Mary Cole, in which they denounced England's ministers as women, 'that are become women', and who should themselves be forbidden to preach. Although the inversion of gender as a literary device was not uncommon, the spectre of two women venturing into print in order to command ordained ministers to be silent is an eloquent example of the ways in which Quaker women were empowered to act. However, this is to see the exchange primarily in terms relating to gender. Two years earlier another Quaker author, one William Tomlinson, denounced England's ministry with the same slur: 'the mighty men of Babylon have forborn to fight, they have remained in their holds; they are become as women, *Jer.* 51.30'.[96] William Tomlinson's gendered language as a means of attacking the national ministry is less celebrated than his co-religionists', but it is significant. Gendered language was not uncommon in much early Quaker writing; and it was a device used by male and female authors alike. Priscilla Cotton and Mary Cole were primarily the authors of a Quaker tract: they wrote as 'prisoners in Exeter gaol for the Word of God', and throughout their writing reflects the hundreds of Quaker tracts which had already been published, and with which they were undoubtedly familiar.

One conclusion to draw from this is that women were empowered by the Quaker movement in very practical ways as well as by the intensity of their religious experience. One of the reasons for the public activities undertaken by Quaker women was that they were enabled by the 'worldly' organization of the early Quaker movement, much of it initiated, it should be remembered, by Margaret Fell herself. Women like Priscilla Cotton and Mary Cole were familiar with Quaker tracts: Priscilla Cotton's husband himself circulated them around his home town of Plymouth. Quaker women were helped in their public preaching and ministry in other ways, too: they received money, support, shelter, and inspiration from the developing organization of the movement.

Wider conclusions force us to reconsider the contribution of women to the development of the Quaker movement as a whole. It has been shown that the doctrinal arguments presented by Quaker leaders to justify women's preaching developed as the movement itself was growing: they were a dynamic part of the movement's development, and emerged out of the pragmatic need to justify and contain the public ministry performed by Quaker women. Rather than examining Quaker women as an interesting but separate sub-plot within the history of the Quaker movement, we should see the origins of Quakerism in more gendered terms. Women were enabled by the organizational structures of the very early movement. Yet the

---

[96] William Tomlinson, *A Word of Reproof to the Priests or Ministers* (London, 1653), p. 28.

explanation that this was due to George Fox's own enlightened attitude is unconvincing. As the Quaker movement consolidated, a wide variety of attitudes towards women were evident, justifying their preaching role in ungendered terms, arguing for a fairly traditional Christian model of family and social relations, and finally denouncing and punishing unruly women. All of these attitudes were developed out of a pragmatic need to respond to the high public profile of women in the movement. Most of them also find some resonance with broader seventeenth-century patriarchal expectations. This paper has deliberately focused on the four earliest and formative years of the Quaker movement, in order to argue that the very creation of church discipline, and the consolidation of recognized Quaker beliefs, were gendered processes. The activities and experiences of Quaker women must be examined in the context of their movement as a whole: conversely, we understand much more about the Quaker movement if we include women in the history of its development.

University College London

GENDER AND THE CLERICAL PROFESSION IN ENGLAND, 1660–1850

by JEREMY GREGORY

T HE relationship between the two co-ordinates of this essay, 'gender' and 'the clerical profession', might be interpreted in a number of ways. It could, for instance, be taken to mean the manner in which clergy articulated and encouraged differences in gender roles. For it is certainly true that the most commonly quoted conduct books of the period – and especially those which prescribed roles for women – were written by the clergy.[1] Clerics like James Fordyce, a Presbyterian minister in London, in his popular *Sermons to Young Women* (1765) advised his presumed audience:

[b]ut you yourselves, I think, will allow that war, commerce, politics, exercises of strength and dexterity, abstract philosophy, and all the abstruser sciences are most properly the province of men. I am sure that those masculine women that would plead for your sharing a part of this province equally with us, do not understand your true interests.[2]

How far, we might ask, did conduct literature such as this demonstrate changes over time in the clergy's understanding of the relationship between the sexes? Moreover, how far were clergy leading those

---

[1] Obvious examples include: Wetenhall Wilkes, *A Letter of Genteel and Moral Advice to a Young Lady* (Dublin, 1740); James Fordyce, *Sermons to Young Women* (London, 1765); idem, *The Character and Conduct of the Female Sex and the Advantages to be Derived by Young Men from the Society of Virtuous Women* (London, 1776); John Bennett, *Letters to a Young Lady on a Variety of Useful and Interesting Subjects*, 2 vols (London, 1795); Thomas Gisborne, *An Enquiry into the Duties of the Female Sex* (London, 1797); and George Horne, *The Female Character as it Ought to Appear when Formed* (London, 1801). Another frequently cited source, John Gregory's *A Father's Legacy to his Daughters* (London, 1774), was written by the professor of medicine at Edinburgh, but his son William was a cleric. Interestingly, 'conduct literature' relating specifically to men was not so common, and when it did occur tended to be targeted at specific groups rather than at 'men' as a whole: for example, T. Gisborne, *An Enquiry into the Duties of Men in the Higher and Middle Classes of Society*, 2 vols (London, 1794).
[2] Quoted in D. A. Johnson, ed., *Women in English Religion, 1700–1925* (New York and Toronto, 1983), p. 38.

changes, or how far were they just reflecting general social assumptions? In any case, interpreting such literature is highly problematic. Rather than mirroring clearly defined and distinct gender divisions which existed in practice, attempts by the clergy to demarcate separate spheres for men and women might indicate that people were not in fact acting in the ways that the literature prescribed, and thus the conduct books written for women could be seen as a clerical (and male) backlash against female behaviour.[3] The paper's title could also refer to male and female attitudes towards the clerical profession: did men and women view the male clergy differently, and, if so, why? The relationship between gender and the clerical profession might further be interpreted as the manner by which the clergy used a gendered language to define and describe themselves. It could also relate to the ways in which the clerical profession itself was a gendered practice. Gender was then both a theoretical and practical factor in the organization of religious life in this period, and all of these aspects of the relationship will be touched on in order to examine how ideas about sexual difference shaped, and in turn were shaped by, ideas about religion.

Much of the most interesting recent work on the period from the late seventeenth to the mid nineteenth century has been concerned on the one hand with questions of gender and on the other with the role of religion in society. Yet remarkably little attempt has been made to bring these two areas of historical interest together. Those historians who have considered the role and position of women in the long eighteenth century, as well as those historians such as Philip Carter who have begun to look at concepts of masculinity, have done so within an almost overwhelmingly secular context.[4] The ways in which the sexes related to each other, and changes in that relationship, have

---

[3] On the problems of interpreting conduct literature, see A. Vickery, 'Golden age to separate spheres? A review of the categories and chronology of English women's history', *HistJ*, 36 (1993), esp. pp. 413–14.

[4] G. Perry and M. Rossington, eds, *Femininity and Masculinity in Eighteenth-Century Art and Culture* (Manchester, 1994) makes no reference to religion, the Church, or Christianity, even in the index; similarly, P. Carter, 'Mollies, fops and men of feeling: aspects of male effeminacy and masculinity in Britain, 1700–1780' (University of Oxford D.Phil. thesis, 1995) discusses masculinity within a totally secular context. But for some starting points, see C. Campbell Orr, ed., *Wollstonecraft's Daughters. Womanhood in England and France, 1780–1920* (Manchester, 1995); S. Gill, *Women and the Church of England. From the Eighteenth Century to the Present* (London, 1994); and G. Malmgreen, ed., *Religion in the Lives of English Women, 1760–1930* (London, 1986).

been accounted for largely in socio-economic terms: the more clearly defined gender roles and divisions which some historians have argued appeared in the period have been seen as reflecting the emergence of a distinctly middle-class ethos, or more generally as a concomitant of the increasing capitalization and modernization of society.[5] In part this concentration on materialist factors behind the formation of gender identity may have arisen because historians of gender have accepted at face-value the commonly received idea that the period after 1660 witnessed a gradual, but inexorable, secularization of society. Religion has been viewed as being increasingly marginal, and thus of little consequence as an explanatory factor for understanding the ways in which gender roles were perceived and defined.

Conversely, the great burgeoning of interest in the role of religion in the eighteenth century, and especially the growth of research into the functioning of the Church of England, has largely been done without reference to questions of gender.[6] The diocesan study, which has underpinned much of this work, has not as yet proved amenable to gender analysis. While we now know more about the structural workings of the Church (in terms of clerical recruitment, education, and training), the role of the Church in politics, and more about popular religious belief, there is little sign that historians of religion in the two centuries after 1660 have addressed themselves to issues of gender: those studies which have been made, for example, of the concepts of 'Christian manliness' and 'muscular Christianity' for the period after 1850, have not been mirrored by scholars working on the period before that date.[7] Neither has the clerical profession in the long

---

[5] K. Shevelow, *Women and Print Culture: the Construction of Femininity in the Early Periodical* (London, 1989); L. Stone, *The Family, Sex and Marriage in England, 1500–1800* (London, 1977).

[6] The most recent collection of essays on religion in the eighteenth century, J. Walsh, C. Haydon, and S. Taylor, eds, *The Church of England, 1689–1833. From Toleration to Tractarianism* (Cambridge, 1993), includes no discussion of gender roles. However, Jane Shaw's forthcoming book promises some discussion of the issue: for the present see her 'The Miraculous Body and other Rational Wonders. Religion in Enlightenment England' (University of California Ph.D. thesis, 1994), ch. 1.

[7] S. S. Pugh, *Christian Manliness: a Book of Examples and Principles for Young Men* (London, 1867); D. Newsome, *Godliness and Good Learning* (London, 1961); N. Vance, *Sinews of the Spirit: the Ideal of Christian Manliness in Victorian Literature and Religious Thought* (Cambridge, 1985); P. Gay, 'The Manliness of Christ', in R. W. Davis and R. J. Helmstader, eds, *Religion and Irreligion in Victorian Society: Essays in Honour of R. K. Webb* (London, 1992), pp. 86–102. See also, E. A. Rotundo, 'Learning about manhood: gender ideals and the middle-class family in nineteenth century America', in J. A. Mangan and J. Walvin, eds, *Manliness and Morality: Middle-Class Masculinity in Britain and America, 1800–1940* (New York and

eighteenth century been subjected to the type of gender inquiry which historians have given to other professions in later centuries, where they have studied in particular the ethos of masculinity in professional and organizational structures.[8] But, on the face of it, it might be worth thinking about the clerical profession in precisely these terms. Clergy of the Church of England between 1660 and 1850 were often the sons of clergy, they were educated at school and university by men, the professional networks in which they operated were totally male, and their professional friendships and contacts were of necessity with men, as witnessed by a range of activities from clerical correspondence to clerical dining clubs.[9] For other organizations, historians might have analysed these elements of the professional life of the clergy under the concept of 'male bonding'. We might also ask how far ideas about the nature of the clerical profession matched more secular notions of masculinity and how far the Church mirrored other masculine organizations in the period, since a favourite metaphor for describing the hierarchical nature of the profession in the eighteenth century was to compare it to other all-male organizations, such as the army and the public school.[10]

The one study which has looked at some aspects of the relationship between gender formation and religion has been Leonore Davidoff and Catherine Hall's *Family Fortunes*, published in 1987. This stimulating book, which has been the starting point for much of the recent work on 'femininity' in the period (though studies of masculinity have been slower on the uptake), has not, on the whole, made such an impact

Manchester, 1987), pp. 35–51, and J. Springhall, 'Building character in the British boy: the attempt to extend Christian manliness to working-class adolescents, 1880–1914', ibid., pp. 52–74. Studies of religion and femininity after 1850 include S. O'Brien, 'Lay-sisters and good mothers: working-class women in English convents, 1840–1910', *SCH*, 27 (1990), pp. 453–66; and idem, 'Terra incognita: the nun in nineteenth-century England', *P&P*, 121 (Nov. 1988), pp. 110–40.

[8] See J. Tosh, 'Domesticity and manliness in the Victorian middle class', in M. Roper and J. Tosh, eds, *Manful Assertions. Masculinities in Britain since 1800* (London, 1991), pp. 43–73; M. Roper, *Masculinity and the British Organization Man since 1945* (Manchester, 1994).

[9] For a clerical dining club, see G. M. Ditchfield and B. Keith-Lucas, eds, *A Kentish Parson. Selections from the Private Papers of the Revd Joseph Price of Brabourne, 1767–86* (Stroud, 1990), p. 10.

[10] 'We may divide the clergy into generals, field officers, and subalterns': Joseph Addison, *The Spectator*, 24 March 1711, quoted in N. Sykes, *Church and State in England in the Eighteenth Century* (Cambridge, 1934), p. 147. For the Church as a public school, see Frances Knight, 'English anti-clericalism, 1800–1850', unpublished lecture, Anglo-American Conference, London, June 1996.

amongst historians of religion. Further it has received a fair amount of recent criticism from Amanda Vickery, who attacked (perhaps rather unfairly) the distinction the authors supposedly drew between 'public' and 'private' spheres.[11] But, in attempting to dismantle this aspect of their thesis, even Vickery seems to accept without question what was in many ways more central to their argument: the importance of the Evangelical Revival in accounting for changes in gender relations, and for providing the ideology behind the notion of separate spheres.[12] Although Vickery challenges their interpretation of the effects of evangelicalism, arguing that the Evangelical Revival gave women a justification for moving into the public sphere, rather than containing them within the home, she, like Davidoff and Hall, contrasts 'serious' Christianity with what had gone before.[13] But such a view not only takes evangelical propaganda at face value; it underestimates the ways in which religious imperatives had shaped gender constructs and practice in the period before 1780. Rather, it can be suggested that although the Evangelical Revival may have intensified the complex nexus of religion and gender, the assumptions it held about male and female roles drew on a long tradition.

Discussion of the relationship between gender and the clerical profession often hinges on the question of female ordination and the roles which women were allowed in public worship.[14] In this sense, the period from 1660 to 1850 can be viewed as something of a non-starter. Part of the post-Restoration backlash against the world which had been turned upside down in the 1640s and 1650s was to equate female preaching and leadership in worship with political and social radicalism, and apart from the Quakers for whom equality in religious matters ensured a strong and continuing tradition of female leadership in religious affairs, even nonconformist groups witnessed a reaction along similar lines.[15] The image of the female Quaker preacher as a symptom of Civil War disorder, as a sign of unnatural behaviour, and even as a comic and ridiculous figure which could be satirized and thus

---

[11] L. Davidoff and C. Hall, *Family Fortunes. Men and Women of the English Middle Class 1780–1850* (London, 1987); Vickery, 'Golden age', pp. 393–401.

[12] Davidoff and Hall, *Family Fortunes*, pp. 21–7, 78–149.

[13] Vickery, 'Golden age', pp. 399–400.

[14] Malmgreen, *Women*; Gill, *Women*.

[15] An example of what has been called 'Thirsk's law': the opening up of opportunities for women and then their repression: D. Hempton, *The Religion of the People. Methodism and Popular Religion, c.1750–1900* (London and New York, 1996), p. 181.

de-radicalized, was a recurring establishment trope, which could be activated at any time when the issue of female participation in the organization of religious matters was mentioned. It was, of course, on hearing of a female Quaker preacher in 1763 that Dr Johnson remarked to Boswell; 'Sir, a woman's preaching is like a dog's walking on his hinder legs. It is not done well; but you are surprised to find it done at all.'[16] And, perhaps more tellingly, one writer in 1739 was concerned that female Quaker preachers were potential professional (and therefore economic) rivals to the clergy of the Church of England, who threatened the united 'interest of the whole Body of Men called Clergymen'.[17]

Such attempts to deny women a valid professional role were not, of course, merely confined to the issue of women being religious professionals. The celebrated osteopath Sarah Mapp, who gained a reputation for being a leading practitioner of her profession, was treated as a freak by her male colleagues;[18] and as late as 1850, as Penelope Corfield has pointed out, there were no female lawyers, physicians, surgeons or army officers.[19] Other historians have maintained that the eighteenth century saw a masculinization of the professions, so that even traditionally 'female' occupations such as midwives were being encroached on by men.[20] The anonymous 'Sophia' who wrote *Woman not Inferior to Man* (1739), which argued that the exclusion of women from the professions was justified only by custom and not by justice, and which claimed that there was no reason why women could not direct an army or teach theology at university, tried to grapple with the exclusion of women from the priesthood:

> With regard, however, to divinity, our natural capacity has been restrained by a positive law of God; and therefore we know better than to lay claim to what we could not practice without sacrilegious instruction. Though, by the bye, let it be observed that the bar which our Divine Saviour has put to our exercising

[16] James Boswell, *Life of Johnson*, ed. R. W. Chapman (Oxford, 1980), p. 327.
[17] 'Bernardus Utopiensis' [J. Rutty], *A Second Dissertation on the Liberty of Preaching granted to women by the . . . Quakers* (Dublin, 1739), p. 13, quoted in P. J. Corfield, *Power and the Professions in Britain, 1700–1850* (London and New York, 1995), p. 108.
[18] Corfield, *Professions*, p. 33.
[19] Ibid., p. 36.
[20] G. Holmes, *Augustan England. Professions, State and Society, 1680–1730* (London, 1982), pp. 178, 182, 201.

any religious functions, neither bars us from any other public offices, nor proves us unworthy or naturally incapable of exercising even them. That he forbad us those functions proves us naturally apt for them.[21]

She went on to suggest that the reason why Jesus had wanted an all male clergy was that 'God undoubtedly knew the general tendency of men to impiety and irreligion; and therefore why might he not confine the function of religion to that sex, to attract some of them at least to those duties they have such a general aversion for.'[22]

Set against this picture of an increasing masculinization of the professions, including that of the clerical profession, is, however, the suggestion that during the eighteenth century religious practice itself became feminized.[23] By this historians have usually meant that at the end of the eighteenth century more women attended church services than men, and this has been accounted for largely in terms of the separation of Church and State and also by the separation of spheres, which meant that church attendance was no longer seen as a public necessity for the male householder, and instead became part of the private sphere, where the female could be dominant. If the religious professional was firmly male, his congregation, it has been claimed, was increasingly female.[24] Some historians have interpreted this move from the public to the private in religious observance as a sign of the

---

[21] Sophia, A Person of Quality, *Woman not Inferior to Man; or a Short and Modest Vindication of the Fair-Sex to Perfect Equality of Power, Dignity and Esteem with the Men* (London, 1739), p. 36. Interestingly the High-Church William Jones of Nayland observed that during a sermon he had recently delivered on the liturgy: 'Among my hearers, to my great happiness, there was a lady of the first liturgical piety in this kingdom, though I say it, that is my own wife. 'Tis pity but her gown had been of the Preaching Sort; she would have done wonders; but the use of her voice is reserved for the Church triumphant': Oxford, Magdalen College Archives, MS 471, fo. 34, Jones to George Horne, 15 Nov. 1791.

[22] Sophia, *Woman not Inferior to Man*, p. 44. This pamphlet produced a male rejoinder: *Man Superior to Woman; or a Vindication of Man's Natural Right of Sovereign Authority over the Woman. Containing a Plain Confutation of the Fallacious Arguments of Sophia* (London, 1739). He made particular fun of her claims for a female role in religious matters, using the image of the fanatical female Quaker preacher to satirize her position: pp. 52–3. Sophia retaliated with *Woman's Superior Excellence over Man, or a Reply to the Author of a late Treatise* (London, 1740).

[23] Malmgreen, *Women*, p. 2; P. Crawford, *Women and Religion in England, 1500–1720* (London and New York, 1993), p. 207. See also R. D. Sheils, 'The feminisation of American Congregationalism, 1730–1835', *American Quarterly*, 33 (1983), esp. pp. 48–9.

[24] H. Mcleod, *Religion and the People of Western Europe, 1789–1970* (Oxford, 1981), ch. 2.

marginalization of religion and women (and indeed of the clergy) from the public realm.[25] A similar development has been noted by historians of Catholicism in France, who, furthermore, have viewed battles between clergy and parishioners as a struggle between a male clergy and the men of France for control over French women.[26] But we must not date this movement in England too early. Statistics of the sexual profiles of congregations, at least before 1850, are not conclusive on this point; and in any case the whole concept is dependent upon the assumption of a general drift towards secularization. But is this a valid hypothesis? An increasing number of nineteenth-century historians have stressed the continuing importance of religion in political life up until at least the 1870s, which makes the overarching suggestion of the transference of religion from the public to the private realm ultimately unconvincing, at least for the period under review.[27] The intention in the remainder of this essay is to look at the ways in which the precepts and practice of gender roles interacted with the precepts and practice of the clerical profession. It begins by looking at the ways in which the clerical profession defined itself, and exploring some of the ways in which we might be able to talk about a gendered language in discussing the clerical profession. It then goes on to consider the role of women in furthering some of the professional duties of the religious functionary.

*   *   *

One way into the relationship between gender and the clerical profession is to look at the language clergy used to describe their own role in society, and especially to demarcate their position from that of their nonconformist and Roman Catholic rivals. As Gillian Perry and Michael Rossington have reminded us, while our critical uses of the terms 'femininity' and 'masculinity' are modern constructions, the labels 'masculine' and 'feminine' were frequently employed

---

[25] J. Obelkevich, *Religion and Rural Society: South Lindsey, 1825–75* (Oxford, 1976), p. 313.

[26] R. Gibson, *A Social History of French Catholicism, 1789–1914* (London, 1989), p. 182. See also A. Douglas, *The Feminisation of American Culture* (New York, 1977); B. Welter, 'The feminisation of American Religion, 1800–1860', in M. Hartman and L. Banner, eds, *Clio's Consciousness Raised: New Perspectives on the History of Women* (New York, 1973), pp. 137–57.

[27] R. Brent, *Liberal Anglican Politics. Whiggery, Religion and Reform, 1830–1841* (Oxford, 1987); P. A. Butler, *Gladstone: Church, State and Tractarianism. A Study of his Religious Ideas and Attitudes, 1809–1859* (Oxford, 1982); J. Parry, *Democracy and Religion: Gladstone and the Liberal Party, 1867–1875* (Cambridge, 1986).

in the eighteenth century.[28] What were the religious associations and assumptions given to these terms, particularly with regard to the religious functionary? It could be argued that the clerical profession has always had a rather ambivalent or liminal position with regard to gender. In the Bible and the Church Fathers, the Church as an organization and as a community was usually depicted as 'feminine', whilst the stress on the masculinity of priesthood, as Christ's representative on earth, ensured a logically complete relationship between a 'female Church' and a 'male' clergy.[29] It might be suggested that the more religious denominations emphasised the Church as a corporate body (as in Roman Catholicism), the more the clerical profession was deemed to be of necessity male. As an analysis of the sermons preached before the annual meeting of the Corporation of the Sons of the Clergy has shown, the clergy of the Church of England prided themselves on being 'pious, charitable', and 'moderate'.[30] This is interesting for our purposes since 'piety', 'charity, and 'moderation' were also deemed in the period to be specifically feminine virtues.[31]

Moreover, in the two centuries after 1660 many authorities considered women to be more inherently religious than men. At the very least, this perception raised some interesting questions about gender difference and gender essentialism. Richard Allestree (1619–81), Professor of Divinity at Oxford (1663), Provost of Eton (1665), and author of the best-selling *Whole Duty of Man* (1658), someone who can thus be taken as an authoritative voice for the Restoration Church, observed in *The Ladies Calling* (1673) that, having made an unsuccessful attempt in his earlier *The Gentleman's Calling* (1660) to convince 'the more impregnable, masculine part of the Gentry' of the importance of

[28] Perry and Rossington, *Femininity and Masculinity*, p. 3.
[29] G. Horne, *A Sermon Preached Before the Sons of the Clergy* (London, 1762), pp. 5–7, likened the Church after the Fall to a widow.
[30] J. Ibbetson, *A Sermon Preached Before the Sons of the Clergy* (London, 1758), p. 9, after praising the learning of the clergy, noted 'the purity of their lives and conversations; if a reverential awe of God and a conscience of keeping all his commandments – if justice, mercy, contentment, sobriety, humility, patience, peacefulness and obedience to governors – be the principal ingredient of a good life'. B. Porteus, *A Sermon Preached at the Anniversary Meeting of the Sons of the Clergy* (London, 1776), p. 16, described clergy as being 'contented, humble, modest, patient and laborious'. A. King, *A Sermon Preached Before the Sons of the Clergy* (1751), p. 9, praised their piety. I am preparing an article on the sermons preached before the sons of the clergy: 'The clergy, sex and marriage' (forthcoming).
[31] For some typical 'female' qualities, see B. Hill, ed., *Eighteenth Century Women. An Anthology* (London, 1984), and V. Jones, ed., *Women in the Eighteenth Century. Constructions of Femininity* (London, 1990).

leading a virtuous and religious life, he would 'now assay the Feminine'.[32] Although he did admit that 'many duties were common both to male and female', he maintained 'that all ages and nations have made a Distinction between masculine and feminine vertues',[33] and as particularly female virtues he listed 'modesty', 'meekness', 'compassion', 'affability', and 'piety' (the longest section was in fact on piety). Indeed for him women had, religiously speaking, a more advantageous position than men, and had reason 'to thank God that made them women, and not men'. In all ages, Allestree believed, Christian virtue had been exemplified by women. 'Nay', he continued, 'to speak an impartial Truth, 'tis not to be denied, that the reputation of Religion is more kept up by women than men.'[34] Statements such as these led some contemporaries to suspect that this cycle of books (published anonymously) was in fact written by Dorothy, Lady Packington.[35] Significantly, Allestree described those who neglected religion as 'our masculine atheists', which indicates that there were possible negative associations between masculinity and religion which resulted in the belief that scoffers against religion were more likely to be male.[36] Similarly, Mary Astell, whose uncle was the curate of St Nicholas's church, Newcastle-upon-Tyne, in her *The Christian Religion; as professed by a Daughter of the Church of England* (1705), maintained not only that women needed a good religious education to help them defend its cause, but, since women had more time for religious contemplation than men, they were more suited to be the Church's theologians[37] – thereby turning the conventional implications of the distinction between private and public on its head.

These textual statements about female aptitude for piety can be matched with real-life examples of pious women. Although much of the work on female spirituality has associated 'the godly woman' with

[32] [R. Allestree], *The Works of the Learned and Pious Author of the Whole Duty of Man* (Oxford, 1726): 'The Ladies Calling', p. 1.
[33] Ibid.
[34] Ibid., pp. vi–viii.
[35] J. Todd, ed., *A Dictionary of British and American Women Writers, 1660–1800* (London, 1987), p. 239.
[36] Allestree, 'Ladies Calling', p. 25. The Revd John Bennett argued that women were more religious than men, because they were more lonely: quoted in Hill, *Women*, p. 22.
[37] M. Astell, *The Christian Religion; as Professed by a Daughter of the Church of England* (London, 1705). On Astell, see R. Perry, *The Celebrated Mary Astell. An Early English Feminist* (Chicago and London, 1986). Also B. Hill, 'A refuge from men: the idea of a protestant nunnery', *P&P*, 117 (Nov. 1987), pp. 107–30.

puritan or later evangelical religiosity,[38] it is clear that we should not be too rigid in linking female piety exclusively with these movements. The practice of the godly woman continued to flourish under post-Restoration Anglicanism. An example of this was Mary Evelyn, the daughter of the diarist, of whom he noted 'piety was so prevalent an ingredient in her constitution'.[39] Rather patronizingly he acknowledged that he had himself 'been assisted by her, both reading & praying by me; and was comprehensive of uncommon notions, curious of knowing everything to some excesse, had I not indeavour'd to repress it sometimes'.[40] Evelyn was also impressed by the piety of Mrs Godolphin, who died in 1678: he recalled that they 'often prayed, visited the sick & miserable, received, read, discoursed & communicated in all holy offices together without reproach'.[41] And in 1725 Edward Mores, the rector of Tunstall in Kent, published *The Pious Example; a Discourse occasion'd by the Death of Mrs Anne Mores* (his mother). After praising her remarkable sense of devotion, he acknowledged that 'although of Late Years by his Office (according to Her earnest Desire in the former Part of her Life, That if She should ever be Mother of a Child, it might be a Son, and that Son a Minister) He became Her Teacher, yet by Her Actions and Deportment, she was truly His.'[42] Both in these instances, and in the general fashion for ascribing to women an inclination for piety, it is striking that religious gifts were liberally assigned to the sex which had no professional standing.[43]

But although the clergy were happy to see women as being generally more religious than men, nevertheless the most noticeable way in which clergy defined themselves against their rivals was to pit their own 'masculine' qualities against the 'feminine' vices of their

[38] D. Willen, 'Godly women in early modern England: puritanism and gender', *JEH*, 43 (1992), pp. 561–80; R. L. Greaves, 'The role of women in early English nonconformity', *ChH*, 52 (1983), pp. 299–311.

[39] *The Diary of John Evelyn*, ed. E. S. de Beer, 6 vols (Oxford, 1955), 4, p. 422.

[40] Ibid., p. 423.

[41] Ibid., p. 150.

[42] E. Mores, *The Pious Example; a Discourse occasion'd by the Death of Mrs Anne Mores* (London, 1725), p. 25.

[43] It is interesting that in the twentieth century's campaign for the ordination of women, it was often asserted that such 'caring' qualities and such 'female virtues' made women supremely suited for ordination. Cf. Clive Field, 'Adam and Eve: gender in the English Free Church constituency', *JEH*, 44 (1993), pp. 663–79, where at p. 678 he observes that women gave higher levels of commitment to religious membership than men.

professional opponents. George Lavington, Bishop of Exeter, for example, in his *The Enthusiasm of Methodists and Papists Compared* (1749–51) called the religious deviants 'peevish' and 'waspish', negative traits long associated with the shrewish woman.[44] Aspects of religious behaviour denoted as particularly feminine could, as we have seen, be positive, and these were appropriated by the clergy to themselves (as in the cases of piety and charity); they could be used as a constraining device (women were expected to live up to these ideals); or they could be negative, and so clergy could castigate their opponents as having vices often imputed to women. This correlation between the defects of the Anglican clergy's rivals and the negative connotations associated with women can be especially seen in the anti-popery propaganda which was such a feature of the period. In some ways it is surprising that there has been no more extended treatment of the gendered and sexual imagery of anti-popery, and of religious stereotypes more generally. Even Jan Albers, who has written sensitively of the religious stereotypes at work in eighteenth-century Lancashire, and has high-lighted the political connotations whereby papists were always seen as Jacobites and Presbyterians as Civil War radicals,[45] has not picked out the sexual and gendered imagery which went hand-in-hand with these labels. Arguably, such sexual and gendered imagery was the most potent way of expressing the social and political abnormality of those groups deemed to be 'other' to the Church of England.

From the earliest days of the Reformation, the Church of Rome was associated with the whore of Babylon (an image full of biblical resonance), and the resulting masculinization of Protestantism versus the feminization of popery was part of that process of binary opposition which, as Peter Lake has shown, was so central in structuring anti-Catholic prejudice in the centuries after 1530.[46] While historians such as Lake have examined the political binary

---

[44] G. Lavington, *The Enthusiasm of Methodists and Papists Compar'd*, 3 parts (London, 1749–51), pt 2, p. 98. In pt 3, at p. 196, he maintained that Methodism appealed to 'persons of a fickle and inconsistent humour', traits also associated with women.

[45] J. Albers, '"Papist traitors" and "Presbyterian rogues"; religious identities in eighteenth-century Lancashire', in Walsh, Haydon, and Taylor, eds, *Church of England*, pp. 317–33. Neither does C. Haydon, *Anti-Catholicism in Eighteenth-Century England. A Political and Social History* (Manchester, 1993) deal at length with the sexual nature of the sentiment.

[46] P. Lake, 'Anti-popery: the structure of a prejudice', in R. Cust and A. Hughes, eds, *Conflict in Early Stuart England. Studies in Religion and Politics, 1603–1642* (London, 1989), pp. 72–106; L. Roper, *The Holy Household. Women and Morals in Reformation Augsburg* (Oxford, 1989), pp. 108–9.

polarities between 'freedom' and 'tyranny' implicit in the distinction between Protestantism and popery, the sexual resonance of the differences between the two religious creeds ought also to be explored. To Protestant eyes, the feminization of Rome was viewed in wholly negative terms. The beguiling 'femininity' of Rome allowed her to be depicted as a blowsy siren, a scarlet woman, or a painted harlot: the surface glitter of popish ceremonies and images appealing to what was most fallen and corrupt in carnal humanity. This image was, of course, not new in the period after 1660: it merely demonstrates the long pedigree behind much eighteenth-century discourse.

One of the complicating factors behind this gendered description of the Roman Catholic Church as a harlot was the fact of the celibate priest. In anti-popish discourse the celibacy of the Church of Rome was an obvious sign of its unnatural essence, and indeed of its perversion, especially since celibacy was usually seen by Protestant writers as a sham and a disguise which hid all kinds of unsavoury behaviour. Of course attacks of this kind on priestly celibacy had long roots within medieval anti–clerical propaganda, only to be refreshed during the Reformation (where the reports of the visitations of the monasteries highlighted a whole range of perverse practices).[47] In the centuries after 1660 this theme continued to be stressed. The *Protestant Almanack* of the late seventeenth century, for instance, claimed that no fewer than fourteen popes were guilty of incest or adultery, and that the papacy had a direct interest in the prostitution racket in the city of Rome.[48] What is noteworthy, too, is how far celibacy was an issue even for High Churchmen of the period. Henry Wharton, for example, the young chaplain of Archbishop Sancroft, who was concerned to defend the catholicity of the Church of England, and who was actually unmarried, published in 1688 a long and detailed history of the errors of celibacy in which he played on a century and a half of anti-popish rhetoric. Although he claimed he did not object to the ideal of celibacy, Wharton wanted to expose 'the pretence and [to] condemn

---

[47] For the accounts of monastic debauchery (and their reliability) see J. Youings, *The Dissolution of the Monasteries* (London, 1971). On the subject of sexuality in religious communities, see E. Donoghue, *Passions Between Women. British Lesbian Culture, 1660–1801* (London, 1994).

[48] [Philoprotest], *The Protestant Almanack for the year . . .* (Cambridge, 'printed for the information of Protestants', 1669). The almanack was printed for various years until 1700. See also the late-seventeenth-century pamphlet, *A Passionate Satyr, Upon a Devilish Great He-Whore That Lives Yonder at Rome* (np, nd).

the imposition of it'.[49] He demonstrated that the Church Fathers were not in agreement about the virtues of the celibate life, and that it had not been instituted by Christ or the apostles. When it did become the rule from the fourteenth century, 'What a deluge of lusts and impurities overflowed the Christian world . . . may easily be imagined.'[50] Likewise, those High Churchmen, George Horne and William Jones, who in Peter Nockles's recent analysis were the key figures in keeping the High Church tradition alive during the second half of the eighteenth century, were not only married, but roundly condemned this aspect of Catholic practice.[51] In this context it becomes more understandable why John Wesley, with his qualified advocacy of the desirability of celibacy, should have been accused by his critics as being a papist in disguise.[52] Further, despite John Henry Newman's insistence in the 1830s that he was merely reviving traditional High Church doctrines and practices, it is clear that his stress on the desirability of celibacy in the religious professional was in fact a radical departure from three centuries of Anglican tradition.[53] One of Newman's severest critics, Charles Kingsley, understood the previous three hundred years of English history as demonstrating the superiority of the monogamous heterosexual couple over what he considered to be the feminine essence of popery.[54] For him, the Reformation had exalted the masculine side of religion. In reply, Cardinal Manning argued that Tractarianism and the associated secessions to Rome were in fact a 'vigorous and masculine' revival within English religious life.[55] Their opposing viewpoints are sugges-

[49] *A Treatise of the Celibacy of the Clergy, wherein its Rise and Progress are Historically Considered* (London, 1688), p. 113.

[50] Ibid., p. 114.

[51] P. Nockles, *The Oxford Movement in Context. Anglican High Churchmanship, 1760–1857* (Cambridge, 1994). Other eighteenth-century High Churchmen such as Henry Sacheverell in his *A Sermon Preach'd Before the Sons of the Clergy* (London, 1713), pp. 2–3, argued that the marriage of bishops and priests was in fact taken for granted in the Bible, and Francis Atterbury in his sermon to the same body in 1709 insisted on the importance of a married clergy.

[52] J. Wesley, *Thoughts on Marriage and a Single Life* (London, 1743).

[53] D. Newsome, *The Parting of Friends* (London, 1966), pp. 93, 104–5, 113, examines the different views of Newman and Samuel Wilberforce on celibacy. See also P. Brendon, *Hurrell Froude and the Oxford Movement* (London, 1974), pp. 75–6, 113; G. Faber, *Oxford Apostles. A Character Study of the Oxford Movement* (London, 1933), pp. 215–32.

[54] C. Kingsley, quoted in *Religion in Victorian Britain, III. Sources*, ed. J. R. Moore (Manchester, 1988), pp. 84–7.

[55] Quoted ibid., p. 77.

tive of the ways in which rival religious professionals used a gendered language for their own purposes: in this case both ardent Protestant and Catholic convert wanted to appropriate the concept of masculinity to their own brand of religiosity.

What is also noteworthy is how far tropes which began as anti-popish discourse could be applied to the Church of England's other rivals. The sexual and gendered stereotypes tended to be easily transferable from one religious group to another, helping to straight-jacket all of the Church's opponents together.[56] Again, this is not surprising. To a culture which believed that it had indeed been Catholic infiltration which had caused the Civil Wars, then popery could be seen behind all religious groups who challenged the monopoly of the Church of England. This meant, too, that any new and rival religious movement in the period after 1660 could be met with the same response: there was a powerful armoury of ideas with which to make sense of such opponents. George Lavington's hostile criticism of Methodism was based on the simple methodological premise that 'the spirit of enthusiasm was always the same, operating in much the same manner, on all sects and Professors of Religion'.[57] Just as Catholics and the nonconformist sects after 1660 were tarred with the same brush of being king-killers, so they were both in some ways viewed as feminine. Indeed, as numerous commentators found, an easy way of stirring up opposition to nonconformity was to highlight its relationship with the female, as a sign of its weakness and irrationality. The decades immediately after the Restoration, for example, saw a range of anti-nonconformist propaganda which noted the weakness of intellect behind the dissenting ministers who were supposedly 'giddy' and 'volatile' in their opinions.[58] This not only played on Anglican criticisms of the unlearned nature of their professional rivals (contrasting their own increasingly Oxbridge-educated background with the unlettered boy preachers of their dissenting rivals) but also linked the nonconformists with women,

---

[56] This is also true of legislation which was first used against papists, and then employed against Protestant nonconformists. It should be noted, however, that after 1689 the suspicion of Protestant nonconformity softened, only to be re-asserted in times of crisis. For an example of the changing relationship between Anglicans and dissenters in one diocese, see W. J. Gregory, 'Archbishop, cathedral and parish: the diocese of Canterbury, 1660–1805' (University of Oxford D.Phil. thesis, 1993), ch. 5.

[57] Lavington, *Enthusiasm*, preface.

[58] Greaves, 'Women in early English nonconformity'.

who were also viewed as being deficient in reason. This is a classic case, perhaps, of the ways in which dominant or hegemonic masculinities have functioned by asserting their authority over others.[59]

These gendered images of popery and Protestant nonconformity were sustained in part by the belief that both Protestant dissenters and papists drew their support preponderantly from women.[60] But, in actual fact, the evidence of a necessary or even a direct link between women and groups which stood outside the established Church is tenuous. Scholars have often assumed that women were particularly attracted to non-establishment groups, since they too were marginal in political, social, and economic terms. But depictions of women as disorderly or deviant tell us more about male anxiety than actual female behaviour. Above all, we should not take at face value hostile observers' characterizations of nonconformist movements as being predominantly female. This supposition was not necessarily an accurate reflection of the actual make-up of groups, but was a way of casting aspersions on the spiritual lives of women and on the religious sect which exploited this.[61] Nevertheless, the appeal of non-Anglican denominations to women was frequently commented upon. In 1753, Horace Mann recounted the story 'of a woman of a certain age, whose friend upbraided her for turning Roman Catholic, and asking what could induce her, was answered, "Why, surely dear Madam, you must allow that the Roman Catholic religion is much more entertaining" ';[62] and Bishop Lavington noted that 'the greater Part of the Dramatis Personae in the Tragi-Comedy of Methodism appears to have been Actresses'.[63] Further, both the Catholic priest and the nonconformist minister were viewed as being particularly skilful in attracting female

---

[59] Roper and Tosh, *Manful Assertions*, p. 13.

[60] For a discussion of how this assumption has sometimes distorted the historiography, see the general comments in S. McSheffrey, *Gender and Heresy. Women and Men in Lollard communities, 1420–1530* (Philadelphia, 1995), pp. 1–15.

[61] But see Clive Field's figures, which suggest that at certain times there was a 'masculinization' of dissent: 'Adam and Eve', p. 667.

[62] *The Yale edition of Horace Walpole's Correspondence*, ed. W. S. Lewis, 48 vols (New Haven, 1937–83), 20, p. 378, Mann to Walpole, 8 June 1753. It is worth remembering Lindal Roper's suggestion that late medieval Catholicism nurtured a peculiarly 'feminine' mode of religious experience which was absent in Protestantism: *Holy Household*, p. 2. It is often suggested that women were attracted to the emotional aspect of dissent, as opposed to the 'rational' nature of Anglicanism. This explanation, with its suggestion of gender essentialism, seems to be rather unconvincing. As a theory, it owes much to Max Weber, *The Sociology of Religion*, trans. E. Fischoff (Boston, 1964), pp. 104–6.

[63] Lavington, *Enthusiasm*, p. 196.

adherents, and Anglican propaganda was not slow in drawing out the most salacious reasons for this. A typical instance of such propaganda is the self-explanatorily titled, *A Communal New dialogue Between Mr G . . .ff, a Pious Dissenting parson, and a Female-Quaker, (A Goldsmith's wife) near Cheapside; whom the reverend Preacher Picked Up. With the Discourse that Pass'd between them, and the treatment he gave her* (*c.* 1705). Similarly, John Wesley was accused of saying things to a girl in Mitchel, Cornwall, 'which were very improper to be spoken to a young Girl, and especially by a Clergyman'.[64] What is also interesting to note is the language used to describe the ways in which females converted from the Church of England to either popery or nonconformity. They were most frequently depicted as being 'seduced' by the Catholic priest or dissenting preacher: a telling indication of the ways in which the language of religion slid into the language of sexuality. Indeed the form and structure of these conversion tales became a stock piece of Anglican pornography, and such stories fed off reports from the continent of young girls being seduced in like manner. In 1764 Mann wrote from Florence to Horace Walpole that 'the subject for about a year has been some Protestant girls who have been seduced by priests to escape from their parents and to change their religion'.[65] In this short report were encapsulated some of the essentials of the anti-papist sexual discourse: priestly seduction of innocent virgins, their conversion, and the consequent break-up of their families. Seeing conversion to popery in terms of seduction played not only upon the sexual motives behind it, but also on the irrationality which sustained it. According to anti-Methodist propaganda, the arts of seduction were not confined to heterosexual relationships. Henry Fielding's *The Female Husband; or, The Surprising history of Mrs Mary, alias Mr George Hamilton, who was convicted of having married a young woman in Wells* (1746) portrayed Methodism as a front for lesbianism and homosexuality, where the anti-heroine seduced women into the sect.[66] Indeed, it may be that seduction narratives, which had a central place in the imaginative literature of the period (such as Richardson's *Clarissa* of

---

[64] G. Lavington, *The Bishop of Exeter's Answer to Mr J. Wesley's Late Letter to his Lordship* (London, 1752), p. 9. See also H. Aberlove, *The Evangelist of Desire: John Wesley and the Methodists* (Stanford, 1990).

[65] *Walpole's Correspondence*, 22, p. 249, Mann to Walpole, 11 Aug. 1764.

[66] This has been called 'the shoddiest work of fiction [that Fielding] ever wrote': M. C. Battestin with R. R. Battestin, *Henry Fielding. A Life* (London, 1989), pp. 411-12.

1747–8), had their origins in part in anti-popish propaganda.[67] This is suggestive of the ways in which modern cultural forms hijacked religious tropes for more secular purposes.[68] Furthermore, in all such seduction literature, the dynamic came from the seducer, whether lover or priest.[69] Moreover, in religious terms, conversion to popery or to nonconformity was not viewed as a positive step in the way in which conversion to Anglicanism was.[70]

Historians of eighteenth-century pornography have often viewed such tales of Catholic priestly and nonconformist ministerial misbehaviour as being rather shallow excuses for erotic writing.[71] This is a moot point. We can never really recover the precise motive behind the writing of such works, let alone how they were interpreted by readers, and it is difficult to know how far they should be seen as serious anti-papist propaganda, or how far they were merely vehicles for titillation. But the tendency to downplay the religious motivation behind these tales may have been misleading. The leading authority on the subject admittedly sees such erotic writing as part of an Enlightenment critique of Christianity and organized religion more generally, but he misses the Anglican and Protestant bias behind these

---

[67] Similarly, Christopher Anstey satirized a highly-sexed Methodist preacher in his poem *The New Bath Guide* (London, 1766), which interestingly drew on Bishop Lavington's criticism of the movement.

[68] For a more detailed treatment of the relationship between religion and new cultural forms in the eighteenth century, see J. Gregory, 'Anglicanism and the arts: religion, culture and politics in the eighteenth century', in J. Black and J. Gregory, eds, *Culture, Politics and Society in Britain, 1660–1800* (Manchester, 1991), pp. 82–109.

[69] My reading of eighteenth-century seduction literature, where females were essentially passive, contrasts with Lindal Roper's suggestion (*Holy Household*, p. 18) that in the sixteenth century women were seen as active and willing accomplices in their seduction to Catholicism. For a similar shift in the secular literature from the sixteenth to the eighteenth centuries, where women were also increasingly seen as passive, see T. Hitchcock, 'Redefining sex in eighteenth-century England', *HWJ*, 41 (1996), pp. 73–90, and idem, 'Demography and the culture of sex in the long eighteenth century' (forthcoming). See also S. Staves, 'British seduced maidens', *Eighteenth-Century Studies*, 14 (1980–1), pp. 109–34; R. Ballaster, *Seductive Forms; Women's Amatory Fiction from 1684–1740* (Oxford, 1992); and R. Rousel, *The Conversation of the Sexes: Seduction and Equality in Selected Seventeenth and Eighteenth-Century Texts* (New York, 1986).

[70] See *The Franciscan Convert; or, a Recantation Sermon by Anthony Egan, Late Confessor General of the Kingdom of Ireland . . . now a Minister of the Gospel According to the Ordination of the Church of England* (London, 1673).

[71] See M. Foucault, *The History of Sexuality*, 1 (New York, 1978), pp. 21–3, 57–8, and idem, 'Literature and sex' in A. Ellis and A. Abarbanel, eds, *The Encyclopaedia of Sexual Literature*, 2 vols (New York, 1961), 2, p. 637. See also D. Foxon, *Libertine Literature in England, 1660–1745* (London, 1964).

works.[72] Yet if, as Linda Colley would argue, anti-popery was the major determinant in fashioning the sense of Britishness in the period covered here, then we ought perhaps to take the denominational implications of such Protestant (and Anglican) pornography more seriously.[73] The numerous tales of sexual transgressions were not merely part of an Enlightenment libertine interest in the erotic, rather they were a reflection of a deep-seated disgust (and perhaps fascination) with the perversions of popery.[74] Indeed these sexual fears help explain the outcry in the early nineteenth century against Catholic emancipation (in which, interestingly, women played a prominent part in petitioning Parliament against the pro-Catholic legislation),[75] and the reaction to the restoration of the Catholic hierarchy in England in 1850.[76] Both events could be interpreted as threats to the professional standing of the Anglican clergy, and both saw a resurgence of such salacious propaganda.[77] The use of overtly sexual imagery to ridicule Catholic and nonconformist rivals is highlighted by the fact that there was a surprising lack of such imagery in the anti-Church-of-England clerical satires of the period. There were, of course, a large number of pamphlets and prints depicting the corrupt nature of the Anglican parson, but overwhelmingly these were economic (prompted largely by concern over tithes) or political, rather than sexual, in their nature. There was actually very little obscene or pornographic satire against the Anglican clergy during the long eighteenth century.[78]

This stress on the abnormal, sexual, and feminine associations of those deemed to be the professional rivals to the Anglican clergy is demonstrated by the ways in hostility to the Tractarian movement was expressed. This was more complex than the usual enmity shown to the opponents of the Church of England, since the revivalists came from

---

[72] P. Wagner, *Eros Revived. Erotica of the Enlightenment in England and America* (London, 1990), pp. 47–86.

[73] L. Colley, *Britons: Forging the Nation, 1707–1837* (New Haven, CT, 1992).

[74] For an analysis of how religious deviants represented people's inner desires, see N. Cohn, *Europe's Inner Demons* (St Albans, 1976), esp. pp. 256–63.

[75] Colley, *Britons*, pp. 237–81.

[76] G. F. A. Best, 'Popular protestantism in Victorian England', in R. Robson, ed., *Ideas and Institutions of Victorian Britain* (London, 1967), pp. 115–42; E. R. Norman, *Anti-Catholicism in Victorian England* (London, 1968); W. L. Arnstein, *Protestant Versus Catholic in Mid Victorian England* (Columbia, 1982); J. Wolffe, *The Protestant Crusade in Great Britain, 1829–1860* (Oxford, 1991).

[77] Wolffe, *Protestant Crusade*, pp. 2, 107, 121, 123–7.

[78] Wagner, *Eros*, pp. 59–60. See also J. Miller, *Religion in the Popular Prints, 1600–1832 [The English Satirical Print]* (Cambridge, 1986).

within the Church. Although the avowed stress by the Tractarians on the catholicity (although of course not on the *Roman* Catholicity) of the Anglican Church made them easy targets who could be attacked with the usual arsenal of insults, what is striking is that alongside the well-worn images of the fear of the confessional as a way of encouraging priestly control over women there was a new fear of 'effeminacy'. The clergy associated with the Oxford Movement were viewed not merely as threats to the traditional masculinity of Protestant culture, but were also seen as representing a de-masculinized religion (perhaps as befitted a movement which avowedly came from within the Establishment). They were depicted not just in terms of being rival men to the Anglican clergy and the Protestant husbands, but as emasculated men who could be accused of effeminacy and even homosexuality.[79]

One of the hardest tasks for the historian is to unpick accurately the resonances of such a gendered language. What we mean by 'masculine' and 'feminine' is not necessarily the same as the meanings given in previous centuries. The gendered language of the past is a difficult source for the historian, depending as it does on images, assumptions, and associations which often developed over a long period of time and which, moreover, may be lost to the modern secular listener. But these images do not merely tell us about attitudes towards popery and nonconformity. Since the Anglican clergy's analysis of popery (and by extension Protestant nonconformity) proceeded through a series of binary oppositions, every negative characteristic imputed to Rome implied a positive counterpart, which Anglicans claimed as their own exclusive property. By highlighting the negative and 'female' attributes of their opponents, such a discourse implicitly cemented the association of Anglican clergy with masculinity. Further, it might be suggested that in the relationship between religion and gender a two-way dynamic is involved. Not only were religious differences defined by reference to a gendered imagery, but conversely, notions of 'masculinity', 'femininity', and 'effeminacy' evolved through use in a religious context. Historians of gender ought to look at the religious

---

[79] D. Hilliard, 'Unenglish and unmanly: Anglo-catholicism and homosexuality', *Victorian Studies*, 25 (1981–2), pp. 181–210, and P. Ingram, 'Protestant patriarchy and the Catholic priesthood in nineteenth-century England', *Journal of Social History*, 24 (1991), pp. 783–97. Similarly, Davidoff and Hall have remarked how the concept of 'Evangelical manhood', with its stress on self-sacrifice and influence, came dangerously close to embracing what some regarded as 'feminine' qualities: *Family Fortunes*, p. 111.

connotations of 'masculine', 'feminine', and 'effeminate', in order to understand the resonances and purchase of these concepts in the past. Indeed it may be that the anti-popery discourse which encouraged people to think in binary terms was instrumental in shaping a binary gendered discourse, so that instead of a continuum of gender roles, which historians of gender claim for the medieval period, increasingly 'masculine' and 'feminine' attributes were sharply polarized.[80]

* * *

Most of the writing about the next main strand of this paper, the ways in which women have related to the clerical profession, has been couched in terms of female oppression and the struggles women had in seeking equality with men in being allowed to undertake the duties of the religious functionary. This, of course, is an important theme, and has alerted historians to the variety of ways in which patriarchy operated by asserting male control over female activity. The two centuries covered by this essay might be seen as being bounded by two attacks on the supremacy of the male religious professional: first, in the Civil War sects which were largely driven underground in the years after 1660 (although, as Anne Laurence has noted, women played a less active part in those sects than both contemporaries or later historians have sometimes believed);[81] and secondly, in the more prolonged and successful attack on the male religious professional which ended in the ordination of women even within the established Church, a movement which Brian Heeney labels 'church feminism', and whose origins can be found in the 1850s.[82] In the two centuries between these movements, historians have used the concepts of 'subordination', 'containment', and 'alienation' to analyse the ways in which women were marginalized from the public sphere. But what is at least as remarkable

---

[80] T. Laqueur, *Making Sex. Body and Gender from the Greeks to Freud* (Cambridge, MA, 1990).

[81] A. Laurence, 'A priesthood of she-believers: women and congregations in mid-seventeenth-century England', *SCH*, 27 (1990), esp. p. 362. See also R. Trubowitz, 'Female preachers and male wives: gender and authority in civil war England', *Prose Studies*, 14 (1991), pp. 112–33.

[82] B. Heeney, *The Women's Movement in the Church of England, 1850–1930* (Oxford, 1988); idem, 'The beginnings of Church feminism: women and the councils of the Church of England, 1897–1919', *JEH*, 33 (1982), pp. 89–109; idem, 'Women's struggle for professional work and status in the Church of England, 1900–1930', *HistJ*, 26 (1983), pp. 326–47. See also O. Anderson, 'Women preachers in mid-Victorian Britain: some reflexions on feminism, popular religion and social change', *HistJ*, 12 (1969), pp. 467–84.

is evidence which to some extent qualifies these categories, which are often derived from an analysis of the prescriptive literature. By concentrating on the textual prescriptions for 'containment' and 'marginalization' there is the danger that we as historians then marginalize the role of women from religious history. As David Hempton has recently pointed out, women were often willing accomplices in their positions, and indeed were able to do more than modern historians' concentration on their passive role would imply.[83] He himself has suggested that we should think about male and female religious behaviour not in terms of separate spheres, but in terms of concentric circles, where women might occasionally move into a wider circle (although, as he acknowledges, they were often pushed back into a smaller one).[84] In any case, even the idea of the separate sphere was, in practice, more flexible than is sometimes allowed; and it was often arguments which stemmed from there being a specific role for women which served as the justification for a more public female role.[85]

Further, although much work has been done to rescue those who have been 'hidden from history', we are in danger of paying more attention to the atypical, to the Ann Lees and the Joanna Southcotts who overtly challenged the male clerical professional, rather than studying the majority of women who, for whatever reason, not only accepted the organizational structures of the Church, but found it more accommodating than the model of subordination usually implies.[86] There is also the danger of suggesting that female fulfilment or even emancipation can come only from those who, in Deborah Valenze's important analysis, showed 'antipathy' to the mainstream established Church, who 'contradicted' and 'reproached' the clergy, and who were 'active rebels'.[87] This is perhaps inevitable given the

---

[83] Hempton, *Religion of the People*, p. 180.

[84] Ibid.

[85] Cf. D. Thompson, 'Women and nineteenth-century radical politics', in J. Mitchell and A. Oakley, eds, *The Rights and Wrongs of Women* (London, 1976), pp. 112–38, and P. Hollis, *Women in Public, 1850–1900: Documents of the Victorian Women's Movement* (London, 1979).

[86] See S. Rowbotham, *Hidden from History: 300 Years of Women's Oppression and the Fight against it* (London, 1973).

[87] D. Valenze, *Prophetic Sons and Daughters. Female Preaching and Popular Religion in Industrial England* (Princeton, NJ, 1985), pp. 7, 22, 138–9. It is also worth recognizing that even Joanna Southcott saw herself as operating within the Church of England: R. Robins, 'Anglican prophetess: Joanna Southcott and the Gospel story', *Anglican and Episcopal History*, 61 (1992), pp. 277–302. See also J. F. C. Harrison, *The Second Coming: Popular Millenarianism,*

types of sources available to us, but just as historians of the early modern period have argued that we should pay attention not merely to the 'godly' or the 'folksy' but also to the unspectacular orthodoxy of the majority of the population,[88] so we need to avoid the impression that only by subverting or challenging male norms were women able to participate as fully as they might wish in the Church. Of course, in some cases, acknowledging the roles that women were able to perform within the Church only reinforces the notion of subordination. As Patricia Crawford has wryly remarked: 'One function which women were always allowed to exercise in the Church was cleaning.'[89] But this statement should not stop us from seeing the full range of work which might exist in practice (from education and pastoral work to writing on behalf of the Church), and from recognizing that despite the male-dominated organizational structure, many women were devoted to the Anglican Church, and demonstrated their affection through leaving gifts and endowments to their parish church, and dutifully attending its ceremonies.[90] Furthermore, even within the male bureaucratic machinery of the Church, women could play key roles as patrons, and thereby achieve wide-ranging influence. The most famous literary example of a female patron, Lady Catherine de Bourgh, is, of course, highly negative;[91] but there were more positive role models such as Lady Betty Hastings (1682–1739), who lived on excellent terms with her vicar and gave away large sums of money for pious uses, and her relation Selina, Countess of Huntingdon (1707–91), whose own religious 'connexion' began by her exploiting the system of aristocratic private chaplains to get together a group of like-minded clergy under her control.[92]

In particular, what needs to be considered is the part played by the

---

1780–1850 (London, 1979) and J. K Hopkins, *A Woman to Deliver her People* (Austin, TX, and London, 1982).

[88] M. Ingram, 'Religion, communities and moral discipline in late sixteenth and early seventeenth-century England: case studies', in K. von Greyerz, ed., *Religion and Society in Early Modern Europe, 1500–1800* (London, 1984), p. 181.

[89] Crawford, *Women and Religion*, p. 56.

[90] Indeed, there seems to be something of a disjunction in the historiography whereby women are at once supposed to have felt alienated from the Church and were also the most active attenders at its services. This last point would suggest that they liked it, or at least were not alienated from it.

[91] Jane Austen, *Pride and Prejudice* (London, 1813). Lady Catherine consistently treats Mr Collins (the vicar) in an authoritarian manner.

[92] *DNB.*

clergyman's wife, sisters, and daughters. These figures remain remarkably shadowy, both in the history of women and in the history of the
Church, although passing reference is often made to them as the
'unpaid' curates of the clergy.[93] However, their roles need more
extended and systematic treatment than is usually allowed. Clergy
wives were the concomitant of a married clergy, and in terms of social
and economic history their existence goes to the heart of the difference
between Protestant and Catholic regimes. Of all the consequences of
the Protestant Reformation, the effects of having a married clergy have
been unduly neglected by historians. Yet it could be argued that the
change from a nominally celibate to an overwhelmingly married clergy
was one of the most far-reaching results of the Reformation. This
transformation did, of course, take time: an example of the lingering
presence of Catholic traditions among the Protestant clergy, and
indeed amongst society more generally. As Mary Prior has demonstrated, it was not really socially acceptable for higher clergy at least to
take wives even in the early seventeenth century,[94] and as late as the
1660s there was still a suspicion that clergy wives did nothing but 'lay
up their estates, and do no good nor relieve any poor'.[95] But by the end
of the seventeenth century married clergy became regarded as the
norm (even for those who chose to remain unmarried). This transformation can be witnessed at the highest levels of the Church. John
Tillotson was the first married clergyman to be promoted to the
archbishopric of Canterbury since the sixteenth century (he married
Oliver Cromwell's niece Elizabeth in 1664),[96] and Thomas Herring
(Archbishop 1747–57) was the last not to be married until the early
twentieth century.[97]

---

[93] M. H. Watt, *A History of the Parson's Wife* (London, 1947), and A. Tindal Hart, *The Eighteenth-Century Country Parson circa 1689 to 1830* (Shrewsbury, 1955), pp. 90–2.

[94] M. Prior, 'Reviled and crucified marriages: the position of Tudor bishops' wives', in eadem, *Women in English Society, 1500–1800* (London, 1985), pp. 118–48. See also the discussion in P. Marshall, *The Catholic Priesthood and the English Reformation* (Oxford, 1994), pp. 165–72. Both would suggest that the statements by E. J. Carlson, 'Clerical marriage and the English Reformation', *JBS*, 31 (1992), pp. 26–8, and R. M. Spielmann, 'The beginnings of clerical marriage in the English Reformation: the reigns of Edward and Mary', *Anglican and Episcopal History*, 26 (1987), pp. 251–63, that clerical marriage was the accepted norm by 1560, are overly optimistic.

[95] *The Diary of Samuel Pepys*, ed. R. Latham and W. Matthews, 11 vols (London, 1970–83), 8, p. 67.

[96] She survived him, living until 1702, highlighting the problem of how clergy widows should be maintained. She was given a £600 annuity.

[97] *DNB*.

Perhaps we should begin by asking what kind of a woman married a cleric? In the diocese of Chichester during the first half of the eighteenth century the vast majority of clergy wives had themselves been the daughters of clergy or gentry; and the same appears true of the early nineteenth century, where Davidoff and Hall discovered that the daughters of clergymen seemed to have had a strong propensity to marry into the clergy.[98] Horace Walpole offered one reason why women might find clergymen a good catch:

> [I]f a girl is in love, how can she secure such a prospect of felicity as by marrying a clergyman. . . . It is almost the only chance they have of not being disappointed. If the bellwether strays after other ewes, the noise he makes betrays him, and [she] is sure of reclaiming him.[99]

It has also been suggested that clergy wives, in some cases, had a sense of a joint vocation with their husbands, which inevitably affected the type of person a young ordinand might marry. The newly ordained William Jones found himself drawn to a woman who gave no thought to religion, yet was attractive and wealthy: 'But what am I doing?' he asked himself,

> am I, as they call it, in love? With what? with my own folly and, it may be my own misery. I fear there is something very mean and base in my attachment to my present object. She seems to be an utter stranger to God; and yet I fondly think I could be happy with her. But how can two travel together, except they be agreed? Were I (as I now think happy enough) to marry her, what distress might it pierce my soul to think that I was embracing in my bosom one who, perhaps, must be after this life everlastingly separated from me. With respect to the training of children, if we had any, and the management of other parts of our family, how distinctly opposite must our sentiments be! . . . Is

---

[98] J. Chamberlain, '"The changes and chances of this mortal life": the vicissitudes of High Churchmanship and politics among the clergy of Sussex, 1700–45' (University of Chicago at Illinois Ph.D. thesis, 1992), p. 65; Davidoff and Hall, *Family Fortunes*, p. 119. The conviction that clergy wives came from relatively genteel backgrounds was one reason which clergy gave in support of clergy widows receiving financial help: they could not be expected to work for a living.
[99] *Walpole's Correspondence*, 25, p. 424: Walpole to Mann, 30 July 1783.

it not time to awake? when I consider matters soberly, I must needs be ensured of enjoying more true happiness in marriage with a pious women, tho' possessed not of a farthing, than with a graceless, gay, dissipated lady, who has a million a year at her command. Guide me, O my heavenly Father![100]

Whatever the reasons for marriage, what is to be highlighted here is the role which clergy wives played in the operation of the clerical profession in practice, and how, despite the largely negative connotations envisaged by female participation in religious organizations, wives of the clergy could, if they chose, exploit their position, and in this sense participate in the male clerical profession. Of course, generalizations are bound to be problematic. Just as there was no single clerical experience, there certainly was no typical clergy wife's experience. But we must be careful not to allow clergy wives to suffer from the 'condescension of posterity'.[101] If, as E. P. Thompson has argued, labouring women had the skill to turn 'customary' practices to their advantage, having the capacity to subvert, or at least find their own strategies within, the legal and cultural limitations of patriarchy, then we might recognize that the same could be true of the wives of the clergy.[102] In any case, it may be that by studying figures such as these, we will get a more accurate way of assessing the impact of women on religion rather than just the other way around.

Part of the power of the clergy wife stemmed precisely from the fact that the home was regarded as a female domain, and she could reach out from this to have influence over the rest of the parish, especially as it was often asserted that the clergyman's home was the model for the houses of other parishioners. In 1697, for example, George Stanhope, a future Dean of Canterbury, made the connection between the cleric as a father to his flock and as father to his family : 'the Care and Abilities of such a Person to instruct and oversee the House of God as a Spiritual father, would best be measured by the condition of his own Family at

[100] *The Diary of the Revd William Jones, 1777–1821*, ed. O. F. Christie (London, 1929), pp. 78–9.
[101] This phrase, which historians are using with regard to any group which seems unduly neglected by historians, is, of course, E. P. Thompson's, *The Making of the English Working Class* (Harmondsworth, 1963), p. 12.
[102] See, for example, his 'The moral economy of the English crowd in the eighteenth century', *P&P*, 50 (Feb. 1971), pp. 76–136.

Home'.[103] This complicates our understanding of the public/private dichotomy, since it was his wife who would be responsible for the family and home. But the clergyman's home was not only a model for the rest of the parish; it was frequently the training ground for the next generation of clerics. Much recent work on the clerical profession in the period after 1660 has stressed the importance of the clerical dynasty in creating a sense of professional ethos and group identity within the clergy, with sons following their fathers and grandfathers into the profession.[104] Clerical dynasties, where the same family provided the incumbent of a parish over three generations, such as the Curteises at Sevenoaks and the Hodsons at Thornham, were not uncommon.[105] And, in some clergy families, more than one son became ordained. In the case of Thomas Porter, rector of East Hoathly from 1752 to 1794, three of his sons became priests.[106] It is sometimes forgotten, however, that clergy had mothers, sisters, and daughters as well as fathers, brothers, and sons. Clearly women were instrumental in creating this clerical tribalism, especially since they were often responsible for the religious education of their children. This gave them a crucial if unmeasurable influence over the upbringing and religious orientation of future clergy. A striking instance of this is Susanna Wesley, the wife of the Anglican incumbent of Epworth, whose system of religious instruction and education was recorded in a letter she wrote later for her son John.[107] She was the mother of nineteen children, of whom only three of her sons reached maturity.[108] It was to be a predominantly female household in which John Wesley grew up and received his religious education. Susanna herself had been well-educated in theology, became converted to the Church of England as a teenager as a result of her reading, and thus demanded a rigorous education for her children. Doubtless Susanna Wesley was not a typical

---

[103] G. Stanhope, *A Sermon Preached Before the Sons of the Clergy* (London, 1697), p. 3.

[104] See Gregory, 'Archbishop, cathedral and parish', ch. 2.

[105] J. Gregory, ed., *The Speculum of Archbishop Secker*, Church of England Record Society, 2 (Woodbridge, 1995), p. xv.

[106] *The Diary of Thomas Turner, 1754–1765*, ed. D. Vaisey (Oxford, 1985), p. 336.

[107] *The Works of John Wesley, vol. 19, Journals and Diaries II (1738–43)*, ed. W. R. Ward and R. P. Heizenrater (Nashville, TN, 1990), pp. 286–91. See also C. Wallace, '"Some stated employment of your mind": reading, writing and religion in the life of Susanna Wesley', *ChH*, 58 (1989), pp. 354–66.

[108] H. Rack, *Reasonable Enthusiast: John Wesley and the Rise of Methodism* (London, 1989), p. 48. On the 'femininity of Wesley's early environment', see V. H. H. Green, *The Young Mr Wesley. A Study of John Wesley and Oxford* (London, 1961), pp. 51–3.

wife of an Anglican clergyman; but neither should we exaggerate her atypicality. Just as some historians would want to remind us of John Wesley's essential links to the Church of England, so too his mother's religious activity ought to be seen within an Anglican experience, and not merely as something which foreshadowed a later nonconformist movement. In any case her behaviour indicated how far the pre-scriptive gender roles might break down in practice. John Wesley himself once commented that his mother 'did not feel for others nearly so much as my father did; but she did ten times more than he did' for the poor and needy of the parish.[109] Samuel Wesley was by all accounts a hopeless manager, and his wife was far more clear-headed: in this relationship at least the traditional gendered distinction between 'feminine' feeling and 'masculine' action was reversed. Famously, Susanna took her duties as a clergyman's wife so seriously that when Samuel was in London during the winter of 1712 acting as a Proctor in Convocation, seeing the shortcomings of the curate he had left in charge she made amends by holding services in her kitchen and reading prayers and sermons to her children. In a letter she explained her actions to her husband:

> As I am a woman, so I am also mistress of a large family. And though the superior charge of the souls contained in it lies upon you, . . . yet in your absence I cannot but look upon every soul you leave under my care as a talent committed to me under a trust by the great Lord of all the families, both of heaven and earth.[110]

Gradually neighbours wanted to join in, listening to her reading out sermons.

> I cannot conceive why any should reflect upon you because your wife endeavours to draw people to church . . . [and] as for your proposal of letting some other person read; alas! you do not consider what a people these are. I don't think one man among them could read a sermon, without spelling a good part of it.

---

[109] Quoted in J. Pollock, *John Wesley* (London, 1989), p. 20.

[110] Wesley, *Journals, II*, pp. 284–6. See also C. Wallace, 'Susanna Wesley's spirituality: the freedom of a Christian woman', *Methodist History*, 22 (1983–4), pp. 158–73, who places her within a 'puritan' and 'revivalist' context, but downplays her 'Anglican' context.

Nor has any of our family a voice strong enough to be heard by such a number of people.

She concluded:

> It came into my mind, though I am not a man, nor a minister of the Gospel, and so cannot be employed in such a worthy employment as they were; yet if my heart were sincerely devoted to God, and if I were inspired with a true zeal for his glory, and did really desire the salvation of souls, I might do something more than I do.

Her justifications for her actions are interesting. First, she claimed, her duties towards her family had encouraged her to take on a more active role in religious matters. Second, there is an intimation of the same kinds of arguments her son John would later use in justifying what his opponents considered to be methodist innovations. Throughout her statement there is an ambiguity which was characteristic of early Methodism: there is acknowledgement of constraint, yet also the possibility of doing something else; but that flexibility occurs within Anglicanism and not just outside it. Interestingly, too, another female supporter of Methodism who took on an active religious role, Mary Bosanquet (1739–1815), became the wife of John Fletcher, the Anglican vicar of Madeley, Shropshire. She too used to hold services in her kitchen, and found that her marriage gave her wider scope and opportunities. On the first Sunday after their wedding, Fletcher introduced his wife to his parishioners: 'I have not married a wife for myself only, but for your sakes also',[111] which is indicative of the ways in which he saw his wife as having a public role. After his death she continued to live in the parsonage and direct the work of the curate, as well as preaching in meeting houses.[112]

By the early nineteenth century, the role of the clergyman's wife was such that manuals were being written for her instruction. The evangelically-minded anonymous author of *Hints to a Clergyman's Wife; or Female Parochial Duties Practically Illustrated* (1832), who hoped that his book might 'prove of some little utility to those Christian females

---

[111] Quoted in Tindal Hart, *Country Parson*, p. 91.
[112] *DNB*.

who are anxious to become true yoke-fellows to their husbands, in the faithful discharge of the high office of the Christian ministry',[113] noted that the distinguishing characteristics of the female – tenderness and compassion – would greatly help clergy in their ministry. Interestingly, these were some of the same qualities which were later put forward as reasons why women should be ordained. The writer separated the role of the clergy wife into three main areas: those where she might co-operate with her husband (such as visiting the sick, distributing charity, and organizing Sunday schools); those where she had a subordinate role (such as the religious instruction of female parishioners); and those where she was independent (the precise details of which he was rather reticent about). Further, her role was seen as crucial in the maintenance of social order in the parish, and this was especially important given the socio-economic dislocation of the early nineteenth century:

> Let her endeavour, in cases of dissension to soften animosity, to assuage anger and irritation; to remove prejudice and its usual concomitant, ignorance; to pour the oil of consolation into the bosom of the agitated and oppressed, and thus gradually to become the general peace-maker in all the little turmoils of a country parish.[114]

Here the clergy wife's role of parish reconciler harks back to John Bossy's depiction of the social role of the clergy as being one of containing faction in the parish.[115] Further, there is a suggestion that the clergyman's wife should look after the physical (and medical) well-being of the parishioners. For Hannah More, the crucial role played by the wife of the cleric is demonstrated in her idealistic depiction of Mrs Barlow in her novel *Coelebs in Search of a Wife* (1809): 'By the large part she takes in [Dr Barlow's] affairs, he is enabled to give himself wholly up to the duties of his profession. She is as attentive to the bodies, as her husband is to the souls of his people, and educates his own family as sedulously as he instructs his parish.'[116] This stress on the importance

---

[113] *Hints to a Clergyman's Wife; or Female Parochial Duties Practically Illustrated* (London, 1832), preface.

[114] Ibid., p. 22.

[115] J. Bossy, 'Blood and baptism: kinship, community and Christianity in Western Europe from the fourteenth to the seventeenth centuries', *SCH*, 10 (1973), pp. 129–43.

[116] H. More, *Coelebs in Search of a Wife* (London, 1809), p. 137.

of the role of the clergyman's wife was not, however, just an evangelical tenet. In the mid-nineteenth century, Francis Edward Paget, a supporter of the Oxford Movement, could claim that the clergyman's wife was the 'adviser, parent, friend of both young and old'; in short she was 'the universal mother'.[117] Interestingly both Paget and the writer of the *Hints* complicated the notion of separate spheres and the distinction between 'public' and 'private' roles. The latter was keen to remind the clergyman's wife that she should not 'stir a step beyond the bounds of her own department of duty', but he also acknowledged that 'much more . . . may frequently be done by the kind encouragement and private instruction of the minister's wife than by her husband's public exercises'.[118] This he suggested might occur at times of confirmation classes: 'the more regular and systematic examination of the candidates will of course devolve upon the minister. But in cases where female bashfulness and timidity often operate as a bar to confidence, the maternal and affectionate instruction of his wife may be most serviceable.'[119]

Wives might, of course, have disturbed relations between the clergy and the wider community,[120] but on the whole they seem to have been important in relating the clergyman to the wider world. It was through being married that the clergyman might have more knowledge of his flock. At the very least, those clergy who were not married might have found it difficult to relate to their parishioners. John Skinner, the rector of Camerton, Somerset, from 1800 to 1839, whose wife died in 1811, lived for the next twenty-five years in an almost perpetual state of battle with his flock.[121] Arguably then, it was the wife who helped the clergyman operate within the public sphere, and by 1851 a monthly journal, *The Vineyard*, was being produced for clergy wives with articles on parish visiting and the organization of Sunday schools. In the late 1840s, Bishop Wilberforce of Oxford occasionally praised the pastoral work of wives in his Diocese Books. Once he even gave a parson's wife most of the credit for her husband's success. This

[117] F. E. Paget, *The Owlet of Owlstone Edge: His Travels, his Experience and his Lucubrations* (London, 1856), p. 30.

[118] *Hints to a Clergyman's Wife*, p. 123.

[119] Ibid., p. 122.

[120] It might be that the need to maintain the clerical family made it even more pressing for the incumbent to collect his tithes, and this was an extra cause of conflict in the parish: Gregory, 'Archbishop, cathedral and parish', ch. 4.

[121] See *The Journal of a Somerset Rector, 1803–1834*, ed. H. and P. Coombs (Oxford, 1981).

occurred at Hillesden, about whose vicar, Revd W. T. Eyre, the Bishop wrote: 'The best part of him is his wife. Raised £20 for the S[ociety for the] P[ropagation of the] G[ospel] & a very good school. Compl[ained] to [the] B[isho]p of Lincoln that his wife would work him to death. She has worked wonders in him. Hillesden is in pretty good order.'[122]

Clergy wives, were, of course, not the only female relatives of clergy who participated in the pastoral work of the Church. Daughters, such as Elizabeth Carter, the eldest child of the rector of Deal in the mid-eighteenth century, not only helped her widowed father in looking after a large family, she also helped him in his cure, and operated on a more national level by writing on behalf of the Church.[123] It is worth pointing out, too, that those women who have traditionally been labelled the 'blue-stockings' of the eighteenth century, such as Catherine Talbot, Elizabeth Montagu, and Hannah More, and who have also been given the label of 'feminists', were either daughters of the clergy, or had strong links with the Church establishment.[124]

It might also be worth thinking about the ways in which being married affected the private lives of the clergy. Although most of this essay has been concerned with what might be called the public face of the clerical profession, it is worth reminding ourselves of the private realm of the cleric. The 'private sphere' has of course been a much discussed, if problematic, tool of gender analysis, and has been used in relation to women, rather than men. But an action is not either public or private in an absolute sense, but rather takes on its character according to context; and we should remember that men had private as well as public lives. We need to ask impertinent questions. How did marriage affect the private lives of the clergy? What was it like being married to a clergyman? These are of course almost impossible questions to answer, although diaries provide valuable insights.

The evidence, not surprisingly, is inconclusive. On the one hand,

[122] Quoted in H. C. Kiener, 'Clergy and community: the Church of England in Buckinghamshire, 1830–1914' (University of Connecticut Ph.D. thesis, 1981), p. 191.
[123] Most notably through her translation of the works of Epictetus which was published in 1758, with the encouragement of Archbishop Secker.
[124] Catherine Talbot was the daughter of a son of the Bishop of Durham and lived in the household of Archbishop Secker. See S. Myers, *The Bluestocking Circle. Women, Friendship and the Life of the Mind in the Eighteenth Century* (Oxford, 1990), and Todd, *Dictionary of British and American Women Writers.* Jane Austen, of course, was also the daughter of an eighteenth-century cleric. See I. Collins, *Jane Austen and the Clergy* (London, 1994), and D. Monnaghan, '*Mansfield Park* and Evangelicalism: a reassessment', *Nineteenth-Century Fiction,* 33 (1978–9), pp. 215–30.

George Woodward, the rector of East Hendred in the 1750s, found a soul-mate in his wife Albinia. He recalled in 1754 how for their winter's entertainment they had been reading Thomas Stackhouse's *History of the Bible* together:

> [W]e have just made a beginning, by going through the Introduction, which is a judicious performance and very entertaining to my wife as well as myself, for (to let you a little into her character) she amongst other great qualifications is a very good Divine; for she is a perfect mistress of the Bible and several books of divinity; which makes the reading of such books much more agreeable to me, than otherwise they would be if she was a person of no taste, and seemed quite indifferent to what I was about.[125]

A similar picture of a meeting of hearts and minds comes from Mary Bosanquet's Journal:

> I have the kindest and tenderest of husbands; so spiritual a man, and so spiritual a union I never had any conception of. . . . Glory! unceasing glory to my adorable Lord! this day we have been married one year. O how does my soul praise God for this gracious Providence! What a help-mate he is to me, and how much better do we love one another this day, than we did this day before twelve months.[126]

Other clergy wives did not necessarily share the views of their husbands. Susanna Wesley, for instance, admitted to John that 'Tis an unhappiness almost peculiar to our family that your father and I seldom think alike';[127] and William Jones of Broxbourne seems to have had a continual round of tiffs with his wife Theodosia, so that he kept 'A Booke of Domestic Lamentations' (which he later burnt). But even here there is a sense of playful badinage, as he calls her 'my old rib', 'my old mate', 'the dear partner of my life', and 'my commanding

---

[125] *A Parson in the Vale of White Horse. George Woodward's Letters from East Hendred, 1753–1761*, ed. D. Gibson (Gloucester, 1982), pp. 61–2.

[126] Quoted in T. Morrow, *Early Methodist Women* (London, 1967), p. 90. See *The Life of Mrs Mary Fletcher*, ed. H. Moore (London, 1818).

[127] Quoted in Rack, *Reasonable Enthusiast*, p. 50.

officer'.[128] More serious was the case of that unfortunate clergyman John Butler, who claimed that his relations with his wife were so bad (something which he blamed on his son having converted to Catholicism) that he had been encouraged to run off with another woman – which led him to defend, on scriptural grounds, the practice of 'honest concubinage to supply the defects of barren and unhappy marriages'.[129]

* * *

This survey of some of the ways in which women participated in the clerical profession raises issues which might be further explored. We should of course recognize, as George Orwell's clergyman's daughter would later do, that some, perhaps many, women resented being a clergyman's wife or child. The role of clergyman's wife is indeed the classic case of a woman being incorporated into her husband's profession, and in this sense subordinated her independence to her partner's requirements. But pastoral tasks taken on by the wives, daughters and sisters of the clergy complicate our picture of clerical and lay relations. Should we count clergy wives as part of the clergy, or as part of the laity? Technically, of course, they were members of the laity (and this point was stressed by the preachers of the sermons before the Corporation of the Sons of the Clergy, to stifle anxiety that by giving to the widows and children of the clergy, money was being transferred from the lay to the clerical estate);[130] but from the parishioners' point of view the clergyman's wife might seem as much a representative of the Church as her husband. Indeed Thomas Turner, the shop-keeper of East Hoathly, complained of Mrs Porter, the rector's wife, who haggled over the prices in his shop: 'If Mrs Porter is neither Turk nor Infidel, I am sure her behaviour is not Christian, or at least not like that of a clergyman's wife.'[131] Furthermore, Turner frowned upon the fact that it was Mrs Porter who often led the revelling in the village community: it was she who headed the party-goers in the well-known incident in which on 23 February 1758 Turner was dragged from his bed at six o'clock in the

---

[128] Christie, *Diary of Jones*, pp. 90, 92, 96, 98, 110, 270; Tindal Hart, *Country Parson*, p. 90.
[129] *The True State of the Case of John Butler, BD. A Minister of the True Church of England: in Answer to the Libel of Martha his Sometimes Wife* (London, 1697), p. 34.
[130] For example, G. Lavington, *A Sermon Preached before the Sons of the Clergy* (London, 1734), p. 19.
[131] Vaisey, *Diary of Turner*, p. 98.

morning and made to dance about wearing his wife's petticoat.[132] His attitude is suggestive of the ways in which ideas about proper clerical behaviour (and in this case proper clerical wifely behaviour) came not only from within the Church as a professional organization, but were also part of the laity's expectations. Perhaps recognizing this, Hannah More's fictional cleric, Dr Barlow, mused:

I often reflect how peculiarly incumbent it is on us to select such partners as shall never cause our emancipation from the old restrictions to be regretted. And we ourselves ought, by improving the character of our wives, to repay the debt we owe to the ecclesiastical laws of Protestantism for the privilege of possessing them.[133]

In conclusion, what were the pastoral consequences of having a married clergy? As early as the 1570s William Harrison, rector of Radwinter in Essex, had been convinced that the support of a wife, rather than any significant improvement in income, had made it possible for ordinary incumbents to do their parish duty.[134] This has led some historians to wonder whether bachelor clergy were increasingly at a disadvantage in carrying out their professional tasks.[135] Moreover, the need to support their families, it has been suggested, may have led many Anglican clergy in the 1640s and 1650s to comply with the new regime;[136] and may also explain why several who were attracted to the nonjuring schism in fact remained in the Church.[137] But we might be able to point to some further effects of the pastoral role played by the clergy's female relatives, which rather belie the often negative connotations of female religious activity demonstrated in the first half of this essay. First, given that clergy wives were often

---

[132] Ibid., p. 138.

[133] More, *Coelebs*, p. 137.

[134] F. Heal, *Hospitality in Early Modern England* (Oxford, 1990), p. 252.

[135] P. Collinson, 'Shepherds, sheepdogs and hirelings: the pastoral ministry in post-reformation England', *SCH*, 26 (1989), pp. 214–15. It is worth recalling that James Woodforde, who remained unmarried, relied on his niece Nancy as a companion and house-keeper. She sometimes found this boring: *The Diary of a Country Parson, 1758–1802*, ed. J. Beresford (Oxford, 1978), p. 451.

[136] I. Green, 'The persecution of "scandalous" and "malignant" parish clergy during the English Civil War', *EHR*, 104 (1979), p. 527.

[137] J. C. Findon, 'The Nonjurors and the Church of England, 1689–1716' (University of Oxford D.Phil. thesis, 1979), p. 100.

deemed to have had special responsibility for women, it may be that, through their wives, married clergy received a better sense of the state of mind of some of the females of the parish. Second, having a married incumbent may have made parish clergy seem more 'normal' to the majority of male parishioners. If, as Patricia Crawford has argued, the Reformation sexualized parish politics by recognizing the sexuality of the clergyman,[138] then having a married cleric might at least have limited the suspicion (which seems to have been prevalent in Catholic countries) that the incumbent was after the wives of the other men in the parish. Is it possible to suggest, therefore, that there was an emerging pastoral difference between Catholic and Protestant regimes as a consequence of having a married clergy? Did the fact of having a wife make Protestant clergy appear more ordinary, so that, despite the general trend towards female-dominated congregations throughout Europe by the nineteenth century, nevertheless (and as recent comparative research on religion and gender in England, France, Germany, and America has shown), there was an apparently growing divergence between Catholic and Protestant experience, whereby Protestant cultures retained a greater hold on their male parishioners than their Catholic counterparts?[139] And if, as Hugh McLeod has recently suggested, factors which heightened anti-clericalism were those which separated the clergy from the bulk of their parishioners, such as distinctive dress and a stress on celibacy, then having a married clergy was perhaps one of the factors which stopped anti-clericalism in England from reaching the levels it did in Catholic Europe.[140] Certainly there is little sign in the period between 1660 and 1850 of that masculinist critique of the clergy which, in the wake of the Tractarian revival, and especially during the Ritualist movement, would be such a feature of English anti-clericalism in the later nineteenth century, where clergy were accused of not being 'real men'.[141] Thus, although the associations between women and religion

---

[138] Crawford, *Women and Religion*, p. 51.

[139] H. McLeod, 'Weibliche Frömmigkeit – männlicher Unglaube? Religion und Kircken im bürgerlichen 19 Jahrhundert', in *Bürgerinnen und Bürger Geshlecterverhaltnisse im 19 Jahrhundert*, ed. U. Frevert (Göttingen, 1988), pp. 134–56. See also his nuanced comments in his *Piety and Poverty: Working Class Religion in Berlin, London and New York, 1870–1914* (New York, 1996), pp. 149–73.

[140] Idem, 'English anticlericalism, 1850–1900', unpublished lecture, Anglo-American Conference, London, June 1996.

[141] Ibid.

were ambivalent, the male clerical professional of the Church of England during the period from 1660 to 1850 profited more than we may have realized from his female relatives.

University of Northumbria

FROM 'THE STATE OF MY SOUL' TO 'EXALTED PIETY': WOMEN'S VOICES IN THE *ARMINIAN/METHODIST MAGAZINE*, 1778–1821

by MARGARET P. JONES

J OHN Wesley's version of evangelical Christianity was distinguished by its insistence on the universal availability of salvation ('Free Grace'), an insistence which rapidly led to the definition of Wesleyan theology as 'Arminian' in contradistinction to the Calvinist evangelicalism of Whitfield, Toplady, and others. Controversy was violent in the 1740s, and flared up again in the 1770s. It was against this background that John Wesley founded the *Arminian Magazine* in 1778. It was to function in defence of Arminianism, and to consist of 'tracts on the universal love of God, wrote in this and the last century',[1] together with 'Original Pieces'. This might seem an unlikely place for women to speak, or even to be spoken about, but Arminianism was not defended solely by means of tracts. By the year of Wesley's death (1791), besides significant amounts of poetry and short anecdotes (the latter characterized by Wesley in 1781 as 'bits and scraps', with which he would scorn to fill up the *Magazine*), there are also fifteen letters written by women, and eleven accounts of women's lives (slightly outnumbering both letters from and accounts of men). Later years show an even greater preponderance of women's 'Lives'. Leaving on one side the value of this source to the historian, this paper seeks only to analyse women's opportunities to speak publicly in their own voice in the *Arminian* (later *Methodist*) *Magazine* under John Wesley's editorship and later.[2]

The *Magazine* was a public space, although increasingly within the self-contained world of Methodism. When, in 1789, Wesley abandoned his original plan of selling it through booksellers in favour of distribution 'At the Methodist Preaching-Houses', he effectively limited its circulation to those in direct contact with the Methodist Connexion and its preachers. This still gave it a wide circulation,

---

[1] *Arminian Magazine* (hereafter *AM*), 1 (1778), p. v.
[2] John Wesley's title was changed in 1798 to *The Methodist Magazine*, but volume numbers continued in sequence.

although figures are difficult to come by (the *Edinburgh Review*'s estimate of eighteen to twenty thousand in 1807, in a strongly anti-Methodist article,[3] should probably carry a health warning). Sharing of copies, well attested for newspapers at a figure of ten families to one newspaper in 1821,[4] and mentioned in the *Magazine* itself, increased the effective circulation. Benjamin Gregory, recalling its appeal in his boyhood, shows how he and other readers were formed by its gender stereotypes of male 'worthies' and sensitive female poets.[5] For the *Magazine*, as a place of publication, was also a gendered place, reflecting and generating male world-views. Men controlled it as editors, as the theologians who wrote its learned portions, and as the preachers who sent in material and distributed copies. A magazine in which the popular short anecdotes portray women as the passive victims of violence, illness, and poverty (unless they are spectacular sinners, The Girl Who Subsisted on Water Alone Almost Four Years, witches, or Queen Elizabeth)[6] might seem an unlikely milieu for women to find space to make themselves heard. Subtle changes within the roles of editor, writer, and preacher did, however, allow women a greater or less amount of space for their own speaking over the years. This study covers a period of forty-three years – long enough to show significant change, and including the long editorships of John Wesley (1778–91) and Joseph Benson (1804–21), as well as the time of transition and shared responsibility in between.

It was clearly John Wesley's choice, exercised through the medium of his complete editorial control, which first made the *Magazine* a place where women might be able to speak. This might be explained by reference to his personality; but this paper argues that there were more general factors at work. Theological controversy at this period did not use solely the male-dominated genres of sermon and theological treatise. Wesley described the 'Accounts and Letters, containing the experience of pious persons, the greatest part of whom are still alive',[7] which feature from the very first volume, as 'the marrow of experimental and practical divinity'. Evidence of prevenient, justifying,

---

[3] Cited in R. Altick, *The English Common Reader: A Social History of Mass Publishing, 1800–1900* (Chicago, 1957), p. 168.

[4] Ibid., p. 392.

[5] *Wesleyan Methodist Magazine*, 6th ser., 1 (1877), p. 11.

[6] *AM*, 4 (1781), p. 375; *Methodist Magazine* [hereafter *MM*], 37 (1814) [for vol. nos see above, n. 1], pp. 629-30; *AM*, 10 (1787), pp. 476-8, 533-5, 601; *AM*, 13 (1790), pp. 46-7.

[7] *AM*, 1 (1788), p. vi.

and sanctifying grace in the lives of believers was just as strong a defence of Arminianism as more formal theological argument. Encouraging correspondents to 'tell their stories' was not simply an expression of personal affection or pastoral concern, or even a desire to encourage, but of theological method. Central to this method is epistemology: 'And how am I assured that I do not mistake the voice of the Spirit?'[8] The answer is experiential: 'By the fruits which he hath wrought in your spirit you shall know the "testimony of the Spirit of God". . . . The immediate fruits of the Spirit ruling in the heart are "love, joy and peace". . . . And the outward fruits are the doing good to all men.'[9] Women and men could testify equally to their experience of such 'fruits', and thus a 'window' was created for women's contributions to be valued equally with men's.

Women's voices are prominent in John Wesley's *Arminian Magazine*. Each volume contains approximately sixty letters written to him over the years (he selected methodically, beginning from 1738 and working through as far as 1783 by the time of his death). And, because Wesley had always used his correspondence to encourage others to tell their spiritual stories, in turning to his letter-books for material for the *Magazine* he found biographical material already to hand. The (auto)biographical content developed rapidly: Wesley wrote to preachers asking for their accounts of themselves, and in 1781 decided to include at least one life of 'those real Christians who . . . have lately finished their course with joy'[10] in each issue. Perhaps surprisingly, in view of the early prominence of preachers' autobiographies, forty per cent of the (auto)biographical material published under Wesley's editorship relates to women, with 113 biographies and nineteen accounts which are to a greater or lesser degree autobiographical, and eighty-seven individual writers identified. Letters and autobiographies of course stand in a different class from biographies; here we may find women actually speaking for themselves rather than being spoken about by others (usually men: there are a mere fourteen accounts of women by women, as against ninety-nine by men).

The first volume of the *Magazine* also included poetry. The suitability of Charles Wesley's poetry for the 'defence of Arminianism'

---

[8] 'The Witness of the Spirit', I, in *The Works of John Wesley, vol. 1: Sermons, I, 1–33*, ed. A. C. Outler (Nashville, TN, 1984), p. 283.
[9] Ibid.
[10] *AM*, 5 (1782), p. v.

is obvious; what is not so immediately obvious is the fact that this decision opened the *Magazine* to a genre in which women were expected to be proficient, if uncommon (seven women poets out of 218, in Cibber's *Biographical Dictionary of Poets* of 1753, may not be many, but at least they are there). The first volume of the *Arminian Magazine* contains fifty-four poems, and fourteen of them are identifiably by women.

John Wesley's *Arminian Magazine* appears, then, to be a place where women were able to find space to make themselves heard in a male-dominated public environment. Closer examination reveals a world with a subtle texture of oppression and freedom, a place of patriarchal barriers with unexpected cracks in them. Women's voices are heard: the tone of women's letters published in the *Magazine* is, on the whole, different to those by men. Women write largely about their 'inner' experience, appearing as those whose focus is internal, private, and emotional, and often referring to their relationship with John Wesley. Men do describe their thoughts and feelings, sometimes in language that might be characterized as 'feminine' (alerting the modern reader to the danger of stereotyping); but they often employ a more detached tone, and are far more likely than women to describe events and to convey news. Taking an example at random, Volume 4 (1781) yields, in consecutive letters, Miss B. (Mary Bishop) writing to John Wesley that 'I had no intent of drawing you to speak more freely: but feeling a strong desire for your soul's prosperity, I just spoke what was upper-most in my heart'; and Mr Thomas Ranken writing, 'God is at work here in a wonderful manner. At first many were much tempted against me for enforcing the Rules of our Society.'[11]

This difference in voice, observable throughout the published letters, may not straightforwardly reflect a gender difference in the writing. John Wesley's *Arminian Magazine* was not freely available to women's self-expression: their appearance in print at all depended on his control, not merely as editor but, maybe years before, as correspondent. On at least three different levels he was able to intervene in what his correspondents had to say, possibly distorting the women's distinctive voice. First, he actively encouraged corres-pondents to write what he wanted to hear, as reflected by the anonymous correspondent (almost certainly, by literary convention,

[11] *AM*, 4 (1781), pp. 217-18.

female) who wrote 'It is not my usual manner to say so much about myself, but as you asked me the state of my soul, I thought it a call to declare what God had done for me.'[12] Secondly, the letter had to be edited for printing. Detailed comparison of Ann Bolton's published letters with the manuscript originals has shown much omission and merging in the interests of 'polish', but nothing materially added.[13] But even 'improved' grammar and syntax modify the voice. Thirdly, there are the criteria of selection. Wesley may have selected letters in accordance with his preconceived notions of what men and women should be writing about, imposing his own stereotypes on the material. It is notable that women's preaching is explicitly mentioned only once under Wesley's editorship, although many known women preachers are represented. The one exception, Sarah Mallitt, is presented as a virtually uncontrollable phenomenon. She gives a vivid first-hand account of the inner conflict occasioned by her call to preach;[14] but the stage is set by her uncle's preface which places her first preaching firmly in the context of a 'fit'.[15] John Wesley chose to publish this version of a woman's call to preach, rather than the more rational correspondence with Mary Bosanquet which was also available to him. On the other hand, not all the stereotyping stems from the editor: women refer to their own preaching and exhorting in an elliptical way which suggests that they were not conditioned to describe their work and achievements in the detailed and self-affirming tone adopted by men.

Women did not, then, have direct access in the *Magazine* to a place of public expression, but indirect access by way of their relationship with John Wesley. This relationship, crucial to the presentation of women in the *Arminian Magazine,* should not be viewed through present-day conventions of friendship and privacy as a case of women exploiting (or profiting from) a private relationship with a man, or vice versa. Rather we are given a glimpse of a world in which the boundaries of public and private are differently drawn, giving women a greater degree of freedom and publicity than they were to have later. (It was only when this paper was nearly written that I encountered Hempson's citation of Amanda Vickery that 'we should

---

[12] *AM,* 11 (1788), p. 216.
[13] J. Banks, *Nancy, Nancy* (Leeds, 1984) p. 2.
[14] *AM,* 11 (1788), pp. 185–8, 238–42.
[15] Ibid., pp. 91–3.

take care to discover whether our interpretation of private and public marries with that of the historical actors themselves'.)[16] This is well illustrated by the case of Sarah Ryan's letters. In 1782 John Wesley published in the *Magazine* letters which dealt with Mrs Wesley's distress at his relationship with Sarah Ryan,[17] recounting how 'Last Friday after many severe words my [wife] left me', and how, after finding Sarah Ryan's last letter in his pocket, 'God broke her heart.'[18] Wesley's decision to publish these letters, twenty-four years on, should be attributed to the conviction expressed in his own words of introduction:[19] 'The following Letters . . . breathe deep strong Sense . . . with a deep, and strong, unaffected Piety.'

Such a story provided eloquent testimony to the work of grace in sanctifying the affections. Randy Maddox argues that Wesley's Lockean framework of psychology is crucial to understanding his practical theology and ecclesiology.[20] In this theoretical structure the affections (better described as 'attitudes') are included in the will, rather than the will acting as a bridle on the affections. The story of the work of sanctification must then include the 'inward' story of the affections or tempers as well as the 'outward' story of correct actions and behaviour. Thus material which we would now regard as essentially private is legitimately part of the public domain. This exposure of the more 'private' areas of human experience in the 'public' sphere would tend to make women more publicly visible. By the long-standing Aristotelian world-view, they were already regarded as creatures of delicate sensibility, and were restricted in their public functions and roles, both in society at large and in Methodism in particular. Wesley's theological anthropology favoured the public discussion of areas of human experience in which women were not only included but even privileged.

The description and analysis of 'holy tempers', although legitimately part of the public world of Methodist formation (or the 'defence of Arminianism'), necessarily began in an inter-personal encounter, whether in the class or band meeting, in private conversation or by letter. Women having a close personal connection with John Wesley

---

[16] D. Hempson, *The Religion of the People: Methodism and Popular Religion c. 1750–1900* (London, 1996), p. 179 and n.

[17] *AM*, 5 (1782), pp. 214–15, 266–9.

[18] Ibid., pp. 268–9.

[19] Ibid., p. 44.

[20] R. Maddox, *Responsible Grace* (Nashville, TN, 1995).

were most likely to have a high profile in his *Arminian Magazine*. His family are well represented at first, with eight of Susannah's letters and seven of sister Hetty's poems in the first volume. Later the voices of his closest friends and spiritual confidantes come into prominence. Nearly half the eighty-seven women whose letters appear in the *Magazine* under Wesley's editorship are represented by only one letter, and a further fifteen by only two. The women who Wesley chose to be represented by more than ten letters each account for thirty-four per cent of the total of women's letters: the voices of Ann Bolton, Mary Bosanquet, Ruth Hall, Elizabeth Ritchie, and Sarah Ryan are very clearly heard.

These women did not actively pursue publication in the *Magazine* as such. They were active, however, in writing to John Wesley, not only about their inner wrestlings and ecstasies, but about their prayer and exhortation, their founding of bands and classes, their travels and conversations. They took the initiative in writing to him (following Baker's judgement that Wesley did not usually initiate a correspondence)[21] knowing that they were writing not only to a friend but to the communications centre of the whole Connexion. Even before the genesis of the *Arminian Magazine*, Wesley disseminated extracts from his letters for the edification of others, taking over from the Moravians the practice of holding 'letter-days' at which encouraging letters would be read out.[22] The eighty-seven women who appear in the *Arminian Magazine* as correspondents have exercised a certain amount of choice and initiative in order to appear in public.

Women were also active in writing and circulating self-contained autobiographical accounts, accessible to those outside their immediate circle. There are nineteen of these in John Wesley's *Arminian Magazine*: not many compared with the fifty-three by men, but his practice (from 1789) of specifically asking preachers for their stories for publication created an instant gender bias. Some of these nineteen accounts are described as being 'In a Letter to Mr. J. W.', such as 'Some Account of Sarah Clay',[23] but others stand alone. Such is Sarah Ryan's 'Account',[24]

---

[21] *The Works of John Wesley, vol. 25, Letters, I, 1721–1739*, ed. F. Baker (Oxford, 1980), p. 34.

[22] *The Works of John Wesley, vol. 19, Journal and Diaries, II (1738–43)*, ed. W. R. Ward and R. P. Heitzenrater (Nashville, TN, 1990), p. 163 (9 Aug. 1740); *The Works of John Wesley, vol. 22, Journal and Diaries, V (1765–75)*, ed. W. R. Ward and R. P. Heitzenrater (Nashville, TN, 1993), p. 213 (26 Dec. 1769).

[23] *AM*, 6 (1783), pp. 528–30, 582–4, 641–3.

[24] *AM*, 2 (1779), pp. 296–310.

the first woman's autobiography to be published in the *Magazine*, written in 1760 in a structured form which is clearly intended to be accessible to those who do not know her personally. These women's autobiographies focus largely on states of soul and mind and, unlike most of the men's accounts, do not provide a narrative of achievements and actions. But they all include the 'social' side of the path to Christian holiness: friends, work, family, society, class, band, and preaching. Friendship in a Methodist context could produce a public document: Martha Thompson's autobiographical story 'is extracted from a short memorandum written by herself . . . at the request of some *intimate* friends'.[25] These women depended on John Wesley's position as editor for their wider publicity, but the stories themselves, with their own distinctive voice, were written in the context of a society which valued what that voice had to say.

Women did take the initiative in providing some material directly for the *Magazine*. The first 'Lives' are extracted from letters, both old and newly-written, the latter showing evidence of requests to write or to add specifically for the *Magazine*. By 1783 unsolicited accounts of holy lives and deaths are beginning to appear, and women contribute nineteen of these. They were particularly well placed to describe the edifying deathbeds of those they had nursed.

'You asked me the state of my soul' seems, then, to provide the paradigm for women's access to the *Arminian Magazine* under John Wesley's editorship: their appearance in print largely dependent on his asking, but the focus on the state of their souls providing an opportunity to talk freely about themselves, a later age's 'public' and 'private' matters being equally valued. Yet by the early years of the nineteenth century, even before Joseph Benson's impact on the *Magazine*, we are in a different world for women, one where the paradigm is 'Her claim to public notice is exalted piety' – a piety defined by the men who shape the stories for print, stories in turn influencing the way women describe themselves, and women's own speaking becoming increasingly rare.

This change began immediately after John Wesley's death. From November 1791 until January 1804 editorial control was shared until Joseph Benson, arriving in London in 1803, 'took an interest' in the *Magazine*, and was formally appointed Editor in 1804. In this period

---

[25] *AM*, 6 (1783), pp. 468–71, 524–6 (emphasis added).

variable editorship results in a style which is ostensibly 'business as usual', but with significant differences due to the removal of John Wesley's all-pervading presence, including some which radically affect women's access to the *Magazine*.

The absence of letters from women is the most striking. Edifying letters were still published, but these were more likely to be from Wesley than to him, with John Fletcher also featuring strongly. Women now appear as the recipients rather than the writers of letters and spiritual counsel: of 151 letters involving women published in 1792 or later, sixty-five are written by women and eighty-six to them. In addition, they appear much less frequently as either recipients or writers of letters; from over fifty per cent of the total before 1791, to a mere fourteen per cent between 1792 and 1803. After 1798 single letters to or from little-known women almost disappear, so that only the well-known names of frequent correspondents – Elizabeth Ritchie, Mary Bishop, Ann Loxdale, Miss Hatton – appear in the *Magazine*. What we have here is not only the loss of John Wesley's vast reservoir of correspondence but, whether as the result of deliberate decision or unthinking assumption, an editorial attitude which does not value the contributions of the unknown and weak-voiced, men as well as women. This represents not merely a different set of personal attitudes and preferences, but a changing theology which, with the growing institutionalization of Methodism, is coming to value authority above experience.

The balance of 'Accounts' or 'Lives' in the *Magazine* was also changed in this period by two decisions of Conference. That of 1792, to publish obituaries of preachers with the Minutes of Conference in the *Magazine*, made the gender balance of material still more unfavourable to women, while that of 1796, to pay preachers an allowance for sending in material, made it more likely that contributions to the *Magazine* would be channelled through them and possibly edited by them. Access to the *Magazine*'s pages was becoming more institutionalized and less accessible to those on the margins. Autobiographical material from women now usually consists of extracts from their journals, used in post-mortem biographies; autobiographies structured by women themselves become rare. There are fifteen 'Accounts' written by women in the twelve volumes between 1792 and 1803, but six of those were sent in one year by Mary Fletcher.

On the other hand, these 'Accounts' do show women active in describing and disseminating the experience of their friends and companions in faith. Sarah Young writes of her friendship with Rebecca Scudamore, describing their hopes and dreams and conversations, and the influence they had on one another.[26] Martha Ward describes the death of Margaret Footte (dying of her fifth child at the age of twenty-four, 'a pattern to wives and mothers') in the context of their shared tenderness and affection.[27] Mrs R. K. writes as, presumably, she spoke to her class, about the 'care of your souls committed to me'.[28] And Mary Fletcher illuminates everything she writes about: the refreshments in the kitchen at Madeley between the times of worship,[29] Martha Clark, the servant who 'adorned her profession' by doing as Mrs Fletcher told her,[30] and above all the illiterate Mary Barnard, who 'frequently exprest herself in a more simple way than others, who have their understanding more improved'.[31] Mary Barnard's vivid imagery, rooted in her daily life, begs to be quoted at length:

> I think the Lord has washed my soul as clean as the stones in the brook. . . . One day I was thinking of how I have seen men climb up trees. . . . Mistress, dun ye know what a mill-post is? . . . Well, when I was young and could carry a *burn* on my head, I used to stop and lean my back against one of these mill-posts. . . . Now – that is just what I feel towards the Lord Jesus Christ.

Mary Barnard's words only appear in the *Magazine* because of Mary Fletcher's sensitive and respectful transmission of them. The latter explains in a footnote that a *burn* is a burden, and adds, 'Mary's own words are preserved in this conversation, as being more descriptive of her simplicity, and Christian sincerity, than any that could be substituted for them.' The educated woman, the spiritual leader, values the exact words of her uneducated sister and sees no need to improve them. Thus women are still able occasionally by their writing to open a window into their world of faith and practice.

When in 1804 Joseph Benson became Editor of the *Methodist Magazine* it became much more organized, each number being divided

[26] *AM*, 16 (1793), pp. 211–18, 254–9, 307–13, 357–62, 418–23.
[27] *MM*, 22 (1799), pp. 167–22.
[28] *MM*, 25 (1802), pp. 83–5.
[29] *MM*, 23 (1800), pp. 219–20.
[30] Ibid., p. 266.
[31] Ibid., pp. 222–3.

into sections with sub-headings: 'The Truth of God Defended', 'The Providence of God Displayed', and so on. Accounts of women's lives and deaths abound (235 'Lives' and 155 shorter Obituaries in eighteen years), all placed in the section 'The Grace of God Manifested'. Of course Wesley had originally included lives of believers because they demonstrated the grace of God; but this use of the sub-heading tends to reduce those described to objectified examples, as earlier editing did not – and the majority (fifty-eight per cent) of those who appear in this section are women. Theorizing, as Booth Newton does in introducing the Life of Mrs Ellis,[32] about 'the utility of sacred biography', has the effect of placing the reader at a greater distance from the subject than John Wesley's unadorned 'An Account of . . .'. In addition, the subjects of biography can be further distanced by the motives that are attributed to their biographers: writing 'to oblige the friends of the deceased'[33] subtly devalues the woman herself.

Distancing is further increased by the increasingly stereotyped description of women's lives. In a circular process, which the *Magazine* itself describes, readers learned to understand their own lives in terms of the stories they read – stories which, after John Wesley's death, and still more after 1804, they had little opportunity of shaping. A 'typical' woman's biography follows the pattern of early life, conversion, spiritual experience, role in the Methodist society, character (especially as evidenced in 'relative duties' 'as a wife', 'as a mother'), last illness, and death, with their attendant spiritual aspects. The conversion story has acquired a new externalized focus, 'joining the Methodists'. Stock phrases recur: 'she was thoroughly convinced of the sinfulness of sin'. Personal attachment to the preachers is highly commended: 'to serve the preachers was what she evidently counted her highest honour'.[34] Description of this attachment makes the women's subservient status abundantly clear. John Wesley's theological anthropology, which had looked for a continual shaping of the will by means of discipline and 'social holiness', is being replaced, in these women's biographies at any rate, by a more individualized piety in which sanctification is experienced as an inner assurance of freedom from sin. Its outward expression is conformity to a series of publicly-accepted norms, focused on Methodist doctrine and discipline. The discipline of the

[32] *MM*, 28 (1805), p. 174.
[33] *MM*, 31 (1808), p. 509.
[34] *MM*, 26 (1803), p. 360.

society thus becomes prescriptive instead of nurturing, and we are not far from the age when Methodists have to be exhorted not to neglect the class meeting.

Despite these caveats, women are still able to make themselves heard, albeit rarely, in the *Magazine*. Preachers still send in women's material written for local circulation (thirty-two pieces in the eighteen years of Benson's editorship). Occasionally a woman, usually a preacher's wife, writes directly to the Editor. Women contribute part of five accounts: in one case a daughter writes about a preacher's private life, and in three others a woman describes the subject's last illness and death. The bulk of the account is thus written by a man, and the woman fills in the gaps by writing about those areas which are judged to be her special concern. There are a few pieces of women's writing which do not fall into the 'Memoirs' category, some expressing decided opinions. Such is the 'Admonitory Letter from a Woman of Deep Thought and Long Standing in the Church' (the title implies the need to win official approval and to fulfil institutional criteria before appearing in print) which attacks the growing opulence of chapels, preachers, and preachers' wives.[35] Most of these pieces found their way into print by being part of letters sent to prominent preachers, the personal relationship providing the point of entry to the public sphere.

Women most commonly appeared in print in this period, however, by the use of their journals to illustrate their Christian experience. Such journals were a commonplace of evangelical spirituality, congenial to women with leisure living in a privatized world. Like letters, they were not regarded as totally private productions even when they were being written. Eleanor Hulett, for example, prefaced her diary[36] with a summary of her Christian experience to date, only necessary for a real or imagined reader. Writers of journals must have been aware of the use that was made of them after the writers were dead, and were in effect writing them with an audience in mind. R. Wood, in presenting an account of Mrs Elizabeth Beecroft 'Extracted chiefly from her own manuscripts', refers to 'what is Commonly experienced by Christians, and daily published to the world'.[37] There are no equivalents after 1804 to the structured autobiographies of the earlier

---

[35] *MM*, 30 (1807), pp. 606–8.
[36] *MM*, 33 (1810), pp. 476–80.
[37] *MM*, 36 (1803), p. 453.

period. The extensive use of journals appears to give direct access to the woman's thoughts and feelings; but the journal material usually forms only part (albeit often a considerable part) of an account written by a preacher, and is thus subject to his selection and editing. William Naylor is explicit about this process when he writes that he has 'omitted what might be considered as superfluous' from Miss Charlotte Pindar's writings.[38]

Despite their apparent prominence, then, women are being squeezed out of access to the *Magazine*. Even their edited voices were heard only two or three times a volume on average in the period 1804–21, and their sometimes lengthy Lives were not shaped by themselves or even by other women. They might be described as filling active roles: Mrs Rebecca Mason, whose 'claim to public notice is exalted piety', had not only been a class leader, a Sunday School teacher, and a visitor for the Benevolent Society, but 'likewise took a very active part in the establishment of the Society for Lying-in Women in Birmingham, of which she was Secretary at the time of her decease'. Nevertheless, she is introduced as one whose 'life was short, her situation private'.[39] Public activity was characterized as private because it had taken place among women, and Rebecca Mason had no opportunity to counteract this judgement by speaking directly to the *Magazine*'s readers. No-one could now overhear her thoughts and assumptions, or those of her sisters, as had been possible at an earlier date. Only in the 'Obituaries' section, normally filled with stereotyped accounts of pious lives and deaths, did one tantalizing crack open up. In 1814 Zechariah Taft sent in the obituary of his daughter, aged ten. Taft's wife Mary (née Barritt) is known to have gone on preaching after the restrictions of 1803. Little Mary Ann is quoted as saying on her death-bed: 'Mother, when I am gone *you must preach* from "The Lord gave and the Lord hath taken away and blessed be the name of the Lord" the same as you did when little Henry died, and my father must preach from "Them that sleep in Jesus will God bring with him".'[40] Even here Mary and Mary Ann could not address the reader directly. Only the combination of a sympathetic husband and father with the relative obscurity of 'Obituaries' as opposed to 'Lives' allows this glimpse of a women's world at variance with the public face of

---

[38] *MM*, 28 (1805), p. 555.
[39] *MM*, 32 (1807), p. 520.
[40] *MM*, 37 (1814), p. 873 (emphasis added).

Methodism. The theology of experience which underlay John Wesley's editorial policy was vanishing; now it was only by the caprice of personal relationship that women might be able to speak publicly in the *Methodist Magazine*.

Wesley House, Cambridge

MINISTERIAL AUTHORITY AND GENDER IN DUTCH PROTESTANTISM AROUND 1800

by PETER VAN ROODEN

I N 1807 Carolus Boers published his *Manual for Young Clergymen*. He started this introduction to the ministry with an overview of prerequisites for theological students. Physical requirements come first. A strong body, a good voice, a hardy constitution are necessary. Bodily disfigurements will expose a minister to ridicule. A weak or sickly clergyman will perhaps be pitied, but certainly not respected by his flock.[1] The body bearing these physical perfections is male. This, for Boers, went without saying. Dutch Protestants did not seriously discuss opening the ministry to women before the twentieth century; and even then it was solely the growing number of women having finished their studies in theology that made this an issue at all.[2] The Dutch minister around 1800 was a man. Yet maleness is not the same thing as masculinity.[3] What kind of man was the minister supposed to be?

The period around 1800 is the first for which this question can be answered in a fairly easy and straightforward manner. Over the course of some thirty years, seven manuals for the ministry appeared, discussing what a good minister was supposed to do. Starting in 1819, there was even a journal – the *Ecclesiastical Councillor* – devoted to the exercise of the ministry.[4] As the main Dutch Protestant Church

---

[1] C. B. Boers, *Handboek voor jonge predikanten* (Leiden, 1807), p. 8; *Kerkelijke Raadgever*, I (1819), pp. 77–8.

[2] Lieke Werkman, *Recht doen aan vrouwen in de kerken* (Kampen, 1993), pp. 5–8.

[3] J. A. Mangan and James Walvin, eds, *Manliness and Morality: Middle-Class Masculinity in Britain and America, 1800–1940* (New York and Manchester, 1987); E. Anthony Rotundo, *American Manhood: Transformations in Masculinity from the Revolution to the Modern Era* (New York, 1993).

[4] J. F. Jakobi, *Reegelen en Voorbeelden voor eerstbeginnende geestelijken, met aanmerkingen van L. Meyer* (Leeuwarden, 1773); B. Bosch, *De geachte Evangelie-arbeider, en welgeraden jongeling* (Amsterdam, 1777); J. G. Herder, *Brieven betreffende de beoefening der Godgeleerdheid* (Amsterdam, 1785); [Fokko Liefsting,] *Gedachten over het Predikamt* (Amsterdam, 1792); idem, *Vervolg* (Amsterdam, 1804); C. F. Sangershausen, *Over de geestelijke stand* (Gouda, 1792); J. Konijnenburg, *Lessen over het Leraarsambt* (Utrecht, 1802); Boers, *Handboek voor jonge predikanten*; G. Bentem Reddingius, *Mijn gedachten over het Leeraars-ambt* (Amsterdam, 1809); *Kerkelijke Raadgever en Raadvrager* (1819–46).

employed some 1,500 ministers, most of them must have subscribed to this journal and bought at least some of the manuals. The manuals share a number of traits. Quite clearly, most authors had read their predecessors. Especially influential was the first large manual, Fokko Liefsting's *Thoughts about the Clerical Office*, the first volume of which was published anonymously in 1792. By comparing the manuals for the ministry published around 1800 with an earlier outcrop of such works, their general characteristics become much clearer. In the first half of the seventeenth century, a number of reviews of the duties and obligations of a minister had been published. Most of these were puritan-inspired.[5] The manuals published around 1800 differ from these works. They are much more interested in the individuality of the minister, in the personal ways in which he can effectively fulfill his office. They do not focus so much on his duties and obligations. Instead, the character, manners, psychological insight, and experience with the world required of the minister are stressed. In so doing, these manuals inevitably, if implicitly, also gender the minister.

* * *

A common motif in the manuals and the journal is a comparison between the ways in which a minister has to act towards his flock and the courses of action open to civil authorities.[6] The main point of the comparison is that the minister, unlike those in positions of civil authority, lacks the possibility of recourse to physical force when dealing with people. He can neither order people about nor judge them. Since he is not allowed to punish, he must instead persuade and exercise moral influence over persons. The comparison with public officials thus serves to stress the minister's need of psychological knowledge and self-restraint. He has to influence people, and work upon them with love and friendship. In his *My Thoughts About the Clerical Office*, Bentem Reddingius, after comparing the minister with the public official, continued his argument with a rhetorical overview of the various ways in which the minister can relate to his parishioners: 'now he implores like a son, now he admonishes like a brother, now he censures like a father'.[7] The point of this simile lies not so much in the

---

[5] The various works are reviewed by G. Voetius, *Politica ecclesiastica*, 3 (Amsterdam, 1669), pp. 213–37.
[6] Liefsting, *Gedachten*, 1, p. 84; Reddingius, *Mijn gedachten*, p. 150.
[7] Ibid., p. 150.

maleness of the various possible roles, as in the family setting from which they are drawn. The minister approaches his parishioners as if they were family, as if there was no difference between his life and his work, as if he lived always and everywhere in a private sphere.

The virtues and abilities of the minister extolled in the manuals all centre on this moral relationship between the pastor and his flock. The minister must have a noble heart. He should be friendly and tolerant of other people's faults, as well as calm, mild-mannered, and gentle. He needs social graces and must know how to deal with different kinds of people. He should be a good judge of human nature. Reading a novel now and then[8] and studying scholarly works about moral characters will help him to acquire this ability. Experience with the diversity of humankind is more important than abstract knowledge, as it enables the minister to operate effectively in daily life. Above all, he must himself be pious. This is necessary, not just because people expect their minister to be pious, but also because it empowers him to bear the insults and misunderstandings to which he will be subjected.

In sum, the Dutch minister around 1800 was supposed to be gentle, suffering fools and detractors gladly, mild-mannered, pious, and treating his parishioners as if they were his family. He is even reading novels – albeit not too many. All in all, his seems to be a highly 'feminine' character. Only his possible vices are clearly masculine – sensuous drives, a wounded pride or anger because of damaged self-esteem.[9] His virtues and idealized comportment, on the other hand, are feminine. Yet nowhere is this made explicit. The gendered identity of the minister is not experienced as a problem – not even as couched in the form of allusions or asides. The Dutch writers of manuals for the ministry – all of them clergymen or professors of theology themselves – are not in doubt about the social usefulness, standing, and import-ance of the clergy. The description of clerical influence as a moral force operating in the private sphere leads neither to self-doubt nor to feelings of marginality. The various aspects of the desired character of the clergyman are nowhere described or experienced as feminine. Nor are they set over against other possible forms of behaviour and feeling, held to be more virile, masculine, or prestigious. It is only the present-day reader who notices the similarities between the virtues and manners desired in a minister and the ideology of motherhood and

---

[8] Liefsting, *Gedachten*, 1, p. 88.
[9] *Kerkelijke Raadgever*, 1 (1819), p. 78.

the importance of women's civilizing role as these were developed in the late eighteenth century.[10]

* * *

It is always a risky undertaking to try to explain something which is not there, but this paper offers some reflections on this lack of self-doubt, or to put it more positively, seeks to explain this remarkable self-confidence of the Dutch minister around 1800. The manuals themselves offer the most important clue. All the manuals depict the mild manners, the psychological insight, and the other 'feminine' traits of the clergyman as tools, subordinated to what is his main task, namely morally shaping the common people. All manuals take for granted the existence of an enormous cultural difference between the minister and his parishioners. He has to transform them to bring them to his own moral and cultural level. The minister is a parent, while his parishioners are children.[11] Liefsting even ended his book with Plato's parable of the cave, in which people are accustomed to shadows and do not believe the reports about the world of light outside. It is the minister who leaves the cave and has seen the light, while his parishioners still live in a shadowy world. He has to persuade them to accept what he tells them he has seen, but this cannot happen overnight. Educating parishioners is a long drawn out process which has to be managed adroitly, for fear of otherwise estranging them.[12]

Curiously, what does not become very clear from the manuals is what in fact the minister has seen outside the cave. Thus, the minister is not disseminating radical enlightened opinions. Liefsting rejects such a charge vehemently, as do the authors of the other manuals. Rather, the minister shares with his flock his loyalty to the main tenets of the doctrine of the Dutch Reformed Church. All the writers of the manuals are, however, very much aware that times have changed, and that the formulations of doctrine are traditional and not products of their own time. They do not base their self-confidence on their role as guardians of orthodox truth. Nor yet is it his introduction to the world of higher learning which establishes the superiority of the

---

[10] Nancy F. Cott, *The Bonds of Womanhood. 'Woman's Sphere' in New England, 1780–1835* (New Haven and London, 1977); L. Davidoff and C. Hall, *Family Fortunes: Men and Women of the English Middle Class 1780–1850* (London, 1987).

[11] Liefsting, *Gedachten*, I, p. 331.

[12] Ibid., I, pp. 336–52.

minister over his flock. His training at the university is clearly important, but abstract knowledge and wisdom gathered only from books are explicitly devalued. Scholarship is no asset in the essentially practical work of the minister, work which consists in stimulating the piety and virtue of his parishioners.

It seems best to say that what the minister saw outside the cave, and what constitutes his superiority over the common people, is the true, contemporary context of piety. He is more up-to-date, more modern than his parishioners. It is this cultural superiority vis-à-vis the common people as such that is the source of his self-confidence: 'I am a teacher of the people, placed in society to spread religion and true virtue among my fellow human beings.'[13] All manuals share this fundamental conviction that the clergyman has to teach the people and is therefore better than the best in his parish.[14] To understand the sources of this self-confidence, we have to relate both the gendered nature of the ministry and the clergy's feeling of cultural superiority to fundamental shifts in the social nature of the Dutch ministry and, more broadly, the place of religion in Dutch society.

* * *

In the last quarter of the eighteenth century the clergy of the Dutch public church became a nationally and socially homogeneous profession.[15] For the first time, ministers regularly changed livings, moving throughout the entire country. A national labour-market for ministers sprang into being. In terms of social class, the clergy became much more homogeneous as well. Recruitment among lower social groups declined. During the whole period of the Dutch *ancien régime*, a large clerical proletariat had existed, made up of students who had finished their training for the ministry but had not yet received a calling. In the last decades of the eighteenth century ministers developed a sense of their collective standing in the nation, and became convinced that the behavior and culture of even the lowest members of their body would reflect upon the reputation of the entire profession. By making it more difficult to enter the clergy, the ministers drastically altered the social composition of their profession. In this way a traditional ministry,

---

[13] Ibid., I, p. 18.
[14] Reddingius, *Mijn gedachten*, p. 30.
[15] Peter van Rooden, *Religieuze Regimes. Over godsdienst en maatschappij in Nederland 1570–1990* (Amsterdam, 1996), pp. 46–77.

which in most aspects had until these years resembled the clerical estate of other early modern European societies, was at the end of the eighteenth century transformed into a nationally and socially homogeneous profession.

This social shift was closely connected with a fundamental change in the way in which religion was thought to be present in society.[16] To put it bluntly, the public church of the Dutch Republic had located religion in the visible, hierarchical order of society. Order had to be preserved, by parents, employers, church councils, ministers, and civil authorities. The monopoly of the Reformed Church on public manifestations of religion had to be safeguarded. Encroachments upon this public religious order by dissenters and Roman Catholics should be resisted. This was an essentially hierarchical view of society.

The public church of the Republic did have a sense of the importance of individual commitment on the part of its adherents. It always upheld rather high standards for full membership. Various pietistic movements, of different forms and inspirations, were active within the Church, almost from the very beginning of the seventeenth century. The practice of distinguishing between the truly converted and merely formal members of the Church grew steadily, becoming an almost invariable feature of eighteenth-century sermons. Yet these widely shared pietistic ideas and endeavours did not replace or directly influence the conception that religion was pre-eminently present in the visible order of society. Public order was supposed to precede private piety. The transformation of inner selves was considered to be something which could be effected by God alone. Social endeavours to strengthen religion ought to focus upon undergirding the social order, not on furthering piety.

In the last quarter of the eighteenth century, this conception was abandoned. Religion became located pre-eminently in the inner selves of believers. The main task of organized religion was henceforth found to lie in bringing about the transformation of moral subjects. Of course, such developments did not take place only in the Netherlands. The peculiarity of the Dutch development is rather to be found in the suddenness of this shift and the lack of any sustained opposition.

---

[16] van Rooden, *Religieuze Regimes. Over godsdienst en maatschappij in Nederland 1570–1990*, pp. 78–168.

Within a single generation, one consensus about what one should do to strengthen religion was replaced by another.

This shift in the social location of religion was closely connected with the emergence of a modern nationalism. Society was no longer thought to be made up of a whole of interlocking hierarchies, but instead became imagined as a moral community of individual, virtuous citizens. The main task of the government was no longer depicted as preserving order, but instead as fostering virtue. Nationalism and the new location of religion were so closely linked that it is probably justified to speak of a religious nationalism.[17] Religion and the churches were generally thought necessary for the creation of virtuous citizens. Conversely, the clergy considered the inner selves that it was their task to transform always as members of the moral community of the nation.

The shift in the social nature of the ministry was interwined with the change in the location of religion. A minister was no longer mainly a local representative of social order, but a member of a national profession engaged in shaping the moral community of the nation. All manuals for ministers share this new conception of the national task of the clergy. Fokko Liefsting explained that he had written his *Thoughts About the Clerical Office* because he observed that 'most ministers in our nation are not very effective in inculcating knowledge and true virtue in their parishioners'. The appearance of so many manuals in these years was, in fact, closely linked to this change in the social composition and self-image of the clergy. In the first number of the *Ecclesiastical Councillor*, the editor offered a list of the various subjects he planned to treat in the journal. This list reads as an overview of the practices entailed by the new location of religion in the inner selves of the nation's members. The journal proposed to deal with the difference between clergy and their parishioners, which he found in the latter's attachment to tradition and the past. This attachment is an obstacle to the introduction of necessary improvements. Other subjects have to do with the change of the context of traditional doctrine: the reduction of theological strife, both within the former public church and between the public church and the dissenters, the various political changes and the emergence of refined cultural sensibilities. A third group of subjects is concerned with the various modern means of educating

---

[17] Peter van der Veer, *Religious Nationalism: Hindus and Muslims in India* (Berkeley, CA, 1994).

the common people: the new national education system, the various nationwide enlightened associations, the home missions of the missionary and Bible societies. The descriptions of various changes in the liturgy, linked with a national homogenization and greater stress on the pedagogical aspect of the services, fall within this category as well.

* * *

It is clear that around 1800 in the Netherlands patriarchal forms of authority in the strict sense of the word were lacking. The masculinity of the clergy was not stressed. Nonetheless the ministry was fundamentally gendered. The close involvement of religion with the nation ensured the public nature of the clergy and by extension its masculine character. The new context of piety was the nation. The nation was, as it were, what the ministers had seen in the light outside the dark cave in which their parishioners dwelt. The piety they were trying to inculcate was, in effect, conceived as an inwardness relating itself to the entire nation. The close involvement of Dutch ministers with what was undoubtedly the strongest cultural and social force in the Netherlands in these years explains their self-confidence. They were creating the nation and, in so doing, were undoubtedly masculine. Images of gender pertain not only to the relation between the sexes, but also to imaginations of the social body and the body politic.

This interpretation seems to be supported by what, avowedly, is only an impression. In the course of the nineteenth century several new forms of dissent emerged within Dutch Protestantism. These new dissenters rejected the close identification of religion with the nation and founded religious groups which formed moral communities that stood apart from the public sphere. The clergy of this New Dissent bore a resolutely male character, stressing their own authority, indulging in a manly ideological aggression, and generally projecting a markedly male appearance. But this implicitly masculinist rejection of an earlier clerical ideal is another story altogether.

Research Centre Religion and Society
Universiteit van Amsterdam

FROM PRIVATE COUNSELLOR TO PUBLIC CHURCH POLITICIAN – THREE FEMALE EXPRESSIONS OF CONSERVATIVE, URBAN LUTHERANISM IN WESTERN SWEDEN, 1810–1910

by ANDERS JARLERT

D
URING the nineteenth century, the High Church revival tradition initiated by Henric Schartau (1757–1825) was widely spread and accepted in western Sweden. According to Bishop Wordsworth of Salisbury, Schartau 'had something of the character of Dr. Pusey in his relation to those who consulted him, but, in his position at Lund, and his general influence, he was perhaps more like his English contemporary, Charles Simeon (1759–1836), at Cambridge'. Wordsworth found great merit in his teaching, being 'strong and spiritual, and without the defects of Moravian or Pietistic sentimentality'.[1] During his Scandinavian journey in 1889, Randall Davidson characterized the followers of Schartau as a High Church party in their emphasis on private confession and their strict rules of conduct. On the other hand he found them to be zealous about the Sabbath, and preaching conversion in a quasi-Methodist way.[2] Here, we shall study this movement through the examples of three women of urban culture. The Schartau tradition has been studied mainly with emphasis on its doctrines and clergy, and as a rural tradition connected to the unchanging values and structures of the old rural society. Through these examples of urban women, the general impact of the tradition is widened, and the emphasis is put on the changes in reception of the tradition among lay people in a changing society.

Essential to all three examples is the teaching of Schartau on the 'helpers of the public priesthood'.[3] The division of life and society into a public and a private sphere is a self-evident prerequisite of his theology, in accordance with the Orthodox Lutheran teaching of the

---

[1] John Wordsworth, *The National Church of Sweden* (London, 1911), pp. 364–5.
[2] London, Lambeth Palace Library, R. T. Davidson Papers, vol. 522, 28 Aug, 9 Sept.
[3] See Tore Hulthén, *Jesu Regering. En studie i Henric Schartaus teologiska åskådning i jämförelse med ortodox, pietistisk och wolffiansk lärouppfattning*, 1 (Lund, 1969), p. 172.

three estates as a functional order giving each member of the society her or his place in each of the estates of ecclesiastical teaching, political government, and economic husbandry.

An important mental prerequisite is the reticent attitude in religious matters characteristic of Schartau's followers on the west coast, in that they avoid personal testimonies and emphasise priestly teaching. A fundamental difference between the women of the Schartau tradition and the women of evangelical traditions in general is that the women of the Schartau tradition – like the men – repudiated all religious associations (except Bible societies and diocesan clerical societies). Instead, they emphasised the legal forms of ecclesiastical work in the congregations.

Essential to the discussion which follows is the gender theory of Linda Alcoff. She asserts that the very identity of women is constituted by their position, and implies that woman herself 'actively contributes to the context within which her position can be delineated'. Alcoff includes the point of Teresa de Lauretis that 'the identity of a woman is the product of her own interpretation and reconstruction of her history, as mediated through the cultural discursive context to which she has access'.[4] Also important is the broad concept of feminism, expressed by Olive Banks, which emphasises the importance of problems arising from within the historical traditions.[5] The importance of Olive Banks's reflections on feminism and evangelism has been expressed by Hanne Sanders, in her study of the early rural revivals in Denmark and Sweden, 1820–50. Her main point is that the revivalist appeal to the sin and faith of the individual made it possible for both men and women to take part. But Sanders also emphasises that the new individualism could succeed because it did not appear as a break, but was built on social structures and ideas, where women already had a position as important as that of men.[6] These open gender theories are combined with an interpretative

---

[4] Linda Alcoff, 'Cultural feminism versus post-structuralism: the identity crisis in feminist theory', *Signs. Journal of Women in Culture and Society*, 13 (1987–8), p. 434. Teresa de Lauretis, 'Feminist studies/critical studies: issues, terms, contexts', in Teresa de Lauretis, ed., *Feminist Studies/Critical Studies* (Bloomington, IN, 1986), p. 180.

[5] Olive Banks, *Faces of Feminism. A Study of Feminism as a Social Movement* (Oxford, 1981), pp. 3–4, 242–3.

[6] Ibid., pp. 4, 13–27, 242–3; Hanne Sanders, *Bondevækkelse og sekularisering. En protestantisk folkelig kultur i Danmark og Sverige 1820–1850* (Stockholm, 1995), pp. 185, 197.

method of the history of traditions organized by prevailing theological structures.[7]

* * *

The first type of female activist might be defined as 'the spiritual counsellor in the private sphere'. Mrs Abela Gullbransson (1775–1822) was the daughter of a merchant in Varberg, and a contemporary of Schartau. She was the child of a certain learned culture, as her mother was née Brunius, and the famous professor Carl Georg Brunius was her cousin; but she was probably not an educated woman.[8] From 1795 she was married to the merchant Laurentius Gullbransson. She gave birth to three sons. There is no evidence that her husband shared her deeper spiritual interests, but he left her considerable freedom for travelling and charity. As was the normal case in Protestantism, her spiritual experiences and activities did not challenge the common view of women as subordinate to their husbands.[9]

Abela Gullbransson represents a form of pre-Schartau church pietism. Though she was familiar with Schartau's teachings and theological position, she tried to find a theological position of her own, which is visible in her extensive spiritual correspondence.[10] She was exceptional in her spiritual counselling, writing traditional sermons in private letters, and thus exceeding the limits of Schartau's theology of vocation as revealed in his views regarding the helpers of the public priesthood. Among her confidants were both men and women. Some of her letters were even intended to be read in small circles. Through the very act of such a reading, her private sphere of counselling was transformed into one of collective privacy, based not on the household as such, but on personal pious interest. This could be connected to a parallel line in Schartau's teaching: the vision of the spiritual priesthood that gets its vocation for singular tasks in the

---

[7] Bengt Hägglund, *Semantik och traditionsforskning. Ett kompendium i metodfrågor* (Lund, 1969), pp. 45–9.

[8] Carl S. Lindblad, *Från sista seklets gryning i Göteborgs stift. Abela Gullbransson* (Göteborg, 1922), pp. 6–7.

[9] Ibid., pp. 113–14; Banks, *Faces of Feminism*, p. 13.

[10] As early as in 1812 she copied Schartau's instructions for a correct reading of the Scriptures, which were not printed until the 1820s, Carl S. Lindblad, 'Författarinnan och hennes skrifter', in Abela Gullbransson, *För hemmets stilla stunder. Betraktelser*, ed. Carl S. Lindblad (Stockholm, 1923), p. VI. The correspondence has been noted by Valborg Lindgärde, 'Ordets kraft', in *Faderhuset. 1800–talet*. Nordisk kvinnolitteraturhistoria, 2 (Höganäs, 1993), p. 195.

private sphere, especially in case of necessity; though Schartau presupposes these tasks to be performed individually, and not in any collective form of privacy.[11] These spiritual letters are still preserved as copies in the University Library of Gothenburg, probably dictated by Mrs Gullbransson.[12]

Abela Gullbransson also wrote many songs, which were published in at least twelve editions between 1823 and 1936. Her mode of expression is traditional, neither romantic nor sentimental. From the perspective of gender concerns, three songs are of special interest. The first is a memorial song for the Chief Court Chaplain Dr Bergsten (d. 1809), who had been rector of the parish of Varberg from 1783 to 1795. The beginning of the song is very unsentimental, almost brutal to modern ears, as she says: 'Thus Bergsten lies stiff and cold' ('Så ligger Bergsten stel och kall') – rather an unexpected way of beginning a memorial song for a close spiritual friend and counsellor. The following verses reveal that Mrs Gullbransson had been a pupil of Bergsten's, who knew the worth of her soul, and nursed her tenderly and well. Her relation to Bergsten is very close. In her song, she exhorts him to sleep in his grave, and soon she will hold out her hand to him.[13]

The second is a farewell song addressed to 'Mari', probably Mrs Maria Sofia Lundström. Carl Lindblad has described Abela Gullbransson as the spiritual mother of the younger Mrs Lundström. At the age of seventeen the latter had married the 47-year-old rector of Örby, a clergyman of a noble but perhaps not very religious spirit.[14] In her farewell song, Mrs Gullbransson expresses her thanks to her friend for their common tears, testifies about her own freedom, and asks for God's blessing for her female friend. She asks her to find her home in the Sacred Wounds, and to be unworried even if she felt cold, dull, or sick, since the Lord knows his sheep. 'Mari' is advised to fight with the sword of the Spirit, and to receive Holy Communion as often as possible.[15]

[11] Hulthén, *Jesu Regering*, pp. 172–3.

[12] Göteborg, Göteborgs Universitetsbibliotek, C. S. Lindblads samling. Cf. Lindgärde, 'Ordets kraft', p. 195.

[13] Abela Gullbransson, *Uppbyggliga Sånger och Böner wid åtskilliga tillfällen jemte ett Bref om Nådetillståndet* (Götheborg, 1825), pp. 148–52.

[14] Lindblad, *Från sista seklets*, p. 128; Carl S. Lindblad, '"Moder och dotter". Abela Gullbransson och Maria Lundström-Torell', in *Julhälsningar till församlingarna från präster i Göteborgs stift* (Göteborg, 1930), pp. 128–53.

[15] Gullbransson, *Uppbyggliga Sånger*, pp. 166–7.

The third song offers a more directly gendered view, because in one of its verses the agony in the human experience of the work of the Holy Ghost is compared to a mother's agony in giving birth to her child.[16]

Teresa de Lauretis's comment that the identity of woman is the product of her own interpretation and reconstruction of her history, as mediated through the cultural discursive context to which she has access,[17] is an apt description of Abela Gullbransson's spiritual and social experience as formulated in her letters and verses. A matter of considerable interest is how Mrs Gullbransson's interpretation of her vocation as a fisher of souls was related partly to her spiritual tradition, and partly to her social position as a merchant's wife. The only known rural examples of spiritual lay counsellors or lay poets from the same period and region were men. The rural women of the more or less Pietist movements were often accused of leaving their families and duties, in order to go and listen to certain revivalist preachers, while their absence for family gatherings like marriages and funerals was left uncriticized. In Abela Gullbransson, revivalism met a woman of a certain learned culture and social freedom of movement – circumstances that opened up the wide sphere of action she created for herself. Thus the observations of Ingrid Åberg, that 'the emphasis on individual responsibility and personal rebirth conferred a strong position on those who had been reborn within the circle of believers and gave them the means of transcending the normal barriers normally imposed by sex and class' are confirmed; but the 'acting out new roles' on this basis was made possible only when the social position of the woman concerned included the necessary personal liberty and culture that could demand 'respect from persons who occupied more powerful positions in society'.[18]

Mrs Gullbransson had no successors, and no lines can be traced from her to modern female preaching; but her songs have been widely read, and some of her private sermons were published in daily portions in a devotional book in 1923. In the 1920s and 1930s, she was interpreted as

[16] Ibid., p. 119.
[17] Lauretis, 'Feminist studies/critical studies', p. 180.
[18] Ingrid Åberg, 'Revivalism, philanthropy and emancipation. Women's liberation and organization in the early nineteenth century', *Scandinavian Journal of History*, 13 (1988), pp. 406–7.

a pioneer of female lay work in church, in contrast to exclusive priestly principles.[19]

* * *

The second type of woman activist in the Schartau tradition is the loyal school-teacher, exemplified by Miss Hilma Christensson (1862–1941). She was the daughter of a tailor in Gothenburg; became a preparatory-school teacher in 1879, and an elementary-school teacher in 1886; and taught until her retirement in 1923. After the deaths of her parents in 1901 and 1909, respectively, she lived together with her three younger sisters, the youngest of whom was also a teacher.[20] An important prerequisite for her work was that she was single. Far into the twentieth century it was considered the duty of female teachers in Sweden to remain unmarried.

Miss Christensson represents a very introversive form of High Church revivalism. She wrote spiritual diaries with inserted personal prayers of varying length and contents (*suckböcker*). Her identity as a school teacher appears to have been completely formed by her vocation to teach religion, and she explicitly emphasised her position as a helper of the public priesthood.[21] In her teaching she did not make any difference between boys and girls. Eva Österberg has recently emphasised that in the teaching of reading and catechism in Sweden in the seventeenth century, no essential difference was made between boys and girls. The girls were examined as much as the boys, and a main point of the descriptions of young girls in funeral sermons is that the clergy wished them to read and understand the Word of God, and meditate on the Bible texts.[22] These observations may easily be applied to later Orthodox Lutheranism, and especially to the Neo-Orthodox tradition of Schartau and its emphasis on catechical education.

Hilma Christensson's diaries make it very clear that the author's identity – using the terms of de Lauretis – is the product of her own

---

[19] Abela Gullbransson, *För hemmets*; Carl S. Lindblad, 'Några blickar in i det andliga prästadömets verk i Göteborgs stift', in *Julhälsningar till församlingarna från präster i Göteborgs stift* (Göteborg, 1933), pp. 47–62, and Gösta Nelson, *Den västsvenska kristendomstypen* [Vol. 1]. *Dess uppkomst och första utvecklingsskede* (Stockholm, 1933), respectively.

[20] Anders Jarlert, 'Och lär mig sucka innerlig . . . En pilotundersökning av personliga privatanteckningar, s. k. suckböcker, i västsvensk folkfromhet', in Anders Jarlert, ed., *Hilma Christenssons suckböcker* (Göteborg, 1987), p. 14.

[21] Ibid., p. 39.

[22] Eva Österberg, *Folk förr. Historiska essäer* (Stockholm, 1995), pp. 215–16.

interpretation and reconstruction of her history, as mediated through the cultural discursive context to which she has access. She finds her self-identity in a balance of the roles of mother and priest. Yet she was in fact neither mother nor priest, and there are no traces of any evidence that she had any wish in either direction; but her interpretation of her position as a teacher is formed by these two offices in the service of the Word of God. Consequently, the two persons most frequently mentioned in the diaries are her mother and her priestly spiritual guide, while three groups are frequent objects for her prayers: her school-children, the confirmands of the congregation, and the future priests. With this follows a decided position in the service of God: in the roles of mother and priest Hilma Christensson found a reference system that gave her opportunities of development and growth in her personal spiritual life as well.[23] This may be taken as a general observation about the whole tradition of Schartau. The balance of the mother and the priest as the pillars of the tradition prevents the feminization of social contact which is often observed in evangelical revivalist movements of the nineteenth century.[24]

The content of these roles of mother and priest was inspired and controlled by the Bible. Of special interest is the vocational experience of Hilma Christensson, as interpreted in the words of Isaiah 55.10–11. She remembers that as a child she experienced a spring day, when the natural rain helped her grasp the promise that the Word of the Lord shall not return void, in its delights and power. These words became of fundamental importance to her whole career.[25]

She co-operated closely with her priestly spiritual guide, the resident chaplain Johan Aron Bogren. She understood the office of the priest first of all as a pastoral office.[26] Two verses from the gospels are often repeated: Matthew 9.38 ('Pray ye therefore the Lord of the harvest, that he will send for the labourers into his harvest'), and Luke 2.8 ('And there were in the same country shepherds abiding in the fields, keeping watch over their flock by night'). The most important task of the pastor is to be the teacher of the congregation. Only the converted teacher is able to teach the Word of God rightly, with the aim of leading souls to God in a true conversion. The place of the

---

[23] Jarlert, 'Och lär mig sucka innerlig', pp. 39–40.
[24] On the feminization, see Åberg, 'Revivalism, philanthropy and emancipation', p. 407.
[25] Jarlert, 'Och lär mig sucka innerlig', pp. 37–8.
[26] On the following, see ibid., ch. 7.

pastor is in the pulpit, in the parlour, and before the altar. The private care of souls is an important part of the pastoral office. In 1926, the Revd Bogren lectured before the diocesan clergy on the ecclesiastical care of souls, emphasising private confession. No absolution is mentioned, as the penitent was probably given consolation by biblical promises only, working in an almost sacramental way as a substitute for absolution.[27]

In the diaries of Miss Christensson, Johan Aron Bogren occupies so much space that it raises the question whether her interest in him did not exceed the limits of his office and concern his whole person. In the diaries we encounter a sublimation, of which the female author herself is unconscious. Since her spiritual guide had been married since 1903, the slightest thought of a personal relation independent of his pastoral office was excluded. The prayers for the pastor's person are continued in prayers for grace and salvation for her own part. Such religious faith-based sublimation has during the centuries supplied the spiritual and caritative culture with some of its most beautiful fruits.[28] The spiritual diaries of Hilma Christensson show examples of a personal, sincere, and emotionally coloured piety on a popular level of the Schartau tradition such as has previously not been found in primary material.

Through the reduction and secularization of religious teaching in public education in the twentieth century, women's opportunities to teach the Christian religion in municipal schools have been lost, and vocations to religious teaching have not been especially taken care of by the Church of Sweden. When priestly offices were opened to women on political initiative in 1958, the Church no longer had its former function as an educating force in society.

* * *

The final type for the Schartau activist is the political pioneer. Miss Tekla Nyberg (1851–1931), of Uddevalla, was probably the very first female fire insurance agent in Sweden. Furthermore, she was one of the first women in western Sweden to occupy a public forum. She spoke at parochial church meetings as early as 1892, and from a most conservative point of view.

---

[27] Johan A. Bogren, *Den kyrkliga själavården. Föredrag vid prästsällskapets sammanträde i Göteborg 14 sept. 1926* (Göteborg, 1926).

[28] Jarlert, 'Och lär mig sucka innerlig', p. 59, and further Hjalmar Sundén, *Religionen och rollerna. Ett psykologiskt studium av fromheten* (Stockholm, 1959), p. 361.

In Sweden, the 1890s were years of women's liberation on different levels from silence in religious life. From 1882 until 1891, Hanna Ouchterlony built up the Salvation Army from nothing to 10,000 soldiers. In 1884, Mrs Booth's apology for women's right to preach the gospel was published in Swedish, followed by sharp criticisms from conservative theologians. In 1895, the women's weekly *Idun* published an interview with the Congregationalist Joseph Parker of the City Temple, on woman in the service of the Church, in which he emphasised female preaching, on the condition that women did not neglect their domestic duties. Mrs Booth and Queen Victoria were held up as examples.[29]

In her younger days, Miss Tekla Nyberg had been a somewhat radical woman. As an art mistress at the school of Eva Rodhe, she was an intimate friend of the radical Miss Maya Nyman, who arrived from Paris in the 1870s, and shocked Uddevalla with her short hair, her black woollen stockings, and her propagation of the radical pronoun of address, 'Ni', instead of titles. The nature and date of Tekla Nyberg's change of mind and direction is unknown, but in the 1890s she was an intimate friend of the conservative Miss Laura Hasselgren (d. 1900). Miss Hasselgren was the owner of a well-reputed inn which served as the hotel of the rural clergy visiting Uddevalla, and as the dining-rooms of the 'homeless' gentlemen of the city.[30] Miss Hasselgren's family had belonged to the Moravian Brethren, but changed to the Schartau tradition during the revival in the 1850s. In due course all her property was bequeathed to the parish of Uddevalla, and has since provided large contributions to the needy.[31] Together with the rector, Tekla Nyberg was responsible for the apportionment of contributions from another large donation to poor women, especially widows.

The positions of Laura Hasselgren and Tekla Nyberg confirm Ingrid Åberg's observations that individual responsibility and personal rebirth confer a strong position, giving those affected 'the means of transcending the normal barriers normally imposed by sex and class'. But it must be observed that both Laura Hasselgren and Tekla Nyberg were single. A married woman could not transcend these barriers so easily. And it is obvious that our examples must be distinguished from Åberg's

---

[29] 'Kvinnan i kyrkans tjänst. En interview med D:r Parker', *Idun* (1895), pp. 91-3.
[30] With the author, duplicated memoirs, 'Signe Hellbergs memoarer', pp. 37-43.
[31] Axel Hellman, *Gället kring Bäveån. 800 års kyrkohistoria* (Uddevalla, 1967), pp. 132, 227, 253.

evangelical women who presented an alternative to 'a male culture based on inns and public houses to which women were not admitted'.[32] Here, the inn was even run by a pious, single woman, who received respectful clerical visitors in her inner room.

The immediate reasons for Tekla Nyberg's appearance at a parochial church meeting in 1892 was that the church of Uddevalla, which could seat 1,200 people, had for a long time been overcrowded at the main services. It was accordingly decided, in December 1890, to duplicate main services each Sunday, as an experiment. The proposition was put forward by the mayor and the leading merchants, with 1,585 votes in favour of the proposal and 502 against – many of the latter from otherwise silent women.[33] On 3 and 17 March 1892, Tekla Nyberg insisted, on behalf of herself and Miss Hasselgren, that the church meeting should express its acceptance of the new order of services on the condition that immediate preparations were made for building a new church. Miss Hasselgren was willing to donate 2,000 Swedish crowns to the building work. About thirty persons were present, and the women's proposal was turned down by the clerical chairman for formal reasons; but their reservation was put on the record, and was therefore read aloud in the main services.[34]

At another parochial church meeting, on 14 February 1893, Miss Nyberg pointed out that the new order of services had brought a reduction of twenty-three service opportunities, since the early morning preaching services had been cancelled because of the duplicated main services. The latter were to be counted as single opportunities only, as they were identical. The young priest Paul Berg of the Schartau tradition spoke in her support.[35]

On 10 October 1893, Miss Nyberg read a written statement before the parochial church meeting. She had found it sad to listen to the (male!) discussion. A proposition had been put forward to build a new church, not now, but in a future that does not belong to us. Instead, we

[32] Åberg, 'Revivalism, philanthropy and emancipation', pp. 406–7.

[33] 'Kyrkostämman med Uddevalla och Bäfve', *Bohusläningen*, 12 Dec. 1890. On the background to the duplicated main services, see Hellman, *Gället*, pp. 87–8.

[34] Uddevalla, Uddevalla Kyrkoarkiv, Uddevalla och Bäve Kyrkostämmoprotokoll 1887–1899 [K IIaa:3; hereafter UKA]; 'Med den nya gudstjänstordningen', *Bohusläningen*, 5 March 1892; 'Klagomålen öfver gudstjenstordningen', 'Frågan om ny kyrkobygnad i Uddevalla', *Bohusläningen*, 19 March 1892.

[35] UKA, 'Kyrkostämma med Uddevalla och Bäfve församlingar', *Bohusläns Annonsblad*, 17 Feb. 1893; 'Kyrkostämman', *Bohusläningen*, 16 Feb. 1893.

should use our time, and quickly do what could be done. It had been said that there was no money, no money for a temple to the Highest One, who has said: 'Whatsoever is under the whole heaven is mine.' Unknown 'people' did not want to give back anything of the good that had been given to us. But there was enough money for other things: for railways, bridges, plantations, and, especially, for schools. How many schools are being supported, but only *one* church! So it is: worldly reason and unbelief are given the ascendancy. It had been said that there was no need for a church, though this need was both known and acknowledged. Many years ago, the town had borrowed a big sum, including 80,000 crowns for a new church. Where was this money? Finally, Miss Nyberg demanded 500 crowns for an investigation of the matter. This came as a surprise, since the parochial church council had demanded 3,000 crowns for the same purpose! This proposed investigation was defeated by 1,928 votes from forty-four persons, against 721 votes from thirty-four.[36]

The right to vote in local elections was at the time connected to the payment of local taxes, so that tax-paying, unmarried women voted together with the men. Married women in Stockholm voted as well as early as in the 1880s; but even in 1904 a married woman was denied her right to vote because she was under her husband's guardianship. The regulations for parochial church meetings matched the regulations for local elections. In some places, for example in Gothenburg, equal rights to vote were assured by local law in elections of incumbents. This was made general law in 1910, when even the wives of the voting men were allowed to vote in these elections.[37]

During the last years of the 1890s, women spoke at parochial church meetings in Gothenburg as well. Male liberals criticized these conservative female pioneers for being sectarian and dominating the elections of incumbents, and for speaking in violation of the apostle's words in I Corinthians 14.34–5.[38] As a Lutheran High Church laywoman, Tekla Nyberg represents a new type of emancipated woman, who was publicly active in church politics, opposing both

[36] UKA, 'Den ifrågasatta nya kyrkan i Uddevalla', *Bohusläningen*, 12 Oct. 1893; 'Kyrkostämman i tisdags med Uddevalla och Bäfve församlingar', *Bohusläns Annonsblad*, 13 Oct. 1893. One person could 'own' several votes.

[37] See Yngve Larsson, *På marsch mot demokratin. Från hundragradig skala till allmän rösträtt (1900–1920)* (Stockholm, 1967), pp. 116–17, 131–2.

[38] [Gustaf Åberger,] *Schartauanismen i lära och lefverne af en svenska kyrkans vän -BRG-* (Stockholm, 1901), pp. 106–8.

the mayor and the rector, with successors of pronounced conservative views even at the end of the twentieth century. Her actions show – in Alcoff's formulation – how women use their positional perspective as a point from which values are interpreted and constructed rather than as a locus of an already determined set of values. This does not necessitate a change in what are taken to be facts, but it does necessitate a political change in perspective, since the point from which all things are measured has changed.[39] However, this position is realized, limited, and directed by the emancipated woman's experience and identity as a Christian.

* * *

Gender positions are dependent on the social environment and the personal initiative of each single human being, and cannot be generalized. In the example of Abela Gullbransson, we have observed the importance of the social position of a married woman of a certain learning, which provided the necessary liberty and culture for personal initiative. In the example of Hilma Christensson, we have noted the duty of the female teacher to remain unmarried, yet her identity was the product of her own interpretation and reconstruction of her history. In the example of Tekla Nyberg we have observed both the voting regulations, which limited the right to vote and speak to tax-payers, and the creation of a new female identity as church politician. The women taken as examples belonged to an urban, middle-class culture. Revivalism provided them with a common ideology, emphasising the Lutheran doctrine of vocation, supplying its followers of different sexes and classes with common limits and positive qualities such as assurance and an alternative, religious class-consciousness.[40]

Concrete examples of more or less emancipated women emphasise the need for awareness of individual positional views, where general gender theories instead could lead to a violation of historical facts. Even moderate, general theories are easily questioned in their encounter with history. For example, Ruth Franzén's theory that revivalist women are generally pushed back to the kitchen when a

---

[39] Alcoff, 'Cultural feminism', pp. 434–5.
[40] See Christer Winberg, *Fabriksfolket. Textilindustrin i Mark och arbetarrörelsens genombrott* (Göteborg, 1989), p. 167.

revival movement is established[41] is open to question, for three main reasons. First, because the gender positions of a movement can often be shown to be dependent on gender attitudes of older ecclesiastical structures in which the movement is integrated. Secondly, because of the ideology and structure of the movement itself. For example, in the Schartau revival there was no need for women to make the coffee, since the movement was not organized as a society. Just as in the Evangelical tradition, the effect of the Schartau revival on feminism was conservative rather than radical; but while the evangelicals led women outside the home in order to bring the domestic virtues into the public domain,[42] Schartau's followers were sometimes emancipated in a more radical way. Thirdly, the theory may be questioned because of the importance of social changes, which thus modify the positions of men and women in revivalism and church life. Unlike experience in the early nineteenth century, in the 1890s the mobilization of women was a mobilization to public life. It was still a 'manifestation of resistance by the two groups, the church and women, which were losing control over important sections of local public life because of the transformation of society'.[43] Our examples have shown the limits and the possibilities of an active, personal contribution to the context within which the gender position can be delineated.

Lund University

---

[41] Ruth Franzén, 'Kvinnoperspektiv på kyrkohistorisk forskning', in *Kirkko ja politiikka. Juhlakirja professori Eino Murtorinteen täyttäessä 60 vuotta 25.11.1990* (Helsinki, 1990), p. 125.
[42] Banks, *Faces of Feminism*, p. 26.
[43] Åberg, 'Revivalism, philanthropy and emancipation', p. 420.

'WOMEN MAY PREACH BUT MEN MUST GOVERN': GENDER ROLES IN THE GROWTH AND DEVELOPMENT OF THE BIBLE CHRISTIAN DENOMINATION

by DAVID SHORNEY

W HEN the Cornish lay evangelist, William O'Bryan, founded the first Bible Christian societies in the late autumn of 1815 he was responding, in the main, to female initiatives. This is not altogether surprising. For several decades before 1815 women had been playing a much larger role in English evangelical Christianity than they had done in the early years of the Evangelical Revival. The informal groupings which came into existence in its second phase, *c.* 1790–*c.* 1830, gave women opportunities to initiate, organize, and exhort on a much more extensive scale. As cottages and farmsteads became centres of worship, women were well placed to play a more important role as initiators and organizers,[1] especially in those areas barely affected by John Wesley, George Whitefield, and their travelling preachers. The more articulate went even further and followed the example of some eighteenth-century Quaker women by speaking in their own localities and further afield. Before the eighteenth century came to an end a number had acquired the reputation of being gifted preachers and 'holy women', 'owned by God', and called to instruct others, both men and women, in the Christian faith.[2] For a short while women were poised in Wesleyan, and later, Primitive Methodism[3] to play a major role in evangelism and church-planting; but it was only amongst the Bible Christians that they, for a time, played perhaps an even more significant role as evangelists than their male colleagues. As such they were in no way inferior to men; but when the denomination acquired a governmental structure copied from Wesleyan Methodism the patriarchal ordering of contemporary society set limits to their Bible-based notions of sexual equality. Though women had a voice in

---

[1] Deborah Valenze, *Prophetic Sons and Daughters: Female Preaching and Popular Religion in Industrial England* (Princeton, NJ, 1985), pp. 26, 35, 52.

[2] Z. Taft, *Biographical Sketches of the Lives and Public Ministry of Various Holy Women*, 2 vols (London, 1825–8; Peterborough, 1992), *passim.*

[3] E. Dorothy Graham, 'Chosen by God: the female travelling preachers of early Primitive Methodism', *Proceedings of the Wesley Historical Society*, 49 (1993), pp. 77–95.

some deliberative assemblies, they were not given a vote. It was axiomatic that though women might preach, men would always govern.

Two factors had hitherto inhibited women from preaching: St Paul's injunction to the Corinthians, 'Let your women keep silence in the churches' (I Cor. 14.34), and the basic assumption that there were two divinely-given 'natures', a male nature fitting men for physical exertion, intellectual activity, and a public role, and a female nature enabling women to exercise strong moral influence in the home.[4] Much more than casuistry and favourable economic and social circumstances were necessary if women were to shake off these age-old inhibitions. Although, perhaps, women enjoyed a special status in the agricultural economy of Devon and Cornwall where small family farms predominated, this in itself does not explain why a hundred or more women (most of whom were in their late teens or early twenties) felt such a strong 'call' to preach in the decade after Waterloo. What is not in doubt is the role they played in converting what had begun as a one-man mission to the people of north east Cornwall and north west Devon into a denomination with hundreds of congregations in a dozen English and Welsh counties.

In May 1815 O'Bryan crossed the Tamar into North Devon to preach in Milton Damarel in response to an invitation from Susanna Rattenbury, a yeoman farmer's wife and a stalwart member of the Church of England. A year earlier she had undergone an evangelical conversion as a result of attending Wesleyan open-air preaching at Warbstow Burrow in North Cornwall while staying with her daughter and son-in-law. Her husband, Hatton Rattenbury, had remained unsympathetic to evangelical religion and bitterly opposed to dissent but eventually, while attending a vestry meeting called by the parson to warn O'Bryan and anyone else who might attempt to preach in the village that they would be arrested by the parish constable, he had a change of heart and dissociated himself from his fellow farmers. On 24 May 1815 both Hatton and Susanna Rattenbury welcomed O'Bryan to their home, and on the following Sunday accompanied him when he preached at the village revels. As evangelical religion took hold of the Rattenbury home it was Susanna who conducted family prayers; but when the first Bible Christian Quarterly Meeting was held on 1

---

[4] Henry D. Rack, *How Primitive was Primitive Methodism?*, 6th Chapel Aid Lecture (Englesea Brook, 1996), p. 22.

January 1816, it was her husband who was appointed a circuit steward. Two years later when O'Bryan drew up the denomination's *Rules of Society*, he decreed that circuit and society stewards 'must be men of piety'. It is possible that the word *men* was used generically, but it is more likely that he assumed that these offices would always be filled by men. Nonetheless, in 1851 at least one woman in Cornwall and four in Devon, describing themselves variously as either 'stewardess' or 'manager', signed the religious census return.[5]

There were many other instances of women introducing Bible Christian preaching into a new locality and sustaining it in its early days: an agricultural labourer's wife in Hartland, a widow in Holsworthy, and a young woman from a fairly well-to-do family in Ashreigney in the Taw valley. In the early 1820s the society at Tredresson in Cornwall was almost entirely sustained by a group of earnest and energetic young women, two of whose number acted as lay evangelists in the surrounding area.[6]

More than anyone else, it was two married women, Mary Thorne and Johanna Brooks, who were responsible for the emergence of the Bible Christian denomination in its heartland of north west Devon and north east Cornwall. Both were Anglicans, and both began their public ministry in the Church of England. Mary Thorne was almost fifty-five when on a Sunday morning in May 1815 she interrupted a communion service at Shebbear parish church to inform the congregation that through the witness of the Holy Spirit she knew that the Lord had forgiven her sins and that they, too, could receive the same blessing if only they would seek it. For three years she and her fellow parishioners had listened to the evangelical preaching of their curate, Daniel Evans, but its Calvinist tenor had produced in her mind, and no doubt in others, the fear of having committed unpardonable sin. One night she became so anguished and distressed that she woke her husband and family to ask them to pray for her. A few days later, when attending a

---

[5] Manchester, John Rylands University Library, Methodist Church Archive, Hatton Rattenbury (Jnr) Diary, MAW, MS 92. 21, *Rules of Society Applicable to All Our Members who Profess to Follow Christ According to the Bible* (Stoke Damarel, nd), p. 7; *Arminian Magazine* [hereafter *AM*], 2 (1823), pp. 151–56, 267; James Thorne *et al.*, *A Jubilee Memorial of Incidents in the Rise and Progress of the Bible Christian Connexion* (Shebbear and London, 1865), pp. 19–20; W. J. Townsend, H. B. Workman, and George Eayrs, eds, *A New History of Methodism*, 2 vols (London, 1909), I, p. 508; T. Shaw, *Methodism in the Camelford and Wadebridge Circuits, 1743–1963* (Camelford, 1963), p. 197; *Devon in the Religious Census of 1851*, ed. M. J. L. Wickes (Appledore, 1990), pp. 29, 108, 131, 139.

[6] *AM*, 2 (1823), p. 149; *AM*, 3 (1824), pp. 9, 368–73; Shaw, *Methodism*, p. 197.

week-night meeting addressed by a visiting evangelical clergyman, she experienced a sense of inner peace. Though reluctant to share her experience with others, she felt a strong obligation to do so. Some were shocked that a woman should address them in the middle of a communion service, but such was her social status in the parish as the wife of a highly-respected yeoman farmer that no one dared lay hands on her.

When Mary Thorne learnt that O'Bryan had been preaching in the vicinity she made several unsuccessful attempts to contact him, and it was not until October 1815, after his final breach with Wesleyan Methodism, that he came to her home at Lake, the Shebbear farmhouse she had inherited from her father three years earlier. That night O'Bryan enrolled twenty-two of those present in a Bible Christian society, but before his arrival the ground had been well prepared by Evans's preaching and Mary Thorne's evangelical activities.[7] With other members of her family she had attended Methodist preaching in neighbouring villages and had in August 1815 invited a Methodist local preacher to preach in a field at Lake. When a Bible Christian society was formed in Shebbear in October 1815 it was the strong moral and financial support given by Mary Thorne and her family which ensured that Shebbear would become, for the next fifty years, the *de facto* headquarters of the new denomination. At the denomination's first Quarterly Meeting on 1 January 1816, she paid from her own pocket the dues owed by the Shebbear society, and for some time afterwards contributed £1 a quarter to the denomination's funds. Though she never held office in the new denomination, she preached extensively in the first years of its history. An extended preaching mission in 1818 took her as far west as Lands End; and in May 1820, when almost sixty, she continued to speak undaunted when a stone struck her cheek while preaching in the open air at Black Torrington, a village some four miles from Shebbear.[8]

Johanna Brooks, a builder's wife and the mother of a four-year-old daughter and a two-year-old son, was only twenty-nine when she astonished the congregation at Morwenstow parish church in north east Cornwall early in 1815 by interrupting the morning service. Unlike Mary Thorne, she had not been subjected to evangelical

---

[7] *AM*, 2, pp. 258–9; John Thorne, *James Thorne of Shebbear: A Memoir* (London, 1873), pp. 8–11.

[8] F. W. Bourne, *The Centenary Life of James Thorne* (London, 1895), pp. 178–9.

preaching in her parish church; but 'some striking texts . . . and pertinent remarks made thereon'[9] by Morwenstow's non-resident curate led her to read an English translation of the seventeenth-century French spiritual classic, Charles Drelincourt's *Les Consolations de l'âme fidèle contre les frayeurs de la mort*.[10] Overcome with fear of death and judgement 'she looked [one morning in church] to see if the flames of hell were coming in through the windows in pursuit of her'. After weeks of acute anguish and mental distress she, too, 'found liberty' and a sense of inner peace. This was soon followed by an over-powering conviction that she should share her experience with her fellow parishioners. She duly summoned up the courage to interrupt the morning service, but after she had delivered a short, impromptu address she was ejected by her husband and one of the parish officers. Amongst those who heard her that Sunday morning were a number who were to become pillars of the Bible Christian denomination. Within eight years a Bible Christian chapel had been built in Morwenstow and 200 members recruited, eight of whom became travelling preachers. Though Johanna Brooks was ostracized by her family, both rich and poor began to call on her for spiritual guidance and advice. Invitations flooded in with requests to address cottage meetings in an area where the Wesleyans and others were just beginning to make an impact. Some of these meeting-places were later to become centres of Bible Christian worship; but almost a year passed before her preaching came to the notice of William O'Bryan. Widowed in 1819 at the age of thirty-three, Johanna Brooks was obliged until her remarriage to support herself and her four children by opening a drapery and grocery shop, but she continued to preach, not only in her own locality but as far afield as Tiverton and South Molton, and even (not long before her death in 1858) on the quayside at Appledore.[11] By that date Bible Christianity had become the dominant social and cultural force in that part of Devon and Cornwall.

---

[9] *AM*, 2, p. 327.

[10] Charles Drelincourt (1595–1669), the French Protestant writer, published *Les Consolations* . . . in 1651; it became a popular work in translation in early eighteenth-century England. More than eighteen editions were published, including one in Exeter in the early nineteenth century under the title *The Christian's Defence against the Fears of Death with Seasonable Directions how to Prepare Ourselves to Die Well* (nd, but a copy exists endorsed '1817' by its first owner).

[11] *AM*, 3, pp. 7–12; Johanna Brooks, *The Handmaid of the Lord* (London, 1868), pp. 10–25, 30–5, 44–5, 68, 82, 85.

It would appear that O'Bryan's original intention was to be a one-man mission evangelizing a rural area in which both Wesleyan Methodism and historic dissent were weak. In so far as he needed assistance, he intended to rely on local preachers and a network of locally-recruited class leaders; but when in the spring of 1816 'the small stream . . . began to run like a torrent'[12] it became imperative to recruit full-time preachers. O'Bryan first looked for assistance to young men, including Mary Thorne's three sons, but when a number of young women proved themselves as exhorters and local preachers he began to look more sympathetically on female preaching. In class meetings and love-feasts a number of young men and women were beginning to speak freely and openly of their spiritual experiences, and, in so doing, unintentionally prepared themselves for a public ministry. O'Bryan was aware that two Wesleyans from Gwinear, near Redruth, Ann Gilbert and Elizabeth Collett, had preached in the 1770s and 1780s, but the only woman he himself had heard was a Quaker. There was considerable antipathy towards female preaching in Cornish Wesleyan circles, and O'Bryan had imbibed the prejudices held by most Cornish male itinerant and local preachers. It was the proven success of his wife's preaching which led him to revise his judgement. In the spring of 1812 she had stepped in to fill the void when the man who was deputizing for her husband was struck speechless. Between 1812 and 1815 she preached and addressed meetings, including a Wesleyan open-air gathering at Warbstow Burrow in the summer of 1815; but long before that she had proved her value as a pastoral assistant by taking spiritual charge of her husband's female converts.[13] From the earliest days of the Bible Christian denomination its founder believed that women should play a major role, but it did not occur to him that they might become full-time itinerants.[14] When he received reports that young unmarried women exhorters and local preachers 'conducted themselves with credit' he became convinced that they 'were owned by God' and could preach on equal terms with men.[15]

In July 1816 a 24-year-old former Wesleyan, Elizabeth Dart, spoke at a love-feast in Milton Damarel and made several converts;[16] and in

[12] *AM*, 3, p. 47.
[13] *Primitive Methodist Magazine*, 2 (1821), pp. 190–2.
[14] *AM*, 3, p. 77.
[15] Ibid., pp. 77, 263, 290.
[16] Elizabeth Dart (1792–1857) joined the Wesleyan society at Poundstock in 1812, began to exhort in 1814, joined the Bible Christians in 1816, and exercised a public ministry as an

the second half of 1816 she addressed a number of meetings in the Shebbear area. Wherever she went she was well received, and her success convinced O'Bryan that it would be right to recruit women as travelling preachers.[17]

By the spring of 1817 O'Bryan had more than sixty local preachers, six full-time travelling preachers, and four who assisted occasionally, including Elizabeth Dart and Elizabeth Gay.[18] Amongst those who addressed the large Bible Christian open-air meeting at Warbstow Burrow in the summer of 1817 were eight females.[19] When that autumn William Lyle was appointed to take charge of the Truro circuit, his sister Mary was appointed to assist him. A correspondent wrote 'Those who never came before . . . now come to hear the woman . . . our young friends are universally approved of.'[20]

At first O'Bryan sent out his young women evangelists in pairs on roving commissions.[21] When Em Cottle was appointed to the Michaelstow circuit in 1818 she was accompanied by O'Bryan's precocious eleven-year-old daughter Mary, and later in the year by Elizabeth Dart when she preached in the Camelford and Boscastle area.

By 1819 O'Bryan had recruited fifteen male and fourteen female itinerants. Of the twelve Bible Christian circuits then in existence, all but two had female preachers, and one of them, Plymouth Dock (Devonport) in the south west's fastest growing town, was staffed by one solitary female itinerant. It is noteworthy, however, that the first baptisms in the circuit were conducted not by Elizabeth Gay, the itinerant stationed in that circuit, but by two visiting male itinerants, William Mason and William Lyle.[22] In 1821 Daniel Lysons's Plymouth correspondent reported that the Bible Christian congregation was served by two women, with only occasional visits from a male preacher. In so far as the denomination had thrived in the area it

itinerant from 1817 until her marriage to J. H. Eynon in 1832. She frequently suffered from ill-health and for a time in 1817 retired from preaching to keep a school. On her marriage she went with her husband to Ontario where it was said of her 'she was the best missionary we ever sent to Canada'. Taft, *Holy Women*, 2, pp. 201–9; Thorne, *James Thorne*, p. 35 and n.; *AM*, 3, p. 48.

[17] Ibid., pp. 42, 77–9.
[18] Ibid., pp. 180, 194.
[19] Ibid., p. 290.
[20] Ibid., pp. 331–3.
[21] Ann Freeman, *A Memoir of the Life and Ministry of Ann Freeman* (London, 1828), p. xvii.
[22] PRO, RG 4/334.

was, he said, because of the novelty of female preaching and its comparative cheapness.[23]

By the early 1820s O'Bryan was frequently using female preachers on solo missions to storm the bastions of urban paganism in towns and cities such as Plymouth, Portsmouth, Southampton, London, Brighton, and Bristol. They were also the shock troops of the Bible Christian advance as it moved out from its West Country base into new, unconquered territory. It was Mary Ann Werrey who introduced Bible Christian preaching into the Scilly Isles, the Channel Isles, and Northumberland. Elizabeth Dart and Mary Ann Soper took the Bible Christian mission into the heart of Bristol. Catharine Reed was the first Bible Christian to preach in London. Ann Mason addressed 500 people at Woolwich and attracted large crowds in the streets of Brighton. Mary Mason and Elizabeth Courtice laid the foundations of what were to become the Kingsbrompton and Weare circuits in Somerset. Mary Toms, Catherine O'Bryan, and Eliza Jew established the denomination in the Isle of Wight. Ann Cory and Catharine Reed consolidated the work begun by James Thorne and William Lyle in Kent, and made some of the most notable converts in that county. Eliza Jew wrote to O'Bryan from the Isle of Wight on 21 December 1823 that 'The Bryanite women is the topic of discourse. Some want to know if we have any men in the connexion, for they say it is altogether a woman's cause.'[24] That same month O'Bryan wrote in the connexional magazine, 'There are at present, I believe, above an hundred females in our connexion who speak in public.'[25] Women were playing a major role in evangelizing cities and urban areas not only as paid itinerants but also as local preachers and exhorters. In 1823 the evangelical weekly *The Pulpit* published a full account of an open-air service on a Friday evening in May 1823 conducted by two young female local preachers in fields between London's City Road and Islington.[26] Thirty years later a Bible Christian minister, appealing for a fresh attempt to evangelize London, looked back wistfully to the days when female preachers in the metropolis preached 'with considerable effect' and had 'many seals to their ministry'.[27]

[23] BL Add. MS 9427, Lysons Papers, fo. 246.
[24] *AM*, 7 (1828), pp. 112–13.
[25] *AM*, 2, p. 423.
[26] Ibid., pp. 281–6.
[27] *Bible Christian Magazine*, 3rd ser., 18 (1853), p. 265.

The Bible Christian denomination shamelessly exploited the sex appeal of its young female preachers. A poster advertizing the opening of the Bible Christian chapel in Shoreditch in April 1826 announced that James Thorne would preach three sermons during the day but in much bolder type added 'a Female will address the congregation in the afternoon and evening'.[28] Thirty-three years later that same James Thorne attempted to lure a young man he met on a train going up from Bideford to London to a service at the Bible Christian chapel in Waterloo Road, London, by telling him that a female, Sister Pollard, would be preaching.[29]

It would be wrong to assume that female preaching had no critics within the Bible Christian denomination. On Sunday, 5 October 1817 James Thorne noted in his journal: 'Sister Ashman spoke at Lake [Shebbear] ... A very good discourse; I query whether these men who speak against women preaching could exceed it.'[30] When O'Bryan summoned his male preachers to a conference in his house near Launceston, Cornwall, in August 1819, heading the agenda was the question 'What are our thoughts on female preaching?' They agreed that God enabled women as well as men to speak 'to edification, and exhortation, and comfort', and quoting Joel 2.28 and Acts 2.17, affirmed that God had declared that females would prophesy in his name. Unlike John Wesley and Zechariah Taft they did not consider that there was anything *extraordinary* in God's call to women to preach.

This was not the end of the matter. O'Bryan, from the very first issue of the connexional magazine in 1822, was at pains to chronicle the role women were currently playing in the Bible Christian denomination and had played in different spheres down the ages. In December 1823, in an article entitled 'A Discourse in Vindication of the Gospel being Published by Females', he asserted that God had stamped female preaching with his authority by convincing and converting sinners through its agency. How could it then be against the will of God if women brought others to a knowledge of him? Women, O'Bryan said, could go where men could not. As men and women were jointly responsible for bringing sin into the world they were both charged with bringing mankind to knowledge of salvation. To oppose female preaching was to oppose God himself. To those who

---

[28] Richard Pyke, *The Golden Chain* (London, 1915), p. 46.
[29] Thorne, *James Thorne*, pp. 271–2.
[30] Ibid., p. 74.

said that women were not intellectually the equal of men he reminded his readers that the first Queen Elizabeth was counted as 'one of the first politicians in Europe'.[31]

Turning to St Paul's injunction in I Corinthians 14.34, 'Let your women keep silence in the churches', O'Bryan contended that the apostle was not condemning female preaching, but was referring to contentious women who sought to stir up controversy in the Church. It was a male prerogative to ask questions on points of doctrine and cases of conscience; and it would be indecorous and wrong for women to contend with men in public, or to usurp man's authority by setting up their judgement in opposition to him. No woman filled with the Holy Spirit would be contentious or guilty of acts of disobedience or arrogance.

That assumption proved to be wishful thinking on O'Bryan's part. Though they addressed him reverentially in their letters as 'Father in the Gospel' and accepted, sometimes reluctantly, his instructions as to where they should minister, some of these high-spirited, Spirit-filled young female preachers were not averse to questioning his spiritual state or the denomination's fundamental doctrines. In July 1819 Ann Mason, having discussed with O'Bryan whether there was any greater blessing to be attained than sanctification, informed him that she had 'a blessing far superior to the being cleansed from all sin', and that as he admitted he had not that gift she knew that his soul was not saved.[32] Others, too, were unwilling to accept male authority unquestioningly. O'Bryan's daughter Mary rebelled against male domination. Having attended a district meeting in the summer of 1825, she described as tyrannical the attempts then being made by her single male colleagues to dictate 'even the colour of our garments'.[33] In 1825 William Mason complained that Mary Ann Werrey, his colleague in the Northumberland Mission, 'refused to take a plan or [in] any way . . . be directed by him, even only once a week, though she often spoke in public . . . when and where she pleased'.[34] Having pioneered the Bible Christian mission in Northumberland she was no doubt unwilling to take orders from a mere male who was reaping where she had sown. It is, perhaps, not

---

[31] *AM*, 2, pp. 405–25.

[32] Freeman, *A Memoir*, p. 25.

[33] T. Shaw, *The Bible Christians* (London, 1965), pp. 110–11.

[34] Manchester, John Rylands University Library, Methodist Church Archive, Bible Christian Journal (1824–52), p. 17.

altogether surprising that both Ann Mason (Mrs Henry Freeman) and Mary Ann Werrey abandoned the Bible Christian itineracy to preach as freelance evangelists in Ireland and Scotland. Others, too, were not prepared to be deferential and submissive to male authority. The 1828 conference censured the highly successful itinerant, Ann Cory, for remarks she had made about O'Bryan.[35]

There is some evidence to suggest that the hardening of attitudes towards female preaching which affected other denominations was having some effect on the Bible Christians. In 1824 the Primitive Methodists had excluded female itinerants from the 'Quarterly Board' unless they were specially called to speak;[36] and the Arminian Methodist Connexion in 1833 decreed that 'the regulation of affairs ... be entrusted only with men excluding females from any vote in its government or concerns'.[37]

In the 1838 edition of *A Digest of the Rules and Regulations of the People denominated Bible Christians*, the denomination affirmed its belief that God, *'in certain circumstances*, calls women, as well as men, to publish salvation to their fellow-sinners ... and ... that ... the Almighty seals their ministrations by the conversion of souls'; but it went on to say 'They do not, however, take part among us in church government; they are entitled to attend meetings for business, but not to vote.'

It is significant that the most radical of Bible Christian male preachers, Henry Freeman (who after his marriage to Ann Mason in 1824 left the denomination to join the Quakers), made a sharp distinction between the functions of preaching and ruling. In his vindication of the ministry of women, published in Dublin in 1824, he wrote that 'Paul suffered not a woman to act for that was usurping authority over the man whom God had appointed to rule. ... Ruling in the church and preaching are distinct, so a person may be a preacher and not a ruler.'[38] This was a view shared, implicitly if not explicitly, by

---

[35] Ibid., p. 49.
[36] Rack, *How Primitive was Primitive Methodism?*, pp. 25–6; Graham, 'Chosen by God', p. 89.
[37] William Parkes, 'The Arminian Methodists, 1832–1837 (the "Derby Faith"); a case study in Wesleyan deviation' (University of Keele M. Phil. thesis, May 1994); William Parkes, *The Arminian Methodists: the Derby Faith, a Wesleyan Aberration in Pursuit of Revivalism and Holiness*, Merlin Methodist monographs, 3 (Cannock, 1995), pp. 23–4, 49.
[38] Henry Freeman, *False Prophets Described, and Thoughts on the Call, Appointment and Support of Ministers, also on Worship and a Vindication of the Ministry of Women* (Dublin, 1824), p. 27.

many, if not all, women preachers. Reporting on Mary Toms's very successful preaching in the Isle of Wight in 1823, her colleague Catherine O'Bryan said she 'is better fitt [sic] to preach than to regulate the affairs of the circuit'. It was with relief that she learnt that James Thorne was on his way to the island to organize the denomination's affairs.[39]

Though women had attended quarterly meetings from the very first days of the denomination, there is no evidence that they were ever summoned to attend annual conferences. They were sometimes there in the wings, and in 1821, during the annual conference, three young female itinerants were amongst the eight speakers who addressed a camp meeting at Shebbear which, it was said, attracted an audience of 2,000.[40] Four women preachers attended the London District meeting on 5–8 July 1825 at the Bible Christian chapel off the Strand;[41] but when the *Deed for Establishing the Identity of the Bible Christian Conference* was drawn up in 1831 it made it clear that male but not female itinerants should attend district meetings. It was not until 1896 that the conference reinstated their right and duty to attend these meetings. 'Female Preachers', it said, 'are expected to attend the District Meetings and take part in the business, without the power of voting.'

Female preachers suffered from other constraints. There was no theological reason why they should not administer the sacraments of baptism and holy communion but there is no evidence that they ever did.[42] The 1821 conference, quoting a judgement in the Court of Arches, asserted that all baptisms 'where water was used as the element, and the sacred name of Father, Son and Holy Ghost' was invoked, were valid. In 1838 the *Digest of the Rules and Regulations* made no distinction between male and female itinerants who, it said, were 'wholly given to the work of the ministry, preaching and administering the Sacraments'. In 1824, in a letter to his daughter Mary, O'Bryan came near to sanctioning lay administration of the Sacrament of the Lord's Supper.

---

[39] Truro, Cornwall Record Office, X241/4.

[40] Thorne, *James Thorne*, pp. 165–6.

[41] Ibid., pp. 203–4.

[42] In the thousands of entries in the twenty-seven Bible Christian baptism registers deposited with the Registrar-General in 1837 and now in the PRO (RG4/100–8, 110–11, 113, 332, 334, 338–40, 873, 880, 1187, 1419, 1694, 2184, 2299, 2428, 2619, 2801, 4162) there is not a single entry by a female itinerant. I have written fairly fully about the non-parochial registers in my PRO Guide, *Protestant Nonconformity and Roman Catholicism* (London, 1996), pp. 30–50.

I believe any church may commemorate the sufferings of Christ
. . . at any time . . . [and] as often as they can . . . not as seldom . . .
[as] there is an administrator . . . Exclude every scruple of man's
account. Women have souls as well as men. As often as you can
make it convenient and the people do [want it, do it] without
hesitation. I doubt not Jesus will be there and that will be better
than all the Bishops in England.[43]

Women preachers exercised many functions in addition to preaching. They formed classes, gave out tickets of admittance, held love-
feasts, organized prayer meetings, and even exercised discipline. Mary
O'Bryan, as a seventeen-year-old itinerant in the Channel Islands,
reproved a butcher for carrying on his business on a Sunday, and
others for drunkenness. On 11 February 1824 she wrote in her diary: 'I
have had to reprove some for improper conduct. I suppose I shall have
to exclude them.' She also joined in discussions about building a
chapel in Jersey, and about the advisability of giving security for £400
to build it.[44]

By August 1826 the denomination was employing twenty-nine
female and fifty-six male itinerants, but the physical strain of itineracy
frequently proved too great for a large number of young females.
Many were plagued with ill-health, and O'Bryan frequently had to rest
them for a year at a time. A number died in their twenties. Only a
small minority made a career of itinerant preaching. By the mid-1840s
the number had fallen to a mere half dozen, but a fair number of
former itinerants continued to make a major contribution as local
preachers and as the wives of male itinerants. Although the denomination failed to recruit any female itinerants in the 1870s and 1880s,
between 1890 and 1907 it employed, for short or long periods, six
women in its home circuits and another eight on its mission stations in
south west China. In 1894 its annual conference decreed that female
missionaries in China should have the right to speak and vote in all
business meetings after they had successfully completed a four-year
probationary period. The 1902 edition of the denomination's *Digest of
Rules, Regulations, and Usages* reaffirmed that God called 'women as
well as men to publish salvation to their fellow creatures'; but by 1907

---

[43] Truro, Cornwall Record Office, X241/8.
[44] Truro, Courtney Library, Mary Thorne (née O'Bryan) Diaries.

only one female itinerant, Lillie Edwards, was employed on its home circuits. Before the Bible Christians merged with the United Methodist Free Churches and the Methodist New Connexion to form the United Methodist Church in 1907, she was given a golden handshake of £135 and appointed 'special agent' in the Hastings circuit.[45] Women in the course of its history contributed in many different ways to the growth and development of the Bible Christian denomination, but they were discriminated against on grounds of gender. Female itinerants were not paid as much as their male colleagues, and were never elected to connexional offices. It was in the early days of the denomination's rapid advance and expansion that they made their most important contribution, but as the Bible Christians gained in respectability and lost some of their early evangelical fervour, women ceased to play so prominent a role as preachers and evangelists.

University of Bradford

---

[45] Oliver A. Beckerlegge, 'Women itinerant preachers', *Proceedings of the Wesley Historical Society*, 30 (1956), pp. 182–4.

METHODIST DOMESTICITY AND MIDDLE-CLASS MASCULINITY IN NINETEENTH-CENTURY ENGLAND[1]

by JOHN TOSH

THE history of the family, at least for the nineteenth century, has reached a certain maturity. Though not yet incorporated into mainstream history – that would be too much to expect – it now boasts a considerable specialist literature and some useful general surveys.[2] Undoubtedly the driving force has been the aspiration of women's history to reconstruct the lives of women in the past. Now that the personal records of women are being studied with such attention, there is a wealth of insights into their experience as daughters, wives, and widows. Jeanne Peterson's account of the Paget family and their circle in Victorian England is a typical example.[3] For the nineteenth-century women's historian, there is the added bonus that this was the period when the claims of women to have the dominant influence in the family were taken most seriously – as witness the persistent appeal of the Angel Mother. Hence to research the history of the Victorian family promises results which will feature women as agents, and not merely as victims of patriarchal oppression.

In many ways, the most impressive thing about the history of the family is the speed and confidence with which it has moved beyond this initial position. The family is not only a women's concern. It is the most important context for the study of childhood (still enormously under-researched); and it is fundamentally about men as well: in the psychological sense that they are emotionally formed by their early domestic experience, and in the social sense that it is men who take the initiative in establishing a family and who must usually shoulder the burden of maintaining it. In short, the family must be seen as a whole,

---

[1] As a newcomer to Methodist studies, I am particularly grateful for help received from Clyde Binfield, Margaret Jones, and John Walsh. For permission to make use of papers in their possession, I am grateful to Manchester Central Reference Library, Bradford University Library, and Mr David Stovin.
[2] See for example John Gillis, *For Better, For Worse: British Marriages since 1600* (New York, 1985), and Rosemary O'Day, *The Family and Family Relationships, 1500–1900* (London, 1994).
[3] M. Jeanne Peterson, *Family, Love and Work in the Lives of Victorian Gentlewomen* (Bloomington, IN, 1989).

embracing all its members – as a field which is constructed in relational terms around generation and sexual difference. That is essentially what the history of gender means when applied to the family. It is already a well established genre, chiefly as a result of the path-breaking work of Leonore Davidoff and Catherine Hall on the English middle class, now ten years old. In their book *Family Fortunes* the family is seen not merely as a private sphere reserved for women and children, but as a central ingredient of men's class identity and of an emerging middle-class culture.[4]

One of the most impressive aspects of *Family Fortunes* is its close attention to religious issues. The authors convey a real sense that the lives of middle-class men and women between 1780 and 1850 were embedded in a religious culture. If historical understanding depends on entering (in some sense) the mentality of our subjects, then this approach to the history of class formation is surely indispensable. It has, however, been rather lost sight of in more recent work. Jeanne Peterson considers the Church as a career which engaged wives as well as husbands, but not the meanings which religious allegiance conferred on family life. James Hammerton's fine study of cruelty and divorce in Victorian marriage tends to play down the influence of religion, in order to do justice to the play of conflicting legal principles.[5] But placing religion on the sidelines in this way is simply not an option open to the Victorian historian. All denominations in this period placed a heavy emphasis on the family. More important for my purpose, they saw the family as a whole, with prescribed and interlocking roles for every member. Of course these roles were not necessarily followed, not least because the various religious traditions taught conflicting lessons. Yet the fact remains that, in the middle class at least, an avid reading public was steeped in a public discourse on family which was articulated almost entirely in religious terms.

That discourse is one obvious focus for research. Sermons and advice literature can tell us much – as Davidoff and Hall showed in their absorbing account of the Congregationalist minister John Angell James, the so-called 'Bishop of Birmingham'.[6] The highly influential

---

[4] Leonore Davidoff and Catherine Hall, *Family Fortunes: Men and Women of the English Middle Class, 1780–1850* (London, 1987).

[5] A. James Hammerton, *Cruelty and Companionship: Conflict in Nineteenth-Century Married Life* (London, 1992).

[6] Davidoff and Hall, *Family Fortunes*, pp. 126–34.

writings of Sarah Ellis, married to a member of the London Missionary Society, are another rich source on family mores.[7] Didactic literature of this kind can supply an analytical frame for studying the history of the family, and it is not difficult to track its influence in particular homes. The problem with this approach is that family experience becomes a means of illustrating a number of general propositions, instead of being treated in its own right. In order to grasp how religion was experienced through domesticity, and how domesticity was understood in religious terms, we need to see the family in something like its actual complexity and integrity, even if this means looking at rather few of them. In this paper, my point of departure is the domestic experience of three nineteenth-century middle-class men: Joshua Pritchard, a Manchester exciseman; Isaac Holden, a West Riding mill-owner; and Cornelius Stovin, a Lincolnshire farmer. Each shows the ways in which religion permeated family life and family decisions. Each man was a Methodist, thus allowing the varieties of family experience within a particular tradition to come into focus. And each case-study concerns primarily the husband or father, because it is still the case that men are under-represented in family studies. The challenge of gender is to study the history of men, not on terms which reinforce their privileged access to the historical record, but from a truly relational perspective. 'Masculinity', so often loosely employed in common speech to indicate a men-only world premised on the exclusion of women, needs to be reclaimed as a historical identity constructed in relation to femininity. There is no better place to start than the domestic sphere, where masculinity is formed through early relations of nurture and discipline, and later articulated every day through identity and conflict with the opposite sex.[8]

* * *

Joshua Pritchard worked for the excise authorities, based in Manchester. He was a man of strong domestic affections towards his wife Mary, whom he married when he was 28, and towards his four children. And, like his wife, he was a devout Methodist, apparently a

[7] Ibid., pp. 180–5, 340–2; Hammerton, *Cruelty and Companionship*, pp. 75–8, 88–90.

[8] John Tosh, 'What should historians do with masculinity? Reflections on nineteenth-century Britain', *HWJ*, 38 (1994), pp. 179–202; Michael Roper and John Tosh, 'Historians and the politics of masculinity', in Michael Roper and John Tosh, eds, *Manful Assertions: Masculinities in Britain Since 1800* (London, 1991), pp. 1–24.

Wesleyan. Occupation, family, and religion were the elements from which a new middle-class identity was forged in the early nineteenth century. Pride of place is often given to the first. Such was the power of the work ethic and of 'calling' in a secular sense, that we might assume that Pritchard was an exciseman first, preoccupied with his reputation as a public servant, and only secondly a husband and a Methodist. Nothing could be further from the truth. His letters and diaries contain almost no reference to his work experience. What they reflect very directly is a painful conflict between work and the rest of his life. Being an exciseman meant being available for sudden postings of several months at a time to other towns, depending on the pattern of illegal distilling.

For Joshua these periods were a painful exile from all he held dear. 'I can assure you', he wrote to Mary from Nottingham in 1835, 'that my mind is continually hankering after you and the children.' The lodgings were comfortable, and they belonged to 'one of John Wesley's hearers . . . a tried stone'. 'But yet I want you to talk with, and the children to play with a bit, to drive dull care away.' He had to content himself instead with buying expensive presents for all the children – including a watch for his eldest boy.[9] After eighteen years of marriage Joshua still found these separations almost insupportable. From London he wrote: 'Bless you Mary, I love to be at home, I now wish you were with me, I am sitting by the fire alone. O bless you my Love, my Dove, my Dear one, my best, my sweetest . . . .' As a saved believer he was confident that he would never be parted in spirit from his wife, but this made the physical separation no easier to bear. From one posting, with leisure on his hands, he wrote in 1836, 'I have now time to talk to my Mary, but no *my Mary* to talk to me. There are 3 Marys in the house but not *my* Mary.' Self-pity sometimes got the better of him. On one occasion he complained, 'O yes, to be sure, Joshua must write long letters, but I wonder who writes long letters to him.' In 1837 he told Mary that, though he no longer had the same 'bloom of youth' as when she had first fallen in love with him, 'thank God our Love is not abated'. That seems to have been the truth. It brought Joshua intense happiness, as well as repeated separations which were less than manfully endured.[10]

---

[9] Manchester Central Reference Library [hereafter MCRL], Pritchard papers, M375/1/4: Joshua Pritchard to Mary Pritchard, 31 Aug. 1835.
[10] MCRL, M375/1/4: Joshua Pritchard to Mary Pritchard, various letters 1835–7, *passim*.

In Joshua's mind there was at times an even stronger tension between family and religion. This was not because the family was at odds with his religion. Mary Pritchard was a Methodist too, and great care was given to the spiritual upbringing of the children. Joshua could sign off his letters home by sending his love to 'all the Class', knowing the message would be passed on. But there was a conflict in his mind about purity. As the rhapsodizing of 'My Dove, my Dear one' suggests, Joshua was a man of strong sexual need. His conscience was not to be satisfied with the comforting notion that marital sex was divinely sanctioned (in the way that, say, Charles Kingsley argued). He believed his passionate nature was a spiritual diversion for his wife. 'I can assure you', he wrote from London in 1835,

> that I very frequently thought, when I was at home, and have also thought so since, that I was a hindrance both to you and the children, & that in consequence of my passionate Spirit, you will be enabled to serve God better in my absence than when at home with you.[11]

Joshua also questioned whether he should be so attached to *any* human being – lest she become 'in the place of Christ' to him.[12] Fourteen years previously, as a newly married man, Joshua had been tormented by an even more disturbing thought: that he had a calling to the ministry which could not be obeyed so long as he had responsibility for his wife and baby daughter. He wrote in his diary:

> Oh that I could for faith incessant cry to the great, the holy, the high! I have almost been ready to beseech the God of love to take my Wife and child to himself and then I would labour for him by his grace and assistance in this world below – and then again when I looked on my child and she of my bosom with whom I had took sweet counsel, I did not like to part with either of them. It is a struggle to me which way the contest will turn.[13]

In the event, Joshua's conscience allowed him to resist the call and remain in secular employment. But he remained a Methodist before

[11] MCRL, M375/1/4: Joshua Pritchard to Mary Pritchard, 15 Aug. 1835.
[12] MCRL, M375/1/4: Joshua Pritchard to Mary Pritchard, 26 June 1836.
[13] MCRL M375/1/3: Joshua Pritchard, diary for 10 May 1821.

anything else – certainly before occupation and sometimes before family.

For Joshua domesticity meant not only the bliss of a happy marriage but also the loving duty due to his children. The standards he set himself were exacting, especially for his first child, Mary Ann, born in 1819. He recorded his successes and failures in a special section of his diary which he addressed to her in the second person, intending her to read it when she was older. For Joshua the most important pointer to his daughter's spiritual state was her attitude to prayer. 'Prayer is a solemn thing which your Father is often obligated to tell you', he wrote. At eighteen months Mary Ann was joining her hands before meals. Her parents tried to get her to kneel down with them at afternoon prayer, and her backsliding was variously attributed to bad influences, playfulness and the machinations of the devil. Blackmail was also attempted: when she was five Joshua told her that, if she was unwilling to pray with him, God 'could affect you & make you unwell'. Shortly before, she had had a dream that God wanted to take her – Joshua told her to keep this in her memory for the rest of her life, just as he surely never forgot his own wish that God would take both wife and daughter in the cause of the Gospel. Mary Ann's life proved short enough. She died before reaching her teens, probably never having read the diary her father had written for her edification. Unfortunately there are no records of that time which might tell us whether she died in morbid repentance of her earlier failures in prayer, or whether she had attained her own assurance of God's grace. Joshua did not believe she was perfect – 'she had her little ways' he later conceded – but he was confident that she was with her Father in heaven.[14]

As often happens when parenting is undertaken too zealously, Joshua was less demanding of his three subsequent children.[15] He allowed himself to take more pleasure in their company, to play with them, and to lavish presents on them. But they could have been in no doubt that life was to be lived in godly earnest. 'Tell the children that their Father had them all up before the throne of Grace', Joshua Pritchard told his wife in 1835 when he was away on business. He

[14] MCRL, M375/1/3: Joshua Pritchard, 'Observations on the deportment of Mary Ann' (1820–4).
[15] A moving Victorian example is the family of Edward and Mary Benson. See David Newsome, *Godliness and Good Learning: Four Studies on a Victorian Ideal* (London, 1961), ch. 3.

urged them to pray themselves, holding up the example of Mary Ann as someone who had attended to prayer and had properly regretted her lapses. He drew particularly pointed lessons for his one remaining daughter, Emma: Mary Ann was interceding for her, and she must emulate her qualities of meekness and modesty.[16] The spiritual destiny of his children, his wife and himself weighed on his mind as ultimately the only real foundation of life.

* * *

With Isaac Holden, my second case-study, the claims of work were much more to the fore. He was not, like Pritchard, at the beck and call of his superiors, but a self-made entrepreneur whose career is a vivid illustration of the new industrial class. Born in Scotland, the son of impecunious English immigrants, Isaac Holden began his working life as a child-labourer in a Paisley cotton-mill. But he came of strongly Methodist stock – his paternal grandparents had been converted by John Wesley himself – and this gave him access to a closely knit, dispersed community, for whom helping one another in business had been explicitly prescribed by the founder.[17] Having briefly considered the Methodist ministry, in 1830 Isaac secured the post of book-keeper in a firm of Wesleyan worsted manufacturers at Cullingworth, near Keighley in the West Riding. This gave him the means to marry Marion Love, who came from a very similar Methodist background in Scotland. Fourteen years of stability followed. The Holdens had four children without mishap, and Isaac became more and more indispensable to the Cullingworth mill. In 1846, however, he left his employment to set up on his own, and Marion died of tuberculosis. At just the time when Isaac's hands were full with what turned out to be a failing business (a mill he had leased in Bradford), his home was without a head and he was deprived of his domestic support. His solution was to marry again, but this time to marry money. Sarah Sugden was a spinster as old as he was, from another Methodist mill-owning family. They were married in 1850, and they set up home near the factory where Isaac could now make an entirely fresh start.[18]

---

[16] MCRL, M375/1/4: Joshua Pritchard to Mary Pritchard, 15 Aug. 1835, 18 Sept. 1836.

[17] Henry Abelove, *The Evangelist of Desire: John Wesley and the Methodists* (Stanford, CA, 1990), pp. 99, 108.

[18] Elizabeth Jennings, 'Sir Isaac Holden (1807–1897)' (Bradford University Ph.D. thesis, 1982); John Tosh, 'From Keighley to St-Denis: separation and intimacy in Victorian bourgeois marriage', *HWJ*, 40 (1995), pp. 193–206.

But this was not quite the whole picture. The new start was made not in Yorkshire, but in France – at St-Denis near Paris. If this seems a move of breath-taking boldness, it is not surprising that Sarah Sugden was not ready for it either. She complained (probably with some justice) that amid all the preparations for marriage Isaac had not dealt plainly with her in this matter. Isaac intended to stay in France for some years in order to give his factories there his full personal supervision. Sarah wanted him to settle in Yorkshire again, and ideally to abandon business altogether for the ministry. Seven months after the wedding she left St-Denis for her family home in Oakworth, with no date fixed for her return. She stayed with her brothers, for whom she had kept house for so many years, until the disagreement could be resolved. There followed a period of intense correspondence, at the end of which it was agreed that the family home would be at St-Denis, but that Sarah would live in Oakworth for two extended visits amounting to three or four months each year. In effect she had two homes, with a managerial role in each of them. This compromise brought to an end the acute phase of their quarrel, but the old tensions regularly resurfaced whenever the couple were separated, up to Isaac's return to Yorkshire in 1860.[19]

The correspondence was not entirely acrimonious. As a couple the Holdens were united by their unquestioning loyalty to the Methodist way of life – the class, the chapel, the preaching, the hymn-singing. Both had been formed in this tradition from birth. In Sarah's family that tradition was reaffirmed by the duly recorded last words of her parents, both youthful converts to Methodism: 'Heaven! Glory! Come!' (her father), and 'I am on the Rock and have firm footing' (her mother).[20] Isaac and Sarah had each won recognition for their leadership qualities – he as a possible candidate for the ministry, she as a class leader. Both took an Evangelical view of the world absolutely for granted. They conducted their social life entirely within the fold of the Methodist community, which was not difficult to do in the West Riding. There Methodists were very thick on the ground: in Bradford the Wesleyans alone amounted to 17.4 per cent of Sunday worshippers in 1851, the second largest group after Anglicans at 23.1

---

[19] Tosh, 'From Keighley to St-Denis'.
[20] R. S. Hardy, *Commerce and Christianity: Memorials of Jonas Sugden of Oakworth House* (London, 1857), pp. 15, 20.

per cent.[21] The devotion of the Holdens to Methodism was a lifelong commitment: in his seventies Isaac was to become a leading lay spokesman for the movement in the House of Commons; Sarah performed a ceaseless round of local engagements which only ended when, aged eighty-six, she caught a fatal chill after opening a bazaar at Haworth.[22]

Furthermore, the nature of Isaac's work – 'masculine' and instrumental though it might seem – was in some ways common ground between them. Their marriage was one of occupational endogamy, like many in the entrepreneurial classes of early industrial England. Sarah's brother, Jonas Sugden, headed the family worsted business in Oakworth; the house was close to the mill, and in her forty-odd years of living there Sarah had acquired much knowledge of the business. Indeed, she would have been failing in her duties as a class leader had she not done so. The Wesleyan leadership paid particular attention to the needs of businessmen, and class leaders whose flocks included businessmen were urged to acquaint themselves with their concerns. By the time she married Isaac, Sarah was well versed in the intricacies of worsted manufacture.[23]

The correspondence also reveals not only shared interests in religion and work, but a mutual physical attraction. This would certainly not have been taken for granted in a marriage between two people in their forties – one of them a virgin – with more than a suspicion of business convenience about it. Yet the letters allow no other conclusion. Isaac was the less inhibited of the two. To 'taste in imagination the sweet conjugal feeling' was not enough, he wrote from St-Denis in December 1850; the memory of her 'spirited and affectionate embrace' made him 'long to squeeze you well'. Eighteen months later he wrote, 'I had to go to my solitary couch thinking of you with heart warm and something else as warm. I feel the want of you more than on any former occasion.'[24]

On her side Sarah was not offended by this overtly sexual language. In the privacy of her bedroom at Oakworth, she imagined herself in

[21] Theodore Koditschek, *Class Formation and Urban Industrial Society: Bradford 1750–1850* (Cambridge, 1990), pp. 253, 255.

[22] Elizabeth Jennings, 'Sir Isaac Holden, Bart (1807–97); his place in the Wesleyan connexion', *Proceedings of the Wesley Historical Society*, 43 (1982), pp. 117–26, 150–9.

[23] Wesleyan Conference Office, *A Class Book* (London, nd), p. 5.

[24] Bradford University Library [hereafter BUL], Holden/21: Isaac Holden to Sarah Holden, 20 Dec. 1850; BUL, Holden/23: same to same, 13 June 1852.

Isaac's arms, 'entwined in each other's embrace', and she longed for the warmth of his flesh. The marriage carried an erotic charge from the beginning – perhaps even earlier (though hardly any courtship letters survive). There is no sign of sexual guilt in either of them, which is interesting in view of Wesley's profound discomfort with carnal desire.[25]

At the heart of this correspondence, however, was a disagreement about the nature of home and its claims on husband and wife. Sarah took her stand on two principles. First, she was alarmed at Isaac's devotion to material concerns. One of the issues which Methodist class leaders were expected to address with 'godly jealousy' was the conflict between business and spirit. With that experience behind her, Sarah did not hesitate to remind Isaac of 'the awful danger there is of being too much entangled with the world'. Any man who was prepared to immerse himself in work in a Catholic country was, in her view, far gone in this direction. 'You may think yourself different from other men and feel yourself adequate for what you engage in', she warned him in 1858, 'but I trust you do not forget that the hand that strikes others is the same that may smite you.' This is surely the tone of the class leader rather than the wife.

In the second place, for Sarah the countervailing influence of home depended not merely on the immediate domestic circle, but on the community of which it formed a part. Sarah felt herself bound to this wider circle by ties of kinship as well as spiritual fellowship. She could not contemplate living without daily access to her brothers and sisters and chapel associates, from whom she derived her 'spiritual enjoyment'. Sarah Holden comes over in this correspondence as self-willed and outspoken, but it would be wrong to interpret her firmness as a bid for independence. Her view of marriage was entirely conventional. When engaged to Isaac, she had looked forward to 'a proper yoke to bear' and disclaimed any wish to be 'a lawless subject'. Her aim in this dispute was not autonomy for herself, but the restoration of the sacred proprieties of life by which they would both benefit. Her sense that his salvation and her own were at stake gave her the power to speak out.[26]

---

[25] BUL, Holden/21: Isaac Holden to Sarah Holden, 20 Dec. 1850; BUL, Holden/23: same to same, 13 June 1852; BUL, Holden/44: Sarah Holden to Isaac Holden, undated (early Nov. 1851); Tosh, 'From Keighley to St-Denis'; Abelove, *Evangelist of Desire*, pp. 49–58.

[26] *A Class-Book Containing Directions for Class-Leaders* (London, nd); BUL, Holden/21: Sarah Holden to Isaac Holden, 4 Dec. 1850; BUL, Holden/52: Sarah Sugden to Isaac Holden, 6 Oct. 1849.

Isaac, on the other hand, was a workaholic in love with his factory. He had only to 'come within the sound of the dear old combing machines' and 'the old passion' came over him, and all other concerns (including his wife waiting for a letter) were forgotten in a moment. The pressing need to 'keep close to the Business' meant that he would not spin out his leisure-time at home, or go on holiday, much less visit Sarah at Oakworth or Blackpool. How he ran his business, and where he located it, were matters between him and Divine Providence. 'As a Man of Business', he told her, 'I enter into the most inviting openings that Providence places before me and remain, with contented mind, till Providence directs my path into a course more desirable' – as comforting a gloss on entrepreneurial ambition as one is likely to find. (In later life Isaac claimed to have been guided to the site of his first French factory by a dream.)[27] Sarah's views were therefore beside the point, however knowledgeable about business she might be. And, while Isaac invoked divine authority for his own preferences, he represented Sarah's attachment to Yorkshire as no more than a selfish desire to have her own way. Providence, it seemed, was profoundly gendered.

But on the question of where Sarah should live, Isaac was more conciliatory. He certainly did not discount the importance of home. His invocation of 'its sweet social intercourse and its reciprocal duties of affection and fidelity' was an impeccably Evangelical sentiment. He knew that he needed a serious Methodist as partner to provide moral ballast to his home, while he got his hands dirty in the business; he needed this both for himself and his two school-age daughters. As far as Isaac was concerned, all this could be as readily created in France as in England. The fact that in France he must do without the wider local community of the godly counted for little in his mind, since the hectic pace of his life at St-Denis left him no time to enjoy it. Isaac also knew that to live in or near Oakworth, as Sarah demanded, would involve more intercourse than he could tolerate with his in-laws, and especially with the head of the family, Jonas Sugden, whom he disliked intensely. But he refrained from ordering Sarah back to France, as was certainly his right. He knew that if she returned to St-Denis, they would probably both be made miserable; whereas if she remained in

---

[27] John Hodgson, *Textile Manufacture and Other Industries in Keighley* (Keighley, 1879), p. 116.

Yorkshire one at least of them would be content.[28] 'I feel willing to allow *you* to decide when you can *willingly* and cheerfully come to me. . . . Therefore my dear Sarah enjoy yourself so long as you can be happier without me, and do not decide on coming till you can be happy with me.'[29] It was a generous gesture and it worked. Within two weeks Sarah was on her way to France, with the bones of a working compromise agreed. Isaac was temperamentally drawn to a companionate marriage rather than a patriarchal one. He believed instinctively that his wife's autonomy should be respected, and he quickly learned that this was also the path to securing her compliance.

We see here two contrasting views of domesticity grounded in the same quite narrow Evangelical tradition. Methodism furnished the materials for a feminine, as well as a masculine view of the world, and even for a measure of challenge to patriarchal authority. Isaac justified his scale of priorities by citing the guidance of Divine Providence which worked through the actions of *men*. In his eyes this justified a devotion to work and a somewhat narrow conception of domesticity, typical of the self-denying work ethic of first-generation entrepreneurs.[30] Sarah took her stand on what she thought were the higher claims of home, founded on divine prescription and example. In this she echoed a generation of women's Evangelical writing, which asserted the moral prestige of women as guardians of the home, and the moral obligation on men to play their part in home life. The uneasy compromise between these two positions lasted for ten years. The tensions were only resolved when the couple moved back to Yorkshire in 1860. By then Jonas Sugden had died. Isaac and Sarah moved into his house, which Isaac drastically remodelled so that its earlier associations were almost completely erased. The Holdens lived together as an exemplary Methodist couple for another thirty years.

* * *

Cornelius Stovin, my third example of Methodist domesticity, was also much preoccupied with the workings of Divine Providence. He could hardly fail to be, given that the prospects of his 600–acre farm at

[28] BUL, Holden/32: Isaac Holden to Sarah Holden, 23 April 1861; BUL, Holden/22: same to same, 10 Jan. 1851; BUL, Holden/21: Isaac Holden to Sarah Holden, 20 Dec. 1850.
[29] BUL, Holden/22: Isaac Holden to Sarah Holden, 10 Jan. 1851. See also Tosh, 'From Keighley to St-Denis'.
[30] Theodore Koditschek, 'The triumph of domesticity and the making of middle-class culture', *Contemporary Sociology*, 18 (1989), pp. 178–81.

Binbrook in north Lincolnshire depended so much on the vagaries of the weather. Judging by his diary for the 1870s, hardly a day went by without uplifting reflections on the operation of Providence in the world. When his barley crop was drenched for the third time, he speculated that Divine Providence intended to drive him through prayer to more humble dependence on God. When the invention of new machinery undercut the bargaining power of his farm labourers, he exclaimed 'What a kind Providence!' His metaphorical view of the natural world tended in the same direction. Every cornfield, with its cycle of germination, growth, and maturity, seemed to him an expression of the Divine plan, and a vivid refutation of the Darwinist heresy.[31]

Unlike Isaac Holden, however, Cornelius Stovin did not need to invoke Providence in order to justify his choice of occupation or his commercial decisions. He was a farmer like his father before him, and his wife, Elizabeth Riggall, was also the daughter of a local farmer. There were no clashes over calling or place of residence. But other causes of friction took their toll. Of the three marriages considered here, this was almost certainly the weakest. Elizabeth came from a wealthier family with expectations which Cornelius could not match. She objected to the poor amenities of Binbrook farm and nagged her husband to demand improvements from the landlord, whereas he would have been content with something 'chastely comfortable'. She complained, as did he, about the poor quality of domestic servants to be found three miles from the nearest village. Elizabeth's health was also poor. She was often not strong enough to nurse her growing family herself and frequently retired to her parents' house twenty miles away for extended periods of rest. Cornelius seems not to have anticipated how much he would miss her – perhaps because he had remained a bachelor until the age of thirty-one. He noted in 1875 that he seemed 'to have become so thoroughly domesticated that my happiness is diminished by their absence'. He found it hard to conceal his frustration. He wrote to her during one bitter November:

> You must not forget that your absence detracts from the
> sweetness and joy of my life. . . . It is cool work entering my

[31] Cornelius Stovin, journal entries for 9 Sept. 1871, 12 July 1872, 22 Aug. 1871, in Jean Stovin, ed., *Journals of a Methodist Farmer 1871–1875* (London, 1982), pp. 33, 73–4, 26.

empty bedroom at night. You may be sure I wrap round me the bedclothes pretty close. . . . It has been comfortless for me through the night by reason of the cold.[32]

There was also a significant difference between them in religious loyalties. Like the Holdens, the Stovins had the satisfaction of living in a region which was strongly committed to Methodism: according to Alan Everitt, some forty per cent of the population of Lincolnshire were connected with it.[33] But whereas Elizabeth belonged to the official Wesleyan church, Cornelius subscribed to the breakaway Free Methodists who (in rural Lincolnshire at least) tended to be poorer and less worldly. She firmly believed that he could have made more of the farm, had he not given beyond his means to the circuit, and spent so much time as preacher and chapel official. In fact the way in which Cornelius interpreted the call of public duty meant that he was away from home much more than might be expected of a farmer. Apart from preaching engagements and circuit meetings, he was also a Poor Law Guardian. These commitments kept him on the road a good deal. He relished the switchback character of his life. 'My career as an agriculturalist is wildly eccentric. One day I mount the pulpit and platform and pour forth a torrent of rude, sometimes incoherent eloquence. Another day I plunge heart and soul into my dear children's amusements'. In 1875 he summed up his objectives in life as '20 more years of hearty service in the cause of Christ . . . while improving my business, making it more profitable, and my house . . . so that my family may have a good start in life both physically, mentally and spiritually.' What made sense to him as an attempt to lead a godly life in all its manifestations caused friction with his wife.[34] Cornelius was mortified by the lack of real communion between them, for he had elevated ideas about marriage. Years later, when giving a speech to mark the golden wedding of his parents-in-law, he observed that the unity of man and woman was like the fingers of a single hand, rather than two railway carriages coupled together.[35]

The vicissitudes of the Stovin marriage were common enough.

---

[32] Cornelius Stovin, journal, 27 Nov. 1874 and 28 April 1875, ibid., pp. 159, 219; Stovin Papers (private collection): Cornelius Stovin to Elizabeth Stovin, 7 and 9 Nov. 1876 (transcripts).

[33] Alan Everitt, *The Pattern of Rural Dissent: The Nineteenth Century* (Leicester, 1972), p. 48.

[34] Journal for 5 Sept. 1872 and 12 Jan. 1875, in Stovin, *Journals*, pp. 96, 178.

[35] Stovin Papers: Journal, 18 March 1890.

More difficult to evaluate is how typical Cornelius's behaviour as a parent was. This was not what we might expect of a Victorian father, much less a devout Methodist. Cornelius conducted family prayers each morning. Like so many fathers, he looked somewhat apprehensively to the future, and he prayed for his children's spiritual as well as their mental advancement. He also looked to their early training in 'self-government', proudly recording how his eldest son Denison began his business career at the age of seven with a commission to spend 4*s*. 6*d*. on groceries in Louth Market.[36] Yet Cornelius's attitude towards his children was anything but joyless and denying. He took an unequivocally Romantic position on the true value of the child. Of his second son Frank, aged two, he wrote in words that might have been inspired by the Lakeland poets: 'He is a splendid divinely constituted ray of sunshine to brighten my lonely hours. He laughs and sings and chatters and enjoys life as if he were on the borders of Paradise.' Cornelius was unperturbed by the demands that babies placed on everyone around them. When Frank was a few weeks old, his father remarked in appreciative wonder, 'He seems to have revolutionised the whole household. Every other interest has more or less to bend to his. At present his sway is almost royal.'[37]

Cornelius regularly stepped into the breach to make life easier for his invalid wife. On one occasion in 1874 when Elizabeth was well enough to go to chapel, he stayed at home with the baby. 'While the saints are honouring God in the chapel I will praise him at home', he wrote. He bottle-fed babies without demur and saw them though the dark watches of the night when they were ill, re-creating the model of the 'nursing father' which had been much more common early in the nineteenth century. He was undismayed by displays of temper in his children, knowing that they would soon be succeeded by laughter and joy. There were punishments (unspecified), but the emphasis was on affection: 'Parental discipline does not in the least interfere with or check their buoyancy.' Cornelius believed in self-expression. 'Every kind of innocent playfulness is encouraged', he wrote, perhaps oblivious that this was in direct contravention of Wesley's killjoy teaching on the subject. Cornelius looked on with pleasure as Frank played with marbles, made 'original and spontaneous remarks', and clambered over the dining-room furniture.

---

[36] Journal, 13 Sept. 1871, in Stovin, *Journals*, p. 36.
[37] Journal, 22 Jan. 1875 and 1 Oct. 1872, in Stovin, *Journals*, pp. 181, 104.

Cornelius was what Americans at that time referred to as a 'frolicking father'. He enjoyed a good romp and was to be seen chasing Frank around the kitchen. He took seriously his children's spiritual and moral development, but 'childlike joyousness' remained at the centre of his vision. Nothing could have been more different from Joshua Pritchard's preoccupation with every detail of his daughter's spiritual training.[38]

Some of this fatherly involvement arose from the pressing circumstances of the Stovin household. Because of the servant problem, there was limited scope for delegating childcare. As a result the little ones were not 'imprisoned in the nursery', and they received much more attention from their parents. But there was nothing forced or reluctant about Stovin's performance as an engaged father. It provided the sparks of joy and vitality in what was all too often a life of toil and anxiety. The emotional costs were high as well. When Denison caught scarlet fever at school in 1874, Cornelius feared the worst (as well he might). 'To see him thrown so far out of my own and his dear mother's reach and to have become so complete a burden to his friends shook my manhood. Tears would rush up from the fountain of grief within me. I still feel myself in a fix.' For good or ill, fatherhood was integral to Cornelius's sense of his divinely ordered place in the world, and inseparable from his masculine self.[39]

* * *

It is sometimes tempting to think of Methodism, like Evangelical Anglicanism, as a 'badge' of class identity. Joshua Pritchard should give us pause. For him the raising of children had little to do with social status and everything to do with his account with God. Domestic life was not a subsidiary interest; it was the very centre of Joshua's emotional and spiritual existence. It was a vital part of that 'recognizable spirituality . . . refined into a recognized culture' which Clyde Binfield has identified as the hallmark of the Wesleyan middle class in

---

[38] Cornelius Stovin, journal entries for 20 Dec. 1874 (Stovin Papers), 12 Jan. 1875, 11 Feb. 1875, 14 Nov. 1874, 12 Jan. 1875 (Stovin, *Journals*, pp. 178, 190, 152, 177). Abelove, *Evangelist of Desire*, pp. 97–8, 101–2; Doreen Rosman, *The Evangelicals and Culture* (London, 1984), p. 107; Stephen M. Frank, 'A frolic with father: play and paternal identity in nineteenth-century midwestern and New England homes', paper presented to Second Carleton Conference on the History of the Family, Ottawa, May 1994.

[39] Cornelius Stovin to Elizabeth Stovin, 14 Nov. 1874, in Stovin, *Journals*, p. 152; Cornelius Stovin, diary, 19 Nov. 1874, ibid., p. 155.

Leeds at this time.[40] Of course the cult of the home in Victorian England was a consequence of work being removed from the domestic environment, and of a profound sense of alienation from the city. But in the long run the convergence between the spiritual and the social was crucial. Evangelicalism ennobled work as a struggle carried on in an ungodly world, while at the same time showing how domestic life could comfort and elevate the worker. The home might no longer be the site of production, but its deeper, more moral purpose now became clear. In drawing religion into the home at the same time as work was being taken out of it, the Methodists greatly intensified the hold of domesticity over the middle class and produced much of its characteristic tone and atmosphere.

Methodism, like other forms of Evangelicalism, had its own theological rationale for locating so much religious observance in the home. Methodism was a 'religion of the heart' which valued the spiritual feelings of the individual. The relative intimacy of the small domestic gathering made space for an atmosphere of spiritual fellowship, in which the soul was bared, guidance sought, and reproof administered. This new dispensation, it has often been pointed out, enhanced the status of women, since it implied a new spiritual dimension to their traditional role as guardians of the hearth. But there were vital implications for men as well. What bound men to the home, in the early Victorian period especially, was not just the popular ethic of companionate marriage, or the emotional and material needs of the bread-winner, but the conviction that home was the proper place to cultivate one's spiritual well-being. The godly household was a corner of heaven on earth. When Methodism became more routinized, it retained its domestic bent by making the class the focus of pastoral care and discipline. The class habitually met in private households for the practical reason that, in the early days, there had been nowhere else for it to convene. But the special spiritual intimacy which was possible in a domestic setting soon became its hallmark. In the homely metaphor of one of Wesley's preachers, 'when live coals are put together, the fire burns vehemently; but, when the coals are scattered, the fire dies away'.[41] Even in the Victorian period the leader of the class

---

[40] Clyde Binfield, '"An optimism of grace": the spirituality of some Wesleyan kinswomen', in Clyde Binfield, ed., *Saints Revisioned* (Sheffield, 1995), p. 68.
[41] William W. Dean, 'The Methodist class meeting: the significance of its decline', *Proceedings of the Wesley Historical Society*, 43 (1981), p. 43.

was often the master or mistress of the house, with the rest of the family (including servants) furnishing the core of the membership. The class which Sarah Sugden had led before her marriage was of this type. In the mid-nineteenth century the chapel tended to become more important than the class – indeed the distinction between them became blurred as class meeetings were increasingly held in chapel (as in Stovin's case).[42] But Methodism continued to be, in part at least, a 'felt' religion, with a pronounced emphasis on domestic religious disciplines.[43]

The implications for marriage were far from straightforward. A shared religion was no guarantee of marital harmony. Church teaching on marriage was shot through with contradictions. It could of course be read as a charter for sexual inequality. The Methodists looked back to the unyielding prescription of John Wesley: 'Whoever, therefore, would be a good wife, let this sink into her inmost soul, "My husband is my superior, my better: he has the right to rule over me. God has given it him, and I will not strive against God." '[44] In the theology of most Evangelicals, the ideal was an earthly father who revealed to his children something of the love and mercy of the Almighty himself. But against this old-style patriarchy must be set the commitment of all the Evangelical churches to the power of the moral mother as the foundation of family life. Once home was recognized as the prime site of 'the religion of the heart', the religious standing of the wife was bound to rise. If the husband reflected the authority of the Father in Heaven (often unseen but ever-present), the wife stood for Christian love and spiritual intuition. It was an open question, for example, whether the bed-time prayer of mother-and-child was not more efficacious than the daily family prayers led by the father.[45]

Religion might therefore inform and justify sharply differing interpretations of the marital relationship, even within the same denomination. The enhanced prestige of women, and above all of

---

[42] See for example, Stovin, *Journals*, pp. 28, 119.

[43] Leslie F. Church, *The Early Methodist People*, 2nd edn (London, 1949), pp. 153–81; Thomas Shaw, *A History of Cornish Methodism* (Truro, 1967), pp. 21–4; David L. Watson, *The Early Methodist Class Meeting* (Nashville, TN, 1985), ch. 4–5. For an instructive American parallel, see Gregory A. Schneider, *The Way of the Cross Leads Home: The Domestication of American Methodism* (Bloomington, IN, 1993).

[44] John Wesley, quoted in Philip J. Greven, *The Protestant Temperament* (New York, 1977), p. 127.

[45] Cf. Colleen McDannell, *The Christian Home in Victorian America, 1840–1900* (Bloomington, IN, 1986), pp. 109, 127, 130–5.

mothers, gave them potentially great leverage within the home. But, in what seems a strange paradox, even Nonconformists, who took a rigorously non-sacerdotal interpretation of the ministry, referred to the household head as 'priest'.[46] Patriarchal values certainly seem to have had some bearing on the cases discussed here. Each of the husbands possessed acknowledged spiritual authority – Isaac Holden as a possible candidate for the ministry, Cornelius Stovin as a local preacher, and Joshua Pritchard as a man who wore his intense spirituality on his sleeve. Consequently the balance of domestic authority was uncertain. Sarah Holden lacked the status of mother, but she had formal religious standing as an experienced class leader. She was also forty-five when she married Isaac. For all these reasons she was able to act independently and force a compromise over where and how they should live. Elizabeth Stovin, on the other hand, received from her husband all the praise and respect due to the mother of seven healthy children. She was less devout than he and had no formal position in chapel, but her views on domestic matters carried weight. Her ill-health and depression were real enough, but they also served to reinforce her case for the radical improvements to the farmhouse which she had set her heart on. Mary Pritchard is an altogether more shadowy figure. Her few surviving letters are short, devout, and practical. She appears to have identified completely with Joshua's spiritual regime for the children, borne along by his passionate enthusiasm. In none of these cases do we find that rivalry and tension between mother and father which was so characteristic of Victorian parenting.[47] The essential precondition was a deeply shared religious outlook, which left something to be desired only in the case of the Stovins.

That same religious understanding should have led to a deep disquiet on the subject of sex. John Wesley had rated purity so highly that he never fully endorsed sex within marriage and was very reluctant to perform marriage ceremonies. Something of the founder's doubts is to be seen in Joshua Pritchard's agonizing about the spiritual threat which his exuberance posed to his wife. But there is no

[46] John Angell James, *The Family Monitor, Or a Help to Domestic Happiness* (Birmingham, 1828), p. 17; Brewin Grant, *The Dissenting World: An Autobiography*, 2nd edn (London, 1869), p. 12.

[47] Claudia Nelson, *Invisible Men: Fatherhood in Victorian Periodicals, 1850–1910* (Athens, GA, 1995); John Tosh, 'Authority and nurture in middle-class fatherhood', *Gender and History*, 8 (1996), pp. 48–64.

trace of this ambivalence in the other two cases. Cornelius Stovin made no bones about hating his empty bed when Elizabeth was away. Isaac and Sarah Holden both employed relatively explicit language to keep their connection alive through repeated separations. There was no sign of sexual guilt. Peter Gay does not make the point in his two-volume study of bourgeois sexuality, but it is worth bearing in mind that a belief in the sacred nature of marriage was not inherently hostile to the enjoyment of sex.[48]

*　*　*

The differences to be found in the three families examined here with regard to child-rearing were even more marked. The nineteenth century is associated primarily with the Romantic idea that childhood is a state which should be enjoyed for itself, and which adults need to remain in touch with if they are to realize their full humanity. From this perspective the Evangelicals have usually had a bad press. They were above all concerned to bring up children to lead disciplined lives and be receptive to God's grace. Unlike the Romantics they attended to the adult in the making, rather than the child in the present. So far from possessing celestial natures, children were born in original sin. The parent's task, as John Wesley and countless others asserted, was to break the child's will by enforcing absolute obedience. Moderate Evangelicals emphasised instead the need for nurture based on gradual principles, rather than conversion with its implied damning of all that went before. They preferred the image of bending and shaping, rather than breaking the child's will, and this perspective led them to attend more carefully to the child's feelings. But each strategy exposed the child to intrusive control, of the kind practised by Joshua and Mary Pritchard.[49] Isaac Holden, like many a Methodist father, anxiously awaited news that each child had given his or her heart to God, thus signalling that his main spiritual duty as a parent had been accomplished.[50]

[48] Abelove, *Evangelist of Desire*, pp. 49–58; Peter Gay, *The Bourgeois Experience, Victoria to Freud*, 2 vols (New York, 1984–6).
[49] Paul Sangster, *Pity My Simplicity: The Evangelical Revival and the Religious Education of Children, 1738–1800* (London, 1963); Greven, *Protestant Temperament*, pp. 32–43, 156–7; Kathryn Kish Sklar, *Catharine Beecher: A Study in American Domesticity* (New York, 1976), pp. 153, 260.
[50] Isaac Holden to Margaret Holden, 26 Nov. 1856, 10 June 1858 and 14 April 1859, in E. H. Illingworth, ed., *The Holden-Illingworth Letters* (Bradford, 1927); MCRL, M478/15/1: Joshua Murgatroyd to Thomas Murgatroyd, 2 Aug. 1870.

The contrast with the teaching of Rousseau or Wordsworth is obvious enough. But the two systems had something in common all the same. Protective seclusion was vital to both: to the Romantics because children needed a playground beyond the reach of the adult world; to the Evangelicals because children's delicate spiritual state was so vulnerable to corruption. The Congregationalist minister John Angell James captured this dual tradition when he included among the 'blissful associations of home' both 'the nursery of virtue' and 'the playground of childhood'. The logic of Evangelical doctrines about man and salvation was to place children near the centre of domestic attention, just as the Romantic sensibility did for quite different reasons. Infant wills could be neither broken nor shaped without a great deal of time and patience. The child in an Evangelical household faced a constant stream of prayers, readings, catechisms, and homilies.[51]

But parent-child interaction was never confined to these serious matters. The reputation for joyless and repressive family life is partly due to the subsequent spread of the externals of Evangelical observance, like family prayers and 'the English Sunday', which could weigh very heavily on the young. At the beginning of the century the Romantic view was still fresh and attractive enough to impinge on the practice of Evangelicals like everyone else. Reminiscences of Evangelical childhood in the heyday of the movement strike a comparatively light note. There was no ban on pleasure for its own sake, only on morally dubious diversions. Parents balanced their inflexible religious routines with playfulness; parties were given and holiday trips undertaken. Evangelicalism was serious-minded but not necessarily killjoy. The eminent Methodist minister Adam Clarke frolicked with his children and wrote them long chatty letters. He was 'both paterfamilias and playmate', as Doreen Rosman has aptly put it. This tradition was still alive fifty years later. G. E. Sargent wrote in 1854 that children's wills needed to be broken, but they should nevertheless be able to invite their father to play with some confidence that he would. Plenty of fathers were happy to follow this advice, though with an ever-decreasing resolve to break wills. Cornelius Stovin's relaxed blend of fatherly guidance and participation in play probably represented the outer limit of what was acceptable.

[51] John Angell James, *Female Piety* (1856), quoted in Davidoff and Hall, *Family Fortunes*, p. 115.

Most Methodists could only have followed his example with considerable strain.[52]

That strain was above all to do with gender, since proper paternal behaviour was an important constituent of manliness. When William Cobbett recalled his years as a conscientious and attentive father in his *Advice to Young Men* of 1830, he felt obliged to add quickly, 'yet I have not been effeminate'. James Stephen, recollecting William Wilberforce's paternal tenderness, denied that it had ever 'degenerated into fondness or . . . caresses'.[53] The truth was that, as the ascribed characters of men and women became more polarized in the early nineteenth century, there was less tolerance for paternal behaviour which seemed to encroach on the mother's sphere. The mother's special qualities – her quickness of sympathy, her emotional insight, and her moral purity – were defined in ways which tended to disqualify men. This increasingly sharp distinction in parental roles was reflected in a revealing change in vocabulary. There was less talk of 'authority' and much greater emphasis on 'influence' – particularly among moderate Evangelicals who stressed nurture over time, rather than the transformative quality of conversion. Because the child's individuality was now more readily recognized, its upbringing had to be carefully adapted to its particular temperament, requiring observation and flexibility from day to day. Once parenting was seen in these processual, developmental terms, fathers were inevitably sidelined. As Sarah Ellis put it in 1843, they lacked 'the nicety and tact to manage the minute affairs of domestic life, and especially those of individual feeling'; they were out of their depth because they lacked the moral resources for the job. It followed that the father who trespassed in these domains was abandoning masculine for feminine traits. The home was suspect as a feminine sphere – the softening power of children its most beguiling threat to manhood. Cornelius Stovin, as we have seen, does not appear to have been troubled by such doubts, partly because of his spiritual certainty, and partly because of his grounding in Romantic ways of thought – not to mention his relative isolation. The redeeming

---

[52] David Newsome, *The Parting of Friends* (London, 1966), pp. 32–6; Standish Meacham, *Henry Thornton of Clapham* (Cambridge, MA, 1964), pp. 49–53; J. B. B. Clarke, ed., *An Account of the Infancy, Religious and Literary Life of Adam Clarke*, 3 vols (London, 1833), 2, p. 38; Rosman, *The Evangelicals and Culture*, p. 107; G. E. Sargent, *Home Education* (London, 1854), pp. 16, 26.

[53] William Cobbett, *Advice to Young Men* (1830; repr. London, 1926), p. 176; James Stephen, *Essays in Ecclesiastical Biography* (London, 1849), p. 273.

power of childhood was to him an article of faith, fully borne out by his daily experience.[54]

Lastly, mention of an unstable or vulnerable masculinity prompts the question of whether this period saw the appearance of a 'new man'. The phrase was used at the time in two distinct senses. It could mean a man newly risen in the social scale, as when Elizabeth Gaskell described the Congregationalist James Watts in 1855 as 'a new man and a new Mayor' of Manchester.[55] Alternatively the term was applied to someone who had undergone an Evangelical conversion, and whose life showed the fruits thereof in piety, domesticity, and a sense of social responsibility. To be a new man in both senses was a passport to respectability and reputation. Leonore Davidoff and Catherine Hall, who use the term without quotation marks, suggest that middle-class masculinity in this period rested on a new conception of 'calling' and a new relationship with the home.[56] At a broad level this was true. But the three case-studies examined here suggest that the relation between these elements was a good deal more unstable than is sometimes assumed. For Isaac Holden, the exigencies of his 'calling' confined the claims of home to a vestigial portion of his life. Cornelius Stovin too was constantly drawn away from wife and family by the self-imposed demands of public life. For Joshua Pritchard, on the other hand, work was an undignified burden, while almost everything of significance in his life took place at home. What seems true in all three cases is that the appeal of home was not just *mediated* through religious idiom; it derived its emotional and spiritual hold from the very distinctive role which Evangelical Christianity accorded to a sanctified domestic sphere. The potential for gender conflict was present here, as it is in any family system. The domesticated religious life both fuelled such conflict, and suggested ways in which it might be transcended or repressed.

University of North London

---

[54] Sarah Ellis, *The Mothers of England* (London, 1843), pp. 27, 160, 366. See also Nelson, *Invisible Men*, pp. 14–16; Steven Mintz, *A Prison of Expectations: The Family in Victorian Culture* (New York, 1983), pp. 27–39.

[55] Quoted in V. A. C. Gatrell, 'The commercial middle class in Manchester, c. 1820–1857' (Cambridge University Ph.D. thesis, 1971), pp. 44–5.

[56] Davidoff and Hall, *Family Fortunes*, p. 113.

'SHE SUCCEEDS WITH CLOUDLESS BROW . . .' HOW ACTIVE WAS THE SPIRITUALITY OF NONCONFORMIST WOMEN IN THE HOME DURING THE PERIOD 1825–75?

by LINDA WILSON

THE role and place of women in the nineteenth century has been the subject of much recent debate. In their influential book, *Family Fortunes*, Davidoff and Hall traced the development of separate spheres, which, they argued, was linked to the process of industrialization and the emergence of the middle class during the period 1780–1850.[1] They emphasised that both nonconformists and evangelical Anglicans had played a determining role in this development. Amanda Vickery, amongst others, has questioned this thesis. She believes that the premises are flawed, and that early modern studies have shown that neither industrialization, nor the development of separate spheres, can be located at the end of the eighteenth century.[2] Additionally, Helsinger and others have pointed out that there was a contemporary debate over the issue of women, with several varieties of ideology under discussion.[3] Whilst these criticisms of Davidoff and Hall need to be recognized, nevertheless, as Helsinger acknowledges, the ideal of the passive, home-based woman was a major influence in mid-nineteenth-century society.

This ideal was epitomized in Ruskin's essay 'Of Queen's Gardens',[4] and in Coventry Patmore's famous poem, 'The Angel in the House', in which he asserts that women's effortless spirituality, as he sees it, is far superior to men's struggles:

---

[1] L. Davidoff and C. Hall, *Family Fortunes: Men and Women of the English Middle Class, 1780–1850* (London, 1987), p. 74.

[2] A. Vickery, 'Golden age to separate spheres? A review of the categories and chronology of women's history', *HistJ*, 36 (1993), pp. 383–414. See also L. K. Kerber, 'Separate spheres, female worlds, women's place: the rhetoric of women's history', *The Journal of American History*, 75 (1988), pp. 9–30.

[3] E. K. Helsinger, R. L. Sheets, and W. Veeder, *The Woman Question* (Chicago, 1989), pp. xiv–xv.

[4] J. Ruskin, 'Of Queen's Gardens', in his *Sesame and Lilies* (London, 1871), pp. 95–158.

Where she succeeds with cloudless brow
In common and in holy course,
He fails, in spite of prayer and vow,
And agonies of faith and force.[5]

This paper investigates how far that passive ideal influenced the outworking of female spirituality within the English evangelical home. Four denominations have been investigated during the period 1825–75: Wesleyan Methodist, Primitive Methodist, Particular Baptist, and Congregationalist. A total of 240 obituaries from denominational magazines were studied and analysed to gain some understanding of these women's lives, with supplementary material from other obituaries and from separately published biographies. As in much women's history, there are methodological problems connected with the sources. Nearly all the obituaries, and some of the biographies, were written by men, although in some cases women may have supplied the material. Many do not mention the woman's Christian name. In addition they had a didactic purpose, in that they were an attempt to represent good Christian lives. Some of the most helpful obituaries, however, quote from women's diaries, giving a glimpse of their authentic voices, and all of them contain useful information about ordinary women's lives which otherwise would be inaccessible.

In the biography of his wife Ann, Baptist minister William Stott portrayed her as dependent on him, 'intensely loving, tender, clinging like the ivy to the oak she loved so much'.[6] This description sounds very patriarchal: she appears totally dependent on him, almost parasitically so, yet he also wrote that she was 'fully, entirely . . . engaged in the Lord's work outside' although not 'negligent or indifferent to home and household duties'.[7] She was an amalgam of an active evangelical woman and a passive 'angel'. Activism, the belief that spirituality should have a practical expression in everyday life, was an essential part of nineteenth-century evangelical spirituality, as Bebbington has shown,[8] whilst the ideals of passivity and submission

---

[5] C. Patmore, 'The Angel in the House', in *The Poems of Coventry Patmore*, ed. Frederick Page (London, 1949), pp. 89–90.
[6] W. Stott, *The Memoir of a Beautiful Life* (London, 1908), p. 15.
[7] Ibid., p. 32.
[8] D. Bebbington, *Evangelicalism in Modern Britain* (London, 1989), p. 3.

were drawn both from contemporary writers, such as Patmore and Ruskin, and from Christian tradition.

The obituaries reveal a similar situation. On the one hand, being active was commended as being spiritual. Sophia Wilson was a Wesleyan Methodist woman whose obituary was published in the *Methodist Magazine* of 1871. Her obituarist described her as living 'in the healthy and bracing breeze of incessant employment and activity' which 'blew away from her life all mist, cloud and stagnation', making a clear link between spirituality and action.[9] There are no 'cloudless brows' in sight. His assumption was that religion led to activity, and activity in turn contributed to a healthy spirituality. This was a common theme in many obituaries published in denominational magazines, and in some longer biographies. Yet on the other hand many also referred to the virtues of 'resignation' and 'submission', particularly in times of illness. Thus some descriptions sound close to Patmore's passive, childlike ideal woman, whilst others sound her exact opposite.

The first responsibility in the lives of most married nonconformist women was running the household, involving many varied tasks. Often imagery of light was used to emphasise the spiritual role of women in this context. The obituarist of Elizabeth Cooper in the *Christian Witness*, a Congregationalist Magazine, commented 'It was especially in the family her virtues shone',[10] and a Methodist writer remarked of Mary Ann Maidment that 'her light shone out bright in the family circle'.[11] These descriptions emphasised the belief that women's role lay primarily in the home, rather than in the wider world. In the narrow sphere of the family their 'light' was seen to better advantage.

A major way married women outworked their spirituality within the home was by supporting and encouraging their husbands. Mary Ward of Tadcaster was a Primitive Methodist who 'proved the genuineness of her religion' by her 'strict attention to her duties as a wife'.[12] One of these duties was to provide a haven from the outside world. Elizabeth Cooper apparently 'encouraged and refreshed' her husband. 'She was', he says, 'of the greatest use to me in reproving me . . .

---

[9] *Methodist Magazine* [hereafter *MM*], 94 (1871), p. 287.
[10] *Christian Witness* [hereafter *CW*], 7 (1850), p. 207.
[11] *MM*, 93 (1870), p. 573.
[12] *Primitive Methodist Magazine* [hereafter *PMM*], 31 (1850), p. 188.

in soothing me when irritated and chafed by the ills of life; and in exciting me to fresh exertions when labouring under depression.'[13] His confession reveals that he was dependent on his wife to quite a large extent and that for him home was a place where the dirt of the world outside could be washed away, and he could be restored and reinvigorated. Mrs Goldsmith, wife of a Baptist deacon in Lewes, was so concerned to protect her husband from the influence of 'the world' that she warned him on her deathbed to 'Beware of the world. There are many temptations and many snares. Keep close to God and He will be near to you.'[14] She felt herself to be, at least in some measure, guarding him from the evils around him. A woman's relationship to her husband thus seemed to be a mixture of subservience and mothering.

A minister's wife could provide a respite from the demands and conflicts of the congregation. Mrs Wigner was married to a Baptist minister in Lynn, and after her death her husband felt that the loss was 'irreparable', as she had often helped him in the midst of 'the corroding cares, the crushing anxieties, the heart's sorrows, which more or less are inseparable from the pastoral office'.[15] She seems to have been vital to his continued ministry; her ability to soothe and advise being just what was required of a good nonconformist wife. Another aspect of female encouragement and support was found in Mrs Cowdy of Romsey, a Baptist woman whose 'great gift in prayer' was put to use in supporting and encouraging her husband.[16] These examples are close to Patmore's ideal in which the wife was a sort of spiritual guardian. Indeed, at first glance the woman's role appears limited to homemaking, providing her husband with moral and emotional support, and bringing up their children. Through philanthropy and church involvement, however, many women were active in more than just the private sphere, and some ministers' wives worked alongside their husbands. Mary Emma Turquand, married to a Congregationalist minister in Walworth, not only kept people away when her husband was studying, but shared the pastoral visiting, chose the hymns for the services, and often the texts for the sermons. She was described by her obituarist as 'almost a co-

---

[13] *CW*, 7 (1850), p. 207.
[14] *Baptist Magazine* [hereafter *BM*], 44 (1852), p. 106.
[15] *BM*, 43 (1851), p. 228.
[16] *BM*, 66 (1874), p. 239.

pastor'.[17] The supportive model of minister's wife was, however, more usual.[18]

Women not married to Christians were in a different position. Some, particularly Primitive Methodists, led their unconverted husbands to Christ. Ann Kirkbride of Hartlepool had been a Christian two years when her husband was converted through her influence, in about 1848.[19] Women like Ann who achieved this were leading the way in spirituality within the home, although there is little indication that the women concerned actually thought of themselves in such terms.

Not all husbands were sympathetic to religion. Occasionally, in order to pursue her spirituality, a woman had to defy her husband, a contradiction not acceptable within the framework of 'angel' ideology. One woman whose faith was stronger than her desire to be submissive was Mary Gore, whose husband strongly opposed her faith. She was converted aged thirty-seven, probably in 1827, when Primitive Methodist preachers came to her home at Wildmoor, near Birmingham. She joined them, and was a member for eighteen years, but her husband was opposed to Methodism and sometimes refused to let her in the house when she had been to the chapel. She had to 'seek shelter elsewhere, or spend the nights in the open air'. Once he seized an axe and threatened to cut her legs off if she kept going to chapel, to which her spirited response was 'Then I will go upon my stumps.'[20] Her action was clearly approved of by the obituarist, who regarded her allegiance to God as more important than her relationship to her husband. For most wives, however, their ultimate allegiance was not tested in this way, and they easily combined loyalty to God with support for their husbands.

Whilst encouraging a husband could be construed as a passive aspect of spirituality, the business of running a home certainly was not. It took a considerable amount of time, as Ann Gilbert, a Congregationalist, discovered. Before her marriage she had with her sister Jane published poems, including *Hymns for Infant Minds* in 1810 which contained 'Twinkle, twinkle, little star'. Once married, for some years she had little time for writing, finding that house, husband, and children absorbed all her energy. In a letter in 1849, she commented,

[17] *CW*, 17 (1860), p. 45.
[18] See L. Sweet, *The Minister's Wife* (Philadelphia, PA, 1983), for a discussion of the role of ministers' wives in America.
[19] *PMM*, 31 (1850), p. 127.
[20] Ibid., p. 62.

on the subject of women and the vote, that 'So long as houses have insides as well as outsides, I think that the female head will have enough to do.'[21] She believed that running a home, not to mention involvement with church and charities, was quite enough for women without them intruding on public life and affairs.

There was a common assumption that a well-ordered house and a well-ordered spiritual life were closely related. Emma Robson was a Primitive Methodist from Hull whose obituary was included in the 1870 magazine. According to her obituarist she came 'near to our ideal of the model wife and mother', partly because she loved order in her home which was 'the picture of neatness'.[22] Creating and keeping order in the home required effort and energy, and for some women, managing on a tight budget. So Elizabeth Brooks, married to a Baptist minister, was eulogized for 'extracting a large amount of domestic comfort from resources always limited'.[23] Christianity thus had a very practical outworking in women's lives, and efficiency in running the home became a measure of their spirituality.

Besides running the household and supporting her husband, a married woman devoted a large amount of her time to her children. She usually had the main responsibility for their spiritual welfare and training, and sometimes their schooling, particularly when they were young, although some fathers did involve themselves in this process. Thus a vital part of the active expression of spirituality was passing on faith to the next generation.[24] This role was encouraged from the pulpit and in the denominational magazines.[25] Typical of these was an article on 'Family Religion' in the *Christian Witness* for 1850, which asserted that 'Pious mothers have done more to people heaven than any other class of persons, next to the preachers of the gospel.'[26] Men and women from the famous to the obscure referred to the importance of their mother's influence on them. This constant re-iteration of a mother's role must have affected women's own evaluation of their work and contributed to the professionalization of motherhood.

---

[21] J. Gilbert, *Memorials of Mrs Gilbert* (London, 1878), pp. 373–4.

[22] *PMM*, 51 (1870), p. 47.

[23] *BM*, 59 (1867), p. 319.

[24] See Davidoff and Hall, *Family Fortunes*, pp. 175, 181, for a discussion of professional motherhood.

[25] See, e.g., John Angell James, *Female Piety* (London, 1852), p. 267 ('Encouragement to Praying Mothers'); *BM*, 42 (1850), p. 745.

[26] *CW*, 7 (1850), p. 60.

Emma Robson followed her own mother's example in training her children. She had 'devoted much time and thought' to the training and 'spiritual welfare' of her children. When Emma herself became a mother, she 'tried to pull weeds and plant "principles of religion"' in the hearts of her boys, teaching them about Jesus and praying with them. Faith was thus communicated through three generations.[27] Like many nonconformist women, she longed to see the conversion of her children and actively worked towards that goal. One way of doing this was in Sunday sessions when a mother taught children about the Bible, and prayed with them. Fathers were hardly ever mentioned in this context. The Baptist writer Marianne Farningham recalled that in her childhood an old family Bible with pictures was brought out on Sunday evenings, and the children would sit or stand around their mother while she told them stories from it.[28] Similarly the preacher Charles Haddon Spurgeon recalled sitting round the table with his mother reading the Bible 'and she explained the Scripture to us'. Then she would ask them about their spiritual state, and pray for them.[29] Her prayers and her instructions made a strong impression on him. Many women passed on the basics of the faith to their children by these methods.

Not only Baptists practised such instruction: one Congregationalist woman, Mrs Spalding, gathered her children together to sing hymns such as 'There is a happy land, far, far away';[30] and another, Mrs Diss, taught her children to paraphrase the Bible and to pray on a Sunday evening.[31] Ann Gilbert chose not to attend chapel in the evenings. She wrote in 1826 to her parents that she preferred 'sowing on a smaller plot at home, where and when I enjoy many a happy hopeful hour, which I would not give up for all the gas-lighted chapels and crowded congregations you could muster'.[32] Although the training of children was very much an expected role for nonconformist women, falling clearly within the private sphere, it was not a passive one.

This was also true of other home-based activities. In houses with servants, for instance, their management was usually the wife's

---

[27] *PMM*, 51 (1870), p. 47.
[28] M. Farningham, *A Woman's Working Life* (London, nd), p. 19.
[29] C. H. Spurgeon, *Autobiography*, 4 vols (London, 1897), 1, p. 68.
[30] *CW*, 8 (1851), p. 462.
[31] *CW*, 11 (1854), p. 305.
[32] Gilbert, *Memorials*, pp. 284–5.

responsibility.[33] Emma Robson was respected by her servants; whilst Mrs Coates, a Wesleyan Methodist living near Grimsby, often spoke to hers of the goodness of God, urging them to pray.[34] Evangelizing the servants was common: Mary Eldridge was a Congregationalist who used Sunday evenings at home in Brixton as an 'opportunity for tender and earnest appeal to the conscience of a domestic'.[35] These women felt that they had a spiritual responsibility towards their servants and actively worked at this. Mrs Spalding, a Congregationalist, felt similarly, and 'combined kindness with authority in the management of her servants; she knew they had souls to be saved, feelings to be consulted, and rights to be regarded with respect'. When she died, they mourned 'as if they had lost a personal friend'.[36] Such women were acting as spiritual guardians for their servants, once again fulfilling an active spiritual role within the home.

Women were less active when it came to family prayers, the devotional heart of the evangelical nonconformist family, when once or twice a day everyone gathered to pray and read the Bible together. Marianne Farningham recalled that in her childhood home 'family prayer was as little likely to be omitted as breakfast or supper'.[37] Bradley argues that in Anglican evangelical homes, the habit of family prayers reinforced patriarchy[38] and in nonconformity too it was usually the man, as head of the household, who took the initiative. Prayers in the Congregationalist household of Sarah Walker's childhood were led by her father. She commented that she attended not just 'to hear a father pray' but to commune with God, and also referred to 'my father's devotions'.[39] She clearly expected her father not only to lead, but to be the sole voice in the proceedings. This was not always the case. Charlotte Lea, a Primitive Methodist in Whitehaven, is described as still praying effectively when she was ill: 'at the family altar her power was remarkable'.[40] It is not clear who led these prayers, but she took an active part in them, reflecting the tendency of Primitives to be more open to the contributions of women.

[33] *PMM*, 51 (1870), p. 47.
[34] *PMM*, 31 (1870), p. 47; *MM*, 94 (1871), p. 289.
[35] *CW*, 18 (1861), p. 116.
[36] *CW*, 8 (1851), p. 462.
[37] Farningham, *Woman's Working Life*, p. 34.
[38] I. Bradley, *The Call to Seriousness* (London, 1976), ch. 10.
[39] *CW*, 13 (1856), p. 13.
[40] *PMM*, 31 (1850), p. 74.

Where the father was unwilling or absent, women occasionally led prayers. Mrs Harris was a Baptist who maintained family worship at home in Leicester while her husband was away because she wanted to please him, and it led to her own conversion.[41] One Wesleyan Methodist woman, Mrs Floyd, conducted family worship both morning and evening when her husband was absent.[42] These women were obviously well able to lead the family in prayer, but only considered it appropriate if the head of the household was absent. Sometimes, however, a woman took the initiative to begin family prayers following her conversion and in this case would lead even if men were present. Mrs Dickson, a Congregationalist who later evangelized her husbands' employees, started family prayer in her parents' house when she was nineteen and 'for several years conducted it with the greatest propriety'.[43] Here it was considered acceptable for a woman to lead prayers even though there was a man present, because she was the 'spiritual' one in the family.

Methodists especially tried to start family prayer, as it was one element in the rules of the Society.[44] Thus Susannah Nichole, who later became a Primitive Methodist local preacher, started such worship in the family home in Hereford as soon as she was converted, and before long her mother, sister, and father were all converted through her.[45] Elizabeth Harris joined the Wesleyan Methodists in 1831 and wrote three years later that she had started family prayers and was hoping for repentance from her mother.[46] It is unclear whether her father was still alive. These examples demonstrate that despite it being considered the male role as head of the house it was acceptable for women to take the initiative on occasions. It is possible, however, to see this as an extension of the 'angel' emphasis that women should take responsibility for spiritual development in the home, rather than as an alternative to it, and therefore as still being within the norm. When it was done against the wishes of the husband this reflection of a stereotype was not so clear. In the *Methodist Magazine* for 1852 the obituarist of Jane Miles of Stone recorded that she prayed with servants every morning and evening, but that this was done for many years in

---

[41] *BM*, 44 (1852), p. 697.
[42] *MM*, 98 (1875), p. 388.
[43] *CW*, 6 (1849), p. 315.
[44] Revd J. S. Simon, *A Manual for Class Leaders* (London, 1892), p. 148.
[45] *PMM*, 31 (1850), p. 131.
[46] *MM*, 95 (1872), p. 92.

the attic because of her husband's opposition.[47] This, however, was a rare exception, and most women left the initiative to their husbands.

Another expression of women's spirituality within the home which linked the spiritual with the practical was hospitality. Giving hospitality to ministers was worthy of special mention in an obituary, especially within Methodism where the ministers itinerated and were constantly in need of beds. Mary Ann Maidment, a Wesleyan Methodist, was glad to offer hospitality to ministers 'feeling that they brought a blessing with them';[48] and the Primitive Methodist Emma Robson seemed to have had a particular gift for being hospitable. Her obituarist quotes a certain Mr J. Wood who, referring to her hospitality to itinerant ministers, says, 'Without any apparent effort on her part she made them feel at home at once.'[49] As well as ministers, frequently relatives would stay with a family for extended periods, and a woman might feel some responsibility towards them. Elizabeth George, a single Methodist woman who lived with her mother, had a cousin who came to stay and he was converted whilst there.[50]

Another aspect of church-related hospitality was being willing to use one's house for meetings. Mrs T. B. Millard, a Baptist woman, started a weekly female prayer meeting in her own house;[51] and Marianne Farningham's weekly girls' Bible Class was held in her home. Methodist and Primitive class meetings were frequently held in homes. Hospitality was an aspect of active spirituality which fulfilled both contemporary expectation and long-standing Christian tradition. As Mary Clare Martin has highlighted, here the division of public and private starts to break down: a busy household, with people staying and meetings taking place, is as much if not more public as a small office, ostensibly in the 'public' sphere.[52]

Much of the expression of women's spirituality within home and family was active. However, when it came to long illnesses obituarists often put stress on more passive virtues, such as patience, resignation, and submission to the will of God. The account of Mrs Dickson, of

[47] *MM*, 75 (1852), p. 112.

[48] *MM*, 93 (1870), p. 573.

[49] *PMM*, 51 (1870), p. 47.

[50] H. Piggot, *Memoir of Elizabeth George* (London, 1858), p. 29.

[51] *BM*, 47 (1855), p. 368.

[52] M. C. Martin, 'Women and philanthropy in Walthamstow and Leyton 1740–1870', *London Journal*, 19 (1995), p. 119.

Bure, near Lancaster, whose obituary was in the *Christian Witness* in 1849, is one which highlights the womanly and Christian characteristics needed during a long illness:

> As Mrs D. [sic] lived when in health, she suffered and died. The temper and bearing of the Christian were ever evinced by her. During the whole of her lengthened illness she never once complained or murmured: the most subdued and cheerful resignation characterised her. She acknowledged the hand of God in the affliction she suffered, and felt assured that the dispensation which had been allotted to her, however painful to flesh and blood, was one of wisdom and love, and she submitted to it with meekness and submissiveness.[53]

The main features in Mrs Dickson's obituary, such as no complaining, cheerful resignation, and a belief that God was in control, are found in many other obituaries. Whilst the obituaries may have been idealized on occasions, they demonstrate that resignation and submission were considered important virtues in nonconformist circles, and probably by women themselves.

The age of the dying woman seemed to make little difference to a sense of resignation to the prospect of death. Hannah Hitchings, a Primitive Methodist dying at seventy-seven, might be expected to be 'quite resigned to the will of the Lord';[54] but so was Catherine McEwan at twenty-four, and Ann Christopherson, a Baptist, at the age of sixteen.[55] A strong belief in Providence tended to alleviate a sense of bitterness, or at least to make it unacceptable to mention such feelings, although sorrow was often expressed. The common belief was that illness and death needed to be welcomed as coming from the hand of God.

Resignation and submission were not always arrived at without a struggle, and the conflict was often to do with 'giving up' relatives, and especially children, into God's care. During her last illness one Baptist woman, Mrs Millard, was 'anxious to be brought into that state of mind' where she would 'be willing to live or to die', but longed to see her children converted, and felt they tied her to the earth. However,

[53] *CW*, 6 (1849), p. 347.
[54] *PMM*, 31 (1850), p. 122.
[55] *BM*, 49 (1857), p. 236.

she believed that God could 'remove all these fears, and give me grace to leave all in his hands'.[56] In other words, she needed to trust God for the future of her children as well as the duration of her illness. A few obituaries also suggested that suffering produced holiness and a readiness for heaven. Mrs Booth, a Baptist, believed that her illness had been sent by God 'to perfect her submission' because she had been rebellious after a child had died.[57] Similarly, May Cowell wrote 'I hope I desire to feel passive in his hands, knowing that he does all things well. . . . I know I need the chastening rod.'[58] These women believed that illness was being used to discipline and train them. A more common view, however, was expressed by Eliza Sanders, a Methodist, who believed that its purpose was to bring her closer to God, but made no reference to discipline as such.[59] What was needed in these cases, they believed, was to be passive and let God work in their lives through the suffering.

Despite the stress on passivity and resignation, women were often practical and active in the outworking of their spirituality, even on the deathbed. Several women, like Charlotte Lea, took the opportunity to evangelize friends, relatives, and servants, sending messages or talking to them, and urging them to turn to God. Her last words were a message to her unconverted son: 'tell him from his dying mother that he must make haste to obtain peace with God'.[60] Another Primitive Methodist, Mary Ann Matthews, continued 'to preach to all around her till within two minutes before her happy departure'.[61] She was eager not to waste a moment. Catherine McEwan, a Congregationalist, made a point during her final illness of buying tracts to send to friends and also organized her finances.[62] Similarly Mrs Bell, a Baptist, arranged her affairs 'like a person who anticipated a journey to some delightsome place, and who wished that every thing might be found in order when she was gone'.[63] These women were still in control of their lives and their affairs, however much they submitted to what they understood to be the will of God, and their spirituality was still practical at this late stage.

[56] *BM*, 47 (1855), p. 370.
[57] *BM*, 48 (1856), p. 166.
[58] *BM*, 42 (1850), p. 500.
[59] *MM*, 93 (1870), p. 284.
[60] *PMM*, 31 (1850), p. 73.
[61] Ibid., p. 250.
[62] *CW*, 7 (1850), p. 414.
[63] *BM*, 46 (1854), p. 111.

The reality is that nonconformist women were both active and passive in the way they expressed spirituality within their homes. The obituarist of Mrs Matthews, a Congregationalist, stressed that she had 'passive graces' as well as 'active virtues',[64] and this was true of many women. The type of spirituality expressed in the home was largely in accordance with behaviour expected of women, showing their devotion to God by their care for their families. There was a little of Patmore's angel about them, but they were also active evangelicals, busy running their houses, training their children, and offering hospitality – and surely not without some effort on their parts! In addition to this women maintained private devotions, and many were involved in extensive visiting and other church activities outside their own homes, moving out from the private sphere. Often busy, not with 'cloudless brow', but with sheer hard work, they brought their spirituality into the everyday world of home and family, working within and rarely directly questioning the patriarchal framework within which they found themselves. Obituaries and biographies, whether written by men or women, bear clear evidence not only that many did consider men and women's worlds to be fundamentally different, but that on occasions women were regarded as the spiritual guardians of the family, an idea that Patmore used and developed.

Perhaps it is unfair, however, to use Patmore's angel as a yardstick for these women. Patmore's ideal was more constricted than the separate sphere ideology proposed by Davidoff and Hall, which itself has limitations. With her 'unclouded brow', she would have been a stranger to the nonconformists whom we meet with in these biographies and obituaries, and who, even when allowance is made for the male writers, some gloss, and a touch of hagiography, were ordinary, hardworking women who cannot be contained within a stereotype.

Open Theological College, Cheltenham

---

[64] *Evangelical Magazine*, ns 4 (1873), p. 467.

A JAMAICA OF THE MIND: GENDER, COLONIALISM, AND THE MISSIONARY VENTURE

by CATHERINE HALL

MARY Ann Middleditch, a young woman of twenty in 1833, living in Wellingborough in Northamptonshire and working in a school, confided in her letters her passionate feelings about Jamaica and the emancipation of slaves.[1] The daughter of a Baptist minister, she had grown up in the culture of dissent and antislavery and felt deeply identified with the slaves whose stories had become part of the books she read, the sermons she heard, the hymns she sang, the poems she quoted, and the missionary meetings she attended. In 1833, at the height of the antislavery agitation, Mary Ann followed the progress of William Knibb in Northamptonshire. Knibb, who was born in nearby Kettering, had gone to Jamaica as a Baptist missionary in 1824 and been radicalized by his encounter with slavery. In the aftermath of the slave rebellion of 1831, widely known as the Baptist War because of the associations between some of the slave leaders and the Baptist churches, the planters had organized against the missionaries, burnt their chapels and mission stations, persecuted and threatened those whom they saw as responsible. Faced with the realization that their mission could not coexist with slavery the Baptist missionaries in Jamaica sent William Knibb, their most eloquent spokesman, to England to present their case. Abandoning the established orthodoxy that missionaries must keep out of politics, Knibb openly declared his commitment to abolition. The effect was electric and his speeches, up and down the country, were vital to the effective organization of a powerful antislavery campaign which resulted in the Emancipation Act of 1833.[2]

Sitting in Wellingborough in 1833, Mary Ann heard the reports of

[1] This essay is part of a much longer study. I am grateful to the ESRC and to the Nuffield Foundation for the support which they have given me.

[2] T. Middleditch, *The Youthful Female Missionary. A Memoir of Mary Ann Hutchins, wife of the Rev. John Hutchins, Baptist Missionary, Savanna-la-Mar, Jamaica; and daughter of the Rev. T. Middleditch of Ipswich; compiled chiefly from her own correspondence by her father* (London, 1840); Mary Turner, *Slaves and Missionaries. The Disintegration of Jamaican Slave Society 1787–1834* (Urbana, IL, 1982).

Knibb's speeches in Kettering and Northampton and longed to be there. 'O, that I had the wings of a dove', she wrote, but being a woman had to make do with reports from her parents and friends. Her dream became to go to Jamaica so that she could make her own contribution, 'teach the EMANCIPATED negroes' herself, play her part in the great experiment which had been launched by abolition.[3]

Mary Ann's identification with Jamaica and the struggles of the antislavery movement on behalf of the slaves represents a powerful element in English society in the 1830s. The empire had its material presence in the everyday lives of the English middle class – the sugar, the tobacco, the tea, the coffee, the chocolate, the Indian shawls, the papier-mâché trays, the host of commodities which had become part of any middle-class home – but it also had another presence, in the mind. In the late eighteenth and early nineteenth centuries it was the British West Indian islands, and particularly Jamaica, the largest and richest of those islands, which dominated the imperial mind; not only because of the debates over slavery and the slave trade, but also because of the slave rebellions of that era. The campaign over the slave trade was successfully concluded in 1807, but by the 1820s it had become clear that this had not resulted in the transformation of the system of slavery itself which the abolitionists had hoped for. In the 1820s the antislavery movement revived, witnessing the launch of the struggle for full emancipation which, it is estimated, involved more English men and women of all social classes in petitioning than any other popular political movement in the early nineteenth century.[4]

The debate on slavery as a system had entered the mainstream of English political and cultural life. It raised questions which could not be contained within a demarcated section of the mind labelled 'empire', for it raised issues as to the nature of Englishness itself. What did England's continued collusion with that system mean; what did it mean to be implicated in such an institution, to eat slave sugar, to allow children to be wrenched from their mothers, men and women to be flogged? What did it say about the English that such horrors continued in 'their' empire? The English men and women who engaged with the struggle over slavery, whether for or against, were constituting their own gendered identities in that process. Jamaica, far

[3] Middleditch, *The Youthful Female Missionary*, pp. 49, 63.
[4] Seymour Drescher, *Capitalism and Antislavery. British Mobilization in Comparative Perspective* (Basingstoke, 1986).

from being an unknown island, remote from the interests of English people, was brought into their daily lives, their dreams, and their fantasies through a process of identification, whether positive, negative, or deeply ambivalent.

Mary Ann Middleditch's thinking about slavery and emancipation, her longing to go to Jamaica, her belief that as a Christian she had a contribution to make there, was rooted in her conception of an imagined place, a 'Jamaica of the mind'. Her 'Jamaica of the mind' was constructed through the narratives of antislavery and missionary enterprise: the books, the sermons, the hymns, the poems, the engravings which poured from their presses. From the late eighteenth century the antislavery lobby had been concerned to counter planter dominance in public debates. They began to publish and publicize their own reports, determined to offer eye-witness accounts (mainly from missionaries) which would challenge the planters' version of slavery. English abolitionists constructed out of these narratives their 'Jamaica of the mind'.

Planters and missionaries were central to the English 'Jamaica of the mind'. It was the slave trade, slavery and emancipation which inspired Jamaica's particular genre of travellers' tales in the 1830s and 1840s. Jamaica never had its Mungo Park or its David Livingstone, for there was no 'dark continent' to explore. The Blue Mountain range never attracted the Royal Geographical Society, for the island was assumed to be 'known', mapped from the seventeenth century after its conquest by Cromwell's forces in 1655, its counties and parishes neatly demarcated with English names, its Maroon population settled as safely as they could be in defined areas. It was the plantation system, the slaves, the whip, and after 1834 the emancipated, that travellers went to see in Jamaica.

The tales written by these travellers, virtually all of whom were men, were central to the struggle over the representation of the British West Indian islands and their peoples in the nineteenth century. But how was Jamaica produced for England, specifically in the antislavery narratives of the 1830s and 1840s? What was the imagined geography of the abolitionist? How was the 'travelling eye' rivetted to the missionary endeavour? What happened when the traveller's tale was mapped on to the missionary story? The men who wrote these accounts were informed by a very particular view of the family and the proper division of labour. Men were to be active in the public world; women were fashioned for the private sphere of the home.

Their encounters with Jamaica, shaped by this lens, were then cross-cut by notions of racial difference. Could the enslaved black men and women whose lives were shaped by the rule of the plantation, with its underlying sexual immorality, become independent working men and domesticated women?

The campaign against 'apprenticeship', the system of unfree labour introduced for a fixed term in the wake of the abolition of slavery, was spearheaded in England by the noted abolitionist Joseph Sturge, Birmingham Quaker and corn-merchant. Sturge decided to go and see for himself how the apprenticeship laws in the West Indies were working, convinced that it was vital to 'awaken the public mind'. Together with his friend and fellow Quaker, Leeds merchant Thomas Harvey, Sturge published an account of his experiences on his return, the first in a series of books which were to be written by noted antislavery advocates in the next twenty years. Their intention was to ascertain 'the actual condition of the negro population of those islands'. Their contacts were antislavery contacts, their hope that their work would stimulate a public campaign in England.[5] The book was an immediate success, provoking sharp controversy and stimulating a campaign. The Jamaican House of Assembly, fearing imperial inter-ference, itself abolished apprenticeship from 1 August 1838.

In the years immediately following 1838 public interest in Britain in the West Indian experiment was extensive, and a series of publications sustained that interest and kept the antislavery viewpoint in the public eye. Sturge, Harvey, and other abolitionists such as Joseph John Gurney who visited Jamaica and published reports, were committed to the view that negroes were fellow-subjects and members of the same universal human family; yet none of them believed in their equality with white people except as a future possibility. England in their view was a civilized society, Jamaica was not. The faith was that it could become civilized with English help; that if only enough good whites, as opposed to the decadent planters of Jamaica, would go and live there, there would be more chance of them learning to be 'like us'. In writing their narratives they constructed a sense of difference, of otherness from black people, as they observed 'the race', made comments and

---

[5] Joseph Sturge and Thomas Harvey, *The West Indies in 1837: being the Journal of a Visit to Antigua, Montserrat, Dominica, St. Lucia, Barbadoes and Jamaica: Undertaken for the Purpose of Ascertaining the Actual Condition of the Negro Population of those Islands*, 2nd edn (London, 1838), p. viii.

judgements on their manners, their 'progress', and their 'improvement', described their dress and customs. Troubling issues, an encounter with wildly dancing women or a myalman, a protagonist of white magic, were marginalized; for such exhibitions disrupted the antislavery orthodoxy that negroes were steadily progressing to become an ordered and industrious peasantry, respectful and respectable, domesticated and familial, learning the ways of civilization and burying two sets of histories – of Africa and of slavery.[6]

By 1841 the existence of these books meant that antislavery supporters had a barrage of evidence at their fingertips demonstrating the first results of the 'great experiment'; a counterweight to the volumes produced earlier by the supporters of the plantocracy which maintained that black people could never be like white. In 1843 a substantial new work was published, *Jamaica: its Past and Present State*, by James Mursell Phillippo. It was published in England and was soon after available in Jamaica. Phillippo had been based in Spanish Town, the capital of Jamaica, for twenty years. His book aimed to unite a missionary's story with a history and topography of Jamaica. It drew on the long tradition of Christian writing associated with conversion, together with a distinctive nineteenth-century sub-genre, the missionary story, which told of the encounter with heathenism and its triumphant defeat. This was then articulated with the antislavery traveller's tale to produce Jamaica for England and the new Jamaica for Jamaica too.

The book was written in England. Suffering from severe ill-health Phillippo had been obliged to leave Jamaica with his wife Hannah and younger son and spend time in Hastings. Too unwell to travel, he found himself with time on his hands, unable to do the usual round of missionary events that were expected of those on leave. He decided to use the time to write a book relying on his memory and 'his own observation and experience', together with the materials he had with him. He had been there; he knew. His eye had seen; he could authenticate. His hope was to 'give a faithful representation of Jamaica as it *was*, and as it *is*', to show the transformation which had taken place from slavery to emancipation.[7]

---

[6] Joseph John Gurney, *A Winter in the West Indies described in Familiar Letters to Henry Clay of Kentucky* (London, 1840); John Candler, *Extracts from the Journal of John Candler whilst travelling in Jamaica*, 2 parts (London, 1840–1), 1, pp. 21, 45, 2, p. 15.

[7] James Mursell Phillippo, *Jamaica: its Past and Present State* (London, 1843), pp. vi–vii.

Phillippo had gone to Jamaica as a Baptist missionary in 1823 and had lived in Spanish Town since then. Born in Norfolk in 1798, the son of a master builder, he was brought up in the Anglican Church. His mother's piety, a factor often mentioned by missionaries and ministers, made a deep impression on him; but having left home to go into farming and trade with his grandfather he became absorbed with the worldly pleasures of country fairs and tea gardens, and together with his young male friends made fun of the worshippers at the local Independent chapel. Stirrings within his conscience, however, drove him to a Baptist chapel despite the prejudices against Dissent which he met all around him and encountered within himself. At fifteen he experienced conversion. 'I felt like Christian when he lost his burden at the sight of the Cross', he recorded; he cast his lot 'with the despised people of God' and became a Baptist.[8]

As a child Phillippo had loved *Robinson Crusoe* and the voyages of Captain Cook. Following his conversion, his birth as a new man in Christ, he became increasingly fascinated by missionary works of travel and adventure, and interested in 'the heathen'. As his biographer Edward Bean Underhill, a later chronicler of Jamaica and for many years Secretary of the Baptist Missionary Society (BMS) put it, 'Stirrings of desire for usefulness among his fellow-men began to be felt, especially among the far-off nations lying in darkness and in the shadow of death.' 'He read the missionary publications of the African traveller Campbell with avidity' and began to train himself in useful skills – 'medicine, brick-making, house-building, cabinet work, the wheelwright's toil, agriculture, and the manufacture of articles of food and clothing, all attracted in turn his serious and ardent attention'. He started to preach and was gradually convinced of his desire to be a missionary, to prove his Christian manhood in imperial adventure of a noble kind.[9] This would be a good vocation for a Christian man.

The BMS had been founded in 1792, and had been sending missionaries to Jamaica since the early nineteenth century.[10] Phillippo was accepted as a trainee missionary by the BMS Committee in 1820.

---

[8] Didcot, Baptist Missionary Society [hereafter BMS], MSS WI/1, James Mursell Phillippo, 'Autobiography', pp. 19–20, 22.

[9] Edward Bean Underhill, *Life of James Mursell Phillippo; Missionary in Jamaica* (London, 1881), p. 8.

[10] See Catherine Hall, 'Missionary stories: gender and ethnicity in England in the 1840s', in Catherine Hall, *White, Male and Middle Class: Explorations in Feminism and History* (Cambridge, 1992), pp. 205–54.

He met Thomas Burchell, who became a lifelong friend, encountered a missionary wife who gave him much valuable information on the life he would lead, and talked to Dr Hoby, a longtime missionary supporter. He was being inducted into the extended network of the mission family at home. He began to preach to small congregations in the Cotswolds. He felt 'a glowing satisfaction at the thought of spending my life in something nobler than the locality of this island will admit'. 'Heathens' and 'savage pagans of the wilderness' in far-flung corners of the empire offered a more enticing and exciting prospect than rural labourers. 'You must remember', he wrote to his parents, 'that I am to be engaged in a glorious cause.' Adopting the language of militant evangelicalism with its call to the faithful to join the Army of Christ, he continued: 'Who would not lend a hand to dispel the darkness of Satan's kingdom and erect upon its ruins the kingdom of God. . . . This world is not a place of repose for a faithful soldier of the Cross.' On moving to Bradford he found preaching in the Yorkshire villages an excellent training for the work ahead – Yorkshire dialect presented him with almost as many difficulties as Jamaican patois and his congregations sometimes had difficulty in understanding him. This 'soldier of the Cross' had chosen an imperial destiny and must face its attendant problems.[11]

Trainee missionaries were well aware that they were expected to marry before leaving the country, securing them against the sexual licentiousness associated with slavery and Africa, and ensuring a 'helpmeet' for the labours of a missionary station. Rumours were rife, however, as to what sort of woman the Committee expected, rumours which reveal the class anxieties as to missionary work and status. Some said she should be mature in age; others focused on useful skills such as laundress or nurse and opined that experience as a servant of all work was really the best preparation. Some claimed that a good personal appearance was quite unnecessary as this would soon deteriorate in tropical climes; others argued that the key qualification was an ardent spirituality. 'It was also understood', recorded Phillippo, 'that some Ministers undertook to select wives for young Missionaries who offered themselves for service', and he told the tale of the efforts made for one young man, including 'the setting up of tea-parties amongst a congregation'. Whilst in the Cotswolds Phillippo had met

---

[11] Phillippo, 'Autobiography', pp. 33, 40, 41, 49, 61.

Hannah Selina Cecil, a young woman to whom he had become engaged, but he heard disturbing gossip as to her likely unsuitability in the eyes of the Committee – she was 'too delicately brought up, had too comfortable a home, had not manifested so much of a missionary spirit as to fit her for so arduous and self-denying position as that of a foreign missionary's helpmeet'. Fortunately, however, the Committee approved.[12]

Phillippo and his friend Thomas Burchell, who had been accepted as a trainee at the same time, were both fully expecting during their training to go to 'the East', as it was called. They were in the forefront, however, of the revived mission to 'the West'. 'I have enlisted as a soldier of the Cross', reported Phillippo, 'and have now received the summons for active duty in a foreign land.'[13] Soldiers took orders; his order was from God. The order went to the man, as employee of the BMS, as trained missionary, as father of the mission station. His new helpmeet was automatically included in that order, her free labour assumed as part of the family enterprise. In October 1823 the newly married couple embarked for Jamaica, and after an enjoyable voyage which included evening sing-songs on deck had arrived in Spanish Town by Christmas.

Their first encounter with black culture was dramatic for it was Carnival, the moment at which slaves were allowed to escape briefly from the plantation and turn the world upside down with bacchanalian festivities:

> There was scarcely any passing along the streets of Spanish town from the heathenish processions encountered at every turn; while the hideous yellings of the multitudes as accompaniments to their still more revolting attitudes in their dances to the rough music of their African ancestry were more than enough to render frantic the animal that brought us thus far quietly on our way, not to anticipate the scenes of dissipation and general wickedness to which these revelries led. Some of the more respectable held their *concerts* but no one certainly unless he has resided many years in the country and discarded all European tastes and predilections could patiently endure their attempts at harmony.

[12] Phillippo, 'Autobiography', p. 52b.
[13] Ibid., p. 64b.

Thus Phillippo encountered and codified difference, defining for himself as he wrote in his journal the moment at which the heathenism of his imagination was mapped on to the sights of Spanish Town, the place which was to be his home for the next sixty years. Here was Africa in all its horror, with the 'revolting attitudes' of the dances the 'sign' of the lasciviousness, the licence of black sensuality rampant – this was the culture which Christianity must transform. Dissipation, wickedness, hideous yellings, and rough cacophanies of sound provided the first engagement with black culture, the culture that was no culture, the proof of the utter depravity of both Africa and slavery. Furthermore, the mission premises were dirty, dilapidated, and inconvenient; but a good clean-up established a new beginning.[14]

The Phillippos' early years in Spanish Town were difficult – a hostile plantocracy who put every obstacle in the way of his preaching, constant difficulties with the law, and three babies lost to Hannah in less than three years. By 1825 the hostility of the authorities had somewhat abated and the imperial government's policy of amelioration, adopted to quieten the critics of slavery by introducing a programme of limited reform, meant that dissenting missionaries could not be persecuted quite so easily. Phillippo was able to preach and had meanwhile established Bible classes, a Sunday school, a day school, and out-stations in nearby Old Harbour and Passage Fort, all of which provided mainly for slaves. Phillippo's initial horror at the heathenism of the African culture which he had encountered at Carnival was tempered by his understanding of the transformation chapel attendance and 'proper' Christian values could bring. Baptism was the symbolic rite of passage, the public statement of transformation, the ritualized washing clean, the crossing from one identity to another. Phillippo made use of a spectacular spot in the river above Spanish Town to fill the minds of both those baptized and the onlookers with 'a mixture of delight and awe'.[15] By 1827 he had raised enough money from England to buy the materials for a grand new chapel which could hold 1,500. Next door was a school, and the mission house, between school and chapel, was enlarged. He supervised the building work which was done by the slaves. The chapel still stands looking much the same as it did in 1827, an impressive building,

---

[14] Ibid., pp. 64b, 78–9.
[15] Underhill, *Phillippo*, pp. 56–7.

constructed, in his writing as well, as a statement of faith and power, suitable for the capital of the country:

> There is something interesting and important in the erection of a place of worship not only as regards the special object of its erection but also in the collateral influence it is calculated to exert. It raises its sacred head with eloquence and power. It speaks of the hallowed purpose for which it is reared. It is itself a call to holiness which will not quite be disregarded even by worldly irreligious men. It shines forth as a beacon and a monument both of Philanthropy and of Prayer.[16]

He might have added, as subsequent events were to show, that it was also a monument to Phillippo, and indeed the church is now known as Phillippo's Church.

In the late 1820s both Phillippo and his wife were involved in raising money in England to purchase the freedom of slaves. Indeed, Hannah became embroiled in a lengthy controversy over the allegation that she had herself owned slaves and she took the unusual step of writing personally to the BMS to vindicate her cause. In 1831 ill-health brought the family to England for a while, so that they were out of the island when the 1831 slave rebellion occurred. Phillippo was, however, soon drawn into the efforts spearheaded by William Knibb to bring the issue of slavery to the heart of British public life. He spoke with Knibb on the celebrated occasion when Knibb first came out against slavery; he did four lectures for Joseph John Gurney in Norwich; he addressed many public meetings for Christian organizations; and caused a sensation in Wales by travelling with Robert Smith, an escaped slave from Jamaica. In Beulah, 'all soon became bustle and confusion. The shoemaker threw down his lapstone, the carpenter his axe, the blacksmith his hammer', business stopped, the townspeople rushed to the doors and windows, 'some never having seen a black man before'.[17]

By the time he returned to Spanish Town in 1834 the Emancipation Act had been passed and 'I was in a new world ... surrounded by a new order of beings.'[18] The celebrations in the chapel were led by black brothers. 'Blessed Lord', said one,

---

[16] Phillippo, 'Autobiography', p. 95.
[17] Underhill, *Phillippo*, pp. 104–6.
[18] Ibid., p. 121.

as dou so merciful pare we, to let we see dis blessed morning, we want word, we want tongue, we want heart to praise de. Debil don't do de good to us, but dou dou de good to us, for dou put it into de heart of de blessed European to grant us dis great privilege! O derefore may none of we poor sinner praise de debil by makin' all de carouze about de streets, but flock like dove to deir window to praise and glorify dy great name.[19]

Freed slaves did indeed flock to the chapels. In the years after 1834 Phillippo was engaged with the struggle over apprenticeship, organizing petitions to the House of Commons, putting pressure on the Jamaican House of Assembly which was five minutes' walk from his mission station, sending regular bulletins to the BMS secretary and the antislavery press, corresponding via the Governor with the Colonial Office, recommending the urgent necessity of 'an immediate attempt to educate the negro in order to remove from his mind and habits of life the pernicious effects of slavery, and to fit him for a life of patient, continuous, and successful toil as a free man'.[20] This was his lifelong conviction – that a Christian education could eradicate the legacy of slavery and make men and women anew. In 1835 he began to buy land to establish free villages, places where the emancipated could live in peace and prosperity.[21] 1 August 1838, the first day of full freedom, was celebrated with huge festivities in Spanish Town. Phillippo, 'the Pastor', together with the Governor, greeted thousands of freed men, women, and children in the main square, a striking illustration of the way in which these senior missionaries were briefly positioned, and a source of fury to the planters who continued to treat them with 'superciliousness and contempt'.[22] Phillippo was convinced that 'the great experiment' would 'prove the most interesting that ever transpired in the annals of the world': hardly a modest vision. He appealed to British Christians for help: 'the fields are ripe and the harvest is great'.[23] Money was required for missionaries, chapels, schools, and land; men were needed too, to be missionaries and teachers.

---

[19] Underhill, *Phillippo*, p. 122.
[20] Ibid., p. 135.
[21] Catherine Hall, 'White visions, black lives: the free villages of Jamaica', *HWJ*, 35 (1993), pp. 100–32.
[22] Underhill, *Phillippo*, p. 181.
[23] Ibid., p. 162.

The years 1838–42 were immensely busy, with many new projects and thousands of members and inquirers flocking to the chapels. In 1841 Phillippo wrote to Dyer, the Secretary of the BMS, describing his workload and asking for help:

> I have been alone in this district for the last seventeen years and upwards. I have eight stations, some of them full twenty miles distant from the central one, each of which requires the services of a regular minister at least once a month on the Sabbath, as well as occasional meetings on a week-day. Eight schools are under my superintendence, and are solely dependent on me for support. I have three new chapels in building, and one being enlarged, the cost of which, full £3000 sterling, I, in some way or other, must meet. I have services to maintain three times on the Sabbath invariably in Spanish Town, and a church-meeting and Sabbath-schools to attend, besides two week-day services, all of which probably involve as much mental labour as in a respectable town in England; with marriages and funerals, visits to the sick, and a thousand other pastoral duties to discharge arising in churches of between two and three thousand members in town and country.

'I have eight stations', 'I have eight schools', 'I have three new chapels': thus Phillippo took possession of the district, its stations, schools, and chapels, occupying the landscape and filling it with *his* enterprises, claiming Jamaica as his, superintended by his imperial eye. Phillippo's vision of himself as 'alone' speaks volumes about the gap between men's reliance on their wives in mission stations (to run classes for women, to teach in schools, to visit the sick, to run the household) and the public invisibility of that work, even to those who benefited constantly from it. In addition to her work as a missionary wife Mrs Phillippo had borne nine children by 1841, five of whom had died. Her health was bad and she frequently had to stay at their house in the mountains at the free village of Sligoville, where the air was better than in the hot plain of Spanish Town.[24]

In 1842 both Phillippo and his wife were exhausted and decided on a trip to England in an attempt to recover their health. It was at this

[24] Underhill, *Phillippo*, pp. 174–5.

point in his life that Phillippo wrote *Jamaica*. He was a man of forty-five, with two houses and eight mission stations, and was one of the most senior missionaries in Jamaica, with thousands under his wing. Baptist fortunes on the island appeared to be flourishing, with twenty-six missionaries and their wives and eighty-two schoolmasters and mistresses.[25] He celebrated this achievement in his book.

* * *

Phillippo was a name well-known to the antislavery public in England. The book was well received in England and 'had a large and remunerative circulation, three editions being rapidly exhausted'. Staunch abolitionist to the last, Thomas Clarkson, the veteran campaigner and by the early 1840s senior surviving figure in the movement, wrote to Phillippo with great enthusiasm, delighted that in his view the book vindicated yet again the great hopes attached to emancipation. Similarly the *Anti-Slavery Reporter* encouraged its readers to purchase the book without delay, and printed relentlessly optimistic extracts which focused on the progress, industriousness, politeness, and improvements in dress of the emancipated classes.[26]

Abolitionist panegyrics over Phillippo's writing, and indeed the calm of his own text, masked some anxious issues which had, however, been disturbing the peace of mind of the BMS and the Baptist missionaries in Jamaica. Fired with the enthusiasm of the heady days after emancipation, when the numbers of Baptist church members multiplied fast, the Jamaica Baptist Union had decided to go independent, and Phillippo was unhappy with this decision. He regretted the cutting of the umbilical cord and the loss of control by the BMS over the thousands of pounds worth of property on the island.[27] Jamaica was still a child as far as he was concerned, still needing succour, guidance, and support from the parental committee and the imperial mother, 'the parent state'. Nor was he personally ready to stand alone, to give up the authority which his long connection with the BMS Committee, with London, with the doings of the metropolis conferred. *Jamaica* was a re-statement of the ties that bound metropolis with colony. His

---

[25] William Knibb, *Jamaica. A Speech to the Baptist Missionary Society in Exeter Hall 28 April 1842* (London, 1842).

[26] Underhill, *Phillippo*, pp. 174–5; *Anti-Slavery Reporter*, 4 Oct. 1843.

[27] On the history of the BMS in Jamaica see Edward Bean Underhill, *The Jamaica Mission in its Relation with the BMS 1838–79* (London, 1879).

vision was one of an infant nation. His love for Jamaica, his conviction that it was his home too, made him anxious to sustain the lines of communication with the imperial government and with the powerful abolitionist public without which, he believed, it would be exceedingly difficult to counter the political dominance of the planters. Since the island had representative government and planters continued to dominate the House of Assembly, 'friends of the negro', as they called themselves, needed to be able to mobilize Colonial Office authority to protect the interests of the black population. Baptist missionaries might have acquired some status but they were still regarded with contempt by much of white Jamaican society. They needed, in Phillippo's view, the protection of the antislavery lobby, the antislavery public. *Jamaica* was peppered with requests for support from the metropolis on particular issues as well as the more general claim for an intimate and continuing connection between 'parent' and 'child'.[28]

Phillippo wanted to remind abolitionists of their continuing responsibilities, and counter the damaging accusations that had been circulating in England about the Baptist mission in Jamaica. The great success of the mission had provoked envy and criticism on a considerable scale. The Baptist missionaries were accused of accepting members who did not properly understand the tenets of the faith and allowing practices which were dangerously close to heathenism.[29] Phillippo was at pains in his book to defend the Jamaican Baptist churches and insist that they were properly supervised by the missionaries.[30]

The book was targeted beyond the Baptists to a much larger public, not necessarily convinced of missionary or abolitionist truths. It aimed to tell much about Jamaica in an entertaining way, using anecdote and dialect, making no claims to 'literary excellence', but hoping to be 'interesting and useful' and provide a comprehensive guide to the island and its peoples. An opening celebration of Christianity was followed by a sketch of the island's history, its physical features, its animals and vegetables, its social and political organization, its

---

[28] Underhill, *Phillippo*, p. 100.
[29] BMS *Circular* (London, 1842); George Blyth, *Remonstrance of the Presbytery of Jamaica with the Majority of the Baptist Missionaries in that Island* (Edinburgh, 1843); Samuel Green, *Baptist Mission in Jamaica. A Review of the Rev. W. G. Barrett's pamphlet entitled A Reply to the Circular of the Baptist Missionary Society* (London, 1842).
[30] Phillippo, 'Autobiography', p. 146.

government and commerce, its population – black, white, and people of colour. This framed the main part of the book dealing with abolition, apprenticeship, and total emancipation, the intellectual, social, and moral condition of black people under slavery, the bringing of Christianity, the work of the missionaries, the transformation of religious and social life which had taken place. It ended with a passionate plea for support for missionary work which had taken a people from slavery to freedom but still had darkness to contend with all over the world. With sufficient support Jamaica could become 'the key-stone to the possession of the New World – a kind of rallying post for the army of the living God', the base for the Christian conquest of South America.[31]

Mindful of his need to convince sceptics as well as friends, Phillippo littered his text with references to authorities, not just the expected antislavery names but Edward Long and the Revd G. W. Bridges (well-known pro-slavery writers from Jamaica), Select Committee reports and the *Morning Journal*, Dr Coke (Wesley's famous associate), and Mungo Park. Afraid of not being believed in his account of slavery (for he was well aware of how highly contested these issues were), he insisted that in case his personal testimony was not enough he would 'adduce representations from historical records', including those of his political opponents, to strengthen his case. No use of the personal pronoun was made, and Phillippo distanced himself by appearing as 'the author', 'the writer', 'the pastor', 'he', his house 'the minister's house'. His wife, who scarcely appears at all, is 'Mrs. Phillippo'. His early chapters on the physical character of the land and its plant and vegetable life are clearly inspired in tone by other texts he had read. In describing the landscape he collapses into conventional rhapsodies over the beauty of the island, forgetting the social relations that he is at pains to describe in later chapters: the 'smiling villages' are unpeopled, the 'numerous cascades' and rivers have nobody bathing in them, no women washing in them, or men and boys fishing. 'Jamaica', he proclaims in language that is not far from a modern tourist brochure, 'may be reckoned amongst the most romantic and highly-diversified countries in the world, uniting the rich magnificent scenery which waving forests, never-failing streams, and constant verdure can present, heightened by the pure atmosphere,

---

[31] Phillippo, *Jamaica*, pp. v, x.

and the glowing tints of a tropical sun.' His account of the vegetable and animal products quotes Linnaeus at the beginning to demonstrate his knowledge of systems and science, but anecdotes break up the listings of strange fruits and animals so that we know, for example, that 'the writer . . . once narrowly escaped having a black snake for his bedfellow'.[32]

Phillippo's glorious narrative is of conquest not by military force but by Christianity, and the total transformation it had brought in Jamaica. This constitutes a particular variety of 'anti–conquest', to use Mary Louise Pratt's term, since he at one and the same time secured his innocence from the history of the slave trade and slavery as perpetrated by the English, and re-articulated Jamaica to her imperial mother through her continued need for 'civilization' European-style.[33] An antislavery version of English history accepting the shame of the slave trade – 'the first Englishman who thus dishonoured himself and his country was Captain, afterwards Sir John Hawkins' – but seeing the country as redeemed by 'the eminent philanthropists Sharpe, Clarkson and Wilberforce' is combined with the notion of a 'British lion' ever ready to take up the cause of freedom. Thus one notion of Englishness is countered with another, and a claim made that the Englishness of liberty, freedom, and antislavery is the tradition to be celebrated and remembered. The relation between England and the Caribbean carried the histories of both slavery and emancipation; Phillippo's task was to soften the memory of the first with the memory of the second, to identify England with the moment of glory, rather than the moment of shame.[34]

Distinguishing between one kind of Englishness and another, one kind of whiteness and another, was essential for Phillippo since his worst enemies in Jamaica had always been the planters, his hope that a particular section of the white public in England would support the missionaries against them. The distancing, objective tone that he had tried to establish in the opening chapters served him well when describing white society on the island, for planters were quite as much a species to him as were the negroes. Whiteness carried no guarantees in Jamaican society, and indeed it was the disarticulation between

[32] Phillippo, *Jamaica*, pp. 35, 38, 46, 59, 122.
[33] Mary Louise Pratt, *Imperial Eyes. Travel Writing and Transculturation* (London, 1992), p. 7.
[34] Phillippo, *Jamaica*, pp. 154–5, 174.

whiteness and Englishness which had ruined white Jamaican society. 'Though the white inhabitants of Jamaica', he writes,

> retained in a considerable degree the national customs, as well as many of the domestic and social habits of their European ancestors, yet in consequence of the peculiar circumstances in which they were placed, they rapidly degenerated in their mental attainments and general accomplishments.

The females 'became addicted to pleasures' and lost their domestic skills, both sexes became proud, avaricious and prejudiced, adultery and promiscuity were everywhere. Small improvements had taken place since 1838, he was pleased to note, but 'revolting as it may be to English feelings' adulterers were still tolerated socially. Meanwhile a darkness 'thick, gross and palpable' still reigned in religion.[35]

While white society remained a disaster, however, black society had been transformed; and it was this which Phillippo was most concerned to demonstrate. Writing as he was within an antislavery discourse which assumed the success of 'the great experiment' in their terms – that negroes had become industrious, domesticated, respectable – Phillippo organized his narrative through the symbolic boundaries of '*before*' and '*after*'. Slavery and heathenism were of the past, emancipation and Christianity represented the future. The break between slavery and emancipation was mapped on to the Christian moment of conversion, the histories *both* of Africa and of slavery eradicated in that moment of emancipation/conversion. So Africa and slavery were connected in his discourse of '*before*', African culture rejected as a part of that savagery. Africa for Phillippo was a place of barbarism – the darkness both of superstition (before Christianity) and of fabled tribes. The enslavement of African peoples and enforced migration to Jamaica brought new horrors: slaves were reduced by their oppressors to the level of 'brutes', 'the dwarfs of the rational world'. Their bodies were possessed and tortured, their minds further corrupted by white wickedness. Their lives were forcibly lived at the level of animals, their songs devoid of poetry, their thoughts 'confined within the range of their daily employments and the wants of savage life'. Slave villages were scenes of degradation, 'every negro hut was a common brothel,

[35] Ibid., pp. 121, 138–9.

every female a prostitute and every man a libertine'. Marriage was not recognized, polygamy was common and customary divorce with a plantain leaf practised. 'Like the inhabitants of all uncivilised nations', wrote Phillippo with the superiority which came from the certainty that nineteenth-century English middle-class forms of marriage were essentially civilized, 'the men treated the women as inferior in the scale of being to themselves, exercising over those who composed their respective harems a kind of petty sovereignty.' Homes 'if such they could be called, were embittered by all the dark passions of the fallen heart'. All were idle in the sense of having no inner drive to work, for the only stimulus was the whip.[36]

An underlying anxiety for Phillippo in his representation of Africanisms was undoubtedly the revival of Myalism, a peculiarly Afro-Jamaican form of syncretic religious practice linking Christianity and West African religion, which had occurred on the island in 1841-2.[37] Phillippo worked hard to provide a rational account of this, no doubt as much for himself as for his readership. The outbreak had centred on the north of the island so had not affected Spanish Town too seriously. Phillippo admitted in *Jamaica* that Myalism had revived but hoped that 'in a very short period . . . few vestiges of the superstition will remain'. He connected the revival with the inadequacy of laws against it, the absence of medical care, and the claim of myalmen to cure assorted ills. He was well aware of the Myalist incorporation of religious phraseology and observances which had taken place. The Baptist missionaries were constantly anxious about a fusion of their orthodox religious practices with those of the Native or black Baptists who had been established on the island long before their arrival. Native Baptists were seen as at the centre of the 1831 rebellion, whilst the missionaries had attempted to distance themselves and their congregations. Phillippo's description of the 'pernicious follies' of the Native Baptists, who he never named as such, was written in the past tense, as if he could will it out of the Jamaica he was representing in his writing. Their actual presence across the island, however, was all too evident. He focused on the ways in which Native Baptist leaders mysteriously blended together 'important truths and extravagant puerilities'. Referring to 'facts which the writer has repeatedly gathered

---

[36] Phillippo, *Jamaica*, pp. 189, 218–19.
[37] On Myalism see Monica Schuler, *Alas, Alas, Kongo. A Social History of Indentured African Immigration into Jamaica 1841–65* (Baltimore, MD, 1980), pp. 32–40.

from lips of some of the parties themselves', he claimed that the preachers and teachers pretended knowledge of the Bible but frequently could not read, tried to mimic the behaviour of John the Baptist, and set great store by dreams and visions. They were not proper Christians.[38]

Terrible superstitions had mingled with the bacchanal of Carnivals. Holiday scenes, such as that recounted on his arrival in Spanish Town, 'were sometimes too disgusting to be looked upon'. Funeral rites involved 'wild and frantic gesticulations', 'strange and ridiculous manoeuvres' together with the claim to speak to the dead. 'The last sad offices' after the burial were scenes of blood and violence, and

> were usually closed by sacrifices of fowls and other domestic animals, which were torn to pieces and scattered over the grave, together with copious libations of blood and other ingredients, accompanied at the same time with the most violent and extravagant external signs of sorrow; they stamped their feet, tore their hair, beat their breast, vociferated.

Nothing could be more shocking to the English middle classes than this absence of restraint, whether in sexual life or dealing with the dead.[39]

After emancipation/conversion, however, all this was changed:

> The crafty Eboe; the savage, violent, and revengeful Coromantee; the debased and semi-human Moco and Angolian, with those of other tribes described by historians as 'hardened in idolatry, wallowers in human blood, cannibals, drunkards, practised in lewdness, oppression, and fraud; cursed with all the vices that can degrade humanity; possessing no one good quality; more brutal and savage than the wild beasts of the forest and utterly incapable of understanding the first rudiments of the Christian religion' – these, thousands of them, are now subdued, converted, raised to the dignity and intelligence of men, of sons and daughters of the Lord God Almighty, and are bringing forth the fruits of holiness, happiness, and Heaven.

[38] Phillippo, *Jamaica*, pp. 261–3, 270–4.
[39] Ibid., pp. 242–6.

Here was the heart of Phillippo's conversion story, that most powerful of missionary stories. Now marriage was spreading and with it the bourgeois family with its demarcated spheres for men and women. Women had learned modesty and a sense of shame and were looking after their homes and children. Men were working on the estates and cultivating their plots. Manners had vastly improved, families were going to church on Sundays dressed respectably rather than in gaudy attire, decent new homes and cottages were being built which facilitated a proper family life, dancing and riotous music were disappearing, funeral practices had been reformed. 'Cunning, craft and suspicion' were giving place to 'a noble, manly, and independent, yet patient and submissive spirit' – the perfect negro man. Perfect because he combined the independence which was so central to an English conception of manhood with patience and submission – characteristics more frequently associated with femininity in England – and marking the difference between white and black manhood.[40]

Phillippo's conception of the family of God was central to his thinking. Such a vision resolved his dual attachment to both England and Jamaica. The richness of the concept of 'family' was that it offered a way of combining inequalities of power with belonging within a family. Just as men and women, parents and children, were both equal, unequal, and different, so white people and black could also be contained within this embracing framework. There was no contradiction for Phillippo in maintaining that

> Children we are all
> Of one great Father, in whatever clime . . .

while believing at the same time that children and fathers had different responsibilities and different levels of authority. He challenged those theorists who argued that negroes could never reach the state of civilized man and argued that the victims of slavery were

> men of the same common origin with ourselves, – of the same form and delineation of feature, though with a darker skin, – men endowed with minds equal in dignity, equal in capacity, and equal in duration of existence, – men of the same social

[40] Phillippo, *Jamaica*, pp. 386-7, 253.

dispositions and affections, and destined to occupy the same rank with ourselves in the great family of man.

That destiny, however, was a long way off in most instances. He asserted his faith 'that our coloured and black fellow-creatures are equally as capable of being conducted through every stage of mental discipline and taught to arrive at as great a height of social and intellectual improvement as has ever been attained by the most privileged Europeans'. The conducting and teaching was clearly to be done by white men of the right kind. Phillippo's overarching conception of the 'family of man', however, allowed for shifts in the balance between equality and difference. At moments his lack of respect for Jamaican whites who had abandoned their English heritage and pride in the reformation (as he saw it) of black people led him to claim that 'the black skin and the woolly hair constitute the only difference which now exists between multitudes of the emancipated peasantry of Jamaica and the tradesmen and agriculturalists of England'. There was still, of course, a line of class division between 'peasants' and the middle classes. Phillippo's father may have been in trade but the son was a substantial professional man.[41]

Phillippo's identification with the new black Christian subject and his desire to give his publics what he saw as an authentic account of their reformation meant that there was a much stronger black presence in his book than in any of the previous abolitionist accounts of Jamaica. This must have been partly the effect of having lived in a predominantly black society for twenty years and having congregations made up almost entirely first of slaves and then freed slaves. Phillippo actually knew black people in a way that none of the visiting abolitionists could possibly have done. Indeed, throughout his life he gave much longer verbatim accounts of conversations with black men and women in his reports and publications than did most other missionaries. This was a risky strategy given the taboos against regional dialect in England, never mind anything more strange. Nevertheless, he included many anecdotes in patois as well as speeches and prayers. Black people had voices in his text, even if always controlled, edited, and monitored by him. However, almost none of them had names and were only distinguished by gender, whereas his

---

[41] Ibid., pp. 150, 154, 201, 208.

white authorities and sources are named, distinguished by occupation and public position.

Phillippo believed that a new age was dawning, that 'The sons of Ethiopia have been too long despised by the proud descendants of a more favoured fortune.' His reading of history showed him that the equality of the African mind had been proved in the past. He was even willing to cite Toussaint L'Ouverture as evidence of heroic African man. Jamaica's future rested with 'the oppressed offspring of Ham', who 'will rise at the life-giving call of Christianity, and meekly array themselves in beauty and in power'. That power rested through Christianity on white (missionary) guidance; it was that which guaranteed the meekness of the race.[42]

In celebrating the missionary cause and the glorious transformation effected in Jamaica, Phillippo was in part celebrating himself. His book not only produced Jamaica for England and Jamaica for the new Jamaica, it also produced Phillippo as new-style imperial man, identified with black people, leading them firmly but kindly to civilization; a man who had won black love and respect, who dreamed of an egalitarian future and yet yoked the emancipated to the parent with new bonds of gratitude for the 'gift' they had been given. *Jamaica* was a paeon of praise to men who had 'sacrificed' themselves, through altruism, to the twin ventures of missionary and antislavery work. At the heart of the book is the description of 1 August 1838, when thousands paid tribute to the part which he had played in the winning of emancipation, and demonstrated by their decorous conduct the truth of abolitionist predictions. A telling vignette, combined with an engraving, described the 'typical' reception of a missionary and his wife in a village – the expressions of respect, regard, and delight, the efforts to entertain, the differences established through dress and seating, the occasion it all provided for a statement about Christian benevolence. Phillippo's account of the success of post-emancipation society is predicated on his own key role, and that of others like him. He represents himself as the supervisory, regulatory patriarchal figure, guarding and guiding the behaviour of his flock, educating them in chapel, in school, in the community, to be an industrious, familial, obedient people. Yet the constant assertions of success, the insistence on missionary work as

---

[42] Phillippo, *Jamaica*, pp. 208–11.

the key to the future, the celebration of 'the pastor' himself, was of course underpinned by anxieties as to the political and economic instability of the island, the character of 'the negroes' as a 'race', and the role of the white man. The distinction between good and bad white people, good and bad black people, was drawn through attachment to religion. But would it be possible to maintain these lines? Was Phillippo himself as secure as he represented himself to be to himself and his public, in his identity as beloved pastor, father of his people?

Phillippo's narrativizing of Jamaica was a structuring of his encounter with that society through the gendered discourses of antislavery and missionary enterprises. His missionary story of conversion provided the structure of his narrative, the before and after of new life in Christ and new life in freedom. The imposition of this binary model allowed him to control his story, to impose a structure which explained why things were going the way he wanted them to go, to marginalize and exclude what could not be dealt with. His *Jamaica* of the mind was firmly in place, regulated by his pastoral/imperial eye, its symbolic boundaries in order. But could this discursive construction hold?

*   *   *

Phillippo returned to Jamaica in 1844 by which time his book, with his vision of the new Jamaica, had appeared there. The missionaries' own paper, *The Baptist Herald and Friend of Africa*, quoted the *Eclectic Review*'s summation: a 'beautiful narrative', 'eloquent' as to its facts, full of generous sentiments and breathing 'universal charity'. The book was announced as on sale in Falmouth as well as being available from the *Herald* office. By September it was noted that nearly one hundred reviews had been published and that almost 3,000 copies had been sold.[43] While Phillippo had been away his missions had been cared for by Thomas Dowson, an English missionary sent out by the BMS. Dowson, who had arrived in Jamaica in 1842, sent regular reports to England which focused on how much 'the Pastor' and his family were missed, how his return was eagerly anticipated. In *Jamaica* Phillippo quoted from these letters and made friendly reference to Dowson. Not long after his return, however, tension erupted between Dowson and

---

[43] *The Baptist Herald and Friend of Africa*, 17 Jan. 1844, 7 May 1844, 24 Sept. 1844.

Phillippo which was to transfix Jamaican society for several years and send waves of agitation to England.[44]

While Phillippo was in England Dowson had married into the Spanish Town congregation and established his own independent relationships with the congregations of the varied mission stations.[45] On his return Phillippo was happy for Dowson to continue preaching in Spanish Town while he convalesced in his beautiful and healthy mountain home in Sligoville. Dowson claimed that Phillippo named him co-pastor in May 1844. By November, however, relations had deteriorated and a schism was appearing in the congregation. Dowson claimed that Phillippo, having offered him the mission house in Spanish Town, had now claimed it for himself and furthermore would not allow him to preach in the chapel. He argued that Phillippo was jealous of him 'on account of the feeling evinced towards him by the people', and that the membership had become increasingly dissatisfied with Phillippo's behaviour, 'in particular . . . on account of his proud and distant demeanour, his neglect of personal attention to the sick, the poor, the ignorant, and the afflicted, and at his non-attendance at the funerals in the families of deceased members'. Furthermore Phillippo had refused to call a church meeting where the issues could be discussed by the membership. Dowson and his supporters set up a temporary chapel, provocatively close to the main one, and consulted a lawyer in order to establish a new trust deed. New trustees appointed Dowson as pastor and held a public meeting at which, they claimed, a majority of the members of the main Spanish Town church voted that Phillippo should no longer be their minister.[46]

Phillippo was shattered. By January he was telling Joseph Angus, the secretary of the BMS, 'my situation and that of my family is painful in the extreme'. Phillippo's version was that he had never named Dowson co-pastor. Dowson, he believed, had set his heart on the Spanish Town mission, 'these valuable premises situated in the most important city of the Island', and would leave no stone unturned to gain control of it. An

---

[44] Robert J. Stewart has written an excellent account of these events in his book *Religion and Society in Post-Emancipation Jamaica* (Knoxville, TN, 1992), pp. 83–94.

[45] The likelihood is that Dowson married a coloured woman (i.e. mixed-race in the Jamaican context), but I have not been able to prove this.

[46] BMS MSS WI/1: James Mursell Phillippo, 'Letters to Joseph Angus 1844–6', 20 Dec. 1844, 27 April 1845; BMS MSS WI/2: Kingston Guardian and Patriot, *Full Report of the Proceedings in Chancery in the Important Case of the Baptist Chapel, Spanish Town, October 1845* (Kingston, 1845), p. 21.

attack on Phillippo's 'ownership' of the church was, in English terms, an attack on his person, since a man's masculine identity was so intimately linked to his property and profession. In March one of Dowson's sisters-in-law, a Miss MacLean, an active member of the chapel, died. Phillippo was asked for the keys to the burial ground and refused to give them up. This enraged Dowson and his supporters since the family of the dead woman 'had largely contributed to the expenses of the said church, which refusal had excited much indignant feeling amongst the people, and a determination on their part to assert their right to the ground, which they believed had been purchased by their money for their use'. A crowd gathered, broke into the burial ground, and began to dig the grave before efforts at negotiation succeeded.[47]

A few days later a more serious episode occurred when the wife of one of the deacons died. Her husband was Richard Bullock, a man who was approvingly quoted by name in *Jamaica*, a rare distinction for a black man. Friends of Phillippo's in the Cotswolds had presented the Spanish Town congregation with a Bible and hymn book for use in the pulpit. Bullock, then a slave and a leader in the chapel, had written to thank them and his letter in patois was included in *Jamaica* as a demonstration of 'the simplicity and fervour of negro piety'. By 1845, however, Phillippo was not so well disposed to Bullock, now a supporter of Dowson. He again refused the keys to the burial ground. A crowd of several hundreds led by Dowson gathered in response, broke into the burial ground, and dug the grave. The body was then buried, according to Phillippo, 'amidst scenes not often exhibited in even a semi-barbarous community'. There was great excitement in the burial ground until well after midnight. Around three in the morning, when Phillippo and his friends thought all was quiet, they attempted to replace the fence and gate but, 'the alarm was given and soon the whole town was aroused by the cry that I had ordered the corpse to be dug up and that I had pulled it limb from limb, and scattered it about the ground' – a fascinating rumour given Phillippo's preoccupation with 'proper' burial rites. A huge crowd assembled and an attack was then made on the chapel, the communion vessels and Bible seized, some damage done. The magistrates had to be called and since they were not confident of being able to maintain the peace the chapel was closed on their recommendation. Phillippo wrote

[47] Phillippo, 'Letters', 7 Jan. 1845, 22 March 1845; Kingston Guardian, *Full Report*, p. 21.

to Angus that '[my] spirits are well-nigh broken and my health and strength prostrated' while Hannah had suffered a breakdown, had been attacked with 'hysterical fits and lost her reason for a considerable time from which she has not yet recovered'.[48]

Varied attempts were made at mediation between the two parties, by other missionaries on the island and by a BMS deputation which was sent out in 1846. The deputation was extremely concerned about the effects of the affair. 'The mischief done by this suit cannot easily be conceived', they concluded. 'It has divided our brethren, alienated most of the intelligent people of the town and has afforded a handle against Dissent.'[49] The brethren were certainly deeply divided, and the BMS was bombarded with angry letters from missionaries. Thomas Hands in Yallahs thought Phillippo had assumed power in ways that were 'utterly inconsistent with the principles and usages of Dissenting churches'. George Evans in Vale Lionel thought that the Baptist denomination in the island would never recover from 'the conduct of one who was looked up to as a guide'; George Rowse from Kingston (which was a centre of support for Dowson) denounced Phillippo as 'a consummate rogue and hypocrite'.[50] Edward Hewett, on the other hand, thought that 'the conduct of Mr. Dowson has been of the basest kind'; while James Hume concluded gloomily that 'the armies of the living God have more to fear from divisions in their own camps, than from the oppositions of their enemies'.[51]

Meanwhile Dowson, to the great distress of the BMS, had gone to the Jamaican Court of Chancery. The legal costs involved were extensive, and after several appeals to the BMS for help Phillippo decided to appeal independently for support in England. A benefactor, Joseph Fletcher, took on most of the work, and an English committee functioned from London, raising money for him and providing advice. This committee's stated concern was that the Spanish Town mission premises had been initially bought with BMS money, that was with public funds and 'British benevolence', and it wanted to protect those original interests and their appointee, Phillippo. The committee was

[48] Phillippo, *Jamaica*, p. 325; Phillippo, 'Letters', 7 April 1845.

[49] BMS: Baptist Missionary Society, 'Notes of Deputation to Jamaica 1846-9', p. 57.

[50] BMS MSS WI/5: Thomas Hands, 'Letter to Angus', 19 April 1845; George Evans, 'Letter to Angus', 20 April 1845; Kingston, Jamaica, Institute of Jamaica, MS 841: George Rowse, 'Letters to the BMS', 8 Oct. 1845.

[51] BMS MSS WI/5: Edward Hewett, 'Letter to Angus', 6 Oct. 1845; James Hume, 'Letters', 28 Aug. 1851.

sharply critical of the way in which Dowson and his supporters had played on what they saw as ignorance. 'The mass of the communicants are untutored and easily excited', it was argued, 'but few of them can either read or write, and many have not long enjoyed the blessings of freedom. They have been told in large and promiscuous assemblies, that their liberties and rights are invaded' . . . no wonder they had been led astray.[52] One of those same communicants, James A. Robertson, wrote angrily to the BMS that he knew exactly what he was doing, that he was not illiterate, and that he was fully cognizant of every decision which he and others had taken.[53] In 1850 the Court of Chancery declared in favour of Phillippo as pastor with rights to the property. This occasioned another riot. A crowd composed mostly of women attacked Phillippo's house which was left 'stoned, damaged, pillaged and gutted of its furniture'. Mrs Phillippo was wounded with a stone and the house was only saved from complete destruction by an appeal to the military. A guard had to be kept on the premises for ten days to prevent further trouble.[54]

The BMS deputation had concluded from their consultations whilst in Jamaica that 'the real and only question is, who is Pastor?' The possession of the very extensive properties, comprising eight mission stations including the highly desirable chapel, school, and mission house in Spanish Town, went with that position. The issue of who was the pastor undoubtedly was important, but perhaps more significant was the question of who had the right to appoint the pastor, or dismiss him. Phillippo had been appointed by the BMS and then, argued sections of the congregation, accepted by the local church. 'They adopted him', they claimed; 'he was not appointed over them . . . the appointment of minister is vested in the leaders, deacons and members of the church.' This crucial distinction meant that the members could also, of course, choose to get rid of a minister they no longer accepted, an issue that was actually being debated in the English courts at the same time. Since dissenting congregations supported their own ministers financially it was clear why they claimed rights to hire and fire. These were the moments when members could turn the patriarchal relation upside down and

[52] BMS MSS HII/2: Joseph Fletcher, *Case of the Baptist Church in Spanish Town, Jamaica, and of its Esteemed Pastor, the Rev. J. M. Phillippo*, BMS printed circular.
[53] BMS MSS HII/3: James A. Robertson, 'Letter to BMS committee'.
[54] PRO, CO 137/310: Sir Charles Grey to Earl Grey, 26 July 1851.

assert their authority over their putative 'fathers'. In Jamaica the situation was muddied by the money which had come from England through the BMS and been invested in property and men on the island. As was expressed in a series of conflicts amongst Baptist congregations across the island in the 1840s and 1850s, Jamaican congregations were for the most part firmly of the view that mission buildings belonged to them since they had provided the money and often built them with their own labour. In the case of Spanish Town they had certainly built it, but Phillippo had raised much of the money in England. Richard Bullock, the Spanish Town deacon, had no truck with this attitude, however. He wrote to the BMS in 1845 complaining about Phillippo. He told them that 700 members of the congregation were opposed to him and wanted him to give up the premises, 'that we may chuse for ourselves the pastor we lik, as it is our property . . .'.[55]

The pastor they liked on this occasion was white just as Phillippo, but questions of 'race' were also at issue in this conflict. From the first signs of schism Phillippo had been anxious to convince the BMS that the respectable and influential in Spanish Town were on his side. Dowson's party included 'the most uninfluential and disreputable characters' he claimed in January 1845; in March they were 'the rabble'; by April 'the very scum and refuse of the religious denominations . . . the basest rabble of the town and neighbourhood'. Dowson's black supporters were at times 'the poor deluded people', corrupted by his lust for power, unable in other words to think for themselves, therefore not to blame. Dowson was fanning their passions and 'exciting the worst feelings'. By July Phillippo saw them reduced to 'demi-savages' and by early 1846 they were denounced as 'infidel . . . wicked . . . profane', the struggle being now one between darkness and light, between the forces of Satan and the army of Christ. The echoes here were of the binary division which Phillippo had made in *Jamaica* between the savage African and the emancipated/redeemed Christian – and those echoes had been picked up by the Spanish Town public.[56] 'We have already found out Mr. Phillippo to be an untrue Pastor, no protector of his people, no comforter to the sick and needy, and another thing an interferer of the dead in the grave', said Joseph

---

[55] BMS: Baptist Missionary Society, 'Notes of Deputation to Jamaica 1846-9'.

[56] Phillippo, 'Letters', 23 Jan. 1845, 12 Feb. 1845, 8 March 1845, 7 April 1845, 6 Feb. 1846.

MacLean, whose relative had been refused burial.[57] Accusations of barbarism did not go only one way.

In March 1845 Phillippo noted that the whole town was in an uproar, and this had bad implications for the new edition of his book. Those people who had been prepared to have their names used for advertising purposes were no longer willing. Among the accusations of Dowson and his friends was the charge, as recounted by Phillippo, 'That I speak well of the black people before their faces, but that I have abused and vilified them on platforms in England, and especially in my Book'. He continued:

> The latter has been one of the most serious charges brought against me. It was first made by Duggan who was in the habit of reading all the portions of it which, though they might be quotations which I introduced in order to disprove what was unfavourable to the black and coloured people, he wished to be believed were my sentiments. Mr. Dowson . . . now denounces the book and has raised such prejudices against it that some of the people are ready to burn it, whilst he has quite succeeded in stopping the sale. The prejudice of the mass, indeed, are so general on this account that many of my own people have expressed their regret that I should ever have written it. . . . Thus the general opinion among the black people is, that I have abused them in a shameful manner in the book and they look upon me as a traitor to themselves and the country.

Furthermore, it was reported to Phillippo that Dowson had been rousing the people against him on varied occasions by using the language of bondage and rights, telling them they would be fools to 'go back to be subjects again to his tyranny and oppression'. 'You were fools to be subjects to him so long as you had been' he chided them, whilst excusing them from foolery because they could not help it for 'you were under bondage'. 'Seek, then for your rights', he urged them. 'The Chapel is yours, and you *shall* have it.'[58]

* * *

---

[57] BMS MSS, HII/3: Joseph Maclean and William James, 'Letter to BMS committee', 17 April 1845.

[58] Phillippo, 'Letters', 8 March 1845, 7 May 1845, 7 June 1845, 6 Sept. 1845.

Phillippo tried to convince himself that *Jamaica* had made enemies for him because of its exposure of the state of the island under slavery. This was not the case in Spanish Town. His critics there were playing on the knowledge that this patriarchal pastor had claimed too much authority, that in representing black people in his chosen image, in splitting so dramatically between good and bad, African and negro, he had transgressed black confidence. As Underhill summed it up in his biography of Phillippo many years later, the events 'greatly affected ... [his] judgement of the negro character'. Phillippo's tale enjoyed considerable success in representing Jamaica to England for, after all, and as the Revd Birrell remarked to a large Baptist audience in England, 'I do think that a pretty accurate idea may be formed of it without leaving our own island.'[59] Phillippo had attempted discursively to construct Jamaican society in a particular way. But Africa had survived; the paternalistic relations which his narrative had tried to set up could not hold; his possessiveness over 'his' chapel and 'his' stations was misplaced. In representing Jamaica to Jamaica, in attempting to produce Jamaica from an imperial and masculine Christian perspective, he provoked a crisis of representation, his fatherhood rejected by large numbers of his 'loving people'. The events in Spanish Town marked the unwinding of those relations of power which his text had attempted to stabilize, the eruption of the excluded, the break-up of a particular 'Jamaica of the mind'.

University of Essex

---

[59] Underhill, *Phillippo*, p. 230; *Missionary Herald*, June 1847; Phillippo, 'Letters', 20 Sept. 1846.

CORONETS AND ALTARS: ARISTOCRATIC WOMEN'S AND MEN'S SUPPORT FOR THE OXFORD MOVEMENT IN SCOTLAND DURING THE 1840s

by ROWAN STRONG

T HE Oxford Movement has been portrayed in its classic historiography as both clericalist and, in so far as all nineteenth-century Anglican clergy were male, a movement of masculine leadership and initiatives.[1] This is not to deny that the movement was largely priest-led and therefore male in its leadership – but 'largely' does not mean 'exclusively'. By looking at the introduction of the Oxford Movement into Scotland, a neglected aspect of its dissemination can be restored, that is, the importance of the laity and of women in the spread of Tractarianism. In Scotland the initial impetus given to Oxford Movement ideals and projects lay not with the clergy but with the aristocratic laity. It also was not the preserve of men, for among its first great supporters in Scotland was a woman, Cecil Chetwynd, widow of John William Robert Kerr, seventh Marquess of Lothian. She would become one of the leading Scottish Tractarians during the 1840s until her conversion to Roman Catholicism in 1851 as a consequence of the Gorham judgement.

During her marriage Lady Lothian's life had been largely that of most of her gender and class – supporter to her husband, bearer of children, her own decision-making largely confined to the domestic sphere. Religiously the Lothians followed the practice of most of the Scottish aristocrats. Although Episcopalian they attended the services of the Church of Scotland on Sundays.[2] This was partly because Episcopalian chapels were still few and, in the south at least, remote

---

[1] The classic account of the movement, R. W. Church, *The Oxford Movement: Twelve Years 1833–1845* (London, 1891), was by a priest and largely about priests, because it recalled the university phase of the movement from 1833 to 1845. This exclusive masculine treatment of the Oxford Movement continues in recent history, as in Geoffrey Rowell, *The Vision Glorious: Themes and Personalities of the Catholic Revival in Anglicanism* (Oxford, 1953), a series of studies of Oxford Movement leaders, all clergy and therefore males.

[2] Edinburgh, Scottish Record Office [hereafter SRO], GD 40/15/70(3), Journal of the 7th Marquess of Lothian, 28 June 1838 to 23 Nov. 1840, for Sunday, 20 Jan. 1841. After family prayers the Lothians went off to the local kirk of the Church of Scotland.

from aristocratic country seats. More importantly, landed families believed in established religion, and were Anglicans when in England and Presbyterians in Scotland. However, by the mid-nineteenth century some Episcopalian aristocrats were beginning to divert funds towards Episcopal church extension, although this did not alter their custom of attending the parish church which, as heritors (or legal property owners), they had a traditional obligation to maintain. So, in 1841, the Marquess, with his more wealthy neighbour the Duke of Buccleuch, was considering financing the building of an Episcopal chapel at Dalkeith along with the stipend of its clergyman. Wives were consulted about this, for Lothian wrote in his Journal that he was 'glad to find that B. & the Dss object to a night service';[3] but the actual decision was clearly the preserve of the Marquess and the Duke, rather than their respective wives. On 14 November 1841 the Marquess died suddenly. This tragedy resulted in his wife acquiring greater autonomous responsibility than would otherwise have been her lot. This new situation not only permitted her to exercise her undoubted talents for estate management, it also allowed her religious views to develop and find expression in unprecedented ways, contrary to previous patriarchal influence.

The major source for Lady Lothian's religious development comes from the memoir written by her granddaughter in 1922,[4] which presents the Episcopalianism of the Marchioness as only a way-station on her ultimate journey to Roman Catholicism. However accurate in hindsight this interpretation may be, it does not represent the confidence of the Marchioness's Episcopalianism during the early 1840s, and therefore the memoir needs to be used cautiously. But this family history does reveal that patriarchal influence had been the determining factor in Cecil Kerr's religious development until her husband's death. Before marriage in 1831, her religious formation was shaped by her father. The influence of Charles Chetwynd, second Earl Talbot, was more direct than usual because her mother, Frances Thomasine, had died when Cecil was eleven, and her father proved

---

[3] Ibid., 20 Jan. 1841, p. 13.

[4] Cecil Kerr, *Cecil Marchioness of Lothian: A Memoir* (London, 1922). This remains the major source for the Marchioness's life despite extensive efforts to trace the diaries and letters used by her memorialist. There is an earlier memorial of her by Fr P. Gallwey S. J., *Salvage from the Wreck: A Few Memories of Friends Departed, Preserved in Funeral Discourses* (London, 1890), pp. 125–63. However, in a funeral sermon for the ex-Episcopalian Roman Catholic Lady Lothian, Gallwey does not dwell upon the Episcopalian period of her life.

an attentive parent.[5] In religious matters, Lord Talbot insisted on regular family prayers and read the Book of Common Prayer to his children, while Sunday was devoted to church going with no music or cards.[6] It was an unremarkable Anglican Protestant orthodoxy which commonly valued the alliance between Church and State epitomized in an established Church. Such Anglicanism was not disturbed by Cecil Talbot's marriage, because her husband was of a similar stamp. Prior to her wedding Lord Talbot gave Cecil a piece of advice about the patriarchal nature of her new life:

> After the Almighty, let your husband reign in your heart. You have now no duty but to obey him. Watch his looks and fulfil all his wishes, conform yourself to his habits and inclinations. Have but one mind, have no secrets from him. Be open, unreserved with him, reserved and cautious with other men. Be cautious with female friends, remember that unless the persons you are thrown with are really good and religious there is no dependence to be placed on them. The married life is either one of happiness or misery, and much depends on the tact and conduct of the wife.[7]

Reliance on the Almighty for the now-married Cecil Kerr in Scotland meant attending the established and presbyterian Church of Scotland in place of the episcopal Church of England, a religious difference which, it is evident from Lord Lothian's journal, bothered no-one.

But these two male authorities in her religious life were radically overturned by the widowed Cecil Kerr during the 1840s as she began to make her own choices. Previously she had exhibited no interest in the upheavals within the Church of England caused by the Romanizing trend of the Oxford Movement and the hostile reaction to it. But, as a consequence of her husband's death, Cecil Kerr began to devour Tractarian material and to correspond with her brother-in-law, Henry Kerr, about it.[8] The Revd Lord Henry Kerr was then vicar of Dittisham, Devon, having matriculated at Cambridge in 1819 and

---

[5] Kerr, *Marchioness*, p. 8.
[6] Ibid., pp. 2, 8.
[7] Ibid., pp. 11–12.
[8] Ibid., pp. 43–4.

been ordained in 1820.[9] Already a mature priest when the Oxford Movement began, he became increasingly sympathetic to it as one of the country clergy whom Newman had in mind as the original audience for the *Tracts for the Times*. That Cecil Kerr turned to Oxford religion as a consequence of her husband's death is also suggested by one of her letters in which she tells Henry Kerr that she has been reading Tract 72 on prayers for the dead.[10] For someone raised in moderate High Churchmanship to become amenable to obit prayers suggests she quickly began to forsake her former patriarchal religion. That this was the direction of her mind is further indicated in her developing scruples about attending the local kirk and instead driving into Edinburgh to an Episcopal church for Holy Communion.[11] Either this was a Tractarian dislike of the Erastianism of established religion or (more likely given her later Roman Catholic conversion) she was developing a characteristic Tractarian denial of the validity of Presbyterian ordination and sacraments. Within a year or two of her husband's death therefore, Lady Lothian had acquired a new exclusive zeal for the voluntary, if minute, Scottish Episcopal Church which contrasted with the attachment to an established Church characteristic of her father and husband.

The result of this new-found Episcopalian consciousness took tangible form in her building and endowing an Episcopal church in Jedburgh, closer to her favourite residence of Monteviot than were the Edinburgh chapels. But this was not just a disinterested example of aristocratic support for Episcopalian church extension envisaged earlier by her late husband and the Duke of Buccleuch. The chapel would give expression to her new-found Tractarian consciousness, and she was determined to maintain her own direction over its development. She wrote in October 1842 to the Duke to encourage him to become one of five trustees, along with herself, the Bishop of Glasgow, and two other male members of the congregation. It was a group she believed susceptible to her continuing influence within the new congregation.

> I am anxious that you should accept this office as I think that having such a quorum as you & I & the Bishop shd make, in the

[9] *Alumni Cantabrigienses: a Biographical List of all known Students, Graduates and Holders of Office at the University of Cambridge from the Earliest Times to 1900*, ed. J. Venn and J. A. Venn, 10 vols (Cambridge, 1922–54), Part 2, vol. 4, p. 29.

[10] Kerr, *Marchioness*, p. 44

[11] Ibid., p. 45.

event of any difference of opinion, as to the choice of Clergyman is most desirable. We are more likely to choose a good man than the other two I sd imagine.'[12]

Kerr evidently appreciated her aristocratic power in her own locality. It was never likely that the other two male trustees, one of whom was Lord Douglas's factor, would have crossed the united wills of two such local grandees as herself and the Duke. Even the aged Bishop Michael Russell of Glasgow and Galloway would surely have thought at least twice before doing so. But neither did Lady Lothian strike out alone in this venture, preferring to ally herself with the traditional patriarchal power of the leading local aristocrat, the Duke of Buccleuch.

Another illustration of her paramount influence in the new congregation, even over the diocesan bishop, was the adoption of the Scottish Communion Office for the new Jedburgh church. This was the eucharistic liturgy used by the Episcopal Church during its nonjuring days of the previous century, and highly regarded by many Orthodox[13] and Tractarians.[14] Bishop Russell, like most Episcopalians in the south, disliked this sign of difference from the Church of England. He expressed himself forcibly on the matter to one of his young priests in Glasgow who was showing signs of wanting to use the liturgy. 'As to the Scottish Communion Office I wish there were no such thing in existence.'[15] So how did Cecil Kerr obtain sanction for the almost unknown use of the Scottish Communion Office in the south of Scotland? Did she exercise power as a landed aristocrat in a poor Church, or was her approach to the ecclesiastical authorities and other interested parties more indirect, in keeping with contemporary masculine attitudes towards women? In the absence of any evidence the answers to these questions will have to remain conjectural. What is known is that the diocese of Glasgow and Galloway had only recently been hived off from Edinburgh when Russell became its bishop in

[12] SRO, Buccleuch Muniments, GD 224/1025/1: Lady Lothian to the Duke of Buccleuch, 20 Oct. 1842.

[13] 'Orthodox' is used here as the more contemporary self-designation of non-Tractarian High Churchmen. See Peter B. Nockles, *The Oxford Movement in Context: Anglican High Churchmanship 1760–1857* (Cambridge, 1994), pp. 25–32.

[14] When the Scottish Communion Office was under threat in the 1850s and 1860s, leading Tractarians were quick to its defence, as in J. M. Neale, *An Earnest Plea for the Scottish Communion Office* (London, 1862).

[15] Edinburgh, National Library of Scotland [hereafter NLS], D'Orsey papers, MS 19325, fol. 54: Bishop Russell to the Revd D'Orsey, 2 Dec. 1847.

1838. In a new diocese experiencing large-scale Irish and English immigration into the industrialized central belt of Scotland, Russell could hardly afford to look this aristocratic gift horse in the mouth, even with the Scottish Communion Office attached to it.

As indicated by the use of the Scottish Office, Lady Lothian's leadership shaped the Jedburgh church so that at its consecration in 1844 it was the first completed expression of the Oxford Movement in Scotland. There were two other contemporary edifices in Scotland usually considered Tractarian – Trinity College, Glenalmond, opened in 1847 but whose buildings were not substantial until the next decade, and St Ninian's Cathedral, Perth, on which work only began in 1849. The new chapel at Jedburgh was therefore the only fully realized Tractarian project in the Scottish Episcopal Church for most of the 1840s. In a period prior to the rise of ritualism Cecil Kerr's attention at Jedburgh focused on the use of the Scottish Communion Office and on building a politically correct gothic church. Gothic was beloved of Tractarians because it provided the potential environment for conducting the worship of the prayerbook in a pre-Reformation manner. While gothic expressed the Tractarian agenda it also attracted more widespread support motivated by a Romantic attachment to the medieval past. Accordingly, the major promoter of ecclesiastical gothic architecture, the Cambridge Camden Society, always enjoyed a wider and more formal membership in the Church of England than did adherence to Oxford Tractarianism. But Cambridge medievalism contained an inherent challenge to the Reformation principles of the Church of England, and therefore provided Tractarianism with indirect support. Consequently, Lady Lothian supervised every detail of her gothic church, large or small, most carefully.[16] The chosen architect was a member of the Camden Society.[17] The interior revealed the sacramental, liturgical emphasis of Kerr's Tractarianism. It included a stone font at the west end, open benches not box pews, a lectern not a reading desk, and a stone altar. In a surfeit of ecclesiological zeal, and probably to the bemusement of the congregation, there was even a fold-stool for the reading of the litany.[18] St John's, Jedburgh, was the first Episcopal church to be built to Camden

---

[16] Kerr, *Marchioness*, pp. 45–6.

[17] A. C. Ryrie, *A Vision Pursued: St John's Church, Jedburgh, 1844–1994* (nd), p. 4.

[18] Thomas Stephen, *The History of the Church of Scotland from the Reformation to the Present Time* (London, 1845), p. 617.

Society principles, and led to liturgical innovations. Considering this, and the fact that Orthodox and Tractarian leaders believed it important enough to be present at its consecration, it is surprising that it has been neglected in contemporary liturgical histories of the period. Peter Anson, Allan Maclean, and Nigel Yates, who have all written on Anglican or Scottish worship in the nineteenth century, make little or no mention of this Scottish innovation.[19]

During this time the Marchioness pursued her new Tractarian education in diverse ways. She attended the most advanced example of Tractarian worship, the Margaret Street chapel, when she was in London in early 1843. She also became friends with Walter Farquhar Hook, vicar of Leeds.[20] Hook was not a Tractarian, but was one of the younger and more dynamic generation of Orthodox. Like others of his persuasion he had looked sympathetically at the Oxford Movement at first, although becoming anxious about its emerging Roman sympathies. As Tractarians and Orthodox drifted apart, Hook would become one of the Oxford Movement's bitterest opponents by the late 1840s. However, during the early 1840s it was still possible to migrate between the two groups, so that in 1843 Lady Lothian was able to learn from both groups what she referred to as her 'High Churchism'.[21] It was the more personal influence of Hook that resulted in her appointment of William Spranger White as the first incumbent of Jedburgh. Kerr's memorialist describes White rather vaguely as a 'thorough-going Churchman'.[22] As current research demonstrates the tensions between Tractarian and Orthodox, this is hardly sufficient.[23] White had been ordained in 1833, prior to the real expansion of the Oxford Movement, so it is likely, given Hook's recommendation and suspicion towards Tractarian extremes, that he also belonged to the

---

[19] Peter F. Anson, *Fashions in Church Furnishings 1840–1940*, 2nd edn (London, 1965), pp. 102–5 (by confining himself to developments in the north east, Anson believes that 'real progress' in the ecclesiological movement in Scotland only began in 1849); Nigel Yates, *Buildings, Faith and Worship: the Liturgical Arrangement of Anglican Churches 1600–1900* (Oxford, 1991) (in an otherwise excellent survey the Scottish innovation at Jedburgh does not rate a mention in a history of 'Anglican' churches); Allan Maclean, 'Episcopal worship in the nineteenth and twentieth centuries', in Duncan B. Forrester and Douglas M. Murray, eds, *Studies in the History of Worship in Scotland*, 2nd edn (Edinburgh, 1996), pp. 107–25, only gives Jedburgh a passing mention despite recognizing that it had a 'particular Tractarian tradition' (pp. 115, 120).

[20] Kerr, *Marchioness*, pp. 47, 49–50.

[21] Ibid., p. 48.

[22] Ibid., p. 51.

[23] Nockles, *The Oxford Movement in Context*, pp. 27–306.

younger generation of Orthodox clergy rather than coming from a Tractarian stable. However, he was always going to have to accept the continued influence of his patron in his new charge. On the very first Sunday of his incumbency, immediately after breakfast, Lady Lothian made sure they discussed the details of the morning's Communion Service.[24]

The consecration of the church on 15 August 1844 witnessed an Orthodox and Tractarian gathering. The incumbent intoned Matins with the choir chanting the responses and the psalm, in what has been reckoned the first choral service in Scotland since the Revolution.[25] Then followed a service of consecration and Holy Communion. Orthodox clergy such as Hook were involved, as also were the Tractarians John Keble, William Dodsworth, and Robert Wilberforce.[26] The Orthodox had for many decades supported the Episcopal Church, which had also seized the imaginations of Tractarians as an unestablished Church retaining apostolic succession. Keble declared that if the Church of England should forsake its catholic nature he would go, not to Rome, but to the Episcopal Church.[27]

But as a supporter of the Oxford Movement Lady Lothian's Tractarianism originated in circumstances different from those affecting other aristocratic Scottish Tractarians in the 1840s. This difference was a consequence of her gender. Unlike her male counterparts she developed a Tractarianism that was at one remove from the immediate source of the inspiration of the Oxford Movement. As a woman she was denied access to Oxford University where the Tractarian leadership was to be found during the 1830s and 1840s. The movement, in its University years, was very much a matter of personal connections. It was as university teachers, even more than as writers, that these theologians most profoundly influenced the lives of the first generation of Tractarian disciples. It was through personal contact that undergraduates saw in men like Newman and Pusey the reality of what they taught. The importance of this direct influence in the lives of undergraduates was how Richard Church remembered the movement spreading at the University.[28] The movement's leadership also

---

[24] Kerr, *Marchioness*, p. 51.
[25] Stephens, *History of the Church of Scotland*, p. 617.
[26] Kerr, *Marchioness*, p. 54.
[27] Marion Lochhead, *Episcopal Scotland in the Nineteenth Century* (London, 1966), p. 89.
[28] Church, *The Oxford Movement*, pp. 156–9.

attached a high priority to their personal influence, as witnessed in the abortive plan by the Tractarian tutors at Oriel to transform their role as tutors into one which encompassed a religious formation over their charges. But Cecil Kerr was excluded from this vital formation of making disciples through human interaction. Her gender confined her to a Tractarian commitment largely derived from the less personal source of Oxford texts and tracts which were an important, but secondary, evangelistic arm of the movement. She did have contact with male family members who had been undergraduates at the university;[29] but important as these personal contacts were they could never match the quality of understanding gained from years spent together with the original Tractarian leadership at Oxford, still a small and close-knit community during these years. Therefore her Tractarianism, originating at second-hand and relying on lesser figures than the leadership, may have been easier to shed for Roman Catholicism when the Gorham judgement severely challenged Tractarian theology.

Her actions during the 1840s suggest that she had not arrived at a self-confident religious position free of dependence on masculine religious authorities. To begin with she fastened on Hook, and then the Tractarian clergyman at the new chapel at Dalkeith, J. C. Robertson, became her spiritual adviser. His secession to Rome in 1847 further undermined her Episcopalian loyalties, already shaken by the departure of Newman.[30] Finally she hitched her religious future to that of Henry Manning, determined to go where he led. 'I have for very long', she confided in her journal, 'all but settled that Archdeacon Manning's course should decide mine.'[31] This indicates that during this decade, while developing her own independent life, she had not finally let go of the need for some patriarchal religious authority.

That Lady Lothian was female deeply affected how her new Tractarianism was inspired and sustained. The link between gender and religion in her case was very different from that connection in the

---

[29] Andrew L. Drummond and James Bulloch, *The Church in Victorian Scotland 1843–1874* (Edinburgh, 1975), p. 205. Family contact or even commitment to the Oxford Movement certainly seems likely, given the Talbot tradition of going up to Christ Church, Oxford. Two brothers were there during the 1830s; an older brother, resident during the 1820s, sent a son to the Anglo-Catholic Keble College; and her youngest brother Gilbert, at Christ Church from 1834–7, later became a Roman Catholic priest: *Alumni Oxonienses: The Members of the University of Oxford 1715–1886*, ed. Joseph Foster, 4 vols (Oxford, 1891), 4, pp. 1453–4.

[30] Kerr, *Marchioness*, pp. 62–3, 73–4.

[31] Ibid., p. 90.

lives of her male contemporaries who were also bringing Tractarianism into Scotland in the 1840s. These men were principally James Hope (later Hope-Scott), George Frederick Boyle (later sixth Earl of Glasgow), and Horace Courtenay (later Lord) Forbes. They were all young Scottish aristocrats zealous to bring to Scotland their new-found catholic Anglicanism. William Gladstone is also usually listed among this advance-guard of the Oxford Movement in Scotland, but I have argued elsewhere that he is an Orthodox Churchman rather than a Tractarian.[32] Both Gladstone and Hope were responsible for the erection of Trinity College, as both a public school for the Episcopalian middle and upper classes and as a seminary for the priesthood. But their correspondence on the project reveals that Hope was the fervent Tractarian and Gladstone the more cautious Orthodox.[33] The other young Tractarian Turks, Boyle and Forbes, provided the impetus for the most extravagant Tractarian project in Scotland, the erection of St Ninian's Cathedral for the diocese of St Andrews, Dunkeld, and Dunblane. Unlike Trinity College, where Gladstone's Orthodoxy ameliorated Hope's Puseyism, St Ninian's was a thoroughly Tractarian foundation.[34] Hope, Boyle, Forbes, and Cecil Kerr were the vanguard and patrons of the first substantial signs of the Oxford Movement in Scotland. But all the men owed their Tractarianism to direct personal exposure to the Tractarian leadership at Oxford University, in contrast to the indirect influence that was all Cecil Kerr's gender would allow her in nineteenth-century Britain. Hope had gone up to Christ Church in 1828 and graduated in 1832, before the Oxford Movement began; but remained at the University as a fellow of Merton College until 1847. Boyle entered Christ Church in 1844 as a gentleman-commoner, graduating in 1847. Horace Forbes was at Oriel from 1846 to 1849.[35]

But while gender differentiated the Tractarian origins of these Episcopalian benefactors, class did not. The upper-class lives of all these Puseyites form a common factor between Tractarians otherwise divided by gender-experience. In the same letter that Lady Lothian wrote to the Duke of Buccleuch about the Jedburgh chapel she also

---

[32] Rowan Strong, 'High Churchmen and Anglo-Catholics: William Gladstone and the eucharistic controversy in the Scottish Episcopal Church 1857–60', *Journal of Religious History*, 20 (1996), pp. 175–84.

[33] NLS, MSS 3667–71, 3672–4 (Hope-Scott papers).

[34] George T. S. Farquhar, *A Short History of St Ninian's Cathedral, Perth, to 1926 A. D.* (Edinburgh, nd).

[35] Foster, *Alumni Oxoniensis*, pp. 1265, 147, 475.

described the rebellious behaviour of her miners at Newbattle, deploring the fact that she had not yet managed to get them evicted from houses which they occupied as her tenants. 'Scotch law is certainly not summary! I do hope this week they will be turned out, but it seems doubtful.'[36] David Cannadine has claimed that 'wealth, status, power, and class consciousness' were in the nineteenth century 'preponderantly masculine assets and attributes'.[37] It is important to recognize the qualification in his claim, for Lady Lothian's influence in the Jedburgh church (not to mention her miners) suggests that she was as ready as any of her male counterparts to use the power of her status in her own interests. Widowed aristocratic women were, therefore, probably one important exception to the masculine preponderance of these qualities among the nineteenth-century British upper class.

The same conscious wielding of upper-class wealth and power which enabled Lady Lothian to dominate the Jedburgh church was also responsible for Hope and Gladstone forwarding their Trinity College project, and for Boyle and Forbes initiating St Ninian's Cathedral. For Trinity College the original sponsors first ensured the committed support of key aristocrats before seeking public subscriptions. Such aristocratic patronage was regarded as crucial. Hope told Gladstone that 'rank and family should, if possible, be put prominently forward'.[38] The public announcement was consequently headed by the names of noblemen who had consented to serve on its committee – the Duke of Buccleuch, the Marquess of Queensberry, the Earls of Errol, Home, and Elgin, and Lord Walter Forbes.[39] Reassured by such heavyweight backing the college project proceeded, despite the initial anxieties of at least one of the Scottish bishops about its viability.[40] The building of St Ninian's Cathedral was even more clearly a project foisted on the Scottish Episcopal Church by aristocratic Tractarians. Boyle and Forbes initiated a committee which raised £6,000. With Bishop Torry's support the cathedral plan went public, proceeding despite angry

---

[36] SRO, Buccleuch Muniments, GD 224/1025/1: Lady Lothian to the Duke of Buccleuch, 20 Oct. 1842.
[37] David Cannadine, *The Decline and Fall of the British Aristocracy* (New Haven, CN, 1990), p. 7.
[38] NLS, Hope-Scott papers, MS 3674, fol. 130: J. R. Hope to W. E. Gladstone, 6 Sept. 1840.
[39] SRO, Buccleuch Muniments, GD 224/998/7(5): 'Proposal for the Foundation of an Academical Institution in connection with the Scottish Episcopal Church' (printed circular).
[40] NLS, Hope-Scott papers, MS 3672, fol. 77: W. E. Gladstone to J. R. Hope, 16 Oct. 1840.

objections to its Puseyite inspiration, and protestations that it lacked the formal agreement of the diocesan synod.[41]

All three initial Tractarian projects in Scotland – St John's, Jedburgh, Trinity College, Glenalmond, and St Ninian's, Perth – were conceived and forwarded by Scottish aristocrats or young Scotsmen of landed families. Their wealth and status gave them the resources to bring their Tractarian innovations to fruition and to overcome opposition or doubts within the Episcopal Church. In regard to using such upper-class influence a female aristocratic Tractarian, Cecil, Marchioness of Lothian, was no different to her male counterparts.

However, by concentrating almost exclusively on the example of just one female aristocrat it may be thought that the Marchioness of Lothian was the female exception who proves the rule of an exclusively male movement. Establishing Tractarian innovation by women in addition to men is difficult to document because even aristocratic women could leave remarkably few records. But there are later examples which suggest the Marchioness was not alone in being a female instigator of increasing Puseyism in Scotland. I have else-where mentioned Lady Frances Kinnaird, who was a prime supporter of the Tractarian Bishop Alexander Forbes of Brechin. She installed a stone altar, redolent of eucharistic sacrifice, in the Kinnairds' new chapel at Rossie Priory.[42] More conclusive proof comes from the 1860s when the Revd James McGregor was appointed in 1862 to the parish of Monimail, Fife, by the patron, Lady Elizabeth Cartwright. But McGregor found that, unlike his predecessors, he could no longer expect Lady Elizabeth and her husband, Mr J. Leslie Melville Cart-wright, to attend the kirk, although other members of her family did so. The reason, he confided to a friend, was Tractarian influence on her ladyship. 'I was glad to see the Melville family at Communion, but sorry to miss Lady Elizabeth. You have no idea how great a loss a person of her influence is to a country church. Bother the Puseyites!'[43] In this case Lady Cartwright's patronage in her own right gave her traditional authority. However, her Tractarianism resulted in her using that authority in a radical way to depart from the traditional

---

[41] George T. S. Farquhar, *The Episcopal History of Perth 1689–1894* (Perth, 1894), pp. 292–4.

[42] Rowan Strong, *Alexander Forbes of Brechin: The First Tractarian Bishop* (Oxford, 1995), p. 72.

[43] Frances Balfour, *Life and Letters of the Reverend James MacGregor D. D.* (London, 1912), pp. 82–111.

alliance in Scotland between the landed classes and the established Church.

The Oxford Movement was led overwhelmingly by men, a fact which reflects that gender's predominance in all the nineteenth-century Churches. But patriarchy did not make it impossible for women to exercise some initiative in Tractarian circles, especially if they came from those upper orders which had long cemented their power in British society. Lady Lothian was a comparatively rare example of female Tractarian sponsorship in the second decade of the Oxford Movement, but women like her would later become more common. While her Tractarianism only developed after the cessation of the influence of her father's and husband's religion, that same masculine dominance meant that her new religion had more indirect origins than was the case among her male contemporaries. That same masculine social predominance meant that it was crucial to her role as a female financier of Tractarianism in Scotland that she remained a widow largely in control of her own affairs. But in adopting that role she continued to exercise power in the same manner as the dominant masculine members of her class. Her feminine Tractarian leadership in Scotland relied primarily on her privileged status and wealth as a Scottish aristocrat. It was as a member of the landed nobility exercising customary influence in her own locality that she initiated her early venture in Scottish Tractarianism. As such, it was a role in which other Episcopalians of her class, male and female, would follow her in Scotland. As they did so, Tractarianism would increasingly loosen the traditional ties between the Episcopalian aristocracy and the established Church. What was not traditional, but ominous for the future of Scottish Tractarianism, was that the Tractarian Cecil Kerr jettisoned her Episcopalianism for Roman Catholicism. It was an apparent connection between Tractarianism and Rome that many Episcopalians, not just aristocrats, regarded as unacceptable.

Murdoch University

MARTHA'S WORK AND MARY'S CONTEMPLATION? THE WOMEN OF THE MILDMAY CONFERENCE AND THE KESWICK CONVENTION 1856–1900

by ALISON M. BUCKNALL

F OR many Evangelical clergy and lay people, the 'annual conference' became a vital feature of Christian life during the second half of the nineteenth century. Dominant among these was the Mildmay Conference, only later rivalled by the convention held at Keswick. The small beginnings of 'conference going' were a group of friends who responded to the invitation of the Revd William Pennefather to meet together in his parish at Barnet in 1856. He had not intended to found an annual gathering, but the momentum of the movement he set off was such that after he left Barnet in 1856 for the parish of Mildmay in London's northern suburbs, the Conference which followed him grew into a powerful organization which not only brought together some three thousand Evangelical clergy and lay people each year, but also involved itself in welfare work which extended beyond the parish boundaries into other areas of London, and supported a wider network of workers in Britain and overseas. The Convention which began to meet at Keswick in 1875 was far removed from the social concerns of Mildmay, and its commitment to a controversial teaching of 'holiness' kept it on the fringes of Evangelical respectability for the first decade of its existence; but by the 1890s the popularity of 'Keswick teaching' could no longer be denied. While other Evangelicals sought to attack or denounce the perceived evils which were creeping into both Victorian Church and society, these conference goers sought to renew Evangelicalism from within in a way that would enable them to speak to that changing world with a new, but still distinctively Evangelical, voice.

This was particularly important in relation to those aspects of Evangelical teaching which had become so closely interwoven with the fabric of Victorian society as to become almost indistinguishable. One such area was that of the Victorian family, where a complex ideology had developed from a fusion of social necessity and Evangelical teaching. In a society where the increasingly competitive sphere of business and commerce absorbed the men of the emerging middle classes, there was an urgent need to maintain religious values in the female world of the home, where women were expected to exemplify the twin virtues of domesticity and spirituality. Evangelical teaching of women's proper role as 'keepers at home' in submission and obedience to men seemed to be entirely supportive of this separation of male and female roles.[1] It was as if the biblical characters of Martha, devoted to the duties of the house, and her sister Mary, absorbed in Jesus' spiritual teaching,[2] were both being projected on to an 'ideal' of Victorian womanhood.

The Martha and Mary typologies of womanhood had long existed in Christian thinking. In very broad terms, it might be suggested that the teaching of pre-Reformation Catholicism had developed a highly spiritualized ideal of woman, which placed its highest value on female virginity and accorded profound reverence to the enclosed life of the cloister and the authority of the female mystic. Mary had found her home in the Catholic tradition. Reformed Protestantism, on the other hand, had taken women out of the cloister only to place them firmly in the home, where respect was derived from their devotion to the care of husband and children under the spiritual leadership of the male head of the household. Martha had seemingly found a secure place in the Protestant tradition, but she was not going to be left alone by the developing ideology of Victorian domesticity and its need to locate spiritual values in the life of the home. Martha must also become Mary, while remaining a creature of the home, always under the authority of her male guide, whether father, brother, or husband.

---

[1] Eph. 5.22–3; Col. 3.18; I Cor. 11; Titus 2.5. All these represented New Testament 'household codes' which were cited as providing biblical support for a pattern of male authority over the women, children, and servants of the household. As a code which gave stability to early Christian society in conformity with the norms of contemporary society, it was especially appealing amid the changes of the late eighteenth and early nineteenth centuries. One of the earliest and most frequently cited attempts to reinstate this teaching appeared in Henry Venn's *Complete Duty of Man* (London, 1763). The appeal was not merely to Evangelicals, but in Sean Gill's opinion reflected a wider need to reinforce a patriarchal political order in the model of the family during the eighteenth century, one which continued to be reinforced by 'The ritual of family prayer – at which servants were also expected to be present', which he believes 're-enacted the hierarchy of the whole spiritual and temporal order in microcosm': Sean Gill, *Women and the Church of England* (London, 1994), pp. 12–14, 66.

[2] Luke 10.38–42. Although the biblical story seems to elevate the 'spiritual' sister over the busy practical one, it implies no denial of the basic female place in the home and her responsibility for its duties. It does, however, insist that the spiritual role is of prime importance.

The strain of attempting to conform to this image was beginning to tell by the middle of the nineteenth century. By then the developing ideology had become increasingly divorced from the reality of women's lives and the Evangelical teaching which was held to sanction it. As middle-class status came to demand that servants should be seen to take over the practical work of the house, 'Martha' had been deprived of her active identity and turned into a 'lady of leisure'.[3] This disconnection from physical activity encouraged the development of a greatly heightened view of the pure spiritual nature of Mary as 'the Angel in the House', expected to exert a 'redeeming' influence on those who came within her sphere.[4] It is difficult to see how this image could be reconciled with Evangelical teaching of universal human sinfulness which could find salvation only through the cross, or with its insistence on an active response of faithful Christian service. Yet, however far it was from reflecting religious or social reality, this image had such a strong grip that many women were indeed 'de-activated'. Inactivity was often expressed in terms of illness, as some simply took to their couches and sought a new identity as the helpless Victorian invalid.[5] Few had the resources to break out of this mould in the first half of the century, because it was constructed around the pattern of female dependence. Yet the mould was under increasing tension, and would not be able to contain the pressure of change in the later nineteenth century. This pressure on the ideal of womanhood was therefore particularly intense during the period when the new conference-going trend emerged, to provide a forum in which Evangelicalism could either attempt to reinforce the earlier image, or find a way of reinterpreting women's role in order to adapt to change. The Evangelical teaching which had been used in support of the restrictive ideology would not retain credence, unless Evangelicals themselves could re-establish an active role and identity for women beyond the confines of the home.

[3] L. Davidoff and C. Hall, *Family Fortunes: Men and Women of the English Middle Class, 1780–1850* (London 1987), pp. 114–15; C. Hall, 'The early formation of Victorian domestic ideology', in S. Burman, ed., *Fit Work for Women* (London, 1979), pp. 15–32; Olive Banks, *Faces of Feminism* (Oxford, 1986), pp. 85–7.

[4] C. Church, 'Victorian masculinity and the Angel in the House', in M. Vicinus, ed., *A Widening Sphere: Changing Roles of Victorian Women* (London, 1982), pp. 146–62; Banks, *Faces of Feminism*, pp. 85–102.

[5] Sara Delamont and Lorna Duffin, eds, 'The conspicuous consumptive: woman as invalid', in *The Nineteenth Century Woman* (London, 1978), pp. 26–56.

The Mildmay and Keswick conferences provided two different environments in which such a re-examination could take place through an exploration of the roles women could play in active ministry. There was no attempt to challenge contemporary expectations. Rather, one leading female writer actually did use the characters of Mary and Martha to identify two contrasting pictures of women involved in Christian work, taking them 'as the portraits of two classes of female workers, as distinctly different now as the sisters of Bethany, and both, like them, "loved" by Jesus'.[6] Curiously, the women of Mildmay and Keswick adopted exactly those roles. The conference at Mildmay was identified with a growing network of 'Martha'-like work in practical service, while Keswick would subsequently draw women into its spiritualized world of 'Mary's' contemplation. Through this apparent conformity to contemporary assumptions about the roles of women, Mildmay and Keswick were both able to adapt and recast the models into a much wider sphere of activity. An examination of the tension and balance between ways in which these conferences followed patterns of conformity, and how far they were able to develop these into 'nonconformity' reveals something of how this process took place.

* * *

William Pennefather, Mildmay's founder, intentionally established a clear separation between the spheres of male and female ministry, as a 'two-fold work' centred first on the conference hall and its teaching, and secondly on the deaconess house and the labours of the women in the service of the Gospel.[7] The Conference was run by men and taught by men. Women were only able to address their separate Ladies' meetings and some smaller afternoon gatherings in which they had special interest, but even this was viewed as controversial and one male CMS leader conspicuously walked off the platform because a woman was to address a missionary meeting.[8] In contrast to this male world of conference, the practical work which grew up around Mildmay, in an attempt to rebuild respectable family life among the poor through an improvement of the conditions in which they

---

[6] Margaret Maria Gordon, *Rights and Wrongs* (London, 1869), p. 229.

[7] William Pennefather, letter of 28 June 1871, published in *Service for the King* (Jan. 1884), pp. 2–3.

[8] G. A. Gollock, *Eugene Stock: A Biographical Study, 1836–1928* (London, 1909), pp. 114–15, cited in Fiona Bowie, Deborah Kirkwood, and Shirley Ardener, eds, *Women and Missions: Past and Present Anthropological and Historical Perceptions* (Oxford, 1993), p. 54.

lived, was regarded as 'emphatically *woman's* work'[9] and the concern of the founder's wife. The call went out to unmarried women 'to carry out into the larger community, the sympathies, the domestic interests, the active administrative capabilities with which God has endowed her'[10] by entering the extended family of the deaconess institution. Founded by the Pennefathers as the 'North London Training Home' at Barnet in 1860, this was arguably the first attempt to introduce the work of the deaconess in Britain, although the title of 'Deaconess' was initially rejected as too controversial.[11] After its removal to Mildmay the work had broadened, but remained focused on the Deaconess house, which adjoined the Mildmay conference hall. Built to receive some thirty ladies 'desiring to devote their lives to Mission work at home or abroad', this home became the centre of a 'vast field for women's work'.[12] By 1876 the wider network included twelve mission houses in other areas of London, as well as a growing complex of work at Mildmay. Here, life was structured like that of a large household, and the qualities looked for in a deaconess were exactly the same as those which were 'essential to the comfort of every household', namely 'A spirit of obedience, diligence, punctuality and order'. A deaconess's life would remain one 'of self surrender and of self-abnegation'.[13] Femininity was still important, with a uniform designed to ensure modest, womanly dress: 'A Mildmay deaconess is always well and becomingly dressed for every occasion.'[14] Practical household skills were also demanded – the rules specified that 'Each young woman [is] to learn thoroughly, and to assist in performing, *every kind of household*

---

[9] Mrs Pennefather, *Woman's Wayside Ministry* (London, 1883), p. 5.

[10] *Mrs Pennefather's Own Account of the Founding of the North London Training Home – What is it?* (London, 1870), p. 29.

[11] The influential Kaiserworth Deaconess house, founded in Germany in 1833, had adopted a distinctive blue gown, but in England much of the violent Protestant reaction to the Tractarians' re-establishment of celibate sisterhoods in the 1840s had become focused on the nun's costume, which was identified with Catholicism, and frequently treated as an object of ridicule rather than respect: see Susan P. Casteras, 'Virgin vows: the early Victorian artists' portrayal of nuns and novices', and Catherine M. Prelinger, 'The female diaconate in the Anglican Church: what kind of ministry for women?', in Gail Malmgreen, ed., *Religion in the Lives of English Women, 1760–1930* (London, 1986), pp. 129–60, 161–92.

[12] *Record of the Mildmay Conference* (London, 1876), p. 208.

[13] Harriette J. Cooke, *Mildmay, The Story of the Deaconesses Institutions or The Story of the First Deaconess Institution* (London, 1892), p. 66.

[14] Ibid., p. 52.

and domestic duty.'[15] The work might take many different forms, but none were incompatible with skills a woman would have been expected to exercise at home, whether visiting the poor, nursing work in the infirmary or cottage hospital, teaching at the night school, or taking flowers and Bible texts to patients in hospital. One American observer, Harriette Cooke, was convinced that the Deaconess house represented a clear, feminine message of 'the ministry and service of women, trained for organised and systematic work in the various branches to which she is by nature especially adapted'.[16] The Mildmay deaconess institution had found a ideal sphere of service for female domesticity.

* * *

Despite the obvious care to observe domestic 'conventions', Mildmay nevertheless called the 'lady of leisure' out from her inactivity. Mrs Pennefather challenged such 'accomplished ladies' living at home: 'What are *you* doing?' Were they 'Reading pretty tales by the fireside, or doing fancy-work to pass away the time, or practising songs for your next evening party?' Would they leave their trifling,[17] and use 'their talents for their lawful Master' in his world outside the home?[18] This would draw them into close contact with the life of the poorest areas of London. Although some remained at the Mildmay Deaconess house, others worked further afield in local mission houses such as that at Bethnal Green, where a substantial hospital was established. There was no thought of danger in going into these areas; rather, it was considered that as women they were especially safe. 'A Christian woman can go where a man would hardly dare, and she will be listened to by many who would not hear a "word from a man".'[19] Because these women walked 'in fellowship with Jesus', their female frailty and weakness would be transformed by his strength, enabling them to go into the very depths of human suffering with him 'to carry the breath of health among the foulness'.[20] It was a call to which many women responded, and during the 1890s Harriette Cooke estimated

---

[15] Rules, listed ibid., p. 46.
[16] Ibid., p. 57.
[17] Mrs Pennefather, *Women's Wayside Ministry*, pp. 6–8.
[18] Ibid., p. 8.
[19] *Service for the King* (June 1890), p. 104.
[20] Mrs Pennefather, *'Follow Thou Me' – Service – The Footsteps of the King (2)* (London, 1881), p. 179.

that there were over eighty deaconesses who regularly visited a hundred thousand poor.[21] This was no small-scale activity.

As the scope of the work of the Mildmay deaconesses widened, so did training opportunities. Women began to learn skills beyond those of domestic life. A separate training home called 'The Willows' was established, where female workers could train for home mission as deaconesses or for work in medical missions overseas. Students at 'The Willows' had to complete a rigorous two-year course which might include a further year of medical education. Others were trained through the nursing branch, which qualified them for paid employment as private sick nurses in different parts of the country. The teaching role of the deaconesses involved with the weekly 'night school' held in the basement of the conference hall was also demanding. Here, working men were taught not simply the basics of reading or writing, but also more advanced skills of shorthand or higher mathematics, in order to qualify for work as clerks, foremen, or reporters. Both for the deaconesses, and for those they taught, Mildmay could provide an opening into new areas of work and independence.

The Mildmay deaconesses also followed a very powerful model of female leadership. Mrs Pennefather retained absolute control over the entire network of work at Mildmay, even during the last years of her life when she lived as an invalid on a couch. This woman would never conform to the conventional picture of the weak, passive Victorian invalid. From that couch she controlled every detail of the work of Mildmay, holding audience like a reigning monarch. It was an impressive scene for one who approached the 'sofa on which she lay like a Queen in the majesty of such intellectual and spiritual grandeur as I have never witnessed'.[22] This active female power of a directive and empowering invalid challenges the Victorian image of weak femininity at its heart. Finally, she could only be overcome by death. 'Truly', lamented the Revd D. B. Hankin, 'this day has fallen a mother in Israel.'[23] The loss of Mrs Pennefather's leadership in January 1893 came at a time when questions were already being asked about the funding of the work she had supervised. A deficit of £5,000 was expected for that year, and despite repeated appeals and large revenue from legacies,

---

[21] Cooke, *Deaconess Institution*, p. 20.
[22] *Service for the King* (Jan. 1893), p. 38.
[23] Ibid., p. 52.

there was little new money coming in. Without Mrs Pennefather's magnetic personality at its core, and with no real successor, the work began to contract.

The picture which emerges of the female workers at Mildmay was thoughtfully drawn. The tension between the attempt to maintain conformity to the domestic ideal of submissive Christian womanhood and the call to women to enter new areas of work outside the home is demonstrated in the carefully balanced descriptions of Mildmay women, which combined gentleness with strength. Of Miss Daniell, whose work among soldiers did not speak naturally of feminine delicacy, it was said that 'In her were combined strength of mind, an intellect of a rarely high order, a power of command and control, a quick readiness of just judgment, with the tenderness, the dignity and the sweetness of a true woman's nature.'[24] Of course, the absolute model of perfection was Mrs Pennefather: 'so tender and yet so strong, so wise and yet so true, so modest, and yet so able'. Her 'splendid intellect', 'sagacity', and 'power of inspiring confidence' were carefully balanced with her more womanly attributes of 'humility' and 'sweet and unaffected submission to His will'.[25]

Such descriptions reflect the care taken throughout the work of Mildmay to avoid offence to contemporary ideas of womanhood, or their domestic role of service in the Victorian family. The activities in which they would engage were strictly limited to those of 'women's work', centred on the homely environment of the Deaconess house. However, the complete separation of the work of Mildmay from the male-administered Conference allowed a very powerful woman to establish absolute autonomy over the running of the work. Under the inspiration and motivating power of Mrs Pennefather, Mildmay banished the image of the 'Lady of Leisure' from its sphere of influence. Single women were called out of their homes into Christian service, and even those with family duties were mobilized into voluntary activity. 'Martha's' domestic skills were to be exercised in the Service of the King, and she would receive new training.

* * *

In contrast to the Mildmay call to action, the remote Lakeland setting of Keswick offered a spiritual home far from the world of daily work.

[24] *Service for the King* (June 1895), p. 140.
[25] *Service for the King* (Jan. 1893), pp. 33–8.

Here, women could join with Mary in quiet contemplation at the Master's feet. Because Keswick teaching focused on the apparently inactive 'rest of faith', it tends to be assumed that this meant Keswick was concerned only with 'other-worldly' matters of inner holiness rather than its expression in Christian service. David Bebbington voices this view: 'Holiness was so much an internal matter of personal consciousness, a trysting of the elevated soul with its God, that the practicalities of everyday living were generally passed over in silence.'[26] Further, this 'rest' was entered only through an act of total surrender and self-abnegation before God which might be seen as an ideal expression of the spirituality of the submissive Victorian lady.

The women of the early Keswick Conventions did indeed accept a very conventional 'spiritual' role. In this they differed from the practice of the American-led 'holiness movement', where women were involved in leadership alongside men, addressing mixed audiences at main meetings of conventions, and contributing a major part of the doctrinal writing on which the teaching was based. Keswick adopted the more conservative Mildmay approach, and did not invite women on to the platform as speakers. Nor did the women attempt to gain a large share in the doctrinal writings of the convention. It does not seem that this reticence on the part of women was the result of any restriction imposed by the male leadership. In 1878 a definitive series of twelve tracts was issued which sought to establish an authoritative basis for Keswick teaching. These included one by Mrs Gordon, on the fundamental doctrine of *Sanctification by Faith*. Despite this apparent indication of male acceptance of women's doctrinal writings, neither Mrs Gordon nor other Keswick women chose to continue in this direction. Instead they preferred to concentrate on devotional and spiritual subjects, in which they found their own distinctive expression of the Convention's doctrinal teachings.

The best known among Keswick's many female writers was Frances Havergal. Already, by 1875, an established and popular writer of hymns, poetry, and devotional works, her name and earlier writings became so quickly identified with the new Convention, that by the time of her death in 1879 it was as if she had been completely adopted by Keswick. Although she spent much of her life as an invalid, she did not follow the recent tradition of sickly 'afflicted women' pouring out

---

[26] D. W. Bebbington, *Evangelicalism in Modern Britain* (London, 1989), p. 175.

sentimental moanings in poetry and hymnody.[27] Keswick spirituality did not encourage her to dwell on her own sufferings. The absolute submission which was the heart of her life enabled her to consecrate even her pain to God's service: 'This terrible pain – I cannot feel that I *wish* it taken away a day sooner than His far-sighted faithful love appoints.'[28] Yet, when told that that day had arrived, her response was eager: 'Come Lord Jesus, come and fetch me. Oh run! run!' After Frances's death, her sister collected her own memories and those of friends in a book which has been described as the 'life record of that blessed saint of our own time, the late Miss F. Havergal'.[29] Elevated to such a saintly role, the life of Frances Havergal provided a defining model for the women of Keswick. In contrast to the active power emanating from the couch of the invalid Mrs Pennefather at Mildmay, the strength of Frances Havergal comes from her passive acceptance of pain and enforced inactivity, as she laid that life down before her Master.

* * *

The return to such a high valuation of the female potential for saintly spirituality during the early years at Keswick seems to be signalling a new emphasis on the image of woman as 'Mary', and perhaps a corresponding move away from the focus on her domestic identity as 'Martha'. At least at Keswick, there was no longer an attempt to hold the two ideals in tension. Was this an isolated change in balance, or did the development at Keswick reflect a wider change in religious thinking during this period?

It is often argued that a 'feminization' of religion took place during the later nineteenth century, partly influenced by the 'holiness movement', and such elevated views of female spirituality as those focused on Frances Havergal.[30] But what is meant by 'feminization', especially in the context of the extreme images of womanhood that were still influential? If it means the purity of womanly virtue effecting 'a

---

[27] Margaret Maison, '"Thine, Only Thine!" – women hymn writers in Britain 1760–1835', in Malmgreen, *Religion in the Lives of English Women*, pp. 20–36.

[28] Maria V. G. Havergal, *Memorials of Frances Ridley Havergal* (London, 1883), p. 173.

[29] Handley Moule, letter to *The Record*, 15 July 1890, reprinted in *The Life of Faith*, 1 Oct. 1890, p. 211.

[30] Lloyd Stevenson, 'Religious elements in the background of the British anti-vivisection movement', *Yale Journal of Biology and Medicine*, 29 (1956), p. 137, quoted in Banks, *Faces of Feminism*, p. 90.

genteel transformation of Christianity from a religion of duty and the conviction of sin to one of benevolence and the conviction of innocence' to produce a 'Sentimental Love Religion',[31] then it surely does not describe developments at Keswick. The ideal of the spiritual woman had emerged as a way of coping with the realities of a society in which the home became the repository of religious values, in contrast to man's secular world of work. Keswick provided a spiritual home for both men and women, where separation began to break down as men reclaimed their place in the sphere of spirituality. Men wanted to be 'holy' and the one mediator of that holiness was Christ, not woman as 'Angel'. Both men and women were called to come in absolute subjection and dependence to Christ, as the only way to receive his holiness. Although it was still thought that such submission would be easier for women, there was no other way into the 'rest of faith' and Keswick men showed themselves willing and eager to humble themselves before God.

Keswick offered no easy 'sentimentalized love religion' based on female innocence. It was a very tough, demanding religion which called for a recognition of both male and female sinfulness, 'equally frail, poor, tempted, partakers of a fallen nature'. It made no allowance for female fragility, as sin could only be purged by God's purifying fire, on the altar of the life laid down in sacrifice. Pain was inescapable, as the 'sacrificial knife' was the only way to cut away the life of sin. Harford Battersby urged those who sought holiness to 'apply the knife unsparingly in the power of the Holy Ghost'.[32] It was by this course that Frances Havergal found sanctification, not through any natural perfection in herself – 'She presented herself as a living sacrifice to the Saviour, and He accepted the offering, worthless as it was.'[33]

'Feminization' is clearly a difficult term. It cannot be said that religion was 'feminized' at Keswick, unless 'feminization' is taken to mean that the Keswick search for holiness through fire marked the beginning of a reintegration of male and female spirituality which had been artificially divided. Much of the ministry of Keswick depended on this reintegration, perhaps most visibly through the man who has been described as the 'poet of Keswick', the Revd Charles Fox, who

[31] Leslie A. Fielder, *Love and Death in the American Novel* (New York, 1960), p. 52, quoted in Banks, *Faces of Feminism*, p. 90.
[32] T. D. H. Battersby, 'Sin that Dwelleth in Me', in *Pathway of Power* (Aug. 1878), p. 123.
[33] Charles Fox, in *Life of Faith*, 1 Sept. 1882, p. 165.

continued his association with Keswick from his first appearance as a speaker in 1879 until his death in 1900. His emotive, impassioned addresses were some of the most challenging at Keswick.

> Nobody touched hearts more truly by exposing his own. The tremulous tenderness of his soul when he opened up the depths was the revelation of an inner man. Certainly, I have never known any case in which the joyous fun of a strong man was so absolutely in harmony with Christian feeling.[34]

Emotion, spirituality, and strength were not regarded as incompatible at Keswick, and much wider implications of such a spiritual realignment would become apparent when active service was resumed.

Keswick's 'rest of faith' did not long remain restful. Confusion seems to arise because there was a period between 1875 and 1886 when there was no specific call to action, and this interlude tends to be treated as defining its character. This period was, rather, intended as a time of preparation, during which it was vital for convention-goers to be quiet and listen to the message. 'The first step to more effective service is not outward toward the world, but inwards towards the Lord.'[35] Only when they had learned how to receive power to live a holy life could that life be expressed in a renewal of active service. But when the new call did come, in 1886, it burst on Keswick with a force which resulted in a sudden explosion of activity. The people were ready: 'They have become transformed believers, – both as to their inner experience and their practical usefulness'; 'Here I am send me.'[36] The image of sitting at the Master's feet only held good for long enough to assimilate his teaching.

Activity found its focus in the groundswell of support for Foreign Missions which grew among convention-goers during the 1880s. By 1887 it became impossible to contain the pressure for missionary meetings, and an appeal from a CMS missionary from Palestine was allowed at Keswick. Significantly, the call was for ten 'Christian ladies with private means' to work among Moslem women, and seventeen

---

[34] J. Elder Cumming, 'The founders and some of the leaders', in C. F. Harford, ed., *The Keswick Convention, its Message, its Method and its Men* (London, 1907), pp. 48–66.

[35] The Revd C. A. Fox, '"Even now!" or Hindrances to Pentecostal lives removed': New Year's Address used as editorial in *Life of Faith*, 1 Jan. 1886, pp. 1–4.

[36] *Life of Faith*, 1 June 1892.

responded. Thus women were uncompromisingly called into action, and into a sphere which had previously been seen as a male preserve. Keswick continued to develop a policy of sending out both men and women as 'Keswick missionaries' through existing missionary societies, but with the financial support of the Convention. Although Mildmay had sent women to work overseas, they were not treated as 'Missionaries' in their own right. Most female participation was restricted to a wifely role. Hudson Taylor of the China Inland Mission had met strong resistance when he wanted to accept women as missionaries as early as the mid-1860s, perhaps, as Peter Williams suggests, because there was still a 'fear of women outside of well-ordered and known relationships within the family'.[37] Taylor stood by his vision of a missionary who would be 'no longer a girl whose place it is to keep back, retired and silent, but His instrument, called to adorn Him who is your ornament';[38] and by the time Keswick declared itself ready for action, the mission field was opening to women. Women had begun to be accepted as missionaries not only by the CIM but also the more conservative CMS, and the rapid increase in female recruitment indicates that the policy no longer posed a threat. By 1900, Williams claims that women had begun to out-number men in some societies.[39] Their influence is even more apparent at Keswick, where a list given in the *Keswick Week* of 1894 of the thirteen 'Missionaries sent forth by the Convention' included the name of only one man.[40]

What is especially interesting is not just the indication that Keswick encouraged these women to serve as missionaries, but that they were treated as equal workers in partnership with men. Outside the confines of English society it had become possible to leave behind some of the restrictions which that society imposed. In the work of Home Mission at Mildmay, the women's sphere had still been separate from that of men. At Keswick men and women were called to work in the same world in the mission field, and by 1888 the Missionary Conference at Exeter Hall could proclaim that 'Women's work had no longer become

---

[37] C. Peter Williams, 'The missing link', in Bowie, Kirkwood, and Ardener, *Women and Missions*, p. 49.

[38] Hudson Taylor, speaking at Broadlands, 24 May 1870, quoted C. Peter Williams, *The Ideal of the Self Governing Church: A Study in Victorian Missionary Strategy* (Leiden, 1993), p. 54.

[39] Williams, 'The missing link', p. 49.

[40] *The Keswick Week* (1894), p. 6.

a mere adjunct, it was itself a power.'[41] The profound nature of this change is illustrated by an address to the Ladies' Meetings in 1892. The speaker enjoined on them the command to 'Be fruitful and multiply'. Previously, this might have been used as a text to justify women's primary role in child rearing. Now, it was taken to apply to the missionary call, and it was believed that God ordered them not into the world of home but to '*Go beyond your sphere*'. God's call was a clear 'charter for all his missionary servants. It is a charter for each of us that are going forth into any service, but it seems to have a special reference to those who are going to the untried life, to preach to those who have not yet heard His voice.'[42]

Early teaching at Keswick does demonstrate a very conventional view of female spirituality which was to be lived out in the home, and it is undeniable that there was a strong emphasis on self-abnegation in the service of others.[43] Later, however, as spirituality began to be expressed in a call to missionary service far beyond the sphere of the home, there are indications of a widening attitude. This is especially apparent in the case of one very vocal woman missionary. At a Keswick meeting in 1892, Miss Gollock launched an attack on languid Christian women. What they needed was the power of Christ's life in them. Did they want to 'be a wet blanket or glow for Jesus?' Would her hearers accept Christ's power to 'overcome their sickly life'?[44] Miss Gollock became one of the leading voices in the call for women to work alongside men, especially in the administration of missions, contending that separate women's societies had 'had their day'.[45] This call for integration of the work of men and women was not simply the view of an idiosyncratic woman, but was also voiced by one of Keswick's leading male speakers: 'The Church will be the better, this world will be blessed, and God will be glorified, if Christians, instead of wrangling, help each other like this, and the men help the women and the women help the men.'[46] This affirmation of mutuality was one of the

---

[41] Augustus R. Buckland, *Women in the Mission Field – Pioneers and Martyrs* (London, 1895), p. 15.

[42] *The Keswick Week* (1892), p. 105.

[43] *Life of Faith*, Oct. 1885, pp. 217–18.

[44] *The Keswick Week* (1892), p. 109.

[45] Minna C. Gollock, 'The share of women in the administration of missions', *International Review of Missions*, 1 (1912), pp. 674–87.

[46] Preb. Webb Peploe, *The Keswick Week* (1894), p. 127.

indications that the worlds of men and women were beginning to be reintegrated through the work of Keswick.

These changing expectations of women's roles at Keswick demonstrate that the Convention was not static, but was part of a movement. Keswick took spirituality out of the exclusive domain of the 'Angel in the House' and created a religious world in which men and women could rediscover something of their equality before God. While this was a humbling experience for the men of the convention, it was a confidence-building time for the women; and when the time of preparation was completed it was among these women that the response of a call to active missionary service was first apparent. Just as male and female spirituality had drawn closer together at Keswick, so did ideas of equality in Christian service. This took place during a period when a much more confrontational 'women's movement' was gaining influence in society, and there would be protests that churches and missionary leaders refused to acknowledge it. It might be argued that the widening role opened up to women through Keswick ensured that attitudes had expanded sufficiently within Evangelicalism to prevent confrontation. Keswick women did not feel a need to join the 'women's movement', and even the vocal Miss Gollock could remain to express her opinions within Evangelical circles.

*   *   *

An exploration of the roles of women at Mildmay and Keswick in the context of the contrasting characters of the domestic Martha and the spiritual Mary reveals something of the tension between conformity to an ideal and a movement towards change. The Mildmay deaconess perhaps experienced more that conformed to conventional ideals of woman's domesticity than she encountered of change. However, it was only through this very careful observance of social expectations that Mildmay was able to gain acceptance for the ministry of women outside the home within the confines of middle class respectability. The later Convention at Keswick did not continue this approach, and might appear to have surrendered to the spiritualized ideal of womanhood; and some who had experienced both conferences expressed concern that Keswick had drawn away from the agonizing work of entering the depths of human society.[47] However, this change

---

[47] Charlotte Hanbury, *Life of Mrs Albert Head* (London, 1905), pp. 54, 113, 226.

reflects a wider shift which began during the last quarter of the nineteenth century. The full-time work at Mildmay was drawing to a close, and the women of Keswick had to find another sphere of ministry. By moving away from the domestic model of women's service, Keswick was able to bring women's ministry out of its separate sphere to join men in their work of foreign mission.

University of Birmingham

HOW MUSCULAR WAS VICTORIAN CHRISTIANITY? THOMAS HUGHES AND THE CULT OF CHRISTIAN MANLINESS RECONSIDERED

by SEAN GILL

ESPITE the enduring popularity of *Tom Brown's Schooldays*, which has never been out of print since its publication in 1857, the reputation of its author, Thomas Hughes, has suffered from the general reaction against Victorian values which characterized the first part of the twentieth century. Even as late as 1965, out of sympathy both with Hughes's Christian beliefs and with his moral didacticism, Kenneth Allsop could dismiss him as a writer 'fluctuating between a facetious smugness and a creepy piety'.[1] However, in recent years scholars such as George Worth and Norman Vance have provided us with a more sensitive and nuanced picture of his thought, and one which severely qualifies the traditional image of Hughes as an exponent of a muscular Christianity which exalted an anti–intellectual credo of schoolboy athleticism and adult male toughness perfectly attuned to the ethos of high Victorian imperialism.[2] This paper examines some of the ambiguities which are to be found in Hughes's attempts to encapsulate and transcend the ideals of appropriate masculine and feminine behaviour within the specifically Christian context from which they arose, and in so doing cast some light on the way in which Victorian Christianity both contributed to, and was influenced by, the construction and maintenance of gender roles for both men and women.

One central problem which emerges repeatedly in Hughes's writing is the tension between his desire on the one hand to emphasise the distinctive and exclusive qualities which he believed pertained to men and women, while on the other to appeal to a common ideal of the Christian life and character with which both could identify. On the

---

[1] Kenneth Allsop, 'A coupon for instant tradition: On "Tom Brown's Schooldays"', *Encounter*, 25 (Nov. 1965), pp. 60–3.
[2] George J. Worth, 'Of muscles and manliness: some reflections on Thomas Hughes', in James R. Kincaid and Albert J. Kuhn, eds, *Victorian Literature and Society: Essays Presented to Richard D. Altick* (Ohio, 1983), pp. 300–14; Norman Vance, *The Sinews of the Spirit: The Ideal of Christian Manliness in Victorian Literature and Religious Thought* (Cambridge, 1985).

face of it, Hughes's commendation of the virtues of what he calls manfulness or manliness would seem to reinforce the gendered polarities operating within mid-Victorian society, and to exalt an ideal of masculine vigour over against what most Victorian Christians would have seen as the more feminine qualities of gentleness and forbearance. As the evangelical *Christian Observer* argued, in terms reminiscent of Ruskin, 'our wise Creator purposed man and woman to hold different positions in the universe . . . man was created for strength, woman for beauty, whether of body or mind; man's life is of necessity active, woman's quiescent'.[3] In *Tom Brown's Schooldays* Hughes delivers a panegyric upon the virtues of conflict waged in a righteous cause which can be read as a perfect example of the uses of such masculine strength. The passage also illustrates the new enthusiasm for Christian militarism which Olive Anderson has suggested derived from the cult of the pious soldier martyr such as Sir Henry Havelock who died at the relief of Lucknow during the Indian mutiny,[4] and which was to reach its apotheosis in the death of General Gordon at Khartoum in 1885:

After all, what would life be without fighting, I should like to know? From the cradle to the grave, fighting, rightly understood is the business, the real, highest, honestest business of every son of man. Every one who is worth his salt has his enemies, who must be beaten, be they evil thoughts and habits in himself or spiritual wickedness in high places, or Russians, or border-ruffians, or Bill, Tom, or Harry, who will not let him live his life in quiet till he has thrashed them.[5]

He then goes on to reject the alternative Christian vision of pacifism exemplified by the Quakers as impracticable.[6] This was the voice of the fervently patriotic Hughes who was one of the first to join the newly formed volunteer movement in 1859 to ward off the supposed threat of Napoleon III's army.[7]

---

[3] *The Christian Observer*, 58 (1865), p. 547.
[4] Olive Anderson, 'The growth of Christian militarism in mid-Victorian Britain', *EHR*, 86 (1971), pp. 46–72.
[5] Thomas Hughes, *Tom Brown's Schooldays* (Oxford, 1989), p. 282.
[6] Ibid., p. 283.
[7] Edward C. Mack and W. H. G. Armytage, *Thomas Hughes: The Life of the Author of Tom Brown's Schooldays* (London, 1952), p. 116.

Nor was Hughes alone in stressing the tougher, more masculine, aspects of the Christian faith; for there was widespread unease at the time that Christianity was appealing far more successfully to women than to men – a concern to which Hughes alludes in the introduction to his 1879 work, *The Manliness of Christ*. Speaking of the lack of success of branches of the YMCA in reaching the young, Hughes comments:

> Their tone and influence are said to lack manliness, and the want of manliness is attributed to their avowed profession of Christianity. If you pursue the inquiry, you will often come upon a distinct belief that this weakness is inherent in our English religion; that our Christianity does appeal and must appeal habitually and mainly to men's fears – to that in them which is timid and shrinking, rather than to that which is courageous and outspoken.[8]

The same concerns had been voiced by the Revd S. S. Pugh in his book, *Christian Manliness: A Book of Examples and Principles for Young Men*, published by the Religious Tract Society in 1867. He complained that

> The Christian life has often been strangely and mischievously misapprehended as to this, so that men have come to think of it as a state of dreary sentimentalism, fit only for women, or for soft and effeminate men, and not calling forth or giving room for the exercise of the sterner and stronger virtues.[9]

Hughes's fellow Christian Socialist, F. D. Maurice, was equally concerned to counteract what he called 'the passive or feminine character which has often been ascribed to the Sermon on the Mount', and which, he believed, had 'been thought to discourage all the qualities which have been most conspicuous in heroes who have struggled for freedom'.[10] With characteristically more bluntness the nonconformist hierarch Charles Spurgeon thundered that 'There has

[8] Thomas Hughes, *The Manliness of Christ* (London, 1879), pp. 1–6.
[9] S. S. Pugh, *Christian Manliness: A Book of Examples and Principles for Young Men* (London, 1867), p. 95.
[10] F. D. Maurice, *Social Morality: Twenty-one Lectures delivered in the University of Cambridge* (London, 1869), p. 461.

got abroad a notion, somehow, that if you become a Christian, you must sink your manliness and turn milksop. . . . Young men, to you I would honestly say that I should be ashamed to speak to you of a religion that would make you soft, cowardly, effeminate, spiritless.'[11]

Norman Vance has argued, however, that Hughes and Kingsley had serious reservations about the label 'muscular Christianity' which was attached to their writings; and he prefers to use the term 'manliness' as a more appropriate way of describing the synthesis of physical and moral virtues which they sought to commend.[12] This view has recently been challenged by Donald Hall, who comments on 'these writers' consistent, even insistent, use of the ideologically charged and aggressively poised male body'.[13]

This problem of interpretation highlights the ambiguity of both Hughes's and Kingsley's attitude towards gender differentiation; and it is certainly possible to find in Hughes's writings a very different attitude towards masculinity and femininity from the one we have so far been discussing. It is important to note, for example, that Hughes sought to stress that the courage implied in his ideal of manliness was primarily not physical but moral. For this reason, he claimed, 'it was as likely to be found in a weak as in a strong body'.[14] Heroism in this sense was not based upon a secularized late Victorian neo-Darwinian vision of human competitiveness and aggression, but rather it echoed the Pauline Christian ideal of warfare against the world, the flesh, and the devil. As such it was equally open to women as well as men to embrace it. Thus, in his discussion of the tests of manliness, Hughes describes what he calls one of 'the most searching of all trials of courage and manliness' as a situation in which 'a man or a woman is called upon to stand by what approves itself to their consciences as true'.[15]

In *Tom Brown's Schooldays* Norman Vance has suggested that the hero's friend Arthur, from whom he learns the value of Christian

---

[11] Quoted in John Springhall, 'Building character in the British boy: the attempt to extend Christian manliness to working-class adolescents, 1880–1914', in J. A. Mangan and James Walvin, eds, *Manliness and Morality: Middle-class Masculinity in Britain and America, 1800–1840* (Manchester, 1987), pp. 55–6.

[12] Vance, *Sinews*, pp. 1–2.

[13] Donald E. Hall, *Muscular Christianity: Embodying the Victorian Age* (Cambridge, 1995), p. 9.

[14] Hughes, *Manliness*, p. 25.

[15] Ibid., p. 36.

standards in life, is associated with the feminine values not of weakness but of gentleness and goodness which turn out to have their own kind of moral strength.[16] In fact the novel contains a far more convincing and direct portrayal of Christian female courage in the figure of Arthur's mother. While Hughes makes it clear that her husband, a young Anglican clergyman working in an economically depressed working-class parish in the Midlands, is the epitome of heroic Christian manliness, the hardships of his life and his ministry are equally borne by her, particularly during a desperate outbreak of typhus to which they both succumb, but from which only she recovers.[17] As Hughes was aware, this was no mere idealized fictional account: the nuns of the newly founded Anglican sisterhoods, for example, served heroically as nurses in the Crimea and in the cholera epidemic of 1866.[18] Nearer home, he once wrote to his close friend the future Marquess of Ripon that he believed that his wife Fanny would 'be a wonderful parsoness', which he regarded as 'the work which was Christ's special work on earth'.[19]

Yet even though both Hughes and Kingsley were keen to advance a notion of manly courage that was applicable to both men and women, neither succeeded in overcoming the dualism which lay at the heart of much Victorian thinking about gender. Thus, in his four sermons of the life and character of David preached at Cambridge in 1865, Kingsley dismissed the notion of muscular Christianity associated with his novels as merely 'a clever expression, spoken in jest, by I know not whom'; but immediately went on to offer his own definition of 'a healthy and manful Christianity, one which does not exalt the feminine virtues to the exclusion of the masculine'.[20] In the same vein, Kingsley's tirade against monasticism rested upon his assertion that it was 'essentially a feminine life', inappropriate for men as it demanded 'gentleness, patience, resignation, self-sacrifice, and self-devotion – all that is loveliest in the ideal feminine character'.[21] Similarly in the

---

[16] Vance, *Sinews*, p. 145.

[17] Hughes, *Schooldays*, pp. 238–41.

[18] Sean Gill, 'The power of Christian ladyhood: Priscilla Lydia Sellon and the creation of Anglican sisterhoods', in Stuart Mews, ed., *Modern Religious Rebels* (London, 1993), pp. 148–50.

[19] Lucien Wolf, *The Life of the First Marquess of Ripon*, 2 vols (London, 1921), I, p. 153.

[20] Charles Kingsley, *David: Four Sermons Preached before the University of Cambridge* (London, 1865), p. 5.

[21] Ibid., pp. 5–6.

writings of Pugh and Spurgeon there is a fear that Christianity will be seen as being an effeminate religion, where effeminacy is defined as the assumption by men of characteristics which are essentially female. When gender differences were as clearly defined as this it was far from easy to appeal to an ideal of human nature which could transcend them.

This difficulty was at its most acute in attempts to portray the life and character of Christ as the perfect exemplar of redeemed humanity who would, in Hughes's words, be 'the Head of every man, woman, child on this earth'.[22] As Daniel Pals has shown, the Victorian era witnessed a significant growth in literature of this kind, designed either to bolster or undermine the traditional accounts of Christ's divinity.[23] Hughes's book, *The Manliness of Christ*, was typical of Broad Church responses to the challenge in its portrayal of a Christ who could command assent by his human qualities rather than by controverted accounts of his miraculous deeds and nature.[24] At the same time, in churches where women increasingly formed the majority of the congregation and often took the lead in a wide range of church activities, including philanthropy and missionary work at home and abroad, it was important that they should be presented with a model of Christ as the pattern for all humanity with which they could identify. Yet it was not easy to maintain such a balance, as the Pre-Raphaelite painter Holman Hunt discovered when he showed his famous portrait of Christ as 'The Light of the World' to Thomas Carlyle in 1853. Carlyle, the author of *On Heroes, Hero Worship and the Heroic in History*, was one of the prophets of the Victorian cult of strenuous moral, intellectual, and physical manhood, and it was by this standard that Holman Hunt's depiction of Christ was judged and found wanting. It was, Carlyle railed, 'a poor misshaped presentation of the noblest, the brotherliest and the most heroic-minded Being that ever walked God's earth', and he urged Hunt to think in future far more of Christ's 'antique heroic soul'.[25] Hughes's own portrayal of Christ attempts to combine the highest attributes of both masculine and feminine nature. For him Christ is without the slightest trace of weakness or cowardice,

---

[22] Thomas Hughes, *Tracts for Priests and People* (Cambridge, 1861), p. 39.
[23] Daniel Pals, *The Victorian Lives of Jesus* (San Antonio, TX, 1982).
[24] Ibid., pp. 19–20.
[25] Holman Hunt, *Pre-Raphaelitism and the Pre-Raphaelite Brotherhood*, 2 vols (London, 1905), I, p. 357.

but is also 'this most tender and sensitive of the sons of men – with fibres answering to every touch and breath of human sympathy', a classic definition of the Victorian ideal of female gentleness.[26] How far such a hypostatic union of gendered opposites succeeded in its intention is another matter. As Anthony Harrison has shown, it enabled the devout High Anglican Christina Rossetti to make a passionate identification with Christ as the pattern for womanly obedience and active compassion;[27] but neither Josephine Butler nor Florence Nightingale believed that women could be spiritually liberated without the aid of a 'female Christ' with whom they could identify.[28]

One possible way of resolving the dilemmas of gender for Victorian Christians was to have recourse to the concept of chivalry, that interplay of masculine strength and feminine weakness which reinforced both and which gave leave for Christ and the Victorian male to be depicted as in some senses tender and compassionate without any loss of their essential manliness. As the Revd Pugh explained to his readership of young men, Christ's gentleness was of a particular kind and in following his example, 'A man who is strong, who in fidelity and courage and self-reliance and self-mastery can keep the even tenor of his ways, can afford to be gentle without fearing to be suspected of weakness.'[29] For Kingsley, too, Christ's example in voluntarily laying down his life revealed 'the true prowess, the true valour, the true chivalry, the true glory, the true manhood' to which we should aspire.[30] As Mark Girouard has demonstrated, the Victorian revival of chivalry had various origins.[31] It owed a great deal to the novels of Sir Walter Scott, and to the revulsion against the materialism and class conflict of nineteenth-century society which sought relief in an idealized vision of the medieval past, both of which influenced Hughes. His grandmother knew and entertained the great novelist at her London home, and Hughes became an avid reader of his works,

---

[26] Hughes, *Manliness*, p. 143.
[27] Anthony Harrison, 'Christina Rossetti and the sage discourse of feminist High Anglicanism', in T. E. Morgan, ed., *Victorian Sages and Cultural Discourse: Renegotiating Gender and Power* (New Brunswick, NJ, 1990), pp. 92–3.
[28] Sean Gill, *Women and the Church of England from the Eighteenth Century to the Present* (London, 1994), p. 140.
[29] Pugh, *Manliness*, p. 123.
[30] Kingsley, *David: Four Sermons*, p. 20.
[31] Mark Girouard, *The Return to Camelot: Chivalry and the English Gentleman* (London, 1981), pp. 1–38.

recollecting that while a student at Oxford he read them to a 'broken-down old jockey' in an endeavour to keep him from the public house – though the outcome of this somewhat rarefied effort to encourage sobriety is not recorded.[32] In *Tom Brown's Schooldays*, the process of the hero's growth towards Christian manhood involves the acquisition of the chivalric virtues of courage, moral purity, and a willingness to defend the weak, as when he champions the cause of a younger boy by engaging in a fight with the aptly named bully, 'Slogger' Williams. This implicit chivalric thread in the novel was recognized and made more explicit in the illustrations provided by the artist Arthur Hughes for the first edition of the work in 1869, most notably in the depiction of Tom as a young Christian knight kneeling in prayer.

In the sequel, *Tom Brown at Oxford*, Hughes refers approvingly to

the old chivalrous and Christian belief that a man's body is given him to be trained and brought into subjection, and then used for the protection of the weak, the advancement of all righteous causes, and the subduing of the earth which God has given to the children of men.[33]

Yet as a mediating concept chivalry did not really succeed in resolving the conflicting ideals of gendered behaviour with which Hughes wrestled. Nowhere is this more evident than in the concluding pages of the novel, where Tom has been saved in time-honoured fashion by the love of a good woman (in this case, Mary Porter). When Tom laments that in marrying her he has unwittingly tied to himself 'a brave, generous, pitying angel', she vigorously rejects the appeal to Coventry Patmore's image of woman as the Angel in the House, insisting that she made a free and conscious moral choice to share his hardships. The ideal of chivalry is also dismissed. 'Life', Tom rhapsodizes, 'should be all bright and beautiful to a woman. It is every man's duty to shield her from all that can vex, or pain, or soil.' To which she replies by asking if women have different souls from men and if not, why they should not share their highest hopes. But in her concluding peroration Mary ultimately returns to a much more conventional view of the relationship between men and women, one very much in the conservative mode of Charlotte Yonge:

---

[32] Mack and Armytage, *Hughes*, p. 41.
[33] Thomas Hughes, *Tom Brown at Oxford*, 3rd edn (London, 1895), p. 99.

Then why not put me on your own level? Why not let me pick my way by your side? Cannot a woman feel the wrongs that are going on in the world? Cannot she long to see them set right, and pray that they may be set right? We are not meant to sit in fine silks, and look pretty, and spend money, any more than you are meant to make it, and cry peace where there is not peace. If a woman cannot do much herself, she can honour and love a man who can.

To which he replies that she has made him 'feel what it is that a man wants, what is the help that is meet for him'.[34]

In his discussion of this scene Peter Gay suggests that it raises some serious questions about the absolute distinctions that we have long thought differentiated the sexes in the Victorian period, though he does not relate this observation to the specifically Christian context in which Hughes was writing.[35] As Hughes was well aware, and later historians have noted, Christianity played a profoundly ambiguous role in the lives of Victorian women, one which both limited them by the stereotypes of pious passive femininity which it often advanced, but also empowered them to undertake much more dynamic and public activities outside the home.[36] By its appeal to transcendent values beyond the structures of patriarchal society, Christianity destablized the category of the feminine in the very act of attempting to define it, and that was bound to have troubling implications for any attempt to construct a coherent notion of Christian masculinity. As Hughes's tortuous wrestling with the problem makes clear, we need to go beyond the oversimplified generalizations implied by labels such as 'The Angel in the House' or 'Muscular Christianity' as if they represent a straightforward mirroring of Victorian Christian understandings of gender, and rather see them in a Foucaultian sense as part of a complex and often contradictory pattern of cultural discourse.[37] At the same time, before we too readily pass judgements on the perceived confusions and failings of a writer such as Hughes, we ought to reflect on the

---

[34] Ibid., pp. 478–9.
[35] Peter Gay, 'The manliness of Christ', in R. W. Davis and R. J. Helmstadter, eds, *Religion and Irreligion in Victorian Society* (London, 1992), pp. 102–16.
[36] For the ambiguous effects of religion upon women's lives in this period, see Gail Malmgreen, ed., *Religion in the Lives of English Women, 1760–1930* (London, 1986), pp. 6–8.
[37] Michel Foucault, *The Archaeology of Knowledge* (London, 1972), p. 23.

fact that the contemporary crisis in masculine identity in our own society suggests that we have not ourselves found answers to the problems with which he had manfully wrestled.

University of Bristol

'KNIGHTS OF GOD': ELLICE HOPKINS AND THE WHITE CROSS ARMY, 1883–95

by SUE MORGAN

A HISTORIOGRAPHER of recent literature on masculinity might be forgiven for assuming that nineteenth-century definitions of Christian manliness were solely the domain of male commentators. The shifting and often conflicting emphases of the manly ideal proposed by critics such as Arnold, Kingsley, Hughes, and Carlyle exerted a prevailing influence upon the Victorian ruling classes – this much is beyond doubt.[1] That codes of manliness were also subject to considerable attention by women, however, is suggested by this preliminary study of the prescriptive writings of the High Churchwoman and leading moral reformer Ellice Hopkins, whose discourse of social purity emerged as a force in the search for regulation of male sexuality during the 1880s and 1890s.

The anti-vice agitation of the social purists provides a relatively unexplored feature of the renewed impetus for social concern evident among the late Victorian Churches.[2] Revelations of working-class immorality contributed heavily to widespread alarm over the material and spiritual impoverishment of the urban masses. Formed in the wake of the campaign against the Contagious Diseases Acts, the movement for social purity (a euphemism for sexual purity), unlike earlier, voluntarist reform strategies, signalled the Churches' preparedness to contemplate increased State legislation in order to control escalating levels of commercialized vice. Hopkins's anti-individualist reading of prostitution as a collective, social sin made her a key protagonist of the new interventionist policies.[3] An innovative rescue worker, she

---

[1] See D. Newsome, *Godliness and Good Learning: Four Studies on a Victorian Ideal* (London, 1961); N. Vance, *The Sinews of the Spirit* (Cambridge, 1985).

[2] E. J. Bristow, *Vice and Vigilance. Purity Movements in Britain Since 1700* (Dublin, 1977), offers the only full-length account I have found on the contribution of the churches to anti-vice crusading. F. Mort, *Dangerous Sexualities. Medico-Moral Politics in England since 1830* (London, 1987), demonstrates the role of evangelical feminist purity discourse in regulating working-class immorality, although religion is not central to his analysis.

[3] Hopkins was a key activist in the passing of the Industrial Schools Amendment Act of 1880, which advocated the removal of prostitutes' children into industrial schools, and the

pioneered non-remedial approaches to prostitution, challenging men to take equal responsibility for their personal moral behaviour. Her demands found practical expression through the White Cross Army (WCA), a society dedicated to the promotion of male purity and co-founded by Hopkins with Bishop Lightfoot. This paper examines the origins and organizational structure of the WCA through which she disseminated her discourse of Christian manliness, and suggests reasons for the widespread appeal of her definition.[4]

Purity campaigns are a noteworthy example of the interdenominational character of the late Victorian social gospel.[5] John Clifford and Hugh Price Hughes, prominent advocates of Josephine Butler's celebrated repeal campaign, secured ongoing Baptist and Wesleyan commitment to purity, as did the Quaker and Congregationalist leaderships. Anglicanism, a good deal more cautious and belated in its approval, eventually produced some of its keenest talent for the cause, notably from the High Church party. Bishop King, Montagu Butler, and the architects of the Christian Social Union – Henry Scott Holland, Charles Gore, and B. F. Westcott – were renowned spokesmen for male chastity, conducting their efforts primarily through the official Anglican agency, the Church of England Purity Society (CEPS).[6] As John Fout has argued, what were outwardly campaigns against vice and obscenity in reality reflected growing ecclesiastical concern over eroding boundaries of gender.[7] Envisioning a divinely ordained moral order which enshrined the heterosexual family model, purity reformers reasserted religious authority over marital and

Criminal Law Amendment Act of 1885, which raised the age of consent from 13 to 16, increased powers of police surveillance over brothels, and criminalized male homosexuality.

[4] White Cross publications and transactions are located at the BL, the Fawcett Library in London, CUL, and the Church of England Record Centre at Bermondsey. This essay is indebted to Sherwin Bailey's seminal article 'The White Cross League', *Moral Welfare* (April 1952), pp. 2–13.

[5] See David Thompson's useful revision, 'The Christian Socialist revival in Britain: a reappraisal', in J. Garnett and C. Matthew, eds, *Revival and Religion Since 1700. Essays for John Walsh* (London, 1993), pp. 273–95.

[6] The CEPS was formed on 25 May 1883 at Lambeth Palace under the presidency of Archbishop Benson. It formed a friendly but more circumscribed counterpart to WCA efforts, organizing on an exclusively Anglican diocesan basis. Sources as for the White Cross collections, plus series of its organ *The Vanguard*, July 1884 – Oct. 1894, thereafter *The White Cross*, held at the BL.

[7] J. Fout, 'Sexual politics in Wilhelmine Germany: the male gender crisis, moral purity, and homophobia', *Journal of the History of Sexuality*, 2 (1992), p. 262.

familial values against an onslaught of secular, progressive critiques. Within this conventional framework of gender relations there was considerable room for subversion. Female purity workers like Hopkins appropriated dominant Victorian ideologies of women as the moral and spiritual superiors of men, creating a language of collective moral outrage which sanctioned their right to enter public debates on sexuality, and sustained a powerful critique of male sexual abuse. In this way a highly successful coalition was forged between religious expectations of male self-restraint and feminist demands for the elimination of the sexual double standard.[8]

Whilst she was not the originator of male purity leagues, Hopkins was responsible for their mass popularization and for procuring the Anglican clergy's approval. Two factors relating to this clerical volte-face should be immediately noted. One was the consolidation of the campaign to repeal the Contagious Diseases Acts with the public outcry caused by W. T. Stead's journalistic exposés of child prostitution.[9] These inflammatory articles gave huge impetus to vigilance work and did much to ensure the legislative triumph of the Criminal Law Amendment Act in 1885. Discussions of sexual morality which had proved highly problematic at Church Congress levels ten years earlier were now a matter of national and international concern – in such a climate the Church was obliged to speak out.[10] Secondly, the enthusiastic backing of Archbishop Benson, his successor at Truro Bishop Wilkinson, and Lightfoot, the Bishop of Durham, should not be underestimated. George Wilkinson, friend and spiritual mentor to Hopkins for many years, proved a persistent advocate in Convocation of a nationwide scheme for male purity.[11] Benson remained similarly convinced of the Church's role in re-educating men along Arnoldian lines of rigorous moral virtue – it is appropriate and certainly no coincidence that the WCA and the CEPS were both established in the first year of his archiepiscopate.[12] Lightfoot maintained active support

[8] See Mort, *Dangerous Sexualities*, pp. 114–19.

[9] W. T. Stead, 'The maiden tribute of modern Babylon', *Pall Mall Gazette*, 6–8, 10 (July 1885), cited in J. Walkowitz, *City of Dreadful Delight* (London, 1992), p. 269.

[10] In 1874, George Butler had been shouted down at the Nottingham Church Congress for raising the issue of repeal of state regulation of vice.

[11] A. J. Mason, *Memoir of George Howard Wilkinson*, 2 vols (London, 1910), 1, pp. 240–1.

[12] Benson's ongoing commitment to social purity, referred to in his farewell address at Wellington College in 1873 and in his enthronement sermon, is a feature of his career neglected by historians.

for purity until his death in 1889. As president of the WCA, his partnership with Hopkins remained one of mutual respect throughout. She referred deferentially to his 'priceless co-operation and approval', whilst his assessment of the moral double standard – 'So long as the violation of purity is condoned in the one sex and visited with shame in the other, our unrighteousness and unmanliness must continue to work out its own terrible retribution'[13] – owed much to her influence. Nevertheless, the success with which the concept of male purity was circulated among the millions remained Hopkins's achievement alone. In a potent mixture of faith, chivalry, and military heroism, she portrayed the White Cross Army as a modern order of knighthood and its crusade, the demise of female ignominy.

* * *

On 14 February 1883, 300 Durham pitmen assembled at the Lightfoot Institute, Bishop Auckland, and pledged themselves to a higher moral standard of living. This, the inaugural meeting of the WCA, was the climax of a lengthy campaign by Hopkins against palliative principles of rescue work. In a paper entitled *A Plea for the Wider Action of the Church of England in the Prevention of the Degradation of Women*, submitted to the Lower House of Convocation in July 1879, she had condemned the Church Penitentiary Association's harsh regime as symptomatic of its indifference to an inequitable system of sexual morality which seemed only to 'cure the evil after it is done . . . and leave the vital factor, *the man,* untouched'.[14] A notebook entry by the Bishop of Lichfield's wife in 1880 recorded Hopkins's orations on the plight of the prostitute as capable of reducing the most forbidding bishop to tears.[15] Her entreaty for 'some agency that would infuse into young men a good strong, passionate sense of . . . the utter unmanliness of crushing and degrading women'[16] created just such a profound impression at the Derby Church Congress in 1882. The following year, the WCA and the CEPS were formed within three months of each other. The White Cross obligations drawn up at Durham attested well

---

[13] Cited in R. M. Barrett, *Ellice Hopkins. A Memoir* (London, 1907), p. 161.

[14] E. Hopkins, *A Plea for the Wider Action of the Church of England in the Prevention of the Degradation of Women* (London, 1879), p. 9. Hopkins had started her own rescue organization, the Ladies Assocation for the Care of Friendless Girls, in 1875.

[15] Cited in F. D. How, *William Dalrymple Maclagan, Archbishop of York* (London, 1911), pp. 223–4.

[16] Hopkins, *Plea*, p. 14.

434

to the idealization of male chivalry and affirmation of a single standard
of sexual chastity :

1   To treat all women with respect, and endeavour to protect them
    from wrong and degradation.
2   To endeavour to put down all indecent language and coarse jests.
3   To maintain the law of purity as equally binding upon men and
    women.
4   To endeavour to spread these principles among my companions,
    and to try and help my younger brothers.
5   To use every possible means to fulfil the commandment, 'Keep
    thyself pure.'[17]

In its very name – 'White standing for purity, the Army for
disciplined strength, and the Cross for the underlying truth that the
fight was for and in Christ'[18] – the WCA typified the militarization of
religious imagery common to the period. From its mid-century origins
Christian militarism had evolved as pre-eminent signifier of the manly
ideal where, as Olive Anderson has noted, the imperialism of late
Victorian culture manifested itself in the increasing 'para-militarism' of
religious work.[19] The WCA never adopted the outward accoutrements
promoted by many Christian youth movements. Yet its discourse and
values were intrinsically militaristic, with members addressed as
'Soldiers', and qualities of self-discipline, duty, and comradeship
perceived as integral to the battle against impurity. Military language
did much to ease the transmission of bourgeois ideals of sexual
respectability to the urban masses. While the CEPS canvassed for the
patronage of the rich, the WCA's cross-class appeal required a complex
presentation of purity to penetrate the barriers of social and economic
division. Middle-class men were encouraged to join through the
rhetoric of chivalrous service to the oppressed. Hopkins wooed working
men with the more radical suggestion that purity might 'protect their
own class from wrong' and form part of a larger demand for political
liberty. Neither she nor Lightfoot viewed the populist approach of the

[17] E. Hopkins, *Damaged Pearls. An Appeal to Working Men* (London, 1884), p. 3.
[18] Cited in Barrett, *Ellice Hopkins*, p. 157.
[19] O. Anderson, 'The growth of Christian militarism in mid-Victorian Britain', *EHR*, 86
(1971), p. 66. Anderson cites the emergence of the Salvation Army, Church Army, and Boys'
Brigade between 1878 and 1883 with military titles, ranks, and drilling procedures as
examples of such para-militarism.

White Cross as 'something set on foot for the improvement of the working-classes . . . alone'. Indeed, she believed purity would ultimately transcend class differences, 'realising a noble brotherhood beneath all class divisions in high thinking and pure living'.[20]

The WCA's ecumenicalism favoured its appeal amongst the urban industrial classes. The Congregationalist and leading northern industrialist, Frank Crossley, became a major benefactor, and Hopkins frequently exhorted Anglican colleagues to organize 'a friendly Conference with . . . the Nonconformist Ministers'. A Manchester purity meeting addressed by her in 1882 provided a model of interdenominational dialogue with Bishop Fraser, Alexander Maclaren, and Bishop Henry Vaughan sharing the same platform. Despite her High Church predisposition, Hopkins was fiercely anti-sectarian. The crusade for purity warranted absolute working flexibility, overwhelming denominational distinctions. 'It is of the utmost importance that "the blessed company of all faithful people" . . . should unite in attacking an evil which . . . will certainly be victorious over one division alone of the great army.'[21] Between 1883 and 1886, Hopkins's nationwide promotion of the White Cross took on revivalist proportions, with gatherings of between 800 and 2,000 men up and down the country.[22] Ever critical of the Church's reticence in discussing purity, she defended these controversial mass meetings as essential to the creation of a righteous public opinion, declaring 'the larger the meeting . . . the sounder and healthier the tone'. The major function of the White Cross was an educational one, seeking to combat the torrent of obscene material with a counter-stream of sound inculcations to a 'higher, purer more knightly type of manhood'.[23] As Hopkins advised her co-workers, 'The mass of the work of educating public opinion must be done by the quiet and unobtrusive agency of good, strong, racy, but carefully worded publications; dull and sermonesque little tracts . . . are not the flora which the fauna we have to deal with is known to feed on.'[24]

[20] Hopkins, *Damaged Pearls*, pp. 5, 2, 7.

[21] E. Hopkins, *The Purity Movement* (London, 1885), p. 17. Many of the 15,000 men who had committed themselves to purity by 1885 were nonconformists. See Bristow, *Vice and Vigilance*, p. 104.

[22] See Barrett, *Ellice Hopkins*, especially p. 181, for accounts of her gruelling itinerary between 1875 and 1888.

[23] E. Hopkins, *Ten Reasons Why I Should Join* (London, 1885), p. 3.

[24] Hopkins, *The Purity Movement*, p. 14.

As its major theorist, she composed all but four of a series of over thirty White Cross pamphlets during the 1880s and 1890s. Combining Christian morality with popular medical science, her dramatic but often dubious polemic dealt with a range of causes and solutions to adolescent male impurity.[25] Her literary output and campaigning successes earned her the open admiration of many Churchmen. Lightfoot described her as having done 'the work of ten men in ten years'.[26] Henry Scott Holland, who had invited her as the first woman to address Oxford undergraduates on the subject of purity, later observed, 'most women are very good speakers, but very few rise to distinct eloquence. She was one of the very few.'[27]

Lightfoot portrayed England in 1886 as 'dotted over with associations, guilds, brotherhoods and the like, enrolled under the White Cross banner'.[28] WCA meetings consisted of a devotional service or medical lecture on purity followed by prayer, after which newcomers were invited to receive the card of membership and pledge themselves to the obligations. The organizational structure of the White Cross was diverse in the extreme, composed of diocesan and municipal societies, university associations, and branches in the services at home and overseas.[29] The sensitivity of the topic and the plethora of current reform agencies made recruitment problematic. Hopkins advocated forming 'inner White Cross bands' within existing Bible classes, temperance societies, or (a particularly successful experiment in Scotland) youth organizations such as the YMCA.[30] Frustratingly for the historian, the strategy of institutional assimilation renders estimates of WCA membership highly uncertain. Hopkins herself noted that 'Scores of Branches are formed, and are quietly at work, and one only hears of them incidentally, or does not learn of them at all.'[31] As Edward Bristow has concluded, however, it is certain that social purity never rivalled numerically the efforts made on behalf of temperance.[32]

---

[25] Topics included the perils of schoolboy masturbation, incest, sanitation, divorce rates, employment conditions of working women, marriage, and motherhood.

[26] Cited in Barrett, *Ellice Hopkins*, p. 103.

[27] Ibid., p. viii of Holland's Introduction.

[28] Ibid., p. 183.

[29] See E. Hopkins, *The Standard of the White Cross* (London, 1885), pp. 5–6 for a summary of WCA administration. See also Bristow, *Vice and Vigilance*, pp. 136–8.

[30] Hopkins, *Standard*, p. 29.

[31] Ibid., p. 5.

[32] Bristow, *Vice and Vigilance*, p. 137. Bristow cites nineteen diocesan branches of the

In 1891 a formal but amicable amalgamation took place between
the WCA and the CEPS, under the eventual joint title of the White
Cross League. The structural eclecticism of the WCA and the loss of its
founders had seriously undermined its initial vitality and practicable
effectiveness by the late 1880s. Lightfoot retired as president in 1888
due to ill-health, and Hopkins's chronic invalidity enforced a reclusive
lifestyle soon after. As Sherwin Bailey has concluded, the WCA's
obvious connections with Anglicanism resulted in only 'nominal
support from Free Churchmen', whilst it suffered from 'want of
official relation to the Church of England'.[33] Ceasing to exist as a
formal institution after 1895, the ideals and spirit embodied in the
obligations of the White Cross Army continued to remain central to
the endeavours of the White Cross League. Hopkins's retirement to
Brighton failed to diminish her prolific publication rate. Requests for
purity literature continued well into the next century, and she
continued to write until her death in 1904. In excess of two million
of her tracts were in circulation by 1907.[34] Overseas demand and the
influential support of the colonial bishops ensured the propagation of
White Cross material throughout Australia, New Zealand, India, the
USA, Trinidad, South Africa, and Japan. Hopkins contemplated the
global diffusion of an English manhood with unreflecting imperialist
confidence, describing the influence of the British WCA over its 'vast
world empire' as 'the most hopeful and inspiring thought'.[35] The
phenomenal sale and distribution of White Cross literature at national
and international levels – the first annual report of the White Cross
Society in 1886 recorded sales of over seven hundred thousand copies
in the first three years – rendered Hopkins's influence in defining late
Victorian constructions of Christian manliness substantial.[36]

* * *

White Cross Society in the 1890s with 120 affiliated parochial associations and 1,150 central
subscribers.
    [33] Bailey, 'White Cross League', p. 6.
    [34] Figure cited in Barrett, *Ellice Hopkins*, p. 182. The White Cross League continued to
promote purity amongst men throughout the early decades of the twentieth century,
publishing books on topics such as contraception, divorce, and sex education for the young.
In 1923 these issues were included in courses throughout theological training colleges. The
League celebrated its fiftieth anniversary in 1933, and in 1939 its work was taken over by the
Church of England Moral Welfare Council. See Bailey, 'White Cross League', pp. 10–13.
    [35] Hopkins, *Standard*, p. 32.
    [36] Figures cited in Bailey, 'White Cross League', p. 5.

Purity remained a constant feature of Victorian definitions of masculinity from the Arnoldian creed of strenuous moral virtue to the robust muscular Christianity of Thomas Hughes, who, in *Tom Brown at Oxford*, declared purity as 'the crown of all real manliness'.[37] Hopkins both confirmed and revised the intrinsic connection between purity and manhood, utilizing a discourse of moral Darwinism which interpreted the individual struggle against the sins of the flesh through an evolutionary schema. Evolutionism suggested that masculinity was profoundly malleable.[38] All men encountered temptation, but with constant vigilance and a civilized environment, the 'true' man could control and redirect his 'lower' instincts for the benefit of society. Hopkins perceived sexual chastity as the ultimate manifestation of man's moral, physical, and spiritual progress. Not surprisingly, she remained unimpressed by medical arguments that excused male sexual urgency in terms of an unavoidable natural animalism. Man was no mere animal, but a 'self-conscious spiritual being' endowed with a conscience, the power of reason and a self-directing will. 'Men are . . . just as modest and full of personal self-respect and delicacy as women' she contested. '[I]n the whole of the animal creation . . . it is reserved for man alone to ill-treat . . . the mother of his children and his devoted companion, and then to turn round and say that in so doing he has obeyed the dictates of nature!'[39] Avowedly Augustinian in her belief that lust represented the enslavement of the higher moral senses, Hopkins was no Manichaean. Her concept of purity was shaped not by the punitive need to subjugate the flesh, but by a passionate desire to elevate and revere human corporeality. Men who defiled the sacramental status of the body by committing impure acts turned 'the temple of the Holy Ghost . . . into the devil's pigsty'.[40]

Aware of the limited appeal that the message of sexual chastity might have for men, the code of chivalry with its exaltation of the feminine provided Hopkins with a perfect symbolic system within which to frame her demands for the elimination of prostitution.[41]

---

[37] Thomas Hughes, *Tom Brown at Oxford* (London, 1889), p. 207.

[38] See Lucy Bland, *Banishing the Beast. English Feminism and Sexual Morality, 1885–1914* (London, 1995), pp. 70–91 for an extensive discussion of the 'multivalency' of Darwinian theories and their relevance to feminist moral reform.

[39] E. Hopkins, *Is it Natural?* (London, nd), p. 6.

[40] E. Hopkins, *The Temple of the Eternal* (London, nd), p. 2.

[41] See Mark Girouard, *The Return to Camelot: Chivalry and the English Gentleman* (London,

Filtered through the language of chivalry, her construal of masculinity as a battleground for purity took on a noble and glamorous heroism, with the contest for self-control depicted as the pre-eminent struggle of the modern knight. When the Dean of Gloucester spoke in 1885 of the consecration of manhood 'to be won by the knightly courage, and ... self-mastery, of the modern Arthurs and the modern Galahads',[42] he had in mind a chivalry equivalent to the Church's general mission to the poor and destitute. Hopkins appropriated the neo-medievalist spirit of ecclesiastical reform and used it to address the plight of women. The ideal knight-errant not only defended the wrongfully oppressed, he dedicated himself to the service of women, performing deeds of valour in their honour.[43] It was for the modern soldier of the White Cross to rescue womanhood anew through a life of sexual purity and heroic self-sacrifice.

This romantic ideal is illustrated in an episode taken from *The Ride of Death* (1883), where a young officer makes a gallant dash to rescue a camp-follower from enemy territory. His dramatic charge across enemy lines, swinging the woman up on to his horse and turning back into the 'ride of death', is brought to a literary climax by the corresponding chivalry of the opposing side who, having seen the gallant objective, 'downed muskets and fired not a shot. Out rang the cheers of the enemy, cheers ... echoed from the British lines as he passed over safely with that living trophy of his noble gallantry stamped true knight of God by the manly deed.'[44]

Hopkins's panegyrical narratives of mythical moral courage are given greater authenticity by frequent reference to contemporary heroes such as General Gordon, whose premature death in the service of God and Empire established him as a cult figure in the soldier-saint genre of religious eulogies.[45] Her portrayal of Gordon as the 'perfect embodiment' of English gallantry made skilful use of current patriotic fervour in articulating Christian manhood, as did her essay, *The National Flag*. Purity was vital to imperial advance, with Britain's rise

---

1981) for the pervasive neo-medievalism of Victorian culture. See also Vance, *Sinews of the Spirit*, pp. 17–26.

[42] 'Address by the Dean of Gloucester at Trinity College, Cambridge', *CEPS Papers for Men* (1885), p. 20.

[43] Girouard, *Return to Camelot*, p. 16.

[44] E. Hopkins, *The Ride of Death* (London, 1883), p. 3.

[45] See Girouard, *Return to Camelot*, p. 29; D. G. Johnson, 'The death of Gordon: a Victorian myth', *Journal of Imperial and Commonwealth History*, 10 (1982), pp. 285–310.

to economic and political supremacy contingent upon the superior chivalry of her manhood. 'Does not all history teach us that the welfare and very life of a nation is determined by moral causes, and that it is the . . . races that respect their women . . . that are the tough, prolific, ascendant races?'[46]

Strong links were forged between national progress, personal morality, and Christian family life. Unlike many critics who considered masculinity in terms of public codes of conduct alone, Hopkins's focus on sexual purity necessarily foregrounded the private, domestic sphere as a site of the formation and culmination of the Victorian manly ideal. In accordance with domestic ideology, female moral guidance was paramount – 'The woman is the heart of the man, the shaping and moulding influence of life', she wrote, 'who weaves . . . the finer tissues of his own character.'[47] Such explicit acknowledgement of womanly influence provides an instructive contrast to accounts that stressed masculine self-image and the feminized affections of home life as mutually exclusive categories. As John Tosh has argued, the 'extreme emotional reticence' of late Victorian manliness was due in large measure to the formal austerity of the disciplinarian father figure.[48] Hopkins interpreted male familial roles of husband and father as those of authoritative, benevolent patriarchs – 'the revelation of God in the pure family'. Yet, in pleading for a new domestic manliness, she also incorporated many corrective features attributed to womanhood, such as pity, compassion, tenderness, suffering, and love. Fathers were encouraged to overt displays of warmth and affection in the shared moral responsibility of teaching and training children.[49] Similarly, without countermanding male jurisdiction, the potential abuse of sexual and domestic power by the husband is mitigated by underscoring the biblical concept of male headship as service. In *Man and Woman; or, The Christian Ideal* (1883), the divine origins of spousal chivalry are explained: 'the man is to "love the woman, and give himself for her, as Christ loved the Church, and gave Himself for it". . . .

---

[46] E. Hopkins, *The National Flag* (London, nd), p. 16.

[47] E. Hopkins, *My Little Sister* (London, nd), pp. 7–8.

[48] J. Tosh, 'Domesticity and manliness in the Victorian middle class: the family of Edward White Benson', in J. Tosh and M. Roper, eds, *Manful Assertions: Masculinities in Britain since 1800* (London and New York, 1991), p. 65.

[49] 'Let your little girl get up on your knee, and nestle her childish head close to your strong heart. No safeguard to a girl like a kind father's love': E. Hopkins, *Little Kindnesses* (London, 1885), p. 8.

Not our idea of the self-sacrificing woman, but God's idea of the self-sacrificing man.'[50]

Commentaries on Christian manliness were primarily concerned to counter dominant perceptions of Christianity as a cowardly, unattractive proposition for men. Hopkins was no exception. 'Our Christianity is so feeble, so negative, so self-circumscribed, so peeping and peering and full of fears for itself, so wanting in bold heroic outlines and strong passions, that it has little power over young men.'[51] She resolved this dilemma by redescribing Christ in terms that proffered an attractive, compelling figure for men whilst simultaneously elevating her own particular definition of manhood to the status of divinity. As the incarnation of perfect manliness – 'He who came quite as much to reveal man as to reveal God'[52] – Christ was both heroic leader of men and loyal friend to women. Inspired by 'His love for His blessed mother, by His great Saviour's passion for the weak and defenceless',[53] Hopkins portrayed Christ as a chivalrous warrior, calling the WCA to a final apocalyptic battle against the Satanic forces of impurity. This representation of God who comes as 'Captain of the Host' with 'sword drawn in his hand'[54] was effectively contrasted with Jesus, the gentle, loyal advocate of women who made a prostitute his closest friend, and suffered women 'to minister to His human needs'.[55] Reverence for womanhood and purity of thought and action characterized his life:

It was to a woman that His last words were offered on the cross, and the first words were spoken of His risen life. . . . Nothing in the life of the true Man on earth stands out in more marked features than . . . His faith in women; as if to stamp it for ever as an attribute of all true manhood, that without which a man cannot be a man.[56]

* * *

[50] E. Hopkins, *Man and Woman; or, The Christian Ideal* (London, 1883), p. 9.
[51] Cited in Barrett, *Ellice Hopkins*, p. 22.
[52] Hopkins, *My Little Sister*, p. 4.
[53] E. Hopkins, *The Man with the Drawn Sword* (London, 1896), p. 8.
[54] Ibid., p. 7.
[55] Hopkins, *My Little Sister*, p. 5.
[56] E. Hopkins, *The Power of Womanhood* (London, 1899), p. 88.

The language of chivalry with its exalted reverence for womanhood owed much to those principal architects of the separate spheres ideology, Coventry Patmore and John Ruskin. Whether as 'angel' or 'queen', proponents of this quintessential Victorian model of gender relations endowed women with a severely circumscribed power-base compensated by domestic deification. From the superior moralizing piety of the wife and mother, social purity workers like Hopkins were able to subvert the constraints imposed upon women by these traditional roles, engaging in public moral philanthropy and adopting a position identical to that of the most radical feminist theoreticians. The demand for a single standard of sexual morality with its vision of transformed relations between women and men is an excellent example of the politicized, gender-based discourse of late-nineteenth-century Churchwomen. Female social purists successfully exerted pressure upon prevailing definitions of manliness, controlling and directing male sexuality in order to eradicate the degradation of women. The metaphor of chivalry lent itself well to this end. The depiction of men as noble, heroic protectors of their mothers, wives, sisters, and daughters was a discursive device seductive enough to inspire action, yet sanitized enough to allay fears of impropriety. Ultimately the ideological language of chivalry did little to challenge women's domestic confinement, and in this sense the liberative potential of its message was limited. Many of the attempts at purity education were undoubtedly excessive, misleading and, despite the inclusive, nondenominational approach of the WCA, plagued by class limitations.[57] Yet Hopkins's desire to speak out frankly on male sexual behaviour and place this discourse firmly within an ecclesiastical orbit was revolutionary indeed. Viewed in terms of the history of gender, her achievement was even more remarkable. In collusion *with* men, a notable cross-class alliance of working-class artisans and leading Church figures, she imposed a gender stereotype *upon* men, persuading them to adhere to a self-restricting construction of masculinity for the benefit of women. Such a feat required the deployment of subversive discourses of enormous subtlety and complexity.

The Churches' involvement in the social purity movement prompts careful revision of interpretations of Victorian masculinity that outline a discernible and relentless shift from piety to secular physicality. The

---

[57] See Bristow, *Vice and Vigilance*, pp. 125–53.

consolidation and expansion of public-school ideologies of athleticism during the second half of the century did indeed demand commitment to sporting activity as a significant means of defining the manly ideal.[58] What Norman Vance has described as the 'tyranny of games'[59] repeatedly displaced religion as the focus of worship. But the firmly Christocentric framework of purity definitions of manhood demonstrates that the shift from 'godliness to manliness' was not absolute. Rather, religious and secular ideologies continued to co-exist in the late Victorian era, overlapping and conflicting in emphases. Both the cult of athleticism and the campaign for male purity coincided in their consecration of the body as a 'living sacrifice', more often than not offered in the service of the Empire. When Hopkins advocated vigorous exercise, fresh air, and stoic endurance against the temptations of sensual indulgence, she echoed the neo-Spartan values of the public-school system. But here the parallels end. Against the tough, self-assured, imperial man trained in the harsh, competitive, Darwinian world of the irreligious English public school, Hopkins offered a self-negating vision of manhood.[60] Chivalrous self-sacrifice for women required total disempowerment before Christ, a heroic self-purging through 'the consuming fire of perfect Love'. A 'flight from domesticity' and denigration of home life was much in evidence in recruitment campaigns for the colonies and popular boys' literature at the turn of the century.[61] Against this trend, and at a time when concern over delayed marriages was increasingly connected with levels of prostitution, Hopkins prioritized Christian family life and the emotionally satisfying roles of husband and father.

Hopkins's concern to purify the public sphere led to a transference of the feminine values of the private realm directly into the public world of male conduct. In championing the feminized, domestic virtues of moral purity and compassion she suggested a Tennysonian ideal of 'manhood fused with female grace'.[62] This was no envisioning

[58] See J. A. Mangan, *Athleticism in the Victorian and Edwardian Public School: the Emergence and Consolidation of an Educational Ideology* (Cambridge, 1981).

[59] Vance, *Sinews of the Spirit*, p. 189.

[60] See J. A. Mangan, 'Social Darwinism and upper-class education in late Victorian and Edwardian England', in J. A. Mangan and James Walvin, eds, *Manliness and Morality. Middle-class Masculinity in Britain and America, 1800–1840* (Manchester, 1987), for a portrayal of the atheistic austerity of the public-school system.

[61] See Tosh, 'Domesticity and manliness', pp. 67–8.

[62] *In Memoriam*, Canto IX.17. See Marion Shaw, *Alfred Lord Tennyson* (New York and London, 1988), p. 83, for this reference within the context of Tennyson's ideal of manhood.

of an androgynous Utopia – the distinction between the sexes was maintained too firmly for that. Rather, the union of 'tenderness with strength' witnessed in her description of Christ anticipates a desire for men to assimilate within a masculine self-image the best qualities of womanhood. Integral to that end was a shared high standard of sexual chastity. To contend for a distinctively feminine definition of late Victorian masculinity would be premature. Yet Hopkins's instrumental didactic role in social purity via the edifice of the WCA suggests that when interpreting nineteenth-century doctrines of Christian manliness both content *and* author must be subject to gender analysis. As the recipients of divergent codes of manly conduct, women too had a stake in their construction.

Chichester Institute of Higher Education

NO MORE 'STANDING THE SESSION': GENDER AND THE END OF CORPORATE DISCIPLINE IN THE CHURCH OF SCOTLAND, c. 1890–c. 1930

by STEWART J. BROWN

I N 1890, the General Assembly of the established Church of Scotland appointed a Commission on the Religious Condition of the People, with instructions to carry out a comprehensive review of the state of religion and morals in the country. The aim was to determine the reasons for non-attendance at church services and for the Church's declining social influence. The Commission visited the presbyteries, and issued a series of reports between 1891 and 1896. These revealed widespread irreligion, non-attendance, intemperance, and vice. Among the most disturbing revelations, however, were the high levels of illegitimacy in many regions of the country. Sexual immorality, according to the report for the synod of Galloway, in the south west of Scotland, was 'a rampant sin in the district, and makes a dark blot on the moral life of [the] community'. In the Presbytery of Strathbogie, in the north east, sexual misconduct 'has so permeated family life, and is so prevalent in the community, that it is difficult to arouse a healthy and vigorous public opinion against it'.[1] The problem seemed to lie in the nature of ecclesiastical discipline within Scottish Presbyterianism. 'The mode of administering discipline', the Commission observed in its final report, in May 1896,

> at present fails to impress the community; it fails to promote repentance in offenders; and it may be asked whether, thus failing, it is not a hindrance rather than a help to the cause of morality. To the more sensitive and delicate in feeling who have yielded to temptation there is a natural repugnance in being obliged to face the minister and elders. . . . To those who

[1] 'Report of the Commission on the Religious Condition of the People', in *Reports on the Schemes of the General Assembly of the Church of Scotland* [hereafter *Reports*] (1895), pp. 746, 766.

447

have no such delicacy, the 'standing of the session' is little regarded.[2]

The administration of ecclesiastical discipline in the national Church, the Commission concluded, 'is only now the remnant of a fact which was once powerful'. The entire system needed revision.

The radical reform of the traditional system of ecclesiastical discipline in the early years of the twentieth century proved to be one of the more important events in the history of the Presbyterian Church of Scotland. For centuries, a defining characteristic of Scottish Presbyterianism had been its system of corporate discipline, by which offenders against a biblically-based moral code were summoned to 'stand the session' — that is, to appear before the kirk-session of minister and elders to be admonished and assigned a penance, which was usually performed in the presence of the entire community. From the Reformation of 1560 onwards, this system of corporate discipline had helped to shape the communal life of rural Scotland. It was a system in which moral authority was rooted in the parish community of believers, rather than in an ordained clergy or ecclesiastical hierarchy. By the end of the nineteenth century, however, the system was failing, and with it the godly commonwealth it was meant to uphold. A major reason for this were changes in attitudes regarding issues of sex and gender in late Victorian Scotland — changes that made it increasingly difficult for kirk-sessions of exclusively male elders to sit in judgement over women in cases involving extra-marital affairs. These changing perceptions about the proper approaches to gender-related issues in disciplinary procedures led after 1900 to the abandonment of the traditional, patriarchal system of kirk-session discipline in the established Church of Scotland, and the introduction of a more private, less gender-specific, and less judgemental system of pastoral counselling. The essay will explore the decline and fall of kirk-session discipline in the context of these changing attitudes to gender issues in late nineteenth- and early twentieth-century Scottish society.

* * *

At the Reformation, the exercise of discipline in the Christian life was given a central place in the national Church of Scotland. In the *Scots*

---

[2] *Reports* (1896), p. 817.

Confession of Faith of 1560, the effective administration of discipline was defined as one of the three distinctive 'notes', or marks, of the true Church — along with the preaching of the word and the administration of the sacraments.[3] The *Book of Discipline* of 1561 set forth a comprehensive programme for the social organization of the country, aimed at transforming Scotland into a godly commonwealth in which the social life of the nation would reflect the glory of God. It abolished the pre-Reformation system of private confession, penance, and absolution conducted by an ordained priest acting with the authority of the Catholic Church. Instead, reflecting the doctrine of the 'priesthood of all believers', the authority for maintaining Christian discipline was rooted in the parish community. The enforcement of discipline was entrusted to the religious leaders of the parish — the parish minister and the elders (usually about twelve in each parish) who together constituted an ecclesiastical court, or kirk-session. The standards of conduct enforced by the kirk-session were derived from Scripture, with every passage of both the Old and New Testaments held as the direct word of God and viewed as equally binding on individual conduct. Those involved in serious infractions, such as blasphemy, murder, and theft, were to be given over to the civil magistrate for punishment. But those involved in less serious offences, such as drunkenness, fornication, failure to observe the Sabbath, or disorderly conduct, were to be dealt with by the kirk-session. Discipline was to be imposed equally on persons of all social ranks and of both genders.

In its ideal, kirk-session discipline was to be voluntary, with offenders coming forward of their free will to confess their offences against God's law. To come before the kirk-session was regarded as a privilege, providing offenders with the opportunity to make their peace with both God and the parish community. In practice, however, discipline very soon took on a compulsory character, with most offences discovered by the minister or elders during their regular visitations, and with offenders summoned to appear before the session. The kirk-sessions would hear evidence and determine the truth of the charges. Once guilt had been established, the kirk-session would

---

[3] For accounts of kirk-session discipline in the Church of Scotland, see I. M. Clark, *A History of Church Discipline in Scotland* (Aberdeen, 1929), pp. 85–186; G. D. Henderson, *The Scottish Ruling Elder* (Aberdeen, 1935), pp. 100–45; A. Edgar, 'The discipline of the Church of Scotland', in R. H. Story, ed., *The Church of Scotland*, 5 vols (Edinburgh, nd), 5, pp. 427–556.

admonish the offender and assign a penance, which generally involved standing or sitting on a special repentance stool before the congregation, sometimes while wearing sackcloth, for a specified number of Sundays. The purpose of the public penance was to impress both the individual offender and the parish community with the seriousness of offences against God's law. Further, it was aimed at reconciling the offender with the community, by allowing the offender to expiate the offence openly and demonstrate contrition.[4] Those who refused to submit to the discipline of the kirk-session were denied the sacrament of communion and placed outside the parish community.

The seventeenth and early eighteenth centuries marked the period of the most vigorous exercise of kirk-session discipline in the Church of Scotland. This was, significantly, the era of the covenants and covenanting language, when many in Scotland perceived of themselves as members of an elect nation, which had entered into a covenant with God. The responsibilities of this covenant included the suppression of all offences against God's law. Secret sins might well bring down the just wrath of God upon the whole society; they therefore had to be brought into the open, confessed, and repented of before the community. Until the eighteenth century the dominance of the national Church over the religious life of Scotland was virtually unchallenged, and kirk-session discipline was applied over nearly the whole of the country. Kirk-session discipline was administered during those periods in the seventeenth century when the Church of Scotland was under Episcopal, as well as Presbyterian government. However, it became most identified with the Presbyterian system of church government, first introduced in the Church of Scotland during the early 1580s and finally established in the Church in 1690. The Presbyterian system of ecclesiastical courts, in which disciplinary decisions could be appealed from the kirk-sessions to the higher ecclesiastical courts — presbytery, synod, and General Assembly — helped to ensure a uniformity of practice among kirk-sessions throughout the country.[5] Kirk-session discipline and the idea of Scotland as a covenanted nation lay at the heart of the Scottish Presbyterian ethos.

In early modern Scotland, kirk-sessions were zealous in the suppression of alternative value systems to the Reformed or Calvinist

---

[4] Edgar, 'Discipline of the Church of Scotland', p. 466.

[5] R. Mitchison and L. Leneman, *Sexuality and Social Control: Scotland 1660–1780* (Oxford, 1989), p. 25.

social theology of the Church of Scotland. As well as acting against traditional folk beliefs and customs, kirk-sessions assumed a leading role in the brutal campaign to suppress witchcraft. But alongside this suppressive role, kirk-session discipline also served to strengthen communal responsibility and preserve basic social order at a time when the civil state was weak at the local level. Many kirk-sessions before the eighteenth century seem to have endeavoured to apply discipline equally to persons of both genders and all social ranks in the community, and to have considered a wide range of offences.[6] Until 1712, kirk-sessions could call upon the civil magistrate to imprison recalcitrant offenders against ecclesiastical discipline.[7]

During the eighteenth century, however, the system of kirk-session discipline grew more narrow and legalistic. The practice of public penance, when offenders appeared at church services before the assembled congregation, became much less frequent, and the repentance stool was removed from parish churches or preserved as an historical curiosity. Penance increasingly assumed the form of a fine levied on offenders, which in many parishes came to form a not insignificant part of the poor relief fund. From the 1730s, moreover, kirk-sessions gave less attention to efforts to regulate general social conduct and focused increasingly on offences related to extra-marital sex.[8] One cause of this change was the adoption of a new code of disciplinary procedures, the *Form of Process,* by the Church of Scotland in 1707. The *Form of Process* brought an increased legality into kirk-session discipline, emphasising the investigation of offences, the collection of evidence, and formal trial procedures. Evidence for many offences was difficult to obtain in the form required by a legal court. For sexual offences, however, the evidence was often obvious, at least for the woman.[9] Discipline therefore became increasingly restricted to sexual offences, and especially to the admonishment of unwed mothers. The communal character of kirk-session discipline was also weakened by the growth of dissent in early eighteenth-century Scotland. Following the Scottish Toleration Act of 1712, kirk-sessions could no longer call on the civil magistrates for support against

[6] J. di Folco, 'Discipline and welfare in the mid-seventeenth century Scots parish', *Records of the Scottish Church History Society*, 19 (1977), pp. 169–83.

[7] Mitchison and Leneman, *Sexuality and Social Control*, p. 20.

[8] L. Leneman and R. Mitchison, 'Acquiescence in and defiance of Church discipline in early-modern Scotland', *Records of the Scottish Church History Society*, 25 (1993), pp. 20–1.

[9] Clark, *History of Church Discipline*, pp. 178–9.

recalcitrant offenders. Those unhappy with disciplinary actions by kirk-sessions found themselves increasingly free to leave the parish church and join a dissenting congregation.

In the first half of the nineteenth century, there was an effort to revive a wide-ranging kirk-session discipline within the Church of Scotland. This movement was associated with a larger Evangelical-led campaign to restore the traditional parish system and expand the influence and authority of the national Church.[10] A number of publications appeared, defining the work of the eldership and calling for renewed supervision of the moral life of parish communities.[11] While most disciplinary action still focused on fornication, many kirk-sessions in the 1840s and 1850s also considered cases of intemperance, disorderly conduct, and unfair business practice.[12] This revival of kirk-session discipline, however, was weakened by the Disruption of the Church of Scotland in 1843, which contributed significantly to the fragmentation of Victorian Presbyterianism.

During the second half of the nineteenth century, kirk-session discipline in the Church of Scotland ceased its broad moral coverage, and again became restricted almost exclusively to cases of extra-marital sex. Kirk-sessions in the Church of Scotland also became reluctant to attempt to discover the fathers, and as a result discipline became more gender-specific, directed primarily at unwed mothers whose 'guilt' was generally obvious. The nineteenth-century Church increasingly took the view that in cases of sexual immorality, the blame lay mainly with the women who became pregnant, and not with the fathers, who were simply acting according to their nature.[13] Further, as children of unwed mothers frequently became burdens on the poor relief rolls, the admonishment of unwed mothers was viewed as necessary for holding parish poor relief costs down. Thomas Chalmers, whose views on poor relief profoundly influenced nineteenth-century practice, had argued that unwed mothers and their children should be denied any

---

[10] R. Buchanan, *The Ten Years' Conflict*, 2 vols, 2nd edn (Glasgow, 1852), I, pp. 333–7. I am grateful to Prof. Hugh McLeod for reminding me of this nineteenth-century revival.

[11] E.g., J. G. Lorimer, *The Eldership of the Church of Scotland* (Glasgow, 1842); D. King, *Ruling Eldership of the Christian Church* (Edinburgh, 1846); J. McKerrow, *Office of the Ruling Elder* (Edinburgh, 1846).

[12] A. A. MacLaren, *Religion and Social Class. The Disruption Years in Aberdeen* (London, 1974), pp. 128–30, 144; P. Hillis, 'Presbyterianism and social class in mid-nineteenth-century Glasgow: a study of nine churches', *JEH*, 32 (1981), pp. 47–64; C. Brown, *The Social History of Religion in Scotland since 1730* (London, 1987), p. 152.

[13] Mitchison and Leneman, *Sexuality and Social Control*, p. 10.

parish poor relief.[14] While this did not become general policy, submission to kirk-session discipline could be seen as a means of becoming one of the 'respectable poor' who were more likely to be treated decently by poor relief authorities and voluntary charity societies. Kirk-sessions exercised considerable authority over poor relief before the passing of the Scottish Poor Law Act of 1845. Even after the passing of that Act and the setting up of new Poor Law districts and elected Poor Law boards, kirk-sessions retained a statutory representation on the Poor Law Boards until 1894, giving them a continuing voice in the distribution of relief to unwed mothers.[15]

By the end of the nineteenth century, kirk-session discipline was clearly failing to achieve its larger social aims. The reports of the Church of Scotland Commission on the Religious Condition of the People in the early 1890s revealed that large numbers did not attend church, and that the traditional Christian social order had largely collapsed. There was widespread intemperance, crime, non-observance of the Sabbath, and social unrest. Perhaps most disturbing were the reported high rates of illegitimacy.[16] Despite the long-standing focus of kirk-session discipline on unwed mothers, Scotland's overall illegitimacy rate (8 per cent) was considerably higher than that of Ireland (1.7 per cent) and England (5 per cent).[17] The rate, moreover, varied considerably from district to district, with particularly high rates in the rural north east and south west of the country. In Banffshire and Aberdeenshire in the north east of Scotland, the illegitimacy rate was nearly 13.2 per cent of all births in 1894. In the south west of Scotland, the presbytery of Wigton reported an illegitimacy rate of nearly 17 per cent between 1885 and 1891, and that of Dumfries had an illegitimacy rate of 14.4 per cent in 1890. Illegitimacy rates were higher in rural parishes than in the towns. A break-down of figures for the presbytery of Dumfries revealed that in 1890 the illegitimacy rate in rural parishes was 18.5 per cent, compared to only 12.6 per cent in town parishes.[18]

[14] T. Chalmers, *On the Christian and Economic Polity of a Nation*, in *Collected Works*, 25 vols (Glasgow, 1835–42), 2, pp. 122–8.

[15] Henderson, *The Scottish Ruling Elder*, p. 233; MacLaren, *Religion and Social Class*, pp. 150–1.

[16] For a discussion of Scottish illegitimacy in the nineteenth century, see T. C. Smout, 'Aspects of sexual behaviour in nineteenth century Scotland', in A. A. MacLaren, ed., *Social Class in Scotland: Past and Present* (Edinburgh, 1976), pp. 55–85.

[17] 'Report on the Commission on the Religious Condition of the People', in *Reports* (1894), pp. 734–5.

[18] *Reports* (1894), p. 762; *Reports* (1895), pp. 751, 766, 788.

For much of the nineteenth century, the Church had argued that the towns and cities, where parish discipline was weakest, were areas of particular immorality, while the rural parishes, where kirk-session discipline was at its strongest, maintained higher moral standards. The reports of the Commission, however, seemed to indicate that the reverse was true, and that kirk-session discipline might well have a negative impact on sexual morals. The Church was also concerned over the large numbers of illegitimate children who were not being presented for baptism in the national Church. In the presbytery of Dumfries, for example, only about 30 per cent of illegitimate children were baptized in the Church of Scotland.[19] Unwed mothers were apparently becoming less willing to submit to kirk-session discipline in order to have their children baptized, and either were joining a denomination in which discipline was not enforced or were giving up all Church affiliation. Thus, it appeared, the system of kirk-session discipline was not only proving ineffective at suppressing sexual activity outside marriage, but was also acting against evangelical priorities.[20] The Commission's reports, moreover, suggested that the existing patriarchal system, by which women were summoned to appear before a kirk-session of middle-aged or elderly men for admonishment on sexual matters, was less than effective. 'Women and girls', the Commission observed in its final report of 1896, 'can be best reached by women. Women alone can freely speak to them, watch over them, fortify them against temptation, and seek to win their lives for Christ.'[21] The system of kirk-session discipline, the Commission concluded, was in need of radical reform.

* * *

In response to the recommendations of the Commission on the Religious Condition of the People, the General Assembly of 1896 instructed its standing Committee on Christian Life and Work to conduct a thorough inquiry into the system of kirk-session discipline. The Committee, accordingly, sent a set of questions on discipline to every parish kirk-session in the Church of Scotland. A summary of responses from 1059 kirk-sessions (about two-thirds of the total number of kirk-sessions in the Church) was presented in the report

[19] *Reports* (1895), pp. 788–9.
[20] *Reports* (1896), p. 818.
[21] Ibid., p. 816.

of the Christian Life and Work Committee to the General Assembly of 1897.[22] The responses revealed that kirk-session discipline was still being administered in the large majority of parishes. Only 118 parishes reported that they had had no cases of discipline during the past five years, while the remainder claimed to have 'a sufficiently large' number of cases. Discipline was now restricted almost exclusively to offences of a sexual nature. While a few cases involved drunkenness, or (less frequently) slander, theft, or quarrelling, the vast majority, 'over 99%', involved extra-marital sexual relations. There was also a considerable variation in the procedures governing kirk-session discipline in the different parishes, with many parishes having departed from the procedures defined by the *Form of Process* of 1707, even though the *Form* remained the law of the Church.

Nearly all cases of discipline now involved communicants or would-be communicants, reflecting the fact that in most of Scotland kirk-session authority had ceased to be recognized outside the congregations of the Church. Virtually all cases, moreover, originated by voluntary confession on the part of the offenders, and only rarely by complaint or information provided by others. The usual evidence of contrition required by the minister and kirk-sessions included humble submission to rebuke and admonishment, promise of 'greater watchfulness' in the future, and regular attendance at church services. Offenders were also required to go through a probationary period of between three months and two years before being allowed to take communion. In two-thirds of the responding parishes, offenders appeared before the full kirk-session for open confession and admonishment. The remaining third of the parishes, however, had adopted a system by which the minister, or the minister accompanied by one or two elders, dealt with offenders privately. Indeed, such private counselling had become the general practice in urban parishes, although it marked a clear departure from the idea of corporate discipline in Scottish Presbyterianism. According to the responses, the effectiveness of discipline in Scotland was being seriously hindered by such diversity of procedures. With each parish evolving its own procedures, the result was confusion in the public mind over the Church's moral standards.[23]

---

[22] 'Report of the Committee on Christian Life and Work', *Reports* (1897), pp. 719–26.
[23] Ibid., pp. 723–4.

Many of the parish responses expressed discomfort with the injustice of an ecclesiastical discipline that had become almost exclusively concerned with sexual offences. Responses from kirk-sessions referred to the 'inconsistency, and perhaps unfairness, of summoning people for discipline only for the sin of impurity', while other equally serious infractions were ignored.[24] There was also uneasiness with the idea of keeping a permanent record of sexual infractions in the kirk-session minute-book, as required by the *Form of Process*, so that persons who went on to become exemplary parents were 'pilloried there for ever'. Further, concern was expressed over the unequal treatment of men and women in disciplinary cases. Some responses observed that male offenders were reluctant to appear voluntarily with their female partners before the kirk-sessions. The kirk-sessions, moreover, which often included the 'daily companions' of guilty men, were reluctant to require male offenders to appear.[25] The result was that men seldom underwent discipline alongside their female partners, and discipline had become largely a matter of young pregnant women appearing before a group of older men to be admonished on their sexual conduct.

Over 300 of the responding parish kirk-sessions called for the radical reform of the existing system of ecclesiastical discipline. This view found support in the Report of the Committee on Christian Life and Work in 1897. The disciplinary procedures, insisted the Report, required amendment 'in light of the changed circumstances of our time'. Discipline needed to be made less a 'mere form' to be got through, which all too frequently served only to harden or embitter the character of the offender. It had to be made more 'gentle, religious and spiritually helpful to those submitting to it, and affectionate and prayerful on the part of those who have to represent the Church in the discharge of it'.[26] In response to the Committee's recommendations, the General Assembly of 1897 appointed a special Committee on Discipline in Kirk-Sessions to formulate reform proposals, and the following year the Committee presented an overture, or motion, for new procedures to govern ecclesiastical discipline. The overture was sent to the presbyteries for approval according to Church law, and of the eighty-one reporting presbyteries, a majority of forty-five approved the act, while twenty-nine disapproved and seven called

---

[24] 'Report of the Committee on Christian Life and Work', *Reports* (1897), p. 724.
[25] Ibid., p. 723.
[26] Ibid., pp. 725–6.

for further consideration. While a substantial minority of presbyteries were clearly unhappy with the reform proposals, the Act for revising Church discipline was formally approved by the General Assembly of 1902.[27]

According to the Act of 1902, accused persons were still to be permitted to appear before the assembled kirk-session for discipline, and this was to remain the norm in most cases. But the Act also specified an alternative, more private procedure. When the accused was unwilling to 'stand the session', the minister and one elder were to meet with the person privately, and then report the results of the meeting to the kirk-session. If satisfied that the case would be better handled privately, the kirk-session could delegate the minister and elder to dispose of the case by a further meeting or meetings with the accused. Instead of judgement and admonition, these meetings were to consist of prayer, questions about the offence, personal counselling, and, if confession was made, a statement of absolution. Minutes of these private meetings were to be kept in a special discipline book, to demonstrate that the minister and elder were acting in the name and by the authority of the whole kirk-session. After five years, however, the names in the discipline book were to be blotted out, so that no permanent record would remain to bring shame upon those who had answered for their conduct, or upon their children. The new Act endeavoured to provide more equal treatment of women and men. In cases involving fornication, if the kirk-session was satisfied that the woman was telling the truth in naming her partner, it was required to proceed against the man even if he denied paternity. Accused persons who refused to submit to discipline within forty days of being summoned were to be suspended from communion and other church privileges.[28] No more was discipline to consist almost exclusively of requiring unwed mothers to 'stand the session'.

The Act of 1902 in effect transferred responsibility for discipline in the national Church of Scotland from the kirk-session to the individual minister. In nearly all parishes, ministers and kirk-sessions took advantage of the provisions of the Act to dispense entirely with the practice of 'standing the session'. Very soon after 1902, discipline cases

[27] H. M. B. Reid, ed., *The Layman's Book of the General Assembly of 1900* (Edinburgh, 1900), p. 143; idem, *The Layman's Book of the General Assembly of 1901* (Edinburgh, 1901), p. 187.
[28] 'Overture on the Form of Process', *Reports* (1899), pp. 1092–4; K. M. Boyd, *Scottish Church Attitudes to Sex, Marriage and the Family 1850–1914* (Edinburgh, 1980), p. 157.

routinely ceased to come before the kirk-session, and instead offenders were counselled by the minister in private meetings. The required minutes of the counselling sessions were generally neglected. By 1935 the special discipline book required by the Act of 1902 was, according to the Church of Scotland minister and historian G. D. Henderson, 'very much of a farce', with few churches keeping a record.[29] The Scottish Presbyterian ideal of confession, admonition, and penance in the presence of the elders of the parish community was given up. For the historian I. M. Clark, writing in 1929, the Act of 1902 represented a turning away from the Presbyterian ideal of communal discipline and a return to the pre-Reformation system of private confession and private penance. 'Thus the history of the Christian Church', Clark observed, 'Catholic and Protestant, seems to point to the fact that a human soul cannot be dealt with by a court, but only by another individual.' However, he added, there was a significant difference between the system of private counselling adopted by the Church of Scotland in 1902 and the private confessional of the Roman Catholic Church. In the Catholic confessional the priest represented the authority of the whole Church. In the system of counselling now emerging in the Church of Scotland, the minister was generally viewed as expressing his own private opinions.[30] There was another difficulty. Few ministers had the training or inclination to enter into the system of private counselling in sexual matters. It was one thing for an inquiry into sexual relations to be carried on by a kirk-session, claiming to represent the moral authority of Scripture. It was something very different for such an inquiry to be carried on privately between a minister and a young woman. As a result, even the Act of 1902, with its provisions for private counselling, was neglected in many parishes.

* * *

Kirk-session discipline within the national Church of Scotland had, by the closing decades of the nineteenth century, become little more than a remnant of a once powerful system. From endeavouring to impose rigorous standards of Christian social conduct on parish communities, the system had narrowed to one of obliging unwed mothers to 'stand the session' in order to receive needed support from the Church and poor relief authorities. The Act of 1902 brought an end to even this

[29] Henderson, *The Scottish Ruling Elder*, p. 289.
[30] Clark, *History of Church Discipline*, p. 211.

remnant of kirk-session discipline. In part, this reflected the waning of the puritan idea of the godly commonwealth, and the introduction of a more individual, private form of religion, impatient with the imposition of standards of behaviour from outside, and more concerned with the free development of personality. The Church was to be more a guide for behaviour than an authoritative source of discipline. Perhaps equally important, the end of kirk-session discipline was a response to new, more positive attitudes toward women in the late Victorian Church of Scotland. Kirk-sessions had grown uncomfortable with a system that had come to place blame almost exclusively on women in matters of extra-marital sex, while regarding men as simply acting in accordance with their more robust natures. For those familiar with stories of wronged women through the realistic novels of Thomas Hardy, George Gissing, and Leo Tolstoi, the idea of a group of older male elders sitting in judgement over a pregnant young woman was increasingly unacceptable. Nor could the elders draw strength from the idea that they were simply declaring the clear moral imperatives embodied in Scripture. The higher criticism of the biblical scholars had demonstrated that the books of Scripture had been composed at different historical periods. They reflected the social and cultural context in which they had been written, and could not be viewed as an infallible authority for gender relations in the modern world. The increasing independence of women meant that fewer women were prepared to submit voluntarily to a discipline conducted exclusively by men. At the same time, the development of secularized social services, including the removal of kirk-session representatives from the Poor Law Boards in 1894, meant that women had less need to 'stand the session'.

The Scottish Reformers had defined the administration of discipline as one of the three 'notes', or marks, of the true Church. The waning of discipline, therefore, raised questions about the nature and identity of the Presbyterian Church of Scotland. Following the loss of their functions in administering discipline, the role of the elders in the Church was no longer clear. Nor was it clear how the national Church could exercise influence over the broader society.[31] Writing on the 'Decline of Discipline' in 1918 at the request of the Church of Scotland Commission on the War, the Church of Scotland minister W. S. Bruce

---

[31] Boyd, *Scottish Church Attitudes*, p. 158.

admitted that few lamented the end of the 'despotic authority' exercised by kirk-sessions under the old system of discipline. 'That system', he observed, 'is gone, never to return' and 'kirk-sessions to-day exercise formal discipline to a very limited extent'. At the same time, Bruce also expressed concern over the decline of Sabbath observance and the growth of crime and immorality, and questioned how the Church could hope ever again to influence the moral standards of society.[32] That question remains unresolved. And yet the end of kirk-session discipline also contributed to the emergence of a less patriarchal and judgemental Church of Scotland, and one in which women could have a more active and equal role.

The University of Edinburgh

---

[32] W. S. Bruce, 'Decline of discipline', in W. P. Paterson and D. Watson, eds, *Social Evils and Problems* (Edinburgh, 1918), pp. 148, 155.

GENDER IN SARAWAK: MISSION AND RECEPTION

by BRIAN TAYLOR

THE interaction of gender and religion affects a developing as much as a developed church. A missionary church raises appropriate issues not merely as they affect those spreading the message, but as they affect the receivers, both immediately and in a later period of establishment. This paper deals with such matters as they appear in the history of the Anglican Church in Sarawak, where the missionary activity began in 1848.

Sarawak lies along the north west coast of Borneo, stretching for some 500 miles, and covering about one sixth of the island. From 1841 until 1946 it was ruled by the Brooke dynasty of Rajahs. Thereafter it was a British colony until 1963, when it joined the new nation of Malaysia. While the focus here is on Sarawak itself, it is not possible totally to exclude developments in Brunei (now Brunei Darussalam), and in British North Borneo (now the Malaysian state of Sabah).

The development of the Anglican Church in Sarawak provides a neatly compact opportunity to offer a case study of the links between gender and Christianity in the missionary context. Within that context, this paper in turn considers the connections between gender and missionary roles amongst the Europeans spreading the Anglican message in the first stages of the missionary effort; the effect of gender relations among the indigenous Iban on their reception of the missionaries' message; and finally the gendered response to attempts to implant Anglican religious orders in the territory in the twentieth century.

* * *

In the north nave aisle of Winchester Cathedral is a modest mosaic wall memorial, made by Powell of Whitefriars in 1864, commemorating Francis McDougall, missionary and first Bishop of Labuan and Sarawak. It also bears the name of his wife, Harriette, who died a little before him, and words similar to ones suggested by the Bishop: 'SHE FIRST TAUGHT CHRIST TO THE WOMEN OF BORNEO.'[1] As

---

[1] Charles John Bunyon, *Memoires of Francis Thomas McDougall . . . and of Harriette his Wife* (London, 1889), p. 21.

the inscription implies, she was more than an accompanying wife. David Bosch, in *Transforming Mission*, has claimed that in America mission auxiliary associations provided women with the first significant opportunity to take leading roles in social life, from the eighteenth century onwards, and then to go further. 'They went out, literally to the ends of the earth, no longer just as the wives of missionaries but as missionaries in their own right', in fact, if not in theory.[2] It was the case in Britain too.

Harriette was born into a family with missionary connections and interest, 'and she had been taught from her early childhood to believe the cause to be a holy one'.[3] Her elder sister, Sarah Frances Bunyon, married J. W. Colenso, who was to become the controversial Bishop of Natal.

A mission to Sarawak was approved by Rajah James Brooke in 1846. Neither the Society for the Propagation of the Gospel nor the Church Missionary Society could undertake this new task, so a committee was formed to raise funds and select the missionaries. The chosen leader was Francis McDougall, who was a surgeon as well as a priest. The missionary party reached Sarawak on 29 June 1848, and within a few weeks the first attempts at starting schools were made.[4] The deacon, W. B. Wright, began a class for men, and Mrs McDougall had a class for women and girls. In August Wright began a day school for boys. Very soon four half-caste children were adopted by the mission, with the encouragement of the Rajah. 'They were running about in the bazaar, and their native mothers were willing to part with them; so Mary, Julia, Peter, and Tommy were housed in a cottage close by. . . . They were baptized on Advent Sunday, 1848, and were the beginning of our native school', the Home School, two boys and two girls.[5] It is not recorded whether

---

[2] David J. Bosch, *Transforming Mission* (New York, 1991), p. 328.

[3] Bunyon, *Memoires*, p. 21.

[4] For the history of the Anglican Church in Sarawak see Graham Saunders, *Bishops and Brookes* (Singapore, 1992); Brian Taylor, *The Anglican Church in Borneo 1848–1962* (Bognor, 1983); from 1909 *The Chronicle*, the magazine of the Borneo Mission Association (the name was changed to *The Borneo Chronicle* in 1934).

[5] Harriette McDougall, *Sketches of Our Life at Sarawak* (London, 1882), p. 20. Further information about the early attempts can be found in this book, and, with later developments, in Brian Taylor and Pamela Mildmay Heyward, *The Kuching Anglican Schools* (Kuching, 1973). For mission schools, not only Anglican, see Ooi Keat Gin, 'Mission education in Sarawak during the period of Brooke rule, 1840–1946', *Sarawak Museum Journal* [hereafter *SMJ*], 42, ns no. 63 (1991), pp. 283–373.

their European fathers, all named in the baptism register, gave their approval, or contributed to their children's maintenance. Before the pattern of schools was established that was to continue, there were various attempts and experiments. Harriette McDougall, despite bearing and burying a child almost every year up to 1853, when they began to survive, took a full share in this side of the Church's work. It had not been part of any contract, 'but', as her brother wrote, 'when anything presented itself to be done which she could deem a duty, she threw herself into it at once and pursued it with all her energy'.[6] She was very ably assisted by the servant, Elizabeth Richardson, who had accompanied the party from England.

Plans were made for professional women missionaries when the McDougalls were in England cn leave, 1852–4. The Borneo Female Mission Fund was established, and two women set sail in 1854. Miss Browne abandoned the cause when they reached Calcutta, and Miss Williams resigned before a year was over, after a suicide attempt. The third and last missionary supported by the fund reached Sarawak at the end of 1856, Elizabeth Woolley, a cousin of Mrs McDougall. She was a formidable woman of extreme Protestant views, who married and managed Walter Chambers, the first priest to follow McDougall to Borneo, and later the second Bishop of Labuan and Sarawak. That same year, mission history took a step forward, when SPG sent abroad its first woman missionary. Sarah Coomes, from Birmingham, arrived in Sarawak in August. She worked hard in the town, surviving the Chinese revolt of February 1857, and later was sent to the mission station at Lundu. She did her best, but she was too old to adapt herself to the life, and soon went to teach in Singapore. She was not used very kindly by Mrs McDougall and Miss Woolley, who treated her more or less as a servant, not accepting her as a *lady*.

The revolt was a serious setback for the mission, particularly with regard to women's work, as trust among communities was damaged. About the end of 1858 Mrs McDougall wrote, 'We have not any place now for a single woman's mission, nor since the Chinese outbreak has there been any definite work for one to do, as the Malay ladies are not so approachable as they were formerly.'[7] Some additional help was given by married women. Not until the early years of Bishop Hose, consecrated in 1881, were more women missionaries recruited; but the

[6] Bunyon, *Memoires*, p. 44.
[7] Ibid., p. 182.

delay was caused by lack of opportunity or availability, rather than by policy.

Wright had considered that boys and girls should be taught together, but Francis McDougall knew that co-education would exclude Malay girls, so separate teaching was the policy in the town, except in the small Christian Home School. Village schools, as they opened with the spread of mission stations, were necessarily mixed – as soon as parents consented to send their daughters. Now, in 1996, only in Kuching are there separate boys' and girls' schools. In other places, such as Linton's Betong (mentioned below), they have been amalgamated. It was not until the episcopate of G. F. Hose that girls' education in the capital became firmly established. Before that there had been no reluctance on the part of the Church to welcome girls, where there were suitable people to teach them. The reluctance was more with the families, who could see no value in education for girls. Equal opportunity was demonstrated in the career of Julia Steward, one of the bazaar children adopted by the mission in 1848. When she was fifteen years old, the McDougalls took her to Dublin, where she entered the Irish Church Education School – the first person from Borneo to go overseas for further education. Two years later, in 1862, she returned to Sarawak and took charge of the classes for girls.

A short summary can do no more than illustrate what is consistently borne out by all the evidence available of nearly a century and a half of Sarawak Church history. Apart from the barrier to ordination, men and women have served the mission and the developing Church according to their abilities. Furthermore their work was equally well reported to English supporters. In the eyes of SPG some of the women may have been only accompanying wives, but that did not hinder initiative when opportunity came. Dr Mabel Allen may not have a place in the index of the official history of SPG, of which she was a mere honorary missionary, and may only be mentioned, without her name, as the wife of G. D. Allen, but she was by far the stronger character, and while they were at Banting in the Second Division of Sarawak, 1904–14, she set up and ran a village hospital.[8] Unmarried women did not work under the shadow of the men, but held their posts with full responsibility, as teachers or parish workers, and later, in health care. Miss Ada Cubitt came as a mission teacher in 1913, but

[8] H. P. Thompson, *Into All Lands* (London, 1951), p. 657.

finished her Borneo Service as matron of the government leper camp, where she was also honorary catechist. It was moved to the offshore island of Satang. 'I am very sorry for her', wrote Bishop Danson.[9] Miss Edith Andrews was head of St Mary's School Kuching from 1916 to 1951, and would be regarded by many as one of the most distinguished missionaries and educationalists that Borneo has known. This is what the people saw, and they responded, with mission schoolgirls, whether Christian or not, growing up to take their place in the life of the country, equally with the men.

A. B. Champion became Vicar of Kuching at the end of 1922. On the lines of the Church of England's Enabling Act, 1919, he very soon set up a church council. It had its first woman member, Miss Chan Ah Soo in 1924 – probably outstripping not a few English parishes.

* * *

The Iban, often called the Sea Dayaks, are the largest native race in Sarawak. They are believed to have entered the present state from the Kapuas river system in what is now Indonesian Borneo, and to have settled in the upper waters of the Batang Lupar and Saribas. This may have been in the eighteenth century, or perhaps as early as the sixteenth. Where they came from before that, whether from Sumatra or elsewhere, is a matter of conjecture. Successive census reports showed that they were about one third of the population, more numerous than the Chinese. More recently the proportion had dropped to 29.6 per cent by 1986, and it was expected that the Chinese would outnumber them by 1990.[10]

The traditional way of life of the Iban was based on growing rice, which provided food as well as nourishment for their spiritual and moral well-being. The annual cycle, from preparing the land to rejoicing in the harvest, gave the framework upon which social and economic life depended. Land given over to hill padi yields very low productivity, and this was the cause of the immigration, looking for new land to farm. The Iban have a very strong sense of local community, and so they have favoured the longhouse rather than a village of separate houses. Because of the need to move on, in the search for new farms, the longhouse of the past was usually not built in

---

[9] *Borneo Chronicle* (Nov. 1924), p. 4.
[10] Joseph Ko Tee Hock, 'A socioeconomic study of the Iban today', *SMJ*, 40, ns no. 61 (1989), Part 4, p. 81.

a substantial way; the posts were flimsy and the floors of split bamboo rather than expensive planks. The search for land also implied the defeat and expulsion of those who already lived there; but this was not regretted by the warlike Iban, and gave them the opportunity for satisfying another need. They were the headhunters of Borneo. Headhunting was discouraged and then prohibited by Rajah James Brooke from the 1850s, but by no means always effectually. From their first settlements in Sarawak the Iban spread eastwards and northwards, and there were some large movements into the north of the state in the first third of this century. With roads and modern communications, Iban families can be found in the towns and all parts of Sarawak.

The Iban are once again the subject of intense study of all aspects of their history and culture, based on the Department of Anthropology in the College of William and Mary, Williamsburg, and a three-volume encyclopedia is soon to appear. Nonetheless the value of earlier writings cannot ever be under-rated, especially those of the English missionary clergyman John Perham, who worked among the Iban from 1868 to 1888, and of the Labuan-born Eurasian priest William Howell, who worked in the Undup for fifty years from 1878.[11]

After considering some other possibilities, Bishop McDougall decided that a mission to the Iban should be the first rural station; and Walter Chambers was taken to Skrang, a tributary of the upper Batang Lupar, in October 1851, seven months after his arrival in Sarawak. This was in the heart of the Iban territory. Quite soon, early in 1853, it was decided that Skrang was in an area far too unsettled for a mission station, and indeed fighting broke out the day after Chambers left. A new start was made at Banting, on a tributary much lower down the Batang Lupar, and this became the centre of Iban work. The first baptisms, of four men, were on Christmas Day, 1854. From this beginning the Church has grown among the Iban. Of the twenty full parishes in Sarawak now, six are in this area, which has always been the principal field for Anglican rural work. There are three other parishes, mainly Iban, in other parts of the state, and Iban families in all the town congregations. Those who settled further east have been in the field of Roman Catholic and Methodist missions.

---

[11] John Perham, articles in *The Journal of the Straits Branch of the Royal Asiatic Society*, 1878–87; William Howell, articles written for the *Sarawak Gazette*, collected in Anthony Richards, ed., *The Sea Dyaks and other Races of Sarawak* (Kuching, 1963); also idem, *Sarawak – Historical Notes* [written c. 1928] (Guildford, 1993).

The evangelizing of the Iban was not easy, much of the difficulty being caused by the attitude of the women. Mrs McDougall recorded this, from the experience of the missionaries.

> Christianity had strong opponents in the women of all the Dayak tribes. They held important parts in all the feasts, incantations, and superstitions. . . . The women encouraged head-taking by preferring to marry the man who had some of these ghastly tokens of his prowess. . . . For many years . . . the women were opposed to a religion which cleared away the superstitious customs which were the delight of their lives, their chief amusement and dissipation, and a means of influencing the men.[12]

The position of women in Iban society is far different from the conception that many people have of Asian life. Hedda Morrison, an experienced observer, wrote, 'The Iban women occupy a position of equality and respect. They take part in discussions and arguments. They work hard but they have considerable independence and in Iban custom their position is in no way inferior to that of their men folk.'[13] That this is no new development is plain from the account of Charles Brooke, a century earlier, who served among the Iban before succeeding his uncle as Rajah in 1868.

> The gentler sex are even more important really. They occupy positions, and are capable of exerting surprising influence . . . in spite of their being so often erroneously supposed by Europeans to rank simply as chattels. . . . In many cases they are more adept politicians than their husbands, and their advice is often followed in serious business. Likewise their assistance and good opinion go a long way to establish a successful result in any negotiation.[14]

There was a division of labour in village life, still continued, but not rigidly, and it has not demonstrated the superiority of either sex. As is commonly found, fetching water is women's work – but this never involves very long walks. On the other hand, men are responsible for finding firewood, and chopping it. In the all–important rice cycle men

[12] McDougall, *Sketches*, pp. 73–5.
[13] Hedda Morrison, *Sarawak*, 2nd edn (Singapore, 1965), p. 217.
[14] Charles Brooke, *Ten Years in Sarawak*, 2 vols (London, 1866), I, pp. 66, 70.

do the forgework, making and repairing tools, felling trees and burning, to open up more land, and dibbling. Women sow the seed, weed, and reap, and deal with the processes of preparing the grain for food. These are less arduous tasks, though more time-consuming. It was not considered appropriate for women to be headhunters, but they had an important part in the reception of newly-won heads into the longhouse community. The essentially feminine task was making cotton blankets, weaving and dyeing the cloth. This was reckoned a dangerous undertaking, for it was a ritual process, involving the spirits in the creation of designs. Valerie Mashman has offered a modern understanding of this:

> Women are able to shift their position in relation to the male prestige system because their gender identity is located outside the system in their knowledge of weaving. As weavers, women play a vital part in protecting the life, health and fertility of the community, objectives shared by men as warriors.[15]

The Iban women's resistance to Christianity, as Mrs McDougall observed, was connected with their prominent part in the traditional religious ceremonies, which they were reluctant to abandon. Even if they were attracted by the message of the Gospel, they would find no comparable role in the sober Anglican worship of the nineteenth century. The Ranee Margaret, wife of Charles Brooke, might play the harmonium in the church in Kuching sometimes, but there was nothing for the village women. Nonetheless the missionaries persevered, and always were as ready to teach and encourage women as well as men, girls as well as boys, and the schools were open to both. The discouragement from conversion that men had from their wives may have slowed down requests for baptism, but it may very well have helped to clarify and refine the understanding of what was sought. Progress was slow, and only with the spread of mission schools did numbers increase. From the 1880s, when a girls' boarding house was opened in Kuching, it became possible for village girls to prolong their education, as boys could at the Diocesan School; but numbers were very low. It was a long time before there were many Christian Iban

---

[15] Valerie Mashman, 'Warriors and weavers: a study of gender relations among the Iban of Sarawak', in Vinson H. Sutlive, ed., *Female and Male in Borneo* (Williamsburg, 1990), p. 246.

families for children to be born into, let alone predominantly Christian longhouses. Now such families are numerous, in the longer-established parishes, and in the towns. By 1980, thirty-seven per cent of the Iban were reckoned to be Christian.[16]

An Iban priest, Fr Dennis Gimang, who was until recently a tutor at the House of the Epiphany, Kuching's theological college, has confirmed from his family experience what all the evidence suggests. He is of the fifth generation from converts of about 1870, a result of the work of the catechist Belabut, whose wife assisted him, teaching Christ to the women, less than a quarter of a century after the arrival of the mission.[17] Dennis Gimang's home is Bangkit Ijok in the Saribas, still a scene of headhunting in 1870, and today the only Christian longhouse in that area.

> In the Iban legends there had been women as leaders, ie. Dayang Ridu a legendary woman . . . who was responsible for raising the social status of slaves. . . . The Iban people have never treated women as Second Class human beings. . . . Today there are women councillors in all many districts in the state. Women in the P.C.C. Women are even more respected due to education.
>
> Christianity has added more roles and responsibilities to women. . . . Generally Iban women are more religious than men. . . . Women are more respected in their faith. Iban may not agree with the ordination of women into the priesthood but their women have always been respected before and after Christianity came to Sarawak.[18]

*   *   *

In the early part of this century, when High Church practices spread in Sarawak, unmarried lady missionaries began to be called sisters, and to wear a uniform similar to that of nurses, but crowned on special occasions with large black veils. They were not bound by any vows or promises, and were free to marry when they left, as Sister Mary Sharp, the sister of the Vicar, A. F. Sharp, did, later becoming Mrs Cronk.

The first mention of hopes for the religious life in Sarawak came in

[16] Ko, 'Socioeconomic study', p. 82.
[17] For Belabut see Peter D. Varney, 'Some early Iban leaders in the Anglican Church in Sarawak', *SMJ*, 40, ns nos 34–35 (1969), p. 276.
[18] Fr Dennis Gimang to the author, 28 Mar. 1996.

1915, when a priest, Wilfrid Linton, was recruited by the Society for the Propagation of the Gospel.[19] The Bishop of Labuan and Sarawak then was W. R. Mounsey, who himself joined the Community of the Resurrection some time after he resigned from Borneo. Wartime conditions delayed Linton's arrival, and he reached Sarawak only in March 1919, by which time E. D. L. Danson was Bishop. Linton was soon sent to work among the Iban in the Saribas. He still hoped to found a brotherhood of priests and laymen to work in the Iban areas, and was clothed as a novice in the Community of the Holy Cross in November 1928. He was joined at Betong by Maurice Bradshaw in 1931 and Jack Sparrow in 1932. Then Linton's health gave way and he could not work in the tropics any more. After losing its founder and only novice the experiment came to an end. Sparrow remained a secular priest and Bradshaw later joined the Community of the Resurrection.

Danson was succeeded as bishop in 1931 by N. B. Hudson, who invited the Community of the Resurrection to work in Sarawak. Five priests were there for varying periods from 1933, in parishes and in a small school preparing senior men for ordination. In 1937 they were withdrawn, as the community had over-reached itself in the activities that it had undertaken.

In 1962 Fr Nicholas Allenby of the Society of the Sacred Mission was consecrated as Bishop of Kuching. For a short while he had with him as secretary Brother Geoffrey Calf of his society; but there is no indication that Linton or the Mirfield or Kelham communities ever intended to attract men from the local Church to join them.

The story of women religious is different. In 1924 Miss Annie Fell Rigby was sent by SPG to Borneo. On leave in 1929 she was admitted to the Congregation of Jesus the Good Shepherd, an institute for teachers founded in 1920, and associated with the Wantage sisters. She returned to British North Borneo as Companion Anne,[20] and was joined by Companion Irene in 1930. So Anglican community life was begun. Companion Alison arrived in 1933, but Companion Anne left for health reasons. The two remained, working in Sandakan, until they were interned in Sarawak by the Japanese. After the war a small group of sisters carried on, responsible for various kinds of work in Sandakan and in the interior of North Borneo.

---

[19] For Linton see Brian Taylor, 'A triumph of patience and purposefulness: Linton of Betong', *SCH*, 28 (1989), pp. 433–44.

[20] With a new constitution, the members were called sisters from 1944.

Bishop N. E. Cornwall, who arrived in 1949, hoped that the religious life would increase. He planned the fourfold Order of the Epiphany: a fellowship for secular priests, a brotherhood and a sisterhood, and a companionship for teachers. The first and the last were started. The brotherhood never began, but in 1957 Prisca Nasa anak Jimbun, an Iban from Bangkit Rembai, Spaoh in the Saribas, went to share community life with Sister Ena Florence, C.J.G.S., in Sandakan. With another Iban postulant, B, she was clothed as a novice on 13 December 1958. Oi Chin, the first Chinese novice, was clothed early in 1960. Bishop Cornwall wrote of the 'embryo Sisterhood of the Epiphany being worked out at Sandakan by Sister Ena Florence C.J.G.S.'[21] However, when Prisca Nasa and Oi Chin were professed, they had come to like the parent community, and so were allowed to belong to it, rather than form a new society of 'little sisters' as had been expected. Novice B had left, being found unsuitable for the sisterhood. Great hopes were held for C, another Iban, but a medical examination discovered tuberculosis, so she could not be accepted for clothing. A few other enquirers came, including a Chinese from Singapore, but they did not persevere in applying for membership.

In 1963, Sisters Prisca Nasa and Oi Chin moved to Simanggang in Sarawak, with Sister Minnie from England in charge of the house. It was thought that Bishop Allenby would be able to encourage development. He wrote, 'It is hoped . . . that other young women will be drawn to the Religious Life and that in due course the Community here will be an entirely indigenous one.'[22] D, a Chinese from Brunei, joined, and was professed after a novitiate in England. At about the same time, Sister Oi Chin returned to her native Sabah, where she now lives in retirement with Sister Margaret, the fourth and last Borneo sister to be professed. Sister Minnie returned to England in 1973, leaving Sisters Prisca Nasa and D in Kuching, where they had moved at the end of 1972. Sister Prisca Nasa died in September 1978. Sister D had already left the community. After trying her vocation with the Sisterhood of St John the Divine at Willowdale in the outskirts of Toronto, she entered the ordained ministry, and is working as a lady priest in a Canadian fishing village.

Sister Ena Florence, who saw much of the story, wrote,

[21] *Borneo Chronicle* (Mar. 1958), p. 4.
[22] *Borneo Chronicle* (Aug. 1963), p. 3.

So why did our prayers and efforts lead nowhere? I think the best answer was given by one of our old girls. . . . She told me that in the early days in Sandakan, a number of them would have joined the Sisters but the fact that they, the Sisters – went home every 3–4 years meant that there was no permanent home. What was needed was a mother house. . . . After the deprivations of World War 2 the western concept of the religious commitment to poverty was not a way of life that commended itself to Chinese culture. . . . Looking back, God had called us to do some basic work for him, it proved it was not the religious life.[23]

A brief comparison can be made with Roman Catholic communities.[24] White Sisters, the Franciscan Missionaries of St Joseph, were brought by the Mill Hill Fathers, and worked in Borneo from 1885 until they were withdrawn in 1972. In 1926 there were the beginnings of local vocations. It was soon decided that they should be formed into a separate congregation, the Little Sisters of Sarawak. From 1950 they worked more independently of the White Sisters, gradually taking responsibility for their activities. After the Second Vatican Council they decided that they disliked the word 'little', and now are the Sisters of St Francis of Sarawak. There are more than eighty professed sisters, with houses in many places in the state. A Carmelite monastery existed in Jesselton in North Borneo from 1930, and a house was opened in Kuching in 1948. 'Both the Jesselton and the Kuching foundations did so well that today [1981] there are few non-Bornean Sisters in either convent.'[25] In 1996, there were fourteen nuns in Kuching. A further house for Carmelite sisters had recently been opened in Miri, with eleven nuns. It may well be that if Bishop Cornwall's aim for a Sisterhood of the Epiphany had been followed, distinct from a European congregation, the Anglican religious life might have grown to match that of the Roman Catholic Church.

With opportunities for the priesthood in both Churches, it is not surprising that vocations to the religious life are less numerous among men. So far there has been one Anglican, Alfred Leong Boon Kong

---

[23] Sister Ena Florence to the author, Mar. 1994.

[24] For further information see John Rooney, *Khabar Gembira* (London and Kota Kinabalu, 1981). Up-to-date details have been received from the Vicar General, Fr John Ha to the author, 2 April, 1 July 1996.

[25] Rooney, *Khabar Gembira*, p. 87.

from Kuching, professed in the Society of St Francis in 1989 in Australia. Three Roman Catholic men have left Sarawak for established Roman Catholic communities: two are professed Franciscans and one is a Redemptorist novice.

Brother Alfred Book Kong has recently reflected on the way things have gone:

> I am afraid I can't say why the religious life had not developed in the Anglican Church in Borneo except that it is not time yet in God's plan! The lack of inculturation may be part of the reason as I remembered the life that I observed of the Sisters of CJGS as very English. . . . However, after meeting the [RC] Capuchin friars from Kalimantan [Indonesian Borneo] where about a hundred friars constitute one province and neighbouring Sumatra had 200 friars almost entirely locals, I have hopes for Sarawak if God is willing!![26]

* * *

These three short studies provide a persuasive illustration of a consistent tradition among the missionaries, and in the growing Church in Sarawak, of even-handed aims and policies, that gave men and women equal place and opportunity, and that this was certainly in accord with the way of life of the Iban, the most numerous native race in Sarawak, and the race that has provided the largest proportion of the Anglican Church membership. The matters discussed here also show that when analysing the relationship between gender and Christian religion in a missionary context, the relations and expectations of the recipient non-Christian society require as much attention as those among the missionaries themselves. The missionaries' ability (or failure) to adapt and respond to the role of gender in the society they are addressing is perhaps one of the more important factors affecting the success of their endeavours. With this in mind, the Anglican experience in Sarawak stands as an illustration of the issues confronted by Christian missionaries through history.

[26] Brother Alfred Boon Kong to the author, 10 July 1996.

'WE INTEND TO SHOW WHAT OUR LORD HAS DONE FOR WOMEN': THE LIVERPOOL CHURCH LEAGUE FOR WOMEN'S SUFFRAGE, 1913-18

by KRISTA COWMAN

T HERE was nothing unusual in the inauguration, in December 1909, of a Church League for Women's Suffrage (CLWS). By January 1914, suffrage had become so expansive that fifty-three organizations competed for or shared a membership divided by tactics, religion, political allegiance, ethnic origin, or metier, but united in their desire to see the parliamentary franchise awarded to women.[1] At the time of the League's formation, the centre stage of suffrage politics was largely occupied by three groups: the Women's Social and Political Union (WSPU), suffragettes whose commitment to direct militant tactics brought them spectacularly into both the public eye and the prison cell; the National Union of Women's Suffrage Societies (NUWSS), whose suffragist members condemned all militancy, describing themselves as 'law-abiding'; and the Women's Freedom League (WFL), militants who had quit the WSPU in 1907 in a dispute over constitutional democracy.[2] Whilst they were often virulently opposed to each other, these three groups shared a commitment to an all-female membership and also the political will to prioritize the franchise above the broader feminist issues which adjoined their public campaigns. By contrast smaller suffrage groups, including the

---

[1] This figure comes from the 'Suffrage Directory', *Votes for Women* [hereafter *VFW*], 6 Feb. 1914.

[2] For the WSPU see, for example, E. Sylvia Pankhurst, *The Suffragette Movement, an Intimate Account of Persons and Ideals* (London, 1931); Roger Fulford, *Votes for Women* (London, 1957); Antonia Raeburn, *The Militant Suffragettes* (London, 1973); Andrew Rosen, *Rise Up Women! The Militant Campaign of the Women's Social and Political Union, 1903-14* (London, 1974). For the NUWSS, works include Ray Strachey, *The Cause: A Short History of the Women's Movement in Great Britain* (London, 1928); Jill Liddington and Jill Norris, *One Hand Tied Behind Us: The Rise of the Women's Suffrage Movement* (London, 1978); Leslie Parker Hume, *The National Union of Women's Suffrage Societies* (New York and London, 1982). For the WFL, which still awaits a published history, see C. L. Eustance, 'Daring to be free: the evolution of women's political identities in the Women's Freedom League' (University of York D. Phil. thesis, 1993), and Hilary Francis, 'Our job is to be free: the sexual politics of four Edwardian feminists from c.1910-1935' (University of York D. Phil. thesis, 1996).

Church League, added extra dimensions to the suffrage campaign. They allowed members of the three main groups to explore issues other than suffrage whilst simultaneously providing alternative arenas for suffrage activity to those who did not feel able to commit themselves to the larger bodies. Thus the Church League did restrict its membership to practising Anglicans, but welcomed both militants and constitutionalists, and men as well as women into its ranks. Whilst the achievement of the parliamentary franchise remained its main aim, it also provided space for those who wished to explore 'the deep religious significance of the women's movement'.[3] This paper uses the example of the Liverpool branch of the Church League to examine in greater detail to what extent, if any, such explorations resulted in an alteration of the gendered nature of space within Edwardian Anglicanism.

* * *

The idea that space is a gendered phenomenon dovetails neatly with the notion of 'separate spheres', the 'middle-class, western and nine-teenth-century variant of the public-private dichotomy'.[4] 'Separate spheres' remains a somewhat problematic concept, and one with which historians of gender have rightly exercised caution.[5] Yet for those of us whose main interest rests with the often forcible entry of women into public life, it remains a convenient yardstick for, as Alice Kessler-Harris acknowledged in her criticism of the concept, 'women and men may function in both [spheres], but gender defines where one's feet are planted'.[6] For Edwardian women, this frequently meant that their feet were planted firmly within the domestic terrain. The popular forms of public speech and their forums had long been conceptualized as 'rational' and 'manly', placing a masculine republic in diametric opposition to a feminine home.[7] Yet this division was frequently

---

[3] London, Lambeth Palace Library, Davison Papers W16, Revd Claude Hinscliffe to Archbishop Davison, 3 May 1912, cited in Brian Heeney, *The Women's Movement in the Church of England, 1850–1930* (Oxford, 1988), p. 105.

[4] Jane Rendall, 'Nineteenth century feminism and the separation of spheres: reflections on the public/private dichotomy', in Tayo Andreasen, Anette Borchorst, Drude Dahlerup, Eva Lous, and Hanne Rimmen Nielsen, eds, *Moving On: New Perspectives on the Women's Movement*, Acta Jutlandica LXVII:1, Humanities Series, 66 (Aarhus, 1991), p. 17.

[5] See Rendall, 'Nineteenth century feminism', for an overview of historiography.

[6] Alice Kessler-Harris, 'Gender ideology and historical reconstruction', *Gender and History*, 1 (1989), pp. 31–49.

[7] The categories of 'rational' and 'manly' come from Nancy Fraser, 'Rethinking the

contested from within the Edwardian feminist movement. Under-pinning all of the movement's political campaigns lay a challenge to the way in which public space was gendered, and a desire to see it become more feminized. This had been achieved in a variety of locations. Educational, legal, medical, and local political institutions had opened up in response to the force of successive crusades. Certain other areas, including the epicentre of the state, Parliament, still remained wholly masculine, barred to women. This was mirrored within Anglicanism, the state religion. Here, even the physical boundaries of public space were gendered in certain churches, where women were 'excluded not only from the priesthood and from the pulpit, but from coming near the altar, singing in the choir – even taking the collection'.[8]

From its founding, the Church League recognized this system of gendered space, drawing heavily on the rhetoric of separate spheres. Many of the men involved in the League used the issue of women's suffrage as a means of promoting their personal views on woman's space and role within the Church. There was nothing new in the association of these views with the suffrage campaign. When the Revd Maurice F. Bell stated in the League's inaugural sermon that it had 'always been the business of Christian women to care for the home', he was following a well-established tradition.[9] As early as 1895, the Central Society for Women's Suffrage attempted to 'remove a fear still to be found in some quarters that the women's suffrage movement is not consistent with the religious aspect of women's work and duty'.[10] Much of the sermons of ministers involved in the Church League could have come directly from the abundance of prescriptive literature concerned with separate spheres and the perpetration of the gendered

---

public sphere: A contribution to the critique of actually existing democracy', in Craig Calhoun, ed., *Habermas and the Public Sphere* (Cambridge, MA, 1994), pp. 109–42. Here, Fraser borrows from Joan B. Landes, *Women and the Public Sphere in the Age of the French Revolution* (Ithaca, NY, 1988). For a similar analysis see Leonore Davidoff, 'Regarding some old husbands' tales: public and private in feminist history', in her collection *Worlds Between: Historical Perspectives on Gender and Class* (Oxford, 1995), pp. 227–76.

[8] Sheila Fletcher, *Maude Royden, a Life* (Oxford, 1989), p. 4.

[9] Maurice F. Bell, *The Church and Women's Suffrage: Sermon before the Inaugural Meeting of the Church League for Women's Suffrage at St Mark's, Regent's Park, Thursday December 2, 1909 by the Vicar, Rev. Maurice F. Bell, M. A.*, CLWS Pamphlet, 1 (London, 1909) [London, Museum of London, Suffragette Fellowship Collection, MOL 50. 82./307].

[10] Central Society for Women's Suffrage, *Women's Suffrage: Opinions of Leaders of Religious Thought* (London, 1895).

public/private dichotomy published in the nineteenth century. The Revd William Temple certainly believed that women's concentration in the private sphere away from the corrupting world had given them 'special' and 'superior' qualities. These qualities, he believed, meant that 'Women have a greater initial facility for worship than men . . . [and] will raise worship to a new place in the life of the whole church by teaching men to revere something which women most easily do.'[11]

However, as an organization dedicated to achieving a greater share in public life for women, it would have been illogical for the Church League simply to perpetuate existing gender conventions regarding access to public space. Within its own domain, therefore, it began to develop a new view drawing heavily on the theological belief that women did have an important role to play within the Church. This was not identical to men's role, but was of equal value and was equally public. As the Bishop of Hull explained, 'the ministry of women is different from that of men but there is no question of superiority or inferiority. Both are needed by Christ.'[12] Hence women within the Edwardian Anglican Church were perceived as 'equal but different'; superior to men but also more restricted in their role and access; more 'godly' yet less able physically to share in the holier spaces. This paradox was unique to neither the Edwardian period nor Anglicanism. Megan McLaughlin has found it to be at the heart of 'Christian rhetoric from the very beginning', whilst Bjorg Seland has noted amongst European Lutherans a prevailing 'pious ideology [which] carried in itself the potential both to conserve and provoke dominant attitudes to female roles'.[13]

For the more radical women involved in the Church League there was no question of allowing any part of the rhetoric of separate spheres to affect their position within both the organization itself and the wider Anglican community. 'Remember what were the conditions of life when the home was the only sphere allowed to women', CLWS

---

[11] Revd William Temple, M. A., 'How the women's movement may help the cause of religion', in *The Religious Aspect of the Women's Movement; being a Series of Addresses Delivered at Meetings held at the Queen's Hall, London, on June 19 1912* (London, 1912) [London, Museum of London, Suffragette Fellowship Collection, MOL 50. 82./205], pp. 57–61.

[12] Right Revd J. A. Kempthorne, D. D., Bishop of Hull, 'Our Lord's teaching about women', ibid., pp. 9–13.

[13] Megan McLaughlin, 'Gender paradox and the otherness of God', *Gender and History*, 3 (1991), pp. 147–59; Bjorg Seland, 'Women's place within the pious Assembly House culture', unpublished paper delivered to 'A Woman's Place' conference, Kristiansand, June 1996 (cited with permission of the author).

activist Mrs Creighton warned the movement in 1912.[14] Christianity did not equate with passivity, and some members of the League were keen to affirm that despite recent advances in society: 'it remained for Christianity to fully declare that the accident of sex is nothing, and that in the Christian Commonwealth there is "neither male nor female"'.[15] One of the aims of the Church League was to see this replicated in the outside world, specifically within the wholly masculine arena of Parliament.

The Church League represented more than simply a way for Anglicans to demonstrate their support for women's suffrage. Christianity had long played an important part in suffrage politics, especially amongst the most militant of suffragettes in the WSPU. Although the suffrage movement aimed at increasing women's equality with men, its own rhetoric could sometimes mirror the paradoxes of that of the Church. Difference was accepted implicitly through the constant stress that was placed on women's innate superiority to men, especially noticeable in the period from 1913 when belief that 'woman's human nature is . . . cleaner, stronger and higher than the human nature of men' led the WSPU to adopt the new campaign slogan of 'votes for women, chastity for men!'[16] This reflected a wider WSPU belief that the intrinsic moral right of their campaign would win over the brute force of their male opposition. 'Fight on', the banner heading Emily Wilding Davison's funeral procession urged her comrades, 'and God will give the victory.'[17]

Many suffragettes drew on their Christian faith to justify their actions. During one of her many imprisonments Emily Wilding Davison scrawled the words 'rebellion against tyrants is obedience to God' on the wall of her Holloway cell, justifying her militant actions in terms borrowed from the civil disobedience of early Christian martyrs.[18] She later became the famous suffragette martyr, dying under the hooves of the King's horse at the 1913 Derby, the WSPU colours pinned to her coat. The self-sacrifice of Lady Constance Lytton, who disguised her identity and her heart condition to undergo

---

[14] Mrs Creighton, 'Effects of the women's movement on the education and ideals of women', in *The Religious Aspect of the Women's Movement*, pp. 46–50.

[15] Revd George Williams, *Women's Rights; a Sermon* (Glasgow, 1914).

[16] *The Suffragette*, 1 Aug. 1913.

[17] Lisa Tickner, *The Spectacle of Women: Imagery of the Suffrage Campaign 1907–14* (London, 1987), p. 138.

[18] Emily Wilding Davison, *VFW*, 3 Sept. 1909.

the forcible feeding that left her an invalid for life, was described by her comrade Dr Mary Gordon as a 'burnt offering' from a 'spiritual movement'.[19] Other suffragettes often described their movement in quasi-religious terms, presenting Christian theology and suffrage rhetoric as interchangeable. Take this early example from a speech made in 1907 by Emmeline Pethick-Lawrence, the WSPU's treasurer. Here, she preaches to her audience in words which would not have been out of place at a Salvation Army meeting:

> The new conception of life which has been given to us is that of the woman, possessor of her own body and soul . . . free to develop within herself the thought and purpose of her Maker, unsubservient to the will or desire of man. . . . The new ideal is not only the cross, it is also the sword. 'I came not to bring peace on earth but a sword.' This word, spoken by the Prince of Peace, is one of the great paradoxes of which life is full.
>
> I call upon [you], those who have vision, to take up the cross, to grasp the sword of this new conception, and with it to wage holy warfare against prejudice and custom . . . which enforce bondage and hold the woman's body and soul in subjection . . . come and join our crusade![20]

For other suffragettes the spirituality of suffrage went beyond Christianity to embrace what Martha Vicinus calls 'a closer union with nature and with religions that gave room for the expression of what they saw as peculiarly feminine characteristics'.[21] For some suffragettes, this involved a departure from 'masculinist monotheism' towards a female trinity, for others it simply involved an acceptance of the iconography of 'Saint Christabel'.[22]

*　*　*

[19] Cited by Martha Vicinus, 'Male space and women's bodies: the suffragette movement', in her *Independent Women* (London, 1985), p. 251.

[20] Emmeline Pethick-Lawrence, *'The New Crusade': a Speech Delivered by Mrs Pethick-Lawrence at Exeter Hall on May 30th, 1907*, WSPU Pamphlet (London, 1907) [London, Museum of London, Suffragette Fellowship Collection, MOL 50. 82./144].

[21] Vicinus, 'Male space', p. 260.

[22] See the religious ideas of Dora Marsden, described in Les Garner, *A Brave and Beautiful Spirit* (Aldershot, 1990), pp. 155–83. A representation of 'Saint' Christabel is reproduced on the cover of David Mitchell, *Queen Christabel* (London, 1977).

The Church League itself provided an obvious forum for debates on the gendered construction of spirituality and organized religion. Thus it provided both a space for those who accepted existing gendered concepts around the idea of public space and also those who challenged them. The remainder of this paper will focus more closely on the Liverpool branch of the Church League, to explore how this contradiction affected the organization in practice.

Although certain radical ministers in Liverpool, mainly within the Free Churches, had long associations with both socialist and suffrage politics, it was not until January 1913 that a local branch of the CLWS was inaugurated, allowing Anglicans a chance to declare themselves simultaneously as suffragists.[23] Like other local suffrage organizations, the branch was called the Liverpool branch, but organized geographically throughout the region which constitutes the present-day county of Merseyside.[24] Nationally, Brian Heeney has noted, there was some public concern expressed over the high number of WSPU members who joined the Church League:

> Despite the insistence of members and leaders that the League was perfectly innocent of political aims, the *Standard* of 25 September 1913 remarked; '[since] no fewer than six members of the elected committee, including the chairman, are subscribers to the Women's Social and Political Union, a grave doubt must arise as to the real character of this outwardly respectable society'.[25]

Liverpool shared the *Standard*'s concerns, but militancy won the day. An early attempt was made to bar 'militants on active service' from membership of the Liverpool CLWS branch, but the majority of the membership opposed this.[26] This first president and secretary, both

---

[23] *Church League for Women's Suffrage Monthly Paper* [hereafter *CLWS Monthly Paper*], Jan. 1913. Pembroke Chapel was the main site of pulpit radicalism in Liverpool. For more details see I. Sellers, *Salute to Pembroke*, unpublished typescript, Liverpool Record Office; also Leonard Smith, *Religion and the Rise of Labour* (Keele, 1993), pp. 145–53.

[24] For an explanation of the way that suffrage politics in Liverpool stretched through into Cheshire, Bootle, and Merseyside, see Krista Cowman, 'Engendering citizenship: women in Merseyside political organisations, 1890–1930' (University of York D.Phil. thesis, 1994).

[25] Heeney, *Women's Movement*, p. 112.

[26] Church League for Women's Suffrage, *Fourth Annual Report* (London, 1913).

constitutionalists, resigned following the membership's decision; but the other branch officials, drawn from both sides, remained. The majority of activists within the Liverpool Church League were predominantly WSPU members.[27] However this did not preclude constitutionalists from joining. A belief that common faith transcended policy differences between political organizations allowed even the most hostile suffragist enemies to combine under the auspices of the League. For example in 1914 NUWSS leader Eleanor Rathbone, whose stated opinion was that the NUWSS should at all times keep their campaign in the public eye over and above that of the WSPU, chaired a CLWS meeting at which the main speaker was Mr Bernard, a prominent local WSPU supporter, without either party appearing to feel compromised.[28]

The denial of difference which was so important to the Liverpool Church League was not simply restricted to policy differences between suffrage campaigners, but reflected the far more radical denial at the organization's heart. At its first reported meeting, the preacher, the Revd J. Coop, took as his text Mark 1.31, explaining that as 'In Christ Jesus there was "neither male nor female" . . . the Church League intended to show those outside what Our Lord had done for women when "he took her by the hand and lifted her up".'[29]

The main campaigning focus of the Liverpool Church League was on education. Membership allowed opportunities to share faith as suffragists during special services where the spiritual dimension of suffrage was discussed. At one such early gathering, some 300 members and supporters heard the Bishop of Hull give his opinion that 'There is not a parish in Liverpool . . . the work of which would not collapse if there were not women workers, and it is little short of a scandal . . . women who do the lions share [sic] of the church's work should not have the privilege of a vote.'[30] This in itself was insufficient for the more radical amongst the Anglican suffrage campaigners, who were

[27] An analysis of the Liverpool members named in the *CLWS Monthly Paper* shows that of the nineteen who had associations with other suffrage bodies, nine were WSPU members, six supported the NUWSS, and four were involved with the WFL.

[28] 'The recent developments of militant policy and . . . the reaction in public opinion . . . make it more important than ever that the . . . methods of the National Union should be kept prominently before public attention': Eleanor Rathbone, 'The methods of conciliation', *Common Cause*, 5 Sept. 1911.

[29] *CLWS Monthly Paper*, March 1914.

[30] *VFW*, 18 April 1913.

seeking a broader debate about the very nature of the work that women did or did not do in the Church altogether. The League remained most committed to developing a critique of the gendering of public space outside the Church. The firmest gendered division of labour, the priesthood, remained 'debarred to women ... a permanent prohibition'.[31] The League appears to have fought shy of this issue. Even Maude Royden, who herself made a 'notorious' speech on the issue in 1915, admitted privately that her support for women priests was 'extreme', and warned her fellow League member, Ursula Roberts, to tread very carefully around the subject.[32]

Outside of the League, as the organization began and increased its activity in Liverpool, there was a marked augmentation in public expressions of spirituality by the WSPU. Following a national campaign, local suffragettes had regularly and enthusiastically participated in the 'prayers for prisoners' initiative, in which church services were interrupted by women praying for suffragette hunger strikers.[33] In Liverpool, the campaign aptly centred around the newly opened Lady Chapel in the Anglican Cathedral. The chapel took famous Christian women as its theme, including Josephine Butler who had a window dedicated to her there, providing a perfect backdrop for militant spirituality.[34] During the first protest, in January 1914, women chanted a suffrage prayer for hunger strikers, 'brave women who are being persecuted for righteousness sake'. The protest culminated in a suffragette unfurling a banner declaring 'I came not to send peace, but a sword.' This was knocked from her hand and the churchwardens with unconscious irony threatened to exclude all women from the Lady Chapel in the future. The following week the prayers were repeated, although the cathedral authorities had hired six policemen and a sergeant to prevent another scene.[35] Such protests did not impress the local church authorities, and a WSPU deputation to the Bishop of Liverpool in April was told that rather than being willing to intervene on the subject of forcible feeding, he 'declined to lift a finger to help ... until ... the women desisted from brawling in the churches'. Members of the deputation, including Dr Alice Ker, an elderly local

[31] Bell, *The Church and Women's Suffrage*.
[32] Fletcher, *Maude Royden*, pp. 143–4.
[33] See Pankhurst, *The Suffragette Movement*, p. 510.
[34] For a short account of the importance of the Lady Chapel to feminism, see *The Vote*, 11 Nov. 1909.
[35] *The Suffragette*, 23 Jan. 1914, 30 Jan. 1914.

GP, 'remarked that it was a grievous matter if women were not to pray for their suffering sisters and added that the Church was in grave danger of losing its chief supporters . . . many women disgusted with the attitude of the clergy had already left'.[36]

Such attitudes were not helpful to women seeking a space in which they could practise their faith without renouncing their political beliefs. Indeed, once again it would appear that they were expected to keep silent in church. Against this background, the Church League did at least offer an area in which political beliefs and faith could run in tandem. It also permitted prayers for suffragettes and allowed the spiritual dimensions of their campaigns to be explored. The 'Cat and Mouse Act', for example, which permitted the authorities to release hunger strikers under licence, only to return them to gaol when their health had improved, was condemned as 'un-Christian' by the Liverpool branch.[37] However, the Church League still supported restricted access to certain functions of the life of the Church, especially the priesthood, which was never really a subject for discussion within the League. For some women, therefore, it was still failing to provide the space that they sought completely. This failure must have appeared most frustrating to suffragettes within the League. They were devoting much of their campaigning activity outside of Anglicanism to an organization in which, as they did not have to compete with men for access to any activity or position, they were constantly able to set, explore, and develop their own agendas. The Church League, however, as a body with a male and female membership, could not replicate this. What this meant in practice was that the women members of the Church League did speak at public meetings, but that the preaching of sermons, the focal point of their regular suffrage services, could only be undertaken by male members.

On Merseyside, the militant suffrage campaign had always been high profile. Local women had shown themselves as capable public speakers and political organizers in its name. Girls in their late teens and elderly women had tackled cabinet ministers, braved imprisonment and forcible feeding, been heckled, stoned, and ridiculed at public meetings, interrupted plays and films, and undertaken a variety of serious illegal actions including bombing and arson in the name of the WSPU. This tradition fostered a sense of independent ability in

---

[36] *The Suffragette*, 3 April 1914.
[37] *CLWS Monthly Paper*, Sept. 1913.

local suffragettes which made them willing to go further beyond what the Church League could offer in an attempt to develop suitable spiritual space for women. In March 1914 a Woman's Church, possibly the only such in the country, was opened at Wallasey. It had no premises of its own, but met in Liscard Concert Hall where two Sunday services a week were held, the afternoon one for women and the evening one mixed. The Woman's Church reflected the dual focus of spirituality within the WSPU. It aimed to recruit both women who, finding the Church 'like a cage ... had come away in sheer disgust at the attitude of the clergy to the things which to them are dearer than life', and also those unattached to any church 'who would ... be eager and anxious to attend a service where the real needs of women were sympathetically understood'.[38] Within the Woman's Church, gendered boundaries of space were not removed. More radically, they were reversed. An article in the *Free Church Suffrage Times* reported:

> Women are to preach the sermons, offer the prayers, provide the music and take the collection. . . . Unthinking people will probably smile, but, after all, there is nothing novel in the idea of a Church governed by *one* sex only: the novelty . . . lies in the fact that it is the sex usually governed which is to govern.[39]

Both local suffragettes and nationally famous Christian feminists supported the Woman's Church initiative. The inaugural service was held by the Revd Hatty Baker, 'one of the pioneer preachers in the Congregational Church' and a co-pastor at Plymouth. Miss Hoy, the Wallasey WSPU Secretary, was a keen attender.[40] It also received publicity within *The Suffragette* and *Votes for Women*. Sadly, the experiment was cut short. The Church appears to have folded during the First World War, a fate shared by many of its contemporary feminist organizations.

* * *

[38] Letter from Miss Hoy, WSPU and Woman's Church activist, *Wallasey and Wirral Chronicle*, 14 March 1914; letter from Miss Brand, ibid., 24 Jan. 1914.

[39] *Free Church Suffrage Times*, April 1914.

[40] For more details on the Revd Baker, see *Free Church Suffrage Times*, Jan. 1917; also Elaine Kaye, 'A turning point in the ministry of women: the ordination of the first women to the Christian ministry in England in September 1917', *SCH*, 27 (1990), pp. 505–12.

From the Liverpool example, it would appear that the Church League for Women's Suffrage did enjoy limited success in directing the spiritual side of the women's movement, and in forming a limited critique of the gendered nature of space within society. However, this critique, which rested on the denial of gender difference inherent within Christianity, did not extend to the separation of space or labour within the Church itself, and hence was insufficient for some spiritually radical women. They were forced beyond the limitations of Anglicanism into the Woman's Church, whose brief experimental forum allowed gender roles within the Church to be reversed, although not eradicated. Within the broader confines of Anglicanism, gendered space remained an accepted fact; and woman's place continued to be largely defined by men despite the impact of the wider Edwardian women's movement. It was to take almost another eighty years before the most rigid gendered division of labour, the Anglican ministry, broke down.

University of York

'I DON'T SING FOR PEOPLE WHO DO NOT SEE ME':[1] WOMEN, GENDER AND THE HISTORIOGRAPHY OF CHRISTIANITY IN SOUTH AFRICA

by GREG CUTHBERTSON and LOUISE KRETZSCHMAR

ONE of the cultural features of South Africa's new democracy is the prolific publication of autobiographical narratives by previously marginalized people.[2] The Truth and Reconciliation Commission, chaired by Archbishop Desmond Tutu, has also focused attention on the plight of oppressed groups under apartheid, and many of the voices being heard are those of women.[3] These personal accounts are breathing life into the sinews of organized political protest and – to mix metaphors – unearthing the 'hidden past' interred in apartheid history. As Alison Goebel also reminds us, life histories or personal narratives have long been identified as 'an ideal feminist method', and have frequently been used in work about African women.[4]

This paper therefore begins with the biography of an African woman and her religious quest, to humanize the historiographical survey which follows. The intention in both is to raise salient issues about religion and culture in South African society in the nineteenth and twentieth centuries. The later part of the paper looks briefly at the lives of missionary women, the changing social identity of Afrikaner women, and finally the spectrum of women's theologies, as expressed in some recent writings. The discussion is informed by the knowledge that all societies are gendered, but in different ways. It tries to explore

---

[1] Margaret McCord, *The Calling of Katie Makanya* (Cape Town, 1995), p. 57.

[2] See, for example, *Natoo Babenia. Memoirs of a Saboteur: Reflections of my Political Activity in India and South Africa, as Told by Ian Edwards* (Bellville, 1995); Frieda Bokwe Matthews, *Remembrances* (Bellville, 1995).

[3] For a literary overview, see M. J. Daymond, 'Gender and "History": 1980s South African women's stories in English', *ARIEL: A Review of International English Literature*, 27 (1996), pp. 191–213. For discussion of women's autobiographies, see Judith L. Coullie, '(In)Continent I-lands: blurring the boundaries between self and other in South African women's autobiographies', ibid., pp. 133–48.

[4] Alison Goebel, 'Life histories as a cross-cultural feminist method in African Studies: achievements and blunders', paper presented at the 'Promoting women's history: local and regional perspectives' conference, Rhodes University, Grahamstown, 6 July 1995.

some of this difference in the context of South African history, by concentrating on the experiences of women rather than men, primarily because the focus of much gender history in South Africa remains 'women'. There is, however, an important emergent literature on gender and homosexuality in South Africa, which is beyond the scope of this paper.[5]

* * *

The 1996 Alan Paton book prize was awarded to Margaret McCord for her biography of Katie Makanya, who was employed by McCord's missionary mother for thirty-five years.[6] It is a moving account of the life of an indomitable African woman. In fact, it weaves together the lives of two women, one black and one white, from interviews recorded in 1954, six years after the apartheid government came to power, and just before Katie Makanya died at the age of eighty-four. Her story is told through excerpts from her oral testimony, occasionally interrupted by comments and introductions to chapters written by McCord.

Katie Makanya was born in 1872 of a Sotho father and Mfengu mother in the mainly Xhosa eastern Cape and was raised to fear the Zulu who were depicted as cruel warriors in her grandmother's tales. As a young woman she sang in the African Native Choir which toured England in the early 1890s. She refused an opportunity to become a leading soprano in Europe because 'I don't sing for people who do not see me'[7] – her response to her agent's comment that those who listened to her sing would not notice she was black. This shows her self-conscious dignity as an African woman and her awareness of the price of trying to maintain her own culture, whilst living under European control in a segregated society.

Katie's early life was spent with her Christian parents and elder sister; later her quest for a Christian husband drove her from 'heathen' Soekmekaar (northern Transvaal), and its arranged 'traditional' marriages, to Johannesburg. Finally, her commitment to the work of

---

[5] See, for example, Nicholas Southey, 'Uncovering homosexuality in colonial South Africa: the case of Bishop Twells', unpublished paper, 1995 (by kind permission of the author); Andries du Plessis, 'Gender studies and homosexuality: where are the histories?', paper presented at 'The future of the past: the production of history in a changing South Africa' conference, University of the Western Cape, Bellville, 10–12 July 1996.

[6] McCord, *The Calling of Katie Makanya*.

[7] Ibid., p. 57.

medical missionary, Dr James McCord, took her to Durban where she became part of the missionary world, tending the sick and counselling uneducated patients in the rudiments of hygiene.

The story is powerful because Makanya begins life on the margins: ethnically alienated, a Christian among adherents of African religions, educated among the uneducated, and later a black woman among whites and a practical person among political activists. Anne Mager, in a sensitive review, remarks on this self-constructed 'otherness' tinged with a certain superiority: 'Katie Makanya knows who she is, and what she wants is "civilised" and proper.'[8] Shula Marks, well-known historian of southern Africa, considers Makanya's story a superb text for showing the paradoxically pro-imperialist and anti–colonial attitudes so common among the African educated elite.[9] Victorian Britain and Queen Victoria were part of her consciousness – distant symbols of protection against a more immediate colonial aggression of white racism in South Africa – and were reinforced by the medical missionary environment of Adams Mission and the doctor's dispensary where she worked as a medical assistant and interpreter.[10] As a domestic worker she also encountered another world – that of the settler 'madams' in whose homes she cooked, cleaned, scrubbed, and cared for white children.

For this paper, *The Calling of Katie Makanya* raises important issues about the interface between religion and culture. The use of 'calling' in the title of the book is itself significant. Was it God who called her to this unsettled but rich and varied life? To what extent was her calling related to her personal social and cultural circumstances? How was she influenced by the perceptions of others about what constituted a call from God? The biography only hints at the answers, but poignantly demonstrates the 'transculturation' of Christianity,[11] without mini-mizing the enormous social and cultural dislocation of conversion, which was partly the result of her being a woman alone in different

[8] Anne Mager, review of *The Calling of Katie Makanya*, *South African Historical Journal* [hereafter *SAHJ*], 34 (1996).
[9] Quoted in Neil Parsons, 'Imperial history in the Ukay – the "South Africa 1895–1921: test of empire" conference at Oxford, March 1996', *SAHJ*, 34 (1996).
[10] Thengani H. Ngwenya, 'The Calling', *Southern African Review of Books* [hereafter *SARB*], 39–40 (1995), pp. 6–7.
[11] A term used in David Attwell, 'The transculturation of enlightenment: the exemplary case of the Rev Tiyo Soga, African nationalist', in Philippe Denis, ed., *The Making of an Indigenous Clergy in Southern Africa* (Pietermaritzburg, 1995), pp. 41–57.

worlds, in search of a Christian husband with whom to raise a Christian family.

McCord's work also raises methodological questions. Can an African woman's life story really be told by a white woman? Did McCord's interpretation shape or distort Katie's reminiscences? McCord was evidently aware of these pitfalls, and claims she only agreed to write the biography at Makanya's insistence. Her interviews formed the basis of the book which raises important questions for social historians engaged in oral history. That *The Calling* took over forty years to produce places it among the pioneers in its use of oral evidence for writing South African history.

Makanya's life spanned major historical moments from the South African War of 1899–1902 and Bambatha Rebellion of 1906 to the World Wars and the advent of apartheid in 1948. She established friendships with politically radical younger women involved in the Industrial and Commercial Workers' Union (ICU), especially Bertha Mkhize.[12] Makanya was instrumental in the formation of the Bantu Women's Society in Durban in the 1930s, but found it difficult to reconcile her religious beliefs with the growing radicalism of the ICU. This came to a head when the ICU leader, Clements Kadalie, raised the cry against discrimination. McCord recalls Katie's anger at his words:

'Even if the angel Gabriel comes down from heaven and tells me not to walk on the sidewalk, I won't obey him. I'll kick him out my way and walk where I want to walk', Kadalie shouted in English. . . .

Katie could not believe her ears. She never permitted anyone to speak against her religion, and no man, white or black, had the right to say he would kick an angel of God.[13]

Her struggle intersected most profoundly with that of other African women when she and 'Mrs' McCord led a march through the streets of Durban protesting against the extension of passes to black women. And

---

[12] For a history of the ICU, see Helen Bradford, *A Taste of Freedom: The ICU in Rural South Africa, 1924–1930* (New Haven, CT, 1987), especially her discussion of 'Separatist Christianity and Garveyism', pp. 123-7.

[13] McCord, *Calling of Katie Makanya*, p. 219.

at this point she also entered the scholarly picture of African resistance to segregation depicted in recent South African historiography.

* * *

African women's resistance to the Pass Laws has been called a struggle 'to define an acceptable balance between domestic duties and income-generating roles either in the formal or informal sectors. It was never a simplistic defence of female domesticity.'[14] It is claimed that black women were neither 'sophisticated politicians nor stumbling feminists', but struggled against economic marginalization as well as the more personal assaults on women as mothers and wives, and on their sexuality.[15] There is now a growing historiography on women in South Africa, using life stories to historicize patterns of social behaviour and the impact of ideology on individual consciousness.[16]

Social historians were perhaps marginally better at reading women into South African history than putting religion back into the meta-narrative, although they have lagged behind European and American scholarship in both areas.[17] It is a valid complaint that, despite the variety of studies of Christianity and its diverse expressions, political and economic factors continue to dominate the historiography: 'Religion, whether serving to channel resistance [to segregation and apartheid] or not, whatever its place in communities, undoubtedly remains firmly in the background.'[18] As for combining gender and religion, Penelope Hetherington's survey of the historiography of women in South Africa, written in 1993, turned up only four articles.[19] Two years earlier at the Durban Conference on Women and Gender

---

[14] Julia Wells, *We Now Demand! The History of Women's Resistance to the Pass Laws in South Africa* (Johannesburg, 1993), p. 10.

[15] Rhoda Kadalie, 'Where's the rock?', *SARB*, 37 (1995), p. 7.

[16] Berlinda Bozzoli, *Women of Phokeng: Consciousness, Life Strategy, and Migrancy in South Africa, 1900–1983* (Johannesburg, 1991); Shula Marks, ed., *Not Either an Experimental Doll: The Separate Worlds of Three South African Women* (Pietermaritzburg, 1987); and Shula Marks, 'The context of the personal narrative: reflections on *Not Either an Experimental Doll: The Separate Worlds of Three South African Women*', in Personal Narratives Group, eds, *Interpreting Women's Lives: Feminist Theory and Personal Narratives* (Bloomington, IN, 1989), pp. 39–58.

[17] See Richard Elphick, 'Writing religion into history: the case of South African Christianity', *Studia Historiae Ecclesiasticae*, 21 (1995), pp. 1–21.

[18] Johannes du Bruyn and Nicholas Southey, 'The treatment of Christianity and Protestant missionaries in South African historiography', in Henry Bredekamp and Robert Ross, eds, *Missions and Christianity in South African History* (Johannesburg, 1996), p. 35.

[19] Penelope Hetherington, 'Women in South Africa: the historiography in English', *International Journal of African Historical Studies*, 26 (1993), pp. 241–69.

in Southern Africa, a mere three of the sixty-four papers dealt with religion, and only one was historical in orientation.[20]

Cherryl Walker's edited volume on *Women and Gender in South Africa to 1945* has three important chapters on women and their ambivalent relationship with Christianity. These, together with Deborah Gaitskell's seminal work on the African women's *manyanos* (the Xhosa word for prayer 'unions') and their economic and political accommodation to urbanization, have became part of the canon of South African social history.[21] Gender was, however, deployed by feminist historians to reinforce rather than eclipse class analysis, often displacing earlier racial explanations.

Gaitskell's analysis of how Christian women coped with the changed division of labour within the family in the wake of migrant labour to the gold mines which spurred industrialization, also looks at the changed ideology of the role of women under a colonial form of Victorian Christianity. At the heart of her work are black and working-class women and a social historian's concern with 'social control'. She therefore shows how a greater responsibility to control adolescent female sexuality fell to mothers as traditional practices of ephemeral sexual intercourse were abandoned among Christians, especially after peer-group education through initiation ceremonies was discouraged by missionaries. In Gaitskell's writing, religious change in African societies is twinned with economic imperialism to produce her damning amalgam of 'God and gold'.[22] Elsewhere, she also explores the different roles of working-class African Christian women as wives, mothers, and domestic workers during South Africa's most rapid period of urbanization.[23]

Gaitskell concentrates on the gender-specific way in which Christianity has spread among Africans and she examines the notion of

---

[20] Norman Etherington, 'Recent trends in the historiography of Christianity in Southern Africa', paper presented at the 'Paradigms lost; paradigms regained' conference to mark the twentieth anniversary of the *Journal of Southern African Studies*, York, England, Sept. 1994, p. 27.

[21] Deborah Gaitskell, '"Wailing for purity": prayer unions, African mothers, and adolescent daughters, 1912–1940', in S. Marks and A. Rathbone, eds, *Industrialisation and Social Change in South Africa: African Class Formation, Culture and Consciousness, 1870–1930* (London, 1982), pp. 338–57.

[22] Gaitskell, 'Wailing for purity', p. 338.

[23] Deborah Gaitskell, 'Housewives, maids or mothers? Some contradictions of domesticity for Christian women in Johannesburg, 1903–1939', *Journal of African History*, 24 (1983), pp. 241–56.

'devout domesticity' in a study of faith among black women in the twentieth century.[24] As her cultural analysis has evolved in the 1990s, she has shifted her focus from class to gender and from consciousness to spirituality. She observes, for instance, that 'what the *manyano* legitimated – despite an increasingly educated female African leadership and one which certainly saw itself as "ordained" – was the eloquence of those tutored only by the [Holy] Spirit'. Participation in ritual, she argues, required no special church training, nor literacy, as women learnt their own hymns by heart, spoke extemporaneously, and prayed spontaneously. The revivalism of these hymns, prayers, and sermons was authorized by their fervour. Gaitskell therefore concludes that 'such longstanding and distinctive spirituality among women as "praying and preaching" seems to deserve a more respectful reappraisal and revalidation, instead of dismissal'.[25]

Recently, Gaitskell has suggested that church women's organizations in the early twentieth century had greater salience for African than for white women. The reasons were that Christianity gave a new primacy to motherhood in the view of many African women; revivalist evangelism was easily accepted by a culture which emphasised orality; and as Christian missions grew, African women were eager to preach, which further established the legitimacy of their own meetings. These African women's organizations are compared with church groups arranged by white women in the colonial churches, to confirm the powerful and distinctive spirituality of African women in a separate religious sphere beyond the confines and control of mixed worship.[26]

Although the focus of much gender history in South Africa is on women, or the areas of social life with which women are closely identified – family and domestic work – in Gaitskell's research there is a more nuanced attention to gender ideology, reconstruction, and disputes around the meanings of femininity and less explored masculinity.[27] A study by Terence Ranger (significantly entitled *Are*

[24] Deborah Gaitskell, 'Devout domesticity? A century of African women's Christianity in South Africa', in Cherryl Walker, ed., *Women and Gender in South Africa to 1945*, 2nd edn (Cape Town, 1990), pp. 251–72.

[25] Deborah Gaitskell, 'Praying and preaching: the distinctive spirituality of African women's Church organizations', in Bredekamp and Ross, *Missions and Christianity*, p. 228.

[26] Deborah Gaitskell, '"The Bantu people are very emotional": comparing churchwomen's organizations in early 20th century South Africa', presented at the 'Promoting women's history' conference.

[27] There is some work on the gendered history of men. For example, T. Dunbar Moodie, 'Migrancy and male sexuality on the South African gold mines', *Journal of Southern African*

We Not Also Men?) looks at gender and the family in Zimbabwe between the 1920s and 1960s. An elegant chapter on 'Making Class; Redefining Gender' considers the role of Methodism in the life of the Samkange family, in which masculinity is redefined in terms of women's participation in Christian organizations.[28]

* * *

Notwithstanding this literature on women, South African history remains androcentric. Ecclesiastical history is no better, despite 'confessions to masculinist sins in introductions or epilogues'.[29] Indexes to text-books on South African Church history and mission Christianity have entries for 'witches and sorcerers', but omit 'women' and 'gender'; thus giving as little space to women and gender as general histories of South Africa.[30] Feminist historians and theologians are therefore engaged in a systematic critique of established scholarship which neglects gender, women, and female oppression. Helen Bradford, most notably, has challenged recent hegemonic narratives of the Cape frontier in the nineteenth century in an indicting taxonomy which classifies texts according to their representations of women, using the categories of 'invisible women'; 'insignificant women'; and 'insignificant women and important men'.[31] Patricia van der Spuy has also taken some historians of colonial South Africa to task for 'adding the word "gender", yet not applying it or taking it anywhere' in their interpretations.[32] Linzi Manicom has also drawn attention to the ghettoization of gender studies; it is overwhelmingly women who

---

Studies, 14 (1987-8), pp. 228-56; and William Beinart, 'Political and collective violence in South African historiography', *Journal of Southern African Studies*, 18 (1992), pp. 455-86, first rendered as 'Violence and masculinity in South African historiography', presented at the conference 'Towards a gendered history of men in Africa', University of Minnesota, Minneapolis, April 1990.

[28] Terence Ranger, *Are We Not Also Men? The Samkange Family and African Politics in Zimbabwe 1920-1964* (London, 1995), pp. 32-62.

[29] Helen Bradford, 'Women in the Cape and its frontier zones, c.1800-1870: a critical essay on androcentric historiography', paper presented at the South African Historical Society biennial conference, Rhodes University, Grahamstown, July 1995, p. 2.

[30] See for example, J. W. Hofmeyr and G. Pillay, eds, *A History of Christianity in South Africa*, Volume 1 (Pretoria, 1994) for Church history; and T. R. H. Davenport, *South Africa: A Modern History*, 4th edn (London, 1991) for general South African history. See also Helen Bradford's critique of William Beinart, *Twentieth-Century South Africa* (Oxford, 1994): 'Not a general history?', *SAHJ*, 32 (1995), pp. 247-9.

[31] Bradford, 'Women in the Cape', pp. 3-36.

[32] Patricia van der Spuy, 'Women in the index', *SARB*, 43 (1996), pp. 11-13.

study gender, and their research is seldom given prominence in the grand narratives of South African history.[33] In the 1990s, religion and gender research is gradually becoming more mainstream, probably influenced by impulses from Europe and the United States, not entirely unrelated to cultural studies and post-modernism which have 'authorized historians to define "history" in a way congenial to the study of religion'.[34] Historians of the private sphere have dealt with intimacy, the body, madness, devotions, personal piety, and conceptions of sin. Those especially concerned with the culture of sexuality have looked to religion for understanding. These trends, coupled with the persuasive argument by Michel Foucault that power relationships permeate all aspects of life in a very complex pattern, have drawn reluctant historians from the material 'reality' of the workplace and state to the constructed realm of the family and church.[35]

Richard Elphick catalogues reasons for the slowness of South African historians to recognize the importance of religion as an analytical category, and links this directly to the tardy development of gender history.[36] This has much to do with the institutionalization of religion in the apartheid state, which portrayed Christianity as white, public, and male; but it is also the result of an obsession with racial and class conflict and secularism in South African history.

Norman Etherington, in a comprehensive bibliographical essay on the growing historiography of Christianity in southern Africa, has remarked that 'lack of interest rather than a lack of documents' accounts for the neglect of gender history.[37] He notes particularly the paucity of studies on the women who accompanied nineteenth-century clerical pioneers to South Africa, an area in which archival collections are extremely rich. This lack is, however, partly filled by recent biographical pieces on Ann Hamilton, Anne Hodgson, and Harriette Colenso (Bishop John William Colenso's daughter).[38]

---

[33] Linzi Manicom, 'Ruling relations: rethinking state and gender in South African history', *Journal of African History*, 33 (1992), p. 442.

[34] Elphick, 'Writing religion into history', p. 18. See also the critical discussion about whether or not feminism and post-modernism are 'natural allies' in Alison Assiter, *Enlightened Women: Modernist Feminism in a Postmodern Age* (London, 1996), especially pp. 4–5.

[35] On state and gender, see Manicom, 'Ruling relations', pp. 441–65; and Jane L. Parpart and Kathleen A. Staudt, eds, *Women and the State in Africa* (Boulder, CO, 1989).

[36] Elphick, 'Writing religion into history', p. 15.

[37] Etherington, 'Recent trends', p. 11.

[38] Karel Schoeman, *'A Thorn Bush that Grows in the Path': The Missionary Career of Ann*

Brenda Nicholls's portrayal of Harriette Colenso, the young anti-imperialist who travelled from Natal to Britain in 1895, brings gender, religion, and ethnicity into play. Her father's unorthodox political and religious views annoyed the Anglican Church, and Harriette's own identification with the Zulu thwarted her attempts as a woman to secure the release of Zulu royalty from its Atlantic island exile. Nicholls avers that 'both in politics and in religion, her sex may have been a disadvantage to her when dealing with the white people in Natal but it may well have been an advantage to her in winning the confidence of black leaders'.[39]

Dana Robert's research on American women recruited from Mount Holyoke College to teach in Dutch Reformed Church schools in South Africa is more concerned with religious motivation. Founded specifically to serve the cause of missions, Mount Holyoke was well-known as 'a "rib factory" where theological students with missionary appointments could count on finding a wife'.[40] Several women from the same school went to Natal as teachers and wives of American Board missionaries.

Etherington has also examined missionary notions of 'proper relations' between women and men that were debated in Natal and Zululand in the late nineteenth century, especially those relating to the encounter between two differently constituted patriarchal societies – one African and the other European. He shows how illuminating the American Zulu Mission archives are on the subject of gender, because of the particular attention which the American Board of Commissioners for Foreign Missions paid to the role of missionary wives. His work provides convincing evidence of an articulate women's critique of the Zulu Mission which contrasts with the attitudes of other Protestants; he argues that 'it was the rule, rather than the exception, for evangelists in Natal to emphasize woman's equality with man and to aim at her liberation'. The degradation of African women was also an insistent theme of missionary sermons to black congregations, and was inextricably linked with European disapproval of conventional

Hamilton, 1815–1823 (Cape Town, 1995); Joan Millard, 'Anne Hodgson – missionary and mystic', *Theologica Evangelica*, 26 (1993), pp. 55–63; and Brenda Nicholls, 'Harriette Colenso and the issues of religion and politics in colonial Natal', in Bredekamp and Ross, *Missions and Christianity*, pp. 173–88.

[39] Nicholls, 'Harriette Colenso', p. 173.

[40] Dana Robert, 'Mount Holyoke women and the Dutch Reformed missionary movement, 1874–1904', *Missionalia*, 21 (1993), pp. 103–23.

Nguni marriage practices. In trying to recover nineteenth-century African women's voices, Etherington admits that we hear them 'at second hand in the writings of missionaries who were mostly men'. And, reflecting on the insights to be combed from the archival record, he asserts that

> the rule of patriarchy, both on the mission and among the northern Nguni communities of the nineteenth century, concealed much of what we would now like to know about the role of women in 'the long conversation' that was religious conversion. It did not, however, suppress the centrality of women's issues in the evangelical enterprise.[41]

Other studies on gender and religion owe a debt to the influential work of the Chicago-based southern Africanists, Jean and John Comaroff, whose *Of Revelation and Revolution* (1991) sparked a renewed interest in the 'study of the colonisation of consciousness and the consciousness of colonisation', and drew attention to the social and cultural backgrounds of both the evangelizers and the evangelized, women and men alike.[42] The influence of missionary ideas of how the body, especially the female body, should be clothed and cared for, as well as the connection between what missionaries thought of as education, and the reorganization of private space, received much attention in the Comaroffs' cultural anthropology of Christian mission among the southern Tswana. Historians like Sheila Meintjies and Heather Hughes have expanded this understanding of women's, especially African women's, religious experience.[43]

One of the most sophisticated and sustained books on gender and

---

[41] Norman Etherington, 'Gender issues in south-east African missions, 1835–85', in Bredekamp and Ross, *Missions and Christianity*, pp. 136, 137, 146, 150. Also see Jennifer A. Seif, *Gender, Tradition and Authority in 19th Century Natal: The Zulu Missions of the American Board*, forthcoming.

[42] Recently the work of the Comaroffs has been criticized by a number of southern Africanists. See, for example, Clifton C. Crais, 'South Africa and the pitfalls of postmodernism'; Leon de Kock, 'For and against the Comaroffs: postmodern puffery and competing conceptions of the "archive"'; Doug Stuart, 'Revelations from neo-modernity'; and Johannes du Bruyn, 'Of muffled Southern Tswana and overwhelming missionaries: the Comaroffs and the colonial encounter', *SAHJ*, 31 (1994), pp. 273–309.

[43] Sheila Meintjies, 'Family and gender in the Christian community at Edendale, Natal, in colonial times', in Walker, *Women and Gender*, pp. 125–45; Heather Hughes, '"A lighthouse for African womanhood": Inanda seminary, 1869–1945', ibid., pp. 197–220.

Christianity in southern Africa unravels the skeins of mission and evangelism in Tswana society even more than the Comaroffs, by concentrating more on Africans than missionaries, especially on African initiative in interpreting the 'Word' of the Gospel in the 'language' of Tswana society. Paul Landau focuses on how Africans constructed a political realm of power, which he shows was predicated upon an alliance between Ngwato royalty, the missionaries and Tswana preachers and, most of all, Tswana women. He argues that:

> As women began visibly and audibly to participate in Christian work, they also embodied the efforts of the king to reorder his kingdom's *thuto* [ideology, culture, consciousness], its institutions, its modes of association. They helped contain and direct elements of the changing world as it pervaded his domain. As communicants in both senses, women configured the norms of loyalty in every town and village. Church became a new forum for reproducing the body politic; it permeated the Tswana town's male political space (the *kgotla*), and behind church walls, took on many of the *kgotla*'s integrative functions. . . . Christianity offered a way to oppose the patriarchal or ethnic domination within villages and homesteads, and often benefited the direct authority of the king, but Christians occasionally fought the kingdom itself.[44]

Landau also measures the contribution of Christian marriage to the construction of monogamous, individuated, and even mutually competitive family units headed by public, productive men and private, reproductive women.[45] His vignette of 'Being a Christian Woman in Serowe' portrays the demographic changes in church membership interspersed with evocative interviews which show the shift of power from men to women, from beer to tea – as a subtitle puts it.[46]

In his epilogue, Landau captures the quixotic nature of history, especially in reconstructing the African past: 'It is an attempt to pin and mount lives on the page of a book, like butterflies or rose petals.' And

---

[44] Paul S. Landau, *The Realm of the Word: Language, Gender and Christianity in a Southern African Kingdom* (London, 1995), p. xvii.

[45] Jean and John Comaroff, 'Home-made hegemony: modernity, domesticity, and colonialism in South Africa', in Karen Tranberg Hansen, ed., *African Encounters with Domesticity* (New York, 1992), pp. 37–74.

[46] Landau, *Realm of the Word*, pp. 93–110.

despite his declared agnosticism, he ends: 'It may be that the only way truly to privilege Christians' own experiences and expressions is to share in their faith.'[47]

*   *   *

The role of women as missionaries in the worldwide missionary encounter is the main theme of a volume in which individual contributions concentrate on the differences between missionary women and women of the receiving cultures throughout the colonial world, including southern Africa.[48] Cecillie Swaisland's short piece on nineteenth-century recruitment of single women to Protestant missions in South Africa looks at mission work as an escape from domesticity, but still construes the value of women to missionary endeavour as closely associated with their gendered training and accomplishments.[49] Missionary women served as models of female behaviour, as representatives and protectors of monogamous Christian marriages, and of the ideals of 'home makers'. And tied to the notion of an exemplary life was also the educational role of missionary women. A perceptive and critical review of this collection points out that 'the desire to reclaim a "lost" history for and of women may have contributed to the sometimes sanitising drift in the treatment of missionary women'.[50] It also questions the conventional assertion that European missionary women, themselves marginalized in their own societies, were sympathetic to colonized women and men.

A conference on 'Promoting Women's History: Local and Regional Perspectives' at Rhodes University in Grahamstown in July 1995 extended the range and depth of historical research on women missionaries and their impact on African communities.[51] Natasha Erlank, for instance, examined the racial perceptions of missionary wives at the Cape in the early nineteenth century. Distinctions were

---

[47] Ibid., p. 219.

[48] Fiona Bowie, Deborah Kirkwood, and Shirley Ardener, eds, *Women and Missions: Past and Present. Anthropological and Historical Perceptions*, Cross-Cultural Perspectives on Women, 11 (Oxford, 1993), pp. xvii–xx.

[49] Cecillie Swaisland, 'Wanted – earnest, self-sacrificing women for service in South Africa: nineteenth-century recruitment of single women to Protestant missions', in Bowie, *Women and Missions*, pp. 70–84.

[50] Carli Coetzee, 'Mission accomplished', *SARB*, 38 (1995), p. 9.

[51] See Julia Wells, 'Putting gender into South African history', paper presented at the 'Promoting Women's History' conference.

mainly based on colour, clothing, language, class, and above all, religion. This was especially true of missionary wives, such as Helen Ross, who encountered the Xhosa on the eastern frontier, and Anne Hodgson, who felt alienated from the Koranna and Tswana of the northern frontier. For them, conversion to Christianity became an index of social status.[52]

Among individual female missionaries, Olive Carey Doke, a Baptist working in Lambaland (Zambia) during the first half of the twentieth century, exemplifies the missionary teacher and administrator. Although limited by her context and, indeed, her theology, she embarked on a wide range of pioneering ministries which Baptist churches in southern Africa have not fully appreciated.[53] An intriguing analysis of the relationship between African American women missionaries with the American Board Mission in Natal and African women between 1880 and 1920 is offered by Sylvia Jacobs. Her hypothesis is that black Americans supported European imperialism in Africa as long as exploitation was not their only goal. She also explains the negative views African American missionaries had of African women in terms of the reversal of labour roles (African rural women were often agricultural workers), disapproval of polygamy, and differences in sexual mores, not to mention nudity.[54]

* * *

Not to be ignored is the white Afrikaner woman and her Pietistic or Calvinistic religion. Again biography is the methodological vehicle as Karel Schoeman describes the world of Susanna Smit between 1799 and 1863.[55] This is a meticulously researched study of a nineteenth-century missionary wife who joined the Boer emigration to Natal in the 1830s when she accompanied her husband, Erasmus Smit, in the service of the Dutch Missionary Society. Although Schoeman's purpose

---

[52] Natasha Erlank, 'Missionary wives and perceptions of race in the early nineteenth century Cape Colony', paper presented to the 'Promoting Women's History' conference.

[53] Louise Kretzschmar, 'Olive Carey Doke: a neglected Baptist pioneer', in Christina Landman, ed., *Digging up our Foremothers: Stories of Women in Africa* (Pretoria, 1996), pp. 141–66.

[54] Sylvia M. Jacobs, 'Give a thought to Africa: black women missionaries in Southern Africa', in Nupur Chauduri and Margaret Strobel, eds, *Western Women and Imperialism: Complicity and Resistance* (Bloomington, IN, 1992), pp. 207–28.

[55] Karel Schoeman, *Die Wêreld van Susanna Smit, 1799–1863* (Cape Town, 1995).

is a literary one – to recover Susanna Smit's diaries written in Afrikaans – he also explores her spirituality. A section from the diary captures the link between Smit's writing and her spirituality:

> I have no money, no possessions to give to you poor, also no vineyard in which to labour. I am a poor woman confined to the intestines of my meagre home, and the sorrows of life oppress the abilities of my soul. I do write on pieces of paper, ponder the wonders of your mercy, and suppose hereby to provide my soul with some solace and thus to praise you. . . . Presented by a spirit lacking in talent, undecorated by any skill in the art of writing . . . it will soon be torn up . . . and so the only glory I attempt to bring my dear Lord in my weakness, will be lost. And thus I walk away from the scene of life where god has blessed me so mercifully, patiently and lovingly, and no trace of your goodness, shown to me in such large measure, is to be found.[56]

Since Smit was one of the few literate Afrikaner women or men at the time of the 'Great Trek' of 'Afrikaners' into the interior of southern Africa, her diaries are naturally a remarkable, if enigmatic, literary product. Schoeman places Smit in the religious and historical context of reveillists at the Cape, and describes her as a mystic, exploring the religious interstices of a white Afrikaner woman's quest for political and personal freedom within the confines of Dutch Reformed Christianity on the frontier.

Christina Landman, in a controversial book on the piety of Afrikaner women, analyses the religious experiences of seven women born between 1768 and 1880. Her main focus is their enslavement and the way in which their self-sacrifice led to complete marginalization. She presents this history as the 'story of white people' and distinguishes between a 'nationalistic' God, the God of men's strong political ambitions, and a 'personal God', the one to whom women pray in private.[57] One critic of such a neat dichotomy claims that it simply acts 'as a way of redeeming white Afrikaner women, since they can be

---

[56] Coetzee, 'Mission accomplished', p. 11: translation of Schoeman, *Wêreld van Susanna Smit*, p. 8.

[57] Christina Landman, *The Piety of Afrikaans Women: Diaries of Guilt* (Pretoria, 1994). See also Landman's response to her critics: 'Responses to *The Piety of Afrikaans Women*', *Religion and Theology*, 2 (1995), pp. 334–42.

written out of their group's history and absolved from the guilt of complicity in what was done in the name of the "nationalistic" God of Afrikanerdom'.[58] On the other hand, Landman's monograph begins the important study of the religious life of pioneer white settler women in South Africa, which she has now widened to include African women.[59]

* * *

A *Festschrift* for Archbishop Desmond Tutu, who ardently supported the ordination of women in the Anglican Church of the Province of Southern Africa ratified at the Provincial Synod held in Swaziland in 1992,[60] appropriately contains chapters on gender and the church.[61] These studies have an historical orientation, but also reflect the current interdisciplinarity of writing about religion. For example, Denise Ackermann writes on violence against women, in which she pays particular attention to the high incidence of rape in South Africa.[62] She offers a theological-pastoral analysis and strategy to deal with this growing problem. Another chapter looks at 'Children, sexism and the church', and shows the effects of the sexist socialization of children in church and society.[63] Gender history therefore also offers insights into the political economy and culture of the family. Libuseng Lebaka-Ketshabile writes about the challenges which face women in South Africa today. In particular, she stresses the need for women to change their outlook from that of dependency to having a mind of their own. She also raises the issue of what constitutes 'women's work', so that an entirely new understanding of the role women play in the economy may be developed and implemented. On women in the church, she points out how ecclesiastical structures and practices have contributed to women's oppression, arguing that women and men should re-think their interpretation of the Bible and Christianity. According to Lebaka-Ketshabile, women's motto should be 'a good life for myself and a good life for others'.[64]

---

[58] Coetzee, 'Mission accomplished', p. 11.

[59] Landman, *Digging up our Foremothers.*

[60] On the ordination of women to the priesthood, see *Report of the Commission on the Ordination of Women* (Church of the Province of Southern Africa, Cape Town, 1989).

[61] Leonard Hulley, Louise Kretzschmar, and Luke Pato, eds, *Archbishop Tutu: Prophetic Witness in South Africa* (Cape Town, 1996).

[62] Denise M. Ackerman, '"For such a thing is not done in Israel": violence against women', ibid., pp. 145–55.

[63] Caroline Tuckey, 'Children, sexism and the Church', ibid., pp. 156–70.

[64] Ketshabile, 'Challenges facing women in South Africa', ibid., pp. 180–1.

Liz Carmichael takes this perspective further in a chapter on 'the spirituality of reconstruction'. While not addressing herself specifically to women, she genderizes the importance of connecting spirituality with social reconstruction, seeing each individual's relationship to God, personal morality, and social rehabilitation as closely interconnected, and all aspects of the Christian faith. Her own experience of retreats for meditation and silence as well as spiritual direction, within the Anglican Church, and the time spent in practical peace and development work in Alexandra township (an African ghetto) in Johannesburg, provide a women's perspective on the nexus between religion and social action.[65]

In the same volume, Beverley Haddad discusses the connection between gender and development in South Africa. She suggests that 'for ordinary African women, talk of liberation, reconstruction and transformation are all premature: for the theology that they live by is a theology of survival'.[66] Using down-to-earth examples, she highlights the plight of economically disempowered women and discusses attempts by social analysts to shift paradigms and design strategies to deal effectively with the poverty of millions of women in southern Africa. She argues that for many women the Church is a 'site of struggle'. Only when the Church itself is transformed can it become an agent of change in the development process and realize its considerable human and material resources to alleviate poverty and contribute to a more just social system.[67]

In her contribution, Janet Hodgson writes on religion and identity. Her keen cultural analysis of the inculturation of Christianity in an African context has many implications for the structures and activities of the church. This, in turn, has implications for women's involvement in the church. Liturgical renewal, for instance, needs to mirror the transformation of Christian theology and the renewal of social structures in the post-apartheid era.[68] Hodgson's focus on the Africanization of Christianity is emblematic of much South African theology, and feminist writers have tried to link this with the feminization of ecclesial structures. Women's experience of culture

---

[65] Carmichael, 'Creating newness: the spirituality of reconstruction', ibid., pp. 182–98.
[66] Beverley Haddad, 'En-gendering a theology of development: raising some preliminary issues', ibid., p. 199.
[67] Ibid., p. 208.
[68] Hodgson, 'African and Anglican', ibid., pp. 106–28.

in Africa is part of this wider debate, since political transformation impinges upon the construction of culture. Mamphela Rampele, the new Vice-Chancellor of the University of Cape Town, provides some personal perceptions about being an African woman in the Anglican communion in South Africa from the 1960s, historicizing her recollections and critique of Anglicanism in terms of the liberation struggle against apartheid.[69]

The key issue for women in contemporary South Africa has been identified by one of the country's leading feminist theologians as their 'need to challenge those aspects of both religion and culture which are oppressive to us'.[70] This also raises the issue of difference, as Africans and women grapple with a variety of experiences and perceptions, sometimes articulated in a range of theologies and ecclesiastical traditions. Because women's experience of God is often mediated through culture, theology, church structures, and ritual, feminist theologians are developing new discourses to reflect and challenge masculinist dogmas and creeds.[71] Denise Ackermann eloquently explores the similarities and differences of women's religious experience and feminist theory in constructing a vision of civil society in a democratized South Africa.[72]

A landmark in feminist theology in South Africa was the publication in 1991 of a wide-ranging book evocatively entitled *Women Hold Up Half the Sky*, shortly after the lifting of the embargo on banned political organizations, itself a key indicator of the beginning of the end of apartheid in February 1990.[73] This was the first major anthology in which a large number of women, from different walks of life and ecclesiastical traditions, collaborated. It covers many themes: women

[69] Mamphela Rampele, 'On being Anglican: the pain and the privilege', in Frank England and Torguil Paterson, eds, *Bounty in Bondage: Essays in Honour of Edward King, Dean of Cape Town* (Johannesburg, 1989), pp. 177–90.
[70] Denise Ackermann, 'Women, religion and culture: a feminist perspective on "freedom of religion"', *Missionalia*, 22 (1994), p. 225.
[71] Louise Kretzschmar, 'The relevance of feminist theology within the Southern African context', in Denise Ackermann, Jonathan A. Draper, Emma Mashinini, eds, *Women Hold up Half the Sky: Women in the Church in Southern Africa* (Pietermaritzburg, 1991), pp. 106–21; Louise Kretzschmar, 'Women and culture: ecclesial and cultural transformation', in Charles Villa-Vicencio and Carl Niehaus, eds, *Many Cultures, One Nation: Festschrift for Beyers Naudé* (Cape Town, 1995), pp. 90–104.
[72] Denise Ackermann, 'From "difference" to connectedness: a feminist view of the question of difference', in J. W. de Gruchy and S. Martin, eds, *Religion and the Reconstruction of Civil Society* (Pretoria, 1995), pp. 261–72.
[73] Ackermann et al., *Women Hold Up Half the Sky*.

and the Bible; theological foundations; spirituality and Christian women; women and the church; women and ministry; and women's experience in the struggle for social justice in South Africa. Among other things, this volume offered a re-definition of women's humanity by women themselves, a critique of patriarchy, and an emphasis on relationality.[74]

Feminist theology, which sometimes privileges white women in the Church and academe, has been challenged by an emerging womanist theology,[75] derived from the experience and writings of black Americans, which pushes the frontiers of Black Theology towards a more inclusive ecclesiology. In 1986, Bernadette Mosala condemned African male theologians for their silence about the oppression of black women in South Africa. With Bonita Bennett and Roxanne Jordaan,[76] Mosala attacked existing ecclesiastical institutions on behalf of African Christian women. Madipoane Masenya has also articulated this challenge in an article on womanist hermeneutics,[77] which racializes feminist scholarship along the lines of Black Consciousness ideology, the midwife of the patriarchal Black Theology of the 1970s.

An even earlier 'womanist' statement about Christian religion, social action, and Black Consciousness is found in Ellen Kuzwayo's biography, which appeared in 1985.[78] Significantly entitled *Call Me Woman*, it encapsulates a kind of female empowerment and separatism associated with Western feminism at a certain stage in its history, but which is profoundly modified by an even stronger separatism of Black Consciousness that proclaims 'blackness' as a distinguishing category. Towards the end of her book, Kuzwayo apologizes for employing a male book-keeper in the Trust she helped to establish; but she feels even more guilt about consulting a white rather than a black doctor.[79] She also redefines the position of women against the power of African

---

[74] See, for example, Denise Ackermann, 'Being woman; being human', in Ackermann *et al.*, *Women Hold Up Half the Sky*, pp. 93–105.

[75] Christina Landman, 'Ten years of feminist theology in South Africa', *Journal of Feminist Studies in Religion*, 11 (1995), pp. 144–5.

[76] See Bonita Bennett, 'A critique on the role of women in the Church', in Itumeleng J. Mosala and Buti Tlhagale, eds, *The Unquestionable Right to be Free* (Johannesburg, 1986), pp. 169–74; and Roxanne Jordaan, 'The emergence of black feminist theology in South Africa', *Journal of Black Theology in South Africa*, 1 (1990), pp. 42–6.

[77] Madipoane J. Masenya, 'African womanist hermeneutics: a suppressed voice from South Africa speaks', *Journal of Feminist Studies in Religion*, 11 (1995), pp. 149–55.

[78] Ellen Kuzwayo, *Call Me Woman* (Johannesburg, 1985).

[79] Ibid., pp. 227, 231 and 207.

patriarchalism,[80] in the context of relating her life in the service of the worldwide Young Women's Christian Association, a predominantly black organization after its rift with the more evangelical and exclusively white YWCAs of Southern Africa in 1931.[81]

As women, black and white, gain formal theological education and greater access to influential positions in churches and the academy, their voices are likely to be heard more strongly, especially once the production of knowledge is also genderized.

* * *

That this paper began with the biography of Katie Makanya and ended with the autobiography of Ellen Kuzwayo was not originally intended; but it does juxtapose two contrasting African women's perceptions about gender, work, politics, and religion under racism in South Africa in the twentieth century. Perhaps the greatest difference lies in the fact that Makanya and Kuzwayo told their stories in 1954 and 1985 respectively. Makanya embraced the missionary world as an educated Christian and was able to say to Margaret McCord: 'I can tell you anything, even those things you do not want to hear.'[82] Kuzwayo, on the other hand, confronted the European missionary world, embraced Black Consciousness but rejected its patriarchalism, thereby consciously refiguring her Christian religion in terms of post-colonial social forces.

Although focused on the construction of African women's religious identities as an integral part of relocating gender more centrally in various renderings of South Africa's past, this survey has also tried to chart the historiographical shifts, inside and outside the academy, which have permitted religion to be written back into that past. Tracing the fault lines between a hegemonic marxisant social history and an emergent, and challenging, cultural history redolent of postmodernist, post-structuralist and post-colonial theory,[83] it appears that gender, culture, and identity have been seismically extruded from this paradigmatical fissure. The contested nature of historical writing in

---

[80] See Dorothy Driver, 'Women and voice in colonial discourse: self-representation in writing by black South African women', paper presented at the Instutite of Commonwealth Studies, University of London, May 1989, pp. 16–19.

[81] See Gregor Cuthbertson and David Whitelaw, *God, Youth and Women: The YWCAs of Southern Africa 1886–1986* (Johannesburg, 1986), pp. 35–40.

[82] McCord, *The Calling of Katie Makanya*, p. 4.

[83] See Paul Maylam, 'Tensions within the practice of history', *SAHJ*, 33 (1995), pp. 3–12.

South Africa should now be confronted with trans-disciplinary and interdisciplinary imperatives which demand a more engaged dialogue between theological, feminist, and historical discourses in an attempt to further rediscover hidden narratives and voices, especially those of women.

University of South Africa, Pretoria

GENDER ROLES, HOMOSEXUALITY, AND
THE ANGLICAN CHURCH IN SYDNEY

by DAVID HILLIARD

I N September 1992 a periodical published by a conservative evangelical campus ministry led by an Anglican clergyman based at the University of New South Wales in Sydney published an editorial under the heading 'Is homosexuality next?' It began with an imaginary dialogue:

'And you know what the next thing'll be?'
'No, what?'
'Gay clergy.'
'What . . . you mean a home for depressed ministers.'
'No, I mean homosexuality. That'll be the next thing. When they've got the women's thing parcelled up, the next big fight will be over homosexuality.'
'Awh, gowarn.'
'No, really. The Yanks are doing it already. Mark my words – within 10 years, we'll have an Australian chapter of MOG (Movement for the Ordination of Gays).'[1]

These comments should be seen in relation to the debate in the Anglican Church of Australia over the ordination of women, which in 1992, after fifteen years, was nearing its climax.[2] The editorial was published two months before the Church's General Synod voted in favour of legislation to allow the ordination of women to the priesthood. This was followed by ordinations in many major dioceses.

But not in Sydney. Since the 1970s the diocese of Sydney has become widely known within the Anglican Communion and beyond for its tenacious and unfashionable opposition to liberal thinking on

---

[1] 'Is homosexuality next?', *The Briefing* (Sydney), no. 99 (22 Sept. 1992), p. 13.
[2] Muriel Porter, *Women in the Church: The Great Ordination Debate in Australia* (Melbourne, 1989), and 'The end of the "great debate": the 1992 General Synod decision on women priests', in Mark Hutchinson and Edmund Campion, eds, *Long, Patient Struggle: Studies in the Role of Women in Australian Christianity* (Sydney, 1994), pp. 161–85.

homosexuality, gender roles, and the ordination of women. In 1985 the diocesan synod approved a report that recommended that known 'practising' homosexuals should not be permitted to exercise any public ministry in the church; in 1986 Archbishop Donald Robinson of Sydney joined the Anglo-Catholic Bishop Graham Leonard of London as one of the two international vice-chairmen of the Association for the Apostolic Ministry. The Sydney diocesan synod in 1987 passed legislation for the admission of women to the diaconate and the first women were made deacons in February 1989.[3] However, majority opinion in the diocesan synod remains opposed to women in the priesthood insofar as this involves a ministry of headship in the congregation and 'preaching with authority'. This paper will explore the relationship between these two issues.

It is not unusual for the diocese of Sydney to stand alone. For much of the twentieth century this large and wealthy metropolitan diocese has occupied a unique position within Anglicanism, proud of its international reputation as a stronghold and guardian of evangelical orthodoxy. In Australia, conservative evangelicals of various denominations often look to Sydney Anglicans for leadership, encouragement, and 'sound' theology. On the other hand, for Christians outside the evangelical tradition the word 'Sydney' (with the derisive term 'Sydney-itis') has often been synonymous with theological and liturgical obscurantism, and tough politicking. In fact Sydney Anglicanism has always been less homogeneous than has appeared from outside. In the 1990s it is more diverse than ever before, with at least four identifiable groupings: Anglican evangelical traditionalists, separatist evangelical radicals, inclusive mainstream evangelicals, and charismatics.[4]

Evangelical Christianity was brought to Sydney by the first Anglican chaplains to the convict colony of New South Wales. By the 1830s, when the first bishop was appointed, the evangelical clergy had become a powerful force. From the late nineteenth century, as Anglo-Catholic influences began to spread elsewhere in the Australian

[3] *Southern Cross* (Sydney), Feb. 1989, pp. 6–7, April 1989, pp. 21–3; Porter, *Women in the Church*, pp. 117–19. The Sydney synod had first passed the women deacons canon in 1985, but on that occasion it was vetoed by Archbishop Robinson.

[4] Stuart Piggin, *Evangelical Christianity in Australia: Spirit, Word and World* (Melbourne, 1996), illuminates many areas of Sydney Anglicanism. See also Stephen Judd and Kenneth Cable, *Sydney Anglicans: A History of the Diocese* (Sydney, 1987), and Marcus L. Loane, *Hewn from the Rock: Origins and Traditions of the Church in Sydney* (Sydney, 1976).

church, Sydney evangelicals became particularly concerned to preserve the evangelical character of their diocese and formed various party organizations to that end. During the interwar years the diocese of Sydney became more isolationist and its militant voices grew louder. They surveyed the world with a sense of battle, hostile to Anglican comprehensiveness, liberalism, Anglo-Catholicism, and Roman Catholicism. From the 1930s the Anglican Church League, the party machine, issued 'how-to-vote' tickets for synod elections to ensure a strong evangelical representation on major committees. In Melbourne, the second largest Anglican diocese in Australia, liberal evangelicalism became an influential force; but in Sydney the conservative wing of the movement gained and retained control.

* * *

The most influential institution in the diocese of Sydney was, and is, its theological college, Moore College, founded in 1856.[5] It was unusual for anyone to be ordained in the diocese who had not been trained at Moore College. Since the 1950s, the systematic theology taught there has been deeply grounded in the Reformed tradition with a strong emphasis on the rational and intellectual content of Christianity.

The principal of Moore College from 1959 to 1985 was David Broughton Knox, son of a prominent (Ulster-born) Sydney clergyman and brother-in-law of Archbishop Marcus Loane (Archbishop of Sydney, 1966–82). He had taught at the college since 1947. Knox linked his high view of the authority of the Bible to the doctrine of propositional revelation. He taught his students that God reveals himself to humanity not through acts and events, but through meaningful statements and concepts expressed in words, recorded without error in the Bible.[6] Knox had enormous influence on the clergy whom he trained; in 1996 these include virtually the entire clerical leadership of the diocese. Until the mid-1980s, whenever moral and doctrinal questions emerged among Sydney Anglicans, he played a central role in articulating and defending a conservative case.

---

[5] Marcus L. Loane, *A Centenary History of Moore Theological College* (Sydney, 1955).

[6] D. Broughton Knox, 'Propositional revelation the only revelation', *Reformed Theological Review*, 19 (1960), pp. 1–9. The main features of D. B. Knox's theology are summarized in Piggin, *Evangelical Christianity in Australia*, pp. 184–8. For a critique, see Robert J. Banks, 'The theology of D. B. Knox: a preliminary estimate', in Peter T. O'Brien and David G. Peterson, eds, *God who is Rich in Mercy: Essays Presented to Dr D. B. Knox* (Sydney, 1986), pp. 377–403.

The relations of women and men in the Anglican Church in Sydney, and its debates over sexuality and gender, have been shaped both by the dominant theological discourse within the diocese and by the wider social context. In understanding gender relations in the church two concepts are useful. The first, developed by the Australian sociologist R. W. Connell, is that of hegemonic masculinity: the configuration of gender practice that institutionalizes the dominant position of men and the subordination of women.[7] The second is the idea of masculinism: the celebration by men of these particular attitudes, values, and behaviour.

In Australia, as in North America, historians of gender have identified two distinct male types that emerged in the late nineteenth century: the tough and the tender. In Australia these cultural types have been labelled the Lone Hand (men who enjoyed, in all-male company, drinking, gambling and swearing) and Domestic Man (churchgoing, abstemious, devoted to home and family). The Lone Hand was the fullest exemplar of masculinism, but Domestic Man – reacting against the suspicion of effeminacy and keen to prove his manliness – was equally receptive to masculinist attitudes and values.[8] This was certainly true in Sydney. Many evangelical clergy were keen to show that, although disapproving of liquor and gambling, they were indeed 'men's men'.

The idea of distinct and separate spheres for women and men in the Church persisted in Sydney for much longer than in other parts of Australian Anglicanism. In women's ministry the diocese of Sydney had led the way, with the ordination of the first deaconess in 1886 and the foundation of an institution for their training in 1891. Many single women from Sydney went overseas as missionaries with the Church Missionary Society, where they outnumbered the male missionaries by two to one.[9] Archbishop Mowll (1933–58) wanted to see a deaconess in every parish to provide a pastoral ministry that was subordinate but

[7] R. W. Connell, *Gender and Power: Society, the Person and Sexual Politics* (Sydney, 1987), pp. 183–8, and idem, *Masculinities* (Berkeley, CA, 1995), p. 77.

[8] Marilyn Lake, 'The politics of respectability: identifying the masculinist context', *Historical Studies*, no. 86 (1986), pp. 116–31; Anne O'Brien, '"A church full of men": masculinism and the church in Australian history', *Australian Historical Studies*, no. 100 (1993), pp. 437–57. For similar trends in North America, see E. Anthony Rotundo, *American Manhood: Transformations in Masculinity from the Revolution to the Modern Era* (New York, 1993), ch. 11.

[9] Piggin, *Evangelical Christianity in Australia*, pp. 72–3.

complementary to that of the rector. During the 1960s, under his less sympathetic successors, the work of deaconesses was more restricted, and they were prohibited from preaching or speaking from the pulpit.[10]

The government and politics of the diocese of Sydney were an all-male concern. It was not until 1972, after several attempts, that the synod voted in favour of the admission of women as parish representatives. This was almost thirty years after the diocese of Adelaide had allowed women synod representatives, fifty years after Perth and Melbourne. From 1979 women were permitted to serve as parish churchwardens. In 1996 the synod's powerful Standing Committee has only five women among its thirty-five elected members.

Evangelicalism was influential in Sydney, but in a city whose population passed the three million mark in the 1980s it was only one of many discrete urban subcultures and minority groups.[11] In the religious life of the city its main rival was the Roman Catholic Church, which comprised one quarter of the city's population, and was closely linked to the Australian Labor Party. There was the bohemian Sydney of the freethinking, anti-religious libertarians. And there was gay Sydney. With its agreeable climate, harbour, and beaches, Sydney gained a reputation among the Australian capital cities for freedom and openness, combined with a distinctive brash vulgarity, which attracted many male artists, writers, and 'outsiders' from places where life was more constrained. By the 1930s, despite the stigma of illegality and regular harassment by the police, there had emerged in the inner city a flourishing though largely hidden homosexual subculture centred on private clubs, coffee shops, hotel bars, and outdoor meeting places.[12] Some of those men who dissented from heterosexuality and the puritanism of conventional evangelicalism gravitated towards the city's two Anglo-Catholic churches which offered both a religious alternative and a sympathetic social environment.[13] Evangelicals did not miss the connection. They liked to contrast their own 'manly'

---

[10] Porter, *Women in the Church*, pp. 44–6.

[11] Shirley Fitzgerald and Garry Wotherspoon, eds, *Minorities: Cultural Diversity in Sydney* (Sydney, 1995).

[12] Garry Wotherspoon, *'City of the Plain': History of a Gay Sub-Culture* (Sydney, 1991), chs 1–3.

[13] The connection is explored in David Hilliard, 'UnEnglish and unmanly: Anglo-Catholicism and homosexuality', *Victorian Studies*, 25 (1982), pp. 181–210.

worship with the appeal of Anglo-Catholicism to women, and men with 'feminine minds'.[14]

Among Sydney Anglicans, before the 1970s, sexuality and gender roles were not subjects of debate. Traditional views on sexual morality and the appropriate roles and behaviour of women and men were unchallenged, seen as part of the common stock of Christian beliefs. In their teachings the churches were generally supported by the popular press. Since the 1970s, however, the diocese has been at the centre of controversy on two issues in particular: homosexuality and the ordination of women. Nowhere in Australian Anglicanism was there a sharper and more intense confrontation between the forces of religious tradition and movements for change, focused on issues of gender and sexuality.[15] A historian of Australian evangelicalism has suggested that an explanation may be found in the two competing masculine types of Lone Hand and Domestic Man. Is it possible, he asks, that Sydney's conservative evangelicals are 'fighting this ordination issue with the reputation of Domestic Man – they are evangelicals after all – but with the attitudes of Lone Hand'? Fearful of women invading their separate sphere, they argue theology as if they were in the male preserve of a pub, and 'they are very strongly committed to defeating their opponents in disputation'.[16]

The late 1960s, in Australia as in the United States, were years of political and cultural ferment. Mainstream magazines and newspapers ran their first sympathetic articles on homosexuality.[17] Conservative Christians were very disturbed by the social and moral changes they saw around them. These were summed up in a new term of abuse – the 'permissive society'. In Australia much of the action occurred in Sydney. In October 1968 Mart Crowley's play, *The Boys in the Band*, opened there, only six months after it began in New York, and enjoyed a long run.[18] In January 1970 a group of women who had been

[14] For example, 'The Oxford Movement and women', *Australian Church Record* (Sydney), 2 June 1932, p. 5.

[15] Denise Thompson, *Flaws in the Social Fabric: Homosexuals and Society in Sydney* (Sydney, 1985), ch. 5; David Hilliard, 'Australian Anglicans and homosexuality: a tale of two cities', *St Mark's Review* (Canberra), no. 163 (1995), pp. 12–20.

[16] Stuart Piggin, 'From independence to domesticity: masculinity in Australian history and the female ordination debate', in Hutchinson and Campion, *Long, Patient Struggle*, pp. 151–60.

[17] Wotherspoon, 'City of the Plain', ch. 4.

[18] John Rickard, '*The Boys in the Band* revisited', *Meanjin* (Melbourne), 52 (1993), pp. 661–7.

radicalized in the anti-war and student movements founded the country's first women's liberation group, and the following year began the first women's liberation newspaper, *Mejane*.[19] In January 1972 Germaine Greer, returning to Australia to publicize her new book, *The Female Eunuch*, addressed an enthusiastic forum on sexual liberation at the University of Sydney where she had once been a tutor in English. Meanwhile in July 1970, following the emergence of gay rights groups in the United States, the Campaign Against Moral Persecution (CAMP) was founded in Sydney by a group of gay men and women to work for social and legal equality. By the end of the following year it had become a national organization, with several thousand members and a monthly paper. In 1971 some members of CAMP who were Christians from various denominations founded a 'church group' called Cross+Section. It sent a circular letter to the clergy of the main denominations in Sydney, questioning the Church's traditional condemnation of homosexual behaviour as always sinful. In the same year the recently-formed Ethics and Social Questions Committee of the diocese of Sydney began a study of homosexuality, and the annual clergy school included a paper on the subject by a parish clergyman who had been a member some ten years earlier of a New South Wales state government committee of inquiry into homosexuality.

It was only a matter of time before there was a confrontation between Sydney evangelicals and the newly-vocal gay movement. This occurred at the end of 1972, when the Australian Broadcasting Commission produced, in a documentary series, a television programme on homosexual relationships. One of the men interviewed, the convenor of Cross+Section, was the full-time parish secretary of St Clement's, Mosman, an Anglican church in an upper-class suburb. He was immediately dismissed from his job, for it was claimed that by publicly acknowledging his homosexuality he had involved the Church in controversy. On Sunday 12 November there was a protest demonstration outside St Clement's during Morning Prayer. Several hundred members of CAMP and their sympathizers with placards and banners were accompanied by newspaper reporters and television cameras.[20]

[19] Verity Burgmann, *Power and Protest: Movements for Change in Australian Society* (Sydney, 1993), ch. 2 on the women's movement, ch. 3 on the lesbian and gay movements.
[20] *Australian*, 13 Nov. 1972.

There was a need for the Anglican Church to justify and defend its position. Early in 1973 Broughton Knox, principal of Moore College, gave a talk on homosexuality on a Church-linked radio station and this was subsequently printed in the diocesan monthly paper, *Southern Cross*.[21] Knox's article was a typically crisp and unambiguous application of his interpretation of biblical teaching on sexuality. God, he said, had created sex to express the relationship of man and woman within lifelong marriage. Homosexual activity, by contrast, because it occurs outside the marriage relationship, is essentially for self-satisfaction and thus contradicts God's purpose for sex. This is why, he said, both the Old Testament and the New Testament were absolutely clear that 'God abominates homosexual acts'. From this it followed that those who deliberately engage in this activity cannot be Christians – 'They may say that they are, but the facts are against them' – and should have no place in the Christian fellowship.

Later that year the Sydney diocesan Ethics and Social Questions Committee issued its long-awaited report on homosexuality.[22] It was very much a product of Moore College. Broughton Knox was one of the ten members of the committee, while its chairman, and the main author of the report, was the Revd Bruce Smith, who taught theology at the college. The report said much the same as Knox's article, though in more detail and supported by substantial appendices. Virtually all of it was on male homosexuality; lesbianism, almost invisible, was discussed in a single page. The report showed many signs of having been written in an atmosphere of panic over what it called 'the homosexual revolt'. The term itself is revealing. Although the principal authors of the report were unfamiliar with the notion of sexual politics, they recognized accurately enough that the gay movement represented a challenge from a subordinated group to the existing gender hierarchy. By demanding equality homosexuals were said to be attacking society at the fundamental level of its sexual definitions:

> The practising homosexual contradicts the heterosexual pattern at its most fundamental level. Fornication and adultery attack the institutional expression of heterosexual relations in marriage very

[21] *Southern Cross*, Feb. 1973, pp. 14–15.
[22] Church of England, Diocese of Sydney, Ethics and Social Questions Committee, *Report on Homosexuality* (Sydney, 1973).

seriously but they do not offer such a basic contradiction. Overt homosexuality defies the polarities of sex. . . . The ramifications of this movement are enormous. It demands nothing less than a radically new society. . . . The threat is reai and not imagined.[23]

Homosexual behaviour, said the Sydney committee, should be punished by the law. Because the homosexual 'way of life' subverts God-ordained patterns of sex and gender and threatens the divine institution of monogamous heterosexual marriage, and because the gay movement had 'almost certainly' increased the number of those who practise homosexuality, it should never be given the status of a legally accepted form of sexual activity. This recommendation was quite different from other Australian Church reports of the period, all of which concluded that the existing state laws against male homosexual behaviour should be repealed.

The Sydney diocesan synod duly received the report on homosexuality. For twenty years it was to remain the cornerstone of diocesan policy. The synod subsequently reinforced its position with further resolutions opposing any legislative moves to decriminalize homosexual activity or to extend to homosexuals the protection of anti-discrimination legislation. In 1977, for example, there was a motion by Broughton Knox, intended to bring wavering moderates into line: 'This Synod is of the opinion that the present laws in New South Wales against homosexual acts are not unjust inasmuch as they reflect the Creator's prohibition of homosexual acts which is so strongly expressed in His Holy Word.'[24] It was hard for the diocese to modify this position without losing face. The diocesan leadership maintained its total opposition to decriminalization until 1984, when the New South Wales Parliament repealed the laws against adult male homosexual behaviour.

During the 1970s Sydney's gay subculture grew more visible; the gay movement through a range of organizations gained a place in the political sphere as a recognized pressure group; and homosexuality became a 'lifestyle'. At the same time conservative Christians mobilized to defend 'biblical' morality against the permissive society and the primacy of the heterosexual family against the various sexual liberation movements. The Australian Festival of Light, modelled on the English

[23] Ibid., pp. 21-2.
[24] Church of England, Diocese of Sydney, *Year Book of the Diocese of Sydney*, 1978, p. 249.

organization of the same name, was formed in 1973 and gained wide support from Sydney evangelicals.

By then the ideological divisions over sexual morality and the family in the public arena had taken on something of the flavour of the sectarian battles between Protestants and Roman Catholics that had been such a prominent feature of Sydney life until the 1960s. On the one side were 'Christians' proclaiming moral absolutes derived from God's immutable laws as the basis for 'community standards'; on the other, the new social movements, gay activists, feminists, secularists, and humanists, challenging patriarchy, heterosexism, and traditional moralities based on religion. Each side saw the other as an aggressive pressure group seeking to impose its will on society, whose political agenda had to be fought at every point. There was no room for compromise.

In this polarized atmosphere the diocese was challenged from within by the formation of the AngGays collective in 1979. It was small in membership but busy and vocal. One of its founders, Fabian LoSchiavo, sat in the diocesan synod, representing an inner suburban parish, and spoke on the subject of homosexuality whenever he could. He was also the leader of the Sydney chapter of the Order of Perpetual Indulgence, an order of gay male nuns founded in San Francisco, whose appearance in traditional-style nuns' habits challenged all received distinctions between male and female, religious and secular. Many people were scandalized. In response to AngGays, a sub-committee of the diocesan Standing Committee published in 1985 a report on 'Homosexuality and Ministry'. This laid down that known homosexuals (defined as 'persons who engage in homosexual acts or follow a homosexual lifestyle') cannot properly occupy any office or perform any ministry within the parish: for example, churchwarden, parish councillor, synod representative, lay reader, Sunday school teacher, youth group leader, organist, choir member, parish secretary, and verger.[25] A few clergymen implemented the report, though in those congregations that had a significant homosexual presence it was a dead letter.

Meanwhile, from the mid-1970s Australian Anglicans had begun to discuss the role of women in ministry and the Sydney debate over sexual morality began to overlap with another, on gender roles within

---

[25] *Year Book of the Diocese of Sydney*, 1986, pp. 245–6, 309–13.

the Church.[26] In the Australian Church, Broughton Knox was the most prominent spokesman for the case against the ordination of women. In 1977, as a member of the General Synod Commission on Doctrine, he submitted an addendum to an official report on the subject which dissented sharply from its conclusion that the 'theological objections which have been raised do not constitute a barrier to the ordination of women to the priesthood'.[27] As with homosexuality, Knox's argument was based on two premises: that God had expressed himself clearly in his written Word, and that the Bible, from the book of Genesis onwards, affirms a particular pattern of relationship of men to women. In this relationship the male has headship and primacy, involving initiative and ultimate responsibility, while the woman is subordinate. As this is a principle on which God has brought the creation into being it is unchanging and universal. It must always operate within the Christian congregation and the family because both institutions are expressions in microcosm of the relationship of Christ and his people.[28]

The debate over the ordination of women in Sydney was conducted against a background of opposition among conservative Christians to secular ('anti-Christian') feminism and the growth from the 1970s of Christian feminist organizations and networks. Lesley Hicks, a regular columnist in the fortnightly *Australian Church Record*, was always critical of feminism and the ideal of female independence. She attributed the rise of divorce among evangelical Christians to the rejection by young women of the plain New Testament teaching on male headship and urged the voluntary submission of wives to their husbands: 'I'm happy as a wife to swim against the feminist tide and accept my dependent state.'[29] She spoke for many middle-aged churchgoing women.

The first Anglican feminist organization in Sydney was Anglican Women Concerned, formed in 1974. In response to the intransigence of the diocese, a broader pressure group, the Movement for the

---

[26] Porter, *Women in the Church*, ch. 3; Piggin, *Evangelical Christianity in Australia*, ch. 9; Ruth I. Sturmey, 'Women and the Anglican Church in Australia: theology and social change' (University of Sydney Ph.D. thesis, 1989).

[27] Church of England in Australia, General Synod, *The Ministry of Women: A Report of the General Synod Commission on Doctrine* (Sydney, 1977), pp. 29–33.

[28] *Southern Cross*, Dec. 1975–Jan. 1976, p. 25.

[29] *Australian Church Record*, 9 Aug. 1982, p. 5; also 28 April 1977, p. 5; 11 July 1983, p. 5; 25 July 1983, p. 5.

Ordination of Women (MOW), was formed in September 1983 and held its first public meeting in March 1984.[30] Its founders were women mainly of evangelical backgrounds; Dr Patricia Brennan, its first convenor and most prominent figure, was a former medical missionary in Africa. MOW soon became a national and ecumenical body. On 4 October 1983, close to the five hundredth anniversary of the birth of Martin Luther, the founding members of MOW Sydney affixed to the door of St Andrew's Cathedral twelve theses, which included:

> we declare to the whole body of Christ that a great wrong is being done to both men and women through the theology of headship and subordination. . . .
> It is our desire therefore to see a reformation of both Head and Body, of priesthood and laity, through a renewed understanding of the unity and equality of man and woman in Christ, and a teaching of mutual subjection one to the other as the basis of relationships, with Christ as their only Head.[31]

In the course of the Sydney debate on the ordination of women the doctrine of male headship, as expounded by Knox and other members of the staff of Moore College, assumed a central position in the conservative case. It also became a distinctive badge of Sydney evangelicalism. The doctrine received little support from Anglican evangelicals elsewhere in Australia, who believed that the ordination of women could be supported from a biblical viewpoint. The outlook and ethos of Melbourne evangelicalism were very different. As early as 1976 Leon Morris, an eminent New Testament scholar who was principal of Ridley College, had argued the case for the public ministry of women.[32] In February 1986 the New Zealand-born evangelical Archbishop, David Penman, ordained the first women deacons in Australia. Scholars from the liberal Catholic tradition were quite puzzled by the Sydney arguments. Meanwhile in Sydney the concern to justify the doctrine of headship against evangelical scholars

<hr>

[30] *Australian Church Record*, 2 April 1984, pp. 1, 12; Porter, *Women in the Church*, pp. 103–4; Piggin, *Evangelical Christianity in Australia*, pp. 208–9.

[31] Julia Woodlands Baird, 'Pigeons, priests and prophets: the politicisation of women in the Anglican Church' (University of Sydney B. A. Hons thesis, 1992), appendix.

[32] Leon Morris, John Gaden, and Barbara Thiering, *A Women's Place* (Sydney, 1976).

who interpreted the biblical evidence differently became something of an obsession. There was little room for disagreement; the other side had to be defeated. In 1985 when some new research was published in the United States that appeared to strengthen the conservative case the *Australian Church Record* triumphantly announced the findings in a front-page headline: '"Head" means "authority over", never "source".'[33]

The lines of division in the Sydney diocese on the ordination of women paralleled, though did not coincide with, the homosexual debate. The conservative leaders of the diocese were strongly opposed to both, while that minority of clergy and lay people who for various reasons were unhappy with the diocese's policy on homosexuality were more likely to be supporters of women's ordination or open to the possibility of change. In the middle was a large group of moderate and liberal evangelicals who had become convinced by the pro-ordination case while still firmly opposed to homosexuality. There was also a tiny group of gay Anglo-Catholics who were appalled by the prospect of women at the altar.

Rebelling against the prevailing ideology of the diocese and its doctrine of heterosexual male headship – hegemonic masculinity – the leaders of AngGays joined MOW. An informal alliance of sympathy emerged between them and the radical wing of MOW. Both wanted to see the Church as a community of equals, without hierarchies and oppressive structures. In 1986 this mutual support led to controversy at the second national conference of MOW in Adelaide. There, after a strong debate, the majority supported a motion ('Through our commitment to justice for all people') deploring the Sydney synod's endorsement of the report on 'Homosexuality and Ministry'.[34]

So homosexuality entered the debate over the ordination of women. It was used by conservatives as a weapon with which to beat evangelicals who were sympathetic to the pro-ordination case. The *Australian Church Record* warned its readers about the implications of the feminist interpretation of Scripture, which undermined the clear teaching of God's Word. If the Pauline restrictions on the ministry of women were to be discarded as accommodations to a particular

---

[33] *Australian Church Record*, 6 May 1985, pp. 1, 12.
[34] *Movement for the Ordination of Women* [Newsletter], Sept. 1986, p. 12; *Australian Church Record*, 6 Oct. 1986, p. 1.

cultural environment, why stop there? Would not this open the way to every kind of ethical and theological relativism?

> Under the principle of the gospel bringing liberation why should not practising homosexuals be the next group to have certain restrictions in their behaviour lifted? ... [The question] *does* need answering because the logic of the liberation hermeneutic could take us there.[35]

Because acceptance of homosexuality was out of the question, for the Bible was absolutely clear on *that*, so the argument went, it followed that MOW's interpretation and application of the Bible must be faulty. Tougher conservatives pressed home their advantage and took every opportunity to make the connection. It was not surprising, they said, that in Churches all round the world – and particularly in the United States – 'acceptance of women's ordination has been closely followed by the legitimizing of homosexuality as a Christian lifestyle and then by the ordination of homosexual clergy'.[36]

*   *   *

In Sydney since the 1970s the gay movement and the movement for the ordination of women have challenged the masculinism promoted by evangelical Anglicans, the theology taught at Moore College, and the structure of power in the diocese. Common to all of these is the idea that gender differences and the subordination of women to men are clearly defined in the New Testament and are part of the God-created order for both family and Church. From this it follows that same-sex relationships and the exercise of religious leadership by women is incompatible with, and subversive of, the divine plan. In response to the demands of the gay movement for homosexual equality, the diocese urged the state to maintain legal sanctions against sexual behaviour between males and attempted to have known homosexuals removed from public roles in its congregations. Against the Christian feminist critique of patriarchy in the Church and the movement to ordain women to the priesthood, the theologians of the

---

[35] Editorial, *Australian Church Record*, 11 June 1984, p. 8.
[36] 'Revision tests', *The Briefing*, no. 100 (6 Oct. 1992), pp. 5–6.

diocese have developed a high doctrine of male headship as a central principle in the Christian revelation. In Sydney more than anywhere else in the Anglican world the two issues have been seen as interconnected and consecutive, with the acceptance of one leading inevitably to the other.

The Flinders University of South Australia

INDEX

Note: Page references in *italics* indicate illustrations.

Compiled by Meg Davies
(Registered Indexer, Society of Indexers)